IN SEARCH OF THEORY:
A New Paradigm for Global Politics

IN SEARCH OF THEORY
A NEW PARADIGM FOR GLOBAL POLITICS

Richard W. Mansbach and John A. Vasquez

COLUMBIA UNIVERSITY PRESS

New York

Library of Congress Cataloging in Publication Data

Mansbach, Richard W 1943–
In search of theory.

Includes bibliographical references and index.
1. International relations.   I. Vasquez, John A.,
1945–   joint author.   II. Title.
JX1395.M285   327   80-19365
ISBN 0-231-05060-7 (cloth)
ISBN 0-231-05061-5 (paper)

Columbia University Press
New York   Guildford, Surrey

Clothbound editions of Columbia University Press
books are Smyth-sewn and printed on permanent
and durable acid-free paper.

For Rhoda and Philomena with love

CONTENTS

PART II. THEORY

FIGURES AND TABLES

FIGURES

TABLES

PREFACE

THIS BOOK is intended to offer an alternative to the dominant realist paradigm in global politics. The result is a theory that focuses primarily upon the role of issues and actors in politics, particularly on how actors are born and change, how issues are conceived and resolved, and how the nature of the resolution process affects behavior. The new paradigm and the companion theory represent the culmination of several years of fruitful collaborative research and teaching at Rutgers University by the two authors. This collaboration and the exchange of ideas it entailed began because both were dissatisfied with the state of theory in the field of international relations in which "nothing seems to accumulate, not even criticism."[1] The continuing dialogue revealed that both authors had separately entertained ideas about the reasons for this paucity of theory that were not only compatible but even parallel.

Despite differing intellectual experiences and substantive interests, both authors had concluded that the fundamental cause of the sorry state of their discipline was the continuing dominance of the realist paradigm and its assumptions about the role of power and nation-states in international politics. In large measure, these assumptions and the theory that emerged from them represented the apotheosis of a political tradition in the West that dates back to the Greek city-states of Thucydides and was nourished by the peculiar history of the sovereign nation-state in Western

Europe. Preoccupation with the nation-state had the important result of shunting speculation about global politics to the periphery and producing two separate areas of enquiry—"domestic" and "international" politics. Preoccupation with the struggle for power reduced the complexity of the global system to a single unidimensional issue. This work began with a rejection of these assumptions and an attempt to remedy their flaws. The actual process of "discovery" occurred by juxtaposing Hans Morgenthau's definition of politics as "the struggle for power," with David Easton's definition of politics as "the authoritative allocation of values," and then moving "deductively" to delineate the implications resulting from the differences in these two definitions.

We decided that the product of this exercise should be a theory of global politics and not just another conceptual framework or even a pretheory, which does not fully elaborate and link propositions. Those exercises were useful in the past, but the needs of the field have moved beyond them. It might be argued that the creation of a theory was premature; this, of course, depends on what is meant by *theory* and how one views its function in science. Unlike some we do not use the word, *theory,* in this book to refer to a body of corroborated propositions, but to refer to a set of linked propositions that purport to explain behavior. This corresponds to our belief that *the only purpose of theory at this stage of the field is to serve as a guide to research.* It is relatively unimportant whether the models presented here are perfect; what is important is whether they are on the right track. A paradigm, as Thomas Kuhn emphasizes, does not provide answers, but only the *promise* of answers. It points the way to knowledge; it is not knowledge itself. The theory and models presented in this book are offered in that spirit. We do not expect them to be above criticism; we hope that they will give rise to a new period of critical thinking about theory. A word of caution should be given here to readers who are unfamiliar with scholarly theories. Unless otherwise stated, most of the statements in this book have been derived from the models we have built. They should not be confused with facts or a body of knowledge that has been corroborated by research. Indeed, many have not even been tested.

This does not mean that the theory and models have been built without care. In developing them we have been guided by explicit principles. First, propositions have always been stipulated so that they have a certain internal logic and seem able to explain behavior, not just predict it or point to correlates. We have tried unabashedly to produce a theory of cause and effect, and we believe that, despite philosophical problems with causality, it is highly useful in building theories to "*think* causally."[2] It is primarily our concern with explanation that led us to use the word, *theory,* rather than the word, *model,* to denote what we have constructed. Second, wherever possible, propositions have been developed and variables and concepts selected in light of existing scholarship. Much of the quantitative research of the last decade and a half has been incorporated within the new paradigm. In particular, the research of the DON project, the Correlates of War, the 1914 studies, and the Simulated International Processes project (SIP/INS) have been invaluable. In a different sense, the pathbreaking theoretical work of James Rosenau, of William Coplin and Michael O'Leary's PRINCE model, and of Kenneth Waltz have served us as essential guides in an uncharted terrain. Finally, propositions were developed with an eye to the principle of falsifiability, a concern for measurement, a belief in parsimony, and an attempt to keep jargon to an absolute minimum.

The significance of this task lies in the present impoverished state of "grand theory" in the discipline, not only among adherents of the dominant paradigm, but among critics as well. Our intent is to go beyond the incrementalism that has characterized much recent scholarship in world politics. While the caution of that scholarship is commendable, it is also suffocating and has prevented its practitioners from boldly abandoning the paradigm which they themselves have repeatedly criticized. After all, whatever the faults of realism, it was a bold and exciting enterprise as it was reconstructed in the 1940s and 1950s and did give rise to a systematic and parsimonious theory.

The book is organized in three parts. The first, consisting of three chapters, presents realism and recapitulates the flaws in it, presents evidence that "actor" and "issue" are key variables that have received insufficient attention, and presents the critical assumptions, logic, and concepts of an alternative paradigm. The second and central part of the book, chapters 4 through 8, develops the theory of global politics that grows out of the new paradigm. The first of these chapters deals with issues—how they are born, altered, and resolved, and how different issue attributes have an impact on these processes—and the global agenda of issues. The following chapter deals with actors and their attributes—how they emerge, coalesce, and fragment—and the conditions, actor attributes, and issue characteristics that produce these processes. The sixth chapter integrates the discussion of issues and actors in explaining the various paths that actors take in reaching initial issue positions and making proposals and the factors that determine which path will be chosen. The final two chapters in this section confront the problem of interaction. The first of these, chapter 7, explains the various dimensions of cooperation and conflict and their relationship to each other and elaborates the factors that predict the nature of interaction, as well as change in it. Chapter 8 provides an analysis of the mechanisms that are available to actors in interaction as they seek to dispose of, or allocate, stakes among themselves. It concludes with an explanation of war, perhaps the most infamous mode of reaching decisions. The final section of the book consists of an application of the theory to the past, present, and future to illustrate the new light which it throws on reality and its relevance for the making of policy. Chapter 9 reassesses the major historical changes in global politics during the so-called classic *Realpolitik* period, 1648 to 1939, through the prism of the theory. The following chapter does the same for the origins and evolution of the Cold War and the genesis of détente. The final chapter entails an analysis of the emerging agenda of global issues and utilizes the new theory for policy prescription.

In the process of writing this book, we have been influenced by a number of scholars as well as by our own students. While not all of these can be acknowledged by name, several colleagues have read portions of the manuscript, or earlier versions of it, and we have been instructed by their criticism, although we have not always agreed with it. Of particular help were Alexander George, Roy Licklider, Thomas Oleszczuk, J. Martin Rochester, T. C. Smith, and Steve Genco. Our thanks to Gerald Pomper and to the Rutgers University Research Council for financial assistance in preparing the manuscript for publication. Our thanks also to our three typists, Cindy Brown, Phyllis Moditz, and Diane Swartz, each of whom in different ways proved invaluable at critical junctures. A special note of thanks must also be reserved for Bernard Gronert of Columbia University Press, whom we first met after spending over two years writing this book, and who welcomed us as if he knew all along we were writing the book for Columbia. Finally, a book of this sort is not completed without the influence and sacrifices of those closest to the authors. For Richard Mansbach, Rhoda has shown not simply the virtues of patience and understanding, but has shared the intellectual wealth of a classicist and the insight and imagination of a novelist. For John Vasquez, Philomena provided the strength and inspiration to write this book, giving wisdom when things seemed desperate, love when all was lost, and companionship when it was needed most. To these two we dedicate this work.

October 31, 1979
New Brunswick, N.J.

CHAPTER SUMMARIES

1 THE DECAY OF AN OLD PARADIGM

The assumptions of the dominant realist paradigm are reviewed and described. Recent criticisms of the paradigm and its assumptions are recalled, and the weaknesses of each assumption delineated. Despite apparent anomalies, there is no alternative paradigm ready to replace realism. However, critics have made a sufficient case to devote the considerable energy necessary to produce and publicize a new paradigm. An empirical exploration of the role of nongovernmental actors and of issues suggests that these factors may be critical for a more profound understanding of global politics and its processes.

2 FROM THE ISSUE OF ITS POWER TO THE POWER OF ISSUES

David Easton's definition of politics as the "authoritative allocation of values" is taken as a starting point for developing an alternative paradigm, the focus of which is not "the struggle for power," but contention over issues. The materials which follow seek to demonstrate the potential theoretical power of issues as an explanatory set of concepts. The literature on issue areas is reviewed. Various issue typologies are then tested empirically, and a number of issue characteristics are found to be significant under certain conditions, while actor relationships are seen to be important under other conditions. The conceptual and empirical problems of each of the issue typologies are reviewed in order to determine which issue characteristics hold out the most promise for developing theory. A new conception and definition of *issue* is offered, and three new issue concepts are presented: issue dimension, type of stake at issue, and nature of stake proposal. These are briefly analyzed in an effort to explain cooperation/conflict. The conclusion is reached that, along with a broader and more flexible approach to actors, issues constitute the building blocks out of which a new foundation for apprehending politics may be constructed.

3 THE ELEMENTS OF A NEW PARADIGM

The assumptions of an alternative paradigm based on issues and actors are listed and explained, and the picture of reality it provides is compared to, and contrasted with, "political realism." Five topics of enquiry, each a separate process requiring theoretical elaboration, constitute the research agenda that grows out of the new paradigm: agenda politics, the formation and decay of actors, the genesis and modification of issue positions, the dynamics of political interaction, and the contexts of authoritative decisions. Theoretical questions of interest within each of these areas are specified in detail, along with an overview of the mid-range theories in each area presented in the second section of the book.

4 AGENDA POLITICS

The agenda process, rarely investigated in global politics, involves such questions as how issues are born, how and why they are placed on the agenda, how they are removed, and how and why the content of agendas change over time. The chapter addresses itself to these questions. The process of issue genesis is described in detail. An overall model of agenda setting is then presented. One key factor which determines whether an issue will reach the agenda is its salience to important actors.

Salience notwithstanding, whether an issue will reach the agenda depends on several other factors that are explained, including the availability of access routes, and the relative resources of contending actors. Agendas themselves are defined by critical issues that pass through a distinctive life cycle, the stages of which may include crisis, ritualization, dormancy, decision making, authoritative allocation, and removal from the agenda. Agenda change is illustrated in the chapter appendix dealing with Indochina, which describes how three different critical issues (colonialism, the Cold War, and the Sino-Soviet dispute over socialism) incorporate yet alter the same set of stakes.

5 THE BIRTH AND DEATH OF POLITICAL ACTORS

Since political actors are significant variables, and since their behavior and even existence is closely associated with the nature of issues that are on the global agenda, this chapter focuses upon processes of actor formation and fragmentation and integrates these processes into a model. Actors are formed in order to influence a collective decision making process. Preconditions of actor formation include the status of individuals or groups which in turn give rise to certain attitudes towards politics, a shared sense of value deprivation, and knowledge of the existence and availability of relevant stakes. These preconditions, along with the organizational context in which individuals or groups find themselves, determine their degree of participation as well as their capacity to communicate effectively with each other. However, membership in an actor ultimately requires the growth of perceptions of interdependence and similarity, processes which are described and explained. In order to carry out the promise to operationalize the concept "actor" without recourse to legal or ascriptive criteria, a set of empirical criteria is elaborated which reveals the variety of actor types that may exist in global politics. This is followed by the presentation of a model of actor coalescence and fragmentation, which highlights the various stages of unity or disunity that may characterize an actor. The conditions for each of the several stages are delineated and explained in terms of variables like issue salience, issue dimension, agreement and interaction patterns, prior patterns of interaction, success or failure of interactions, and organizational context.

6 DETERMINING ISSUE POSITIONS

This chapter presents a model of the factors that determine why actors adopt the positions they do toward issues under contention. A review of foreign-policy research by behavioralists indicates how far they have strayed from this focal area of enquiry. The model presents three distinct calculi that actors may use to develop a position toward an issue or toward the proposals of others—a cost-benefit calculus, an interdependence calculus, and an affect (positive or negative) calculus. The selection of one or another of the calculi is explained in terms of the paramount variables of issue dimension and issue salience. The sources of the latter having been delineated in chapter 4, the sources of issue dimension are now examined in detail. These are perceived similarity, prior pattern of interaction, and status of the contending actors. The ways in which these variables combine to condition the issue dimension and the manner in which issue dimension and salience combine to determine the issue calculi and the prospects for eventual agreement are explained theoretically.

7 THE LABYRINTH OF CONTENTION

With this chapter, attention is turned toward the concept of contention itself and the factors that determine the nature and characteristics of interaction processes. Contention, commonly conceived of as a single cooperation/conflict dimension, is distilled into its distinctive components—agreement-disagreement, positive-negative acts, and friendship-hostility. Acquaintance with the multidimensional nature of contention facilitates an understanding of how hostile or friendly spirals originate and persist. The key factor is whether the components of cooperation/conflict are congruent or not and consequently reinforce or counteract one another. This is determined principally by the issue dimension and secondarily by other issue characteristics—salience, type of stake(s), and the nature of issue proposals. A negative actor dimension produces symbolic and transcendent stakes which are highly salient and encourage proposals to distribute costs and benefits unequally. This process promotes disagreement, which in turn encourages the exchange of negative acts which produces hostility. Hostility tends to spread beyond the single issue at hand and reinforces the negative actor dimension which comes to characterize the relations of actors on all issues in which they are participants. A vicious circle ensues as a result of the complex feedback loop. Two key variables exist, however, that may impinge upon the circle and act as agents of change—cognitive dissonance and the success/failure of interactions. The sources of each and their potential impact are described and explained in detail, as is the manner in which they may combine and promote change in the relations of actors. The chapter ends with a discussion of the prospects for leaders consciously to induce such change and manipulate dissonance, a topic of considerable importance for policymakers.

8 THE COHERENCE OF CONTENTION

Contention is not a random or purposeless process. It is undertaken in order to increase value satisfaction by value allocation, and it serves as a mode of decision making. It is given coherence by the presence of four allocation mechanisms—force, bargains, votes, and principle—which are differentiated along a number of dimensions. These mechanisms combine in various ways to form gamelike patterns of interaction, each with its own typical rules for decision making. The genesis of interaction games occurs by means of special sequences of informal and formal rule-making games. But three additional theoretical questions remain: Which game is selected when more than one is available? How and when do actors switch games? And, how are new interaction games created? Each of these questions is treated in detail, and one game—war—is analyzed in depth. War is seen to be the result of the failure of previous games to produce authoritative allocations. Such failure encourages actors to turn to unilateral games of force, which produce insecurity and compel them to reduce that insecurity by combining into alliances. Such arrangements accentuate existing tendencies toward arms races and other modes of self-help, and these often conclude in war, owing to an inability to halt escalation during one of the series of acute crises that ensues. War itself may be fought for any of three different reasons—to overcome disagreement, to satisfy frustration/anger, or to change or enforce particular versions of systemic rules—and the actual war is likely to reflect the reasons for which it is fought.

9 REASSESSING THE PAST: GLOBAL HISTORY FROM A CHANGED PERSPECTIVE

One way of assessing the utility of the new paradigm and the theory that is constructed from it is to determine the extent to which it helps clarify the past. Thus, key developments in global history from 1648 to the outbreak of World War II are reinterpreted in light of some of the major elements of that theory. Emphasizing the movement among critical issues, changes within actors, and the models of interaction and interaction feedback elaborated in the previous chapters, a number of critical periods are identified and analyzed. These include the era of "classical balance of power," the collapse of the balance, the Congress of Vienna, the Concert of Europe, the collapse of the Concert, the Bismarckian hegemony, the descent to World War I, Versailles, and the rise of fascism and nazism.

10 THE COLD WAR

The transformation of World War II into the Cold War and the subsequent erosion of the latter reflect a fairly rapid movement among interaction games. This chapter constitutes an explanation of those phenomena through the lens of the new paradigm with application of the theory deduced from it. The pattern of events and ad hoc games that produced the Cold War are explained by reference to the three key background variables of prior pattern of interaction, perceptions of similarity, and status change. Although the prospect existed for avoiding this outcome by manipulating cognitive dissonance and shaping the postwar agenda, the opportunity was sacrificed after the death of President Franklin D. Roosevelt. With the onset of the Cold War, a new critical issue came to dominate the agenda, and a negative actor dimension served to attract numerous stakes toward it. This critical issue is described, and the stages through which it passed—crisis, ritualization, dormancy, and decision making—are reviewed. The interaction models, it appears, do explain the emergence of a détente interaction game, as tentative as it may be, and shed light on the old debate over the origins of the Cold War.

11 THE FUTURE

If the theory presented in this book has explanatory power, it also is predictive and has normative applications. The final chapter illustrates this point by utilizing these normative implications to discuss détente and predict the emerging political order in global politics. Détente is defined in terms of its interaction rules and expectations, and the growth of new system rules is explained. The genesis and likely role of new issues and actors are posited and justified, and some of these are defined and described in detail.

IN SEARCH OF THEORY:
A New Paradigm for Global Politics

PART ONE

FOUNDATIONS

CHAPTER ONE

THE DECAY OF AN OLD PARADIGM

SINCE THE birth of the modern nation-state in Western Europe, a single paradigm has held sway over efforts to theorize about global politics. Variously called "power politics," the "billiard ball model," "political realism," and the "state-centric" model, this paradigm assumes global politics to be a contest for power among sovereign nation-states in an anarchic environment.[2] Its key tenets have been passed down from generation to generation by historians and political theorists as varied as Thucydides, Machiavelli, Hobbes, and Ranke. In the United States, its basic ideas were reinforced and systematized during and after World War II by a group of scholars including Nicholas Spykman, E. H. Carr, Hans Morgenthau, George Kennan, and Robert Osgood, who were reacting to what they saw as the errors made by advocates of "idealism" with their emphasis on national self-determination, international law, political community, and morality during the interwar period.[3]

The Peace of Westphalia of 1648, which brought to an end the religious wars of Europe, must be regarded as the crucial historical step in the evolution and acceptance of a paradigm of global politics which features "power" and "state" as core concepts. Although a process of intellectual ferment had been underway for several centuries, Westphalia is said to have "legislated into existence" the system of states that has provided a focus for much of the discipline.[4] Westphalia signified the victory of secular princes over the imperial pretensions of Pope and Holy Roman Emperor, and the localist pretensions of feudal barons, and provided the basis for the growth of a detailed system of international law that legitimized the authority of these monarchs within their own territories. The law transformed the reality of the monarchs' personal property into the legal fiction of the sovereign state with the ascribed legal characteristics of independence and equality. It also gave rise to the corollary of nonintervention in the "internal" affairs of such sovereign kingdoms. Hans Morgenthau summarizes the impact of the doctrine of sovereignty as referring "in legal terms to the elemental political fact of that age—the appearance of a central political power that exercised its lawmaking and law-enforcing authority within a certain territory," as elevating "these political facts into a legal theory," and giving them "both moral approbation and the appearance of legal necessity."[5] The basic image of global politics, the product of a particular age and set of historical conditions, has survived the passing of the reality which gave birth to it.

While there has been little research of a systematic sort on the role of paradigms in international relations enquiry, a belief that the power politics approach has been the guiding intellectual force in the modern period is widely accepted. Yet if such a claim is to be meaningful, it is important to understand what a paradigm is and what it is not. According to Thomas Kuhn, a paradigm is a set of fundamental assumptions that form a picture of the world that the scholar is studying; it is a shared example among practitioners of a discipline, which instructs them about how to view the object of their enquiry.[6] A paradigm, then, is very broad and somewhat nebulous. It is, by definition, broader than a conceptual framework, because it is what gives rise to concepts. It is also much less specific than a theory or a model, both of which are systems of propositions that relate concepts to be found in the paradigm. Nor is a paradigm, in the Kuhnian sense, synonymous with a method or an epistemology. For Kuhn, the scientific method is simply something that all the natural sciences share, and the concept of paradigm is intended to distinguish the various substantive perspectives within a field; if this were not the case, then physics, geology, chemistry, and biology would all share the same paradigm!

The realist paradigm can be said to consist of three fundamental assumptions:

(1) Nation-states and/or their decision–makers are the most important
set of actors to examine in order to account for behavior in international politics.

(2) Political life is bifurcated into ''domestic'' and ''international''
spheres, each subject to its own characteristic traits and laws of behavior.

(3) International relations is the struggle for power and peace. This
struggle constitutes a single issue occurring in a single system and
entails a ceaseless and repetitive competition for the single stake of
power. Understanding how and why that struggle occurs and
suggesting ways for regulating it is the purpose of the discipline.

The key insight underlying these assumptions relates to the realist understanding of power. Nation-states are seen as the critical actors, because
they alone are sovereign and can marshal the necessary resources to wield
power. For Morgenthau, they are ''the ultimate point of reference of contemporary foreign policy.''[7] In domestic politics a single actor, the government, has sufficient power to regulate the activities of all other entities in
society, producing a certain measure of order and tranquility; in the international arena, there is no such leviathan. Consequently, in such an ''anarchic'' environment, each nation-state must struggle to maintain, if not to
increase, its power; otherwise it will be crushed.

These assumptions have provided a core of beliefs about world politics
that has been shared by scholars as diverse as A. F. K. Organski, Thomas
Schelling, J. David Singer, Inis Claude, Karl Deutsch, E. H. Carr, and
R. J. Rummel. To say that the realist paradigm has dominated the field
means only that its three fundamental assumptions have been widely
held, and not that there is no disagreement over various conceptual
frameworks, theories, or even methodology. Nevertheless, agreement on
assumptions is not a trivial matter. The assumptions provide a cognitive
map of the world that scholars are investigating; it informs them of what
is known about that world, what is unknown, and how to view the world
if one wants to know the unknown.*

---

* The use of Kuhn's concept of paradigm can be very problematic given the ambiguity of
his definition, and must take account of revisions suggested by various critics: see Dudley

CRITIQUES OF THE REALIST PARADIGM

In recent years, the intellectual hold of realism has been weakening, and an increasing number of scholars have come to challenge the dominant paradigm and each of its assumptions from a number of perspectives. Their verdict is that the attractively parsimonious picture of world politics painted by the paradigm—a system of nation-states, sovereign at home, struggling to gain power while avoiding total war—provides a narrow and incomplete description and explanation of world affairs. The decline of the Cold War and the emergence of a new agenda of issues, many of which are only peripherally related to "national security" as traditionally defined (e.g., the rise of significant nongovernmental actors like multinational corporations; the survival of interstate communities like the European Economic Community; the growing incidence of civil wars and separatism; the phenomena of interdependence, transnational, and transgovernmental penetration; and the successful challenge by the previously weak of the strong as in Vietnam and energy), pose complex questions upon which the old paradigm can shed little light. As a result of the criticisms of this rising generation of scholars, many of the basic concepts of global politics like "nation-state," "international organization," "international system," "power," and "security"—the very vocabulary on which the discipline had come to rely—appear increasingly nebulous and polemical.

Increasingly, each of the three fundamental assumptions has been seriously questioned. The first, that nation-states are the most important actors, was the earliest to come under direct attack. In 1971, Robert Keohane and Joseph Nye, Jr., explicitly called for rejection of the state-centric paradigm, because it failed to recognize the importance of what

Shapere, "The Paradigm Concept," *Science* (May 14, 1971) 172(3984):706–709; Imre Lakatos and Alan Musgrave, eds., *Criticism and the Growth of Knowledge* (New York: Cambridge University Press, 1970); Stephen Toulmin, *Human Understanding* (Princeton, N.J.: Princeton University Press, 1972), 1:93–130, 478–503. The definition employed here reflects a revision of Kuhn's concept. The justification of that revision, the applicability of Kuhn's framework to account for the intellectual history of the field of international relations, as well as an elaboration of the argument that the realist paradigm may not be as scientifically useful as another paradigm can be found in John A. Vasquez, *The Power of Power Politics: An Empiricial Evaluation of the Scientific Study of International Relations* (New Brunswick, N.J.: Rutgers University Press, 1981).

they identified as "transnational behavior," activities that cross national frontiers without being mediated by governmental agents and directed by nonstate actors.[8] Their volume, *Transnational Relations and World Politics,* by focusing on such varied actors as multinational corporations, churches, foundations, terrorists, and labor unions, revealed how the state is not necessarily "the gatekeeper between intrasocietal and extrasocietal flows of action."[9] Their work reinforced Oran Young's observation that the dominant paradigm had prevented "the analysis of a wide range of *logically* possible and empirically interesting models of world politics."[10]

Although highly suggestive, the Keohane and Nye volume suffered primarily from the fact that case studies do not permit their thesis to be easily falsified, and consequently the editors could be accused of "ransacking history." To eliminate this potential criticism, the Nonstate Actor project of Mansbach et al. collected event data to investigate empirically the emergence and behavior of nonstate actors and "to understand these newly recognized phenomena in the context of a changing global political system and its processes."[11] The authors hypothesized the existence of six types of actors in global politics (interstate governmental, interstate nongovernmental, nation-state, governmental noncentral, intrastate nongovernmental and individual) that undertake global tasks in one or more of four issue areas (physical protection, economic development and regulation, residual public interest tasks, and group status). Utilizing event data, they showed that significant actors exist in each category and that significant interaction has occurred between each logically possible combination. Comparing Western Europe, the Middle East, and Latin America, they documented the existence of profound regional differences in the quantity and quality of nonstate activity and provided hypotheses to account for this. In effect, they "move one step further away from the 'billiard ball' paradigm" and "have begun to break the *internal structure* of the 'billiard balls' into pieces."[12]

It is clear, in light of this work, that nation-states are not necessarily the only or even the most important actors under all circumstances. However, the more dramatic implication of Keohane-Nye and Mansbach et al. is that the very notion of a unitary nation-state may be inadequate. Not only may governments be unable to control all groups in their societies when it comes to foreign policy, but the government itself may be fragmented. Karl Kaiser, for instance, has suggested that various "parts" of nations or governments may come together to form transnational coalitions or entities that have primary loyalty to each other (if only in functional terms) rather than to their respective nation-states.[13] These units may, in turn, give rise to international regimes that act as supranational decision-making loci.[14] From a different perspective, Graham Allison and Morton Halperin challenge the unitary nature of governments, because they see bureaucracies and individual officials acting independently or even competing with the central decision maker, even if they do not form transnational coalitions.[15] They reveal how bureaucracies are not always the handmaidens of central decision makers and can produce inconsistent *national* policy, an observation that reduces the realist assumption that nation-states "act" to the level of triviality which reflects a misunderstanding of the nature of collective action. The belief that governments aggregate individual perceptions and interests into a single coherent "national interest" seems less plausible than previously imagined because of the sheer difficulty of such a task. Ultimately, the realists confuse alleged descriptions of rationality with prescriptions for rational behavior and impose an observer's version of such behavior upon a singularly uncongenial reality. Efforts to develop deductive theory from such assumptions, as in formal game theory, have been unsuccessful, and such failures have spawned a variety of competing models of collective decision making that share a rejection of the simple rationality described in utility models.[16]

These weaknesses in the first assumption of the paradigm stem from a tendency to collapse the distinction between governments and the societies for which they are surrogates, a confusion that has been buttressed by an ill-founded determination to compare actors on the basis of accessible quantitative *national* data, instead of elusive data that may be more relevant. Sovereignty, the concept still employed to retain the above distinction, is a legal fiction and ascriptive characteristic, not a descriptive and empirical one. Reliance upon it neglects the fact that not all governments can control "their" societies. This is not to say that governments are *never* unitary actors, that they *never* exercise control over their societies, or that it is *always* incorrect to postulate an international system. Rather it is to suggest that actors in world politics are variables, too, and must be defined and operationalized by behavioral rather than legal attributes. A fixed cast of actors cannot be *assumed* to exist. As it is demonstrated that nation-states sometimes behave as unitary actors and at other times do not, then it will be necessary to develop a theory that delineates the conditions under which unitary behavior in foreign policy will occur.[17] Thus, what was once a postulate of the field must now become a focus of investigation, both theoretical and empirical.

The validity of the second assumption of the paradigm, that political life can be divided into "domestic" and "international" spheres, has become less obvious as the world has been brought increasingly closer, owing to revolutions in communication, transportation, and military-economic technology.* "Linkages" among issues in both arenas have become endemic, thereby rendering the distinction meaningless. According to James Rosenau:

> Almost every day incidents are reported that defy the principles of sovereignty. Politics everywhere, it would seem, are related to politics everywhere else. . . . One can no more comprehend the internal political processes of a Latin American country without accounting for the United States presence (or, more accurately, the multiple United States presences) than one can explain the dynamics of political life in Pakistan or India without reference to the Kashmir issue.[18]

In order to comprehend this breakdown, Rosenau employed the concept of "penetration," which entails a recognition that in some "sovereign" nations foreign actors have a significant, if not determining, voice in critical domestic decisions.[19] When someone's domestic policy is shaped by someone else's foreign policy, then to what extent are there two separate spheres? Conversely, changes in domestic politics may have profound effects on global politics, often altering the very course of world history, as evidenced by the French and Russian revolutions.[20] For these reasons, John W. Burton called for a new paradigm, suggesting that the study of international relations be replaced by the study of world society. He goes so far as to argue that the concept of world society would be more properly understood "if we were to map it without reference to political boundaries, and indeed without reference to any physical boundaries."[21]

If absolute sovereignty over the territory, resources, and people of a society, and the insularity of domestic politics from international politics,

---

* See John H. Herz, *International Politics in the Atomic Age* (New York: Columbia University Press, 1959) for an early argument that these changes rendered the "hard shell" of national frontiers "permeable."

cannot serve as justification for the domestic/international distinction, neither can the proposition that domestic politics is different from global politics because government prevents domestic anarchy and lessens the probability of violence. The frequency of civil war and strife within states makes it impossible to distinguish the two spheres on the basis of centralized versus decentralized systems.[22] Just as realism underestimated the impact of collaborative arrangements in global politics, both formal and tacit, to allocate values peacefully, so prevailing approaches to domestic politics have overstated the conflict-management capacity of governments.* The nature of political behavior is not as causally affected by the existence of national boundaries as it once appeared to be. With proper qualifications and caveats, there seems to be no pressing a priori reason why a theory of politics must be different for domestic and global behavior.

The final assumption, that international relations can be treated as a single unidimensional issue—the struggle for power—has been most severely challenged by scholars who see the world as consisting of several different issue areas. Rosenau has argued that world politics is not confined to a single elite of nation-states that struggle for power, but that who are significant actors in world politics, and the kind of behavior they will engage in will vary according to the issue area.[23] This belief stems from research in American politics that reveals that power varies by issue area[24] and that different types of issues affect different interests, thereby producing different sorts of coalitions and decision-making processes (e.g., pluralist versus elitist).[25] It is not surprising, therefore, that when Keohane and Nye call for a new paradigm they show as much concern for issue areas as for nongovernmental actors:

We are suggesting an approach to the study of world politics through analysis of different types of issue areas . . . and of the relationships between them. The elaboration of this paradigm suggests three foci for research; (1) analysis of issue areas, (2) research on transnational and transgovernmental actors, and (3) studies designed to illuminate relationships between issue areas.[26]

---

* For example, Cobb and Elder state the the paradigm of liberal democracy "directs our attention to the consensual basis of conflict management and the incremental character of normal political decision-making" and "ignores or treats as an aberrant condition violence and the threat of violence." Roger W. Cobb and Charles D. Elder, *Participation in American Politics: The Dynamics of Agenda-Building* (Boston: Allyn & Bacon, 1971), pp. 8–9.

Empirical research has lent some credence to this view. Michael K. O'Leary has demonstrated that world politics is not unidimensional and that behavior does vary according to issue, and he has pointed out the dangers of collecting and analyzing data without controlling for issue.[27] Likewise, Mansbach, et al. demonstrate at a regional level that actors and their behavior vary by issue.[28]

Despite the wide attention paid to issues, much of the research on the topic has employed it only as a control variable, much as Rosenau first suggested. The effort to move beyond this and to treat issue area as a more forceful topic of theoretical enquiry is associated with the PRINCE simulation of William D. Coplin and Michael K. O'Leary. They argue that preoccupation with the struggle for power has made scholars neglect explaining, in a scientific manner, the substance of foreign policy, and they try to correct this by demanding that one of the major dependent variables in the field be the position of actors on various issues on the global agenda. They proceed to elaborate a theory that purports to explain and predict an actor's issue position by employing such concepts as issue salience, power (in an issue-specific sense), and friendship–hostility.[29] Coplin's and O'Leary's preoccupation with issues led them to call explicitly for a new paradigm, what they termed the "world policy process" paradigm, as an attempt to overcome the more obvious shortcomings of the realist paradigm.[30]

The issue challenge to the realist paradigm stems from the claim that the single issue of power fails to account for the existence of a global community, primitive as it may be, and the patterns of cooperation and peace that are actually more characteristic of it than war and conflict. It suggests that the power politics approach to the field rests upon a concept that eludes both definition and measurement and leads to a research agenda that is at once narrow and arbitrary. The belief that the struggle for power is the dominant issue fails to accommodate the multiplicity of values and stakes for which actors both cooperate and compete. These values and stakes can be perceived as distinct but often are perceptually related to one another in a variety of ways to form identifiable issues. Issues, in turn, may be more or less closely related to one another, and each issue, in time, changes in terms of substance, the patterns of behavior that characterize it, and the cast of actors that interact over it. When described in this way, issues become a central theoretical focus perform-ing a role once played by the concept of power.

But is a new paradigm really necessary? Have the critics made their case? More importantly, what kind of case must be made in order to reject the old paradigm? Thomas Kuhn argues that a paradigm is only re-placed when it confronts a major anomaly that it cannot resolve.[31] Imre Lakatos further argues that rejection of a paradigm is a decision that must be made by a field as a whole, and he offers some rules for making the decision in a rational manner. He suggests that one paradigm may be rejected in favor of another if the latter produces a better theory. For a rival paradigm to be accepted, its theory must: (1) explain everything the old theory explained, (2) explain at least part of what the old theory failed to explain, and (3) have at least some of its explanations (under [1] and [2]) empirically corroborated by research.[32] These criteria are reasonable, even though they are weighted in favor of the old paradigm. They entail recognition, as Kuhn has demonstrated historically, that scholars are hesi-tant to discard basic guiding principles unless something much more promising is at hand. Can the case against the realist paradigm be made on the basis of Lakatos's criteria? It cannot *at this time,* because there is no alternative paradigm or theory that can explain as much as realism did in the past. Thus, Kenneth Waltz correctly points out that students of transnationalism have to date failed to develop a "distinctive theory of their subject matter or of international relations generally."[33] This does not mean that the old paradigm wins by default. Rather, the case that must be made is that there are sufficiently serious questions about the old paradigm to devote the energy necessary to create a rival paradigm and theory that can stand the scrutiny of Lakatos's criteria sometime in the fu-ture. Critics have succeeded in making *this* case, and their arguments may be summarized as: (1) the realist paradigm has failed to account for and to predict recent political events; (2) it has failed to guide adequately empirical research; and (3) research on actors and issue areas has revealed that these two variables produce significant effects on behavior. A review of each of these points will show that the paradigm is indeed undergoing decay.

Since international relations enquiry has not been a very rigorous science, anomalies have been produced not so much by laboratory find-ings as by inexplicable and/or unexpected events. The onset of World

War I was instrumental in giving rise to the idealist paradigm, and the failure of the League of Nations, the collapse of governments in Central Europe, and the coming of World War II, brought about that paradigm's demise. While there have been no dramatic events of this sort to bring about the summary rejection of the realist paradigm, there has been a series of events that have raised gnawing doubts in various sections of the discipline. Among some scholars, America's participation in the Vietnam War was inadequately explained (as opposed to justified) by the paradigm's theory, and they sought other explanations, often from a Marxist perspective. For others, the formation of integrated units, transnational activities, the "rise" of multinational corporations, and the need for and emergence of institutionalized functional regimes in economics, the environment, food, and the sea, provided an impetus to question realist assumptions. For still others, the erosion of the Cold War and the coming of détente posed a problem of explanation to the extent that it implied that the struggle for power was ending and lasting peace was indeed in sight. Finally, there were those who saw the 1973 Arab oil embargo as the beginning of a new era in which questions of equality, resource scarcity, and race would introduce profound ideological battles that could not be explained adequately from the realist perspective. But, as with the scholarly research on assumptions, these events only raised questions. None were of such a cataclysmic nature as to produce outright rejection.

In addition to serving as a guide to contemporary history, the realist paradigm must, from a scholarly perspective, be a guide to fruitful research. In a very fundamental sense, the realist paradigm has failed to do this. Employing data-based techniques, John Vasquez demonstrated that of 7,678 hypotheses that were statistically tested between 1956 and 1970, those that accepted rather than rejected the three realist assumptions were more frequently falsified (93.1 percent vs. 83.1 percent).* In addition, he found that the proposition that had the poorest record was a central one of the realist paradigm, namely that national power is related to inter-nation cooperation/conflict (91.7 percent of these (n = 2,994) had measures of association of less than $|.34|$).[34] Finally, he demonstrated that of the

---

*John A. Vasquez, "Colouring It Morgenthau: New Evidence for An Old Thesis," *British Journal of International Studies* (October 1979), vol. 5, table 9. Falsification was operationalized as having a measure of association below .50; 7,158 hypotheses were realist and 520 were nonrealist. See also John A. Vasquez, *The Power of Paradigms*.

statistical findings that did exhibit high correlations, the realist ones tended to contain more trivial findings* than the nonrealist ones (69.5 percent to 54.2 percent; n = 157 and 24 respectively).[35] This review suggests that the realist paradigm has not produced hypotheses that are able to survive empirical tests as well as hypotheses that reject realist assumptions.

There is reason to believe, then, that the realist paradigm is failing both as a guide to politics and to political science. But do the means of overcoming this failure lie in a focus on variation in actors and issue areas? Are these phenomena as important as the critics claim? These questions must be addressed by empirical research.

THE LIMITS OF THE DOMINANT PARADIGM: AN EMPIRICAL EXPLORATION

In order to assess the contribution that nongovernmental actors and issue variety can make to understanding behavior, a data set of event interactions between American-based and West German-based actors between 1949 and 1975 was collected.† The American-West German dyad was

*Triviality was operationalized as hypotheses that correlated measures of the same thing with each other, which were highly idiographic and lacked generalizability, and which did not entail nonobvious explanations of behavior.

† The data were collected by a content analysis of the *New York Times* for 780 randomly selected dates between 1949 and 1975 as part of the *Nonstate Actor (NOSTAC) II Project.* Only reports that included both the Federal Republic of Germany (F.R.G.) and the United States as actor and/or target were coded. However, since other actors often participated in the same event (e.g., a treaty), other dyads besides F.R.G.–U.S. and U.S.–F.R.G. were included in the data set. Forty advanced political science majors at Rutgers University were employed as coders, and their work resulted in an intercoder reliability score of .893. The sample yielded 1,026 dyadic events, with each event being coded for initiator, direct target(s), and indirect target(s) (if any).

To determine the role of nonstate actors, nongovernmental as well as governmental actors were included (such as interstate organizations, corporations, interest groups, and so forth). Additionally, government actors were classified wherever possible as specific bureaucratic agencies and subagencies and, for purposes of comparison, could be readily reaggregated into unitary nation-states.

To determine the effect of issues, each event interaction was coded according to the substantive stake(s) over which the actors were contending (e.g., access to Berlin). Since a dyadic event might contain more than one stake, each stake in the event was said to produce one "issue interaction" within the dyad. Thus, one protest note between the U.S. and the F.R.G. on four separate stakes would constitute four "issue interactions" or "issue events." Each dyadic event had to be classified into at least one stake, but some were clas-

selected for two reasons. First, as large, economically advanced states with lengthy histories, the United States and the Federal Republic of Germany (F.R.G.) are the sort of units that should best reflect the realist paradigm and its assumptions. Unlike many newer, more feeble, and less stable nation-states, they possess strong and experienced governments, considerable acquaintance with theories of "national interest," and a capacity to regulate behavior within their frontiers as well as behavior crossing those frontiers. Second, in the period covered, the American-West German dyad has often been described in terms of the evolution of a basic set of Cold War issues with West Germany as a pivotal player and stake in the Cold War. Therefore, the actors and issues in the dyad should be amenable to realist analysis in terms of power and unitary actors. Indeed, previous research suggests that such issues were in fact quite "state-centric" in the Western European context.[36] The selection of this dyad, therefore, provides a stringent test of the explanatory utility of an alternative paradigm.

sified into as many as four. This task was performed by three of the principal NOSTAC investigators with an intercoder reliability of .932. In this manner the 1,026 dyadic events generated 3,399 issue events.

Such a procedure obviously increases the number of events in an analysis, and caution must be employed when using such data in certain kinds of analyses, such as making inferences about the *number* of stakes in an event (which is an artifact of the coding scheme). For the purposes of this analysis, the procedure is valid, however, since the "issue events" are employed (1) to see how behavior in a dyad changes when controlling for stake and (2) to examine the frequency of initiations of governmental and nongovernmental actors. In the first instance, the number of stakes controlled for is not going to affect the type of behavior to be found in a dyad. Also, there is nothing in the coding scheme that makes it more likely that dyadic events with nonstate actors would be coded as having more stakes. Even though that is not the case here, if it were, it could be argued that it would constitute an authentic empirical finding and not a coding artifact.

Finally, behavior in the data set was coded in terms of a fivefold classification of cooperative deed, cooperative word, participation, conflict word, and conflict deed that was derived by Stephen A. Salmore ("National Attributes and Foreign Policy: A Multivariate Analysis," Ph.D. dissertation, Princeton University, 1972) from a twenty-two-fold classification initially developed in the WEIS Project. (Charles A. McClelland and Gary Hoggard, "Conflict Patterns in the Interactions Among Nations," in James N. Rosenau, ed., *International Politics and Foreign Policy,* rev. ed. (New York: Free Press, 1969), pp. 711–24.) A discussion of the behavior classification as it has been employed in NOSTAC, and of the scoring techniques to which it has been subjected, may be found in Richard W. Mansbach and Donald E. Lampert, "The Nonstate Actor Project: An Interim Report," *International Studies Notes* (Fall 1975), 2(3):2–6. Complete coding rules for the data set are available from the authors.

The realist paradigm ignores nongovernmental entities as actors (i.e., initiators) because it does not believe, in theory, that they have sufficient power to affect global behavior in a significant fashion. This assumption has been criticized because: (1) it ignores the fact that some nongovernmental actors do have sufficient resources to participate in world politics; (2) it overlooks the possibility that nongovernmental actors may play theoretically significant roles in world affairs, so that to ignore them may result in a failure to comprehend global dynamics; and (3) to treat nation-states as unitary actors rather than as a collection of separate bureaucracies and other players may obscure some important differences in behavior as well as make assumptions of control that are not borne out.

A rank order of the data (according to frequency of behavior) reveals that nongovernmental actors can be initiators in a "big-stake game" (table 1.1). Of the thirty initiators in the subsystem, nine were nongovernmental, two of which (individual U.S. congressmen and West German political parties) ranked eleventh and twelfth.* Their appearance demonstrates that there are important domestic/international linkages that may be overlooked by focusing exclusively upon "executive" decision makers. And the mere fact that these groups appear in a subsystem that is confined to relatively few nation-states indicates that nongovernmental actors cannot be ignored on an a priori assumption that they are irrelevant because they lack power.

Of course, mere participation alone does not mean that nongovernmental behavior is theoretically significant for explaining world politics. In other words, despite their participation, it may still be possible to apprehend international relations without including these actors. Table 1.2, a

* Nongovernmental actor is operationalized as actors outside the executive. Individual legislators when acting on questions of foreign policy are considered nongovernmental, because they cannot legally (under international law) represent their states and, in practice, usually are unable to speak officially for the executive. Congress as a whole or one of its bodies should only be seen as committing the state when under the Constitution it could legally override the president, as the Senate did to Wilson on the Versailles treaty. Such situations tend to be rare; Congress tends, at best, to be only one of several influences on the executive. Indeed, the literature suggests that Congress tends to be controlled by the executive on foreign-policy matters, with the major exceptions being domestic related questions, such as tariff policy. See James A. Robinson, *Congress and Foreign Policy-Making: A Study In Legislative Influence And Initiative* (Homewood, Ill.: Dorsey, 1962), pp. 54–70; Aage R. Clausen, *How Congressmen Decide* (New York: St. Martin's Press, 1973), chapter 8, and Randall B. Ripley, *Congress: Process and Policy* (New York: Norton, 1975), pp. 282–84.

Table 1.1 Rank Order of Actors by Number of Interactions Sent[a]

Actor	N	Percent	Rank
U.S.	915	26.9	1
F.R.G.	518	15.2	2
U.K.	238	7.0	3
France	228	6.7	4
USSR	185	5.4	5
Netherlands	91	2.7	6
Belgium	84	2.5	7
Italy	82	2.4	8
Canada	73	2.1	9
Switzerland	60	1.8	10
Individual U.S. congressmen	57	1.7	11
F.R.G. political parties	55	1.6	12
F.R.G. subnational	50	1.5	13
Luxembourg	49	1.4	14
Japan	46	1.4	15
Common Market[b]	43	1.3	16
Norway	39	1.1	17 tie
Denmark	39	1.1	17 tie
Iceland	39	1.1	17 tie
Jewish groups	39	1.1	17 tie
Portugal	36	1.1	18
U.S. business	33	1.0	19
Turkey	28	0.8	20 tie
American-European Commission	28	0.8	20 tie
West Berlin	28	0.8	20 tie
Greece	27	0.8	21
G.D.R.	26	0.8	22 tie
U.S. subnational	26	0.8	22 tie
F.R.G. business	24	0.7	23
Sweden	21	0.7	24

[a] Percentages are based on 3,399 acts. Actors with less than 20 are not reported.

[b] This includes an aggregate of Council of Europe, American-British Commission, Euratom, EEC.

rank order of actors in terms of the conflict they initiate and receive, raises serious questions about the validity of this argument. Nine of the ten most conflict-prone actors in the subsystem are nonstate, and eighteen of the twenty-five nonstate actors are conflict-prone. Conversely, only eight of the twenty-six governments were involved in any conflict at all.

Because nongovernmental actors alter the distribution of conflict in the subsystem, it may be a sterile enterprise to try to explain conflict without including them. It is probably no accident that an earlier study of quantitative research in international relations found that, on the whole, the field was more successful in explaining *internation cooperation* than it was in explaining *internation conflict*. [37]

Table 1.2 Rank Order of Actors by Percent Conflict Sent and Received[a]

	Sent		
Actor	Conflict	Cooperation	(N)
Arab terrorists	100		(18)
East Berlin	100		(12)
French Parliament	100		(8)
* Czechoslovakia	100		(2)
Other individuals	100		(1)
F.R.G. police	60.0	0.0	(5)
F.R.G. subnational[b]	44.0	22.0	(50)
U.S. Congressmen[c]	43.9	35.1	(57)
F.R.G. courts	42.9	28.6	(7)
U.S. subnational[d]	38.5	26.9	(26)
* USSR	38.4	18.9	(185)
* G.D.R.	30.8	11.5	(26)
U.S. individuals	30.0	30.0	(10)
Jewish groups	25.6	35.9	(39)
* Israel	23.1	76.9	(13)
U.S. business	21.2	54.5	(33)
* U.S.	20.7	51.6	(915)
F.R.G. individuals	17.6	23.5	(17)
F.R.G. political parties	16.4	21.8	(55)
U.S. courts	14.3	42.9	(7)
* F.R.G.	10.8	57.1	(518)
F.R.G. business	8.3	33.3	(24)
West Berlin	7.1	67.9	(28)
NATO	6.3	43.8	(16)
* Switzerland	5.0	86.7	(60)
* France	4.4	59.6	(228)
* U.K.	1.7	68.5	(238)
13 nations and 17 nongovernmental actors with no conflictful acts initiated[e]	0.0	–	–

Table 1.2 (*continued*)

Direct Target	Received		
	Conflict	Cooperation	(N)
Arab terrorists	100		(5)
Intnatl. Red Cross	100		(5)
*Poland	100		(3)
*China	100		(2)
W. Berlin individuals	100		(2)
*Yugoslavia	100		(1)
F.R.G. police	100		(1)
Other European business	100		(1)
EEC	57.1	28.6	(7)
*USSR	55.9	18.2	(143)
U.S. subnational [d]	50.0	50.0	(8)
F.R.G. business	38.5	7.7	(13)
*G.D.R.	37.5	42.4	(40)
Other individuals	31.3	68.8	(16)
F.R.G. individuals	30.8	30.8	(13)
U.S. Congressmen [c]	30.8	26.9	(26)
F.R.G. political parties	30.0	20.0	(10)
NATO	27.3	54.5	(11)
U.S. individuals	23.1	46.2	(13)
F.R.G. subnational	20.0	80.0	(5)
*U.S.	14.4	49.3	(536)
*F.R.G.	9.9	65.8	(444)
*U.K.	9.1	55.9	(340)
*France	9.0	58.3	(324)
West Berlin	7.9	31.6	(38)
*Luxembourg	3.1	96.9	(65)
*Belgium	2.0	96.0	(101)
*Italy	1.9	98.1	(106)
*Japan	1.9	98.1	(53)
7 targets	0.0	100	(1)
4 targets	0.0	–	(2)
3 targets	0.0	–	(3)
3 targets	0.0	–	(6)
Western powers "big three"	0.0	71.4	(7)
F.R.G. Bundestag	0.0	6.7	(15)
*Sweden	0.0	100	(21)
*Turkey	0.0	100	(26)
*Greece	0.0	100	(28)
*Portugal	0.0	100	(38)

Table 1.2 (*continued*)

Direct Target	Received		
	Conflict	Cooperation	(N)
* Norway	0.0	100	(39)
* Denmark	0.0	100	(39)
* Iceland	0.0	100	(39)
* Switzerland	0.0	96.2	(53)
* Canada	0.0	95.1	(82)
* Netherlands	0.0	99.0	(100)

* Nation-states.

a Percentages are based on total cooperation, conflict, and participation. Row percentages do not add to 100, because participation percentages are not reported.

b These include F.R.G. media, students, labor, and education-cultural groups.

c The U.S. Senate sent out 50.0 percent conflict of 46 acts and the U.S. Congress undifferentiated in news reports sent out 0.0 percent conflict of 4 acts.

d These include U.S. educational-cultural-scientific groups, state and local governments, other miscellaneous domestic groups, labor, and the media.

e The nations with no conflict are: Austria (1), Uruguay (2), Israel (6), and the 10 nations listed at the end of the table. The nongovernmental actors with no conflict are:

U.S.-German Chamber of Commerce (1)
Japanese business (1)
Nazis (1)
F.R.G. Bundestag (1)
Western powers Big Three (2)
World Bank (2)
U.K. business (2)
F.R.G. finance (2)
Belgium business (3)
U.S. sports (4)
F.R.G. sports (4)
West Berlin (5)
EEC (9)
National Catholics (11)
U.K. parties (12)
Council of Europe (21)
American-European Commission (28)

The role of nongovernmental actors gives rise to two theoretical propositions. First, it may be the case that certain nongovernmental actors behave as "triggers" for interstate conflict, particularly over certain types of stakes. Palestinian guerrilla groups, for example, appear to have played such a role. This proposition suggests that not only may nongovernmental actors be responsible for much of the general conflict in the subsystem, but also, indirectly, for interstate conflict. Second, comparison of the nongovernmental actors that engage in conflict with those that do not, reveals that actor type and stakes may be significant variables for explaining nongovernmental conflict. For example, intergovernmental organizations like the EEC and NATO, the surrogates of nation-states in this context, tend to be less conflict-prone than subnational or transnational groups. Within the latter categories, groups based in the U.S. and F.R.G., the major Cold War disputants in this region, tend to be more conflictive than similar groups based in states that are less involved in the Cold War. The latter phenomenon suggests that stake may be a significant variable in explaining the behavior of conflict-prone nongovernmental actors. For example, nongovernmental conflict in the subsystem was related to four issues: Cold War German disputes, Nazis and Jews, the Middle East, and routine civil strife (police, courts, etc.). What probably tied these issues together is that they are all highly salient to the nongovernmental groups that act on them.

Finally, the realist map ignores bureaucratic actors by aggregating them into their respective national governments. Recent work on bureaucratic politics reveals that bureaucracies have different interests from each other and consequently behave differently. The findings in table 1.3 tend to support this hypothesis. Since there are significant deviations from the conflict score of specific agencies of a government and the aggregate score for the national government as a whole, the result of not looking at individual agencies is that the overall picture provided of a nation's behavior is misleading. For example, if aggregate actors are taken alone, then the United States was the most conflict-prone nation-state in the data set, with a score of 20.7 percent conflict. A breakdown of the data, however, shows that U.S. bureaucracies accounted for most of this conflict and that the American central decision maker was relatively nonconflictive with a score of 11.6 percent. The same was true of the United Kingdom. For the Federal Republic and France, the exact opposite was the case. This finding suggests that event data analysis of unitary actors may shield not only the sources of conflict but its meaning and impact as well, since conflictive statements by a central decision maker must be regarded as more significant than those of lower level bureaucrats. Lastly, while the discrepancy between the bureaucracies and the American central decision maker cannot be stipulated as undermining a president's policy, the

Table 1.3 Bureaucratic Conflict and Action[a]

Actor	Percent Conflict	Percent Cooperation	(N)
U.S. Government	20.7	51.6	(915)
Dept. of Agriculture	100		(2)
Dept. of Commerce	57.1	28.6	(7)
propaganda radio	50.0	0.0	(4)
Intelligence	50.0	0.0	(2)
Dept. of Defense	33.8	33.8	(77)
High Commissioner	27.1	37.1	(70)
Dept. of State	24.1	45.7	(352)
undifferentiated	15.5	62.5	(200)
central decision maker[b]	11.6	58.9	(146)
Dept. of Treasury[c]	1.8	83.6	(55)
F.R.G. Government	10.8	57.1	(518)
undifferentiated	17.6	57.6	(170)
central decision maker	2.7	53.8	(173)
Finance Ministry	7.4	70.4	(54)
Defense and Intelligence	0.0	77.3	(22)
Foreign Ministry	0.0	50.5	(99)
France Government	4.4	59.6	(228)
central decision maker	16.7	75.0	(12)
undifferentiated	13.1	49.2	(61)
Defense	0.0	0.0	(3)
other executive agencies	0.0	0.0	(8)
Finance Ministry	0.0	100	(24)
Foreign Ministry	0.0	60.8	(120)
United Kingdom Government	1.7	68.5	(238)
undifferentiated	3.8	70.0	(80)
Foreign Ministry	0.8	63.2	(125)
Defense	0.0	0.0	(2)
central decision maker	0.0	57.1	(7)
Exchequer[c]	0.0	100	(24)

[a] All percentages are based on 2,864 acts. While participatory acts are not reported they are included in the computation of percentages.

Nongovernmental targets (232 acts) have not been reported; hence the target total does not equal the actor total. This table is based on all actors (nations and others) and includes 3,399 cases.

[b] This includes "White House staff" and U.S. Executive.

[c] These also include the national bank, e.g., U.S. Federal Reserve.

data is not inconsistent with such a hypothesis, and it merits further investigation. The point here, of course, is that such a "clue" would not turn up if discrete bureaucracies were not examined.

In addition to ignoring the diversity of actors, the realist paradigm ignores *issue* as a significant variable. An examination of the role that issues play in American-West German relations shows that several important distortions result from this omission. If specific stakes or types of stakes are not significant variables, then it would be expected that there would be little correlation between them and cooperation/conflict. This is not the case. Seventy-eight specific stakes were identified in the data, and a correlation between them and a fivefold measure of conflict/cooperation produced an eta of 0.635.* This is quite high considering that the stakes had not been grouped into a theoretically significant typology. If stakes were clustered in such a manner, or if variables that tap various issue characteristics (such as salience) were employed as predictors, an even higher correlation might be expected. This simple correlation suggests that behavior does vary by stake and that ignoring the diversity of stakes leads to important distortions when drawing a map of global behavior. The extent to which behavioral variation occurs by issue is revealed in table 1.4. The possibilities for distortion can be appreciated by comparing the conflict scores for individual issues with the aggregate conflict score for the entire subsystem.

The implications of such distortion for describing cooperation/conflict, not to mention explaining it, are made clear when a map is drawn of dyadic conflict between nation-states, controlling for stake. The result is that the picture of the world is, in Yeats' words, "All changed, changed utterly." Tables 1.5 and 1.6 reflect this analysis for the U.S.-F.R.G., F.R.G.-U.S., U.S.-USSR, and USSR-U.S.† The U.S.-F.R.G., F.R.G.-U.S. dyads, when treated as aggregates, have respective scores of 13.9 percent conflict and 14.6 percent conflict. Controlling for issue, however, reveals that the level of conflict between these two actors varied considerably from a high of 66.7 percent conflict (U.S.-F.R.G. on Nazi-related

---

*The use of eta assumes that the dependant variable is interval and that there is a nonlinear relationship. Employing a more conservative assumption, that all the variables were nominal, yields a lambda asymmetric of 0.46. All calculations were based on 3,399 cases.

†Only two dyads were selected because of limitations of space. These two were chosen because they were representative of conflict between and within blocs.

Table 1.4 Rank Order of Top Fifteen Stakes by Conflict[a]

Issue	Percent Conflict	Percent Cooperation	(N)
All (aggregate of seventy-eight issues)	14.3	60.0	(3,399)
World War II conference agreements	39.0	28.8	(82)
Access to Berlin	32.6	25.8	(89)
Middle East questions	32.0	62.1	(103)
F.R.G. integration into NATO	23.3	52.4	(103)
East-West strategic balance	22.5	25.4	(71)
Other	15.8	52.6	(76)
German unification	14.6	20.7	(198)
Western commitment to Berlin	11.4	33.6	(149)
U.S. commitment to Western Europe	11.0	35.6	(73)
European Defense Community (EDC)	7.1	86.4	(140)
International monetary questions	2.6	89.9	(228)
Commodities and energy questions	2.0	93.6	(202)
Troop levels and NATO organizational questions	1.9	92.8	(473)
World trade questions	0.8	99.2	(121)
Third World questions	0.0	98.3	(117)

[a] Percentages are based on all 3,399 cases.

questions) to a low of 0.0 percent (U.S.-F.R.G. on West German entry and integration in NATO). In addition, the distribution of conflict is considerably more asymmetrical than the aggregate score would indicate; i.e., while both sides behaved hostilely toward the other 14 percent of the time, this "symmetry" holds only in the aggregate and not for specific stakes.*

When the U.S.-USSR and USSR-U.S. dyads are treated as aggregates (see table 1.6), they have respective scores of 63.6 percent and 42.9 percent conflict. Again, when controlling for stake, the level of conflict varied dramatically from a high of 85.7 percent conflict (U.S.-USSR on Soviet threat to West Germany) to a low of 0.0 percent (USSR-U.S. on

*For example, the U.S. was conflict-prone toward the Federal Republic on matters relating to the EDC which would have provided for the rearmament of Germany, but the Federal Republic was predictably cooperative. Conversely, on the question of German integration into NATO, which the U.S. vigorously supported, the U.S. was cooperative towards the Federal Republic while the latter was relatively conflict-prone, obviously not finding the NATO formula an ideal one.

Table 1.5 American and West German Conflict by Stake[a]

U.S.-F.R.G.		F.R.G.-U.S.		
Percent Conflict	(N)	Percent Conflict	(N)	Stake
13.9	(251)	14.6	(212)	Aggregate total (no control)
20.0	(10)	0.0	(3)	EDC
0.0	(14)	21.4	(14)	F.R.G. integration into NATO
10.0	(10)	18.8	(16)	Troop levels and NATO organizational questions
33.3	(3)	37.5	(8)	Cost sharing and balance of payments
0.0	(7)	14.3	(7)	NATO strategy questions
0.0	(7)	25.0	(4)	East-West strategic balance
0.0	(13)	0.0	(6)	West commitment to Berlin
8.3	(12)	0.0	(8)	German unification
0.0	(10)	0.0	(3)	U.S. military aid to F.R.G.
33.3	(6)	0.0	(1)	U.S. economic aid to F.R.G.
40.0	(5)	66.7	(3)	U.S.-European trade
–	–	28.6	(7)	Middle East
66.7	(6)	50.0	(1)	Nazi-related questions
0.0	(2)	28.6	(7)	Arms control: nuclear weapons
50.0	(2)	20.0	(5)	Arms control: conventional weapons
8.3	(12)	20.0	(20)	International monetary questions
33.3	(3)	20.0	(5)	Independent France
14.3	(14)	0.0	(4)	Commodities and energy questions
28.6	(14)	0.0	(3)	F.R.G. economic reconstruction
20.0	(5)	0.0	(2)	USSR threat to F.R.G.
0.0	(7)	22.2	(9)	Western commitment to F.R.G.
6.7	(15)	11.1	(9)	Routine diplomatic interaction
28.6	(7)	18.2	(11)	German nationalism
20.0	(5)	0.0	(9)	U.S. commitment to Western Europe

[a]Only issues with five or more interactions on either the U.S.-F.R.G. or F.R.G.-U.S. dyad are reported. Percentages, however, are based on all 3,399 cases.

Western commitment to Berlin). Unlike the U.S.-F.R.G. analysis, however, there is not as much distortion in the aggregate asymmetrical pattern of conflict. Except for one issue, World War II conference agreements, the U.S. consistently "overreacted" to the Soviet Union. Nevertheless, controlling for issue is important even here, because it makes clear that American-West German behavior was subject to crosscutting pressures, whereas American-Soviet behavior was not. Since a number of scholars

Table 1.6 American and Soviet Conflict by Stake[a]

U.S.-USSR		USSR-U.S.		
Percent Conflict	(N)	Percent Conflict	(N)	Stake
63.6	(107)	42.9	(63)	Aggregate total (no control)
40.0	(5)	25.0	(4)	East-West strategic balance
77.8	(18)	57.1	(7)	Access to Berlin
66.7	(15)	0.0	(1)	Western commitment to Berlin
75.0	(4)	16.7	(6)	All-German peace treaty
50.0	(18)	25.0	(12)	German unification
100	(1)	20.0	(5)	Arms control (conventional weapons)
85.7	(7)	50.0	(2)	USSR threat to West Germany
81.8	(11)	83.3	(6)	World War II conference agreements

[a] Only stakes with five or more interactions on either the U.S.-USSR or USSR-U.S. dyad are reported. Percentages however are based on all 3,399 cases.

have argued that crosscutting is related to conflict, the omission could be of theoretical significance. Obviously, as these brief examples illustrate, the failure to control for issue blurs the sources of conflict within dyads, and thereby encourages the scholar to ignore possible issue-related variables that might predict conflict patterns.

The analysis presented to this point strongly suggests that the neglect of actor and issue variation and diversity within the realist paradigm leads to distortions that not only make that paradigm something less than complete, but also theoretically unsatisfactory. An alternative paradigm will be scientifically promising only if it can offer variables that will be more fruitful than those encountered in the power politics paradigm in explaining global behavior. While a demonstration of this sort would require a number of pieces of research, at this point it is possible to show the promise of an alternative approach by two simple tests. If the data inclusion rules are broadened to incorporate bureaucratic and nongovernmental actors, as well as the various stakes within global politics, then it would be expected that various actor and stake types would, at minimum, predict cooperation/conflict. To test this possibility, two sets of analyses were attempted. The first tested the relative potency of actor variables by correlating actor with cooperation/conflict controlling for issue, and the second tested the relative potency of stake variables by correlating stake with cooperation/conflict controlling for actor.

Both tests produced encouraging results. When controlling for stake, eta ranged from |.09| to |1.00| with a median correlation of |.748.| Furthermore, most of the weak correlations were those with very few cases. Selecting only issues that accounted for 2 percent or more of the cases, the range was reduced to |.453| to |1.00| with a median eta of |.750|. Controlling for actors, eta ranged from |.112| to |1.00| with a median eta of |.809|. Similarly, selecting only actors that initiated 2 percent or more of the cases, the range was reduced to |.594| to |1.00| with a median eta of |.750|. These findings demonstrate that the two control variables may be potent predictors of cooperation/conflict.

Criticism of the dominant paradigm, then, has taken its toll and demonstrated that an alternative paradigm that avoids the pitfalls of the three fundamental assumptions of realism may provide a better guide to enquiry. However, an alternative paradigm must consist of something more than "serious questions" and isolated challenges to individual assumptions. Critics must make explicit an alternative theory as great in scope and explanatory power and as rich in policy implications as the power politics theories. Otherwise, little guidance will be afforded scholars or practitioners. The pressing need in the field is not for further criticism but for new theory. The purpose of this book is to elucidate such a theory.

The agenda of interstate relationships consists of multiple issues that are not arranged in a clear or consistent hierarchy. This absence of hierarchy among issues means, among other things, that military security does not consistently dominate the agenda.
—Keohane and Nye [1]

CHAPTER TWO

FROM THE ISSUE OF POWER TO THE POWER OF ISSUES

THE FINDINGS presented in the previous chapter suggest that a new paradigm and a new theory elaborated from it may be necessary to resolve some of the persistent questions that have been raised by critics of the dominant paradigm. For scholars to reconstruct their conceptual and theoretical universe, they must return to fundamentals. And, since the realist definition of politics as a struggle for power has been found wanting a good place to begin the search is with an alternative definition of politics. One widely accepted alternative, other than Marx's,* is David Easton's idea of politics as the "authoritative allocation of valued things." [2] Insufficient attention has been paid to the extent to which the realist and Eastonian definitions clash in terms of their scholarly and prescriptive implications. Yet definitions are critical, for the promise of any stipulative definition is not that it is "true" or even "correct," but that, if it is

Our thanks to Marie T. Henehan, whose ideas and work greatly contributed to the first three sections of this chapter.

* The Marxist paradigm is the major alternative to realism in contemporary thought. See Tony Thorndike, "The Revolutionary Approach: The Marxist Perspective," in Trevor Taylor, ed., *Approaches and Theory in International Relations* (New York: Longman, 1978), pp. 54–99.

adopted, it will clarify what has previously been confusing and assist in reconstructing what has previously been misunderstood. An uncongenial starting definition will produce a flawed paradigm. Research directed by that paradigm will then be misguided, since the paradigm itself points to peripheral or erroneous phenomena or leads to the wrong questions being asked.

The Eastonian definition moves the analysis of global politics away from conceptions of power and security and toward the assumption that demands for value satisfaction through global decision making must be at the heart of any theory, and must be the central process that awaits explanation. As Easton expresses it: "Demands may be conceived as a central variable for the simple fact that without them, there would literally be no occasion to undertake the making of binding decisions for a society."[3] Indeed, there would be few occasions to make decisions of any kind. For theorists of global politics, Easton's definition reorients attention away from questions of cooperation/conflict and power struggles and toward still more basic questions of how dissatisfaction is generated and the processes that respond to it, including the creation of new actors and the disappearance of old ones. The phenomena of conflict and power do not disappear altogether but are relegated to a place *within* a theory of allocation, expressing variations in the relations of actors as they participate in the decision-making process.

If the Eastonian definition is assumed as the basis for a new conceptualization, then global political behavior becomes the process of allocating values in an authoritative fashion (though the notion of "authority" and the manner in which it is operationalized undergo subtle changes). Instead of global politics being conceived of as a single unceasing contest among a set cast of actors which determines the ebb and flow of a single value (power)—as in the case of realism—global society is conceptualized as the scene of many different decision games, characterized by numerous and changing casts of players, involving different issues and different allocation mechanisms.[4] Few of these games are centralized or hierarchical (though there are exceptions), and most decisions are reached (if at all) in the absence of formal "government."

The source of authority in global politics is, of course, not that of legislation or statute, as is the case with centralized societies. It is more elusive (as is international law itself), and it can be found largely in precedents and habits of compliance created and sustained by expediency and common need. It is not simply that decisions are reached in the global arena, but that some of them at least are accepted by key actors as proper (even though they may have initially been imposed by force). If active consent of the governed is demanded as a criterion of legitimacy, most contemporary governments and their decisions would have to be regarded as illegitimate.

Easton stipulates that decisions flow *from* an authoritative source, whereas the process described here is one of reaching decisions which *are then in search of authority;* and, though few acquire it, it is also the case that far fewer "domestic" decisions are initially regarded as authoritative than Easton implies. Despite decentralization a decision in global politics may become authoritative if it is regarded as legitimate by key actors who willingly obey it and carry it out.

Politics from this perspective consists not so much of a struggle for power, but of contention over issues. If the previous chapter raised questions about the utility of the power approach, this chapter seeks to demonstrate the theoretical power of issues as an explanatory variable. Only once this is accomplished will it make sense to switch the focus of the field from *power* to *issues*.

THE NATURE OF ISSUES

Within the literature, there are several typologies and analytical discussions of issues that offer the promise of providing the elements of a new theory of the role of issues in politics. The seminal work on the impact of issues is James Rosenau's "pretheory" of foreign policy, which was written precisely because "foreign policy analysis lacks comprehensive systems of testable generalizations that treat societies as actors which produce external responses."[5] Although Rosenau was not the first scholar to suggest that global behavior varies by issue, he was among the first to realize that this insight, taken directly from the literature in American politics, would avail little unless a deductive typology of issues was developed, one which clearly delineated the theoretically significant characteristics of issues. His preliminary typology of four issue areas was constructed "from an impression that the motives, actions, and interactions of political actors are crucially related to the degree of tangibility of both the values which have to be allocated and the means which have to be employed to effect allocation."[6] The four types he identified are "status area" (intangible ends/intangible means), "human resources area" (intangible ends/tangible means), "territorial area" (tangible ends/intangible means), and "nonhuman resources area" (tangible ends/tangible means).[7]

Rosenau reasoned that the more tangible were the *means* employed in interaction, the clearer the costs would be in allocation, and hence the more strongly motivated and persistently active the participant actors. And, as ends became less tangible, more actors would perceive themselves as effected and become involved because of the lack of clarity as to what is at stake. The lack of clarity presumably encourages actors to "read in" their own interests. Finally, "the presumption was made that the greater the tangibility of both the *ends* and *means* involved in an allocative process, the more the tendency to bargain among the affected actors would increase."[8] Rosenau saw the tangibility of issues as importantly related to three key behavioral variables—actors' strength of motivation and persistence of action, the number of actors involved, and the readiness of actors to bargain. Thus, "the status area, being composed of both intangible ends and means, is likely to evoke more uncompromising political behavior on the part of more actors than any of the other three; on the other hand, the nonhuman resources area, being composed of both tangible ends and means, is likely to evoke more bargaining on the part of fewer actors than any of the other areas."[9]

A second influential issue typology is that of Theodore J. Lowi. Attempting to resolve the debate in American politics as to whether the system can be best conceptualized as an elitist, pluralist, or decentralized-logrolling process, Lowi suggested that all three processes were present in varying degrees, depending upon the type of issue under contention. Initially, Lowi described three types of issues—distributive, regulatory, and redistributive.[10] Lowi initially conceived of foreign policy as a separate fourth issue area but later asserted that "foreign policy issues" could be distributive, regulatory, or a separate elitist area in response to a crisis or a noncrisis routine situation that involved no domestic resources. With the possible exception of monetary devaluation, Lowi did not think that foreign-policy issues could be redistributive.[11]

Lowi argues that each issue area will develop its own "political structure, political process, elites, and group relations."[12] Crisis decisions and noncrisis decisions that do not involve the expenditure of domestic resources, he declared, will be elitist; conflict will be absent, and the process will lack the participation of interest groups or the general public. The elitist pattern in crises is the product of a need to make rapid decisions in secrecy under conditions of stress that are conducive to consensual behavior.[13] Under these conditions, it is not possible for domestic interests to mobilize and impinge upon the decision. At the other end of the spectrum of elitist decisions are noncrisis issues that involve little or no expenditure of domestic resources, such as the routine and noncontroversial recognition of governments. According to Lowi, an elitist pattern is present in these cases, because they do not affect the interests of domestic groups.

Regulatory issues are those which involve the allocation of a privilege by officials to some elements of society. The essence of a regulatory issue is that the number of privileges that can be distributed is limited, so that there are identifiable winners and losers. Such decisions must be made by the application of a general rule and according to the broader standards of law.[14] Regulatory issues, like tariffs, involve the competition of domestic groups for governmental favors and hence generate conflict in a pluralist pattern. Distributive issues differ from regulatory ones principally because the stakes at issue can be sufficiently disaggregated so that all contenders may enjoy some profit. Any individual or group with the "power" to frustrate a decision can be bought off by being given a "piece of the action." For this reason, distributive issues are said to be characterized by logrolling and minimal conflict and lack identifiable losers.*

William Zimmerman reconstructed Lowi's classification scheme and elaborated its theoretical rationale.[15] In particular, he sought to extend Lowi's suggestion that crisis and routine issues would be characterized by elitism by combining it with Arnold Wolfers' earlier distinction between

---

* Redistributive issues, which Lowi believes are uncharacteristic of foreign policy, are similar to regulatory issues in that there are identifiable winners and losers. However, the potential impact of redistributive issues is greater, because they may lead to the deprivation of one major sector of society in an effort to satisfy another. In the presence of such expectations, conflict will become intense.

the "pole of power" and the "pole of indifference." [16] Crisis, for Wolfers, involves a situation "in which both the external and internal factors—a dire and unmistakable threat to national survival, plus the fear it engendered among those responsible for state action—would place statesmen under the influence of almost irresistible compulsion" to behave according to the dictates of power politics. [17] But, argued Wolfers, "a similar degree of conformity may be found where danger and compulsion are at a minimum," at the pole of indifference. [18] Where only minor values are involved, "governments usually find it expedient to act according to established rules, since their interest in seeing others do likewise exceeds their interest in winning an occasional and minor advantage." [19] Like Wolfers, Zimmerman argued that both types of issues tended to produce a unitary, rational decision-making process that is influenced principally by external rather than internal factors. [20] According to Zimmerman, nineteenth-century global politics was largely confined to a bimodal distribution of issues at these two poles, but this has changed during the twentieth century so that issues increasingly impinge upon the values and interests of important domestic groups, though what these values are, Zimmerman does not specify. [21] If he is correct, the nature of the policy process becomes a critical factor, and Lowi's distinction among distributive, regulatory, and redistributive issues acquires relevance for comprehending foreign-policy behavior.

In order to combine the insights of Lowi and Wolfers, Zimmerman posited that both tangibility *and* domestic impact produce theoretically significant distinctions among issues. This yields the fivefold classification of issues depicted in figure 2.1. Although similar to Lowi's original scheme, Zimmerman's reformulation makes two contributions to issue-area theory.

First, unlike Lowi, Zimmerman argues persuasively that not only do redistributive foreign-policy issues exist, but that they are among the most important issues that affect domestic life (e.g., limited war). In such cases, he argues, part of society is deprived while others profit. The extent to which the domestic impact of a foreign-policy issue is symmetrical or asymmetrical becomes, therefore, an important variable affecting behavior. Second, like Rosenau, Zimmerman sees tangibility as a major issue characteristic. However, any classification based on tangibility is

Figure 2.1 Zimmerman's Issue Typology

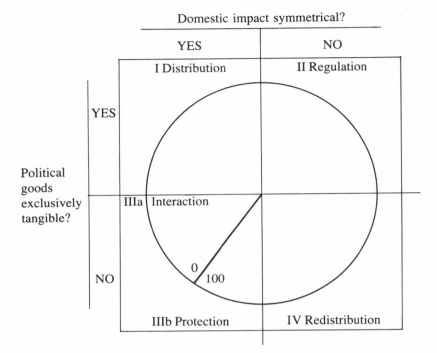

Source: William Zimmerman, ''Issue Area and Foreign-Policy Process.''
American Political Science Review (December 1973), 67(4): 1208.

not easily made mutually exclusive, because most issues reflect a mix of
tangible and intangible means and ends, and can only be distinguished by
whether they are exclusively tangible or not.

Zimmerman's integration of domestic impact and tangibility reinforced
the theoretical foundation of Lowi's typology, because it elucidated more
clearly the causal factors that may lie behind the proposed types of issues.
Thus, though Zimmerman does not elaborate the causal dynamics, it
would be expected that issues are distributive because the political goods
are exclusively tangible and can be divided symmetrically. The political
goods that comprise regulatory issues, while tangible, can only be di-

vided asymmetrically. Similarly, the political goods that underlie redistributive issues can only be divided asymmetrically, and such issues, unlike those that are distributive or regulatory, also include intangible goods like "status." Finally, protection and interaction issues entail political goods that have a symmetrical impact, because they either threaten survival of the collective or involve no internal resources, and these goods are not easily divided because they include such intangibles as "security."

In addition to the efforts of Rosenau, Lowi, and Zimmerman to construct issue areas and "arenas of power" on the bases of tangibility and domestic impact, attempts have been made to classify issues according to their substantive focus. Those attempts emerge from the suggestion, made by Rosenau among others, that issues could be differentiated according to the cluster of values they entail. In fact, Rosenau formally defined an issue area as "(1) a cluster of values, the allocation or potential allocation of which (2) leads the affected or potentially affected actors to differ so greatly over (a) the way in which the values should be allocated or (b) the horizontal levels at which the allocations should be authorized that (3) they engage in distinctive behavior designed to mobilize support for the attainment of their particular values."[22] The reasoning underlying this definition was presented by Robert Dahl, who argued that the resources (power) relevant to the allocation of an issue will vary in part as a function of the values being allocated.[23]

Although Rosenau does not provide a formal typology based on the values being allocated, others have sought to do so. Among the earliest and best known of such efforts was that of Michael Brecher and his colleagues.[24] They classified issues into four types: military-security, political-diplomatic, economic development, and cultural-status. The key problem with such a typology, however, is that the categories are neither mutually exclusive nor logically exhaustive. Most troublesome, perhaps, is the category of political-diplomatic if only because military or economic issues can also be highly political. The only way in which the latter are made distinct is to exclude in arbitrary fashion from the political area "violence, material resources and cultural and status relations."[25] In light of such exclusions, the political category becomes no more than a residual or miscellaneous cell. Although this technically permits the typology to meet the criteria of exclusiveness and exhaustiveness, it does so at the cost of identifying an artificial fourth category, the content of which is undefined.

AN EMPIRICAL ANALYSIS OF ISSUE TYPOLOGIES

While the above typologies are familiar in the discipline, there have been few efforts to test them empirically. Even though Rosenau's pretheory has generated a good deal of empirical research, particularly the Inter-University Comparative Foreign Policy project,[26] the issue-area concept has not received adequate attention.[27] One exception to this is a study by Thomas Brewer of American policy toward West European integration and the Atlantic Alliance.[28] Although Brewer was concerned primarily with issue area as a control variable in explaining foreign-policy decision making and not with comparing and evaluating the various typologies, his study provides a focus to begin an assessment of the scientific utility of the concept.

Brewer tested the utility of the Rosenau and Lowi typologies in predicting four dependent-variable clusters—domestic participation in foreign policy-making, intellectual and political activity in the policy-making process, and external behavior toward other actors.* On the whole, he found that Charles Hermann's situational variables (threat, time, and surprise)[29] and contextual variables, such as prior involvement and the existence of concurrent issues, are more potent predictors than the issue typologies. Nevertheless, the findings on the issue variables do provide some interesting results. Brewer's test of Rosenau's typology found the tangibility of an issue affected neither the level nor scope of domestic group participation in foreign policy-making.† Brewer also found that the two issue types do not produce different performances in intellective tasks

---

* Brewer's data base consisted of 65 cases involving threats to "American objectives concerning European integration or the Atlantic Alliance during 1949–1968." Thomas L. Brewer, "Issue and Context Variation in Foreign Policy," *Journal of Conflict Resolution* (March 1973), 17(1):89.

† Brewer operationalized level of participation as the number of acts of: executive, congressional, other political, business-labor, academic, communications, and executive agency groups; whereas, scope of participation was measured by how many different types of elites were involved. Since the two variables were highly correlated, only data on level of participation were reported.

(e.g., attention to U.S. objectives and capabilities, other nations' objectives and capabilities, feedback), nor do they produce differences in levels of conflict among domestic participants. It should be made clear, however, that these results do not disconfirm any of Rosenau's hypotheses, since he only claimed that external foreign-policy behavior would vary by type of issue. For this reason, Brewer's analysis of output behavior is of particular interest. The results here, however, were not very encouraging; only one hypothesis involving output behavior was modestly supported by the research. Brewer found a slight relationship (.35) between the Rosenau issue types and the number of actions they trigger. The other findings included the relationship between the issues and whether "any action" was taken (.24); whether the action was "nonsupportive" (.24), "verbal" (.12), "comments" (.09), "supportive" (.08), and whether the action involved "consultations" (.09).[30]

An important caveat must be kept in mind when interpreting these test results; Brewer identified only two out of the four Rosenau issue areas in his data set—status and nonhuman resources. Both of these are pure types, with status characterized by intangible ends and means, and nonhuman resources characterized by tangible ends and means. The absence of the mixed cases (territory and human resources) limits the general applicability of the test. In addition, he appears to have had some difficulty in classifying issues on the basis of tangibility, so that the "names" of the issue were employed as the coding rules.[31]

Brewer's tests of the Lowi typology were confined to three issue types—crisis or crisislike issues, distributive issues, and regulative issues—since Brewer apparently accepted Lowi's claim that there are no redistributive foreign policy matters. On the whole, Brewer found stronger measures of association for the Lowi than for the Rosenau typology, but almost all associations are less than $|.30|$. There are only weak relationships between the three issue types and the level and scope of domestic elites, with the strongest associations being .25 (all types of participants), .27 (executive actors), .25 (other political), and .28 (business-labor groups). Nor did Brewer discover strong relationships between the three issues and intellectual or political activity. This last finding explicitly undermines Lowi's contention that issue areas are a major determinant of domestic conflict, since political activity was operationalized as the amount of conflict and consensus among participants. Finally, Brewer uncovered only a weak relationship between Lowi's issues and the nature of external behavior, but on the whole these were slightly superior to the Rosenau issue types with associations of .31 (number of actions), .28 (verbal), .28 (supportive), .26 (comments), .25 (nonsupportive), and .20 (consultations).[32]

Brewer's investigation of issue areas, though highly suggestive, is hardly conclusive. His is a single test with a narrow data base of sixty-five cases that deal only with European integration and the Atlantic Alliance. Moreover, only two of Rosenau's issue areas were identified, so that Brewer's work must be regarded as only a partial investigation of that typology. There must be a number of tests based on a variety of data before one have confidence in his conclusions. The Brewer test is only a first step.

In order to shed more light on this question, the data described in the previous chapter were recoded to classify the stakes according to the typologies of Rosenau, Lowi-Zimmerman, and Brecher et al. Three tests were conducted. The first entailed a comparison of the ability of the three typologies to predict cooperation/conflict. The second entailed an investigation of whether actor attributes are more potent predictors of cooperation/conflict than issue variables.* The third involved examining the ability of the most potent issue typology to predict dependent variables other than cooperation/conflict in an attempt to delineate other issue-related

* For a discussion of the coding rules for the issue typologies, reliability tests, and a listing of the issue data, see John A. Vasquez and Marie T. Henehan, "Issue Area as a Variable in the Study of Foreign Policy Behavior: A Quantitative Test of Alternative Typologies," paper delivered to the annual meeting of the Mid-West Political Science Association, 1979. The data on issue area were derived by taking the NOSTAC II data, which coded events on the basis of the stakes over which actors were contending, and classifying the events' "issue" stakes into the broader issue areas of Brecher et al., Lowi, Rosenau, et al. For example, in the NOSTAC II data, the stake of "Access to Berlin" generated a number of events. That stake and all the events associated with it would be classified in the typology of Brecher et al. as "military-security." To evaluate the Brecher et al. typology the 3,399 events were classified on the basis of their cooperation/conflict traits and on the basis of the inclusion of their "issue" stakes into the four issue-area traits of Brecher et al. The issue-area traits of the events were then cross-tabulated with the cooperation/conflict traits of the events to see if the issue areas could discriminate successfully the cooperation/conflict traits the events exhibited. The cooperation/conflict data are compatible with Brewer's, in that he employed World Events Interaction Survey (WEIS) categories, and this set employed a scheme derived from the WEIS categories.

characteristics that might act as intervening variables in explaining cooperation/conflict among actors.

The first set of findings is reported in table 2.1. Of the three typologies, Rosenau's fared best. It was operationalized in two different ways—tangibility of ends and means and the four substantive issue "names."* The first produced a gamma of −.483 with cooperation/conflict as the dependent variable, and the second an eta of .415.† It ap-

Table 2.1 Issue-Area Typologies by Cooperation/Conflict

Typology	Gamma*	Eta*	(N)
Rosenau—tangibility	−.483	.402	(3,251)
Rosenau—substantive categories	−.249	.415	(3,235)
Lowi-Zimmerman	.227	.161	(3,230)
Brecher		.300	(3,315)

*(p < .05, X^2)

peared that the more tangible the issue, the less conflict it produced. The substantive typology of Brecher et al. was considerably less potent, producing an eta of only .300, and the least potent was the Lowi-Zimmerman typology with a gamma of .227. Of the three, the Rosenau typology is the most promising in explaining external cooperation/conflict, and it appears to be the dimension of tangibility that is theoretically significant rather than the four substantive "names." Further exploration suggested that tangibility of means is more important than tangibility of ends.‡

* As Brewer found, it was difficult to code tangibility directly, because there seemed to be a mix of tangible–intangible characteristics in most goals and means. To solve this problem, the predominant characteristic was chosen as the basis for making coding decisions. In addition, the more easily identifiable issue names were coded. The correlation between the two different measures was low, lambda = .356, indicating that Rosenau was really tapping two different theoretical aspects of issues.

† Gamma is appropriate to test the ordinality of tangibility, whereas eta is more suitable to test the nominal substantive categories. Treating the first (tangibility) classification as nominal produces an eta of .402.

‡ This appears to be a function of the fact that territorial issues are more important than human resources issues. When tangibility is ordered with ends as the most important, gamma is −.483; whereas, when the opposite is assumed, gamma drops to −.477. The same procedure for the issue-names typology produced respective gammas of −.249 and −.071.

Such bivariate findings reopen some significant questions about the typologies that were tested. First, tangibility may indeed be a theoretically important characteristic in explaining interstate behavior. Second, the attempts to develop substantive foci, such as that of Brecher et al., seem less promising both conceptually and empirically. Third, the work of Lowi and Zimmerman is simply too broad and imprecise to generate explanations of interstate behavior. Furthermore, its utility varies depending upon the nation-state in question. But it may be useful for explaining at least part of the dynamics of domestic participation and conflict.*

Despite the contributions of existing issue typologies, it is clear that additional variables require investigation, including other issue characteristics, in order to explain behavior in a more satisfying fashion.† One obvious set of variables includes dyadic actor characteristics of the sort identified by R. J. Rummel.[33] In order to determine where such dyadic characteristics are more potent than issue-area variables, the data were analyzed to control first for dyad and then for issue area.‡ The findings are consistent with those presented in chapter 1, revealing that actor and issue variables are both important, but in these findings it becomes clearer under what conditions these various characteristics are more potent.

If issue were more significant than dyad, it would be expected that the association between dyad and cooperation/conflict would be low when controlling for issue. A low correlation would mean that in that issue area all dyads were behaving in the same manner. Rosenau, for example, would argue that issues with tangible means and ends will produce cooperative behavior regardless of dyad. If that is not the case, some dyads will behave cooperatively whereas others will not, and the correlation between dyad and cooperation/conflict would be high. Such clear results, however, are only produced when one of the relationships is spurious. If

*Preliminary findings indicate that it does better when it tries to predict these dependent variables. With the exception of distributive issues for the U.S., regulatory and protective-interaction issues for the U.S. and the Federal Republic and distributive issues for the F.R.G., other dyads exhibit conflict levels that correspond to Lowi's propositions. The findings on domestic participation are more mixed.

†It was found that the correlation (eta) between the individual stakes at issue (prior to their being grouped into typologies) and cooperation/conflict is .636, a result which suggests that there are other characteristics of these issues that, if identified, would produce stronger correlations than the variables isolated by the four typologies.

‡Eight dyads were selected for analysis—U.S.–F.R.G., F.R.G.–U.S., U.S.-USSR, USSR-U.S., U.S.-U.K., U.K.-U.S., U.S.-France and France-U.S.

both variables are significant, then for some dyads the correlation would be high, and for others it would be low when controlling for dyad. In this manner, the specific mix of the two variables can be identified, and relative potency of each weighed.

Table 2.2 reports the results for each typology and shows, with few exceptions, that dyadic characteristics are more important than issues in predicting American-Soviet and American–West German behavior, but that issue variables are more important in predicting American-British and American-French behavior. This may imply that the influence of issue variation is greater in the case of older and more stable relationships, such as those among the longtime Western allies, than in the case of newer and more tentative relationships. These differences notwithstanding, controlling for issue reveals that issues characterized by tangible ends and means, that involve human or nonhuman resources, that focus on economic development or culture-status, or that are distributive, override the effects of dyadic characteristics. Such issues, moreover, tend to promote cooperative rather than conflict behavior. Thus, while the impact of dyadic characteristics varies among dyads, certain types of issues defy this variation. The issue characteristics delineated above are sufficiently potent that even the hostile U.S.–Soviet dyad during the Cold War temporarily manifested cooperation. This finding suggests that the overall affect of a dyadic relationship is probably highly correlated with the type of issues that engage the actors, so that changes in the characteristics of issues under contention will alter the nature of the overall relationship.

The foregoing analysis encourages two conclusions. First, the issue typologies in and of themselves are deficient. Only the Rosenau typology produces a respectable correlation, but, being below .50, this does not explain even 25 percent of the variance. If the issue-area variable is not to be relegated to the periphery of attention, the dimensions underlying the typologies must be substantially reworked so that their causal effect on behavior becomes demonstrable. Second, the control tests show that although the typologies themselves do not fare well, certain specific issues do. It remains to be explained theoretically why this is the case. Each of the typologies that have been discussed contributes some insight. As Rosenau and Lowi suggest, tangibility of ends and means facilitates the division and distribution of political goods, thereby encouraging bargain-

Table 2.2 Comparison of Dyad and Issue Variables

Rosenau Typology—Tangibility

Control for Dyad		Control for Issue	
1. U.S.-F.R.G.	eta = .109 (364)*	1. Intangible/intangible	eta = .377 (400)*
2. F.R.G.-U.S.	.079 (33)*	2. Intangible/tangible	.588 (37)
3. U.S.-USSR	.128 (109)	3. Tangible/intangible	.424 (392)*
4. USSR-U.S.	.206 (63)	4. Tangible/tangible	.192 (384)*
5. U.S.-U.K.	.289 (102)*		
6. U.K.-U.S.	.381 (69)*		
7. U.S.-Fr.	.304 (109)*		
8. Fr.-U.S.	.258 (66)		

Rosenau Typology—Substantive Categories

Control for Dyad		Control for Issue	
1. U.S.-F.R.G.	eta = .093 (362)*	1. Status	eta = .424 (374)*
2. F.R.G.-U.S.	.132 (329)*	2. Territory	.449 (364)*
3. U.S.-USSR	.179 (108)	3. Human resources	.215 (128)
4. USSR-U.S.	.286 (63)	4. Nonhuman resources	.207 (340)*
5. U.S.-U.K.	.295 (102)*		
6. U.K.-U.S.	.394 (69)*		
7. U.S.-Fr.	.244 (108)*		
8. Fr.-U.S.	.217 (65)		

Lowi-Zimmerman Typology

Control for Dyad		Control for Issue	
1. U.S.-F.R.G.	eta = .103 (364)*	1. Distributive	eta = .188 (185)*
2. F.R.G.-U.S.	.178 (315)*	2. Regulatory	.220 (89)*
3. U.S.-USSR	.049 (109)	3. Protection-interaction	.368 (930)*
4. USSR-U.S.	——	4. No redistributive	
5. U.S.-U.K.	.176 (104)		
6. U.K.-U.S.	.210 (70)*		
7. U.S.-Fr.	.244 (110)*		
8. Fr.-U.S.	.109 (67)*		

Brecher Typology

Control for Dyad		Control for Issue	
1. U.S.-F.R.G.	eta = .149 (381)*	1. Military-security	eta = .409 (563)*
2. F.R.G.-U.S.	.144 (340)*	2. Political-diplomatic	.333 (352)*
3. U.S.-USSR	.050 (110)	3. Economic development	.218 (256)*
4. USSR-U.S.	.087 (65)	4. Cultural-status	.218 (80)
5. U.S.-U.K.	.294 (105)*		
6. U.K.-U.S.	.409 (71)*		
7. U.S.-Fr.	.214 (111)*		
8. Fr.-U.S.	.294 (68)*		

*($p < .05$, X^2)

ing and compromise. Such issues tend to involve economic and cultural matters. Human resource issues also tend to produce cooperation, because they involve visible costs but are less salient than issues involving tangible ends—such as territory—thereby encouraging bargaining rather than escalation. These inferences are buttressed when the kinds of issues that do *not* alter dyadic behavior are identified. Such issues are characterized by intangible ends and means or intangible ends but tangible means. They involve status, territory, and military security. In general terms, they are issues that are highly salient and in which political goods can be disaggregated and divided only with difficulty. The issue typologies, then, do point to some things of importance, but these are obscured by the overly simplistic classifications. With the possible exception of tangibility, the typologies do not elucidate specific characteristics that are potent. Instead, they appear to have classified issues in a manner that groups significant and insignificant characteristics together. What needs to be done is to use the typologies to delineate a set of issue-related variables that, in addition to predicting behavior, can explain it in a theoretical fashion. To further this task, the tangibility typology, which is the most potent and theoretically useful, was investigated in more detail to see how it relates to other potential variables that might help account for cooperation/conflict.

An investigation of the tangibility typology is facilitated by the fact that Rosenau suggests several other variables through which tangibility affects cooperation or conflict, although these relationships are not fully elaborated. A close reading of Rosenau's "pretheory" reveals at least four propositions that might be tested with the data available. The first deals with the number of participants. He argues that tangible means tend to limit the number of actors, because such means are more costly than those that are intangible. This presupposes a second proposition, which is that tangible means will necessitate more costly resources than intangible means.

A third persuasive proposition is that tangible goals tend to produce less intense and less persistent behavior than issues featuring intangible goals. This is because intangible ends tend to include moral and ideological aspirations which generate greater intensity and persistence than tangible ends. A final proposition, which incorporates these effects, involves the concept of issue linkage. As issues become linked to one another, they become less easy to resolve because they (1) are less able to be disaggregated, (2) command more attention, (3) are probably of greater scope and domain and thus not as amenable to compromise, (4) involve more participants, and (5) attract more costly resources. Each of these propositions is important theoretically, because each points to other issue characteristics that may interact with tangibility to explain behavior.

Interaction was examined first by relating tangibility to the cooperation/conflict measure while controlling for each of the other issue characteristics (participation in the issue, number of resources utilized in interaction, resource type, persistence of behavior, issue salience, and linkage to other issues) and second by relating each of the issue characteristics to cooperation/conflict while controlling for tangibility.* The tests of each of the propositions provided intriguing findings, not only because a number of Rosenau's suggestions find support, but also because, even where they were not supported, the tests uncovered theoretically interesting relationships.†

The findings that were produced by controlling for the other issue characteristics suggested that, as an issue acquires intangible aspects, it will generate more conflict when *any* of the following six conditions are present: the issue is of high salience (gamma $= -.905$); it is not linked to other issues ($-.601$); behavior in the issue is persistent ($-.587$); economic or diplomatic resources are employed ($-.497$, $-.573$); only one resource is employed ($-.448$); or there are many participant actors ($-.345$).† Conversely, as tangibility increases, conflict decreases under

* Participation was operationalized by classifying each stake within an issue according to the total number of actors (as opposed to targets) which contend over it, according to the following scale: three actors or fewer, five to ten, ten to fifteen, and fifteen or more. Number of resources employed was confined to dividing stakes into those that employed only one resource and those that employed two. Three types of resources were classified: diplomatic, economic, and military. Persistence was operationalized by classifying stakes according to the number of years they appeared in the data set: less than five, five to ten, ten or more years. Salience was measured by classifying stakes according to the number of acts they evoked from the contending parties: less than 50 acts, 60–150 acts, 200–230 acts, 480 acts. Finally, issue linkage was operationalized as no links with other stakes, one link, two links, or three links.

† A summary of only the most interesting findings are presented here; for a complete report, see Vasquez and Henehan, "Issue Area as a Variable," 1979, table 4.

‡ All the gammas are negative, because they relate an increase in tangibility with a decrease in conflict.

the above conditions. These six conditions form a pattern that needs to be explained theoretically. While this is not a simple task, it is facilitated by the fact that the list *was not derived inductively* but rather from propositions that already have a theoretical rationale. The key lies in tangibility, and a comparison of the effects of the six conditions on cooperation/conflict while controlling for tangibility helps elucidate some of the theoretical relationships underlying the findings.

When controlling for tangibility, it was found that each of the other variables has a separate effect, depending on the type of issue. Table 2.3

Table 2.3 Six Variables with Cooperation/Conflict—Controlling for Tangibility[a]

	Partici-pation	Number of Resources	Resource Type	Persis-tence	Salience	Linkage
Intangible/ intangible						
Intangible/ tangible	.562		−.664	.562	.562	
Tangible/ intangible		−.572	−.353	.348		
Tangible/ tangible	−.473		.381		−.580	.649

[a] Gamma

Effects produced by ends   Effects produced by intangibility

summarizes the most potent of these effects. From the summary, it appears that the six variables are more useful for understanding issues that feature tangible means rather than intangible means. But what is interesting is that the effect of these variables will change, depending upon the nature of the ends involved in the issue. Thus, when tangible means are employed to obtain intangible ends, an increased number of participants produces increased conflict. When tangible ends are sought, the inverse occurs—an increase in the number of participants is associated with a decline in conflict. A similar pattern was found for salience. High issue salience is associated with a high level of conflict when tangible means are used for intangible ends, but is associated with a low level of conflict when tangible ends are sought. The nature of the goals must be producing these changes, since the means remain constant.*

Finally, tangible-tangible issues tend to be very conflict-prone if they are linked to other issues. This is probably the case only when they are linked to a different type of issue, although none of the findings speak directly to this question. The other three types of issues are not affected in the same manner, most likely because they are *already* conflict-prone. The linkage proposition reflects a contamination process, suggesting that tangible-tangible issues are somewhat unique. Such issues reveal different patterns than the other two types that produce strong findings, and what distinguishes them is their tendency to produce cooperation.

While a good deal has been learned about issues that are resolved by tangible means, less is known about issues that attract intangible means for their resolution. Some propositions are suggested by the limited findings about issues with tangible ends but intangible means. Intangibility of either ends or means has an impact on the patterns of resource use and persistence of behavior, and that impact implies that the infusion of intangibility makes an issue more difficult to resolve and hence more conflict-prone.

The effect of intangible means also is to eliminate the role of actors and salience, a pattern that holds for intangible-intangible issues as well. In addition, there is a slight tendency for these issues to persist. Other than this, little can be learned about intangible-intangible issues from

---

*The relationship between tangible ends and conflict tends to be more "correlational," than causal; that is, conflict engenders reduction in activity. On the other hand, when issues have intangible ends, the increase in the number of actors and the frequency of their interaction (high salience) seem to be more "causal." This reflects the fact that issues with intangible ends are more difficult to resolve, and are fundamentally different than those with tangible ends *even if* they can be resolved by tangible means. Thus, the longer these issues persist, the more conflict they engender. No such relationship is found for issues with tangible ends. The differences in the way these issues can be resolved is illuminated by the findings on resource type. Tangible-tangible issues have a slight tendency to produce more conflict as more costly resources are employed, while intangible–tangible issues have a strong tendency to produce less conflict as more costly resources are employed. What this means is that tangible-tangible issues tend to be resolved by recourse to economic resources, and that if military resources are employed, conflict increases. Conversely, issues with intangible goals do not seem to be resolvable by economic means, and this leads to a great deal of diplomatic conflict. However, as military resources are employed, there is a sobering effect, reducing conflict, but probably without resolving the issue. (Whether the issue is resolved is not reported in the data set).

table 2.3. However, certain tentative inferences can be drawn. Such issues will entail conflict; that much is known from the bivariate association between tangibility and cooperation/conflict. Since none of the six issue-related characteristics can account for the pattern, it is possible to infer that a variable which is not issue-related is at work.

Here, earlier findings that were produced by controlling for dyad provide a critical insight. It was found that issues that were more intangible tended to be more sensitive to the relational characteristics of the contending actors than to issue characteristics. There is, of course, a large body of research which deals with the relational characteristics of actors and cooperation/conflict.* The research presented here suggests that those actor variables are most relevant for issues that manifest both intangible means and ends. Issues of this sort are fundamentally different than the other three. They have a dynamic all their own, and that dynamic is determined by the affect among contenders. When the object of contention is intangible, "who" is contending becomes more important than "what" is the object of contention. When these conditions are satisfied, the stage is set for a conflict pattern of interaction. Clearly, these findings are useful for reformulating the theoretical bases not only of the Rosenau typology but that of Lowi-Zimmerman as well. An in-depth review of some of the problems inherent in these two typologies, along with a review of some of the rest of the issue literature, may provide insights that can be employed to develop a new set of issue concepts.

A CRITIQUE OF THE ISSUE LITERATURE

A. The Rosenau Typology

In light of the previous analysis, Rosenau's most intriguing proposition is that the tangibility of ends and means increases the readiness of actors to

---

* Three research projects, Dimensionality of Nations, Correlates of War, and Comparative Research on the Events of Nations (CREON) have all shown that differences in the attributes of nations (what is usually called status) play an important role—R. J. Rummel, "U.S. Foreign Relations: Conflict, Cooperation, and Attribute Distances," in B. Russett, ed., *Peace, War, and Numbers* (Beverly Hills, Calif.: Sage, 1972), pp. 71–115; Michael Wallace, "Status, Formal Organization, and the Onset of War, 1820–1964," *ibid.,* pp. 49–69; Maurice East and Charles F. Hermann, "Do Nation-Types Account for Foreign Policy Behavior?" in J. N. Rosenau, ed., *Comparing Foreign Policies* (Beverly Hills, Calif.: Sage, 1974), pp. 269–303.

bargain. This seems to be the case, particularly in light of Lowi's analysis, because tangible issues can be disaggregated and thereby distributed in a compromise fashion. But just because such distributions are possible does not mean that they will occur. The question of why they are more likely to occur is not answered by Rosenau.

A possible answer may be provided in two other propositions he suggests. He argues that tangible means tend to limit the number of actors, because such means are more costly than those that are intangible. While this may be generally the case, the link between tangibility of means and cost is probably not as strong and direct as he implies. The costs involved in disposing of the stakes at issue are more likely a function of the distribution of capabilities and the nature of relations among participant actors than they are of the issue itself. If affect is strong, stakes will take on a different coloration and meaning than if affect is moderate or weak. If capabilities are evenly distributed among participants, the costs in bringing about the resolution of an issue will be greater than if distribution of capabilities is dramatically unequal. Finally, the costs of acting will be greater for an actor that has limited tangible means than for one which possesses plentiful amounts of them. The costs for an actor to employ tangible means such as money or troops depend less on the issue itself than on whether the *other* major contenders are OPEC and the Soviet government or Mali and the Dominican Republic, and whether the initiator possesses sufficient amounts of those resources so that their expenditure does not entail dislocation and lost opportunities. Tangible means tend to limit participants because such resources are less widely available and less equally distributed than intangible means.

Limiting participation is important, because it increases the prospects for compromise, owing to the possibility of distributing the stakes to a finite set of contenders.* Thus, tangibility of ends increases the *possibility* of bargains through disaggregation and distribution of stakes, while tangibility of means enhances this prospect by limiting the number of contenders and making each "piece of the pie" that might become available

* This proposition conforms to the notion of "minimum winning coalition," propounded by William H. Riker. See Riker, *The Theory of Political Coalitions* (New Haven: Yale University Press, 1962); and "A New Proof of the Size Principle," in Joseph L. Bernd, ed., *Mathematical Applications in Political Science* (Dallas, Tex.: Southern Methodist University Press, 1966).

larger and more attractive to the few who can afford to participate. In addition, failure to bargain requires the continued expenditure of scarce tangible resources, which provides an additional incentive to resolve the issue.

Another proposition that is persuasive is that tangible goals produce less intense and persistent behavior than issues featuring intangible goals. Intangible ends that turn upon moral concerns and/or are enshrouded in

Table 2.4 Tangibility of Means and Ends

	Means	
	Intangible	Tangible
Ends		
Intangible	Many participants	Few participants
	Less costly resources	More costly resources
	More intense/persistent (ideological)	More intense/persistent (ideological)
	Nondisaggregation	Nondisaggregation
Tangible	Many participants	Few participants
	Less costly resources	More costly resources
	Less intense/persistent (mundane)	Less intense/persistent (mundane)
	Disaggregation possible	Disaggregation possible

ideological myth and symbol tend to generate more intensity and persistence than tangible ends that are divisible and of more easily calculable value.* Tangible ends like territory produce greater commitment and intensity if they come to symbolize some greater intangible goal, such as colonial independence, national unification, or rectification of past humiliation.† The relatively lower intensity produced by tangible ends permits actors to show greater flexibility, which facilitates the proposal of compromise solutions. Table 2.4 provides a summary of the hypothetical effects of tangibility.

*See Richard N. Rosecrance, *International Relations: Peace or War?* (New York: McGraw-Hill, 1973), pp. 88–106 for a discussion of this question in terms of the "environmental supply" of different types of ends.

†This implies that it is the intangibility of moral-ideological ends rather than their substantive content that is the key causal determinant of intensity.

B. The Lowi-Zimmerman Typology

Of the typologies tested, the Lowi-Zimmerman scheme was the least potent in predicting external behavior. This seems to be the consequence of at least five problems with the typology. First, the scheme arises largely from an American policy-making context, so that foreign-policy issues are regarded almost as an afterthought. Most of these would be placed in Zimmerman's additional "interaction-protection" categories of crisis-routine action, which reflects Lowi's original view that (real) foreign-policy issues are "not part of the same universe."[34] But, if Zimmerman's claim is correct that interaction-protection issues dominated nineteenth-century global politics, is such a typology sufficiently precise and can a single dimension account for subtle distinctions among all such issues? The sole reason to expect such a typology to be useful would be if it were exclusively a typology of issues confronted within a domestic context. Yet, there is no compelling reason why this should be the case.

This introduces a second major problem. Lowi's typology is not of sufficient general applicability, perhaps because it is not truly theoretical. In the words of one recent critic:

Unfortunately, while Lowi's categorization possesses considerable intuitive appeal, the lack of any rigorous theory underlying his framework makes it somehow less than compelling on its own merits. Lowi's issue areas are not really distinct conceptual types at all; rather, his idea of a definition consists of little more than a cataloguing of attributes that appear to cluster together.[35]

In his initial discussion, Lowi argued that the internal decision-making process was *the* dependent variable. But, if he purports to offer a typology of issues, then it should account for issues at *any* level of politics. Distributive issues, for example, should exist and produce cooperative behavior at the interpersonal, intergroup, and global levels. Lowi largely ignores this problem, and Zimmerman's effort to reformulate Lowi's scheme by utilizing Wolfers' continuum of the pole of power to the pole of indifference misses an opportunity to alleviate this problem. If there are issues which, as Wolfers claims, are resolved through power-politics behavior and others that are reconciled through compliance with regime norms, the issue characteristics that produce these different patterns of behavior are worth investigating on both the internal and external levels. Yet this was not done. The entire second problem stems largely from omission rather than commission and points to a logical limitation rather than an explicit error.

A third problem has to do with the internal-external distinction. If Lowi and Zimmerman insist on maintaining distinct domestic and international spheres, then it is incumbent upon them to explain how, if at all, the internal process affects the external behavior of actors and vice versa. Do redistributive issues, for instance, make actors more intense in their motivation externally but less persistent because of internal divisions? How does wider participation in the internal policy-making process affect external behavior? Is the mood theory of the effect of public opinion in foreign policy relevant only for some issues rather than others, and, if so, does this mean that the role of the public in Lowi's original three issue areas is somehow different than the episodic public participation in protection issues that so concerned Walter Lippmann and George Kennan?[36] In short, what indirect effects do tangibility and domestic impact have upon the decison-making process that in turn affects external behavior?

A fourth problem has to do with whether or not there is something inherent in political goods that determines the manner in which they must be distributed. Zimmerman implies, as does Lowi, that a political good or stake will have either a symmetrical or asymmetrical domestic impact, that is a zero-sum, variable-sum or positive-sum quality. This conforms to Mancur Olson's distinction between "collective goods," which cannot be withheld from any member of a group if it is provided to one member, and "private goods," the benefits of which can be distributed in any number of ways.[37] Yet, as Robert Salisbury points out, the extent to which an issue is zero-sum or not depends largely on the perceptions of the contenders.[38] If this were not the case, how could Lowi assert that the tariff issue in the United States has been transformed from a distributive into a regulatory issue?[39] It would appear that actors have considerable leeway in defining issues. In fact, the capacity of the Soviet and American governments to redefine issues from zero-sum to variable-sum is a central aspect in the evolution from Cold War to détente. Ultimately, any theory of issues must address itself to the variables that lie behind such issue redefinition.

Finally, there is a problem with the belief that a political stake can have a symmetrical domestic impact. Symmetry is not a dichotomous variable. It constitutes a continuum with asymmetry, and is best measured ordinally. Even with this caveat, there remains a real question as to what is meant by symmetry. Does it refer to the scope of impact (how many individuals are affected) or the equality of impact (distribution of impact among only those who are affected)? It is difficult to discern which criterion is used in the Lowi-Zimmerman typology. Not all members of a collectivity benefit, for instance, from distributive issues, and the benefits are not necessarily distributed equally among those who do benefit. In what sense, then, is the domestic impact of distributive issues symmetrical? Indeed, using the scope criterion, few issues appear to have a symmetrical impact. And, even a collective good like security, which has an impact upon most members, apparently fails on the equality critierion. Thus, though all individuals may derive *some* benefit from national security measures, measures such as military expenditures tend to cost some members *more* than others and to benefit some *more* than others.

The last comment makes clear that the notion of domestic impact, and by inference symmetry, actually has two faces—costs and benefits. The Lowi-Zimmerman focus is almost exclusively upon benefits, but benefits cannot be evaluated without reference to costs. The entire issue-area of redistribution depends upon this distinction. How, then, can symmetry of impact be assessed and measured? If an issue offers equal benefits but unequal costs or the reverse is its impact symmetrical or asymmetrical? This problem, too, seems to call for an ordinal scale and precludes the use of a dichotomized variable.*

Despite the very considerable problems associated with the work of Lowi and Zimmerman, a number of valuable insights about issues emerge from analyzing their efforts to combine tangibility and domestic impact. As in the Rosenau classification, the discussion of domestic impact in particular provides a basis for several propositions. First, different issues

---

* An effort might be made to construct such a scale by measuring costs and benefits separately and then aggregating them in some fashion. At best, however, this is a dubious procedure, since the costs and benefits relating to a particular set of stakes commonly arise in separate issues. Thus, issues concerning taxation are generally separate from (though related to) those concerning how tax revenue will be spent. The two sets of issues commonly arise in different contexts, at different times, and with distinct casts of contenders. Like the distinction between zero- and variable-sum contests, that between costs and benefits depends less on the political good or stake at issue than on what contenders want from the issue itself, that is, how they define it in the first place.

trigger different internal decison-making processes, various levels of participation, differing levels of internal cooperation/conflict, and therefore probably produce different forms of external behavior (though these differences remain to be understood). Second, "who" participate in decision-making and their relative level of participation are better understood by the predicted distribution of costs and benefits among members than by simple symmetry of domestic impact. Third, these costs and benefits do not inhere in the issue itself but in the perceptions of members who decide whether or not to try to participate. In particular, such perceptions are produced by the articulation of specific proposals to dispose of stakes. Finally, as Wolfers suggests, efforts to resolve issues range from resort to power politics to obedience to regime norms in those cases where the stakes at issue are not deemed worth the costs of using vigorous techniques.

C. Substantive Typologies

Unlike the previous typologies, that of Brecher et al. was not offered as an original theoretical contribution, but simply as an attempt to classify issues on their substantive basis. In this sense, the Brecher et al. typology reflects an entire genre, and its poor performance raises serious questions about the very definition of issue that is employed in the field. A brief review of some of the other efforts will elucidate the problems with this approach.

The first is encountered in the effort to develop a logically exhaustive list of the major types of issues. The Brecher et al. effort has not produced any consensus. William D. Coplin, for example, while not seeking to provide a formal typology, argued that four issue areas are critical for analyses of foreign policy—national security, economic, ideological-historical, and procedural.[40] Coplin's ideological-historical category is somewhat more precise than Brecher's political-diplomatic, in that it at least specifies criteria of inclusion, but it, too, remains uncomfortably close to being a miscellaneous category.[41] Of greater interest is the procedural category, which is often overlooked by scholars. It contains issues concerning "the way foreign policy objectives are pursued rather than the nature of the specific objectives,"[42] which Coplin argues are of great importance in world politics. However, its addition introduces "means" into the typology that is otherwise based on "ends."

Since the elaboration of only four substantive foci does not exhaust issue possibilities, a number of scholars, particularly those using event data, have sought to identify them inductively. Among the first to control for issues was Edward Azar in his massive data set of events in the Middle East.* Azar identified a number of specific Middle Eastern issues and then reduced them to four major types—territory-security, capability, political-ideological, and refugees.[43] A broader effort to identify issues by using the "generally available events data sources" was undertaken by Coplin, Michael K. O'Leary, and their associates. By recoding the WEIS (World Event Interaction Survey) data of Charles D. McClelland, they identified large numbers of substantive topics like "nonproliferation treaty," "hijacking" and "population control," which they then distinguished by controlling for geographic area.[44] The employment of the geographic variable was based on an assumption that regional factors have an impact on defining the issue. Even more inductive was the approach of Mansbach and Vasquez, who in collecting "issue events" from the 1975 *New York Times* identified some 350 different specific issues, such as "Arab unity," "unrest in Yemen," "Third World Assistance" and "Israeli participation in the UN system."[45]

These efforts reveal that while substantive focus is important, it is extremely difficult to aggregate discrete issues into a few major categories that are sufficiently precise to capture all the key differences that distinguish the political goods being allocated. There is some consensus that national security issues (including territorial and capability questions) and economic issues are two important and distinct categories, but how many other types exist, and how they can be distinguished from these two, as well as what to make of procedural issues remain unanswered questions. The deductive substantive typologies have been found to be wanting whenever efforts have been made to utilize them, the result of which has been to encourage inductive efforts to identify issues. These efforts, while providing lists of specific issues that are precise, lack theoretical rigor and do not specify how any issue can be objectively and reliably distinguished from any other.

The problems which such research has encountered might be minimized by distinguishing among the various *stakes* over which actors con-

---

* For a description of the data set, see Edward Azar, "Analysis of International Events," *Peace Research Reviews* (November 1970), 4(1):1–113.

tend, such as the Golan Heights or the Sinai Desert, and the manner in which these stakes are linked into *issues,* such as the Middle East. Attempts to answer these questions deductively have largely missed the point made by Keohane and Nye, as well as others, that issues are fundamentally perceptual in origin, so that the stakes that are seen to cohere into issues will vary as actors, and their relations with one another, change.[46]

An adequate typology based on substance requires a two-step process—a listing of the stakes at issue, followed by an empirical analysis of the perceptual bases that fuse them into issues for contenders. Perhaps the most successful efforts to delineate issue areas empirically are those which have used such an approach to identify underlying dimensions by employing mathematical techniques, such as Guttman scaling and factor analysis to analyze UN and U.S. congressional voting. Their assumption is that, if actors perceive a set of objects or a set of resolutions about a set of objects to be part of a single issue, then they will vote on the basis of a single attitude. With this assumption, the identification of such a single attitude in voting upon a series of discrete resolutions can be used to infer the presence of a single issue. In this manner, Alker and Russett "showed that three major dimensions or 'superissues' could be identified in each of four different Sessions" of the UN between 1947 and 1961.[47]

They were characterized as "cold war," "colonial self-determination," and "supranationalism" issues, and among them they regularly accounted for more than half the total variance in all roll-call voting. Two other superissues, concerned with problems of intervention in southern Africa and of Palestine, were found in three of the four Sessions. The four or five factors appearing in any Session always accounted for between 59 and 70 percent of the total variance in that session.[48]

Permitting actors to define issues themselves, as do Alker and Russett, appears to allow the construction of exclusive and logically exhaustive categories and takes account of changes in these categories through time. Since their approach is based on examining the perceptions of participants, it can also overcome the potential problem of actors defining the same set of stakes differently or including different stakes in the same issue. Thus, oil is a stake that is perceived by different actors as impinging upon different issues. Arab regimes perceive it as part of an Arab-

Israeli issue; Third World producers see it as central to economic redistribution; and Western governments see it as a vital stake in a set of environmental and energy issues. Even a single actor may perceive a single stake as part of several issues, which, though complexly related in some fashion, remain sufficiently distinct to call for different responses on its part. Typologies developed in this fashion would result in identifying issues that produce unique forms of interaction, as Rosenau and Keohane and Nye have proposed. Of course, it remains unclear whether such typologies would explain or simply predict such behavior.

Regardless of the theoretical value of a substantive typology of issues based on actor perceptions, deductive efforts of the sort exemplified by Brecher et al. will not produce such a typology. Is the effort, then, to construct a powerful deductive classification of substantive issues hopeless? The answer is probably no if scholars return to the original definition of issues that was offered by Rosenau, namely, that an issue consists of a cluster of values that are to be allocated.* To date there has been little effort to classify stakes according to the values they represent. Though a single inclusive list of values is difficult to compile, such a list could be constructed, which would be logically exhaustive and in which each value could form the basis of a different type of issue.

Three difficulties stand in the way of such an approach, though these are probably not insurmountable. The first is that stakes may represent more than a single value, or that actors may seek the same stake in the name of different values. In such cases, this distinction becomes an additional basis for classifying stakes. The problem of multiple values can be resolved either by classifying stakes only according to their principal value, or according to all the actual values under contention. A second problem is that each value may not produce *distinct* modes of behavior, which is why Rosenau speaks of clusters of values. The problem is fundamentally empirical and can probably be overcome inductively, in order to combine the individual values and so reduce them into groups that do produce distinct modes of behavior. Finally, some stakes may be sought

---

* Coplin, Mills, and O'Leary define issues in similar fashion as "a proposed allocation of values which can be achieved only through collective action." William D. Coplin, Stephen L. Mills, and Michael K. O'Leary, "The Prince Concepts and the Study of Foreign Policy," in Patrick J. McGowan, ed., *Sage International Yearbook of Foreign Policy Studies* (Beverly Hills, Calif.: Sage, 1973), 1:75.

for their intrinsic worth; that is, for the values they represent, whereas others may be sought for the instrumental purpose of acquiring values that are actually associated with other stakes. As in the case of multiple values, this problem could be overcome by regarding the distinction as an additional basis for classifying issues.

Investigating efforts to develop substantive typologies of issues has provided a number of insights. First, there is a distinction between the actual objects under contention and the values to be satisfied by their allocation. A deductive typology, based upon values, is possible, because the number of values is finite. Typologies based upon the objects at stake require induction, because of the virtually infinite number of such objects and the rapidity with which they change through time. Second, what cause different stakes to cohere into individual issues are the perceptions of participant actors in particular historical contexts. Consequently, issues are dynamic phenomena. Finally, the stakes at issue can be sought for one or several values, and for either intrinsic or instrumental reasons.

Any future analysis of issues must address itself to the host of conceptual problems that have been described above. These can be summarized into three major tasks that need to be performed in any issue analysis. First, how are issues to be defined? Second, what is the effect of tangibility? Third, how are issues related to costs and benefits? The work on substantive typologies is useful for the first task; Rosenau provides insights for the second; and Lowi-Zimmerman for the third.

TOWARD A NEW CONCEPTION OF ISSUES

Since all of the typologies have been found wanting, none of them will be employed, and an alternative set of concepts will be developed, which will delineate the effects of specific issue characteristics and the theoretical rationale behind these propositions. The three key concepts are issue dimension, type of stake, and the nature of stake proposals. The first two are new, and the latter is fairly well-known in political science, although not widely employed in international relations inquiry. Before investigating these concepts, it is necessary to elaborate more fully the issue perspective on politics, so that a formal definition of *issue* can be offered.

Politics, as Easton suggests, involves efforts to allocate *values*. Since values are abstract and intangible ends, they cannot be attained directly and must be sought through access to, or acquisition of, *objects* that are seen as possessing or representing values. These objects are then regarded as *stakes* for which actors contend. Politics stems from the quest for value satisfaction. Values are subjective constructs that express human aspirations for improving their existence. Although an inclusive list of such values would be difficult to construct, some of those which have been identified and sought through time and across space are wealth, physical security, order, freedom/autonomy, peace, status, health, equality, justice, knowledge, beauty, honesty, and love.[49]

While there may be semantic differences among definitions of specific values and variations among the lists of values that have been compiled, there does seem to be a consensus as to what are the key values.* *Wealth* refers to the acquisition of goods and services from the environment, in contrast to *physical security,* which means the safety of one's person and goods from external danger. *Freedom/autonomy* connotes independence of the environment and of others. *Peace* means the absence of physical or psychological violence, and *order* refers to the widespread acceptance of procedures, norms, and roles, so that behavior in society follows certain patterns and fulfills widely held expectations. *Status* refers to the relative worth or respect one is accorded by others. *Health* connotes physical well-being. *Equality* refers to evenness and impartiality in the distribution of other values, whereas *justice* emphasizes fairness and equity, particularly in receiving rewards that are equivalent to one's effort and ability. *Knowledge* means enlightenment and acquaintance both with reality and the ways of changing reality. *Beauty* refers to the aesthetic appreciation of selected qualities of physical phenomena, people, or ideas. *Honesty* refers to the telling of truth, and *love* refers to affection and warmth of feeling.

Values are sought for themselves, but, as consummatory ends, they are never achieved in any "final" fashion. Value satisfaction serves *intrinsic* needs. However, the satisfaction of one value can enhance the prospects

* The list of values that follows is based on a perusal of several lists that have been offered. See Harold J. Lasswell and Abraham Kaplan, *Power and Society* (New Haven, Conn.: Yale University Press, 1950), pp. 55–56; Ted Robert Gurr, *Why Men Rebel* (Princeton, N.J.: Princeton University Press, 1970), pp. 24–26; as well as Roger W. Cobb and Charles D. Elder, *Participation in American Politics* (Boston: Allyn and Bacon, 1972), p. 40; and Lowell Dittmer, "Political Culture and Political Symbolism: Toward a Theoretical Synthesis," *World Politics* (July 1977), 26(4):559–61.

for satisfying another, preferred value, so that when actors seek peace as a means of acquiring wealth or security, value satisfaction is also *instrumental*. As this suggests, though all values are desired in and of themselves, each actor has a value preference schedule which changes in time in accordance with the conditions in which that actor finds itself.[50] Two basic criteria exist for assessing value satisfaction. The first entails measuring such satisfaction in terms of the future, present, and past; and the second involves a comparison of self versus others. Utilization of the first criterion produces fewer perceptions of relative value deprivation (defined by Gurr as "actors' perceptions of discrepancy between their value expectations and their value capabilities"),[51] because it involves perceptions of absolute gain or loss. The second criterion, in contrast, produces interactor conflicts if perceived differences are great.

Once an object is sought and becomes a political stake actors seek to divide or acquire it. To this end, actors formulate and debate proposals for the disposition of stakes. *Proposals* are statements of, or claims for, potential outcomes toward which each contender develops and articulates, either explicitly or tacitly, a position of support, opposition, or neutrality. As this process continues, actors interpret the implications of proposals for present and future value satisfaction, assess the relationships (if any) among stakes and among themselves, and modify their positions accordingly. It is the perceptions of contenders concerning the way in which these various proposals about stakes are related that shape issues. Proposals that are seen as related (either because actors consciously claim that they are or behave as though they were) are perceived to constitute an issue. Consequently, the stakes that are the subjects of these proposals are necessarily seen to be linked in some fashion. Stated more formally: *An issue consists of contention among actors over proposals for the disposition of stakes among them.** An issue includes both the characteristics of the stakes involved *and* the particular relationships among the actors participating in the process. The definition reflects the research findings reported earlier that suggest that both actor and stake characteristics are important and are interrelated.

Having placed the concept of issues at the center of enquiry, it remains necessary to delineate the key issue-related variables that explain the na-

---

* This definition is consciously designed to reduce the centrality of "conflict." Cf. Cobb and Elder, *Participation in American Politics*, p. 82.

ture of contention. The most important of these is *issue dimension* which refers to the manner in which actors perceive and define the issue before them. Which stakes do actors identify as part of an issue, and how are they seen to be linked together? This variable is the key to unlocking the puzzle of how to determine what constitutes an issue. Issue dimension* is discerned by examining the proposals which actors make.[52] It is a dimension because it describes the underlying linkages among stakes. There are two types of perceived linkages that fuse stakes into issues—stake and actor.

A stake linkage entails a perception that proposals involving two or more stakes represent the same preferred values to actors or are instrumental to such values. Such linkages mainly involve tangible stakes and encourage a consciousness of interdependence that permits trade-offs and compromises. An actor linkage entails a different sort of self-conscious interdependence, which involves a heightened realization that competition for different stakes involves the same friends or foes. Participants focus upon the effects that the disposition of stakes will have on the value satisfaction of others and on their capacity to compete for other stakes in the future. In the presence of an actor linkage, trade-offs and compromise are discouraged, because they are seen as strengthening or weakening friends and foes.

A stake dimension reduces the centrality of affect in the allocation process and increases the possibility of disposing of specific stakes by means of agreement rather than pressure. In contrast, an actor dimension increases the role of affect and reduces the prospect of disposing of stakes by agreement. If dispositions do occur, they will do so through the exertion of superior influence. Greater time and energy is spent on rewarding friends and punishing foes than on achieving an absolute increase in value satisfaction for oneself.†

* Discerning dimensions of this sort may be possible by using Guttman scaling, cluster bloc analysis, or factor analysis. For examples of such efforts to identify issues, see Hayward Alker and Bruce M. Russett, *World Politics in the General Assembly;* Bruce M. Russett, *International Regions and the International System;* Leroy N. Rieselbach, "Quantitative Techniques for Studying Voting Behavior in the UN General Assembly," *International Organization* (Spring 1960), 14(2): 291–306; and Arend Lijphart, "The Analysis of Bloc Voting in the General Assembly," *American Political Science Review,* (December 1963), 57(4):902–17.

† John Foster Dulles tended to see issues in terms of an actor dimension and examined proposals to determine whether they strengthened or weakened the USSR, refusing to alter

The Cold War illustrates how this process works. The issue was the product of growing postwar perceptions of linkages among numerous stakes that brought about a fusion among many formerly different issues. As World War II drew to a close, issues involving stakes such as control over the governments of the countries of Eastern and Central Europe and their future political and economic orientation were viewed by the governments of the United States, Britain, and France in terms of a stake dimension, on the basis of common stake values like freedom, independence, and security. In seeking to dispose of each stake, the Western governments found their proposals confronted by Soviet opposition and resistance, and Soviet leaders saw the same process in reverse. In this way, a strong actor dimension began to grow up among the issues at stake until a single Cold War issue emerged. In the following years, issues in Asia, Africa, and Latin America acquired a Cold War coloration as they too were infected by the central actor linkage. It seemed to make little difference whether such issues were basically economic, social, or technological. Even as new stakes emerged, the total number of separate issues remained constant.

The second theoretically significant variable is the type(s) of stake(s) under contention. Stakes vary in the type and amount of value that are attached to them, and in the number of values that are attributed to them. For the most part, actors contend for stakes in the belief that access to them will afford immediate value satisfaction. These are *concrete stakes*. A concrete stake is one the object of which is tangible and divisible and which would, if disposed of, immediately confer value satisfaction, because the value is inseparable from the object itself. The value of such a stake can be calculated rather accurately in advance. As Francis I is reputed to have replied when asked whether he had differences of opinion with Charles V: "We agree perfectly. We both want control of Italy."[53] "Italy" was both tangible and divisible, and its conquest promised either ruler immediate access to greater security, wealth, and status.

There are, in addition, *symbolic stakes* which are seen as representing

his image of Soviet leaders regardless of whether a proposal promised to benefit the United States. See Ole R. Holsti, "The Belief System and National Images: A Case Study," *Journal of Conflict Resolution* (September 1962), 6(3):244–52. For a general description of the relationship between hard-liners and soft-liners on the one hand, and the actor dimension and the stake dimension, on the other hand, see Glenn H. Snyder and Paul Diesing, *Conflict Among Nations* (Princeton, N.J.: Princeton University Press, 1977), pp. 301–2.

other stakes of greater value. Their acquisition or loss is viewed as a step toward value deprivation or enhancement. American policymakers, for instance, did not believe that the loss of West Berlin or of an obscure country like Laos promised any *immediate* threat to American security. Nevertheless, they considered these areas to be highly valuable because Berlin was symbolic of Germany and Western Europe, and Laos of all of Southeast Asia. The "domino theory" was fundamentally a rationale for a high-risk and costly policy to contend for a relatively minor stake that was seen as symbolic of a much greater one. However, because a symbolic stake does not automatically lead to the acquisition of the stake it represents, it can, unlike a concrete stake, lose its value if the opponent declares, "take it, it doesn't matter."

Finally, there exist *transcendent stakes* which are entirely abstract and nonspecific, and which concern beliefs, prescriptions, or norms about how people should live or behave. As such, their connection with any specific objects is at best tenuous. Should the economy function according to the norms of socialism or private enterprise? Shall individuals or groups of different racial stock be regarded as inherently equal or as unequal? Transcendent stakes are usually to be recognized by contention over fundamental rules that are intended to produce order, while concrete and symbolic stakes are less grandiose and always require the use of empirical referents that point to tangible objects.

The existence of an actor dimension tends to produce symbolic stakes, because attention is shifted from *what* is being disposed of to *who* is acquiring it. Issues with little in common are therefore linked by the presence of common contestants. Objects without inherent value take on symbolic importance because they are viewed as instrumental to other stakes or as indicators of commitment and will. Their acquisition produces psychological victories and defeats. For example, the Soviet Union sought for many years to force the West to admit the People's Republic of China to the UN and to recognize de facto the German Democratic Republic. Symbolic stakes also tend to arise as substitutes for conflicts that, for one reason or another, cannot be waged openly, as has been the case during the nuclear era. As the actor dimension intensifies, concrete stakes disappear or are transformed into symbolic ones.

The existence of a strong actor dimension or its reinforcement also increases the probability that transcendent stakes may emerge. As the actor dimension persists, actors often find a "higher" rationalization for it and infuse it with ideological justification, which provides ideational cement to fuse the disparate issues under contention, as well as moral suasion to command loyalty. As issues fuse, a single "artificial" ideological cleavage may gain dominance, and new issues are made to "fit" the existing ideological division as they are added to the agenda. Thus, in the 1950s, the numerous newly emerging Third World and economic issues, although radically different in content and participants from the early European Cold War issues, were integrated by the superpowers into the existing East–West contention. Although efforts were made by UN Secretary-General Dag Hammarskjold and others to "forestall the competitive intrusion of the rival power blocs" into these new issues or to decouple them from the Cold War, these efforts were unsuccessful until the transcendent East-West issue began to break down. Nowhere was this difficulty more manifest than during the Congo crises of 1960 through 1964.[54]

Both symbolic and transcendent stakes tend to be perceived by key participants in zero-sum terms. This is because they lack concrete or easily divisible objects of which to dispose. Consequently, there is little over which to compromise or bargain; one either acquires the value at stake or does not. Owing to this, an increase in symbolic and transcendent stakes will affect the final issue-related variable, the nature of stake proposals. The nature of stake proposals refers to the probable manner in which the costs and benefits associated with a proposal will be distributed. Although precise allocations can only be determined by interaction, certain stakes must be divided equally if they are divided at all, whereas others permit inequalities in costs and/or benefits. Although there are many specific outcomes possible, the two dimensions can, for simplicity, be collapsed into the four quadrants depicted in figure 2.2: equal benefits/equal costs (collective goods), equal benefits/unequal costs, unequal benefits/equal costs, and unequal benefits/unequal costs.

The costs and benefits promised by proposals that make up the issues named in the first quadrant cannot easily be divided among contestants, and the quadrant is akin to Lowi's "constituent arena." Although proposals promising completely indivisible costs and benefits are rare, those associated with the U.S.-Soviet nuclear test ban treaty were viewed in this manner by American and Soviet government bureaucrats. A more

Figure 2.2 Nature of Issue Proposal

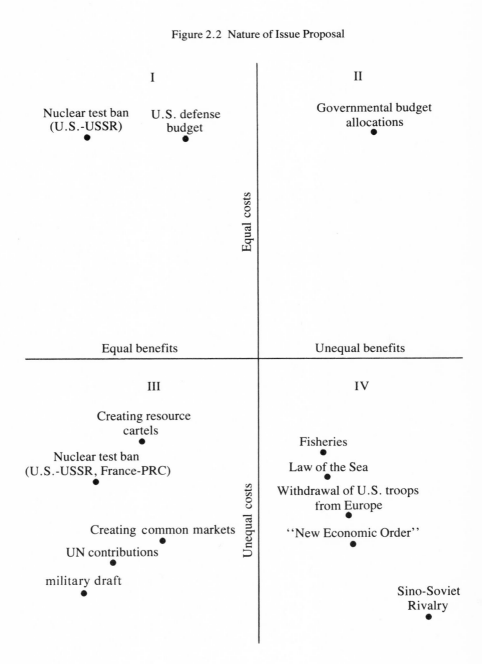

common type of proposal is that which is associated with defense expenditures that entails relatively equal costs to members (taxpayers) but affords disproportionate benefits to select subgroups like the Department of Defense and stockholders, workers, and managers in defense-related industries.[55] Issues that consist of proposals that promise relatively equal costs but disproportionate benefits appear in the second quadrant and are similar to those which Lowi describes as "distributive."

The third quadrant includes issues that consist of proposals that typically promise equal benefits but unequal costs. An example of such an issue is military conscription from which all citizens gain some measure of security but for which costs are disproportionately borne by males between the ages of 18 and 26. From a global perspective, at least, another example is that of banning nuclear testing. Again, major participants gain relatively equal benefits owing to reduced tension and a cleaner atmosphere, but the costs have to be borne by actors that lack a nuclear capability or whose capability remains relatively unsophisticated. As this example illustrates, the nature of the issue proposals may be altered by the inclusion of different actors in the cost-benefit analysis.

The final quadrant features issues that consist of proposals that promise both unequal costs and benefits. Issues that imply a global redistribution of wealth, such as petroleum pricing, or the creation of the Special United Nations Fund for Economic Development (SUNFED) and the United Nations Conference on Trade and Development (UNCTAD), consist of proposals that seek disproportionate gains for resource producers and poorer actors respectively, and that threaten disproportionate costs for resource consumers and wealthier actors. Such issues resemble those which Lowi terms "redistributive" as well as those he labels "regulative." The issue of international fishing rights appears in this quadrant because coastal and deep-sea fishermen would receive disproportionate benefits and bear unequal costs depending upon specific proposals and agreements.

It is in the fourth quadrant that most symbolic and transcendent stakes will be found; the more their zero-sum quality, the closer to the lower right-hand extreme. The existence of such stakes promote strong disagreements among contestants who are divided by profound cleavages that cannot easily be bridged. Such disagreements are very difficult to bargain away, owing to the polymorphic character of the issues and the

Figure 2.3 Summary of Issue Variables and Cooperation/ Conflict

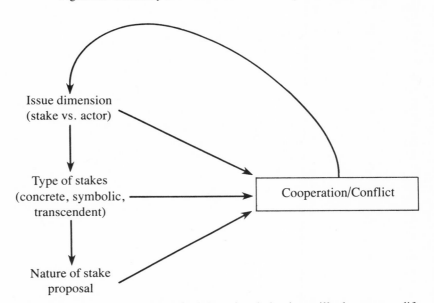

scarcity of divisible stakes. Collaborative behavior will also prove difficult because the nondivisibility of stakes eliminates the prospect of "spoils" resulting from collaboration. Collaborators will necessarily have to be like-minded and share a common major adversary. Their collaboration cannot easily rest on concrete common, or complementary, interests. This is why, if disagreement does occur among them, as in the case of China and the Soviet Union, that disagreement is liable to be intense.

Figure 2.3 summarizes in a very general manner the relationship among the three issue variables and cooperation and conflict. Issue dimension affects the types of stakes under contention, with an actor dimension producing more symbolic and transcendent stakes, and a stake dimension producing mostly concrete stakes. The type of stakes under contention, in turn, affects the nature of proposals that are made to dispose of these stakes. Symbolic and transcendent stakes tend to produce proposals that offer to distribute costs and benefits in an unequal manner, even if not in zero-sum terms. Conversely, concrete stakes tend to produce proposals that promise a more equitable distribution. An actor dimension then tends to produce conflict, because it gives rise to stakes which engender proposals that make for disagreement. Disagreement leads actors to behave toward each other in a negative fashion, which in turn produces or intensifies hostility. Such hostility reinforces an actor-dimension approach to issues, thereby producing a vicious circle.

The three issue variables capture in systematic fashion several of the features of the issue-area literature. The importance of tangibility and its impact, for example, are incorporated in the distinction between concrete stakes on the one hand, and symbolic and transcendent stakes on the other. The fact that stakes lack inherent qualities, but that perceptions of costs and benefits are important, is incorporated in the nature of stake proposals, which also clarifies the underlying dynamic of Lowi's typology. Finally, issue dimension captures the perceptual basis of issues and is at the center of the relationship between actor and stake.

Although flawed in many respects, the literature on issues and the subsequent empirical analyses of hypotheses drawn from it has pointed the way toward a new conceptualization of global politics. Along with actors, issues constitute the building blocks with which a new foundation for understanding interaction can be constructed. The next chapter will make more explicit the assumptions that will be employed to convert these building blocks into a new paradigm for global politics.

In the absence of a paradigm or some candidate for a paradigm, all of the facts that could possibly pertain to the development of a given science are likely to seem equally relevant.
—Thomas Kuhn [1]

CHAPTER THREE

THE ELEMENTS OF A NEW PARADIGM

HAVING DESCRIBED the history and assumptions of realism and having analyzed some of their flaws, this enterprise has reached the stage where it is necessary to summarize the assumptions of an alternative paradigm, and explain the logic that lies behind them. Once this task is completed, how these assumptions provide a different picture of the world will be delineated along with a review of the new research agenda of the paradigm and an overview of its theoretical components.

ASSUMPTIONS OF AN ISSUE PARADIGM

The issue paradigm being offered here consists of four assumptions:

(1) Actors in global politics may consist of any individual or group that is able to contend for the disposition of a political stake.

(2) The fundamental causal processes that govern political interaction are the same regardless of whether contention occurs between or within groups. A single theory of politics, domestic and global, is therefore possible.

(3) Politics can be defined as the authoritative allocation of values through the resolution of issues; i.e., through the acceptance and implementation of a proposal(s) to dispose of the stakes that com-

pose the issue under contention. Substantive issues lie at the heart of politics, providing not only an overall purpose to contention, but having a major impact on the way in which contention is conducted. Politics, then, consists of the raising and resolving of public issues. To explain and regulate that process are the empirical and normative goals of political enquiry.

(4) The shape of political contention is a function of three general factors—the characteristics of the issues on the agenda, the pattern of friendship-hostility among contending actors, and the nature of the institutional context in which allocation decisions must be made.

The first assumption of the alternative paradigm means that the actors in global politics may range from individuals acting on their own behalf to large collectivities bound by common purposes and functioning in collaborative fashion. Actors are not determined on the basis of some legalistic ascription, like sovereignty, but empirically. Actors must have a measure of autonomy, unity, capability, and conjoint purpose. Since the resources necessary to contend over an issuue can vary by the type of issue under contention, which will be the most important actors on an issue can vary by issue. It is possible to identify these actors by identifying those who are responsible for most of the contention on the issue. Variation in the number and types of actors are assumed to be partly a function of variation in the number and types of values and stakes that are on the agenda and pursued at any point in time. While the variety of values is relatively permanent, the stakes and issues of which they are part are in flux. Actors may purposely or accidentally create stakes and raise issues, and their existence, or changes in them, encourage the formation, reformation, and even the decay of actors.

The second assumption leads to a rejection of the alleged dichotomy between "international" and "domestic" politics. A theory of politics can be elaborated that reunites the disparate and artificial divisions among international, comparative, American, or other national theories of politics. In part, this assumption arises from the original definition of actor and the elimination of confusion between that concept and other terms like "state," "society," "polity," and "government." It admits of the logical necessity to distinguish between political processes *within* actors and *among* actors but sees an unbreakable connection between these two types of processes. But the variability of actors precludes the existence of an a priori set of levels, like "international system" or "domestic system." A number of levels may be said to exist at any point in time, but they must be defined and identified *only* in reference to the actors that are being scrutinized at that moment. The "within-among" distinction is retained in this paradigm by recurrent reference to "members" and "actors," with the former describing the interaction of individuals and groups within still larger entities, and the latter describing interactions among these larger entities themselves.* It should be kept in mind, however, that "members" may themselves acquire the characteristics of "actors."

The third assumption is critical. It maintains that people are moved to engage in politics by perceptions of relative value satisfaction or deprivation. This assumption raises questions concerning how ends are selected and why some are chosen in preference to others. Realism evades these prior questions by assuming the pursuit of power as the single end of political man. Politics, seen here as contention over a variety of values and stakes, cannot be reduced to the means of acquiring them. Ends are important not only to give purposive meaning to politics, but because the way ends are embodied within issues affects behavior both directly and indirectly. A paradigm that focuses on issues must develop a theory of issues that explicitly states the characteristics of issues that are critical for explaining behavior in a scientific fashion. To understand why issues arise, how actors contend over them and resolve them (if they do), and the way the consequences of resolution affects value satisfaction is to understand all that is interesting or worth knowing in politics.

The final assumption points to the three most important phenomena for explaining political behavior once an issue perspective is adopted. While the specific variables that will explain behavior need to be found, this paradigm assumes that the most promising places to search for these theo-

---

* This conceptualization conforms closely to Ludwig von Bertalanffy's classic definition of a system as "sets of elements standing in interaction." "General System Theory," *General Systems* (1956), 1:3. It takes seriously Charles A. McClelland's claim that the main task of empirical theory and research is "to identify, portray, measure, and relate the characteristics of the performances of the system down through the tiers or levels of the subsystems" without identifying behavioral systems either in a priori or de jure fashion, and without assuming that nation-states or groups of states constitute separable systems with identifiable boundaries. McClelland, *Theory and the International System* (New York: Macmillan, 1966), p. 21.

retically significant factors are among the characteristics of the participating actors, the issues under contention, and the institutional context in which allocation decisions are made. The first two clusters of factors are the more variable and can include such phenomena as the relative status and similarity of actors, their prior relations, the type of stakes under contention, the nature of the underlying dimension that fused the stakes into an issue, and the types of proposals offered to dispose of the stakes. The third factor is less variable in that it is at once more structural and systemic, but nevertheless is critical because it embodies the written and unwritten rules of political intercourse, thereby making certain kinds of behavior and resources more effective than others and hence more likely to occur. It includes such phenomena as the type of allocation mechanisms available, the degree to which these mechanisms are institutionalized, legitimate, and hierarchical, and the nature of the systemic rules.

When taken together, the assumptions outlined above provide the bases for a dramatically different, though still parsimonious, paradigm and theoretical framework from that of the dominant paradigm described in the first chapter. An alternative paradigm will also provide a new prism through which to view the reality of global politics, a prism of value to both practitioners and scholars. For the former, it promises to highlight key factors that were formerly ignored or omitted, and to deemphasize others like "power" that dominate the way they continue to think about the world, often to the detriment of the citizens they represent. For the latter, an alternative paradigm counsels a rather different research agenda from that employed in the past, directing attention toward elements of change rather than a static contest among a relatively fixed cast of actors.

AN OVERVIEW OF THE NEW PARADIGM AND ITS RESEARCH AGENDA

A paradigm contains within it a fundamental view of the world, and its assumptions act as lenses through which that world is perceived. "Facts" rarely speak for themselves and make sense only when interpreted in the light of the basic assumptions of a paradigm. More importantly, a paradigm serves to make some facts salient and meaningful at the cost of other facts, which may actually be of greater significance. Relevant information may be right before scholars' eyes, yet they may fail to apprehend it because their gaze is fixed upon other phenomena that are highlighted by their initial assumptions. These assumptions, both those that are articulated and those that are implicit, express a general view of the world, stand behind theories that are constructed about it, and guide the behavior of those in high position who share them. Yet precisely because they are assumptions, they are not regarded as suitable subjects for empirical study; indeed, it is probably not possible to study a number of them at all in this manner. In view of this, it is not surprising that equally competent observers may look at the same "reality," yet see dramatically different worlds if they are guided by different paradigms. Thus, Marxists will "see" an economic dimension in all social activities and begin to theorize from that point, while realists will assess the same phenomena in terms of "power" which they believe defines politics. No clearer expression of this natural propensity to theorize about reality from a set of initial assumptions is to be found than in Robert Osgood's definition of a realist:

The Realist, because he is skeptical of the ability of nations to transcend their self-interest, sees the struggle for national power as the distinguishing characteristic of international relations. He tends to view international conflict as an inevitable state of affairs, issuing from man's tenacious patriotic instincts and conditioned by relatively immutable influences, such as geography or some primordial urge, like the drive to dominate.[2]

The assumptions of an issue paradigm bespeak an equally different view of the world. From an issue perspective, the view of realists is seen as a distortion of "reality" because of an overgeneralization and exaggeration of certain kinds of behavior that are confined to particular interpretations of certain issue areas. These are produced by a peculiar mix of specific kinds of actor relationships, issue types, and institutional contexts. An issue paradigm looks first at how issues are defined, what values they are supposed to embody, the proposals that are being made for their resolution, and the issue position each actor takes on the various proposals. It then looks at the interaction process. How and why do actors contend over the competing proposals, what types of techniques are employed to achieve resolution, and how does the process itself influence the relationship among actors and the way they define the issues? Finally, it looks at how resolution is accomplished and what factors encourage or impede resolution. The picture of politics painted by the issue paradigm is not one of struggling for power, but one of struggling to make a collective decision for the purpose of allocating values in an authoritative manner. In the same way as different assumptions provide different pictures of the world, they also provoke different research agendas.

A realist research agenda, for example, would focus primarily on the following questions: What are the ingredients of power, and how do they change? How do changes in the distribution of power affect the behavior of nations? What is the most suitable policy for an individual nation depending upon its power status? What means are available to moderate the perpetual struggle for power? How is it possible to assure that national leaders are undisturbed by "irrelevant" factors, so that they can formulate policy that is prudent, conscious of the realities of power, and governed by selfless patriotism?

The questions suggested by an issue paradigm are quite different. Since the focus of the new paradigm is on issues and how they affect behavior, the first research question that arises is how objects are converted into political stakes; that is, the manner in which value is attributed to objects. The assumption of diverse and multiple values encourages the analysis of diverse stakes, the impact of differences among them on actors' perception and behavior, and the manner in which they are tied into discrete issues. Thus, the first aspect of a new research agenda is the investigation of agenda politics; that is, the processes by which issues are formed, placed upon a global agenda, and taken off that agenda. To undertake such research requires identification of the factors that enable actors to raise issues and to be heard, or that thwart such efforts. It is also necessary to identify the key differences among issues in order to enable their comparison. Variables like the scope of issues, their salience, the nature of stakes that constitute them, and the manner in which these stakes are linked, will provide important clues to the researcher.

Moreover, issues go through rather distinctive stages, in which behavior assumes different characteristics. Certain stages appear to be more amenable to resolving the issue than others. Yet little is known of this cycle or about the factors that produce movement from one stage to another. Before prediction and explanation of the different stages are possible, richer description of them is necessary. As issues change, the rules governing interaction may also change, and actors may resort to different techniques to bring about allocation.

Chapter 4 provides some preliminary theoretical answers to these questions. It postulates that objects of value (political stakes) arise from two sources—the environment and the actors themselves. The first process occurs when previously ignored objects are seen to be valuable, usually because of technological innovation, or when new threats from the environment emerge, such as air pollution, which require collective action to maintain existing levels of value satisfaction. Actors are the source of issues when some of them seek to alter the existing distribution of stakes, an event that often coincides with a change in the status hierarchy. Whether a stake which is thus "born" will occupy a place on the political agenda depends on a number of variables, including the salience of the issue of which it is part, the availability of access routes to the agenda, and the resources of contending actors. Once on the agenda, issues pass through a cycle.

Although the cycle is poorly understood, it appears that critical issues (those that dominate the attention of actors and shape the political order) go through the following stages. First, a new critical issue generates a series of crises, because it provokes changes in interaction and alignments. As actors discover how to contend with each other over the issue, this stage gradually merges with a second—ritualization. If the issue is tractable, it may move directly from ritualization to some form of decision-making, which produces an authoritative allocation and removes the issue from the agenda. Normally, however, critical issues prove difficult to manage, and actors cannot agree on, or do not abide by, decisions over how to resolve them. Before they can be resolved, they may have to lie dormant for a time until issue positions soften and become less uncompromising. During this stage, the issue may reawaken on occasion, during which time incremental decisions are made and interim dispositions of stakes take place. When the issue is intractable and the dormancy stage is omitted, war and/or coercive diplomacy are likely to characterize decision-making.

Since an array of actors may contend for stakes, and since such contention may affect them in numerous ways, it is necessary to enquire into how actors emerge and become participants in politics, and how they change and disappear. Unlike the realist paradigm, an issue paradigm assumes that actors are a central independent *and* dependent variable. A second major task of the new research agenda, therefore, involves delineating factors that permit or obstruct the emergence of autonomous actors, and that encourage or discourage their formation, reformation, or demise. Such research will inevitably entail a search for factors that condition and shape individual motivation and loyalties, and that anchor loyalties in some cases while producing shifts in loyalties in others. By placing questions concerning actor coalescence and fragmentation at the foundation of enquiry, pervasive assumptions of a fixed cast of actors in global politics and a dichotomy between "international" and "domestic" politics are discarded. The actor is regarded as a variable, the analysis of which will facilitate efforts to identify attributes that may provide the most potent comparisons and contrasts.

Another item on the new research agenda is the investigation of the impact of actor unity upon cooperation/conflict. Since one of the assumptions of the new paradigm is that actors are variables—and that a major source of variation is unity—it is necessary to enquire into how this may dilute or intensify dominant patterns of relations. Where unity and coordination among agencies of government—or other groups within actors—are low, their separate activities may produce incompatible patterns of relations with identical competitors. Actor attributes like unity are also regarded as possible intervening variables.

Chapter 5 suggests that the process of actor formation and fragmentation is closely connected to the issues on the agenda. Individuals and groups seek to form political actors, because alone they cannot manipulate the political process to resolve issues in a manner they find desirable. Potential members of actors always suffer from perceptions of value deprivation, but whether they will seek to alleviate that deprivation through political participation depends upon their attitudes toward politics, the availability of stakes suitable to alleviate their deprivation, and the organizational context of the political system (the number of organized interests and the extent to which the environment facilitates or constrains the formation of organizations). Not all potential members will actually join a new actor. Whether they do is a function of two variables—the extent to which they need others to achieve a desired outcome (interdependence) and the extent to which they trust others (similarity).

In the literature, the concept of actor has been regarded as a dichotomous variable; either an actor exists or it does not. This is inadequate to explain the degree to which members coalesce to form an actor or with-draw to fragment an existing actor.* Hence, actors are classified according to their degree of coalescence or fragmentation—unitary actor, coalition, faction, divided into competing actors. Once an actor is formed, the degree to which members coalesce depends on seven variables: whether the issue under contention features an actor or stake dimension, the salience of the issue to members, the prior and concurrent patterns of interaction among members (the extent to which they agree and engage in positive behavior toward one another), their consequent friendship or hostility, the success or failure of the actor in providing value satisfaction to members, and the organizational context.

Since it is assumed that actors and issues are interdependent in some fashion, a third characteristic of a new research agenda is the investigation of the means by which issues (as well as other factors) condition the perceptions of actors toward stakes, as well as toward each other. The central question here concerns factors that determine the manner in which elites think about issues and approach the problem of formulating proposals for the disposition of stakes. What is the process by which actors assume issue positions and when, how, and why do these positions change? Is it possible to identify different ''calculi'' that actors might utilize to formulate issue positions? How do these calculi differ in their effects, and what factors predict resort to one or another of them?

Chapter 6 attempts to answer these questions in a systematic fashion by developing a model to explain the calculi actors will employ and the likelihood of these calculi producing ultimate agreement among them over how to resolve an issue. Actors are conceived as utilizing one of three calculi to determine their issue positions: a cost-benefit calculus (which focuses solely on the value to be derived from the stake under contention), an interdependence calculus (which looks at the need to derive support from other actors for concurrent issues), and an affect calculus (which determines issue positions primarily on the basis of hostility or

---

*The literature on integration as ''process'' is something of an exception to this generalization. See, for example, Leon N. Lindberg and Stuart A. Scheingold, *Europe's Would-be Polity* (Englewood Cliffs: Prentice-Hall, 1970), and Philippe C. Schmitter, ''Three Neofunctional Hypotheses about International Integration,'' *International Organization* (Autumn 1970), 24(4):161–66.

friendship toward the other actors contending for the stakes in question). Other factors being equal, a strong stake dimension encourages a cost-benefit calculus; a strong actor dimension encourages an affect calculus; and a weak stake or actor dimension encourages an interdependent calculus. Such an analysis is not explanatory, however, because, to be so, it must delineate the conditions under which a stake or actor dimension will emerge. The latter is determined by four variables: the salience of the issue under contention, the similarity of the contending actors, their relative status, and their prior pattern of interaction. Actors that are relatively equal in status tend to be competitive, but the degree to which this competition will be regarded as threatening is determined by the other three variables. Similarity reduces threat because it engenders trust, whereas dissimilarity increases the sense of threat by producing suspicion. Perceived threat also increases as the salience of the issue grows, and as the prior pattern is more one of conflict. An affect calculus is likely to arise when negative affect is present, and this condition is probable when there is equal status and dissimilarity, high issue salience, and a history of antagonism. Other factors being equal, a cost-benefit calculus is apt to be employed when an issue is of high salience but negative affect is absent. An interdependence calculus is used when the salience of issues and the status of contenders are intermediate. Other factors are not, of course, always equal, and the specific relationships are detailed in the chapter. For the moment, it is sufficient to note that the use of an affect calculus in the presence of positive affect produces agreement; and in the presence of negative affect produces disagreement. An interdependence calculus permits considerable agreement, and a cost-benefit calculus permits disagreement.

Questions of actor agreement lead to the analysis of interaction patterns and the concepts of cooperation and conflict, which constitute the fourth major topic of enquiry on the new research agenda. Of course, much of the study of international relations has featured these as central dependent variables, and the assumptions of realism reinforced this propensity. Such research has not been misguided, but it has been hampered by the assumption that cooperation and conflict constitute two ends of a single continuum and that behavior is unidimensional. Recent research suggests that this assumption is incorrect, and that both cooperation and conflict are complex and multifaceted variables that feature affect and observable behavior. In addition, the two may be distinct variables, rather than functions of each other.

More significantly from the perspective of an issue paradigm, relationships among actors may vary by individual issue, so that it is misleading to describe them in terms of any single mix of cooperation and conflict. The existence of separate issues with separate arenas of competition produces the possibility of crosscutting effects as well as reinforcement of dominant patterns of behavior. A major task of the new research agenda is the analysis of the ways in which linkages among issues serve to dilute overall cooperation or conflict among actors, or produce spirals of one sort or another. Indeed, if issues are sufficiently encapsulated, several apparently contradictory patterns of interaction may exist at one time among the same contending actors.

Finally, while the various aspects of cooperation/conflict may constitute suitable dependent variables, the assumptions of the new paradigm also permit them to function as independent variables, in their turn, in producing significant alterations in such key variables as issue linkage, actor characteristics, and issue-position calculi. It is not only cooperation/conflict that feeds back into prior processes; these patterns of interaction produce success or failure, and consequently positive expectations of hope or negative expectations of frustration. A key aspect of the new research agenda entails a search for the manner in which these consequences feed back directly or indirectly into prior processes.

Chapter 7 addresses these questions by beginning with a reconceptualization of cooperation/conflict. It is separated into three related dimensions: agreement–disagreement (a behavioral expression of differences over issue positions), positive–negative actions (a measure of behavioral punishments and rewards), and friendship–hostility (a measure of psychological affect). A model is presented that delineates and explains hostile spirals and distinguishes them from patterns of cooperation. At the heart of the model lies the notion of issue dimension. An actor dimension tends to produce disagreement because of the competitive nature and distrust usually associated with this dimension. In addition, an actor dimension tends also to produce issues that consist of symbolic and transcendent stakes. These types of stakes encourage disagreement directly, as well as indirectly, by producing proposals for their disposition that tend to allocate benefits and costs in an unequal manner. The three issue variables have a strong impact on the agreement pattern. Disagreement, in turn, tends to make actors employ negative actions as a way of influencing issue positions and proposals. These actions have no direct impact on issue positions, but do have an immediate effect on friendship–hostility. Negative actions engender hostility, which in turn feeds back on the issue dimension, encouraging contenders to develop an actor dimension. This produces an amplifying effect, making the stakes appear still more symbolic and transcendent, which makes proposals still more unreasonable.

Chapter 7 concludes with an examination of how such hostile relationships can be changed. The two critical variables that determine whether such a relationship is susceptible to change are the success or failure of the interaction process in overcoming value deprivation and the amount of cognitive dissonance or consistency arising from behavior. Of the two, the former is more important. Other factors being equal, success tends to make actors repeat behavior whereas failure leads to change (usually escalation). Cognitive dissonance, which is produced by mixing cooperative aspects (such as positive actions) with elements of conflict (such as disagreement or hostility), tends to produce change (usually deescalation) whereas consistency encourages the status quo. The ways in which these various combinations may bring about changes in interaction through a change in the issue dimension are specified.

These considerations require scholars to give greater weight to the cognitive processes of elites within actors than has traditionally been the case under the assumptions of realism. Rejecting the assumptions that these processes are fixed or that interests are "self-evident," the new paradigm encourages research into the prospects for restructuring cognitive maps and the possibility that such restructuring will intrude upon existing patterns of relations. Failure and success of existing cognitive maps, for instance, disturb or reinforce the elements of those maps, though in ways that have not been specified by political scientists. Cognitive maps provide actors with prescriptions concerning what they should do under different conditions. What processes are initiated if the maps in fact lead to unexpected destinations? Under what conditions are existing maps altered or reinforced?

Cognitive maps themselves are the products of expectations, not only about what results will flow from different courses of action, but also about how other actors will respond to different initiatives. What are the consequences when such expectations are violated? Since the relations of actors are considerably more complex than realists had assumed, and since cooperation/conflict does not adequately describe this complexity, there exist numerous possibilities for cognitive dissonance, both of an individual and collective nature. Indeed, leaders may purposely introduce such dissonance into relations out of conviction or idealism or for reasons of expediency. The prospects for such dissonance in global politics have been poorly explored, and its possible effects have been virtually ignored. Since different interaction games are conducted according to different sets of tacit or articulated "rules," a key question concerns the effects of dissonance upon these "rules." Will unanticipated behavior or unexpected consequences be treated as heinous violations or as opportunities? In a more general sense, what are the various means by which cognitive consistency can be restored, and under what conditions will there be resort to one or another of these means?

Answers to these questions require investigation of different types of games and rules, in order to determine which are more susceptible to change and what conditions are conducive to it. Variation in such characteristics of interaction games as institutionalization, legitimacy, and hierarchy may provide some clues for such an enquiry. These clues may help to generate cumulative theory when observed with the aid of elements in learning theory as applied to persistent patterns of success and failure, rewards and punishment, and benefits and costs. Such analysis, however, will inevitably be complicated by actor variables, such as internal unity, because it is not always clear to which individuals or groups the patterns apply. Whatever the success of the enquiry, it will focus upon change itself, breaking out from the static analyses of realism, and will be directed toward penetrating the essence of development and decay in global politics as a whole.

The final aspect of the new research agenda concerns the manner in which authoritative decisions about issues are reached. Under what conditions are final allocations of disputed stakes possible, so that an issue may be removed from the agenda once and for all? How and when can these conditions be satisfied, and when will allocations prove merely tentative and temporary (interim dispositions of stakes), thereby threatening to reappear on the agenda in perhaps a more threatening guise than before?

Such questions direct enquiry to different possible mechanisms for allocation. These mechanisms may be classified according to several dimensions, including their reliance on unilateral strength as opposed to collaborative norms. On the basis of these dimensions, the various techniques may be characterized as reflecting one of four "pure" allocation mechanisms—force, bargains, votes, and principle. Each of these contain different criteria for making decisions, determining "victory," and therefore achieving final allocations. Though any of them may produce final allocations, it appears that they vary as to their capacity to do so. Therefore, careful investigation of these mechanisms is necessary in order to determine their association with different outcomes, and in order to identify the conditions that provoke resort to one or another mechanism.

Since there is more than one mechanism, this raises questions of how they are related and whether actors can and will switch from one combination of techniques to another. Such combinations may be thought of as interaction games. Of fundamental importance is how new games are created and integrated into the system. War itself, as a mode of arriving at decisions, must be treated in terms of the different mechanisms; in this fashion, different types of wars can be identified. Each type has its roots in different sets of conditions, is waged in different fashion, and may produce different consequences, particularly in yielding authoritative allocations.

Chapter 8 explores in detail the association between allocation mechanisms and the genesis of interaction games. As actors seek to dispose of stakes and reach decisions, they engage in behavior that forms patterns and gives rise to mutual expectations. In this way, interaction games with informal (though occasionally formal) rules arise. The "rules" in these games inform actors of how to behave if they wish to reach a decision and have their proposals prevail. Such games usually feature mixes of the allocation mechanisms that must be employed in various sequences (e.g., force among equals is usually employed only after other techniques have been tried). Games of this sort can be created consciously, as the Congress of Vienna created the Concert of Europe; or in an ad hoc manner, as the Cold War developed between 1945 and 1947.

Since more than a single interaction game usually exists in any political system, it is necessary to explain which will be employed by actors to dispose of a given stake. If all factors were equal, actors would struggle with one another to select the game that promised them the highest probability of winning; that is, the game for which their resources were best suited. This tendency is limited by two other variables—the dominant issue calculus that is used among the contenders and the strength of the systemic rules. The use of a particular issue calculus places limits on the choice among allocation mechanisms, and hence the selection of games, because certain calculi favor certain mechanisms over others. A negative affect calculus, for instance, encourages force and bargains and excludes principle and votes. The reverse is true in the case of a positive affect calculus. Within these constraints, actors favor games that maximize their chances of winning. However, as a pattern of behavior becomes more institutionalized, rules regarding the sequence of games that *should* be played for different types of issues grow up and become accepted. These "systemic rules" inform actors of how they should behave in order to achieve allocations of value at acceptable cost. In societies where "government" is the dominant game, systemic rules are often embodied in a written constitution.

Governments and constitutions are largely absent in global politics. One result of this is that war has been commonly used to dispose of stakes and resolve issues. The theoretical section of the book comes to a close with a discussion of how and why this interaction game is selected. Employing a status inconsistency model, and adopting insights from learning theory, a model of the onset of war is presented. War is most likely to erupt when a change in the status hierarchy makes one actor equal in status to one that was superior to it in the past but which is also perceived as being dissimilar. Under these conditions, competition and mistrust usher in an actor dimension in the presence of a highly salient critical issue. The actor dimension promotes relationships that are prone to the types of hostile spirals described in chapter 7. Negative affect will make it difficult to dispose of the stakes at issue amicably and their consequent symbolic and transcendent quality will increase this difficulty. Systemic rules will determine the sequence of games that will be played; but each game is "doomed" to failure, owing to the presence of the other factors. Repeated failure, coupled with the consistency of hostility, will promote an escalation in negative acts, defections from or misunderstandings about rules, and a tendency to favor games that rely on force and coercive diplomacy. As each game fails, actors will increasingly behave in unilateral fashion and form or join alliances to protect themselves from perceived threats. These processes encourage a sense of mutual threat which promotes arms races—and arms races are highly correlated with the onset of war. The alliance polarization–arms race–hostility spiral syndrome is, in effect, a final interaction game prior to war.

With the conclusion of this chapter, the realist paradigm, with its flaws and their consequences, and the issue paradigm, with its assumptions and elements, have been portrayed. The following section of the book presents in detail the theory that emerges from the assumptions of the alternative paradigm.

PART TWO

THEORY

The process by which demands of various groups in the population are translated into items vying for the serious attention of public officials can appropriately be called agenda building.
—Roger Cobb et al.[1]

CHAPTER FOUR

AGENDA POLITICS

INSOFAR AS almost every political organization from a school club to the United Nations General Assembly has an agenda, it is surprising that processes of agenda setting and change are not better understood and more widely studied. The need to do so has become more pressing in light of the growing centrality of the concept of issue in politics, because agenda processes reflect the treatment of issues and indicate both the relationship among them and the relative importance accorded them. Yet the literature on agendas is scant in general and practically nonexistent in global politics.* Roger Cobb and Charles Elder define agenda as "a general set of political controversies that will be viewed at any point in time as falling within the range of legitimate concerns meriting the attention of the polity."[2] With this as a starting point, a number of questions arise that any theory of agenda politics must address: Where do issues come from? Why do some reach the agenda whereas others do not or are consigned to its periphery? How are issues removed from an agenda? Under what conditions do agendas change?

Although some tentative answers have been suggested in the area of American politics, the questions have been largely ignored at the global

---

*In the case of global politics, this is partly a result of the emphasis by the realist paradigm on anarchy rather than society and the consequent failure to see in world politics a political system that seeks to arrive at authoritative decisions.

level.[3] This omission is partly a result of the conventional overemphasis by scholars on global anarchy and their consequent failure to see world politics as a process, part of the purpose of which is to arrive at authoritative decisions. The contemporary world is conceived better as a global society than as an anarchic state of nature, if indeed anarchy ever existed for any length of time.[4] Even in the absence of formal government, there are identifiable patterns of behavior, an agenda or set of agendas, and, from time to time, authoritative decisions. With these as working assumptions, this chapter will sketch the outlines of a theory of agenda politics in the global arena by scrutinizing three related processes—how a global issue emerges, how issues reach an agenda, and the life cycle of issues.

GENESIS: THE SOURCES OF ISSUES

There are two basic sources of issues—the environment and the actors themselves. An issue emerges from the environment when opportunities for increased value satisfaction, or fear of value deprivation, is occasioned by factors not directly associated with the behavior of actors. Such factors make their presence felt slowly and reveal themselves gradually, during which time the salience of old stakes changes and new stakes are perceived. The two types of environmental issues are "opportunity issues," which are the consequence of science and technology, and "disaster issues," which are the product of common problems that threaten existing value satisfaction.

"Opportunity issues" involve stakes which are generated by the capacity of humans to transform previously valueless objects into objects with value, or to "invent" stakes with greater value than those that had previously existed. The increasing technological capability to exploit the seabed, for instance, has made such territory an object of contention, thereby shifting the content of the law of the sea issue away from stakes that were the traditional subjects of international law. From the Truman Declaration of September 28, 1945, "we can trace," declares Wolfgang Friedmann, "both the technological revolution that is opening up the oceanbeds to exploitation of both mineral and biological resources at an ever-increasing pace, and a new phase in international relations, in which the oceans, hitherto free to all for navigation and fishing, are subjected more and more to exclusive and competing national interests, and widening portions of the oceanbed . . . are partitioned between rival states or groups of states."[5] Although legal theorists since Hugo Grotius have concerned themselves with the law of the sea, few have considered the seabed itself. Similarly—as air and space travel develop—territorial airspace, the moon, and even other extraterrestial bodies, become political stakes. Technology is also making it possible to harness the seas and the sun for energy, as well as to "harvest" the seas for food in previously unimagined ways.

As technology yields new stakes, the values they reflect undergo significant change as well. The seas, for instance, traditionally regarded as providing security from attack, are now seen as dangers to security, owing to the advent of missile-launching submarines. Such developments reopen such old issues as the limit of territorial waters, which was traditionally determined by the range of shore-based gunfire.[6] In the same fashion, the "First World War made suddenly evident the vital importance of the legal status of the air. . . ."[7] For the most part, "opportunity issues" initially have the effect of increasing the size of the total "pie" and hold open the possibility of common gain, thereby resembling "distributive" issues, which Theodore Lowi argues are characterized by logrolling and coalitions of uncommon interests.[8] Whether this occurs depends on the extent to which the new opportunities are equally available to potential consumers and the willingness of actors not to preempt them unilaterally. Global inequality is fostered when only selected actors have the capability to exploit new stakes. Seabed resources, for instance, are currently accessible only to the few Western governments and corporations that control the technology to take advantage of them. Similarly, developments in fishing techniques have enabled certain governments and their industries, notably those of the USSR and Japan, to acquire more than their "fair share" of this valuable resource. Problems such as these feature importantly in current Law of the Sea negotiations.[9] As inequality increases, an issue may assume a regulatory character, as disadvantaged actors seek to exert control over the privileged few.

"Disaster issues" emerge from the environment in the sense that no actor, or set of actors, is responsible for having created them intentionally. The outbreak of plague is an example; others include water or atmospheric pollution, overpopulation, changing climatic conditions, and depletion of key resources such as oil. These issues tend to be regulatory in Lowi's sense, because they involve regulation of the physical environment and/or the behavior of actors in order to overcome the problem. They threaten a common (though not necessarily equal) deprivation of value and a shrinking of the total pie. Only if the issue is resolved will net benefits remain the same (as in the case of plague) or possibly increase (as in the case of regulating air traffic). These issues encourage collective problem-solving techniques * as long as there is a prospect that all actors will be victimized relatively equally by the threat (as in a hypothetical invasion from space). However, they can become extremely dangerous if they afflict actors asymmetrically, thereby sharpening perceptions of relative deprivation.†

This last problem is illustrated by the "limits to growth" controversy.[10] Analyses of world population trends, food production, industrial growth, depletion of raw materials, and pollution have suggested to some Western economists and ecologists that human survival may be threatened unless growth is limited and a steady-state world economy introduced. The major burdens of such a decision, however, would be borne by Third World populations that would be deprived of the opportunity to achieve a standard of living equal to that of the West. They are called upon to limit population growth, industrial pollution, and energy consumption in order to overcome dilemmas that they view as having been caused by the prodigality of the economically wealthy. Such attitudes, if they persist, become a second source of issues as Third World actors seek a New International Economic Order.

Actors are the source of issues when it is their purposeful behavior that creates a new stake, revives an old one, or alters the values ascribed to an existing stake. Issues are commonly raised to the agenda by actors that seek to redistribute a set of stakes that other actors control, or to acquire greater access to stakes the benefits of which they already enjoy to some extent. These might be called "deprivation issues" because they threaten

*For the distinction between collective problem-solving and competitive bargaining techniques, see William D. Coplin, *Introduction to International Politics,* 2nd ed. (Chicago: Rand McNally, 1974), pp. 258–323.

†Colonialization offers many instances of an outside power—instead of being viewed by elites as a common threat—being seen as promising potential allies against indigenous enemies. In both North America and Africa, the result of such perceptions was the eventual conquest and domination of an entire native population.

to deprive another actor of some stake. Imperialism in its classical mode is an example of such an issue. Able to defeat major competitors,—as Rome did Carthage—or to come to some amicable division of the spoils—as did France and Britain prior to World War I—the imperial power simply strips others of the stakes. Related to this process is the reverse one engaged in by revisionists or revolutionaries who seek to end their status as "have nots." Germany's effort to overthrow the Versailles Treaty and Stalin's attempt after World War II to reincorporate the territory lost by the Brest-Litovsk treaty are exemplary cases of this. But revisionist and imperial powers may not confine themselves to concrete stakes. They may also seek to impose a "new order" in the process, such as Trotsky described in *The Permanent Revolution*. When they do, considerable strain is placed on global society and its distribution of values.

"Deprivation issues" are produced when there is a change in the global status hierarchy. As "haves" weaken or "have nots" grow stronger, the appetite of the deprived is whetted. Revolutionary behavior not only becomes a more possible but a more attractive option once authorities have begun to experience setbacks. In Russia, the Bolsheviks sought to seize power at a time when the old regime had been crippled by its defeats in World War I, and in Germany positions of authority were surrendered to the Nazis only after the Weimar Republic had been paralyzed by successive crises that grew out of inflation and depression. Such cases suggest that revolutionary conditions arise in the context of *less* than normal coercive control by authorities. The same would appear to be true in a global context. Prior to World War I, the appetite of various South Slav groups was whetted by the growing enfeeblement and fragility of the Ottomans and the Habsburgs, and the crumbling of those empires domestically and internationally. Similarly, once France and Poland had been defeated militarily by the Nazis, Mussolini and Stalin took the opportunity to satisfy their own claims. As Winston Churchill declared: "The rush for the spoils had begun. . . . To join the Jackal came the Bear."[11] And, the defeat of France offered Italy "a chance which comes only once in five thousand years."[12] In other words, the weakness and decline of some actors provide incentives for others to challenge an existing order.

When stakes become available owing to the eroding status of their possessors, or to the strengthening of challengers, a leveling process ensues as the dissatisfied compete for stakes previously thought to be beyond them. Such a process seems to be taking place today in relation to critical raw materials in a context of rising demand, increased dependency of industrial societies upon external sources, and innovative political tactics (such as cartelization) by the suppliers of commodities like oil tin, and copper. As C. Fred Bergsten declares:

A wide range of Third World countries . . . have sizeable potential for strategic market power. They could use that power against all buyers, or in a discriminatory way through differential pricing or supply conditions—for example, to avoid higher costs to other LDC's or against the United States alone to favor Europe or Japan.[13]

As existing mechanisms of global political and social control break down, the variety and number of stakes are increased. However, as new mechanisms are perfected, the total number and variety of stakes are reduced as they are removed from "the market." Over time, then, the number and variety of issues on any agenda are variable.* As the environment generates stakes, the number and diversity of groups becoming actors will grow, because there exist greater opportunities for value satisfaction. As their number and diversity increase, some of them will place still other issues on the agenda. In particular, those that are frustrated by the distribution of environmental stakes will explore new avenues to achieve value satisfaction and challenge status quo actors that have expropriated prior stakes. But not all potential issues reach the agenda; and, of those that do, some are regarded more seriously than others. If the agenda process is to be understood, it is necessary to explain how these outcomes are produced.

FROM INDIVIDUAL AGENDAS TO A GLOBAL AGENDA

Cobb and Elder stipulate several phases through which an issue passes on its way to an agenda. These include initiation (articulation of a grievance by a small group), specification (translation of grievances into specific demands), expansion (the attraction of support for issue positions and the growth of recognition that an issue must be dealt with), and entrance (the movement of an issue from a "public agenda" to a "formal agenda"). In

* Variation is also caused by the manner in which the stakes are perceived to be linked.

addition to the original participants in an issue, other groups that may become involved include an "identification group" (those who feel strong ties, often on the basis of shared traits, to the aggrieved), "attention groups" (those who see themselves as having a direct interest in the outcome of the issue or disposition of the stakes), the "attentive public" (groups and individuals that are generally aware of and commonly involve themselves in public issues even in the absence of a perceived concrete interest), and the "general public" (other groups or individuals that tend to remain uninvolved and unaware).[14]

While Cobb and Elder provide the best analysis of agenda building in the literature, their work remains incomplete, because they do not develop a clearly specified model of how and why an issue gets on an agenda. Their work, moreover, is in many respects limited in its application to the American polity. Indeed, the elaboration of a model of agenda processes is hampered at the outset by the general conceptual impoverishment that afflicts the discipline of international politics as a whole. To construct such a model, it is best to begin by seeking a common and inclusive set of definitions and descriptions.

An *agenda* consists of proposals for allocating stakes in issues over which actors are contending. Cobb and Elder suggest the existence of two agendas in a political system—public and formal. An issue exists on a public agenda when those who make proposals for allocations gain the attention of those who can carry out such allocations. An issue is part of a formal agenda when those who can make an authoritative allocation take it under consideration. However, the diffuse nature of global structure and the absence of explicit authorities to whom supplicants might turn reduce the value of this distinction for global politics. The distinction at the global level is better made by simply recognizing the difference between gaining the attention of those who are capable of making a decision and the actualization of that capability to resolve competing claims, rather than positing two separate agendas, which implies two different causal processes underlying each of them.*

---

*Since the UN is not a world government, its agendas cannot be considered as formal. In relatively tranquil domestic societies, the public agenda can be found in the reports of the major media—or its equivalent in closed societies (e.g., underground reports)—and the formal agenda can be found in the agendas of the various government agencies and legislative bodies that make authoritative decisions. The conceptual definitions provided here are in-

There is, of course, no official single agenda in global politics. Instead, each actor in global politics has its own "foreign-policy" agenda that is a list of external issues with which it is concerned. These lists can be culled from official documents such as the president's state-of-the-world speech and statements of UN representatives or from the official, semi-official, and prestige media of the actor. The relative salience of issues and their rank order on the cognitive maps of leaders can be determined through content analysis of these sources. Some actors like the United States government have agendas of considerable scope and domain, whereas others like the PLO are "single-issue" actors. Actors rarely have identical agendas, and their relative ordering of issues by importance varies considerably.

Though subtle and diffuse, however, a single global agenda can be identified and can be defined as those issues and associated proposals that attract serious attention from either a large number of actors or from those capable of resolving the claims. In other words, the global agenda consists of those elements of individual actors' agendas that overlap. *Among the most challenging of foreign-policy tasks for any actor is to determine the issue agendas of other actors and to persuade them of the legitimacy of one's own agenda and the hierarchy of issues it incorporates.* These tasks are logically prior to and prerequisites for obtaining the acceptance of preferred proposals. In this manner a global agenda evolves and comes into existence. The dependent variables of this analysis are how individual actors inject issues of concern to them into this agenda-building process and what happens to issues once they have been added.

Since the procedures for resolving issues are not fixed in the global arena and since those who are capable of making decisions among com-

tended to be sufficiently broad to apply to political systems with or without formal governments.

If two agendas were posited, an important question would be why some issues exist on the formal, but not the public, agenda. In global society this possibility is manifested in the secret treaty and agreement. In domestic society, it may be seen in the "gentleman's agreement" or the "old boy network." An insufficiently recognized question is why societies differ in the extent to which they are characterized by issues on a formal, but not a public, agenda. The ratio of issues on the formal agenda to those on the public agenda may be an untapped measure of societal "openness." Employing this measure, it appears that, although global society is elitist and lacks formal government, it is often more "open" than many domestic societies.

peting claims, if they exist at all, may differ according to the type of issue (military security vs. economics vs. law of the sea), or the geographical source of the problem (Latin America vs. Sub-Saharan Africa vs. Eastern Europe), the identification of a single global agenda, as opposed to several unrelated issue-area or regional agendas, is an empirical question. This question can be answered by examining the extent to which actors share the same issue concerns, communicate with each other about these concerns, and offer and contend over proposals to resolve the issues. Clearly some issues will not have great scope or domain and may only be bilateral (illegal aliens from Mexico in the United States) whereas others will attract many actors (the Cold War or the Law of the Sea). In part, the number of actors contending on an issue is a measure of the salience of that issue in the system as a whole, and each issue need not be interpreted as having an existence separate from the global agenda just because the cast of actors varies from issue to issue. If there is little or no overlap among actors in these issues or regional subsystems then the global system and agenda may be said to be subsystem dominant, if not nonexistent. In the ancient world, for example, the Roman political system was isolated and distinct from the Chinese, not to mention other self-contained systems in North and South America. The concept of global agenda, then, is an analytical device for identifying interaction processes among actors, and the more tightly knit the system the greater the probability of finding an overarching global agenda.

Determining the extent to which there is a single global agenda poses the same kind of conceptual and measurement problems as does the problem of whether there is a single global political system or a series of subsystems. These two problems are essentially definitional and can be resolved instrumentally. Whether one posits a single system or agenda depends primarily on what one wishes to study. For the purposes of this analysis, the empirical question of a single agenda is a tangential concern, since it is assumed that the agenda-building process is essentially the same (in terms of causal patterns) for a global, regional, or even domestic agenda.

If the global agenda consists of overlapping issues from the agendas of individual actors, then the agenda-building process can be approached by asking two questions: 1) how do actors gain the attention of other actors who are not concerned about these issues, and 2) what makes an issue of concern to actors in the first place. The first process involves questions of influence and the second, salience, the topics of the next two sections.

ACCESS ROUTES TO A GLOBAL AGENDA

Actors who, owing to their resource base behave or are regarded as authoritative decision makers, have almost immediate access to the global agenda, just as authoritative decision makers, like the president, do in developed domestic societies. Such global actors can be defined as high-status actors. Theoretically, high status refers to the overall reputation of actors for resolving issues. This reputation is derived from the actual ability of actors to dispose of political stakes in the past because of their resource base. High-status actors constitute an elite in two ways: first, they have the capacity to make substantial decisions about issues by themselves or with one another, and, second, collectively they can confer legitimacy upon most decisions or dispositions in the system.* In this manner high-status actors provide for the global political system, at least in part, some of the traditional functions of government.

The status of an actor in global politics determines the means and ease with which it may place an issue upon the agendas of other actors (or raise them higher upon those agendas). High-status actors have easy access to much of the world's media since whatever they do "makes news" owing both to the weight of their actions and the attention paid to them by others. They also have easy access to international organizations of all kinds owing to the factors just cited, as well as their control over the financial and other resources necessary for the operation of such organizations. As a result, their advocacy of a specific proposal or program will receive serious consideration by others, though not necessarily acceptance; and, if an issue is high on the agenda of one or more of them, it is likely to appear somewhere on the agendas of other actors as well. This is the case even if the latter are fundamentally unconcerned about the issue, because the attitude of high-status actors toward issues about which they are concerned may be decisive in terms of outcomes. Lesser actors

---

* Whether global politics has a ruling elite or a series of elites in different issues with limited or no overlap among them is an important empirical question without immediate relevance to this analysis. Presumably the degree to which there is a single elite will vary historically.

must be minimally prepared to accord attention to the concerns of the powerful if only in order to attract the attention of the powerful to the issues with which they are preoccupied. Weaker actors are often prepared to "feign" interest in the issues that preoccupy the strong, or to redefine issues in such a way that they appear to be part of a key issue which concerns the strong. Thus, many actors sought to influence the United States or the Soviet Union during the Cold War either by supporting one of the superpowers in the Cold War or by presenting the issue that was really important to them as though it were an element of the Cold War.

Since high-status actors are key determinants of the global agenda and since their favor is crucial to obtaining acceptance of proposals, a major task for most actors is to bring issues of importance to them to the attention of those of high status and then to persuade the latter to act on them. However, bringing issues to the attention of the strong and getting action on them is no mean task. High-status actors tend to be status quo actors, prone to suppressing or ignoring issues that threaten to "rock the boat." Generally, those who are well-disposed to a status quo enjoy structural advantages over those who would change it.[15] Many issues never reach the global agenda because those who are satisfied resist their inclusion.[16] Status quo actors seek to limit the agenda to "safe issues":

(D)emands for change in the existing allocation of benefits and privileges . . . can be suffocated before they are even voiced; or kept covert; or killed before they gain access to the relevant decisionmaking arena.[17]

The capacity of elites to keep items off an agenda is primarily a function of the nature of formal and informal access points, a structural variable. These access routes determine what resources are necessary to get an issue on the agenda.

Access to a system requires an understanding of the rules of the game in that system, a willingness to follow them, and the skill to do so—assets that can only be acquired with experience. These requirements are not unlike those that are associated with successful lobbyists in a domestic context. Indeed, research concerning access to the public agenda in the United States is relevant to the development of global theory as well. Access usually depends on whether the structure of the system gives groups the opportunity to acquire information and communicate effectively, an opportunity which grows out of sustained and long-term interaction. In domestic society access is correlated with the opportunity to acquire the education and skills necessary to participate in politics. Research on political participation reveals that certain skills and attitudes are prerequisites to participation. Sidney Verba and Norman Nie argue persuasively that those who are of high socioeconomic status (determined by job, education, and income) develop certain civic attitudes (sense of political efficacy, a belief that politics are important, and a sense of obligation to participate), and are affiliated with voluntary organizations will have a greater tendency to participate than others.[18] Although the specific skills and attitudes necessary to participate in global political life might vary, by definition the greater the extent to which a system encourages the proliferation of skills necessary to utilize communication channels, the greater will be access to the agenda.

However, for these skills to be relevant, some communications infrastructure must exist—media, places to petition, or other channels between those who wish to make demands and those who can deal with them authoritatively. The contemporary revolutions in communications and transportation systems and the globalization of the mass media have made it possible for groups, even in remote areas, to bring an issue to public attention. Access to television, radio, or the press permits groups that would otherwise remain unknown or isolated to bring their grievances to the public eye by behaving in a sensational or disruptive manner. The media also provoke a sense of immediacy and urgency toward issues that formerly would have been absent. Thus, the issue of emergency food relief was forcefully brought home by televised footage of Cambodian refugees. These developments have increased both the pressures by new groups to be heard and the opportunities to gain a hearing.[19]

Of course, it is easier to achieve access in some systems than in others. Access to an agenda is facilitated when it is widely known *who* can make authoritative decisions and where procedures exist for making them. Societies with effective governments tend to provide specific mechanisms for such access—nomination procedures, elections, party congresses, political parties, and so forth. Access becomes still easier if there exist a variety of legitimate ways to influence decision makers. To the extent that these conditions are absent, access is limited.* Such channels are not en-

---

*One of the ways in which the U.S. and USSR are "developed" politically (in Samuel Huntington's sense) is that they both provide explicit, albeit very different, access channels

tirely absent from the current global system. One might view the global system as a middle arena between fully developed, and decaying or collapsed polities.

The most traditional access route in societies without formal government is to structure or alter the agendas of high-status actors. Such efforts are facilitated to the extent that a weaker actor occupies a strategic position in relation to the stronger. If, for instance, it can play an important role in some other issue of importance to the strong, an opportunity for trade-offs exists. Or, as a result of past friendship, existing patterns of communication, high transaction or interaction levels, or personal ties, the petitioning actor may find itself or its surrogates strategically located near access points of the strong. Such was the condition of the "special relationship" between the United States and Britain which was in reality as much a special relationship between influential elites in the two countries as it was the situational interdependence of the two actors as a whole. Thus, the host of formal and informal bonds that grew up between the two societies provided British leaders in all fields with relatively easy access to American attention, even after Britain declined as a significant force in world politics. The British could bring matters to the attention of influential Americans with some ease, thereby increasing the prospect that these would be placed on the agenda of the U.S. government. Currently, a similar relationship characterizes the United States and Israel.

An alternative, though indirect, route for raising issues to the agenda of high-status actors in global politics is through international organizations. Less likely to be effective in altering the agenda of key actors than is direct access, this path is taken largely by those who lack this direct access. International organizations may act as "transmission belts" between the agendas of different actors. Third World actors that lack direct access to the U.S. or Soviet systems, for instance, may raise issues of importance to them (economic development, racism, and colonialism), but of lesser importance to the mighty, in the General Assembly and other UN organs. The effects of ensuing rhetoric and resolutions upon the

to the formal agenda. See Samuel P. Huntington, *Political Order in Changing Societies* (New Haven, Conn.: Yale University Press, 1968), pp. 1–3. Conversely, unstable societies in which coups are common do not provide easy access to the formal agenda either because (1) it is not known how long leaders will be in charge and therefore whether allocations are really authoritative, (2) access may not exist or (3) no one is capable of making allocations.

agendas of high-status actors is far slower than direct access but can be cumulative if the existence of opportunities or the presence of threat to them is made clear. Of course, this alternative was not always available in global politics, and it arose only with the advent of universalistic organizations. Prior to that time, elite institutions like the Concert of Europe or the Big Three determined the global agenda on their own. Even with the creation of international organizations, access increased only gradually. Neither the League of Nations nor the United Nations ever became a "conscience of mankind," in part because powerful members kept embarrassing issues off of their agendas (e.g., the Vietnam War for the most part). Nevertheless, with decolonization and with universal membership and equality of voting in the General Assembly and other organizations, weak actors have acquired unprecedented access to the global agenda. And, from time to time they do evoke a significant response, as the World Food Conference and, to a lesser extent, the New International Economic Order talks, illustrate. Moreoever, international organizations have been valuable mechanisms for the weak in providing their representatives with the skills and experience that are necessary for direct access, and some UN institutions like the United Nations Conference on Trade and Development (UNCTAD) have as their major function the articulation of Third World demands.[20]

Although the United Nations on rare occasions provides access to revolutionary groups, like the Palestine Liberation Organization, nongovernmental actors have generally had to rely on informal access. One route has been through the organizing of nongovernmental and transnational groups, which, in turn, have contact with the UN through the specialized organizations (like the International Labour Organisation) and the Economic and Social Council (ECOSOC), one function of which is to maintain contact with such groups. On the whole, only the more "functional," as opposed to "political" groups, have managed to gain access by this route. Yet in the cases of population control, women's rights, pollution control, and the law of the sea, these actors have played important roles in raising issues in the first place.[21] The UN has even established major nongovernmental (NGO) forums at important conferences to solicit ideas and information from these actors.

Since many politically oriented nongovernmental actors lack even this avenue of access, they may resort to violence or other forms of disruption.* Roger Cobb and his associates hypothesize that:

a) the more important the issue, b) the more isolated the original grievance group, c) the longer the issue has been on the public agenda, and d) the lower the likelihood that the authorities will consider the issue on their own, the more likely that the entrance strategies will include the use of violence or threats of violence. . . .[22]

Political "parvenus" can in this fashion focus the attention of "haves" upon previously ignored grievances. The threat of continued disruption may convince elites that ignoring the dissatisfied will be more costly than dealing with the issue they raise. (Such was the effect of riots in America's urban ghettos in the late 1960s.) Violence may be used to tempt opponents into overreaction, thereby creating sympathizers and new victims; it may be used to provide martyrs, to discomfort third parties, or to attract the attention of the media. Whatever their tactic, previously ignored groups like blacks, Indians, Chicanos, and feminists in the United States; ethnic groups like the Kurds, the Philippine Moslems, and the Ulster Catholics; as well as revolutionary groups in countries like Italy and El Salvador, have succeeded in placing issues on the global agenda by violating existing norms and expectations.†

The most dramatic contemporary example is that of the Palestinians who, since 1967, have employed hijacking, assassination, and even random terror to awaken "the audience that is irresistibly attracted to the scene."[23] El Fatah and other Palestinian groups became increasingly active and autonomous after the Six-Day War, when it appeared that neither existing Arab regimes nor outside powers were prepared to press the Palestine issue vigorously. Their major contribution since that time has been to raise the salience of this issue to the point where it has become a focus

---

* Those who have been frustrated in their efforts to air grievances or prohibited access are more prone to use violence or the threat of violence to gain a hearing. See H. L. Nieburg, "The Threat of Violence and Social Change," *American Political Science Review* (December 1962), 56(4):865–73.

† James Q. Wilson argues that such protest groups resort to violence and/or disruption, because they have nothing else to "trade" in order to gain satisfaction of their demands; *Political Organizations* (New York: Basic Books, 1973), pp. 281–300.

of global attention,* and to stimulate proposals by other participants for resolving it.[24]

The use of such tactics and their consequences reveal that the vulnerability of global society to disruption makes access to an agenda always possible for those who are prepared to accept the risks that are involved. Violence, of course, may be unnecessary in order to raise an issue to an agenda if organized and articulate opposition suffices. It is with this in mind that Robert Dahl writes of the tremendous "slack in the (American) system."[25] There are resources that are untapped and can be utilized if the "right" issue comes along. Opposition in the United States to the Vietnam War and, earlier, to racial segregation illustrates this. New groups formed and marshaled resources. They developed innovative ways of attracting attention and pressing their demands. Access to an agenda, at the global or local level, is often a matter of hard work and imagination, except in the most closed and repressive societies.

In general, it is becoming increasingly difficult for "gatekeepers" in global politics to keep items off their agendas and to disregard issues that are of importance to others. The rapid movement of people and ideas across political boundaries compounds this difficulty; issues cannot easily be "quarantined" any longer. The various ways in which an issue may gain access to the global agenda from the agendas of individual actors are depicted in figure 4.1.

However, the analysis of access routes to the agenda does not provide a complete picture of the agenda-setting process, because it does not answer the question of why some issues are regarded as important in the first place. It is this question that must now be addressed.

THE DETERMINANTS OF ISSUE SALIENCE

The most potent factor in determining whether an issue will reach an agenda is its salience to key actors. Salience refers to the importance of an issue to an actor,† and it is the product of five factors: the degree to

---

* Ironically, the tactics of the Palestinians resemble the tactics of Zionist groups after World War II, when they sought to bring the issue of an independent Jewish state to world attention.

† Issue salience should be kept analytically distinct from the degree of awareness of an issue within a society or group.

Figure 4.1 Access Routes to the Agenda

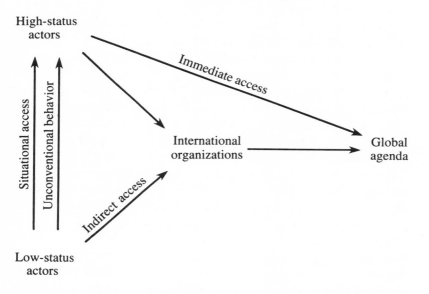

which an issue involves deprived—as opposed to satisfied—values; the status of the stake(s) at the outset (whether controlled or unattached); the type of stake(s) (concrete, symbolic, transcendent); the number and diversity of values associated with the stake(s); and the extent to which these stakes are sought for intrinsic or instrumental purposes.

The first factor determining the salience of an issue to an actor is the degree to which its leaders and members collectively feel themselves to be deprived of the value(s) associated with the stake(s). Although all values are, in the abstract, equally desired, at any moment actors have rough value preference schedules that are the product of collective perceptions of existing or threatened deprivation and the possibility of alleviating that deprivation. Thus, while an actor may have no a priori preference between, let us say, peace and wealth, it will, ceteris paribus, focus on issues which include stakes that are associated with the value of which it is most deprived, or of which it fears it will be deprived. This is why those who are desperately impoverished are willing to sacrifice peace and gamble their lives to overcome poverty. Although there may exist a hierarchy of human needs, as Marx and Maslow maintain (with self-actualizing needs arising only after physical needs are somewhat satisfied), once nonphysical needs emerge they will take precedence over other needs to the extent that they are unsatisfied.* Thus, even though the relevance of a value to political autonomy or survival may contribute to its salience, such a value (if satisfied and unthreatened) may be risked for more elusive values like status.

This last observation points up a key flaw in realist thinking, the assumption that "national security," defined in terms of political survival, motivates the foreign policy of all actors and is at the core of their national interests. Derived from realist assumptions about the role of the unitary national actor in global politics and the function of power in political life, this view of national interest, defined by Morgenthau as territorial integrity and national sovereignty,[26] tells only a part of the story. Actors do strive to enhance security as defined in this narrow sense, but they are not so much interested in surviving as in surviving well. Thus, what was intended as an explanation becomes more of a prescription.† Global actors seek not just survival-related values, but any value of which they are deprived, or fear they will be deprived, and that seems obtainable or defensible through political means.‡ Moreover, the realist notion of survival, meaning the maintenance of the "political and legal personality" of a collective unit, is rather different than the physical survival of the individuals who constitute it. Since it is assumed here that issues which embody deprived, as opposed to satisfied, values are more salient

* See A. H. Maslow, "A Theory of Human Motivation," *Psychological Review* (1943), 50:370–96. In Marx, this distinction is used to separate prehistory and history, the latter being the new human nature that will arise after economic cleavages are overcome. See Vernon Venable, *Human Nature: The Marxist View* (Cleveland, Ohio: Meridian, 1966), pp. 74–97.

† But even this is of limited use, because it does not provide any specific recommendations as to how to identify national interests. See Arnold Wolfers, "National Security as an Ambiguous Symbol," in Wolfers, ed., *Discord and Collaboration* (Baltimore, Md.: Johns Hopkins University Press, 1962), pp. 147–67.

‡ Once this is recognized, much of the American government's economic activity and subsequent diplomatic moves to protect itself during the several months prior to U.S. entry into World War I become easier to understand. In 1917, the U.S. government insisted on maintaining its right to trade with belligerents. The effort to maintain "the balance of power" had little to do with America's actual survival in terms of territory or sovereignty but a great deal to do with perceptions of what it meant to survive *well*. For a similar and more controversial argument against the war with Japan in World War II, see Bruce M. Russett, *No Clear and Present Danger* (New York: Harper and Row, 1972).

to an actor, survival-related issues may not always be central, although actors may seek to paint some issues this way in order to gain internal support.

A second factor that determines the salience of an issue to an actor is the initial status of the stakes that compose it. At the time an issue is introduced, the stakes that it entails may be (1) outside the control of any actor (a "free" stake), (2) in the hands of one or several actors (a "preempted" stake), or (3) already shared by all actors (a "collective" stake). Free stakes tend to produce less salience than preempted or collective stakes, because fear of losing that which is already enjoyed generally produces more passionate involvement than the prospect of acquiring something in addition and the "possessor's valuation may even increase by his knowledge that it is coveted or by an attempt to extort it from him."[27] For this reason, issues that threaten the loss of stakes that are being enjoyed generate higher salience to an actor than issues that revolve around stakes that are controlled by others or that no actor controls. The fear of loss produces perceptions of relative gain and loss more commonly than does the prospect of gaining something new. The phenomenon of "backlash" reflects the powerful emotions that may be unleashed by perceptions of relative loss.

Perceptions of potential relative deprivation increase to the extent that an actor enjoys access to, or control over, a stake that is being challenged. The psychological predisposition described above is reinforced by the generally higher level of legitimacy accorded to the status quo than to challenges to that status quo. An actor which is challenged may react with great vigor if its resources permit it to do so, as did Great Britain when its naval dominance was challenged by imperial Germany in the first decade of the twentieth century. Perceptions of relative deprivation are less striking for issues in which the stakes are in someone else's control (though such perceptions will be high for the latter). Perceptions of loss for the actor in question (as opposed to the possessor of the stakes) are muted—though awareness of inequalities in value satisfaction may still be high—and envy or jealousy, rather than fear, is the motivation. Finally, perceptions of loss and inequality are weakest in the event that the stakes are outside of anyone's control. In such cases, greater attention is paid to alternatives that promise the highest absolute return to an actor than to those that promise value deprivation for others. Whatever an actor finally obtains for itself (even if not as much as originally hoped) is seen as an absolute step forward. Such issues may, however, prove unstable in the long run once allocation gets under way. As some actors begin to enjoy access to the "free" stakes, they will also begin to fear their loss unless agreement can be reached regarding their authoritative disposition.

A third factor that conditions the salience of an issue is the type of stake which constitutes its central focus. Does the issue revolve primarily around concrete, symbolic, or transcendent stakes? Symbolic stakes usually are more salient than concrete ones, because they are seen to represent other stakes, and/or are connected to the images actors have of themselves on the status hierarchy. Transcendent stakes are still more salient because they reflect fundamental philosophical and moral beliefs that provide social and political cohesion. To challenge such stakes is to threaten the elemental social fabric of other actors and their world view.

Realism's great contribution was to inveigh against the efforts of idealists to transform reality into utopia by pursuing transcendent stakes. Ideological wars tend toward total war, so that to seek transcendent ends as the basis of foreign policy is likely to provoke unrestrained responses which may threaten survival itself. The wisdom of the national interest dictum lay precisely in pointing up the paradoxically "immoral" consequences of a foreign policy based on the rigid moral views of individual actors. The realist definition of "prudence," which it regarded as the highest virtue, was the elimination of transcendent stakes from politics. Unfortunately, political actors from the ancient past to the present have not taken this presciption seriously enough.

The final two variables that determine the salience of an issue are the number and diversity of values associated with stake(s), and the degree to which those stakes are sought for intrinsic or instrumental purposes. First, the greater the diversity of values associated with an issue, the higher is its perceived importance to contestants. Moreover, issues that are broad in the sense that they consist of diverse and numerous values will be viewed as more valuable than those that are narrow. Second, issues that involve intrinsic stakes for all participants are more salient than issues which promise instrumental stakes to all or some. This is because intrinsic stakes promise immediate and direct value enhancement. Under certain conditions, however, an issue may be more salient to an actor which is seeking instrumental stakes than to one which is seeking intrinsic stakes if the instrumental stakes are viewed as necessary to acquiring other stakes that are themselves of extremely high salience. Figure 4.2 summarizes the effects of the five factors just discussed on the salience of an issue.

The foregoing discussion leads to two questions: (1) which stakes will be sought first, and (2) which issues will be most salient as they come upon the agenda. With regard to the first, dissatisfied actors seek stakes that they can most easily obtain. These include stakes that have not previously been allocated, that are not firmly controlled by their possessors, that are not held legitimately, and that the actor's resources are best suited to obtain. Assuming a rational cost-benefit analysis, an actor will initially seek to acquire stakes that are not under anyone else's control, because such efforts will arouse less resistance and appear more legitimate to observers than if directed towards the acquisition of stakes already claimed by some other actor. Once "free-floating" stakes have been exhausted, the attention of an actor will turn to stakes that are only weakly held by others. Stakes that are firmly held will be challenged only after other avenues have failed to produce satisfaction, and only if the challenger believes it has sufficient resources to defend itself from the challenged.*

The salience of different issues becomes clearer when the status of the stakes is examined in relation to a cast of actors rather than a single actor. Assuming for convenience a dyadic universe, the most explosive issue will be one involving stakes to which both actors enjoy some access and where proposals threaten their loss by one and monopolization by the other. Such situations are inherently competitive, because neither contender can gain without harming the other, thereby assuring issue proposals that promise unequal costs and benefits. Clashes between actors which fear they are declining relative to one another typify such situations; for example, relations between Russia and Austria-Hungary between 1890 and 1914.

Next in salience are issues involving stakes to which at least one major actor enoys access, and where that access is challenged by a second that

---

* The major exception to this proposition would be the case of a challenge made to punish or warn another actor, as in Israeli raids into Lebanon and the Chinese assault on Vietnam in early 1979. Such challenges are only partly serious in that they are undertaken to acquire "bargaining chips" and do not really contradict the proposition.

Figure 4.2 Salience Conditions

HIGH SALIENCE		LOW SALIENCE
Deprived values		Satisfied values
Joint fear of relative loss	Joint fear of absolute loss or promise of relative gain	Joint prospect of absolute gain
Transcendent stakes	Symbolic stakes	Concrete stakes
Broad scope	Intermediate scope	Narrow scope
Joint intrinsic stakes	Mixed intrinsic-instrumental stakes	Joint instrumental stakes

stands to benefit from any further disposition. In this classic redistributive setting, one participant perceives the issue in terms of unequal costs and benefits, while the second discerns tempting opportunities for enhanced value satisfaction. The next most salient issue involves stakes to which all participants have access, but where their enjoyment is threatened by collective deprivation. Issues of resource depletion are of this sort. Perceptions of cost make the issue salient, but the collective character of the threat mutes perceptions of relative gain or loss. The least salient issues in terms of preferred values are ones where stakes are outside anyone's control. Where stakes are divisible, perceptions of interdependence may result if background variables permit them to do so. In a few cases, it may prove impossible to divide the undistributed stake, which can only be enjoyed collectively. This is the "public good" for which no single actor will strive energetically because none can be deprived of access to it.*

Figure 4.3 suggests that salience is the key intervening variable in agenda setting. Other key variables are the nature and variety of access routes and the status of actors. Each of these variables is more potent than the one which follows it in the sense that it reduces the number of cases that remain to be explained.

Salience is the most potent variable, because only issues that are at least salient to one actor can reach an agenda. This proposition escapes the risk of tautology, because the foregoing analysis specifies the characteristics of issues that will *not* be sufficiently salient. But, it must not be assumed that all issues of high salience *will* reach the agenda. Whether they do, depends on the status of the stakes. Stakes that are initially beyond anyone's control are likely to reach the agenda, because this may be the only acceptable manner to allocate them. Conversely, when a stake is initially under some actor's control, that actor will oppose its inclusion

---

* See Mancur Olson, Jr., *The Logic of Collective Action* (New York: Schocken, 1965), pp. 9ff., and Norman Frohlich, Joe A. Oppenheimer, and Oran R. Young, *Political Leadership and Collective Goods* (Princeton, N.J.: Princeton University Press, 1971), p. 3. Although individual actors tend to see such issues as low salience ones because each hopes that others will bear the costs involved in producing the collective good, the issue may grow more salient in time if it remains unresolved and touches a core value. In other words, issues involving collective goods can become highly salient because of other variables in the model, but the collective quality of the stakes inhibits them from becoming salient easily or quickly.

Figure 4.3 Agenda-Setting Model

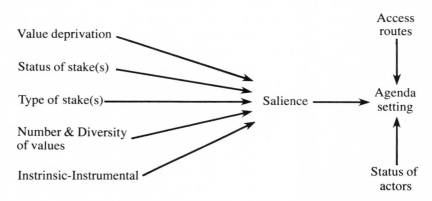

on the agenda, unless its loss appears inevitable. Whether challengers succeed in raising an issue to the agenda depends on the availability of suitable access routes and on their capacity to outwit or outfight opponents.

The *relative* salience of issues on the global agenda is also important, because it provides a way of comparing the concerns of individual actors and ranking them according to the significance that they have for global society as a whole. In this manner the global agenda gains structure and helps shape interaction into identifiable patterns. Ceteris paribus, all actors try to get the issue that is most salient to them to be salient to others. Thus, a major part of the agenda-building process is a struggle over salience rankings. The most important of these struggles is over which issue will be at the highest ranking, thereby taking precedence over all others.

Issues that have the highest salience in the political system can be referred to as *critical issues*. These are issues that are initially at the apex of the individual agendas of all or most of the high-status actors and that, in time, tend to draw in or redefine other issues. Such issues dominate and shape the agendas of lesser actors and, consequently, the global agenda. These issues come to form the bases of political identification in global politics and the axes of major coalitions. In American politics such issues have included slavery, populism, and the Great Depression.* In global

* For a review of this literature, see Gerald M. Pomper, *Elections in America* (New York: Dodd, Mead, 1968), and the classic V. O. Key, Jr., "A Theory of Critical Elections," *Journal of Politics* (February 1955), 17(1):3–18.

politics such issues have included the rise of Islam, the French Revolution, imperialism, fascism and, more recently, communism (the Cold War).

Critical issues define an agenda by conditioning the most important alignments in a system and shaping basic affect (friendship-hostility) among actors. They have this impact because they determine who will agree and disagree, a major source of affect. It is through critical issues that the political order acquires ideational direction. In American politics, the concept is employed to explain how party identification is generated and how it changes. Critical issues are so salient that they force political parties to realign on the bases of the new cleavages they reflect. Once the parties have regrouped, contention among them, particularly at elections, centers on the critical issue, thereby providing a focus for policy as well as for interaction.

Critical issues tend to operate in a similar fashion in global society, once the obvious structural differences are taken into account. When a critical issue such as the French Revolution or communism emerges, it establishes alignments among actors. The system can be "realigned," in which case friends become enemies and enemies become friends, or "maintained," in which case the alignments remain the same, but the reasons for their existence change.

Critical issues usually produce an actor dimension (perhaps differing from ordinary issues in this regard), and one consequence is a reduction in the fluidity of alignments over time, so that the possibilities for realignment are restricted to their initial stages. If the issue is dominated by two principal actors, the alignment of minor actors is dictated to them. Minor actors tend to become "stakes," "pawns," or "clients" in the course of contention between the principals, whose alignment policy (the product of a negative actor calculus) is directed toward depriving the adversary of friends and preempting allies (rather than seeking an accretion of strength). If minor actors passively acquiesce in this process, the principals may assume a policy toward them based on a positive actor calculus. But efforts to defect will prove difficult, owing to weakness, and will be treated by the principals as acts of betrayal—an attitude summed up in Cleon's speech about the Mytilenian effort to abandon the alliance with Athens during the Peloponnesian War:*

* Snyder and Diesing depict the relationship between unequal allies of this sort in a game they call "Protector." See Glenn H. Synder and Paul Diesing, *Conflict among Nations*

Now, to act as they acted is not what I should call a revolt (for people only revolt when they have been badly treated); it is a case of calculated aggression, of deliberately taking sides with our bitterest enemies in order to destroy us. And this is far worse than if they had made war against us simply to increase their own power.[28]

Realignment, even in the presence of critical issues, is a more viable prospect, if alliances consist of a number of actors of approximately equal status.*

Clearly identifiable critical issues are unusual; therefore, it is important to delineate the characteristics that differentiate them from more common issues. James Sundquist, in his review of critical elections in the United States, argues that the potency of an issue and hence the probability of its becoming a candidate for a critical issue is a function of four factors: the breadth and depth of the underlying grievance that gives rise to one issue, the extent to which the issue crosscuts prior alignments, the strength of attachments to prior alignments, and the ability of leadership to defuse the issue.[29] The *breadth* of a grievance describes the number of stakes that are involved and the diversity of values associated with them.† *Depth* refers to the extent to which stakes are infused with symbolic and transcendent qualities. The extent to which an issue *crosscuts* defines the degree to which enemies find themselves in agreement with each other and in disagreement with friends. Crosscutting produces cognitive dissonance; the more encompassing the crosscutting, the more drastic the shift in affective bonds because the entire world is turned upside down. The *strength of prior alignments* may deflate a new critical issue, if it produces considerable crosscutting. However, the strength of such align-

(Princeton, N.J.: Princeton University Press, 1977), pp. 145–52. Their overall discussion of alliance games has considerable heuristic value (pp. 129ff.) Their utilization of games is based on Rapoport's and Guyer's analysis of 2 x 2 games. See Anatol Rapoport and Melvin Guyer, "A Taxonomy of 2 x 2 Games," *General Systems* (1966), 203–14.

 * As Snyder and Diesing point out (*Conflict among Nations* p. 429), alignment questions are more significant and the prospects for intra-alliance bargaining are greater where there are a number of actors with substantial resources. Then, there will be tension between the general interests of partners in maintaining the alliance and their particular (often differing) interests in the specific stake at issue (pp. 429–40). Snyder and Diesing depict bargaining among allies in these contexts as games of "Leader" and "Hero," which are variants of the game of "Chicken" (pp. 131–45).

 † The definitions of these variables, while derived from Sundquist, are based upon the larger theoretical framework being developed in this analysis.

ments is a function of the extent to which prior critical issues have been resolved. If they have been removed from the agenda, as fascism was in 1945, the bases of prior alignments will be undermined. Finally, *leadership* refers to the extent to which existing leaders can defuse or encapsulate an issue. Franklin Roosevelt, for instance, played an important role before his death in preventing communism from becoming a critical issue.

While the above variables may explain the potency of a critical issue in the United States, another factor must be added to explain it in global politics—the *stability of the status hierarchy*. Changes in status hierarchy often result from the enfeebling of actors that were on the losing side of the previous critical issue, thereby reducing old attachments among victors. In addition, if new actors emerge, they may have little concern with the old issue, as in the case of Third World actors in recent decades.

Some of these characteristics suggest a set of operational criteria that can be employed to identify the specific critical issue in a system and its relative potency. A critical issue must meet two basic criteria. First, actors that are able to make authoritative decisions must devote more of their attention and behavior to this issue than to any other. Second, the outstanding pattern of agreement among actors and the bases of the major coalitions in the system must be determined by and be explicable in terms of actors' issue positions on this issue. Because critical issues are so important and because so little is known about what happens to issues once they reach an agenda, the following analysis will seek to delineate the stages that these issues may pass through during their life cycle.

THE ISSUE CYCLE

Of the many issues that exist on an agenda, relatively few are subjects of active contention at any time. Many are pushed aside temporarily or are eclipsed by the emergence of other issues. In some cases, contention persists but remains highly stylized, subject to standard operating procedures and practiced initiatives and reponses leading to incremental change. Other issues, however, may find themselves the subjects of rapt attention and frenzied activity.

During its life, an issue may be characterized by changes in stakes, fluctuations in perceptions regarding those stakes, and variation in the cast of actors that are contending for them. Despite such changes, the issue continues to represent a contest for the same or for similar values. For example, "neocolonialism" is really a continuation of the older issue of "colonialism." Its core value remains freedom or independence for Third World populations, but the key stake is no longer political control of local governments. Instead, stakes like commodity prices, control of multinational corporations, and tariff concessions are centers of attention. The core actors, moreover, are no longer the governments of Britain, France, Spain, Portugal, Holland, or Belgium—or their colonial representatives—and aspiring nationalist elites. Instead, Third World leaders, international organizations, corporations, and the governments of the United States, the Soviet Union, and China occupy center stage in the issue.

Such shifts give rise to the suspicion that there exists an "issue cycle" or series of stages through which an issue passes before it may be resolved. Unfortunately, little is known of these. Different kinds of issues probably pass through different stages, particularly those that are salient to only a few in society. Anthony Downs has described an issue cycle for typical issues (those that affect primarily a minority rather than a numerical majority in the United States).[30] The issue cycle that will be elaborated here refers to issues that dominate the attention and energy of the major actors—critical issues.*

Critical issues usually pass through at least four, and sometimes five, stages once they have reached the global agenda: crisis, ritualization, dormancy, and/or decision making (as alternative paths off the agenda), and administration. These are summarized (except for administration) in figure 4.4.

Once a new issue reaches the agenda, it passes through a *crisis* stage. First, there is a crisis owing to an atmosphere of urgency: the issue must be resolved or disaster will ensue. As Charles McClelland has shown, crises are associated with palpable increases in the frequency of interaction.[31] Second, there is a crisis in the sense that alignments and the focus of political activity change, and thus the very basis of the political order may be transformed. Memories of agreement and positive acts that had characterized relations in other issues may no longer be relevant to the

*The extent to which noncritical issues follow this cycle is a subject that should be investigated empirically.

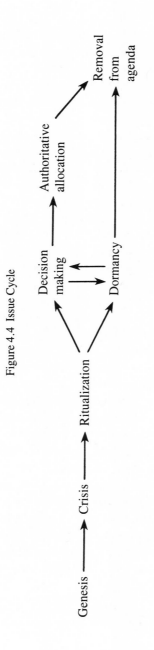

Figure 4.4 Issue Cycle

new critical issue, thereby permitting misunderstandings and misperceptions, with protagonists coming to believe that the other party is defecting from existing understandings when, in fact, those understandings are no longer germane. Existing expectations become invalid, and the future becomes unpredictable. Third, there is a crisis in that shifting alignments and the emergence of the new critical issue may coincide with dramatic changes in the status hierarchy. This often occurs because a prior critical issue was resolved through the destruction or enfeebling of a major actor, as in the cases of Napoleon's France and Hitler's Germany. If this is the case, actors simply do not know how to deal with one another nor what is expected of them. They will then test each other, and a series of crises in the narrow technical sense (high threat, short time, and surprise) will ensue.[32] Finally, the crisis may exist in the sense that some aspect of accepted morality is seen to be threatened.*

The crisis stage may be analyzed as three phases. During the first, the new critical issue struggles to dominate the agenda, either by eclipsing a prior critical issue or overshadowing other potentially critical issues. An awareness of the threat posed by the new issue characterizes this phase until it supersedes its rivals for attention.

Realignments are produced in the next phase, and cognitive dissonance ensues as actors withdraw from old alliances and as earlier commitments are openly questioned. Such was the case when France pulled out of NATO, or the United States abrogated its mutual defense treaty with Taiwan. Meanwhile, the new issue produces new friends and, more importantly, new interests. Gradually, the actor dimension present in the old issue is dissolved into a stake dimension, while the new critical issue results in other stakes being fused along a new stake dimension that may later produce another actor dimension, once the realignments are completed. By the time this occurs, the new issue dominates the agenda.

The more changes in actor relationships that are produced during the realignment phase, the more difficult will be the final phase of the crisis stage—the development of a new pattern of expectations regarding how to interact and to contend over the new critical issue. For structured poli-

---

*James Sundquist is one of the few scholars who emphasizes this, and he seems to be correct in doing so. He argues that a realignment can only occur when the crosscutting issue is intrinsically moral (like slavery) or is basically nonmoral but becomes infused with moral overtones as did populism.

ties, this last phase may be of short duration, though some unconventional behavior may occur. (Slavery produced the American Civil War, and populism ushered in agrarian radicalism.) In societies that are poorly structured, realignments often destroy the institutions that were produced by the old issue. For example, in the absence of the Napoleonic threat, the Concert of Europe collapsed in eight years; and with Hitler gone, the Big Three could not institutionalize their pattern of behavior into an effective United Nations Security Council. New institutions must be created, and shifts in power must be accommodated. These factors, along with an absence of prior experience with the issue, tend to produce crises (in the narrow sense of high threat, short time, and surprise). Lacking established repertoires of measures and countermeasures, actors may respond to one another's initiatives in a "tit-for-tat" sequence which threatens escalation and undermines stability.[33] Since mutual expectations are minimal, the prospect of surprise is great, and this fuels mutual fear and heightens concern for relative gain and loss that might provide one, or the other, side with a decisive advantage.

Ad hoc interaction eventually produces a patterned set of expectations concerning how to interact over the issue. At this point, the issue has entered the stage of *ritualization*. But there is no clear demarcation between crisis and ritualization, and, for at least a transitional period, an issue is in both stages. The length of this transition depends upon how disruptive the new issue has been to the prior pattern of interaction. If there are only minor changes in alignments, no significant changes in the status hierarchy, and a fairly institutionalized and stable set of procedures for making decisions, then the crisis stage will be minimal and the issue will be ritualized at an early time.

Ritualization involves the continuation of competition and repetitive probing, but within mutually understood limits, and governed by tacit rules in accordance with standard operating procedures that the actors develop to prevent surprise and uncertainties from leading to renewed crises.[34] Ritualization also entails the continued threat of force and bargaining from strength, and is dominated by a climate of negative affect. Hostile moves are undertaken by adversaries, but such moves are expected and so can be parried. These moves may range from minimally irritating gestures to more sharply provocative acts, such as the East German inspections of allied convoys to Berlin in the 1950s and 1960s, or the exchanges of artillery fire and low-level military incursions between Mainland China and Taiwan in the 1960s. However, competition remains stablized, so that crises will not recur unless one party violates newly formed expectations in a major way, as did the Soviet Union when it secretly implanted missiles in Cuba in 1962. Such violations, if they occur, may be the consequence of a felt need for internal consensus building by one actor (Austria-Hungary's ultimatum to Serbia in 1914), the catalytic behavior of a subgroup or third party (Palestinian terrorism against Israel that precipitated the Israeli occupation of southern Lebanon in 1978), fear that the adversary is on the verge of violating understandings (Israel's preemptive attack on Egypt in 1967), or some combination of these.

Ritualization is not a prelude to the final resolution of an issue, although it *permits* the onset of the sequence of events that may bring about such resolution. While key actors may be conscious of how their fates are linked, this instrumental tie lacks positive affect to cement them. Thus, the Cold War did not suddenly end after the Cuban missile crisis, and, in fact, the USSR at that time launched a significant program to modernize and enlarge its strategic military capability. Final resolution is made doubly difficult during ritualization because actors are fearful of "rocking the boat." Thus, decisions tend to be highly incremental. Such incrementalism precludes the altering of basic assumptions by participants about the intentions and motivations of one another, so that negative images remain intact. Even a generous proposal might be destabilizing if the other side interprets it as a sign of weakness or as a ruse.

Crisis and ritualization, then, tend to go hand in hand; each crisis elaborates existing rituals, or creates new ones, and gradually institutionalizes behavior patterns, so that coercive diplomacy is no longer needed to attain interim or tacit agreements. Since outcomes can be anticipated, the need to play high-risk games is obviated when suitable rituals or "charades" may produce the same results. In this process, zero-sum games become "Chicken" games, and eventually positive-sum games. Such a process occurred during the emergence of nuclear deterrence as a dominant mode of diplomacy in the late 1950s and early 1960s; the institutionalization of deterrence and the doctrine of "mutual assured destruction" in SALT; and the grudging effort to substitute détente for deterrence in the 1970s.

Once interaction is ritualized, it becomes possible to remove an issue from the agenda, but the manner of its removal may be complex. Figure 4.5 depicts the three major paths leading to the removal of an issue from the agenda.* One prominent path (rarely taken in global politics) is for ritualization to lead directly to some determinant decision. This path often entails a prolonged process during which *interim dispositions* of stakes (incremental and partial allocations of stakes that are not accepted as legitimate) are made, eventually resulting in an authoritative allocation and a final resolution. The second and third paths require that an issue first become dormant. Dormancy is a stage during which an issue is relegated to the periphery of public attention. The dormancy stage may, after a time, lead directly to the decision-making stage (the second path), or it may result in an atrophy of the issue without resolution (the third path). Which of these paths will be taken is a subject that must be investigated.

An issue may travel directly from ritualization to decision making if decision-making structures are well-established and accepted, and if one side is capable of winning within the rules. Dormancy is more likely to result when, as in global politics, decision-making structures are so amorphous that actors can contend over how to make a decision and thereafter demand an alternate procedure if the outcome is unfavorable.†

An issue may also become dormant when an interim disposition of stakes has been made, and the decision-making process cannot continue without mutual harm ensuing. Continued stalemate may be costly and frustrating, yet it is not feasible for either actor to eliminate or defeat the other without irreparably damaging itself. This is a situation in which

---

* A major stage in the issue cycle that does not appear in figure 4.5 is that of "administration." Since global society is decentralized, the implementation of decisions or "administration" of an allocative formula is less common than in more structured societies. It is not included because stakes at this stage are usually not on the agenda. Administration does, of course, occur in global politics and is a major task of UN functional agencies and informal "international regimes." Although administration often leads to the removal of an issue from the agenda, that issue may reappear if those who are displeased by the allocation regain strength (Germany after 1933) or as the administration of a decision provokes new opposition (Second and Third Law of the Sea Conferences).

† The various decision-making games in global society are spelled out in detail in chapter 8. For present purposes, the reader can appreciate the global decision-making structure by imagining that a bill in the U.S. could be passed by the Congress, President, Supreme Court, or constitutional convention without any rules existing which delineated the relationship among these institutions.

conditions are not yet conducive to resolution, but in which continuing attention and resource expenditure offer few prospects for success. It was under such conditions that a number of the issues that divided European "liberals" and "conservatives" became dormant during the nineteenth century. According to Richard Rosecrance, the fact that ideological divisions dissipated "was a tribute both to the weakness and strength of the two camps."[35]

Finally, an issue may become dormant because it is robbed of its salience. This may occur in three ways. One of these is for environmental change to render the stakes less important than before. Technological change may render less salient, even irrelevant, stakes that formerly had been the objects of fierce competition by making them obsolete, or by replacing them with substitutes that are not as scarce. Thus, advances in military technology have reduced the importance of formerly critical military installations or geographic locations. Issues involving the distribution of raw materials may disappear as new sources of them, either natural or synthetic, are found, or as different resources are substituted for them. Natural changes in demography may reduce population pressures thereby eliminating land hunger, or new methods of cultivation may permit the exploitation of previously unfertile land and so have the same effect. A second route to dormancy is for the environment to create a major common threat to the participants under which circumstance the original issue seems relatively less important and is relegated to the periphery, at least for the time being. Finally, reduced salience may ensue when key competitors are confronted by challenges on other issues, or are faced by major new enemies that require a reallocation of attention and of scarce resources. Thus, a number of European issues became dormant as Soviet leaders began to perceive China to be a major source of threat, and as the United States government became increasingly preoccupied with Vietnam.

Regardless of its source, dormancy rids an issue of the passions that have been attached to it. Stakes that feature ritualized delay may slide almost imperceptibly into dormancy. Thus, Leonard Woolf strongly endorsed those conferences which prevent "excitement by being so intolerably dull" as a prelude to agreement.[36]

In this manner, dormancy reduces the prospect of renewed crisis and may facilitate the final resolution of an issue. Even if final resolution does not occur, dormant issues are shunted to the periphery of the agenda, where they no longer strain actors' relations. Stakes tend to lose their symbolic or transcendent quality, thereby contributing to a softening actor dimension, and making it easier for issue encapsulation to follow. It may then prove possible to open negotiations aimed at resolving discrete issues according to their merits, rather than regarding them as vestiges of actors' past hostility and augurs of their coming relations. In other words, when issues become dormant, it becomes possible to disentangle them from the central fused relationship so that they may lie quiescent until the opportunity arises for them to reappear on the agenda under conditions more conducive to their resolution. Thus, a number of issues that reappeared on the agenda at the time of Anglo-French negotiations that culminated in the 1904 Entente Cordiale had been dormant for a prolonged period. If the key tacit rule entailed in issue ritualization is for actors to abide by interim dispositions of stakes, then dormancy may be regarded as part of the transition toward legitimizing such interim dispositions and transforming them into final allocations (second path). Alternatively, the issue may simply be forgotten without ever being decisively resolved (third path).

Dormany may entail its own perils. The relegation of an issue to the periphery by mutual consent of major participants may raise the frustration quotient of individuals or subgroups within one of the leading actors or of third parties that see their interests being sacrificed to the interests of leaders. A smouldering sense of injustice may lead dissidents to forge new links with one another, or with other actors, or to try to accumulate sufficient resources in order to catalyze a crisis that would force the issue to be "reborn." The assassination of Archduke Francis Ferdinand and his wife in Sarajevo by Bosnian students in 1914 and the murder of French Foreign Minister Louis Barthou and King Alexander of Yugoslavia in Marseilles in 1934 by Macedonian terrorists were efforts to trigger crises over half-forgotten issues. Likewise, Chinese polemics against the USSR and United States after the Soviet Union refused to provide a "blank check" to China during the 1958 Quemoy crisis, and Palestinian terrorism after 1967, have also entailed efforts to place "pet" issues back at the top of the agenda. Such issues, then, may once again flare up in still more frightening forms, owing to the violation of expectations of leading participants by dissidents. *Tacitum vivit sub pectore vulnus!* [37]

If dormancy is skipped, the decision-making process is just as complex and somewhat more dangerous, because passions have had little opportunity to subside. While the variety of decision games cannot be discussed in this chapter, resolution may be produced either by eliminating contenders, or by finally allocating by agreement. The first process has historically taken place on the field of battle and may be referred to as the "war route" for the elimination of issues. The destruction of the German, Austro-Hungarian, Ottoman, and Russian imperial regimes during World War I brought an end to a series of contentious issues, including the disposition of the provinces of Alsace and Lorraine and the status of ethnic and national groupings in Eastern and Central Europe. Similarly, the collapse of the Axis at the end of World War II effectively ended the issue of fascism. The "war route," however, leads to final allocation *only* if the conflict is effectively terminal. Otherwise, the result is likely to be an interim disposition brought about by force, as a result of which the loser seeks to reverse the verdict at a later time and sets about to rearm, or to find allies, so that the issue can once more be joined. So it was that the allied failure in World War I either to crush Germany decisively prior to the armistice, or to reach a mutually satisfactory agreement with the Germans at Versailles, set the stage for early German resistance to its stipulations and, ultimately, to Hitler's efforts to revise the outcome. Since the results of war are rarely final, they are likely to exacerbate the actor dimension, so that conflict over an issue will become either "episodic" (as in the case of Alsace-Lorraine between 1871 and 1919) or "continuous" (as in the case of contemporary Palestine).[38]

The "peace route" can achieve the final resolution of an issue only when the preferences and perceptions of the key contenders change. One way this occurs is through a proposed allocation that all regard as optimal. Such arrangements may be manifested in treaties and customs, or in the setting up of authoritative international agencies and regimes to implement distributive agreements. The Concert of Europe, constructed after the defeat of Napoleon, was such an agency that enjoyed only limited success. Commonly, interim dispositions of stakes occur through "satisficing" outcomes that are temporarily accepted, thereby postponing efforts to achieve final solutions.

More often, the "peace route" requires the dissolving of large complex issues into smaller component issues, each consisting of a limited number of divisible concrete stakes. Additionally, it requires that participants grow able to trust one another and, therefore, the agreement they have reached. This necessitates the disappearance of a negative actor dimension and movement toward a stake dimension that permits the decoupling of issues and the growth of mutual respect and positive affect. Large and complex issues tend to remain on the agenda for extended periods, as contention persists even after interim dispositions take place, the tentative nature of such dispositions reflecting an incremental process. The global agenda is commonly lengthened by the presence of dormant or partly solved issues that have existed for considerable periods of time, and which under certain circumstances may become again the subjects of controversy. Although many stakes may be disposed of, the issue itself continues to survive until contention over *all* its stakes ceases and their disposition is accepted as final and legitimate by all the major contenders, or until these issues decompose into simpler fractions that can be negotiated with less risk.

Critical issues tend to dominate an agenda for definite periods of time. In American society, this period has been estimated to be from twenty-eight to thirty-six years.* In global society, this cycle seems—at least in modern eras—to be slightly shorter, around twenty-three years. Frank Denton found that every 22.27 years there occurred large systemic wars that produce major changes in the global political order. These periods tend to coincide with Richard Rosecrance's different historical systems.[39] What seems to occur is that one issue is resolved and another emerges in its place.

The fact that American society takes longer to resolve a critical issue is probably a function of the fact that violence, with one historical exception, has not been employed, and resources have been distributed more widely and equitably then in global politics. To delineate the number of years, however, does not explain *why* it takes that long, particularly when violence is employed and enemies defeated. The causal dynamic is probably associated with some generational factor. Among the possibilities are

---

*The critical elections which mark the birth of a critical issue have been 1800, 1828, 1860, 1896, and 1932. Walter Dean Burnham argues that their life is approximately thirty years—"Party Systems and the Political Process," in William N. Chambers and Walter Dean Burnham, eds., *The American Party System: Stages of Political Development* (New York: Oxford University Press, 1967), p. 288.

that it may take this period for socialized attitudes (including friendship and hostility toward other actors) to weaken so that the grandchildren of the original combatants are receptive to new issues and alignments; it may require a new generation to have sufficient energy, or numbers, to begin a new battle; or, the converse, it may require a new generation to forget the pain and waste of millennial struggles.

Whatever the generational factors, at some time during this period a new critical issue will emerge. Often it is an older issue that was dormant or was resolved in (what is now seen to be) an unsatisfactory manner. The seeds of critical issues can usually be traced back to events that occurred while another critical issue made them appear relatively insignificant. The Cold War, for instance, harks back to the 1918 Allied interventions in Russia. The Sino-Soviet dispute harks back to 1945 and before that, to the 1927 Canton incident and the Long March when, in both cases, the USSR told the Chinese Communist party to enter a United Front. Agenda change, then, is a dynamic, almost dialectical process. The exact nature of how agendas change is best understood by tracing a single stake as it moves from different issues on the global agenda. The appendix on Indochina provides such a case.

APPENDIX

Indochina: The Evolution and Transformation of a Political Stake

The subtlety with which agendas change is dramatically revealed in the history of Indochina. During the present century, it has played a role in three different major issues and agenda shifts—colonialism, the Cold War, and the Sino-Soviet cleavage. From the last quarter of the nineteenth century until the outbreak of World War II, the issue of colonialism constituted a key item on the global agenda, and Indochina was one among many stakes in Asia and Africa that were acquired by European actors during this era. Indochina, therefore, has been a major stake in global politics for well over a century. France initially colonized Vietnam in 1867, and Laos and Cambodia became French protectorates in 1883, as the French Empire valued Indochina for its products—mainly rubber and rice. By the time of World War II, the French Empire in Indochina consisted of four protectorates—Laos, Cambodia, Tonking, and Annam—and one colony, Cochin-China. The key stakes were under exclusive French control.

The rise of Japan during the first third of the twentieth century and the formation of the East Asia Co-prosperity Sphere during World War II reflected Japan's effort to emulate the European imperialists and share or seize the Asian stakes from declining powers. In some respects, the war with Japan was a struggle to resolve the colonial issue in the East.* The Japanese invasion and conquest of Indochina in 1940 simply replaced one colonial ruler by another. However, the Japanese victory over France in Indochina—like the rapid Japanese conquests of Malaya, Singapore, Hong Kong, and Indonesia—destroyed the myth of European invincibility and so encouraged anti-European nationalism throughout Asia, including British India. With the defeat of Japan in 1945, the Asian stakes were, for the time being, outside any actor's definitive or legitimate control, thereby encouraging indigenous leaders to believe they were at the threshold of independence.

The struggle for them was already an old one. Ho Chi Minh had sought unsuccessfully for many years to raise the question of Indochinese independence to the global agenda. During World War I, he had journeyed to Europe and had sent a memorandum to the conferees at Versailles to which they paid little heed.[40] Seeking to satisfy their perceived deprivation of national independence, Ho and other Vietnamese nationalists then joined the Communist party and spent the 1920s and 1930s in China and the USSR, at the same time as French administrators in Indochina increasingly resorted to force to suppress nationalist claims. During the Japanese occupation, Tokyo governed through collaborating French officials, and Ho proceeded to organize the Viet Minh on Chinese soil. Toward the end of the war, the Viet Minh began to engage the Japanese and sought to create conditions that would facilitate the achievement of Vietnamese independence.

The French were unable to reenter Indochina at the moment of the Japanese surrender to reclaim their "possessions." French collaborators had

---

* This issue became linked with that of fascism in Europe owing to the formation of a coalition of expediency between Imperial Japan and Nazi Germany. Fascism, as a separate issue, was partly a product of Germany's own challenge to the existing division of the colonial stakes.

been disarmed and interned by the Japanese in the spring of 1945, and the latter had set up pro-Japanese governments in Laos, Cambodia, and Annam (the last under the emperor Bao Dai). The weakness of both the French and Japanese provided the opportunity for which the Viet Minh had been waiting. There existed at this time one highly organized and tightly welded actor prepared to lay claim to Indochina—the Viet Minh, which had been organized by Ho in 1941, consisting of a coalition of nationalists led by the Vietnamese Communist party. In August 1945, even as the Japanese surrender was being negotiated, the Viet Minh overthrew Bao Dai, and on August 29 in Hanoi declared the Democratic Republic of Vietnam. However, under the orders of the supreme commander, General Douglas MacArthur, the Japanese north of the sixteenth parallel surrendered to the Chinese Army while those to the south surrendered to the British. Although the latter withdrew quickly, the Chinese did not do so until the French agreed, in February 1946, to abandon claims to extraterritorial rights within China itself. The Chinese finally withdrew at the end of May. During this period, the Viet Minh in Tonking had established their authority, including the holding of elections to a national assembly.

The stage was set for the first major postwar crisis in Indochina as Ho Chi Minh demanded Vietnamese independence, while the French were prepared only to consider a settlement which would ensure their continued domination of foreign and defense policy. In addition, Ho argued that a unified Vietnam should include Cochin-China as well as Annam and Tonkin, while the French sought to perpetuate their colony's special status. The overall French policy was to restore the prewar colonial empire through the overarching framework of an Indochina Federation of the French Union.*

Disagreements between the French and Viet Minh were initially papered over but were exacerbated when the French High Commissioner sought to move ahead unilaterally in creating a separate government for Cochin-China. In April 1946, Ho Chi Minh entered into negotiations with the French government at Fontainebleau, but these abruptly ended when the French High Commission announced the formation of a provisional government of Cochin-China and the convening of a conference of repre-

---

*Cambodians and Laotians generally supported French pretensions owing to their suspicion of the Vietnamese and to French support for the recovery of territories that had been seized by Thailand during the war. In Laos, however, the Viet Minh did have a significant ally in the Communist Pathet Lao.

sentatives of Cochin-China, Laos, and Cambodia to construct a Federation of Indochina. The initial Indochina crisis came to a head on December 19, 1946 when Viet Minh forces launched a major attack upon Hanoi, thereby signaling the beginning of war. French efforts took two forms. The first was political, involving support for Emperor Bao Dai, who, in June 1949 after prolonged negotiations, was declared head of state of a united Vietnam that included Cochin-China. The second was military, as the French sought to smash guerrilla resistance under Ho.

Thus, the Indochina stakes became available largely owing to the defeat and weakening of French power in World War II. This provided the opportunity for nationalists of many hues, motivated by a growing sense of deprivation of freedom, to coalesce around Ho Chi Minh. French resistance to a loss of status and determination to overcome the humiliations of the war made agreement and resolution of the issue nearly impossible. It was salient to both sides; the French resisted the loss of a stake which they believed was exclusively theirs, and the supporters of Ho were even more strongly motivated by the brief period during which they had tasted the fruits of independence. From the mid-nineteenth century to the mid-twentieth century, the issue remained the same—colonialism. The definition of the Indochina stake and its place in the issue did not change, only the actors able to contend seriously for it changed—from France to Japan to the Viet Minh to France, once again.

The transformation of the stake only occurred with the emergence of a new critical issue on the global agenda—the Cold War between the capitalist/democratic West and the communist East. But the transformation was gradual, since colonialism was not removed from the agenda but only shunted to its periphery, to be dominated by greatly weakened powers and their colonial subjects. During World War II, F.D.R. viewed Indochina and the other Western colonies that had been lost to the Japanese as colonial stakes. He suggested to Molotov that after the war many of these colonies should be placed under international trusteeship and then granted independence.[41] The Truman Administration inherited this perspective, even if the trusteeship plan proved abortive. Indochina was seen as a "French problem," and the administration's attitude toward it could be deduced from its general position on imperialism:

President Truman was prompted from time to time by the State Department to approve statements that seemed to me little more than reiterations, of the long-standing American attitude against "colonialism."[42]

As the Cold War began to spread outwards from Europe and to fuse an increasing variety of stakes, American perceptions began to undergo change. As Dean Rusk recalled in testimony before the Senate Foreign Relations Committee concerning the seeds of American involvement in Indochina:

I think the first involvement was the assistance that we provided to France during the period of the Marshall Plan at a time when France was faced there with the Viet Minh movement, a very large part of which was nationalist but which also had within it a very strong Communist increment.[43]

Rusk's comment reflects the dualism in American perceptions of Indochina that evolved gradually from the early years of the Cold War, during which time American leaders viewed Indochina as only indirectly related to the Cold War issue as a consequence of American interdependence with France and the need to trade for French support of American efforts in Western Europe. This perception was, however, transformed into one of a direct relationship once Mao Zedong came to power in China and the Viet Minh were granted Chinese "sanctuaries" in their war with the French. By 1949, Secretary of State Dean Acheson described Ho Chi Minh as an "outright Commie."[44] In January 1950, Ho's government was recognized by the Soviet and Chinese governments, and a month later the United States recognized the French-supported government of Emperor Bao Dai. By this time, the Soviet and American governments were divided by intense negative affect, so that each was behaving less in response to its interests in the stake itself than to the issue position and behavior of the other. Increasingly, Indochina came to be viewed in Washington as a symbolic rather than concrete stake. The "domino theory" was articulated as early as February 1950, when the National Security Council announced the extension of military aid to the French in Indochina.[45] "In consequence, the Truman Administration began to take an increasing interest in the success of France, and in May 1950 economic and military aid began to flow to Indo-China."[46] The real transformation came with the Korean War. American assistance to the French was seen as part of a larger effort to contain communism. As time went on, American assistance assumed still greater proportions, so that by 1954 the United States was underwriting over three-quarters of the cost of the war.

But the connection with the colonialism issue still dominated the actions of the major combatants. In France, the Indochina war, like the later Algerian war, divided society on the basis of those who supported the empire and those who did not, a division that usually ran along the right-left cleavage. As the war continued, the French military position began to deteriorate, while the home front became increasingly fractured by the issue. French unity reached its nadir during the decisive battle of Dien Bien Phu. On April 5, 1954 Secretary of State John Foster Dulles received an urgent cable from America's ambassador to France, Douglas Dillon, in which Dillon reported a French request for "immediate armed intervention of U.S. carrier aircraft at Dien Bien Phu" as "necessary to save the situation."[47] The U.S. government rejected the plea, and French forces at Dien Bien Phu capitulated on May 7.

Shortly before the surrender, on April 26, representatives of all interested parties assembled in Geneva to discuss Indochina. By this time French will to continue the apparently endless colonial struggle had dissipated.* The government in Paris was rocked by scandals concerning speculation in Indochina currency and the leaking of military plans. Continued external failure rendered it increasingly difficult for any coalition cabinet to govern effectively, if at all, and one after another was formed only to collapse within days or months. On June 12, a government was formed under the socialist Pierre Mendès-France, who announced two days later that he would seek an end to the war within four weeks and would resign if no settlement were reached by July 20. Mendès-France ended the war in four weeks and a day.

If the French were for the most part relatively untroubled by the Cold War issue, so too, albeit to a lesser extent, were important leaders in the United States, including President Eisenhower. Eisenhower resisted the advice of Dulles and the Chairman of the Joint Chiefs of Staff, Admiral Arthur W. Radford, to heed the French call for intervention. In an action which may have been intended to undercut these two advisers, Eisenhower instructed them to solicit the advice and support of congressional leaders. Several of these, particularly among the Democrats, raised serious questions, such as the attitude of America's allies, which led the

---

* The government had never dared employ French conscripts in Indochina for fear of repercussions at home, so that the war had been largely waged by mercenaries in the foreign legion.

administration not to seek authority to intervene at Dien Bien Phu.[48] Eisenhower later rationalized in his memoirs that the strongest reason for America's refusal to respond to French pleas for intervention "was our tradition of anticolonialism."

The standing of the United States as the most powerful of the anticolonial powers is an asset of incalculable value to the Free World. . . . Never, throughout the long and sometimes frustrating search for an effective means of defeating the Communist struggle for power in Indochina, did we lose sight of the importance of America's moral position.[49]

Eisenhower's statement suggests that for him Indochina was a stake that *linked* two separate issues, and that he felt it more important to take an anticolonial position to gain the support of nascent nationalist movements than to abandon the field to the Communists. In this regard, Eisenhower's position was not unlike that of Senator John F. Kennedy's on the Algerian war.

In Eisenhower's linkage of the two issues, Indochina was primarily connected to colonialism despite a concern about "falling dominoes." Others in the United States, in particular John Foster Dulles, placed the emphasis more on the communist (Cold War) issue than colonialism. This is not surprising, since Dulles was guided primarily by ideological considerations, whereas Eisenhower was obviously concerned with military implications as well. Dulles was strongly of the opinion that Indochina had become a key theater of the Cold War—an opinion that French leaders had sought to reinforce when requesting American aid at the moment of Dien Bien Phu's agony, when they cited evidence of Chinese intervention and declared that "for good or evil the fate of Southeast Asia now rested on Dien Bien Phu."[50] Disturbed by the promises of Mendès-France, Dulles feared a French "sellout" at Geneva and with the National Security Council urged Eisenhower "to inform Paris that French acquiescence in a Communist take-over of Indochina would bear on its status as one of the Big Three" and that "U.S. aid to France would automatically cease."[51] From the moment Mendès-France became French premier, Dulles' and French perceptions of the war in Indochina perceptibly diverged. Britain, America's ally, sought unsuccessfully to reconcile Dulles to a solution that would place part of Vietnam under Communist control, but the secretary of state (who had refused to shake hands with Chinese Premier Zhou Enlai) would not participate in the final phase of the conference at which agreement was reached (July 21).

The Geneva agreement constituted a final resolution of the Indochina stakes *from a French perspective* (i.e., the issue of colonialism) but only an interim disposition *for Dulles* (i.e., the Cold War issue) and *the Viet Minh,* who had won only part of what they had fought for. The accord divided Vietnam temporarily along the seventeenth parallel, forbade the introduction of fresh troops or new bases into either zone, and provided for an armistice commission—to be staffed by Canada, India, and Poland—to supervise the cease-fire and prepare for national elections, to be held throughout Vietnam in July 1956. Separate agreements were reached for Cambodia and Laos. The former was to be "neutralized," and all foreign troops withdrawn. In Laos, a small contingent of French officers could remain to provide training for the Laotian army, while the Pathet Lao was permitted to regroup in the northeast provinces of Samneua and Phongsaly. In this way, the overall Indochina question was divided into several more specific issues, with each agreement reflecting concessions to the realities of the local situation.

As far as the resolution of the colonial issue is concerned, France was the major loser. That a reasonably graceful compromise was reached, which provided Paris with a continued presence in South Vietnam and Laos, appears to have been largely the consequence of Soviet pressure upon the Viet Minh to limit their claims for the time being. In this sense, though the Vietnamese achieved independence and therefore victory, the Viet Minh were frustrated in their efforts to unite Vietnam under communist leadership. The Soviet interest in Indochina as a stake in colonialism was marginal, but Soviet leaders did see its instrumental relationship to the Cold War and apparently modified Viet Minh demands in return for French rejection of the European Defense Community (EDC) which was then under consideration before the National Assembly in Paris, and which represented the Eisenhower Administration's preferred means to rearm West Germany. The colonial issue, of course, remained salient to the Viet Minh. However, Ho Chi Minh was persuaded for the time being to establish his regime in the north and await the promised elections in 1956.

In Dulles' eyes, Geneva was an unqualified "disaster" that "completed a major forward stride of Communism which may lead to the loss of Southeast Asia."[52] From the perspective of the Cold War issue, North Vietnam had been lost, but the other stakes in Indochina (and Southeast Asia) were still very much up for grabs, so that—in Bernard Fall's words—the "struggle now began to rebuild a truncated land into a viable non-Communist Vietnamese state."[53]

Although the struggle became temporarily dormant, the two sides began preparations for the next round, when Indochina would again return to the top of the agenda—on this occasion as a central stake in the Cold War. For the Eisenhower Administration, these preparations took two forms, one public and one covert. The former included the creation of a Southeast Asia Treaty Organization (SEATO), at Dulles' urging, in Manila in September 1954 to include the governments of the United States, Britain, France, Australia, New Zealand, Pakistan, and the Philippines. Although the treaty was subsequently cited to justify American intervention in Vietnam, this interpretation is dubious, owing to a clause in the agreement that required the consent of all the signatories before action could be taken. The covert preparations were in violation of the Geneva accords and aimed to bolster the South Vietnamese regime of Ngo Dinh Diem, an anti-communist, nationalist and Catholic, who was strongly supported by liberal and Catholic elements in the United States. As early as August 1954, President Eisenhower approved a National Security Council proposal to provide direct assistance to Diem without reference to French authorities, who were no longer seen as relevant to the issue. In addition, the Pentagon had already dispatched an American team under Colonel Edward Lansdale to begin secret operations against North Vietnam.[54] The United States also provided assistance to Diem in building up an authoritarian regime in the South, a process which included the suppression of the Hoa Hao, Cao Dai, and Binh Xuyen sects, and which climaxed in Diem's "fraudulent" electoral victory in the autumn of 1955.

The final integration of the Indochina stakes into the Cold War occurred against a backdrop of anti-communist hysteria in the United States. It was this atmosphere that provided an opportunity for opponents of Ho Chi Minh in the South to gain American backing. The rise of Diem is an intriguing story of the forging of a transnational link in which organized groups both in Vietnam and the United States, operating as factions within their countries, were able to tie domestic and foreign stakes together into a single issue. Diem was first tapped as a possible non-communist alternative in 1950 by Wesley Fishel, a political scientist from Michigan State University, who arranged for Diem to come to the United States.[55]

Diem proceeded to develop ties with the American Catholic hierarchy through the good offices of his brother, who was a Catholic bishop. The key individual was Cardinal Spellman, who provided Diem with solid anti-communist credentials. Such credentials, during the era of Senator Joseph McCarthy, made Diem an appealing figure to liberal elements in the United States "who felt it mandatory to show their anti-communism" and who were "still quaking from the shocks of the loss of China, the Korean War, and the conviction of Alger Hiss."[56] Diem was placed in contact with, and derived considerable support from, Justice William O. Douglas and Senators Mike Mansfield and John F. Kennedy among others. Spellman and Joseph Kennedy, the senator's father, were instrumental in bringing Diem to the attention of the Eisenhower Administration at a time when it was still smarting from the Geneva accords. Colonel Lansdale convinced CIA Director Allen Dulles to support Diem, and Dulles was an ideal link to the Secretary of State, his brother.[57] In time, the pro-Diem lobby organized itself as the American Friends of Viet-Nam and proved a potent actor in mobilizing political support for South Vietnam and presenting the issue to the American public as part of an anti-communist crusade.

Between 1954 and December 1960, when the National Liberation Front (NLF) was formed in South Vietnam, the issue of a united Vietnam remained dormant. Both sides violated the Geneva agreements but sought to mask their violations. The scheduled national elections were thwarted by Diem's refusal to negotiate with the leaders of North Vietnam, and American leaders encouraged this posture, fearing that a free election would almost certainly result in a communist Vietnam. Diem seemed to have established his position in the South, while the North remained silent. To American officials, this was a hopeful omen:

It seemed for a while that the gamble against long odds had succeeded. The Vietminh were quiescent; the Republic of Vietnam armed forces were markedly better armed and trained than they were when the U.S. effort began; and President Diem showed a remarkable ability to put down factions threatening the GVN and to maintain himself in office.[58]

Paradoxically, the Vietnam issue began to return to the center of the global agenda not as a consequence of the behavior of Diem's external enemies but as a consequence of his own behavior. Using as an excuse the rationale of a threat from the North, Diem increasingly imposed upon the South a ruthless and brutal dictatorship while ignoring the host of economic and social problems that beset the country. In this way, he added numerous new recruits to the legions of disaffected both in the cities and the countryside, so that a rural insurgency resumed in 1957 and continued to spread and grow until it reached civil war proportions. The more severe Diem's behavior, the greater the threat of fragmentation became. Diem's response was to jail political opponents, isolate potential military figures who might become the foci of coup attempts, and repress ethnic minorities like the hill-dwelling Montagnards. In 1963, the Catholic Diem finally turned his police and military loose against the Buddhist majority of the country, and they sparked an internal political crisis by firing upon Buddhist demonstrators in the city of Hue and occupying Buddhist temples.

Diem's American allies either could not, or did not wish to, comprehend the sources of South Vietnamese instability, because they were convinced that what was taking place was another effort by Ho Chi Minh, supported by the USSR and China and using the Maoist strategy of "national revolutionary war," to unite all of Vietnam under communist rule. The problem was seen as an extension of the Cold War. In line with this assumption, the Eisenhower Administration, and later the Kennedy Administration, provided ever larger quantities of military assistance to the Diem regime. In the spring of 1961, President Kennedy authorized the dispatch of 400 Special Forces troops to South Vietnam and the beginning of covert operations by the CIA against the North, all of which violated the Geneva accords. By 1963, some 16,000 American troops were in Vietnam. Certainly, the North was prepared to take advantage of instability and unrest in the South, particularly as covert operations were launched against it. Yet, until the issue was transformed—largely through American actions—the key problem remained Diem himself. It was not ignorance on the part of successive administrations that was responsible for promoting the view of Vietnam as a stake in the Cold War which could be retained by military means. Contrary information existed and was available to administrators in Washington:

Over the years, secret intelligence reports had told of the corrosive effects of such methods (Diem's) on military morale. Periodically, they also described the gulf between the mandarin ruler and the apathetic peasantry, or the alienation of an urban middle class resentful of overbearing military controls and of its lack of real political voice.[59]

The secret Pentagon study of the Vietnam war says the United States Government's official view that the war was imposed on South Vietnam by aggression from Hanoi is "not wholly compelling". . . . The war began largely as a rebellion in the South against the increasingly oppressive and corrupt regime of Ngo Dinh Diem.[60]

What seems to have been responsible was a mind-set in Washington that had grown accustomed to interpreting symptoms of unrest, wherever they might arise, as stemming from efforts by the Soviet Union, China, and their proxies to expand communism. Vietnam was seen in the early 1960s much as was Cuba or Berlin; that is, as a stake symbolic of American credibility in the Cold War. Thus, Assistant Secretary of Defense John T. McNaughton wrote in March 1965 that in Vietnam "70 percent" of the American objective was "to avoid humiliating U.S. defeat [to our reputation as a guarantor]."[61] Local events from this perspective acquired global meaning and could be dealt with according to procedures developed for the Cold War as a whole.

Laos and Cambodia, though separated as stakes from Vietnam at Geneva, were also regarded in Washington as linked to the Cold War. The Cambodian settlement had permitted that stake also to become dormant. Viet Minh forces had withdrawn from the country, and the government of Prince Norodom Sihanouk successfully pursued a policy of Khmer nationalism and nonalignment. But the settlement in Laos proved ephemeral, and that country was quickly drawn once again into the vortex of the Cold War. Fighting between the government and the Pathet Lao under Prince Souphanouvong continued in 1955. Agreement was reached between the two sides in August, and for three years the government of Souvanna Phouma pursued an uneasy policy of nonalignment, even while accepting American Aid. Souvanna, however, was caught in the middle as right-wing and left-wing factions in the country eagerly accepted the patronage of foreign sponsors. Laos, once more closely tied to the Cold War, was the arena of ritualized conflict between the Soviet and American governments, with both sides quietly providing aid and comfort to local allies. Finally, in June 1962, a coalition government was formed in Laos, and agreement concerning Laotian neutrality was reached the following month, thereby establishing explicit guidelines to regulate continued contention.

Nevertheless, the Kennedy Administration continued to view the Laotian problem in the context of a fused Indochina issue, which itself was seen as representative of the Cold War as a whole. By late 1962, American arms shipments were being sent to the Laotian government in violation of the agreement which had been signed, and in 1964 secret bombing raids were initiated against Pathet Lao forces. All of this served increasingly to fuse the Indochina stakes into a single issue to a degree which had not been the case since 1954.

The key stake once again was Vietnam. Kennedy himself specified its symbolic quality in citing the "loss of China" as analogous to the Vietnam situation. As military assistance to the Diem regime increased, Vice-President Lyndon Johnson was dispatched to Saigon and reported to Kennedy in May 1961 that "the battle against Communism must be joined in Southeast Asia with strength and determination to achieve success there—or the United States, inevitably, must surrender the Pacific and take up our defenses on our own shores."[62] Despite continuing reports about the civil war quality of the situation, the Kennedy Administration persisted in regarding North Vietnam as the principal source of aggression.

On November 22, 1963, President Kennedy was assassinated and was succeeded by Johnson, whose earlier visit made him see Vietnam as inextricably tied up with the Cold War, symbolizing American will to resist aggression. Since Johnson saw the Vietnam conflict as an integral element of the Cold War and, like other postwar American presidents, perceived the Cold War as analogous to the crises of the 1930s, he was drawn easily into assuming that the strategies of deterrence and containment, having been so successful in Western Europe in the 1950s, could be applied equally effectively in Vietnam. He sought to engage in the same interaction games in Asia that the United States had employed in Europe, hoping that reliance on pressure and force would compel America's Asian adversaries to join Washington in ritualizing this conflict as America's European adversaries had done.

Details of the American effort to resolve the Vietnam issue by force need not concern us here. The Johnson Administration did not, in fact, think in purely military terms but rather in terms of coercive bargaining that would lead to a resolution based on trade-offs. Gradually, however, reliance on force became so great, and the Administration's negotiating position so narrow, that the elements of bargaining were virtually forgotten. The expansion of the war was largely piecemeal as "no one really foresaw what the troop needs in Vietnam would be" and the resilience of both North Vietnam and the National Liberation Front (NLF) was grossly underestimated.[63] Ultimately, more than a half-million American troops found themselves mired in a military conflict that promised no end. The confusion in Washington was mirrored by conflicting and unclear objectives. Was the North being bombed to force Hanoi to the negotiating table, to interdict supplies moving south, to strengthen the morale and will of the Saigon regime, or some combination of these? What was the relationship of the bombing campaign to the conventional war being waged in South Vietnam? Under these conditions, questions were increasingly raised concerning the manner in which the issue itself was being defined. By October 1967, "the war's major incongruities were being intellectually understood, or at least intuitively sensed, by a growing number of Americans."[64] Leading officials continued to argue, nevertheless, that not only was the issue an integral facet of the Cold War, but that the struggle was being waged specifically to combat China's model of communist expansionism. For example, on October 12, Dean Rusk declared

Within the next decade or two, there will be a billion Chinese on the mainland, armed with nuclear weapons, with no certainty about what their attitude toward the rest of Asia will be . . . . Peking has nominated itself by proclaiming a militant doctrine of the world revolution and doing something about it.[65]

There was apparently not a gleam of recognition of the burgeoning Sino-Soviet dispute, which was already undermining assumptions elsewhere concerning the "communist monolith." Out of step with reality, officials of the Johnson Administration had convinced themselves that the issue could be resolved militarily on favorable terms, since the United States was by far the stronger contender and that the key problem they faced was the maintenance of internal unity. To them Moscow, Peking, and Hanoi were all of a piece.

The advent of the Nixon Administration in 1969 brought to power in the United States a group of officials whose personal commitment to Vietnam was less than that of their predecessors, and whose perceptions were to permit the beginning of a process of decomposition of the Cold War. Nixon and Henry Kissinger were prepared to deal with a Vietnam separate from the Cold War issue, and to formulate negotiating positions on the basis of perceptions of American interdependence with other key actors, like China and the Soviet Union.

The key step in this process was the visit of Nixon to China in February 1972 and the initiation of a normalization of relations between the Chinese and American governments. As early as 1969, Nixon had asked Kissinger, then National Security Affairs advisor, to reassess Sino-American relations. By 1970, quiet negotiations between Americans and Chinese were resumed in Warsaw, having been interrupted by Chinese opposition to American intervention in Vietnam. The Nixon Administration unilaterally made several unmistakably conciliatory gestures that were understood by the Chinese, who reciprocated. In April 1971, an American table-tennis team was invited to visit China. Kissinger then arranged contacts with the Chinese through Pakistan and in July flew secretly to Peking. For the Nixon Administration a reconciliation with China offered several possible advantages, including leverage against the Soviet Union, assistance in achieving a graceful exit from Vietnam, and possible trade gains. In addition, after years of failure in Vietnam, it offered the prospect of an external success that might contribute to internal unity and to Nixon's personal political fortunes. Indeed, Kissinger is quoted as recalling that Nixon's "political ass was on the line."[66] For Mao Zedong the reconciliation offered the prospect of support against the increasingly threatening prospect of the USSR, as well as trade advantages and an infusion of technological know-how for China.

Regardless of the reasons for Nixon's journey, it symbolized the end of American assumptions concerning the unity of the communist bloc and the unidimensionality of the Cold War. Additionally, it pulled the rug from under American rationalizations for the war in Vietnam. If China were to be courted, the Chinese model of wars of national liberation could not be regarded as unduly threatening. Despite the continued savagery of war, "Vietnam was a 'cruel side show' in the Administration's new worldwide policies."[67] Kissinger himself declared in 1971 that what was taking place with China was "so great, so historic, the word 'Vietnam' will be only a footnote when it is written in history."[68]

American participation in the Vietnam War continued until 1973, going through alternate phases of intense and lower levels of violence and activity. Nixon gradually withdrew American troops and sought to replace them with South Vietnamese—a program called "Vietnamization." In April 1970, the Cambodian and Vietnam issues were tightly fused when the United States undertook an invasion of Cambodia aimed at eliminating the North Vietnamese who were using that country as a sanctuary and base of operations. Laos was added the following year when the South Vietnamese invaded that country with American assistance. In reality, however, the three stakes had been fused for some time, even though the conflicts in Laos and Cambodia had been waged in a limited and ritualized fashion. The most significant effect of the Cambodian invasion was to fragment American society further, and to galvanize those groups and organizations in the United States that opposed the war. Even as the ground war in South Vietnam was de-escalated, however, the air war in the North grew. Haiphong harbor was mined in the spring of 1972; and after Nixon's reelection in the autumn, the United States launched a final spasm of bombing against the North.

All the while, Kissinger was conducting secret negotiations with the North Vietnamese, which had begun in 1969 and intensified in 1972. Finally, on January 27, 1973, a cease-fire was agreed upon, and the United States government agreed to withdraw all its forces within sixty days. The Paris peace accords constituted movement toward a major interim disposition of the Indochina stakes at a time when the Nixon Administration expected significant Soviet and Chinese concessions as part of détente and a general decay of the Cold War issue.

Yet the Paris accords did not signal the end of the drama. American advisers continued to violate the accords surreptitiously; and North Vietnam, first cautiously and then more openly, began to apply military pressure upon the South Vietnamese regime of President Thieu. Nixon and Kissinger, having twisted Thieu's arm to accept the accords, were prepared to continue bombing Laos and Cambodia to force North Vietnamese forces from those countries.[69] Nixon, moreover, assured Thieu "that if Hanoi fails to abide by the terms of the agreement, it is my intention to take swift and retaliatory action."[70] Whether the President would have honored this commitment if he could have cannot be known, because the Congress precluded this possibility by circumscribing the President's war-making powers in the throes of Watergate. As Congress and President became increasingly engaged by a negative actor dimension, presidential policy in Vietnam became something of a hostage in the political struggle that was raging in Washington. Kissinger had hoped for Soviet and Chinese assistance in tempering North Vietnamese aggressiveness, and had assumed that the possibility of American aid to Saigon would remain a bargaining chip to deter the leaders in Hanoi. But, as Snepp suggests, "He could not have known at the time that the very underpinnings of these policies and premises would be destroyed by Watergate."[71] Deprived of American aid, the Thieu regime moved rapidly and inexorably toward collapse—a collapse facilitated by a number of inexplicably foolish military decisions—and, in April 1975, Saigon fell. Almost at the same time, the communist Khmer Rouge and Pathet Lao triumphed in Cambodia and Laos respectively.

These events marked the second major postwar disposition of the Indochina stakes, the first having occurred in 1954. Although severed from the Cold War, the stakes were not removed from active contention. Even before the heirs of Ho Chi Minh could institutionalize their rule in the South, the Indochina stakes had become the objects of fierce contention between the Soviet Union and China; and were fused into another major issue, the successor to "colonialism" and the "Cold War." As stakes in the Sino-Soviet competition, they came to be treated as parts of an issue which might be termed "the proper road to socialism." Symbolic of the credibility of their commitments elsewhere and of their relative status in the communist world, the Indochina stakes once more assumed prominence after 1975. Closely aligned to the Soviet Union (with which it signed a mutual defense pact in November 1978), a united Vietnam asserted its ascendancy over Laos, sought to bring to heel the xenophobic and radical Pol Pot regime in Cambodia—which, in turn, came to serve as a proxy for China—and harrassed ethnic Chinese in Vietnam (many of whom fled as "boat people").

In 1978, Cambodian-Vietnamese tension exploded in a brief but savage "proxy war."[72] Finally, in early 1979, Vietnamese forces—armed with Soviet and Chinese weapons received during the war against the United States and American weapons recovered after the fall of Saigon—

rolled into Cambodia in a lightning strike and crushed the Pol Pot government, indirectly humiliating the Chinese as well (whose advisers were forced to flee in haste to Thailand). Indochina was once more the focal point of a major global issue. The Chinese sought to salvage what they could from the Cambodian debacle by flying former Cambodian head of state, Prince Sihanouk (who had spent 1970 to 1975 in Peking), to New York and the United Nations to denounce "Soviet-Vietnamese" aggression; and the world media were treated to the spectacle of a rhetorical clash between the prince on behalf of China and the Cuban foreign minister on behalf of the USSR.

For its part, the Carter Administration found itself caught between the two communist adversaries and its friendship became a stake in the emerging Sino-Soviet confrontation. Recognizing the government of the People's Republic of China in January 1979, the United States government sought to assure the USSR that this action was not directed against Moscow. Nevertheless, Soviet suspicions were fueled by the rhetoric of Chinese Deputy Prime Minister Deng Xiaoping, who took the opportunity of his visit to the United States to press Washington publicly to adopt a "harder line" against the Soviet Union. Throughout early 1979, Chinese-Vietnamese border tension heightened, and, even as the Chinese concentrated military forces along the Vietnam frontier, the Soviet Union continued to strengthen its forces along the Chinese border to the north. Then, on February 17, Chinese military units struck in force against the Soviet proxy to the south in an effort to teach Vietnam "a lesson," and as a challenge to the Soviet commitment to Vietnam.

The current status of the Indochina stakes reflects the acute negative actor dimension in Sino-Soviet relations. Tensions were apparent even before the end of the American presence (as the Chinese severed the movement of Soviet supplies to Hanoi from time to time in order to increase their political leverage in North Vietnam) but had been masked behind the Cold War issue. The use of force by Vietnam in Cambodia, and by China against Vietnam, reveals the ending of a ritualized phase in the Sino-Soviet conflict and the initiation of ad hoc games to determine interaction rules in the future. Until the Sino-Soviet issue begins to decompose, the Indochina stakes are likely to remain the objects of fierce contention, even though the cast of featured players has again changed dramatically.

The history of Indochina since 1945 illustrates how issues are born as actors attach value to them in efforts to alleviate value deprivation, or to prevent such deprivation. It also illustrates the manner in which the same or similar stakes may remain the objects of contention for prolonged periods, during which time they become associated with one, and then another, issue—or indeed several issues at the same time—that may be characterized by different actors that are related to one another in different ways. The Indochina stakes were on occasions closely "packaged" together, while at other times they remained separate. These same stakes have been part of the issues of "colonialism," "Cold War," and currently are associated with "the proper road to socialism." It is, of course, not for the observer to impose his version of these linkages upon reality; instead, the links among stakes that define issues are the product of leaders' perceptions. Put simply: if they believe that a set of stakes are sufficiently related to be regarded as part of a single issue, they *are* so related, because leaders will presumably behave as though the links they assume to exist, do exist.

The Indochina case reveals, moveover, the manner in which changes in the global agenda and the definition of issues are produced by the addition of key actors—or their absence from—ongoing games, and by changes within such actors. It shows how the availability of stakes, or changes in the status of stakes, may mobilize new groups, which are galvanized to become actors in their own right. Finally, it reflects how efforts to dispose of stakes, and the success or failure of actors in achieving objectives at home and abroad, may actually produce profound changes within the actors themselves—in their membership, aims, tactics, and philosophies. It is this subject that the next chapter will address.

CHAPTER FIVE

THE BIRTH AND DEATH OF POLITICAL ACTORS

THE GENESIS of political actors is a topic that has fascinated political thinkers since ancient civilization. Whether speculating about the *polis,* the state, or transnational units, they have sought to understand how and why people seek to organize for collective purposes; why some succeed in doing so while others do not; how and why some groups cohere, prosper, and endure while others shine briefly and are extinguished; and how and why some groups, adapting to changing conditions, are transformed into larger and more encompassing organizations or divide and redivide into smaller and more specialized units. The theme of change and evolution in political associations is a preoccupation of the most memorable of political philosophers, whether Aristotle writing of the growth of political associations, Thucydides describing the decline of the Athenian Empire, Machiavelli pondering the development and decay of states, or social contract theorists like Hobbes and Rousseau seeking to imagine the conditions of political birth.

Since two major criticisms of the realist paradigm are that it pays insufficient attention to the variety of actors in global politics, and that it tends to treat nation-states as components of a "billiard ball" model, theoretical questions related to the nature of actors are of paramount importance. In particular, three questions must be answered in the course of evolving any comprehensive alternative theory of politics. The first is, Why do individuals participate in political activity and how are these individuals aggregated and transformed into political actors that may be regarded as greater than the sum of their parts? The second is, How can political actors be identified and distinguished from one another (and therefore compared): Is there a permanent cast of actors in a political system, or does this cast vary as a consequence of factors like different issues?* Finally, once actors emerge, what factors encourage their cohesion (i.e., foster coalescence), and what cause their debilitation and fracture (i.e., foster fragmentation)? This chapter will approach each of these questions in turn.

THE FORMATION OF POLITICAL ACTORS

Politics is an avenue that is traversed by those who cannot unilaterally manipulate an outcome. Their collective behavior with regard to specific issues reflects the fact that they need something from other actors or from the world in general—even if it is merely to confer legitimacy upon their actions. The fact that individuals or groups require the acquiescence or cooperation of others in order to achieve value satisfaction indicates that politics is, at root, a process of interdependent decision making, in which the fates of individuals and groups are in some respect linked. Polybius, the Roman historian, expressed this succinctly when he observed that "political societies" originate in man's "natural weakness."[2]

What distinguishes political actors from other groups is that they seek to enhance the value satisfaction of their members through use of a politi-

---

* The concepts of "actor" and that of "system" continue to be confused in the discipline. Actors are often regarded as systems themselves and as subsystems of larger international systems. Realists went so far as to identify systems, actors, and states, thereby eliminating the theoretical distinctiveness of the systems approach. Systems do not have purposes; actors do, and they pursue goals and objectives. Systems are analytical constructs for ordering a particular segment of reality and have no existence apart from the perceptions of scholars who create them; actors, in contrast, are units that exist apart from the perceptions of observers, and whose behavior leaves traces that are empirically discernible. Finally, all actors may be analyzed through a systems framework if the scholar's definition of system is suitable, but all systems are certainly not actors. See Donald E. Lampert, Lawrence S. Falkowski, and Richard W. Mansbach, "Is There an International System?" *International Studies Quarterly,* (March 1978), 22(1):146; and also Ernst B. Haas, "On Systems and International Regimes," *World Politics* (January 1975), 27(1):147–74.

cal system.[3] Any group can perform a political *function* and therefore become a political actor, even if its primary function, or purpose, is religious, social, or economic. Formally defined, a *political actor* is any individual or group that seeks to enhance its value satisfaction through making, or contending over, proposals for the authoritative allocation of values. Clearly a single individual may be a member of many groups, or a group may join several political alliances and, in this manner, satisfy a variety of political as well as other needs. In doing so, of course, not only are multiple loyalties created, but political awareness and interest may be generated.

Individuals or groups will not always seek to form actors to alleviate value deprivation, because this may often involve more energy and resources than participating directly in politics or using existing organizations. New groups will be created in the presence of old ones, however, if the latter will not, or cannot, take political positions that members believe will alleviate their value deprivation. The process that leads to fragmentation of existing groups, or the withdrawal of members, will be treated in detail in the last section of this chapter, but before the fragmentation process can be explained, it is necessary to understand why individuals participate in politics and how political actors are created in the first place.

Political participation has been studied extensively in political science, and a body of knowledge is gradually being accumulated, although many of the studies are based only on observation of the American case.[4] The first model of political participation that received wide attention was one that suggested that high socioeconomic status in an individual creates certain "civic" attitudes (efficacy, involvement, duty) that then increase the likelihood of participation. As this model was applied to developing nations, it was found that lower-status individuals could participate as frequently as individuals with high socioeconomic status—and *without* the proper civic attitudes—if they belonged to organizations (including mass organizations).[5] The recent work of Verba and Nie has revised the standard socioeconomic model to include other factors that will increase the likelihood of participation. They classify the independent variables (as they are relevant to the U.S.) into two categories—the social circumstances and the institutional situations of the individual. The former involve socioeconomic status, position in the life cycle (e.g., age), and race; while the latter include the effects of three institutional structures—party affiliation, type of community, and membership in voluntary organizations. These last three variables are a refinement of the organization effect delineated by Nie, Powell, and Prewitt. Verba and Nie argue that there are many different routes to participation, so that the effect of lower socioeconomic status and "inappropriate" civic attitudes can be "overcome." Among the more interesting contributions of their research are the propositions that group consciousness and ideology can overcome the normal effect of race on participation in the United States, and that institutional structures are just as important as status. These findings are then compared with findings on participation from six other nations.*

In global politics, participation has also been a subject of enquiry, though nation-states, rather than individuals, have been the units of analysis. Much of the research in comparative foreign policy has concluded that the *size* of a nation (an indicator of "power," usually measured by population, but often also by area or GNP) is the single most important variable accounting for participation, and that *economic development* is the second most potent variable.[6]

James Rosenau and Gary Hoggard found that size and development, as well as type of polity, were critical variables. Although not intending to investigate participation, they found that a rank ordering of nations on these three attributes correlates highly with cooperation ($-.952$) and conflict ($.928$).† Unfortunately, Rosenau and Hoggard did not separate the

---

* Also of general interest, but of less direct relevance to global politics, is their finding that there are different types of participation (citizen-initiated contacts, voting, campaign activity, and "cooperative" activity—citizens working with each other). This is of interest because then it becomes possible to examine whether different aspects of their model account for different types of participation. See Sidney Verba, Norman H. Nie, and Jae-On Kim, *The Modes of Democratic Participation* (Beverly Hills, Calif.: Sage Professional Paper, 1971); and *Participation and Political Equality* (New York: Cambridge University Press, 1978).

† James N. Rosenau and Gary Hoggard, "Foreign Policy Behavior in Dyadic Relationships: Testing a Pre-Theoretical Extension," in James N. Rosenau, ed., *Comparing Foreign Policies* (Beverly Hills, Calif.: Sage, 1974), pp. 117–51. The negative sign is produced because Rosenau and Hoggard hypothesized that small, underdeveloped, open nations would be more cooperative than large, developed, closed nations. In fact they found the opposite—the larger, more developed, and closed a nation, the more cooperative *and* conflict-prone it is; that is, the more *active*. Some caution must be exercised with this and other tests that employ media sources from large nations rather than regionally oriented news sources. The media from large nations (so-called global media) tend to underreport the

effects of the three variables, therefore making it impossible to determine the exact influence of each of them. In a more elaborate analysis of the Rosenau classification, Maurice East and Charles Hermann controlled for each variable and tested various interaction effects.[7] Their study, part of of the CREON project, examined the behavior of thirty-three nations as reported in *Deadline Data* from 1959 to 1968. They found that size was the only statistically significant variable when controlling for the effects of the other variables (beta = .4582, R^2 = .210).[8] However, because of the way they measured size, they also tapped economic capability, and therefore did not establish that economic capability (if not economic development) is unrelated to participation.* The findings of earlier research, that economic development is the second most potent variable, then, cannot be discounted. Despite this caveat, East and Hermann do report some important findings that show that the effects of size, development, and accountability vary when controlling for type of participation. They find that size, accountability, and development interacting with accountability are the most important predictors of diplomatic events (respective betas = .6139, −.2813, and −.2693) and of economic events (−.5058, .3253, and .3327). Military events are not explained by any of the variables. When controlling for the source of participation within the nation, they find again that size, development, and development interacting with accountability best explain the percentage of bureaucratic involvement (−.5323, .3013, and .3035). However, participation by the head of state is predicted only by the interaction between size and accountability (.4978).[9] These findings, when interpreted with attention to the operationalized measures that were employed, lend support to the conclusions that size is the most important variable; that economic capability is probably still, as found in earlier research, the second most potent predictor;

actions of small, underdeveloped nations. See James Kean and Patrick J. McGowan, "National Attributes and Foreign Policy Participation: A Path Analysis," in Patrick J. McGowan, ed., *Sage International Yearbook of Foreign Policy Studies* (1973), 1:246.

* Size was measured as a dichotomized variable based on a discriminant function analysis of four indicators: total population, total GNP, total land area, and total KWH. More clearly than the Rosenau and Hoggard study, which employed only the first indicator, the East and Hermann study is measuring *overall* capability. The inclusion of the last three variables, however, cannot but tap some aspect of economic capability, including industrialization (because of the KWH indicator). For their operational definitions, see the note to table 1, p. 284.

that accountability, as suggested by Rosenau, can indeed have an effect on certain types of participation when controlling for size and development; that the interaction effects of size, development, and polity do *not* have an impact on participation, but that, on occasion, development and accountability will interact in a significant manner to predict slightly the type of participation.

James Kean and Patrick McGowan argue that the correlation between participation and size and development is spurious. They maintain that "resources," which is correlated with size, and "needs," which is correlated with economic development, explain participation. Resources, which they operationalize as Gross Domestic Product (GDP), measures a states's capability to influence the environment; hence the greater an actor's resources, the greater the range of events it can affect, and the greater its potential impact. "Needs" is operationalized as the per capita dollar value of the state's total trade and refers to the degree to which an actor "must interact with its environment to maintain its economic, political, social, and cultural institutions."[10] Looking at four separate modes of global participation—international organization involvement, international involvement, foreign policy focus, and regional involvement—their tests produced mixed results. Their model was only supported for international organization involvement.* International involvement and foreign policy focus were strictly a function of resources, with needs playing no role. Finally, regional involvement was negatively related to needs, and the correlations of size and modernization were not found to be spurious, as in the other findings.

Since these findings are inconsistent, it would not be appropriate to reject the earlier findings, and to accept Kean's and McGowan's contention that the size and development correlations are spurious. Rather it is more reasonable to treat each of the four indicators—size, development,

---

*Organization involvement was operationalized as headquarters or subsidiary offices of international organizations, which means that needs and resources are more important in attracting office location than size or development. This kind of measure is more sensitive to status than more typical measures of organizational participation, such as the number of international organizations to which a nation belongs. Their other measures of participation are for international involvement—total acts reported in the *New York Times* as recorded in the World Events Interaction Survey (WEIS) data—for focus—the number of targets for which a state had five or more WEIS acts—and for regional involvement—the number of WEIS acts a nation initiated within its own geographic region.

resources, and needs—as measures of different aspects of the same concept—relative overall capability. When regarded in this light, Kean and McGowan are correct in pointing out the need to explain the correlation of participation with size and development. The research on individual participation seems to provide precisely the theoretical rationale that is needed, and has the additional virtue of providing the bases of a theory that is generalizable on the individual, national, and global levels.

Kean's and McGowan's finding that size is in various ways (direct and indirect) related to participation can be incorporated under the status variable in the Verba and Nie model. Although groups such as nations do not have a socioeconomic status the way an individual does, a status hierarchy does exist among global actors, and there is an extensive literature on the effect of status on global behavior.[11] Size, development, resources, and needs can be seen as different aspects of the overall capacity that determines the status of actors. Global actors that have high status would tend to have the proper "civic" (i.e., political) attitudes and thus participate more frequently. As with individuals this is probably due to the fact that they benefit from participation more consistently than actors of low status. Figure 5.1 depicts a model that attempts to integrate this insight and the research on individual and nation-state participation, in order to develop a unified explanation of participation and actor formation.

The model presented here is based on the assumption that the formation of a political actor occurs as a two-step process. The first is the decision among the deprived (potential members) to communicate with one another about the prospect of forming a group, and the second is the actual formation of an actor from among potential members. Whether communication will occur, and among whom, is a function of five variables. The three that are most important are value deprivation, attitudes toward politics, and availability of stakes. When these variables fail to encourage communication, then little will occur; if they do encourage communication, then the probability of communication (and with whom) will be determined by the organizational context of potential members. The status of potential members of the group will condition the extent to which they experience value deprivation, have "correct" attitudes toward politics, and have stakes available to them. The last variable also conditions the extent to which value deprivation is felt. Finally, the organizational context of individuals has an effect (after a time lag) on their atti-

Figure 5.1 Political Participation and Actor-Emergence Model

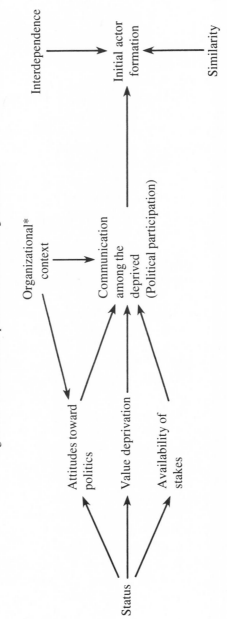

*There is a time lag between organizational context and attitudes toward politics.

tudes toward politics. Once communication is established, the interdependence and similarity of potential members will determine who will become part of the new actor. Each of these variables will now be analyzed in detail.

Communication is a critical precondition, because it permits the growth of a sense of mutual relevance among otherwise isolated individuals. The prerequisite for such communication is the existence of a set of individuals who share a common value deprivation, or who fear such deprivation. Whether the communication will actually develop, and will persist if it does develop, depends on the availability of stakes that can alleviate value deprivation, and on the prevailing political attitudes among potential members. If no stakes exist that can alleviate value deprivation, then there will be little incentive to communicate, since political activity will appear futile. Thus, the availability of stakes has an effect on value deprivation to the extent that the clear absence of stakes will reduce the sense of value deprivation that is relevant to political participation and lead to resignation. Conversely, the presence of stakes can increase a sense of value deprivation because it highlights the *relative* nature of that deprivation.

Value deprivation and the availability of stakes provide the setting for political participation. However, whether individuals and groups become involved depends very much on their *attitudes toward politics*. While the exact set of attitudes that will be critical should be identified by research (particularly in global and cross-cultural contexts), Verba and Nie found three attitudes that are relevant here—the degree to which individuals are interested in and attentive to politics, the degree to which they think politics is important, and their sense of political efficacy.* Interest in and attention paid to politics are important, because they provide information that makes potential members aware of their interests—awareness providing an incentive to participation. In addition, information provides understanding of the political situation, which no doubt increases the sense of

---

*See Norman H. Nie and Sidney Verba, "Political Participation," in Fred I. Greenstein and Nelson Polsby, eds., *Handbook of Political Science,* vol. 4: *Nongovernmental Politics* (Reading, Mass.: Addison-Wesley, 1975), pp. 17, 32; and Verba and Nie, *Participation in America,* 1972 pp. 13, 126. Other attitudes they examine but that are not directly applicable to groups in world politics (although they are certainly relevant to individuals within those groups) are: a sense of civic duty, strength of partisan identification, and sense of contribution to community welfare.

efficacy and the belief that politics is important. The absence of a sense of political efficacy or belief that politics is important is characteristic of members of traditional societies, for whom permanent value deprivation is a "given,"* an expected and accepted way of life that cannot be changed.[12] Only after individuals have been made aware of the *possibility* of change in their environment, and have come to believe that conditions are manipulatable rather than the "natural order of things," will it become possible for them to consider participating in politics.†

The presence of these attitudes, along with a sense of value deprivation and an awareness of the availability of stakes, is associated with the *status* of an individual or group. Status is primarily a perceptual variable that refers to the reputation or prestige of an individual. Individual status, however, can be deduced from objective criteria like education, income, and occupation. In global politics, there are also widely shared criteria of status, and these are related to overall political capability, which in turn seems to be based on such objective criteria as size (both demographic and territorial, including resource base), economic capability, and military strength.‡ These objective factors have been employed to explain

---

*Such individuals correspond to "parochials" and "subjects" as described by Gabriel A. Almond and G. Bingham Powell, Jr., in *Comparative Politics: A Developmental Approach* (Boston: Little, Brown, 1966), p. 53.

†It should be noted that an individual or group will not participate in politics, even if all these conditions are met, if they can attain the stake in question through a channel that may be less costly than politics, e.g., economic activity or crime.

‡R. J. Rummel, "A Status-Field Theory of International Relations," p. 213; and J. David Singer, Stuart Bremer, and John Stuckey, "Capability Distribution, Uncertainty and Major Power War, 1820–1965," in Bruce M. Russett, ed., *Peace, War, and Numbers* (Beverly Hills, Calif.: Sage, 1972), pp. 25–26, look at status in these terms. Singer and Melvin Small have tried to measure the reputational aspect of status directly by dividing states into total system and central system. See J. David Singer and Melvin Small, "The Composition and Status Ordering of the International System, 1815–1940," *World Politics* (January 1966), 18(2):236–82; and J. David Singer and Melvin Small, *The Wages of War, 1816–1965: A Statistical Handbook* (New York: Wiley, 1972), pp. 19–30. Two problems exist with these criteria, however. The first is that the economic aspect should be refined. There are at least three theoretically significant aspects of economics that might be employed—economic wealth, level of industrialization, and the Marxian notion of means and mode of production. The literature in global politics has been remiss in not defining which of these aspects are more important for explaining behavior. Second, the status criteria have tended to focus solely on nation-states. Since other actors have become increasingly involved in global politics, some objective criteria for determining their rank in the status hierarchy must be found. Certainly for corporations and international organizations, economic capability would be a feasible measure. The functional equivalent of size, however, is unclear.

participation in terms of status. Indeed, it has been stated that "one of the most thoroughly substantiated propositions in all of social science is that persons near the center of society are more likely to participate in politics than persons near the periphery."[13]

This relationship is probably not that direct; rather, higher status most likely provides groups with the skills and sophistication necessary to manipulate the political system to their own advantage. Consequently, they develop favorable political attitudes because they tend to achieve their ends. Those of lower status develop less favorable attitudes in part because politics proves unfruitful for them.* Thus, William D. Coplin and J. Martin Rochester find that Third World actors tend to cease participating in the International Court of Justice—and develop negative attitudes toward it and international law—after they have sought to avail themselves of them. This is because they lose, and Coplin and Rochester point out that they learn quickly that the legal system does not work to their advantage.[14]

Further research is required to identify the particular attitudes that encourage participation at a global level, but it can be presumed that these would include individual decision makers having a sense of efficacy, believing global politics to be important, and being able to pay attention to global developments.†

In addition, actors of high status are more aware of available stakes and, owing to this, have higher aspiration levels and seek greater value satisfaction than those of lower status. Awareness of available stakes whets the appetite, and high status means that an actor has a major investment in the existing distribution of stakes—the status quo. Nevertheless, individuals of lower status who belong to voluntary organizations tend to

---

*In the 1960s, political efficacy was often viewed as a personality-related variable with the implication that something was "wrong" with a person who viewed himself as "inefficacious." However, it is more likely a product of socialization that has been reinforced or changed by experience. As lower-status individuals or groups are defeated, it is natural for them to develop negative political attitudes. To feel inefficacious in such a situation is realistic.

†How well decision makers perform this task for the groups they represent will no doubt affect their attitudes and those of their members if not their behavior. Maurice East, for example, hypothesizes and finds some evidence that many small nations simply do not learn of global issues in time to have a significant impact on the decision-making process and often respond to this dilemma when the issue is salient to them by initiating highly conflict-prone behavior. See Maurice A. East, "Size and Foreign Policy Behavior: A Test of Two Models," *World Politics* (July 1973), 25(2):558–60.

participate more and presumably, at some point, develop favorable attitudes and skills.[15]

The organizational context may encourage participation if social conditions are such that others promote expectations of participation, or if participation is made easy by institutional structures and access channels to
the agenda. In contemporary world politics, the rapid growth of universalistic international organizations[16] has produced an organizational context for Third World nations that not only has encouraged, but practically
required, their participation. If such a context produces success, then
lower status groups will be able to develop the same attitudes as those
with high status. Until that happens, however, the organizational context
will encourage participation, and will mobilize a set of actors who may
lack "correct" political attitudes. On the other hand, if the organizational
context produces defeat, as it has for Israel and South Africa, negative
political attitudes and an eventual reduction in participation may develop,
as indeed has occurred in the United Nations with respect to both Israel
and South Africa.

The organizational context is also important in another sense. Whether
potential members *will* form a group depends upon their ability to identify
and communicate with each other; that is, the extent to which the social,
physical, and political environments permit communication and organization. Awareness of linked fates and a capability to function jointly are
prerequisites for group formation. The critical place occupied by communication in generating a sense of mutual relevance appears to be the
same, whether one is describing the relations among individuals in group
formation, or among collective actors in the formation of alliances and
expanded political collectivities. The political constraints may prevent individuals from participating in politics. In ancient as in Maoist China, for
example, the organization of the family was manipulated to prevent its
formation into a politically relevant factor.* In certain societies, the

---

* Writing about the extended kinship group in third century-B.C. China, one observer described the way in which the regime sought to prevent such groups from becoming actors
that might imperil the existing order: "What power they (the clans) retained was blotted out
in the Ch'in unification of the country. Clan organization or anything resembling it was
anathema both in Legalist principle and in Ch'in practice. Ch'in even attacked small-scale
extended families by doubling taxes on households where more than two mature sons lived
with parents; its aim was to fragment society into nuclear family units, which could not
hope to oppose state authority. Moreover, Ch'in organized families into mutual-sur-

regime deliberately tries to keep political participation, especially for certain categories of individuals, at a low level; this is especially true for "authoritarian" regimes.[17]

Whether such communication will actually bring individuals and groups together as an actor depends upon the *level of interdependence* and the *similarity* of those who communicate with each other. Interdependence refers to the extent to which individuals or groups need each other's resources to bring an end to their joint value deprivation, or to prevent further deprivation. Actor formation will take place *only* among those who perceive that they have something to "offer" one another which "links their fates," and only if it appears that their joint contributions will aggregate sufficient resources so that there is a possibility of ameliorating their joint condition.

Expediency alone is not sufficient to produce more than a temporary coalition. An actor will come into existence only when some "affective" bond is produced by communication among potential members.* Only if such bonds grow and deepen will the group come to mean more to its members than a transitory interest coalition based on fleeting but limited motives. Such a collectivity lacks any social basis for community and is no more than a Hobbesian commonwealth, "a purely mechanical contraption with its springs and gears visible to an embarrassing degree" without "any natural dependency among the members."[18] The Stalin-Hitler coalition following their 1939 nonaggression treaty, and the later "Grand Alliance" between the United States, Great Britain, and the Soviet Union, were collectivities of this sort. Such coalitions are fragile and usually crumble after the immediate threat or opportunity that gave them life disappears. Trust is a minor factor in such coalitions, and egotisms remain untamed. Since they are not what Karl Deutsch calls "security

veillance, mutual responsibility teams of fives and tens to establish loyalty to the state as the supreme value"—Charles O. Hucker, *China's Imperial Past* (Stanford, Calif.: Stanford University Press, 1975), p. 58. In 1958, Maoist China initiated "a great leap forward" in which large numbers of peasants were brought together in agricultural communes whose "double aim was to destroy family ties and to tighten the regimentation." "The Chinese Legalist School some two thousand years earlier had advocated a similar regimentation."—O. Edmund Clubb, *Twentieth-Century China* (New York: Columbia University Press, 1964), pp. 361, 357.

*Leon N. Lindberg and Stuart A. Scheingold distinguish between "utilitarian" and "affective" bases of support. See *Europe's Would-Be Polity* (Englewood Cliffs, N.J.: Prentice-Hall, 1970), p. 40.

communities,'' they are unable to endure, and so members continue to compete for later stakes.[19]

An affective bond will grow if communication fosters recognition that the individuals are suffering the same, or similar, deprivation, which they all view as great. The more salient the issue to potential members of a group, the more intense the sense of value deprivation and ''suffering'' that each member experiences. When such individuals encounter others who are experiencing similar suffering seen as originating from a common cause, affective bonds of identity may grow, because the individuals share something in common which is of great significance. They tend to empathize with one another, and this leads to a sense of understanding, trust, and ''we-ness.''[20] Mutual responsiveness encourages a capacity for agreement, which promotes further assimilation.

The likelihood that mutual ''suffering'' will be transformed into an affective bond that is sufficient for the growth of strong psychological identification, even in the absence of sociocultural similarity, is increased if individuals learn that their joint deprivation is due to some trait that they share (e.g., race, sex, class, education, language, or religion), which distinguishes them from others who enjoy greater satisfaction. The deprived are then more likely to see themselves in the ''same boat.'' This increases their capacity to trust one another and, in that respect, may generate harmony among them.

The existence of similar deprivation by itself simply means that individuals have a joint problem, one which, without further encouragement, they might be tempted to solve at each other's expense. Similar traits alone are *not* likely to produce trust unless individuals share a great number of them that are mutually reinforcing. After all, any two individuals will probably have some trait in common. What creates a consciousness of ''similarity'' is the sharing of some trait which is seen as *the reason* for their joint deprivation. In that event, individuals will focus upon the common trait (thereby seeing themselves as similar) rather than focusing upon traits that they do not share (thereby seeing themselves as dissimilar). Such is the case among Jewish groups that see anti-Semitism as the cause of their deprivation, and among black and feminist groups that perceive race and sex, respectively, to be the sources of their deprivation.

Of the various potential traits that can serve to establish similarity, the most important are sociocultural, because the differences here tend to produce different expectations and misunderstandings over the meaning of acts. On the personal level, it is known that one's "silent language" (nonverbal behavior and customs) can produce negative impressions and hostility of the sort implied in anecdotes about "ugly Americans" and "boorish Russians," or in the culturally biased reports of early colonizers and missionaries.[21] On the societal level, misunderstandings may be more severe. Without a shared culture it becomes difficult to understand communication, not only because the connotation of words are different, but because the very foundation of what gives language meaning is different—its *Weltanschauung,* ideology, meaning of values, and expectations about the world and life in general.[22] Thus even such "similar" actors as the United States and the USSR can, because of their ideologies, mean very different things by "democracy," "free elections," and "human rights."

To recapitulate briefly: the existence of communication among deprived individuals is necessary for the process of actor formation to begin. A sense of interdependence is necessary to supply "rational" motives for cooperation and so serves to trigger the process. Without the addition of affective identity bonds, which may be produced by recognition of mutual suffering reinforced by perceptions of similarity, resulting coalitions will only be expedient and short term. Once these conditions are satisfied, autonomous actors will form. Autonomy denotes a condition in which an actor has "an independent capacity to solicit and receive information, to process and refine it, and finally to respond to it."[23] Actor formation begins when members self-consciously develop a common issue position toward a proposal, or set of proposals, for the disposition of stakes that they have identified as important to them. This issue position, however, relates only to the disposition of stakes between the group and outsiders. For the group to be considered a unitary actor, as opposed to a temporary coalition, it must also have achieved agreement about how the resulting payoff (or loss) will be distributed (or borne) among the members themselves, or at least have accepted a legitimate procedure or principle for determining how such an agreement might be reached. As this caveat implies, the group must evolve some accepted structure (leaders, rules of procedure, a division of labor, and the like), and members must assume recognizable performance obligations on behalf of the group; i.e., provide some resources.[24]

In this fashion, roles will develop, and what had previously been no more than an agglomeration of individuals will become an organization. Though they may range from rudimentary to highly complex, such roles reflect both hierarchical and functional distinctions. In their absence, it is unlikely that a group will endure beyond the single issue at hand. Their presence reflects the growth of individual interests in the survival of the group itself, as opposed merely to the grasping of the stake it is pursuing at the moment. The formal and informal positions within a group, themselves, become stakes to be sought after or retained. However, individuals or groups can be members or parts of more than one actor. It is therefore necessary to develop explicit criteria for identifying actors.

THE IDENTIFICATION OF ACTORS IN THE GLOBAL ARENA

After the birth and institutionalization of territorial nation-states in Western Europe and the acceptance of a "state-centric" view of political life, it was generally believed that nation-states as a type of actor represented the culmination of political history. The burning question was how individual states might compete successfully with their brethren. In the field of international relations concepts like "balance of power," "reason of state," and "power politics" or realpolitik characterized this newer orientation of mind. In the tradition of realpolitik, war was seen as the basic engine of political change, and, since sovereign states alone could wage wars, only the most powerful states had to be analyzed to comprehend world politics. Other states or actors could be viewed either as their pawns or as irrelevant. Power was the key, and the combination of military capability and legal sovereignty made the identification of actors coterminous with an elite of dynastic states.

Since World War II, a concatenation of factors has revived scholarly interest in identifying global actors. One factor was the destructiveness of the war, which led to renewed interest in international organizations like the United Nations, world government, and world federalism, as means of ridding global politics of its "anarchic" characteristics, which allegedly are the causes of war.[25] Another factor was the growing recognition of functional problems that individual governments were seen as incapable of handling in the absence of transnational and international cooperation, and which problems stimulated transnational "functional linkages." Peace, it was argued, could only be assured by coping with the economic and social issues that were sources of conflict, so that the foundations of peace "must be laid by piecemeal international efforts in commonly recognized transnational problem areas which are readily acceptable to the procedures shaped and accepted by modern man." [26]

A third factor, closely related to the preceding one, which induced renewed interest in the development and decay of political actors was the emergence to independence of large numbers of former colonial territories in Africa and Asia, which were experiencing birth pangs unprecedented in global politics since the territorial state had first emerged in Western Europe in the seventeenth century. Scholarly interest in development tended to focus upon the difficulties confronted by these new entities as they strived for "nationhood." [27] In addition, these new states seemed only nominally comparable with the established states of the West,* meeting few of the internal or external criteria generally associated with "sovereign independence." [28]

Finally, concern with the origins and evolution of political actors was fostered by a growing recognition that there exists a rich galaxy of units "out there," other than sovereign nation-states, that interact with one another for political ends. As sociologists and political scientists have long recognized in the context of domestic politics, an individual may belong to several units and become active in them for different purposes. These units are not congruent with national frontiers, so that "it seems desirable to think increasingly in terms of world systems that are heterogeneous with respect to types of actors (i.e., mixed actor systems) in the analysis of world politics." [29] Students of realpolitik and realism generally failed to appreciate that the actor itself (and not only its behavior) is a variable, and instead assumed that global politics could be *defined a*

---

* The peculiar difficulties inherent in comparing new and old states is evident in the study of comparative politics, where the comparison of specific countries is giving way to the comparative analysis of "bureaucracies," "corruption," "judicial processes," and the like, with attention focused upon homologous functions and patterns of behavior, rather than upon formal institutions. Cf. Roy C. Macridis and Robert E. Ward, eds., *Modern Political Systems: Europe,* (Englewood Cliffs, N.J.: Prentice-Hall, 1963) and Joseph La Palombara, *Politics Within Nations,* (Englewood Cliffs, N.J.: Prentice-Hall, 1974).

priori as the interaction of sovereign states which were designated by ascriptive and legal criteria. When analyzing foreign policy, they assumed that they could compare the behavior of these territorial units, which were "givens" from which they could work backwards. The actors were inevitably seen as independent variables, and only rarely were they thought of as dependent or intervening variables. Consequently, the tendency was to approach the problem of comparing foreign policy as though it were a problem of knowledge, rather than of method. For the application of a comparative methodology in global politics, it is necessary initially to identify *empirically* the population of units that exists as the "substantive basis" of the inquiry. It must not be assumed, as did the realists, that "proper names" like the "United States," "the Soviet Union," or "China" are the independent variables that explain foreign-policy behavior.[30]

For these reasons, it is both unprofitable and unsatisfying to *define* global politics at the outset as the interaction of sovereign nation-states, as so many scholars do, thereby ignoring the variable quality of the actors themselves. Instead, it is necessary to elaborate an explicit set of criteria for identifying what entities constitute actors. Operationally, a group will appear as a political actor when it first undertakes autonomous behavior aimed at achieving a favorable disposition of the stakes, usually by offering or discussing proposals relevant to the issues. To engage in autonomous behavior, a group—even if it is a "government"—must enjoy centralized access to, and control over, members' resources; and must be the recipient of their loyalty. The collectivity may be regarded as an actor in an issue only if its members fulfill their performance obligations, publicly adopt and consciously support a group position, actively communicate and interact with fellow members in such a manner as to encourage general satisfaction, reinforce group identities and loyalties, and facilitate the development of a single group strategy.

Applying these criteria reveals that many units that are generally considered to be global actors may not in fact be so, and that other units, which are often ignored or overlooked, can and do play conspicuous roles in the disposition of stakes and the resolution of issues. The term "satellite" is applied to governments that are scarcely independent of other actors; other governments are inert; and still others are little more than aggregates of independent and competing actors so that "government behavior'' represents merely the competitive initiatives of coteries of individuals holding formal positions within them.

Unlike the illusion of relative permanency conveyed by the doctrine of sovereignty, these criteria imply the virtual impossibility of delineating a single inclusive universe of political actors at any time. As issues are examined, it is clear that the actors vary. Depending upon their value preference schedules, the number and type of stakes perceived to be available, and their own resources, some actors may participate in many different issues, while others limit their involvement to a few, or even a single, issue. Furthermore, actors may reassemble themselves in different issues. As issues shift and the contexts in which they arise change, the same actors are liable to command varying sets of loyalties and be characterized by new goals, identities, and expectations. Where the reassembly process is sufficiently extreme, new actors emerge and former actors are eclipsed temporarily or permanently. For example, a set of government representatives may operate so closely together that they begin to constitute an international organization or ''regime,'' the proposals and issue positions of which are different from, and independent of, those of the separate governments. In still other contexts, the individual governments may again reassert their individuality and autonomy. Or, the governments themselves may dissolve into component agencies, or subagencies, to function as actors in their own right. Thus, during the Nigerian civil war, the White House and President Nixon, in particular, were sympathetic to the Biafran cause, while the Department of State and the American Embassy in Lagos were strong advocates of the federal position. Consequently, when the White House attempted to initiate mediation efforts in August and September 1969, it kept these secret from the State Department, even while America's representatives to the United Nations were publicly denying any such United States' attempts. Mediation at that time was supportive of the Biafran cause, because the Biafrans were then on the verge of military defeat. Similarly, when widespread famine engulfed Biafra following its collapse, the American Embassy was the last to admit that any such catastrophe was taking place—a position contrary to that of Biafra's sympathizers—while the White House, and eventually the State Department, put pressure on the embassy to get aid to Biafra.[31]

No actor is permanent in the sense of maintaining readily distinguishable boundaries between its internal and external environments. Such boundaries are not the product of geographic or legal ascription. They are determined by the division between those who advocate and pursue one issue position, as contrasted with those who pursue a contradictory issue position; and, though some groups tend to retain their unitary character over time, and in a variety of issues, by virtue of their greater interdependence and profound affective bonds, there is a tendency for the character and number of actors to vary by issue, since different issues touch different values and stakes, thereby having a different effect upon individuals and subgroups. Thus, as recent studies of bureaucratic behavior suggest, different agencies compete with one another for a share of budgetary resources; for which issues, they are each actors whose opponents constitute part of the external environment. When they are jointly threatened, however, as in the event of a threat from abroad, they coalesce once more.[32]

Such a conceptualization requires abandoning the image of two autonomous spheres of political life—"domestic" and "foreign"—so that "the political unit is simply assumed to have an environment to which it responds and with which it interacts."[33] The sovereign nation-state is not characterized by "impermeability,"[34] but is instead a "penetrated political system."[35] Citizens of one country may have more in common with fellow-citizens than with foreigners, but for the purposes of specific issues or issue-areas, they may identify more closely with foreigners. Penetration of this sort is dramatically seen in superpower relations with client governments. In Eastern Europe, the leadership of the Communist party of the Soviet Union (CPSU) makes critical economic decisions on behalf of, and provides political support for, the ruling elites of those nations. In the West, the World Bank (particularly the IMF and IBRD), elements of the U.S. government, and various multinational corporations and banks, often make the critical economic decisions for Third World nations that are in financial difficulty, and that have a significant amount of Western economic investment or are deeply in debt to Western banks.[36] The phenomenon of penetration shows that an actor is a unit that makes proposals and behaves in a unitary fashion; it is not an aggregate of individuals who live in a limited geographic space or speak the same language (though such characteristics may facilitate conjoint behavior).

It should be clear that this analysis rejects the assumption that nation-states are fundamentally different from other actors because they are sovereign, or because they are characterized by a bureaucratic apparatus. In fact, nation-states are themselves not actors at all (though governments may act in their name). The assumption of state-as-actor entails a peculiar confusion between the concept of actor and that of social system. The inhabitants of established nation-states are linked to one another by history, language, and shared norms; but it is necessary to differentiate between the passive social links of citizens and the mobilization of actors (including governments) to contend for stakes. It is only on rare occasions that the entire population of a society is mobilized in support of an issue position; more often it is the case that large numbers of citizens either do not care about an issue, are unaware of it, or oppose the government's position. The only time it is possible to speak of the state-as-actor is when the active collectivity embraces the entire social collectivity.

Governments, which may behave as actors, vary in terms of their access to the resources of the society they represent. The Soviet government, by virtue of its control of the economy, enjoys greater access to the material resources of the USSR than the American government commands over similar resources in the United States. One cannot imagine a Soviet leader being confronted with the sort of limitations that President Truman discovered when on April 8, 1952 he issued an executive order directing the Secretary of Commerce to seize the steel mills in order to prevent a threatened strike that would endanger production during the Korean War. The Supreme Court, in this case, upheld a lower-court decision which declared that the President did not have the constitutional right to take over private property in this manner.[37]

In addition to differences in access to social resources, the degree of loyalty that a government enjoys, and the willingness of citizens to contribute resources, vary by issue, as is apparent in contrasting public support in the United States for World War II and Vietnam. In the former, public support was sufficiently great that one could speak of ''a nation in arms,'' and the active collectivity closely resembled the social collectivity as a whole. In the latter, the American public was well-informed about the issue and held very strong views about it,[38] but large segments of youth refused to serve in the armed forces or deserted; so that in 1970 the desertion rate was 142.2 men per 1,000 in uniform, whereas in 1944 the rate was 72.9 per 1,000. Moreover, between 1967 and 1971, over

350,000 American servicemen deserted; and more than 61,000 were granted "conscientious objector" status in 1971 alone, in contrast to only 17,000 in 1960.[39] Not only did citizens object to what the government thought was their performance obligations; many people of all ages actively opposed American participation in the war, and the antiwar movement proved a powerful constraint on presidential freedom of action, as both Lyndon Johnson and Richard Nixon discovered.* During the war, the government was forced to employ several illegal and "undemocratic" devices in order to maintain even a facade of public unity, a fact well-documented during the Watergate revelations.[40] In the wake of the Vietnam debacle, the government could no longer count on automatic public, or even congressional, support for its foreign policy—a fact supported by the refusal of Congress to supply the CIA with funds for Angola. As James Nathan and James Oliver remark:

> It is true . . . that during peak moments of international tension or crises . . . the public has, in the past, closed ranks behind Presidents. But observers began noticing in the mid-1960's that "as each crisis receded, national unity diminished." By the time of the military alert during the Yom Kippur War of October 1973, national unity did not even begin to coalesce. . . . No future administration can be certain that support can be mobilized in any given instance. . . .[41]

Even where governments are powerful and united, observers must distinguish between them and the social systems they putatively represent. Both within and across social systems, governments, and the bureaucracies of which they are composed, are potential competitors of one another (as well as potential allies) as are a host of nongovernmental actors.[42] Rarely, if ever, is a single actor coextensive with the society, or societies, in which it is anchored. Since the state itself is not an actor, it follows that the "state"/"nonstate" dichotomy is invalid. Indeed, all actors vary in their degree of "stateness,"—a set of characteristics that include legal supremacy over a defined territorial area and group of people living in that area, as well as a set of loyalties and membership traits anchored in the territorial characteristic. The exclusive focus on the state-as-actor is the confused product of a Procrustean tradition in political

---

* For a causal explanation of how members of the antiwar movement became disassociated from the nation's foreign policy and, in effect, were desocialized from the political norms of American society, see John A. Vasquez, "A Learning Theory of the American Anti-Vietnam War Movement," *Journal of Peace Research* (1976), 13(4):299–314.

theory that regarded the international realm as an "untidy fringe of domestic politics"—a tradition encrusted by legal doctrine and historical myth that sought the ideal-type state.[43] The notion of a unitary nation-state is best regarded as an ideal type as well. As for sovereignty, it is properly associated with resources of authority and legitimacy as well as their trappings, and provides symbolic influence that is reflected in the prerogatives of bureaucrats that are instrumental to attaining preferred values. To the extent that groups are transformed into actors, they all acquire some of the marks of "stateness," even though the imprimatur of sovereignty may elude them. But sovereignty, even though a resource, should not be confused with influence. Unfortunately, "political scientists," as Karl Kaiser argues, "have acted as if the ideal type of international politics were a reality and, in fact, the only reality."[44] Even the government of a "sovereign" nation-state may not always be an actor, and even when it is, it may dissolve at times into competitive actors, or become part of a still more encompassing actor. This raises a final question concerning actors: under what conditions will the members of *already existing* actors continue to coalesce or fragment.

THE COALESCENCE AND FRAGMENTATION OF ACTORS

The extent to which a group is a unitary actor is best understood as a question of degree. Table 5.1 portrays the coalescence/fragmentation continuum and identifies four key points of qualitative or step-level change: unitary actor, coalition, faction, and competing actors. A unitary actor is distinguished from a coalition in that the latter is based solely on a shared issue position; whereas, the former also develops a set of affective bonds among members that produce a sense of "we-ness" and a level of trust that serve as a basis for a long-term commitment to each other. A unitary actor begins to come apart when disagreement erodes the affective bonds that produced "we-ness." Once this occurs, the sense of identification weakens, even snaps, and the actor at best will only be a coalition of psychologically independent members. A coalition begins to break down once agreement can no longer sustain the pattern of interaction. Disagreement on a high salience issue necessitates factionalization if members are going to pursue different policies to attain a stake. If such action produces feelings of hostility because members feel betrayed, an environment of

Table 5.1 The Coalescence/Fragmentation Continuum

Level of Unity[a]	Indicator	Adequate Scholarly Conception
High coalescence	5. High positive identification with group	
Low coalescence	4. Satisfaction with group behavior	Unitary actor
	Threshold	
Strong agreement	3. Active support of group's position (high positive communication)	
Weak agreement	2. Public adoption of position (low positive communication)	Coalition
	1. Fulfillment of performance obligations	
	Threshold	
Weak disagreement	1. Abdication of performance obligations (low negative communication)	
Strong disagreement	2. Public disagreement with group's position (high negative communication)	Faction
	Threshold	
Low fragmentation	3. Active support of independent position	Competing actors (New unitary actors)
High fragmentation	4. Creation of counter-group or expulsion of dissenting members and attempt to seize their resources	

[a] Since each step up or down the scale is a prerequisite for the next, a Guttman scale can be used to assess the degree to which a group may be considered a unitary actor for any issue.

distrust and withdrawal from the group may ensue. Since feelings of betrayal are a function of the presence of affective bonds, the higher the sense of "we-ness," the greater the subsequent hostility once fragmentation occurs. In this sense, unitary actors are less likely to break down into factions or new groups; but *if they do,* they are apt to do so with considerably more hostility. As in marriage, love is closer to hate than mutual self-interest. Each of these transitions involves distinct changes in the psychological attitudes of members, the nature of their communication, and their organizational structure. These three variables yield an eightfold typology that can elucidate the different levels of coalescence and fragmentation of groups.*

The psychological attitude that is the most important is satisfaction with the group—i.e., with the group norms, the performance of the group, and the interactions within the group. Such satisfaction determines the extent to which the actor is legitimate in the eyes of its members; this quality is revealed in public support for group positions, reflecting conscious recognition of a "group interest" in issues. A second factor in the coalescence/fragmentation continuum is group organization. The more hierarchically the collectivity is organized, the more likely that conjoint activity will be elitist (with passive membership support). In contrast, the more egalitarian is the organization of the group, the more active will be the membership as a whole, and the more easily can affective bonds become deeply rooted. Consequently, egalitarian structures tend to be characteristic of groups that are relatively new and have failed to develop a sense of "we-ness" and trust that will permit them to develop a greater specification of roles and a division of labor.

Frequent and positive communication is a third factor. Continuous, rather than episodic, communication reinforces group loyalties and facilitates the coordinated application of collective resources. In addition, it encourages the elaboration of a common set of ideas, the meaning of which is understood by all members. A common set of symbols for those ideas promotes a language of mutual understanding, complementary habits and routines, and, above all, a common issue focus and discern-

---

* The eightfold typology is introduced here primarily for heuristic and explanatory purposes so that the different types can be "identified" in an illustrative fashion. Methodologically, however, coalescence-fragmentation is best measured on an ordinal scale using an index composed of the various indicators suggested in table 5.1.

ment of salience among issues. All of these factors help the group differentiate itself from outsiders, thereby going well beyond the similar interests that gave rise to the group in the first place and intensifying the "we-they" consciousness.* High levels of positive communication among members stimulate the institutionalization of roles and behavior, so that each member is increasingly able to anticipate how others will behave in different situations and all members can acquire an understanding of collective procedures. As common cognition is fostered, patterns of member interaction become predictable.

Figure 5.2 depicts the eight variants, assuming that satisfaction is the most important indicator of coalescence, followed by organization, and then communication. Point 1 reflects high membership satisfaction, hierarchical structure, and frequent communication as in American society during World War II. This is a mobilized unitary actor, as opposed to one directed by an elite (cf. point 2). Points 3 and 4 represent two different types of coalition. Both have satisfied members and an egalitarian structure, but the first type is "active" (i.e., the Big Three at Teheran and Yalta); and the second is latent (i.e., England and Russia in the Triple Entente). Points 5 and 6 depict types of faction in an hierarchically organized actor. The first does not communicate very frequently with the elite and can be characterized as an "estranged potential faction"; whereas the second, because of its frequent communication, can be viewed as the "rebellious faction." Finally, points 7 and 8 distinguish between the faction that has separated from the group and is estranged and the one that has separated and is hostile.

The question that remains is, Under what conditions will these various types of actors emerge? When are the boundaries of actors altered to the point where previously identifiable actors disappear or rearrange themselves into new ones, i.e., the extremes of coalescence/fragmentation? When will a government command the rest of society? When will part of the society split off to oppose a government? When will a government itself divide, with bureaucracies doing one thing and the executive an-

---

* It is for this reason that the relative intensity of communications and transactions among members, in comparison with their exchanges with outsiders, is a more significant indicator of integration than the absolute level of such exchanges. See the discussion of the index of relative acceptance (RA) in Donald J. Puchala, "International Transactions and Regional Integration," *International Organization* (Autumn 1970), 24(4):738.

Figure 5.2 Group Variations

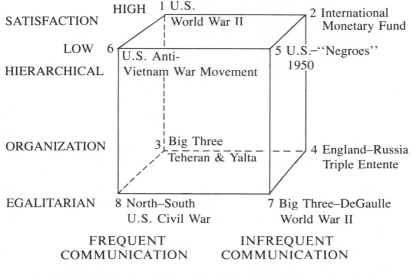

SATISFACTION

HIGH   1 U.S.
World War II   2 International
Monetary Fund

LOW   6   U.S. Anti-
Vietnam War Movement   5 U.S.–"Negroes"
1950

HIERARCHICAL

ORGANIZATION   3 Big Three
Teheran & Yalta   4 England–Russia
Triple Entente

EGALITARIAN   8 North–South
U.S. Civil War   7 Big Three–DeGaulle
World War II

FREQUENT
COMMUNICATION   INFREQUENT
COMMUNICATION

1 (High Satisfaction, Hierarchical, Frequent Communication)
Unitary Actor (mobilized)
2 (High Satisfaction, Hierarchical, Infrequent Communication)
Unitary Actor (elite directed)
3 (High Satisfaction, Egalitarian, Frequent Communication)
Coalition (active and committed)
4 (High Satisfaction, Egalitarian, Infrequent Communication)
Coalition (latent)
5 (Low Satisfaction, Hierarchical, Infrequent Communication)
Estranged Potential Faction
6 (Low Satisfaction, Hierarchical, Frequent Communication)
Rebellious Faction
7 (Low Satisfaction, Egalitarian, Infrequent Communication)
Estranged Faction
8 (Low Satisfaction, Egalitarian, Frequent Communication)
Competing Hostile Actor

other? Finally, when will a society divide with factions fighting each other for control of the governing apparatus?

Any satisfactory model of the coalescence/fragmentation process must take cognizance of factors both external and internal to the collectivity. The principal external factor is the nature of the issue which the actor is called upon to confront. The two variables that are critical here are issue dimension, which summarizes the collective perception of the actor of its relationship both to the stakes for which it seeks to compete and to other major actors, and issue salience.

As can be seen in figure 5.3, issue dimension has a direct impact on the level of friendship and hostility among members of a group. It also affects the nature of current interaction among members of the group (the extent to which they agree and, hence, whether they tend to send positive or negative acts toward each other), which in turn directly conditions friendship–hostility. Whether the level of current interaction will ever become sufficiently frequent to generate enough friendship or hostility to produce coalescence or fragmentation is determined primarily by the salience of the issue. Issues which are of the highest salience to all the major contenders in a system—i.e., critical issues—invariably fragment old groups and produce new ones. Issue salience therefore has a direct impact on coalescence/fragmentation as well as an indirect one through issue dimension.

The ease with which issue salience will produce or destroy actors depends on three other variables: prior pattern of interaction, group and member success/failure, and organizational context. The prior pattern affects coalescence/fragmentation both directly and indirectly through friendship–hostility. It is a powerful variable because it represents the cumulative effect of previous interactions. Thus a group whose members have enjoyed a long and fruitful relationship will not be divided easily by the disagreement introduced by a new issue. Success/failure affects coalescence directly, although slowly. A group which persistently fails to overcome the value deprivation of its members will decline in numbers and lose support, particularly if there are competing successful groups. Finally, the organizational context will have some impact on the ease with which the other conditions bring about coalescence or fragmentation. If members belong to many groups and the group structure is egalitarian, they are less likely to move beyond the coalition stage; whereas if

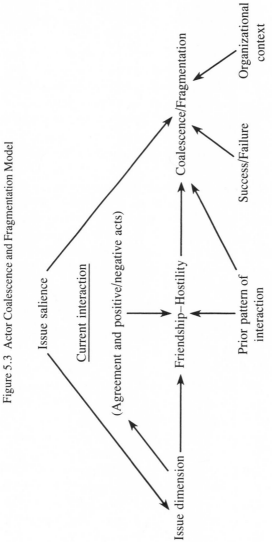

Figure 5.3 Actor Coalescence and Fragmentation Model

they are "bound" to a single group that has a rigid hierarchical structure that is effectively enforced, they may not be able to withdraw even if they desire to do so.

Clearly, not all the variables in the model are of equal importance. The two most potent variables are issue dimension and issue salience. The effects of these variables are then accentuated or attenuated by the prior pattern of interaction, success/failure, or the organizational context. Finally, current interactions and friendship–hostility act primarily as transmission belts for the more fundamental issue characteristics.* The way in which each of these variables operate must now be explored in more detail.

The issue dimension is of critical importance, because it constitutes the manner in which the collectivity views the links among issues on the agenda and determines whether members view the external world as fundamentally threatening and nonmanipulative or nonthreatening and fluid. An issue which is highly salient often tends to produce an actor dimension (positive or negative). A negative actor dimension leads to the fusion of issues that involve the same competitors, thereby encouraging a collective perception of value deprivation as the consequence of external malice. If the individuals, whether they be members of an actor or not, perceive their external environment to be dominated by the presence of such a common adversary, pressure will grow to see themselves as sharing common interests in the variety of stakes at issue (no matter how objectively dissimilar those stakes are), and "personal antagonisms remain subdued because of a felt need for ultimate consensus."[45] As Irving Janis observes: "It has long been known that group solidarity increases markedly whenever a collection of individuals faces a common source of external threat. . . ."[46] Such internal positive affect, if it persists, encourages coalescence when the issue is seen as a critical one. Thus, members of revolutionary parties that had to fight for power—as in China, Yugoslavia, and Algeria—developed deep bonds of friendship and fellowship because of the life-and-death struggles they waged together, and became more cohesive and autonomous actors than parties such as those in Poland or Mali, which had power handed over to them.

The fact that an actor dimension tends to fuse issues means that the

* The interrelationship among the independent variables, particularly the last two, with the various issue characteristics is elaborated in chapter 6.

collectivity only needs to adopt positions on a single issue which most members see as central to their values. Loyalty is demanded and returned because of the sheer scope of the issue and its relationship to core values. The attention of members is focused on the competitor's motivation as the central feature of their common environment, and the source of existing and future value deprivation. In addition, the fusing of issues is associated with the disappearance of concrete stakes and their reappearance as, or transformation into, symbolic and transcendent stakes. These give rise to ''zero-sum'' proposals that stimulate external conflict, make the stake more salient to members, and encourage members to cherish still more greatly the collectivity which promises to acquire or protect them.*

In practice, the heightened salience and sense of threat (which is common to all members) encourage agreement among individuals on collective proposals and the exchange of positive actions, including performance of group obligations; that is, they encourage cooperation among members in a common task of ensuring survival. Though individual members may resist the fusion of issues and continue to dissent as a consequence of their dissatisfaction over the treatment of other issues, their concerns will be seen as ''parochial'' at best and ''treason'' at worst. Thus, during World War I, those Irish who continued to oppose British rule were viewed as pariahs, and their demands vigorously silenced for the duration of the conflict.[47] For cohesion rather than divisiveness to occur, however, the threat must be perceived as a common one, rather than as directed at only some members. During the early phases of the German blitz of London during World War II, much of the damage was to the city's working-class East End, and there was considerable bitterness among inhabitants of this area, who believed they were not being adequately protected. Once the city's wealthier districts had been treated in the same fashion by German bombers, these divisions disappeared.†

* If members of the group do not share the group view, they may be purged and seen as dangerous allies of the enemy. Most of the American Left was treated in this fashion during the McCarthy era. Hence the great ''need'' of those who had shared previous issue positions with the Left (i.e., liberals such as Reinhold Niebuhr and Hubert Humphrey) was to ''prove'' their loyalty by vigorous anticommunism.

† Writing in his diary on September 17, 1940, Harold Nicolson noted:

''Everybody is worried about the feeling in the East End, where there is much bitterness. It is said that even the King and Queen were booed the other day when they visited the destroyed areas. Clem (Davies) says that if only the Germans had had the sense not to

In the presence of a stake dimension, on the other hand, the agenda of issues will be viewed as less tightly linked, and the pressure of external threat as a spur to internal unity will be less. No one issue is so salient as to swallow up the others. The NATO alliance, for example, remained cohesive as long as its members perceived key issues as linked by a negative actor dimension, arising out of a Soviet military threat to Western Europe. Although the ebbing of that threat was by no means the sole cause of the malaise which afflicted the alliance in the 1960s, the subsequent reduction in salience of the Cold War issue in an "atmosphere of détente removes the previous urgency for Allied cohesion."[48] To the extent that an actor was originally organized to confront a single "superissue" (as in the case of NATO), the bonds of its members are susceptible to weakening, and the collectivity may even lose its raison d'être as the issue decomposes or is resolved. At that point, the continued existence of the organization itself may become an issue, as has happened to NATO.*

Where stakes are loosely linked, actors are forced to adopt a variety of positions toward the several issues of concern to their members. Under such conditions, the collectivity will be held together by less intense bonds, because individuals and subgroups may accord different salience to the several issues and the values they represent—a condition that encourages crosscutting interactions and trade-offs among members. If members perceive the collectivity to be adopting proposals that are inimical to their personal preference schedule, they may reduce or withhold support for the collectivity. And if they can identify other members or outsiders who share the same sense of dissatisfaction, and with whom they can communicate, they may form competing subgroups, even com-

---

bomb west of London Bridge there might have been a revolution in this country. As it is, they have smashed about Bond Street and Park Lane and readjusted the balance." Nigel Nicolson, ed., *Harold Nicolson: The War Years 1939–1945* (New York: Atheneum, 1967), pp. 114–15.

* Samuel P. Huntington declares: "If over a period of time an organization has developed a set of responses for effectively dealing with one type of problem, and if it is then confronted with an entirely different type of problem requiring a different type of response, the organization may well be a victim of its past successes and be unable to adjust to the new challenge." Thus, one of the criteria he examines to determine the stability of a group is its ability to *adapt* to changing circumstances—*Political Order in Changing Societies* (New Haven, Conn.: Yale University Press, 1968), p. 13. A good example of successful adaptation is the case of the March of Dimes, which turned its resources to overcoming birth defects after polio had been "conquered."

peting actors. What is taking place is the growth of a sense of interdependence among dissenters of the sort described earlier in the context of initial actor formation. As long as their rivalry with fellow members of the original collectivity is not infected by hostility and a stake dimension remains dominant, bargaining and logrolling—both among members within the collectivity and between members and outsiders—may persist, as in cases of "transgovernmental" behavior, where buraucrats in different governments assist one another against other bureaucrats in their own government on issues in which they share common interests.[49]

The explicitly pluralist setting is conducive to weaker affective bonds both within an actor and among actors, and the heightened consciousness of expediency as the basis of collective behavior permits the penetration of the collectivity from without. If collaboration between dissatisfied members and outsiders occurs on issues that are salient to both—and if it proves rewarding—they may develop bonds of positive affect, thereby eroding their loyalty to the original collectivity or at least diluting it. In this manner, the preferences which members have for values other than those which gave rise to the original collectivity, while not having an immediate effect, may have consequences over time as new issues emerge or old issues assume a new face. Highly committed or ideological members of political parties, for instance, tend to withdraw their support or surrender their membership if the party as a whole compromises its original issue position, or attempts to adopt positions on issues outside the narrow range which originally inspired its "true believers." Changes in the dominant issue dimension—if combined with suitable membership variables—will promote the reorganization of a collectivity or stimulate the birth of yet new politicized groups by tapping the interests of the collectivity as a whole. Consequently, the original "social contract" may be undermined.

As the foregoing analysis suggests, issue dimension and issue salience work hand in hand with interaction variables (both current and prior interaction) and friendship–hostility. The highly salient "critical issue" generates an actor dimension, which, if it poses a common external threat, will unify the group by producing agreement, positive acts, and friendship within; but disagreement, negative acts, and hostility without. Conversely, if the critical issue divides the group, the actor dimension will promote disagreement, negative acts, and hostility within, and lead members to withdraw and seek allies elsewhere. Stake dimensions, on the other hand, are produced by less salient issues and rarely produce consistent agreement patterns and strongly anchored friendship–hostility. They rarely produce new unitary actors or fragmentation of existing ones. Rather, less salient issues linked by a stake dimension tend only to result in coalitions of factions. The two issue characteristics are determinative. Nevertheless, two other variables will have some impact—the organizational context in the short run, and the success/failure of the group in the long run.

The immediate effects of the two issue characteristics are attenuated or accentuated by the organizational context in which individuals and groups find themselves. Individuals that belong to only one or a few groups, or to hierarchically organized groups, are less likely to be separated from those groups in case of disagreement than individuals who belong to many groups, or to groups that have an egalitarian structure. The organizational context can be of great importance when issues are fused on a stake dimension and are not as salient as the critical issue. When critical issues do appear and provoke an actor dimension, the organizational context provides only a temporary delay to an overriding force.

The success/failure variable only enters the picture once an issue has been on the agenda for some time. The time it takes to have an effect depends on the level of salience of the issue and the nature of the issue dimension. Critical issues will not be affected for a long time; less salient issues linked by a stake dimension will be more susceptible to its influence. Success/failure occurs at two related levels—for the group as a whole, and for each member of the group. Collective success refers to the adoption of proposals made by the actor, or acceptable to the actor, and the subsequent acquisition, or safeguarding, of stakes valued by the actor. From the point of view of members, such success is equivalent to the provision of "collective" or "public" goods. Individual success is equivalent to the provision of "private" goods or benefits.[50] Consistent with Mancur Olson's "logic of collective action," collective success alone, though strengthening affective bonds among members, provides only limited inducements for enthusiastic participation in collective action, as the benefits it brings—such as security from external attack—are available to all members regardless of their contribution to the collective. Thus, though all citizens may aspire for collective victory in time of war, individual citizens will generally be prepared to let "others" do the fighting necessary to achieve victory. In the absence of coercion or moral suasion, enthusiastic participation will occur only when members are provided with private benefits; that is, with benefits that are available only to them. These may include financial benefits, status, and position, and even a personal sense of achievement; and their acquisition promotes a consciousness of individual success. The more widely available private benefits become, and the more they are seen to be distributed "fairly," the more probable is actor coalescence. In all cases, a favorable interim disposition of stakes heightens morale and generates enthusiasm for the collectivity by illustrating its worth and capacity to members. The legitimacy of leaders is increased, and members' appetites are whetted for further successes on the path toward a final favorable resolution of issues. Such, for example, was the effect of Hitler's initial foreign policy successes:

The aggressive . . . foreign policy which Germany began to follow under Hitler's leadership . . . gave expression to the long-smouldering rebellion of the German people against the defeat of 1918 and the humiliation of the Peace settlement. Through the sense of national unity which it fostered, it served to strengthen the political foundations of the regime in popular support. . . .[51]

Indeed, it is not unusual for governments that are the objects of public dissatisfaction to "search" around for an external triumph, as did Tsardom in the Balkans after its 1905 defeat in the Russo-Japanese War.

The issue dimension is of some significance in the case of group failure. If an actor dimension is dominant, interim failures produce coalescence, at least in the short run, owing to perceptions of external threat. If it persists, however, frustration and defeatism arise, and members may seek to save themselves at the expense of the collectivity. Enthusiasm for the collectivity will begin to wane once it appears that victory is beyond its reach, and "privatism" will grow, which may be followed by overt opposition in the form of demonstrations, assassinations, coups, or even revolutions. As the general frustration level rises, fears spread that ultimate defeat is inevitable, and the weakness of leaders becomes manifest. Illustrations of this process include the "generals' plot" against Hitler in 1944 when it became obvious that World War II was lost, the Bolshevik overthrow of the Kerensky government in Russia in 1917 when the latter refused to abandon the alliance with Britain and France, and growing discontent in the United States during both the Korean and Vietnam Wars.

In the presence of a stake dimension, the effects of group failure on cohesiveness are likely to be substantially different. The existence of many issues on the agenda, and their crosscutting quality, reduce the affect generated by either success or failure, so that the process is unlikely to become extreme. But unlike an actor dimension, interim failure will not produce coalescence, because the ingredient of threat will not be as sharp. Instead, interim failure with a stake dimension (the consequence of disagreement) will breed dissatisfaction among those elements of the collectivity that evaluate the issue as important to them. They will rationalize their dissatisfaction by claiming that the collectivity or its leaders are not as serious about "their" issue as they are about other issues on the agenda, and that the issue is being sacrificed.

The success or failure of the collectivity as a whole only tells part of the story as far as membership satisfaction or dissatisfaction is concerned. In the context of group life, individuals and subgroups assess their own private success or failure in terms of the *individual* psychic and material costs and benefits the group affords them. As the collectivity as a whole succeeds or fails, members' level of satisfaction is affected by whether the costs and benefits associated with the collective effort are distributed in equal or unequal fashion; and their resulting sense of individual success or failure cannot be predicted by the fate of the group as a whole. Inequality by itself may not produce widespread dissatisfaction as long as some benefits are available to all, or as long as some costs are borne by everyone, at least until a consciousness of inequality becomes widely felt and communication among deprived individuals takes place.

For analytic purposes, it is possible to distinguish three stages that are reached and then passed as the collectivity moves toward coalescence or fragmentation. In the case of fragmentation, the first is that of individual alienation and anomie, which Gurr views as indicative of "men's loss of faith in, or lack of consensus about, the beliefs and norms that govern social interaction."[52] At this stage, the sense of private failure is particularly responsible for perceptions of relative deprivation and a resulting dissatisfaction with the collectivity. The intensity of such dissatisfaction may range from mild to acute, and may manifest itself in withdrawal of attention from the political process, nonvoting, desertions from military service, general nonperformance of obligations, and anomic violence (mobs, assassinations, crime). Unless increased communication among the dissatisfied takes place, the fragmentation process will cease, and the second stage, during which subgroups publicly espouse proposals and issue positions contrary to those of the collectivity, will not be reached.

During the second stage of fragmentation, coherent subgroups will articulate their positions in the form of election campaigns (if possible), denunciations, organized demonstrations, recall movements, and the like. In striking contrast to the previous stage, the collectivity will be characterized by the emergence of factions, each of which—in James Madison's words—consists of "a number of citizens . . . who are united and actuated by some common impulse of passion, or of interest, adverse to the rights of other citizens, or to the permanent and aggregate interests of the community."[53] At this stage, private failure is likely to combine with a growing consciousness of collective failure (as occurred during the Vietnam War in the United States). Additionally, increasing numbers of individuals will be prone to conceive of issues in terms of a stake dimension, so that the sense of external threat is not seen to be sufficiently sharp that public dissension is regarded as "unpatriotic" or impermissible. Thus, many of the groups which organized to oppose America's continuing involvement in Vietnam did so not merely because their members believed that the war could not be won, or that it was immoral, but also because they felt that the war was absorbing collective resources and skills that could be more profitably expended elsewhere. Where a stake dimension is present, then, perceptions of "opportunity costs" are prevalent.

Finally, the appearance of public and organized vocal opposition to collective issue positions reflects a growing capacity on the part of dissatisfied members to communicate with one another, thereby leading to the further spread of dissatisfaction. As long as divergent issue positions are communicated only episodically, the awareness and depth of disagreement may be contained. This was the purpose of imposing the ideal of "bipartisanship" upon the American government's conduct of foreign affairs in the early years of the Cold War. Episodic disagreement within a group, even if severe, need not degenerate into endemic conflict, and as Coser suggests, "may help to establish unity and cohesion where it has been threatened by hostile and antagonistic feelings among the members,''—particularly if such conflict revolves around goals that ''do not contradict the basic assumptions upon which the relationship is founded,'' because it allows for norms and influence within the collective to be adapted to changing conditions and expectations.[54]

Whether or not a fragmentation process moves into the final stage of organized discontent depends upon the degree to which the prior articulation of dissatisfaction is successfully met by the collectivity. An organized sense of relative deprivation can be satisfied by redistributions of existing stakes, or the provision of new stakes as substitutes by the actor to its members. Or, the process can be aborted by the imposition of overwhelming constraints which prevent continued communication and organization among the dissatisfied, and which will return the process to the first stage. Thus, cross-national data suggest an inverse relationship between civil violence and government control of economic resources.[55] Repression does not end dissatisfaction; it merely renders difficult the organization of the dissatisfied necessary for them to become threats to an existing order. Where dissatisfaction persists, repression actually increases frustration, so that when the opportunity to communicate and organize reappears, dissident behavior is likely to arise once more, as in the case of Irish Republicanism after the 1916 Easter Rebellion.

Like the fragmentation process, coalescence can be seen as proceeding through three stages. During the initial stage, individuals, though satisfied with group performance, tend to behave in passive fashion without emotional commitment. Members carry out their performance obligations but are unwilling to do more than ''their share'' for the common good. Communication is vertical and tends to be from the top down, rather than from the bottom up. The second stage features an expansion in communication from the bottom to the top, as well as more intense enthusiasm, which leads to spontaneous or planned demonstrations of support for the positions of surrogates and leaders. Such behavior is likely in the event of collective success (as in the case of a military victory) or in the event of common external threat. It is the latter, however, that is responsible for movement to the third stage of coalescence, which is characterized by enthusiastic participation in collective ventures that goes beyond the ''letter'' of performance obligations. As has been noted, an increase in external threat associated with the development of a rigid actor dimension, as in the case of ''crises,'' tends to deepen affective bonds within the group; thereby giving rise to the unitary actor, at least for the issue before it.

Having delineated the conditions under which actor coalescence and fragmentation are likely to occur, it is now possible to demonstrate the utility of the model by applying it briefly to answer two questions that have been of recent concern: (1) why do alliance and coalition patterns change periodically? and (2) how important are the various observations made by the bureaucratic politics approach? The first question has been of concern since France's withdrawal from NATO, and has assumed greater importance as the U.S. government rethinks the various military commitments it made during the 1950s.[56] The second question has been a concern raised by academics who have participated in government and have been troubled by problems of rationality and accountability.

The model presented here provides an explanation of the first phenomenon by pointing to a change in the issue-dimension variable. The Cold War is no longer held together by a negative actor dimension, but a stake dimension. This has meant that disagreement and crosscutting is more likely. In coalitions that are based primarily on agreement and have not developed strong affective bonds, disagreement and the weakening of an external threat tend to promote dissolution, especially as other issues become more salient. Thus, the People's Republic of China is more important to the United States, and Taiwan must suffer. Likewise, some commitments are just too costly or risky in light of the fact that they no longer provide any benefit since the demise of the actor dimension. Certainly Korea and even Berlin fit into this category. The change in the underlying issue dimension of the Cold War takes a heavy toll on alliances based on expedience; but in the absence of strong affective bonds, it is naïve to think that the strong will continue commitments that are no longer in their interest, and that might stand in the way of resolving issues that have been under contention for over thirty years.

Alliances have been placed under even more strain, because as the Cold War has waned, other issues have sought to replace it as a critical issue. The Sino-Soviet dispute and the North-South conflict provide new highly salient issues that not only introduce new areas of disagreement into existing groups (particularly among Communist actors with regard to the first issue), but provide foundations for the genesis of new coalitions and groups. Thus, the Soviet-Cuban-Vietnamese coalition emerges as an important new grouping centered around the Sino-Soviet dispute. Likewise, OPEC and the International Energy Agency (IEA) are new powerful actors in the North-South conflict.

The waning of the Cold War and the erosion of its issue dimension, as well as the rise of other salient issues, have provided a major dynamic for change during the current period of history. Their force is irresistible, and little can be done to prevent shifts in coalitions without manipulating these two issue variables. Nonetheless, other variables can have a mitigating effect. Prior pattern, success/failure, and the organizational context all play a part in determining whether the transition from an actor to a stake dimension and the more fundamental, yet still emerging change within agendas will be smooth or rough. Thus, the prior pattern of interaction made it likely that France, Russia's traditional ally, would be the first to break the coalition as the actor dimension waned, while Britain would probably be the last. Similarly, the ancient conflict between China and what is now Vietnam made it probable that as the Cold War actor dimension loosened, and the Sino-Soviet dispute intensified, Vietnam would be drawn toward the USSR, regardless of ideological preferences, because of vestigial hostility and distrust left from prior interaction with China.

Organizational context and success/failure have also played important, even if minor, roles. Throughout the Cold War, French governments sought to keep their organizational options as plentiful as possible by trying to create and lead coalitions that would buttress French independence. The French role in the Common Market, its special relationship with Germany, its abortive attempt in the 1973 oil embargo to establish an alternative to the IEA, and even its attachment to the French Empire and later the French Union, reflected efforts to facilitate French maneuverability. Likewise, success/failure has had a role. Actors that have found alliances rewarding, usually the weak in the "Free World," have been the most reluctant to give them up; especially, as with Taiwan, when their organizational context leaves them few viable alternatives.

These examples serve to illustrate that while the current global situation is in flux and undergoing fundamental changes, these can be explained and even predicted by a relatively parsimonious model. In addition to being able to explain such macrobehavior as global change, the model can also explain coalescence and fragmentation at the microlevel.

For the purposes of illustrating the utility of the model at this level, the question of bureaucratic politics and its role in foreign policy-making will be examined.

The bureaucratic politics approach[57] has raised several interesting questions about foreign policy-making but is criticized for failing to specify in rigorous fashion the conditions under which the phenomena it describes will actually occur. In the words of Charles Hermann:

Little effort has been devoted to establishing the limiting conditions under which the effects of bureaucratic politics occur. Assuming that bureaucratic politics does not operate with equal force on all issues for all countries, what are the circumstances under which it becomes an important source of explanation? This question remains largely unexamined.[58]

Hermann's point is well taken. Even if bureaucratic politics plays a role in something as important as the Cuban missile crisis, the observer wishes to know how and why it comes to play it and what factors condition that role. In this way, science can not only find patterns of behavior but account for them as well.

The model presented here would assume that for the United States (but obviously not for other actors) the amount of bureaucratic influence would be at its low point in a situation like the Cuban missile crisis. In other situations, considerably more bureaucratic involvement would be expected. This is because the American government is hierarchically organized, with fairly positive affect among its members. The attack on Pearl Harbor was a highly salient problem held together by a negative actor dimension. Under these conditions the bureaucracy was encouraged to coalesce with the executive by agreeing with it, and by exchanging with it positive acts more frequently than the prior pattern of interaction might indicate.

The prior pattern is very important in assessing the influence of bureaucratic factors, because it sets a base line for determining how accommodative the bureaucracy will be with the other variables, either pushing accommodation above or below the line. In this sense, prior pattern is really more correlative than explanatory, but it reflects incremental tendencies in human behavior. Thus, as salient issues, an actor dimension, and other factors encouraging coalescence come into play, the bureaucracy can be expected to exceed the cooperative behavior level indicated by the prior pattern. Conversely, as less salient issues, a stake dimension, and other factors encouraging fragmentation come into play, the bureaucracy can be expected to be less accommodative than might have been predicted by the prior pattern.* Prior pattern of interaction, as a repository of the effects of the other variables at an earlier time, provides a means of assessing the overall impact of bureaucracies on foreign policy, and of measuring the extent to which that impact will be accentuated or decreased in varying situations.

After the two issue variables, the success/failure variable is the most potent. Other factors being equal, bureaucracies will follow prior patterns that have been successful and avoid those that have failed. If following executive orders, rather than standard operating procedure, has brought success in the past, then that tendency will be continued; if it has been unrewarding, then it will tend not to be repeated despite orders from above. Obviously, the most critical element of success/failure is whether deviation from the letter and/or spirit of an executive instruction was successful in the past, where success is operationalized as the value satisfaction enjoyed by specific bureaucracies.

The final variable is the organizational context of a group. For bureaucracies, the two most significant aspects for determining independence are multiple memberships and organizational structure. The first refers to the number of other coalitions to which a bureaucracy "belongs." Does it, for example, have allies in the legislature, interest groups, the media, or even in other nations, that can influence central decision makers in its behalf? The more coalitions to which it belongs or the more allies it has, the greater the possibility of factionalism in the face of disagreement. The second aspect, structure, refers to whether the government is organized in an effective hierarchical manner or whether it is egalitarian. If the bureaucracy has an independent political or legal base, even if only in certain areas, then it is more apt to factionalize in the face of disagreement.

If the above assumptions are correct, then bureaucratic "deviance" will be *least* when: (1) the issue before the government is a critical one (high salience and held together by an actor dimension); (2) following executive orders both in letter and spirit has proved rewarding to the bu-

* For these purposes, the prior pattern can be seen as similar to Azar's *normal relations range*. See Edward Azar, "Conflict Escalation and Conflict Reduction in an International Crisis: Suez, 1956," *Journal of Conflict Resolution* (June 1972), 16(2):183–201.

reaucracy in the past, and not doing so has been painful in terms of the overall value satisfaction of the members of the bureaucracy, and of the bureaucracy as a whole; and (3) the organizational context prohibits the bureaucracy from belonging to other groups, and the government is hierarchically organized and able to enforce effectively that structure. In such circumstances, the "bureaucracy" will coalesce with the rest of the government—particularly the executive—at a level "higher" than its previous pattern of interactions.*

As these conditions change, so will the level of coalescence. Of particular importance are the two issue variables, because they may change rapidly from situation to situation and are the most potent variables in the model. Issues that are of less salience, and/or held together by a stake dimension, are going to produce less coalescence than could be expected from the prior pattern. As certain issues come to predominate, they will give rise to a new prior pattern. Under the following conditions bureaucracies may be expected to behave *independently:* (1) the issue before the government is of low salience to it, of high salience to the bureaucracy, and is held together by a stake dimension; (2) following its own inclinations in past situations similar to this has been rewarding to the bureaucracy; and (3) the organizational context encourages or permits deviation.†

The specification of these conditions indicates that the model can elucidate contemporary events and the intellectual problems they pose. Its applicability to both macro- and microbehavior demonstrates its generalizability. The next problem for the new paradigm is to clarify what produces agreement or disagreement among actors, the main factor in determining whether actors will move toward coalescence or fragmentation. To understand agreement patterns among actors, it is necessary to develop a model that will delineate the factors that underlie an actor's issue position.

* Obviously, such a prediction does not mean there will be no bureaucratic deviation or that a rational actor model will be followed.

† For some highly suggestive propositions related to structure, see Hermann, "Decision Structure and Process Influences on Foreign Policy," especially pp. 83–91, 96–100.

Instead of trying to explain politics as the struggle for
power among individuals or groups, this . . . (approach)
seeks to study politics from the perspective of policy
analysis. It focuses on how and why policy outcomes
occur, rather than how and why political actors seek to
dominate each other.
—*Coplin, Mills, and O'Leary* [1]

CHAPTER SIX

DETERMINING ISSUE POSITIONS

THE HEART of any paradigm that takes issues as its primary focus is to explain why actors adopt the positions they do toward the various questions on the political agenda. Theoretical analyses of this problem are rare in political science. Until recently, the concept of "issue position" did not even exist as a focus of enquiry; instead it was obscured by more general concepts like "goals" and "objectives," both in domestic public policy and foreign policy. Consequently, the literature on policy, especially foreign policy, has largely failed to explain in a nomothetic sense why particular policies are adopted. A review of this literature suggests that this failure is, in part, the result of the dominant realist paradigm and, in part, the result of the insufficient attention behavioralists devoted to the dependent variable of their analyses.

The study of foreign policy, like all of international relations, has passed through two distinct phases since World War II—the "realist" and the "behavioral." Both have suffered from serious conceptual deficiencies of the most fundamental sort. Realism obfuscated the difference between the normative and empirical realms in its reliance on the concept of national interest as its chief tool of analysis, and committed a number of errors for which the scientific method was offered as a corrective—nonfalsifiability, lack of precision, susceptibility to ad hoc explanations and post hoc inferences, and failure to provide adequate controls for drawing inferences from evidence. Nevertheless, the realists sought to explain an important question: Why does a nation pursue the foreign policy it does? However, the very nature of the question tempts investigators to idiographic analysis, particularly when policy concerns motivate them, and little attention is paid to methodology. Area specialists abounded, who, by acquiring substantive knowledge and subjecting it to introspection and retrospection in order to place themselves in the shoes of decision makers, and by employing the simple realist hypothesis that nations act to protect their national interests, thought themselves able to explain and predict foreign policy. But their explanations were narrow and particularistic.

The behavioral approach, in an effort to generalize and to overcome some of the conceptual and methodological confusion which realism entailed, expended considerable time and effort in identifying and assessing the potency of independent variables; but, in doing so, lost track of what the discipline really sought to explain—the foreign policy of actors—and instead shifted attention to "foreign-policy behavior," an amorphous and poorly defined concept. The shift in this direction was provoked by Snyder, Bruck, and Sapin, who elaborated a framework that offered a "checklist" of variables that could be used to explain the decisions of any actor at any time.[2] Reliance upon the foreign-policy decision as the dependent variable retained some connection with the major realist query, but it was difficult to operationalize in a generalizable manner. Consequently, it tended to give rise to case studies of why a single decision had been taken, or to quantitative studies, which—rather than seeking to explain decisions—shifted to describing and explaining the "decision-making process." Snyder's and Paige's study of American intervention in Korea, and Paige's later enlarged study of this case, are the examples of the first genre; while the work of Charles Hermann on crisis decision making, as well as the 1914 analyses of decision makers' perceptions during the outbreak of World War I, exemplify the second.[3]

In the midst of this development, other scholars were attracted by the Snyder et al. independent variables, particularly those which reflected the traditional idea that different types of states had different foreign policies. Adopting this approach, James Rosenau called for a new field, "comparative foreign policy," and developed in his seminal "pretheories" article a set of propositions to explain which *kinds* of states behave differently and why.[4] Influenced by Snyder et al., Rosenau sought to overcome the single-minded dependence of realism on the attribute of power for prediction, while remaining alert to the need for a theory of foreign policy that could incorporate both actor attributes and decision-making variables. His effort emphasized differences among national attributes producing different patterns of foreign policy. The use of the latter as dependent variables resulted in analyzing something called ''foreign-policy behavior,'' which presumably included anything one actor did to another. The need to operationalize the concept, however, forced scholars to identify what they meant. As a result, foreign policy came to mean participation (as opposed to isolation) in world affairs and cooperation/conflict among states. The Comparative Research on the Events of Nations (CREON) project, which has worked closely with the Rosenau pretheory, reflects this tendency.[5]

The study of foreign-policy behavior as participation and cooperation/conflict is a far cry from explaining why actors have the foreign policies they do. While the shift is understandable in view of the extreme difficulty of operationalizing a concept like national interest, with its strong normative and policy components, it nevertheless produced more of an interaction than policy focus among scholars of foreign policy. A major effort to overcome this focus took place when Coplin and O'Leary conceptualized foreign policy as the issue position of an actor on any global issue.[6] The addition of this concept permits a clear distinction between the prescriptive question of what is really in the interest of an actor; and the empirical questions of what is the position of that actor on an issue, and why it holds that position. This revision of the dependent variable encouraged the study of foreign policy to return to the question that the field, as a whole, had initially sought to answer.

An *issue position* is the stand (in favor, opposed, or neutral) an actor adopts toward any proposal that is intended, either directly or indirectly, to dispose of a stake and thereby allocate value. Issue positions always evolve in reference to proposals which are, at least potentially, specific and observable outcomes. An issue position is as broad as the proposal under discussion. It may specify something quite narrow, such as the movement of troops behind a certain line in the Sinai, or something very broad, such as a permanent peace settlement of the entire Middle East question. The latter, of course, would presumably involve a set of more specific outcomes—concerning the Golan Heights, the West Bank, Gaza, the status of the Palestine Liberation Organization, the Sinai, and the recognition of Israel—that would be linked together in one package. In this conceptual framework, a *foreign policy* consists of a set of interrelated issue positions on a set of interrelated proposed outcomes.

An issue position must be distinguished from the variety of tactical negotiating positions or "nonnegotiable demands" that an actor may express for purposes of bargaining. The issue position reflects an actor's attitude toward the proposals that other actors put forward, and conditions its own proposals. Foreign policy analysis involves determining how an actor develops its policy when an issue first attracts its interest, what is called here *initial issue position(s)*, and how it changes its policy in light of further interaction that modifies its initial positions and attitudes regarding its own and other actors' proposals.

Coplin and O'Leary pioneered in this area by developing the first testable theory of how and why actors change their issue position. Their framework consists of five concepts: *issue position* (measured on a scale from +10 through 0 to −10), *salience* (the importance of an issue to an actor), *affect* (the overall pattern of friendship–hostility), *influence attempt* (verbal and behavioral actions directed toward actors for the purpose of getting them to change their issue position), and *power* (the ability to prevent an outcome from occurring).

Coplin and O'Leary try to explain shifts in issue position by determining first the likelihood of a shift, and then its probable direction.* The likelihood of a shift is a function of the affect among actors and the salience of the issue. One actor is more apt to respond to another's demand for a shift in issue position if there is either *strong* positive or negative affect. Extreme affect, regardless of the direction, encourages some response; but this is tempered by the salience of the issue. An actor is *more* likely to shift on an issue that is of low salience to it, and *less* likely to shift on an issue that is of high salience to it. Coplin and O'Leary add, however, that if an actor does change its issue position on an issue that is of high salience to it, it will do so in an extreme (rather

---

*The hypotheses in this section are drawn from William D. Coplin and Michael K. O'Leary, "A Simulation Model for the Analysis and Explanation of International Interactions" (paper presented to the International Studies Association, San Juan, Puerto Rico, 1971).

than incremental) fashion. The direction of the shift is hypothesized to be a matter strictly determined by the affect level. The more positive the affect, the more likely an actor will moved toward the issue position of the actor requesting a shift; while the more negative the affect, the more likely an actor will move away from the issue position of an actor demanding a shift.

The above model raises the question of what are the determinants of affect. For Coplin and O'Leary, affect is determined by three factors—the number of influence attempts sent, salience, and power. The greater the number of influence attempts in a given period, the more likely is a change in affect. While an increased number of acts can alter the affect pattern, affect is also likely to change when these influence attempts are directed toward an actor on an issue that is of high salience to it. The direction of the change will depend on whether the influence attempts are positive or negative. These last two propositions offer an important insight; namely, *influence attempts are intended to change issue positions but instead they change affect.* Punishments and rewards do not change policy stances but only actors' attitudes toward one another. This makes political contention highly complex and difficult, because affect is the critical intervening variable that makes it impossible for influence attempts to accomplish directly the purposes for which they are being employed. Finally, actor A is likely to change its affect toward actor B when actor B has more power on the specific issue than actor A.

The inclusion of these hypotheses concerning affect make the Coplin and O'Leary model persuasive in explaining shifts in issue positions, as well as in providing insights about the dynamics of cooperation and conflict. What it does not explain is where the issue positions come from in the first place. The authors also do not explicitly elaborate whether the end result of the issue-position shifts will produce ultimate agreement on a decision to allocate value. This chapter seeks to build on their work by answering these two questions. To accomplish this, it is necessary to delineate the several decision-making calculi that an actor may adopt in reaching an issue position, and the conditions under which the various calculi will actually be utilized. Finally, the question of whether an actor's initial issue position will lead to agreement or disagreement will be broached.

DERIVING ISSUE POSITIONS

Realists were able to "predict" and explain foreign policy, at least in post hoc fashion, by determining the facts of a situation, examining what would be in the interests of the actors, and then assuming that actors "rationally" pursue these interests.* While such a deductive procedure may prove informative, particularly when employed by experts, the assumptions of rationality and interest-based-on-power leave considerable room for error, because of the imprecision of these concepts.

The traditional use of capability analysis, which was popularized by realism, runs into considerable difficulties. There is, in the first place, uncertainty as to which factors contribute to power and how they are related to each other. Thus, David Vital argues that "small" states are those with populations of 10 to 15 million that are economically developed, as well as those economically less-developed states with populations in the 20 to 30 million range.[7] Such definitions are at best imprecise, and the factors of size and economic development cannot easily be combined.[8] In the second place, such measurements once more confuse the society in which actors find themselves with the actors themselves, so that comparisons remain fruitless unless we are able to compare accurately the access that different actors—both governments and others—enjoy to the resources within their societies, or for that matter, within other societies as well. In the case of governments, the nature of the regime, its popularity and style, its unity, the customs and traditions of its leaders, and other factors determine the degree to which it has access to the resources of a society; and only such knowledge makes it possible to distinguish between probable future influence and maximum potential influence.

The use of rationality also runs into difficulties, because no distinction is made between the short and long term, and because the interest of an actor may call not only for gaining the greatest part of a stake under contention but also for denying an opponent a strategic advantage, or not alienating an ally. While the notion of employing a calculus to explain an

* "Rationality" was behavior in accordance with the logic of the power position of actors. See Hans J. Morgenthau, *Power Among Nations,* 6th ed. (New York: Knopf, 1978), p. 40; and Arnold Wolfers, "The Role of Power and the Pole of Indifference," in Wolfers, *Discord and Collaboration* (Baltimore, Md.: Johns Hopkins University Press, 1962), pp. 81–102.

actor's foreign policy has merit, its particular embodiment in the national interest calculus needs to be made less impressionistic. It also must be dissociated from the assumption that actors have consistent interests that dominate their collective consciousness.[9]

The search for a deductive calculus is facilitated by separating the different possible aspects of a self-interest calculus to form three analytically distinct calculi—the cost-benefit calculus, the participant interdependence calculus, and the participant affect calculus. The first determines issue positions solely on the basis of trying to derive the most value from the stake under contention; the second determines issue positions on the basis of trying to derive support from actors on other issues; and the third determines issue positions on the basis of hostility or friendship toward the other actors contending for the stakes in question.*

These calculi provide an explanation of any actor's initial issue position, although they may not be able to provide precise predictions of every issue position, owing to the almost infinite variety of potential proposals. Until more refined measures are found, prediction must rely upon an intuitive analysis of the calculi to "deduce" the specific issue positions by getting into the shoes of the decision maker and employing one of the calculi to determine the issue position of an actor. This procedure is an advance over the single national interest calculus, not only because it provides a more precise explanation of an actor's foreign-policy positions, but, more importantly from a scientific perspective, because it makes it possible to specify the conditions under which the different calculi will be employed—thereby increasing understanding of the causal processes underlying the foreign policy-making process. Before turning to this theoretical question, the nature of the three calculi and the manner in which they can be applied require fuller elaboration.

The cost-benefit value calculus has an economic logic and leads to an issue position based on predictions of immediate value enhancement, or deprivation, associated with alternative proposals for allocation. For those who employ such a calculus, the key questions are: Will a given proposal enhance or reduce value satisfaction and to what extent? The calculus emphasizes conceptions of *absolute* loss or gain unencumbered by "noneconomic" factors like envy, jealousy, or hostility; that is, it excludes

---

*These three calculi incorporate in explicit fashion the difference, in Coplin's and O'Leary's model, between salience (cost-benefit) and affect (participant affect).

"nonutilitarian strategy preferences."[10] If such a calculus is in use, stakes are in the main regarded as concrete; and the issues they constitute, limited in scope. In other words, the economic predilection minimizes perceptions of nontangible linkages among separate stakes. An issue position is adopted solely on the basis of whether or not a given proposal minimizes the loss, and/or maximizes the gain, of a core value; and the actor is prepared to adopt its position regardless of whether it diverges from the position of friends or corresponds to that of enemies. The outcomes of such a calculus are implied in examples like Soviet proposals for arms control in the early 1960s, which alienated the People's Republic of China; and, more recently, Egyptian President Anwar el-Sadat's recognition of Israel, which alienated other Arab governments and groups.

Where a cost-benefit calculus is at work, an actor seeks to mobilize allies, whether friends or not, in order to obtain sufficient support for its proposals to gain acceptance. In other words, it is the highly valued stake(s) (rather than the other actors) that constitute the focus of attention. The stakes are seen as having inherent value for actors regardless of their relations with each other. Resulting alliances may resemble William Riker's conception of "minimum winning coalitions" when there is a specific concrete stake under contention, such as the division of spoils after World War II.[11] Despite the fact that twenty-eight governments declared war, the Big Three made the key decisions. France and China had to be "taken care of" by other powers—mainly the United States—a fact that was evident in the divisions of Germany, where the Soviet Union insisted that any French zone of occupation must be carved from Anglo-American shares. A cost-benefit calculus will tend to limit participation only to the players necessary to produce resolution of the issue. For this reason, weak actors may try to mobilize only one powerful patron, as when the governments of Taiwan and South Korea relied primarily on the US, rather than all the SEATO powers, during the 1960s.*

Determining the issue position of an actor when this calculus is in use is not unlike determining the positions of labor and management in collective bargaining situations. Initially, each side demands more than it can possibly get—a position that is, in effect, an upper limit. At the

---

* This policy is particularly effective if the patron is using an affect or interdependence calculus.

lower limit are positions which are totally unacceptable, because they deprive the actor of more of the value of the stake than it thinks it is capable of attaining. The latter position is determined by the willingness of an actor either to fight, or to risk nonresolution, rather than accept such a disposition. Within these two limits, there is a range of acceptable positions which can be rank-ordered in terms of the value they afford each contender. All sides will seek the outcome that gives them the most value, but so long as there is an issue position for all sides that is above their respective lower limits, agreement may be reached on a mutually satisfactory position. The logic of game theory is relevant here. Notions of equity and merit—merit being based on power and status—play important roles in identifying such an issue position. Thus the mathematical division of the North Sea seabed by the International Court of Justice for purposes of oil exploration is accepted by all littoral states, because claims are relatively equal and no one "deserves," or can get, more than the others. Conversely, a mathematical division of German territory in 1945 was not acceptable for a number of reasons, one of which was that the French government had surrendered in 1940 and contributed little to the defeat of the Nazis.

In utilizing this calculus, the more highly motivated actor may approach the issue as though it were the only one on the agenda—ignoring, or pretending to ignore, other issues. This approximates the behavior of regimes in the Third World as they seek to eliminate vestiges of neocolonialism, rapidly initiate a process of economic development, and secure the loyalty of nonmobilized groups within the state's frontiers. It is also similar to the behavior of highly integrated bureaucracies that have a clear conception of role and interests, and that function according to standard operating procedures. In effect, they come to consider the issues to which they are assigned, and with which they are equipped to deal, as either the most important, or the only, issues on the agenda; and they try to convince others that this is the case. In such instances, a cybernetic approximation to rationality of the sort described by John Steinbruner may operate. The decision maker "does not resolve value conflicts; that is . . . he does not seek to produce an optimally balanced return to competing objectives. Rather, the cybernetic decision maker breaks such problems into separate decision processes and operates at any one time in terms of a single objective with a single expected outcome.''[12] Unable, or unwilling, to grasp the relationship among competing objectives and issues, bureaucracies and operators—even within a single government—may find themselves working at apparent cross-purposes; as was the case in the USSR after the Bolshevik assumption of power, when the Foreign Office under G. V. Chicherin strove to normalize relations with capitalist regimes while the Comintern sought to overthrow them: "One strained its utmost to overthrow the governments with which the other tried to maintain friendly relations.''[13]

Rarely, however, is an issue position adopted without its being infected by some degree of affect, or without some consciousness of the relative status of other contenders. The position of the American government toward Chiang Kai-shek, for instance, was colored by the general idea that one should help a proven friend, regardless of whether or not its proposal will be immediately beneficial to one's interests. Where an actor's affect toward other participants strongly conditions its issue position, a participant affect calculus is operative. Whether a participant is for or against a proposal depends less on what and how the proposal purports to allocate, and more on who made it. Thus, the second calculus is based on the predicted impact of a proposal for the value satisfaction of other actors, viewed as *relative* to one's own value satisfaction. Whether or not the actor's issue position promises to minimize its losses, or maximize its gains, in an absolute sense is regarded as secondary to whether or not "friends" or "enemies" will benefit from it. The key questions are: Will a given proposal enhance or deprive *other* participants, and will a given issue position satisfy or spite them? By answering these questions, an observer who is familiar with the facts of a situation, and who knows that the actor is employing the affect calculus, should be able to predict and explain the actor's initial issue position.

Where positive affect is dominant, an actor will adopt its issue position with empathy and sensitivity of the sort that was evident in Charles de Gaulle's comment to Dean Acheson, during the Cuban missile crisis, that "a great government such as yours does not act without evidence.''[14] When negative affect is dominant, the actor will adopt an issue position that promises to do harm to another participant, as in Kaiser Wilhelm's decision to enter World War I, which was influenced by his animosity toward England: "If we are to bleed to death, England shall at least lose India."[15] Strong feelings of affect will influence actors to search for solutions that promise relative rather than absolute payoffs (or losses), and to view the issue as akin to a zero-sum or constant-sum game.

In situations dominated by a participant affect calculus, the issue positions of actors will change as those of other actors are modified. If a friend alters its issue position, the actor will move toward that friend, regardless of whether the new position promises as positive an outcome as did the old one. If an enemy offers a new proposal, the actor may reject it even though objectively it entails concessions. Such a process was evident in Soviet-American disarmament negotiations during the 1950s when both governments tended to abandon their own proposals once they had been partly accepted by the other side. Positions as these are the consequence of strongly held attitudes rather than expediency and tend to become embedded in closed images.

In the participant interdependence calculus, both cost-benefit and affect considerations are present, and issue positions are adopted as a consequence of both. The actor seeks to determine how, and in what ways, a given proposal will have an impact upon its own satisfaction, *and* upon the satisfaction of others, in the issue at hand and in the other issues that constitute the agenda. Expediency is present in the sense that close attention is paid to the relative power of participants in this issue as well as in others, and to how power ratios are likely to predict outcomes. However, affect, too, is present, in that an actor seeks to assist those who are friendly and able to render assistance, and to oppose those who are unfriendly and likely to adopt contrary issue positions.

In this context, the concept of interdependence refers to a recognition that the reception which an actor's proposals meet on one issue is related to its performance on other issues. Attention is paid to an actor's relative influence in gaining acceptance of its proposals for each issue under consideration.[16] Issue positions are adopted which are seen to maximize the actor's chances of getting a favorable hearing on other issues of equal or greater importance. The key question posed is: Will a given issue position generate support and favorable issue positions from other participants on other issues or will it alienate them? The logic of the calculus leads to the following sorts of propositions, which can be used to "deduce" the initial issue positions of actors employing this calculus: (1) If the issue at hand is unimportant, adopt a position beneficial to actors which are influential on other issues or follow the lead of those actors which are likely to be powerful and friendly on important issues. (2) If the issue is unimportant, and if other actors which are equally powerful in other issues and equally well disposed to you are divided, remain neutral. (3) If the issue is important and you are weak, ask influential actors for a "loan" in return for support elsewhere or for "collateral." (4) If the issue is important and you are sufficiently powerful to gain acceptance of your preferred proposal, disregard other actors and develop an issue position in accord with the cost-benefit calculus.

As these propositions suggest, conceptions of logrolling are present when the interdependence calculus is in use and trade-offs among issue positions are contemplated. Since relative power is issue-specific, even the least influential actor, in an overall sense, may have something to offer on specific issues in return for support in other issues. If such trade-offs prove to be mutually rewarding to partners and are repeated, ties will be reinforced by positive affect. As such patterns are institutionalized and become habitual, a patron–client relationship may evolve. However, if trade-offs prove detrimental to one or both partners, ties of expediency are likely to crumble under the pressure of negative affect. An illustration of such an unsuccessful trade-off occurred in September 1908, when the Austro-Hungarian and Russian foreign ministers agreed to support one another's proposals for the disposition of Bosnia and the Straits at Constantinople, respectively. It turned out to be "a day of dupes" however, because only Austria-Hungary benefited from the bargain, and relations between the two governments were deeply embittered by the ensuing controversy.[17]

A MODEL FOR DETERMINING ISSUE POSITIONS

From the description of the three calculi, it should be clear that there is a continuum underlying them, so that it is only possible to move from a cost-benefit to an affect calculus by passing through the interdependence calculus. The underlying continuum is provided by the issue dimension, which, it will be recalled, refers to the manner in which actors link stakes into issues. Stakes are linked through either an inherent quality (stake orientation) or because of who contend for them (actor orientation).*

A stake dimension entails recognition that proposals will affect the same desired value(s), or that, where the values are different, no one value can be satisfied without immediately affecting the others. A common milieu, for example, may impose a stake dimension upon an issue because of the apparent impossibility of distributing any single stake located within it without distributing others as well. Territorial issues are commonly of this sort. The stakes which actors may be seeking include arable land, subsoil minerals, control of strategic military locations, and so forth. The various stakes may be sought to enhance different values, but it is difficult for any one to be distributed without dividing others simultaneously, because they are tied together by the common territory in which they are located. The issue of the Law of the Sea Conference exhibits a stake dimension. Actors seek access to fish in the sea, and to mineral resources both upon and under the seabed; they seek access to the sea lanes for trade and military security; and they seek to protect their coasts from ecological damage. Here a variety of stakes and values are linked together by a common milieu—the sea itself—and control of the sea by any actor, or group of actors, provides access to all these stakes. The sea may be regarded as a ''superstake'' because of the way it ties together the specific stakes that constitute the issue.

* This distinction was aptly made by Hans Morgenthau in a letter written to the *New York Times* (April 28, 1978, p. A24) about the SALT negotiations:

''*Dangerous Quip*
''To The Editor:
''In your issue of April 2 you quote a member of the House Armed Services Committee, visiting the Soviet Union: 'If the Russians want it—a treaty limiting nuclear arms—it must be bad for us.' May I suggest that this quotation reveals a basic attitude which is not only obsolete but also fraught with mortal danger for the United States and all mankind.

''It is obsolete because it is unaware of the new fact of interdependence in which the advantage and disadvantage of one can also be the advantage or disadvantage of some other nation. It is fraught with danger because if the nuclear arms race and nuclear proliferation cannot be controlled the prospects for the United States and all mankind are grim indeed; for without such controls a nuclear world war appears to be inevitable.
''Hans J. Morgenthau
''New York, April 5, 1978''

An actor dimension links proposals together not by perceptions of the interdependence of the stakes themselves, but by the perception of a link among the participants in the issue—a link rooted in strong affective feelings. The same, or a similar, cast of actors is contesting the various stakes, so that proposals which benefit or deprive other actors in any one of them are likely to condition the proposals which they make about the disposition of other stakes for which they are common competitors. The fact that the same actors are in contention for the different stakes transforms a series of games into a single "supergame" which defines the issue.[18]

Figure 6.1 Issue Position Model

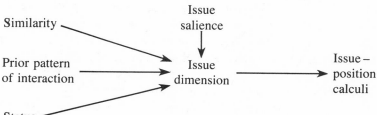

The issue dimension provides the means of predicting which calculus will be selected by an actor. A cost-benefit calculus will be selected when the stake dimension is dominant; an affect calculus is employed when the actor dimension is dominant; and an interdependence calculus is utilized when the two dimensions are present in mixed form. Which issue dimension will dominate is, in turn, determined by the salience of the issue, the similarity among actors, their status, and their prior pattern of interactions. This model is depicted in figure 6.1.

A stake dimension tends to produce the use of a cost-benefit calculus, because concrete stakes are likely to predominate. These are most susceptible to a cost-benefit analysis, because they are divisible and tangible, and usually lack the emotional commitments associated with symbolic and transcendent stakes. This makes the question of who is involved (other than oneself) less important to contenders. Consequently, cross-cutting cleavages are often produced, and new issues, particularly those that are salient, tend to be linked by a stake dimension. Current discussions on the Law of the Sea reflect such an issue, and a cost-benefit calculus seems to predominate among actors. Not only is the older Cold War cleavage broken by the U.S. and Soviet governments often sharing the same position on navigation (in particular military) rights against others; but the North-South cleavage is also broken, with landlocked states turning against coastal ones, and mineral-producing states wary of non-mineral-producing states. Likewise, political actors within societies are divided, each seeking its own parochial goals. American tuna fishermen were against extending the U.S. fishing zone to two hundred miles; while coastal fishermen, like those who worked the Grand Banks off Cape Cod, lobbied in Congress for such a provision. The U.S. Environmental Protection Agency was in favor of extending sovereign control into the free seas as a way of assuring responsibility for pollution and assigning authority for its regulation. The Pentagon, however, felt any extension of sovereignty would begin to destroy the very principle of freedom on the high seas, and therefore threaten navigation rights for military and national security purposes, such as electronic surveillance.[19]

Resort to a cost-benefit calculus is usually of limited duration, ignoring the long-term effects of selfish behavior. But as actor-oriented considerations enter the picture, the stake dimension no longer remains the sole basis for linking stakes, and there is a propensity to move toward the interdependence calculus. As with the cost-benefit calculus, however, the interdependence calculus can only survive when patterns of affect are relatively moderate, and when stakes are seen as concrete rather than as symbolic or transcendent. The appearance of the latter promotes the loss of identity for individual issues, so that trade-offs become more difficult. Such stakes and the consequent fusing of issues tend to generate "all or nothing" proposals; after which, haggling over specific stakes loses its crosscutting logic, because each stake is believed to represent other stakes, or because the process is infused with an ideological quality that heightens perceptions of fear or amity. It is because the conditions for interdependence calculi existed in eighteenth-century Europe that realists recall fondly the era of the "classical balance of power" as a halcyon age of cosmopolitan diplomacy, enlightened expediency, and limited objectives. Modern nationalism did not exist, so that "we-they" barriers were weak, and diplomacy was unhindered by implacable hatreds of a personal or national nature. Diplomats shared common characteristics and were personally empathetic to one another.* Conditions in which "the goals of statesmen are not fully set and in which there is no rigidly established priorities among objectives"[20] are conducive to the conclusion of bargains, because commitments to established issue positions are shallow. What is not commonly recognized by students of balance of power is that the system thrived because power—though relatively equally distributed through the system as a whole—was *unequally* distributed by issues, so that incentives for trade-offs existed. Nowhere were these trade-offs more common than in Europe's division of imperial claims in Africa and Asia in the late nineteenth century. When Bismarck was offering France Tunisia—"a ripe plum ready to be plucked"—in exchange for French acceptance of the status quo in Alsace-Lorraine, and the British, French, and Russians were concluding bargains "in Egypt, Persia, and in the Far East,"[21] the atmosphere was one of interdependence.

As actors engage in such bargains, they become preoccupied not only with the net worth of what they receive from the stakes, but with what others have received as well. Once value satisfaction or deprivation is measured in relative terms, stakes no longer have inherent value but change value according to who receives them. Consequently, there is an increase in the perception of symbolic stakes. Thus, if an actor's ally receives a stake, it is almost as if the actor received it. It is also permissible for a neutral or weak third party to obtain a share; but if an enemy takes control, the actor's deprivation is doubled; it has been denied the stake while the competitor increased its relative value satisfaction.

Issues that are linked by an actor dimension must of necessity give rise to an affect calculus for determining issue position. If symbolic stakes, in turn, assume a transcendent quality—involving disputes over fundamental belief systems like communism, democracy, and fascism—then the actor dimension is anchored and rigidified. Disputes actually begin to revolve around the relative worth of the different fundamental values. The intensity of issue positions becomes a key variable as well. Strongly held issue positions will change less easily and more slowly than those which are not as deeply rooted. Other things being equal, they will also induce larger expenditures of scarce resources—and riskier policies in pursuit of

* Realists have often expressed their preference for the "traditional diplomacy" of the eighteenth and nineteenth centuries. See, for example, Hans J. Morgenthau, *Politics in the Twentieth Century*, abridged ed. (Chicago: University of Chicago Press, 1971), pp. 390ff.

favored proposals. In this fashion, intensity of issue position partly predicts the probability of change in an actor's issue position and the level of its commitment to that position.

Concern by the Carter Administration, in 1978 and 1979, regarding Soviet and Cuban influence in Africa reflected a return to an affect calculus in issues involving the Soviet Union, after the Nixon and Ford Administrations had made strides toward converting the relationship from a single- to a multi-issue system, based on both stake and affect dimensions. Growing American and African expressions of alarm over Soviet and Cuban influence combined with reduced sensitivity to the local realities in Eritrea, Greater Somalia, Angola, Mozambique, Rhodesia, South Africa, and Zaire. Actor competition, rather than the inherent value of the stakes, began to become the fulcrum of contention. In Africa, there continues the irony that China seeks to be the leader of the world's revolutionary forces by siding with American-backed groups like UNITA (National Union for the Total Independence of Angola), and conservative and corrupt regimes like Mobutu's in Zaire. Meanwhile, Cuba and Neto of Angola are placed in the awkward position of having to defend the raiders of Shaba province in Zaire, who are the remnants of Moise Tshombe's Katanga, one of the most neocolonial regimes in the short history of postcolonial Africa. These anomalies occur because the outside parties base their decisions on an affect calculus centered on an East-West issue, whereas local participants are really motivated by tribalism, an issue which is unrelated to that which perturbs the interventionists. Nevertheless, the local participants are sophisticated enough to phrase their struggle in the "proper" ideological rhetoric, so as to gain the support of strong patrons, who in a real sense risk being duped by the weak.

The relationship between issue dimensions and the calculi which underlie issue positions, so stated, however, simply asserts a psychological propensity in the issue-position process and does not really provide a non-tautological explanation. To provide such an explanation, it is necessary to delineate the conditions that determine why actors perceive the issues before them in terms of a stake or actor dimension. The manner in which actors perceive issues, and the calculus which they adopt, are the consequence of a concatenation of four key factors: *prior pattern of interaction* among contenders, their *similarity* in the sense of overlapping or incongruent identities and roles, their relative *status,* and the *salience* to them of the issue at hand. As these indicate, the perception of an issue by an actor does not occur in a vacuum but, instead, is conditioned by the way in which the actor is related to the issue before it, other issues that have been or remain on the agenda, and other actors that make their interest in the issue known. Additionally, attention must be paid to both the internal and external environments of the actor, in order to comprehend what lies behind the growth of perceptions by its decision makers concerning the stakes which they are seeking. In other words, a central concern is "about what governs a perception rather than a decision."[22]

With the exception of salience, which is specific to the issue at hand, and which comes into play only when the issue is on the agenda, the other variables transcend specific issues and constitute a background matrix of relations among actors on any issue. Salience summarizes what communications theorists consider to be current information available to an actor, while the background variables are like elements of collective memory.[23] The latter predispose actors toward certain types of relationship. They tend to be more potent the less available is current information about an issue, and appear in the form of simple analogies to the past or comparisons with past issues. In a sense, background variables tend to inhibit "objective" analysis of any set of stakes and set the stage for "selective recall," thereby encouraging idiosyncratic interpretation and definition of a situation by each actor, and making it difficult for the actors to perceive any issue in identical fashion. The two types of variables combine on each occasion to determine the calculus an actor will employ to arrive at an issue position.

BACKGROUND VARIABLES AND THE GENESIS OF ISSUE DIMENSION

A. Prior Pattern of Interaction

A prior pattern of interaction consists of the experiences of contending actors in dealing with one another in past and concurrent issues, especially their history of agreement–disagreement, positive and negative acts, and friendship–hostility.* Actors may generally agree, disagree, or

---

*These three concepts are defined at length in the following chapter. They reflect different aspects of cooperation/conflict. Agreement-disagreement refers to the compatibility or incompatibility of issue positions and proposals. Positive and negative acts include all be-

find that their agreements and disagreements occur with roughly equal frequency (what is called technically "crosscutting"). They may engage in relatively aggressive behavior toward each other by exchanging un-negative acts, and may perceive one another in a hostile fashion. Or, their relations may reflect some alternate mix. Whatever the prior pattern, it will tend, all other things being equal, to be carried over into the issue at hand.*

The influence of prior pattern of interaction is potent for reasons that are evident to any student of human behavior. Neither group nor individual behavior is random but is a product of expectations, which are usually created by previous patterns of interaction. This is particularly the case with behavior that deviates from highly ritualized forms of interaction such as exchanges of greetings, standard operating procedures, role performances, and etiquette, where the group has set up detailed rules governing behavior and speech.

Prior behavior tends to govern current behavior, particularly in interpersonal relations. Individual behavior toward others is not only dependent upon past interactions, but most persons will reserve entire classes of behavior for only selected types of relationships, in order to avoid excessive familiarity. Individual relationships come to be characterized not only by discernible patterns, but by stages or thresholds that add dimensions of behavior (i.e., what is called intimacy, closeness, or familiarity) as the relationship grows. Consequently, arguments, intellectual discussions, sexual behavior, jokes, and so forth, assume different forms among friends, acquaintances, or strangers. The best way to explain and predict such behavior, according to social psychological research, is to know the nature of the prior relationship among the individuals.[24]

This insight is equally applicable to behavior among collective actors, even though leadership and generational change may render memories of previous behavior patterns imprecise. Once prior relations are known, even apparently similar actions acquire different meaning, because such

havioral interactions, verbal and nonverbal, encompassing what is commonly measured as cooperation/conflict by event data, including such concepts as punishments, rewards, and influence attempts. Friendship–hostility denotes a psychological dimension that is attitudinal in nature; it is therefore similar to what is called affect.

*This variable has much in common with the "history" of an actor, which is often identified by integration and attribute theorists as a key factor in integration and coalition behavior. Unlike that variable, prior pattern of interaction refers to the dyad.

meaning exists only in the context of previous actions.* Thus, a kiss between a husband and a wife does not mean the same thing as a kiss between a husband and wife who are not married to each other. Similarly, a protest note sent to the Soviet Union by the U.S. government at the height of the Cold War has implications which are very different from a similar note sent by the United States to Great Britain in 1941. Minimally, the latter would have been unusual and unexpected, given the relationship and the way the actors had learned to behave toward each other.

Integration research and interaction analysis of event data have measured the impact of the prior relationship between states. Cobb and Elder, for instance, found the most potent predictor of continued, or further, integration to be the existing level of integration.[25] Likewise, interaction analyses have found that patterns of cooperation/conflict are best predicted by previous patterns of cooperation/conflict, as are previous levels of hostility and violence.[26] While these findings may appear trivial, they verify certain patterns which cannot be ignored if more theoretically nonobvious explanations are to be generated.

Two pieces of research that have moved in this direction are the crisis studies of Charles McClelland and Edward Azar. Working separately and with different data, both have shown the importance of what is here termed prior pattern of interaction for understanding and predicting behavior. Analyzing the various Berlin and Taiwan Straits crises, McClelland was able to show that not only the frequency but also the variety of acts between the United States and the USSR and China respectively changed with the onset of a crisis, only later to return to the previous pattern once the crisis had dissipated. McClelland classified acts into five broad types: conflict deeds, confrontation, attempts to settle, settlement acts, and comment. He found that there exist identifiable patterns of communications between actors, not only in terms of frequency of action type but also in terms of the amount of behavior within each category. For instance, the United States *typically* sends a certain number of acts of different types to the USSR, which constitute a certain percentage of its total behavior toward the Soviet Union.[27]

---

* For a justification of this interpretation from the viewpoint of analytical philosophy, see J. L. Austin, *How To Do Things With Words* (Oxford: Oxford University Press, 1965); and Ludwig Wittgenstein, *Philosophical Investigations,* G. E. M. Anscombe, tr., 3d ed. (New York: Macmillan, 1958).

Azar's research on the Middle East produced a similar finding, which he terms the "normal relations range," a level of cooperation/conflict as measured on a thirteen-point scale.[28] Some actors typically engage in a high level of conflict, whereas others engage in much less. To determine whether a specific action is "cooperative" or "conflictive," Azar compares it to the initiator's normal relations range; if it falls within the range, it is "normal," but if it is above or below the range, it is considered "conflictive" or "cooperative."

If the techniques developed by McClelland and Azar were applied to longer periods of interaction, then a prior pattern of interaction would include not only a normal relations range, but also the *pattern* of deviation from that range (e.g., how frequently do crises emerge? how long do they last? do they always manifest the same mix of actions? are they always resolved in the same manner?). Such an extensive empirical map could capture the full meaning of the variable being described here.

The explanatory power of the variable prior pattern of interaction can be explained theoretically by recourse to learning theory. O. Hobart Mowrer, for instance, argues that prior relations become significant because not only are they associated with punishment or reward—and concomitant frustration or satisfaction—but they also produce expectations of fear or hope concerning other actors.[29] Thereafter the drive for value satisfaction stimulates further initiatives, but it is the affective factor which determines which type of behavior will be selected. John Raser sums up the results of a relationship in which punishment has generated fear:

With the Mowrer model a new factor has been added, the affective, with fear as its dominant element. It becomes evident that *future responses will be made from this* affective condition, not from a sort of *tabula rasa.* . . . Thus, once this relationship has been established, all interaction between actor A and actor B will be carried on within a context of fear, fear based on expectations on the part of A that any given behavior *vis-à-vis* B will result in punishment by B.[30]

There is no reason to assume, as Mowrer implies, however, that fear and hope are the *only* emotions generated in the course of interaction. The past relations of actors with one another, as well as their mutual experiences in other issues, condition their expectations and evaluations of one another and may foster other sentiments, such as trust or mistrust. Where prior relations have proved highly rewarding, trust may become habitual, and a positive actor dimension may be generated. This prospect becomes increasingly likely if the provision of rewards does not appear to be patently connected to the acquisition of some immediate advantage, or if a "loan" is not recalled and gratitude is not demanded. Under those conditions, a sense of altruism may develop which may foster trust. Where past agreements and disagreements have occurred with roughly equal frequency, a stake dimension will be encouraged, or at least permitted, owing to the absence of strong affect. Finally, if the prior pattern of relations has been consistently negative (disagreement and negative acts that appear to be the product of something other than coincidence or chance), mistrust will come to characterize the expectations of actors about one another, and a strong pattern of mistrust will tend to produce a negative actor link among the proposals made by actors. Each actor will be conditioned to see the proposals of the other as motivated by a general effort to cause harm, a motivation which is seen to link disparate proposals. Negative affect may then prove a potent source of issue position as responses are fashioned in order to harm other actors who are seen as malevolent in intent. Indeed, it may be hypothesized that even if only one actor perceives the issue in this manner, its perception is likely to prove infectious as its behavior alters the perceptions of target actors, so that something akin to self-fulfilling prophecy takes hold.

In this manner, the prior pattern of interaction helps shape the issue dimension. It should be kept in mind, however, that this variable is actually a feedback loop which reinforces or mitigates existing relationships. To ignore its influence is to fail to understand reality, but to remain satisfied with what it explains is to miss the fundamental causal factors that initiated the spiral in the first place—similarity, status, and issue salience.

B. Similarity

Similarity refers to the extent to which actors perceive that they share the same political, economic, cultural, religious, linguistic, demographic, geographical, ethnic, racial, or other significant characteristics. The concept as employed here does *not* merely refer to homogeneity among traits, as in the case of conventional attribute analysis. Similarity in that sense is a purely passive, albeit multidimensional, factor. Instead, as used here, similarity denotes the degree to which actors identify and focus upon common characteristics, or subidentities, that they view as providing them with common ground on some issue, or issues, in which they are jointly involved.[31] In brief, similarity refers to the degree to which actors focus upon traits that encourage them to identify with one another.

Generally speaking, any two actors are likely to share *some* common characteristics which *could* serve as a focus of identification. It is equally probable that any two actors will also be divided by other traits—traits upon which they might focus as well. The larger the number of recognized shared traits, and the greater their centrality to the political culture of the actors' memberships, the more likely it is that they will focus upon one of them. It is the situation in which actors find themselves that encourages or discourages the allotment of attention to specific traits. The mere existence of common attributes in a passive sense will not evoke mutual identification unless third parties have focused, or are focusing, upon them as a means of identifying adversaries—as in the cases of Hitler and the Jews, or the Bolsheviks and capitalists—or unless the stakes at issue are closely related to traits that are common to the actors. Thus, the governments of capitalist societies had not identified with one another on the basis of this trait (Marxist theory notwithstanding) prior to the 1917 Revolution and did not do so until Bolshevism appeared as a common threat to them, and even then only in those contexts where the USSR or international communism were perceived to be involved. Ironically, Stalin's failure to distinguish between the Western democracies and the fascists until quite late was one consequence of the untenable assumption that all capitalists are natural allies.

Despite the complexity of the determinants of similarity, it is important to define the variable, in any situation or historical era, in an explicit and *falsifiable* fashion. Otherwise, the notion of similarity may become the source of ad hoc explanations that will never permit the theory to be refuted. In this context, awareness of the agenda and the critical issue (or set of highly salient issues) that dominate(s) it becomes very important. *The traits that will constitute "similarity" are those that are most relevant to the critical issue on the agenda.* With this in mind, recognition of the bases of similarity should be possible, with only the periods of agenda change posing a major problem.

The proposition that similarity affects attitudes and behavior has had wide currency in the social sciences generally, as well as in international relations enquiry. Early studies of social distance and prejudice, such as those of Bogardus, emphasized differences between individual characteristics as significant in explaining interpersonal behavior.[32] Similarly, group homogeneity and heterogeneity have been seen as crucial in determining the harmony of a group.[33] In international relations theory, Lewis Richardson believed that group differences accounted for the onset of deadly quarrels at both the individual and national levels.[34] More recently, integration theorists have argued that similarity is an aid to integration,[35] though bivariate tests of this hypothesis have produced few significant results except for fairly obvious demographic and geographic characteristics.[36] Both Richardson's analysis of deadly quarrels and Cobb's and Elder's tests of integration hypotheses produced null findings. Other provocative efforts have involved characteristics like political culture, ideology, internal cohesion, and type of regime, but in large measure the results must be judged as disappointing, leading Michael Sullivan to conclude that the "effect of national attributes on foreign policy is limited, and thus the potential impact for decisionmakers is also limited."[37]

These findings should not prove surprising in view of the simplistic manner in which hypotheses have been posed. They leave too many questions unanswered. For example: Does similarity always produce cooperation and never conflict? Does it produce all kinds of cooperation/conflict or only certain types? Is similarity directly related to cooperative and conflictive behavior, or does it work through intervening variables? What constitutes similarity? Which attributes are significant, and do these change with the situation and in time?

The work of R. J. Rummel and his associates in the Dimensionality of Nations (DON) project suggests some tentative answers to these questions.[38] Rummel began his work by investigating whether a single attribute—internal conflict—was associated with external conflict, and he found that it was not.[39] He then investigated whether the political, economic, societal, military, cultural, and geographical attributes of a nation were related to conflict, and found that they, too, were not.[40] Others within the discipline also tested for such relationships, using a variety of attributes and in different combinations. With the exception of demographic characteristics and violence; economic characteristics and support of supranationalism in the United Nations; and demographic and geographic characteristics and internation integration; the findings were either weak or null.[41]

On the whole, this research indicated that attributes do not, in themselves, determine behavior; and that, where strong relationships exist, they involve specific attributes and only certain kinds of behavior. Such inductive research guided Rummel to develop "field theory," which owed much to the work of Kurt Lewin and Quincy Wright.[42] Field theory maintains that it is not attributes per se, but *differences* in attributes, that are significant; and a test of the theory, in the context of American foreign policy, produced some provocative findings concerning the questions raised earlier about similarity.[43] First, distances or differences between attributes were able to explain 50 percent of the variance of all types of foreign-policy behavior; a very strong correlation and highly impressive in terms of most findings in the field, but one which still leaves 50 percent of the variance unexplained. This suggests that other variables play a part. Second, different attributes are correlated with different types of behavior. For example, the more open and the more non-Catholic a culture (i.e., the more like the United States on these two attributes), the less frequent was Cold War behavior. Thus, it is necessary to specify, or at least determine inductively, which characteristics are associated with which behavior types, and then to explain why this variation exists. Thirdly, the analysis is dyadic, which raises the question of how the analysis might be altered by third, fourth, and nth parties. Finally, the analysis was limited to the United States', and later the People's Republic of China's, foreign policy. That raises the question of whether there are actor-specific variables that are hidden by the sample selection.

The use of similarity in the model presented here is an attempt to incorporate these findings, and to answer the questions raised by the research in the field, in a new manner. To begin with, similarity is not seen as directly related to cooperation/conflict, but as affecting it in a rather indirect fashion, namely as one of three potent variables that determine the issue dimension, which in turn has an impact on the selection of the issue-position calculus, and on the likelihood of agreement. This stipulation helps account for the 50 percent of the unexplained variance of Rummel's very important finding. Second, it is the assumption of the theory presented here that different attributes will, in fact, correlate with different types of behavior, and that the explanation for this finding lies (as Rummel suggests) in the notion of issue area. This proposition relates to the earlier question of which characteristics are significant in determining similarity and what is similar. This problem must be treated in detail, because it is complex and is related to the problem of third and nth parties.

What constitutes a "significant" attribute is closely related to the nature of the issue system under consideration. An issue system refers to (1) the issue dimension that links numerous stakes together; and (2) the actors which contend for them. Significant attributes are determined by these two aspects. The first source of similarity, the ability to dispose of stakes, makes some characteristics significant in some issues, and not in others, because capability or power varies by issue. When an agenda is dominated by economic issues, as in tariff talks, economic characteristics become salient; when religious issues dominate an agenda, as in the Reformation wars, then religious characteristics are salient. Since the ability to dispose of a stake varies by issue, what is seen as similar will change as issues change, and will be as broad or narrow as the variety of issues under contention. At minimum, the issue naturally makes salient selected attributes that predict whether other participants *can* share an actor's issue position and interests.

When a new issue arises, or an old one grows in salience, the process brings in its train new conceptions of similarity, as it emphasizes new or different attributes. For example, with the revitalization of the Law of the Sea negotiations in 1974—coupled with the seabed as a new stake—new characteristics, such as size of navy, level of marine and deep-sea mining technology, access to the sea, and fishing fleet quality become important for determining which actors are similar. This is because these characteristics become relevant in shaping whether actors have a conflict of interest or a common interest. Landlocked states and states with a long continental shelf and naval power discover they have common interests and are in conflict with dissimilar actors—coastal states, and states with no continental shelf or small navies.

The Law of the Sea illustrates that other issues on the agenda besides the critical issue can condition perceptions of similarity. This is possible, however, only to the extent that these other issues remain uncoupled from the critical issue. If they become linked to a critical issue, they no longer serve as important determinants of similarity. This was apparent at the 1972 Stockholm Conference on the Human Environment when the question of the seating of an East German delegation (a Cold War stake) led the Soviet Union to boycott the conference, though it had assumed a leading role in preparing and planning it. The intrusion of the Cold War dissipated the effect of any attribute except regime type.

The second but related source of similarity, the context of the actors, refers to the number and variety of participants in the issue system. Similarity, it must be remembered, is both a relative and a relational concept. Germany and France have traditionally been seen as dissimilar, but this has been only in the context of classical Western European issues, such as the balance of power and imperialism. When viewed in the context of the Cold War or North–South relations, they appear very similar, because competing actors have very different characteristics. In this manner, third and nth parties have a major bearing on the content of this independent variable. This is particularly true in light of agreement-disagreement patterns. Actors that are faced with a common opponent will tend to see each other as more similar, even if they must define themselves in terms of negative characteristics, such as antifascist, antiwar, or anti-imperialist. Such definitions, which reflect shared issue positions (i.e., agreement) and an interdependence calculus, have a way of slowly evolving into *perceived* attributes rather than just agreement. To be antifascist or antiwar is, after a while, not simply to agree but *to be something,* to share a fundamental experience or traumatic crisis that shapes part of one's essence. Such shared experiences lead to conceptions of "we-ness" and to definitions of similarity.

Similarity is a theoretically significant variable in determining the selection of an issue-position calculus, because it encourages actors to form or mitigate certain attitudes or relationships. Perceptions of starkly similar or dissimilar characteristics encourage actors to respond to one another's proposals with a view to the actor dimension: I will adopt this issue position because he is a fellow democrat or because of our shared experiences in the war; I will oppose his proposal because his regime is authoritarian. Returning to the origins of the Cold War, it should be recalled that the fact that the USSR and the United States emerged from World War II as the two most influential actors in global politics contributed to the growth in competition between them. Social, ideological, and cultural dissimilarities fostered suspicion and misunderstanding. The combination of parity and dissimilarity, combined with a prior pattern of disagreement, makes it less than surprising that an actor dimension began to color those issues in which they were jointly involved.

Actors that are similar tend to trust one another, identify with one another, and be drawn toward each other.[44] They see one another as sharing similar aspirations, hopes, and fears that are the consequences of, and are grounded in, their similar attributes. Where trust and sympathy are engendered by homogeneity, fear is reduced even in the event of parity. Each actor views with greater equanimity the prospect that the other may acquire a disproportionately large share of the stakes, and they are less apt to view one another's status in relative terms. Similarity may permit actors to become reference groups, and, as Coplin, Mills, and O'Leary suggest, the result is that:

An actor moves closer to the issue positions held by those other actors which it considers to be positive reference groups, and it moves farther from the issue positions of those actors which it considers to be negative reference groups.[45]

C. Status

The third key variable that determines issue dimension—and, thereby, the issue-position calculi—is status. Status refers to the perception by others of the general overall influence enjoyed by actors; that is, the differential influence enjoyed by actors relative to one another. It includes attitudinal notions like prestige and reputation and also a recognition that such attitudes are, at some point in time, derived from the observed ability of an actor to transform its resource capability into the acquisition of stakes. The status of actors can be relatively equal (parity) or unequal, and it is possible to identify a status hierarchy, or "pecking order." Although such influence is ultimately rooted in the resources and skills commanded by an actor, it is different from an aggregate of the power enjoyed by an actor in specific issue contexts. Status is attributed to an actor by others as a result of past performance, which conditions their expectations of how the actor can perform in the issue at hand. Nevertheless, it is not uncommon for a highly regarded actor to lack the specific resources that are suitable for creating leverage, or for a weaker actor to control precisely what is needed to place it at an advantage in a particular context. Overall weakness may not prevent an actor from occupying a decisive position in a given issue.

The concept of status combines aspects of sociology and political science in order to overcome some of the problems associated with the concept of power.[46] One problem with the concept of power is that it has been used to refer to several analytically distinct, and sometimes empirically uncorrelated, phenomena, as well as being employed ambiguously and inconsistently. A key task here is to distinguish among capability, influence, victory, authority, force, and coercion.[47] Capability usually means that an actor possesses resources which appear to permit it to achieve certain ends. Capability, however, may not be used effectively and so fail to bring influence or victory.* It was this realization that enabled Ho Chi Minh to predict correctly that "in the end the Americans will kill ten patriots for every American who dies, but it is they who will tire first."[48] Force, coercion, and authority are all means of transforming capability into influence or victory. Since each of these terms have specific and different referents, they cannot be adequately distinguished by a single concept.[49]

The fact that power distinctions have tended to be collapsed into a single term raises a further problem, which is that the concept has tended to be used as a latent synonym for *cause*.[50] The tendency in social science has been to answer the question of why something was caused, by looking at *who* caused it or was capable of causing it. While this is evident in all the words used to convey the different aspects of power, it is most problematic in the concept of influence. This is because it is impossible to infer causation of this sort without very precise measures of influence that would permit one to infer not only whether influence exists, but as is more often the case, the *extent* and *nature* of influence. This is not unlike the problem of determining the relative potency of different variables for explaining behavior. But even if this problem were solved so that it would be possible to determine who had what percentage of influence in any single decision or outcome, that would at best only provide an idiographic and genetic explanation,† and not a nomothetic (i.e., sci-

---

* Influence constitutes a psychological relationship between actors, in which capabilities are applied to achieve some impact. See I. William Zartman, ed., *The 50% Solution* (Garden City, N.Y.: Anchor, 1976), p. 17. In contrast, victory means that an actor attains its objective (even though it may not have had influence or exercised what it did have).

† A genetic explanation is one which answers the question "why" by recounting the events that preceded the event and are believed to have brought it about. It assumes a chronological approach to explanation. Conversely, a nomothetic explanation delineates the con-

entific) explanation like Newton's law of gravity.[51] An observer would not know the variables or fundamental causes that resulted in a certain outcome, but would know only the roles of characters in a play that were moved by these more fundamental causes. Any theory which uses a substitute concept for power must make sure that if it strives for nomothetic explanation, it employs that concept in a manner conducive to understanding causes and not merely actors' roles.

Still another problem has to do with resort to two invalid assumptions in the making of inferences. The first, already referred to, is the assumption that capability can, or will, be utilized effectively. The second, closely related to the first, is the assumption that capability is general and fungible and does not vary by issue.* This is an empirical question and cannot be assumed. Indeed, such an assumption inevitably leads to anomalies, as when American military power fails to have any effective influence on economic questions among Organization for Economic Cooperation and Development (OECD) nations, or when American nuclear

ditions under which any phenomenon is likely to occur and does not specify, except in very general causal terms, the particular events preceding the phenomenon. A genetic approach is less preferable for understanding causality because it presupposes general causal relations; otherwise it would be unable to decide which event(s) out of the numerous ones that preceded the phenomenon to be explained were the important ones. On the question of explanation, see Robert Brown, *Explanation in Social Science* (Chicago: Aldine, 1963), pp. 40–44.

*The different meanings of power and its variation in general, as oppose to issue-specific, contexts have received wide attention in the literature, particularly in studies of community power structure. Overall influence can be measured by a combination of general actor resources, what Morgenthau and others call the "elements" of power, and by reputation, a technique employed by Floyd Hunter to delineate community "power." See Hans Morgenthau, *Politics Among Nations* (New York: Knopf, 1978), ch. 7; and Floyd Hunter, *Community Power Structure* (Chapel Hill: University of North Carolina Press, 1953). There should be a strong correlation between the general resource distribution among actors and their reputation. What "counts" as a resource, however, is related to the substantive type of issues dominating the agenda and the type of decision games used to dispose of stakes. Thus, where there is an absence of central and legitimate authority, and territory is a stake, military strength and the factors that produce it will "count" as key resources. However, in a city such as that which Hunter studied (Atlanta, Ga.), what "counts" as a resource is different, because the issues and nature of decision games are different.

Actor interdependence was defined in the first section of this study. It refers to the resources necessary to dispose of the stake(s) under contention. Note that neither definition employs Dahl's concept of "influence," which is a phenomenon that *both* overall influence and interdependence would predict. See Robert A. Dahl, "The Concept of Power," *Behavioral Science* (July 1957), 2:201–215.

strength is unable to produce victories over nongovernmental actors like the PLO or the NLF (Vietnam).

The use of the concept *status* attempts to overcome each of these problems by precise definition. First, status refers to a reputation for capability being translated into both influence and victory. It is a complex concept, derived from defining power as a psychological relationship, which refers primarily to the attitudes of others. This makes it possible to overcome operational difficulties, and makes it amenable to empical analysis concerning whether such a reputation is deserved. "Power is what people think it is," declares John Spanier, and a "reputation for power will confer power."[52] Second, status is not issue specific (unlike influence), but is an overarching characteristic.* While it cannot be assumed that high status leads to victory on every issue, it can be predicted that high status leads to the widespread *expectation* of victory in many issues; and, if this expectation is not fulfilled, the status of an actor will decline.[53] Although high status may not lead to victory on every issue, it does increase the likelihood of greater participation across issues—and therefore of having some "influence" even though the issue-specific capability of an actor may not be great. The concept in this theory that refers to issue-specific capability is *actor interdependence*. Status differs from similarity in that the former is a systemic quality determined in the context of all issues and all actors, whereas the latter is an attribute determined in the context of specific issues and the specific group of actors contending for them. The inclusion of these three concepts—status, actor interdependence, and similarity—maintain a clear distinction between overall and issue-specific "power."

The concept of status has been chosen because it has demonstrated theoretical significance. It has not only been able to explain phenomena but has passed empirical tests; and, in combination with the concept of similarity, makes it possible for the model offered here to incorporate much of Rummel's status-field theory, which has already woven together sev-

* Status can vary by *type* of issue, so that Japan, for example, is looked upon as more important when economic matters are at stake than when military questions are central. There is, nevertheless, a tendency to aggregate separate status orderings into a single ordering as part of evaluating the overall past performance of actors. In addition, according to the status-equilibration hypothesis, there is a tendency for changes to make statuses in different structures similar if the same actors are involved. See Morton Deutsch, *The Resolution of Conflict* (New Haven, Conn.: Yale University Press, 1973), pp. 80–81.

eral theoretical strands of international relations theory. Research in social psychology and sociology has employed the concept to explain considerable interpersonal and intragroup behavior. In his review of this literature, Rummel suggests that the hypotheses most relevant to international relations are those that are related to stratification.[54] According to status theorists, every social system can be conceived of as a stratified system with individuals having some rank within it. Their insight is that an individual's rank will determine how he behaves toward others, and how they behave toward him. Research has found that the higher the status, the greater the interactions; high-status individuals interact more than do those of low status, and low-status individuals tend to direct their actions toward those of higher status. In addition, status inconsistency (high status on one dimension, like wealth; and low status on another, like social standing) will lead an individual to resolve the inconsistency in terms of high status. Attempts by members of a group with inconsistent status to raise their rank often lead to conflict with higher-status members and, consequently, produce high frustration among status-inconsistent individuals. In fact, much of the research finds that status-inconsistent individuals make up much of the pool of "potential suicides, radicals, aggressors, or innovators."[55] Although this conclusion does not provide a complete explanation,* it does make the point that status is a significant determinant of individual behavior.[56]

Variations of these hypotheses have been utilized to explain aspects of international relations. The most notable theorist in this area has been Johan Galtung, who has used status to explain aggression and imperialism.[57] Galtung's earliest work dealt with rank and its impact on interaction. He found that by employing rank, not only could East–West relations and summit conferences be interpreted in a theoretical fashion, but so could individual attitudes of a foreign policy elite.[58] Despite generalizing across levels of analysis, Galtung has argued that rank-determined behavior varies with context, and that it is more prevalent in *inter*-nation behavior than in *intra*-nation behavior.[59] In his works on aggression and

* It is not complete because it is not precise, may not be falsifiable, and ignores other independent variables. It does not, for example, specify whether an individual will become an innovator or an "aggressor" (whatever that may be). Consequently, it is too open to ad hoc explanation in the face of contrary evidence. Finally, it has a tendency to commit the fallacy of affirming the consequent; that is, of assuming that suicides or aggressors have a disequilibrated status, when in actuality there may be other factors at work.

imperialism, he suggests that status quo can be measured by looking at its various dimensions and seeing when an actor is topdog or underdog (T or U) so that it can be described as TTT or UUU if it has consistent status, or TUT if its status is inconsistent.[60] He then goes on to postulate a relationship between status inconsistency and conflict. This may help to explain why revolutions tend to erupt when the conditions of the deprived are actually improving.[61]

Rummel has integrated the status approach within field theory to develop status-field theory. Whereas field theory sees "distances" between actors as determinants of behavior, status theory views "stratification" as the determinant. The two can be united by recalling that status is the distance between specific attributes; in particular, according to Rummel, economic development and military power are the most important determinants of status in contemporary global politics.[62] According to Rummel, actors desire upward mobility and try to raise their status by concrete measures to hasten economic development, by augmenting military power, and by directing interactions toward those of higher status.[63] Like other theorists, he, too, maintains that actors characterized by status disequilibrium suffer from cognitive dissonance and seek to restore balance to their status. Such motivations are strong because elites closely identify with their actor's rank and status. Actors, moreover, emphasize their dominant status and the subordinant status of others in interaction. High-ranking actors support the existing global order; and high-ranking dyads tend to be cooperative, particularly if they are similar in terms of economic development. Common status provides actors with common interests and a "communications bridge." In contrast, dyads characterized by status incongruency or inconsistency tend to be uncertain about how to behave toward each other and manifest unstable expectations about one another's behavior. Status inconsistency is, therefore, correlated with conflict behavior. Rummel goes on to postulate that the cooperation and conflict behavior of economically developed actors toward others is a function of their military power incongruence; whereas the cooperation and conflict of economically underdeveloped actors is a function of their economic development incongruence.

The aspect of Galtung's and Rummel's propositions that has received most attention is the posited relationship between status inconsistency and conflict. Galtung has maintained that the status inconsistency hypothesis is confirmed by East-West interactions.[64] In his test of status-field theory in the context of American foreign policy, Rummel found that equal status leads to high cooperation and that status disequilibrium leads to conflict, a finding with a correlation of .94.[65] This is not unlike Maurice East's finding that the greater the status discrepancy within a global system, the greater the occurrence of conflict.[66] Likewise, Wallace found that status inconsistency in a system is related to alliance aggregation; which in turn is associated with arms races, which correlate with the onset of war.[67] Conversely, status inconsistency in a system is negatively correlated with the creation of intergovernmental organization, which, in turn, is negatively correlated with arms races. Wallace's findings, then, suggest that status, though important for understanding war, is not *directly* linked to its outbreak at the system level. Finally, Manus Midlarsky* has found a strong association between status inconsistency and "years in war," "number of wars," and "battle deaths" at the actor level.[68]

The concept of status that is employed here is derived from the literature discussed above, but, unlike some of the sociological literature, it places more emphasis on the capability and influence aspects than on the deferential connotation. In this sense, the use of the concept *status* is meant to capture many of the insights about behavior provided by the realist theory, particularly by the propositions associated with national power and the balance of power. Governments, and other actors as well, do on occasion follow the three policies that Morgenthau saw as the essence of foreign policy: maintaining power (policy of the status quo), increasing power (policy of imperialism), or demonstrating power (policy of prestige). When they undertake any of these, they are engaging in status behavior, and the major disagreement between this model and that of Morgenthau is that the former does not assume that actors always engage in such behavior, or that it is the essence of world politics. Rather, this model sees status-seeking behavior as a function of the kind of stratification structure in existence, and the nature of the issues under

---

* Since both East's and Wallace's research designs are based on a systemic level, care must be taken to avoid the ecological fallacy by inferring that a status inconsistent actor will engage in conflict. Their findings merely indicate that status inconsistency in a system makes that system conflict-prone. Which actors engage in such conflict is another question requiring additional investigation, a process that Midlarsky's work begins.

contention. Classic power-politics behavior is simply one type of behavior that must be explained.

The principal impact of status in world politics is not as a direct effect on cooperation and conflict, but as one of three significant variables that link issues either in a stake or actor dimension. Equal status means equal capability and influence, in general; and hence, that actors are able to compete vigorously with one another for the stakes under contention. Such a situation can be potentially threatening to participants. It can produce either mutual respect or fear,[69] because the actors *can* harm one another. Equal status then tends to heighten perceptions of an actor linkage—in the classic balance-of-power sense. Participants are likely to perceive a negative actor dimension with those who are feared, and a positive one with those who are respected. A corollary of this is that "conflict between parties who mutually perceive themselves to be equal in power and legitimacy is more difficult to resolve cooperatively than conflict in which there is mutual recognition of differential power and legitimacy."[70]

Unequal status means that actors cannot compete effectively with one another across issues. It encourages deferential behavior, where actors seek protection if they are weak and seek pawns if they are strong. The weak may fear the strong, but the strong only fear those who are as strong as they, and who threaten to become stronger. A strong actor will be relatively unconcerned about a weaker one "whose leaders consider that it can never, acting alone or in a small group, make a significant impact on the system."[71] The weaker actor "recognizes that it cannot obtain security primarily by use of its own capabilities, and that it must rely fundamentally on the aid of other states, institutions, processes, or developments to do so" and so is not feared by the strong.[72] Status, then, is an important shaper of attitudes, a major factor in establishing the issue dimension among separate stakes, and an indirect cause of competitive behavior.

Status, like capability, changes over time. An actor of high status is expected to participate in a wide range of issues—if only because its presumed resources are regarded as permitting it to do so. If, over time, a high-status actor fails to participate in many issues or fails to manifest its presumed influence in specific issues, its status will decline, as was the case with Great Britain after 1945. By contrast, if a low-status actor succeeds in having a persistent impact on a number of issues, its overall status will increase. While status constantly lags behind the realities of power in specific issues, there is constant movement between status and issue-specific capabilities toward a rough equilibrium.

The notion of status change is evident in the sociological concept of status inconsistency, and in the realist idea of upward mobility in the power structure. Both of these traditions suggest that competition will be different if the contending actors are undergoing changes in status. This is because a secure actor of high status will find the lack of deference exhibited by a rising power insulting and "uppity" and, in a real sense, a deprivation of value—or at least, an omen of potential deprivation. The tendency in such a situation is for the higher-status actor to try to put the challenger "in its place." Such was the British mood toward Imperial Germany at the turn of the present century and South Africa's policy toward Namibia today.

An insecure or declining power, on the other hand, will find the challenge of a rising power to be threatening. This perception is particularly acute if the challenger has been previously defeated and is seeking revenge or a redistribution of key stakes. Certainly, the Soviet government feared German rearmament after World War II precisely for this reason. The challenger, in turn, is governed by similar attitudes. If the status quo power is secure, the challenger will regard withholding of recognition of its new status as frustrating—especially if the increase in its capabilities, which *should* result in increased status, was attained legitimately according to the rules of the game. Wilhelmine Germany's struggle for its "rightful" place in the sun, and Imperial Japan's hostility toward Western efforts to thwart its efforts to emulate Western imperialism in China, are obvious examples of such frustration. If a status quo power is insecure, the challenger is apt to realize this, and it will whet its appetite to press harder. Germany's attack on France in the Franco-Prussian War, Hitler's demands on the West in the late 1930s, and Khrushchev's challenges of Kennedy in the early 1960s were of this sort. The effect of status on behavior is considerably more potent when the stratification structure is in the midst of change.

DETERMINING ISSUE CALCULI

Status is only one of three important variables which determine the issue dimension and, hence, the selection of issue-position calculi. The nature of the competition posed by status will be either mitigated or reinforced, depending on the similarity of contending actors. Indeed, the combination of similarity and status largely determines the overall relationship of any two actors. The four logically possible combinations—equal status-dissimilar, equal status-similar, unequal status-similar, and unequal status-dissimilar—produce four types of relationships if the participants interact on a regular basis: "enemies," "friends," "patron-client," and "topdog–underdog."

In practice, there are many more possible relationships in the world than these four. They are four ideal types along two continua that help to clarify the impact of each variable in determining issue-position calculi. The many variants that exist in reality are reflected by the relationship of the American government with its various clients. Israel, Taiwan, South Korea, and Greece, for instance, must be considered clients if one *has* to choose among the four categories. However, the Israeli-American relationship is clearly different from the Greek-American relationship or the United States' relationship with Taiwan and South Korea. As long as status and similarity are properly regarded as continua, then the richness and uniqueness of individual relationships are preserved. This is particularly true when the bases of similarity (religious overlap, ethnic composition, and so forth) and status (military, economic, and the like) are examined in detail. The four types of relationships are in actuality illustrative of important tendencies.

The reason status and similarity are able to yield the four ideal types is that they interact to produce the attitudes that predispose actors to the kinds of behavior that will result in such relationships. For example, equal status tends to make participants conscious of each other, while the extent of similarity will contribute to positive affect (if the actors are similar) or negative affect (if they are dissimilar). Positive affect removes the threatening aspect of equal capability because it produces trust. Hence competition occurs in an atmosphere of mutual respect, much like competition among "friends." Participants can select a cost-benefit calculus and not fear the consequences of possible disagreement or even the loss of a particular stake. The existence of positive affect permits actors "to agree to disagree" and conditions both to be responsive and sympathetic to one another's substantive interests. They do not expect one another to deny their self-interest; what they do expect is that disagreement will not arise as a consequence of malice. If disagreement does result from actors' using a cost-benefit calculus, it is possible that they will move to an inter-dependence calculus as a result. Conversely, negative affect in the presence of equal status makes the competition quite threatening because of the mistrust engendered by the differences in attributes. Mistrust serves as the catalyst for an actor dimension and the use of a negative affect calculus in decision making. This situation can become so aggravated that actors may reject one another's proposals—even if they are conciliatory in substance—because "tricks" are anticipated, whatever the actual nature of the proposals. Indeed, were one actor to agree with the other, considerable anxiety would result owing to the violation of deep-seated expectations.

The combinations of unequal status give rise to perceptions lying between the pure actor dimension and stake dimension. When actors are characterized by unequal status but similarity, a potential patron–client relationship exists. Unequal influence suggests that the actors cannot be direct competitors much of the time, and that their interests may be regarded as, at least, congruent. Indeed the weak tend to be "attracted" to the strong.[73] The existence of trust owing to similarity encourages the parties to employ their respective influence in a manner beneficial to both, thereby giving rise to an interdependence calculus. Whether the potential patron-client relationship is actualized depends upon previous interactions. If over time the parties reappear as participants in the same issues and continue to reach agreement, a patron–client pattern will emerge. Since the pattern of agreement reinforces the explicitly expediential aspects of the weak–strong relationship with positive affect, the actor dimension is somewhat more potent in the patron–client case than it was before the relationship arose.

The unequal status-dissimilar relationship gives rise to mistrust even in the absence of repetitive direct competition. The "underdog" tends to behave deferentially as a consequence of fear while remaining psychologically resentful. The "topdog" is likely to ignore the "underdog" and to remain largely indifferent to it—and, if they do interact, prone to behave arrogantly. As in the previous combination, the parties are apt to mix stake dimension and actor dimension though tending toward the former, with the "topdog" indifferent to the "underdog"—and the "underdog" seeking to avoid casting the issue in actor terms, because then it will inevitably lose.

In general, regardless of trust, unequal status tends to mix the stake dimension and actor dimension and give rise to an interdependence calculus. In the patron–client relationship, the interdependence calculus takes the form of the client deferring to the patron when an issue is of equal salience to both, or of higher salience to the patron, in order to protect the future of the relationship. In return, the patron will defer to the client on issues that are of higher salience to the latter. They defer to each other in those cases of mutually low salience, again in order to reinforce the relationship itself. Even where there is a lack of trust in the unequal influence–dissimilar relation, a variant of an interdependence calculus will be used as the "underdog" defers to the powerful on those issues that are salient to the latter, in order to avoid providing the strong with incentives for retribution on other issues which are not as salient to it. If negative affect were to govern the calculus of the "underdog," it would invite retaliation by those who are more powerful and would suffer still greater value deprivation.*

Although the background variables of prior pattern of interaction and status-similarity provide incentives for using one or the other calculus, the salience of specific issues is also a potent variable. High salience, other things being equal, pushes actors toward a cost-benefit calculus as they tend to focus on the issue before them to the exclusion of other issues on the agenda. Indeed, if physical survival is threatened, neither the affect nor the interdependence calculus may play any role at all in determining issue position.† In effect, high salience pushes background variables aside for the issue at hand. As salience is reduced, prior interaction patterns, status, and similarity can increasingly impinge, thereby enabling the affect or interdependence calculus to dominate. Reduced salience is particularly important if an interdependence calculus is to be adopted, because it requires that an actor look for other issues that are of equal or greater salience than the issues at hand in order to press for trade-offs.

The manner in which these three variables interact to produce an issue-position calculus is summarized in table 6.1. The equal status and dissim-

---

* In such cases, the weak power would seek the protection of an influential partner which can protect it in a classic "power-pawn" alliance.

† If high salience is reinforced by strong negative affect, then both the cost-benefit and affect calculi are likely to produce identical issue positions although the affect calculus may be dominant psychologically.

ilarity that characterize enemies usually result in a negative affect calculus regardless of the salience of the issue, so that malice comes to substitute for rationality. Unequal status and similarity, which characterize a patron–client relationship, cause the strong to use a cost-benefit calculus when the issue is of high salience to it. The strong will use a positive affect calculus when the issue is of high salience only to the weaker actor and an interdependence calculus if the issue is of low salience to them both. In the meantime, the weaker actor will employ an interdependence calculus if the issue is of high or low salience to both, a cost-benefit

Table 6.1 Specific Predictions of Issue-Position Calculi

Salience	Equal Status/ Dissimilarity	Unequal Status/ Similarity	Unequal Status/ Dissimilarity	Equal Status/ Similarity
Both high	Negative affect	Strong: cost-benefit Weak: interdependence	Cost-benefit	Cost-benefit
Mixed one high one low	Negative affect	High: cost-benefit Low: positive affect	High: cost-benefit Low: interdependence	High: cost-benefit Low: positive affect
Both low	Negative affect	Interdependence	Interdependence	Positive affect

calculus if the issue is of high salience to it alone, and a positive affect calculus if the issue is of high salience only to the stronger. Such a relationship features a high degree of rationality, tempered by elements of friendship. The unequal status and dissimilarity combination of topdog–underdog relationships leads to cost-benefit calculi if the issue is highly salient to both and to interdependence calculi if the issue is highly salient to neither. When the issue is of mixed salience, the actor for which it is of low salience will adopt an interdependence calculus. This, is the most "rationalistic" of the four relationships. Finally, "friends" produced by equal status and similarity will employ a cost-benefit calculus when an issue is of high salience, and a positive affect calculus when an issue is of low salience. In this happy situation, neither party wishes nor expects the other side to sacrifice something which is truly important to it, and both actors are free to try to maximize their share of the stakes.

Although additional participants increase the complexity of determining probable issue-position calculi, they do not alter the logic derived from the dyadic case. The issue-position calculus of any single actor can be predicted by examining each of its dyadic links and aggregating them. For example, if there are four contending actors, then one predicts actor A's issue position by looking at the issue position that would result from the dyadic relationships between A–B, A–C, and A–D. One then predicts the issue position on the basis of how important the three relationships are, and whether the three predictions of issue position produce the same issue position. Assume for the moment that the three relationships are equal, that the issue is of low salience to actor A, and that an analysis of each of the dyads suggests that actor A will adopt issue position X. Each dyadic prediction of actor A's issue position can be interpreted as a vector influencing A's position. Since the relationships are equal and the three analyses produce reinforcing vectors, actor A's issue position will be issue position X, and the likelihood of that changing is small, since there are no cross-pressures. The use of a vector analysis for more than one dyad makes it possible not only to predict final issue position, but also the intensity with which it is held and the likelihood of its changing. This is important because relationships involve not only external actors, but also the members and groups within an actor. An actor's policy on a given question is a result of efforts to satisfy not only members of the executive, but other domestic actors, as well as external forces. To determine an issue position, one aggregates the various dyadic force on the decision maker(s).

The hypotheses to this point are in the nature of probabilistic explanations, so that at times they will not hold. When they do not, actors' expectations will be violated, and they will suffer from cognitive dissonance. Such dissonance, if strong and persistent, may encourage a change in their relationships of actors and the issue dimension, thereby overriding the impact of the similarity variable. In other words, persistent agreement or disagreement, *when unexpected,* can lead to either trust or mistrust (conditions usually determined by similarity). Therefore, crosscutting or persistent agreement (initially improbable) will cause any enemy relationship in which a negative affect calculus is used to move toward a situation in which a cost-benefit calculus is used instead and an actor dimension begins to give way to a stake dimension. Similarly, a patron–client relationship that does not result in the expected deference, and that produces crosscutting agreement instead, is likely to become quickly a topdog–underdog relationship, in which interdependence calculi are employed, and in which the respective attitudes of indifference and resentment ensue. In contrast, persistent agreement in a topdog–underdog relationship can change it to a patron–client relationship, whereas persistent disagreement may transform it into an enemy relationship; in which case, the underdog will need to seek a powerful patron for protection. Finally, a relationship between friends may become one of strangers if agreement is consistently crosscut on issues of low salience. On the other hand, if continuous agreement takes place over issues of high salience, their typical employment of a cost-benefit calculus may be replaced by a positive affect calculus. This is a special situation that requires intensive long-term agreement and strong positive affect due to great similarity. In such a case, mutual sacrifice could convert the relationship from one of "friends" to one of "lovers," ultimately even producing their coalescence into a single actor. Such sacrifice is particularly impressive because it focuses on altruism as a source of motivation.[74] On occasions in past years, the Anglo-American "special" relationship bore some resemblance to this case, particularly between 1939 and 1942.

The importance of a relationship is difficult to measure, but could presumably be discovered through either content analysis or survey research. Nevertheless, it is a function of two variables—actor interdependence for the given stake (the extent to which one actor needs another to get its proposal accepted) and the *intensity* of friendship-hostility. The weight of each dyad on the ultimate issue position adopted can be determined through aggregation, with consistent vectors making the issue position less likely to change. The more an actor is needed to get a proposal adopted, the more influence that dyadic relationship will have in determining the final issue position. For example, in U.S. foreign policy making, the President's views have the most weight, when they are forcefully expressed. Likewise, in international organizations that give selected members vetos, relationships with these actors are crucial, owing to actor interdependence. Such "power," however, is not the only source of influence. Every actor has its own reference group, which is a source of advice, even if it has no direct capability to affect dispositions. The *intensity* of friendship–hostility felt for this actor determines the extent to which it is an influential force. It is assumed that hostility, because it can give rise to more irrational behavior, is—all other factors being equal—a more intense force than friendship.

Having delineated the manner in which the issue-position calculus may be determined, the question remains as to the extent to which third parties may directly affect which calculus is selected. While the logic remains the same, there is some impact. Friends, when confronted with enemies, will not employ a cost-benefit calculus as predicted in the dyadic case, but will instead employ a positive affect calculus among themselves, and a negative affect calculus against their enemies. Coalitional behavior of this sort is likely to produce bipolar tendencies for strongly motivated actors. Likewise, an underdog which is a client of a powerful patron that is the enemy of the topdog (e.g., North Korea and the U.S.) will not behave as an underdog, but as an enemy (assuming it feels secure in the protection of its patron). Indeed, in its behavior toward the topdog it may be less restrained than the patron itself would be, because the latter is seen to bear ultimate responsibility. Third parties, of course, increase the use of interdependence calculi; the weak (as opposed to clients) are prone to take neutral issue positions when the strong disagree, lest they give offense. The difficulty in maintaining neutral positions, as well as the little capital it produces among the strong, encourages the actualization of "potential" patron–client relationships in time.

THE DYNAMICS OF AGREEMENT

The issue-position model can also be employed to determine whether two or more actors are likely to agree on a given issue, because agreement levels are affected by the issue-position calculi employed, and hence by the issue dimension that is dominant. Positive affect usually produces agreement, and negative affect disagreement. Interdependence produces considerable agreement, and the cost-benefit calculus permits disagreement. These are, of course, only initial levels of agreement. Over time, the continued use of cost-benefit calculi will tend to result in agreement through some type of bargain or compromise. A negative affect calculus will not result in agreement; it will instead tend to produce ever-increasing hostility, and the issue will fester so long as both sides continue to employ that calculus. It must be noted, however, that, although the employment of these calculi result in such outcomes, the calculi do *not* cause them. The cause lies in the issue dimension and the four key variables—similarity, relative status, prior pattern of agreement, and issue salience.

Some of this can be illustrated in the case of American foreign policy toward Rhodesia-Zimbabwe and Biafra. To predict and explain agreement, it is necessary first to determine the salience of these two stakes to the U.S. government and to delineate the relationship between that government and other contending actors. Neither stake was particularly salient to the United States, and policy was shaped, not by the President and White House staff, but by the bureaucracy.[75] Rhodesia proved more salient to elements in the United States than Biafra, because it was linked to domestic businesses which were denied access to chrome, owing to the UN embargo, and because of its close relationship with South Africa. The Rhodesian case involved primarily Great Britain, the white Ian Smith regime, the Black Africans in Southern Rhodesia, Zambia, South Africa, the other African border states, as well as the rest of Africa and the Third World. The Biafran situation involved primarily Great Britain, the Nigerian federal government, Biafra, the Soviet Union, France, bordering African states, and other African states.

In both cases, the U.S. government followed British policy but tried to indicate that it also supported Black African and Third World aspirations, while at the same time not needlessly alienating the major local contenders. A review of each of the variables shows that American policy was determined by employing a positive affect issue position with Great Britain, and an interdependence calculus with everyone else.

In Rhodesia, the low salience of the issue, coupled with the traditional tendency to follow the British line in the former British colonies, led the U.S. government to condemn officially the unilateral declaration of independence by Ian Smith. This policy was adopted because, among the contending parties, the relationship with Britain was the most important. In terms of actor interdependence, Britain—as the colonial power—had the only legitimate authority in the area; and in terms of the intensity of American friendship–hostility, among the contending actors, friendship was highest with Britain. Finally, the prior pattern between the two actors had been dominated by friendship; and British support and noncriticism of Lyndon Johnson's Vietnam policies increased the tendency to defer to

British interests, in light of the fact that American interests were minimal.[76]

American interests were seen to be minimal, because the issue was viewed as a problem of colonialism, and the American government's position throughout the postwar period had been one of opposing colonialism while encouraging its allies to grant their colonies rapid independence. Successive American administrations sought to win favor among the second most important group of actors in the situation—Black African and other Third World actors—while not alienating NATO allies. A few of the former were potential clients, but most were regarded as weak third parties, which could have an impact upon the United States only by collective action. It was this last possibility that led the U.S. government to adopt an interdependence calculus toward these actors, in hopes that deferral of the issue—or partial support of their position on an issue of high salience to them (colonialism)—would win capital for the United States on an issue of high salience to its leaders (the Cold War). Consequently, the United States sought to present itself as somewhat in advance of the British position in trying to end white supremacy in Rhodesia, an image easily fashioned by rhetoric in the UN or abstentions on votes where Britain was in opposition.[77] As a whole, since African and Third World governments lacked the capability of Britain and remained unified on few issues, and since positive affect was less toward them than toward Britain, U.S. administrations assumed positions of relatively low visibility and avoided assuming a leading role. Local participants exercised the least influence on American policy, primarily because the United States had had few significant prior contacts with them. Finally, though the American position was at odds with that of the government of South Africa, the U.S. government wished to avoid radical steps that might alienate South Africa by threatening that government's vital interests. In all, the American issue position, and subsequent changes in it, appear to be explicable in terms of the model that has been presented here.

The attempt by Biafra to secede from Nigeria is a more complicated case than that of Rhodesia, because it produced a number of crosscutting cleavages among major powers and African governments. Again, the U.S. government supported the British position and followed the British lead, but again it hedged its position by seeking influence with selected

Third World governments. On this occasion, the Soviet Union sided with Britain, providing arms to the federal government in Lagos; and France supported the Biafran secessionists, at least informally; as did China and several key African governments, such as those of the Ivory Coast and Tanzania. Despite these crosscutting cleavages, American policy is explicable by the model in terms of the same factors that operated in the Rhodesian case, which was coterminous. Despite the intervention of the Soviet Union, the U.S. government did not view Biafra as a Cold War issue but rather as one rooted in colonialism. France's position exerted little influence on the United States, because it remained unofficial and was perceived as a function of France's former rivalry with Britain for influence in Africa. This view reinforced American perceptions of Biafra as a colonial question. Finally, American support of the British position—itself one of support for the federal government—was compatible with the position of major African governments and of the Organization of African Unity (OAU) that tribalism and challenges to existing national boundaries must be opposed, owing to the fragility of African societies and the prospect of controversy over almost all African frontiers. Nevertheless, as the conflict dragged on, the United States failed to increase its support of Nigeria and provided extensive "humanitarian" relief to Biafra. The latter was in response both to world public opinion and domestic critics.

The application of the model in these cases suggests that, while multilateral situations are complex, this apparent complexity is reduced by the effects of coalitional behavior. As the model predicts, the prior patterns of relations and the relative salience of the issues provide important insights into which relationships are more important to key actors. Such concerns lead immediately to interaction itself.

*When two or more entities behave vis-à-vis one another,
and there is a sequence of at least two discernible acts
such that the first can "reasonably" be interpreted as
partly responsible for the second, we may speak of*
interaction. *Before and after, as well as during, a given
interaction sequence, the entities continue to be* related
in some fashion, however distant and remote.
—*J. David Singer* [1]

CHAPTER SEVEN

THE LABYRINTH OF
CONTENTION

THE CREATION of issues and the selection of initial issue positions by actors are merely the first steps in the complex process of value allocation. Much of the subsequent process occurs under conditions in which the outcomes of individual actors are determined not only by their own behavior but by the choices and actions of other participants. In other words, it is fruitless to seek explanations of allocations only in the motivations and attributes of individual actors, because such allocations are a function of the interplay of actors with their environment. To apprehend the manner in which the claims of individual actors are transformed into issue outcomes, it is necessary to delve into the effects which initial issue positions and actions have upon the motivations and attributes of other participants, and how their positions and actions further modify joint prospects.

It is rare that actors maintain the same positions they start with in the course of interacting with one another, as they adjust their own proposals and attitudes in response to the proposals and behavior of other participants. It is through interaction with one another that actors seek to win acceptance of preferred proposals, or at least those that are satisfactory to them, and ultimately to dispose of stakes in authoritative fashion. This process includes the revision of initial issue positions and the formulation of new issue positions, articulated as new proposals, as well as actions designed to influence fellow participants.*

This chapter presents a model to explain the way actors contend over issues. In doing so, it elucidates from a new perspective what has been a central concern of the realist paradigm—cooperation/conflict. From this perspective, cooperation/conflict is almost an epiphenomenon of the attempt to get actors to shift their issue positions.

Shifts in issue positions and in proposals are a function of changing evaluations of both what is feasible and what is desirable. The feasibility of various outcomes varies, owing to the degree of resistance or acceptance by others, and to their relative capacity and skill in pursuing their own preferences. Variation in what is desirable occurs as an actor's situation is strengthened or weakened in the course of competition, so that its "base line" for evaluation changes. An actor may enter the competition for a stake confidently proposing that it be surrendered and arrogantly rejecting as "humiliating" any counterproposals to share the stake. However, if its behavior produces the threat of a war that the actor is unlikely to win, or if a war occurs that it may lose, the actor may dramatically scale down its objectives to the point of seeking merely to avoid the threatened conflict or to salvage what it can from the debacle. Its initial situation has so deteriorated that the matter of value enhancement takes on a very different coloration than at the outset. Feasibility and desirability are obviously closely connected, and perceptions of them tend to move in tandem.† Hence, as an actor's situation improves, both what is seen as feasible and what is seen as desirable may grow; whereas, as an actor's situation deteriorates, that which is viewed as feasible and desirable may diminish. Indeed, a major difficulty in wartime negotiations is the tendency of those who are temporarily winning to increase the scope and domain of their objectives, a phenomenon that was painfully evident in both world wars as well as in the Korean conflict.

Even stalemate does not ensure a congruence of views by participants as to what proposals are feasible and desirable, because of changes that

---

* The distinction between proposals and actions as "moves" is consonant with Thomas Schelling's distinction between strategic and real moves. *The Strategy of Conflict* (New York: Oxford University Press, 1963), pp. 119ff.

† In the long run, desirability is a function of feasibility, and perceptions of the former must be brought into line with the latter or else disaster may ensue.

occur—in the course of interaction—in the attitudes of actors toward each other, and in their perceptions of what is in fact at stake; that is, their definitions of the issue. Rather than scaling down objectives when failure looms, actors are apt to scale them up in order to justify the decisions, sacrifices, and investments that have been made. In this way, the very nature of the issue may be redefined as concrete stakes are seen to be symbolic or transcendent, and as the issue is expanded to bring in new stakes. Changes in affect are, of course, closely tied to this process, so that what begins as a strictly limited competition for a concrete stake may be transformed into an effort to eliminate a dangerous adversary in a life-and-death struggle. And, even if escalation of conflict does not take place, obsolete proposals and issue positions may assume a life of their own, owing to the vested interests of particular subgroups or bureaucracies within the various actors. As the ebb and flow of competition proceeds, partial or preliminary dispositions of specific stakes occur; but the issue, in one form or another, will remain on the agenda until a disposition of stakes takes place that is viewed as legitimate by the key participants, so that it meets no challenge and ends contention.

Although the complexity of such interactions has long been recognized, political scientists—particularly in quantitative analysis—have tended to reduce the entire process to a study of the frequency and intensity of cooperation/conflict.* This oversimplification could be justified in that it emphasizes one aspect of interactions for purposes of research. Yet even this aspect of interactions has not been clearly conceptualized. The development of a new model of contention must begin by reevaluating this old concept.

RECONCEPTUALIZING COOPERATION/CONFLICT

Many scholars think of global interactions in terms of cooperation and conflict. Charles McClelland and Gary Hoggard define interactions as all nonroutine verbal and nonverbal communication among actors, and using the WEIS data set, empirically delineate three types—cooperation, participation, and conflict.[2] Other scholars have seen cooperation as a single

---

* For an interesting exception, in that he looks at "resolution," see James Harf, "Inter-Nation Conflict Resolution and National Attributes," in James N. Rosenau, ed., *Comparing Foreign Policy* (New York: Halsted Press, 1974), pp. 305–29.

continuous dimension that can be scaled.* Some of the later event data projects, such as that of Edward Azar, have followed in this tradition of developing a single scale.[3]

There is growing empirical evidence to suggest, however, that—like the phenomenon of cancer—the cooperation/conflict conceptualization is entirely too broad to produce a satisfactory typology of behavior, and that more precise concepts must be developed to replace it. Rummel, for example, showed that conflict and cooperative behavior are distinct dimensions that are uncorrelated and hence require different variables to explain them.[4] John Vasquez's review of statistical findings in international politics research indicated that, while quantitative research has enjoyed some success in explaining cooperation, it has largely failed to explain conflict.[5] Richard Mansbach et al. showed that the type of actors which engaged in cooperation were different from those which engaged in conflict.[6] Finally, in chapter 2 it was found that the dynamics of cooperation tend to be a function of issue-related characteristics, especially the tangibility of stakes, whereas the dynamics of conflict tend to be a function of actor-related characteristics. All these studies suggest that cooperation/conflict is not a continuum but constitutes at least two separate dimensions with their own dynamics.

Separating the two dimensions, as is done in the CREON project and by Rummel, does not solve the problem however.† Separating the "scale" into three types of behavior (cooperation, participation, and conflict) does not really provide a new conceptualization. Each of these concepts, individually, is crude, because each combines very different phenomena that should be kept analytically distinct. For example, a relationship is generally thought of as cooperative if it is characterized by easy and honest cross-communication, perceptions of similarities, benevolent attitudes, and a division of labor in search of mutually beneficial outcomes. In contrast, a conflict-prone relationship is characterized by poor or guarded communication, perceptions of dissimilarities, hostile or even malevolent attitudes, and self-help behavior aimed at achieving indi-

---

*An early and notable attempt to do this is the work of L. T. Moses, R. Brody, O. Holsti, J. Kadane, and J. Milstein, "Scaling Data on Inter-Nation Action," *Science* (1967), 156:1054–59.

†For the findings on cooperation and conflict that have been produced by the CREON project, see Maurice A. East and Charles F. Hermann, "Do Nation-Types Account for Foreign Policy Behavior?" in Rosenau, ed., *Comparing Foreign Policies*, pp. 269–303.

vidual benefits even if they are at another's expense. In each case, the characterization of cooperation/conflict includes several different variables, some cognitive, some attitudinal, and some behavioral. What must be done is to separate the most theoretically useful analytical distinctions within each concept and show how these can be recombined to provide the same linguistic functions as the old continuum. Finally, if this new conceptualization can be employed to develop a theory that explains not only how the dynamics of cooperation are different from the dynamics of conflict, but how they are related, then the field will begin to understand what it is trying to explain.

What distinguishes good from bad theory is that the former will delineate from the numerous logically possible distinctions *only* those that adequately explain behavior and that pass empirical tests. "A fact," according to David Easton, "is but a peculiar ordering of reality according to a theoretic interest."[7] According to the theory being presented here, the three most significant aspects of cooperation/conflict are: (1) agreement versus disagreement (an expression of opinion reflecting differences in issue positions), (2) positive versus negative acts (a measure of behavior that reflects the use of punishments and rewards), and (3) friendship versus hostility (a measure of attitude reflecting emotional reactions and psychological tendencies).

Agreement–disagreement refers to the extent to which actors share common issue positions, and to the extent to which there is overlap among their proposals. It reflects their respective positions toward each other's proposals for disposing of stakes. This variable is especially susceptible to crosscutting, owing to the high probability that actors will participate in a number of common issues, some of which will elicit complementary proposals—and others, contradictory proposals. The larger the number of common issues in which two actors participate, the greater the probability of a crosscutting pattern of agreement–disagreement unless the generalized affect of friendship–hostility becomes so dominant (as reflected by resort to an affect calculus) as to make agreement–disagreement a function of it. Under such circumstances, randomized agreement–disagreement will be replaced by obsessive agreement or disagreement. Unless this occurs, there will be no necessary congruence between friendship–hostility and agreement–disagreement (though a likely correlation). Actors that are generally hostile may find themselves in agreement on particular issues, as was the case with the United States and Soviet governments during the 1956 Suez crisis, and is currently the case on the issue of nuclear proliferation. Conversely, generally friendly actors may find themselves in strong disagreement on specific issues, as did the American, British, and French governments in 1956. As these examples illustrate, friendship–hostility and agreement–disagreement are distinct and distinguishable variables.

A second commonly ascribed aspect of cooperation/conflict, and perhaps the most visible, is that of positive–negative acts in the sense of behavior that furthers, or thwarts, one another's objectives. The very visibility of this factor has led to its being exaggerated in analyses of cooperation/conflict, particularly where event data are used. The tendency has been to construct operational scales of cooperation/conflict, based on the observed acts that are exchanged, with little regard for the other key variables. Although there is likely to exist a strong correlation between the three types of variables where sustained patterns of positive-negative acts appear, much must be left to the imagination where such patterns are absent. In addition, the use of such scales has contributed in no small way to the assumption that cooperation/conflict constitutes a unidimensional continuum. Visible behavior of this sort (both its magnitude and direction) contributes to the creation of expectations about status and capability, and, in the absence of information about motivation, may be used to predict that as well. Nevertheless, positive-negative acts are not necessarily or inevitably congruent with the other cooperation/conflict factors. Actors which are friendly and in agreement may *not* behave in ways that are seen as mutually beneficial. During the Cold War, for instance, the United States government—particularly during John Foster Dulles' tenure as secretary of state—tended to act in ways which its allies considered to be rash or unwise, even though the Western alliance was characterized by friendship and common issue positions.

Friendship-hostility reflects actors' affect towards one another; do they like or dislike each other? Unlike the other cooperation/conflict variables, however, friendship–hostility characterizes actor relationships *across* issues and acts as a setting for the other variables, which are specific to individual issues. Nevertheless, it is intensified or weakened as a consequence of relationships with third parties. For instance, friendly feelings toward another actor will be diluted if that actor is also friendly towards a third party to which the initial actor is hostile. Friendship-hostility is also closely related to similarity and therefore identities; intensive friendship generates a focus upon similar attributes, but if diluted by third-party relationships the effect will be to "point up" attribute differences.[8] Finally, of the three cooperation/conflict variables, friendship-hostility is probably the most important in producing generalized expectations concerning the *intentions or motivations* of other actors. Actors that are generally friendly will tend to explain away one another's misdeeds (if not persistent) in terms of misunderstanding, accident, or impulse, whereas hostile actors are prone to explain one another's positive deeds as misleading and even treacherous.

Once the multidimensional nature of cooperation/conflict is appreciated, it is no longer possible to view either aspect as merely intensifying or moderating along a single continuum. Both destructive spirals, and constructive, cooperative spirals, require that all three variables move in the same direction and reinforce one another. The former process is characterized by a sequence of disagreement, the exchange of negative acts, and the intensification of hostility. Stakes tend to become linked by a negative actor dimension, so that the scope of conflict grows, and issue positions are increasingly determined by a negative affect calculus, thereby preventing even random agreement from occurring. The stakes tend to assume symbolic and transcendent proportions, making compromise more difficult to achieve and readying actors to bear greater costs than they had expected, or were willing to bear, at the outset of the sequence. Each additional commitment produces more elaborate justifications and stimulates similar commitments and justifications by the adversary. To reverse the process, a change in direction must occur in at least one of the key variables, or it must be mitigated by exogenous factors like the threat of a third party or the growth of new, and more critical, issues. It is unlikely that such a change can begin in overall friendship–hostility, since such general affect is mostly dependent upon behavior. A change might come initially in the agreement variable, perhaps owing to the specter of mutual destruction, as was the case during the Cuban missile crisis of 1962; but this too is unlikely, since hostility will generate efforts to avoid agreement. Thus, the brightest prospect for terminating a vicious cycle is likely to be the exchange of positive acts (or at least reduction of negative ones), which can be initiated by individual leaders.

One problem here is that, in the presence of hostility and disagreement, leaders are prone to see their own actions as defensive, legitimate, and necessary, and those of the adversary as aggressive and unnecessary—a propensity that encourages grave misperceptions. Regardless of where the change begins, the reversal of at least one of the variables is a necessary (though not sufficient) condition to halt such a spiral.

Most situations of cooperation and conflict are not pure ones, so that it becomes important to identify which of the variables is the key one in order to alter the existing relationship. Where disagreement is the central element in conflict, resolution must emphasize the manipulation or packaging of stakes, so that proposals can be offered that will satisfy disputants. Such situations offer the most dramatic possibilities for third-party intermediaries, which are seen as impartial and knowledgeable, and which may devise new ways of looking at existing stakes. Such efforts may be fruitful if the intermediary points up overlap in proposals, the spuriousness of perceived links among stakes, or the existence of other links that had not been seen but which could be the bases of trade-offs. In cases when the exchange of negative acts is the key to conflict, resolution depends upon manipulating the behavior of adversaries. Again, third parties may be useful, particularly in performing communications, supervisory, interposition, or inspection functions. Often it may prove necessary to show actors how their behavior harms others or contributes to misunderstanding, in order to overcome the natural assumption of each that its behavior is purely reactive. Where conflict is directly rooted in hostility, it will be very difficult to remedy the existing situation, because this requires changes in the fundamental attitudes of participants toward one another, and so runs into the sorts of deep prejudices that are highly resilient. Cases of racial or religious enmity illustrate the difficulties inherent in coping with them directly. In such instances, the specific disagreements or negative acts that gave rise to enmity may be forgotten or distorted; or the attitudes may have become deeply embedded in the social fabric or the psyches of members. At best, such a "Hatfield-McCoy" conundrum will defy rapid solution.

Rarely will a relationship that is dominated by cooperation or conflict be the consequence of only one variable, so that every effort at conflict resolution requires identifying that which is most easily manipulated and most likely to have powerful effects on the others. Almost inevitably, hostility must be approached indirectly through agreement–disagreement and positive–negative acts, as the latter are issue-specific. In the absence of manipulation, there is a tendency for the three elements of cooperation/conflict to become balanced and congruent. Unfortunately, unless the elements of cooperation are deeply anchored and considerably stronger than those of conflict, the latter are likely to dominate in the long run—"a 'Gresham's Law of Conflict' " that suggests that "the harmful and dangerous elements drive out those which would keep the conflict within bounds."[9]

In summary, it is only by distinguishing among the three aspects of cooperation/conflict that scholars will clarify the underlying causes of what is a multivariate phenomenon. But as stated earlier, cooperation/conflict is really only an epiphenomenon of contention over issues. This is because what triggers positive and negative acts is agreement and disagreement over proposals to dispose of stakes. More important than providing a reconceptualization of cooperation/conflict, the three new variables delineate the most significant aspects of political contention. It is primarily this process, and how it relates to the allocation of values, that must be explained.

A MODEL OF POLITICAL INTERACTIONS

The way in which actors contend for issues and the causes of their behavior are depicted in figure 7.1. As described in detail in the previous chapter, similarity, prior pattern, status, and salience determine the issue dimension, which in turn affects the agreement pattern. The background variables (similarity, prior pattern, status) determine the overall relationship of actors that conditions their interaction in specific contexts; they change relatively slowly as a consequence of a series of interactions. The interactions themselves are determined by the four issue-related intervening variables, which can change more quickly—and are more manipulatable—than the background variables. These are centered around the issue dimension which, in addition to affecting agreement directly, also impinges upon the agreement pattern indirectly by its influence on the type of stakes which are raised, and on the nature of the proposals that are offered. Finally, the agreement pattern, along with status, determines

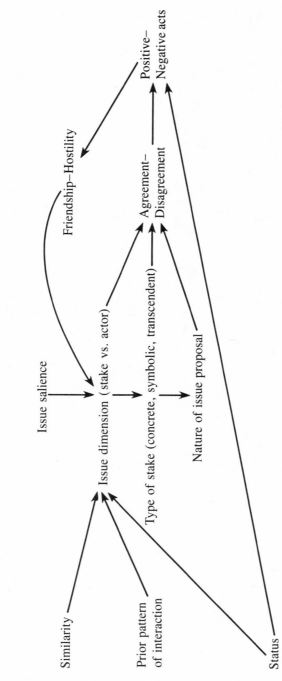

Figure 7.1 Interaction Model

the mix of positive and negative acts that actors will send each other in the attempt to alter each other's issue positions. Briefly, agreement tends to engender positive acts, whereas disagreement gives rise to negative acts. The frequency with which these will occur depends on the relative status of the contending parties, a finding which has been well established empirically, and which was discussed in the previous chapter.[10] Positive–negative acts, as Coplin and O'Leary point out, do not directly change issue position but instead alter the attitudes actors hold about each other (friendship–hostility).[11] The resulting affect then feeds back into the issue dimension.

Of the intervening variables, issue dimension is the most critical, because it transmits and integrates much of the important past and current information regarding relations that feeds back into the process to generate long-term adaptation, learning, and development. Issue dimension directly conditions agreement-disagreement by the fusing or decoupling of issues on the agenda, the consequence of which is to "define" or "redefine" the issues. Where an actor dimension is present, individual issues in which the same contenders are participants tend to merge into single large issues that are defined or "named" after the adversarial or collaborative relationship that is involved. The variety of (possibly crosscutting) issue positions that exist when a stake dimension is dominant is eliminated by the imposition of a single issue position based on an affect calculus. No longer may issues be resolved without regard to *who* gets what, as in the case of the stake dimension, and consequently a more consistent, even rigid, pattern of agreement–disagreement results, possibly leading to extreme polarization between "friends" and "enemies." Under such conditions, it is no longer possible for conflict to be moderated by a pattern of overlapping issue positions that might encourage trade-offs among issues.* Instead, alliances are formed against the "enemies of one's enemies," and they are apt to evolve and decay only slowly, because of their nonexpediential character. Since affect, rather than complementary issue positions alone, is the glue of such alliances, they tend to take on an ideological coloration. In contrast, where a stake

* For evidence and insights from anthropology concerning the significance of crosscutting possibilities, see R. A. LeVine and D. T. Campbell, *Ethnocentrism: Theories of Conflict, Ethnic Attitudes, and Group Behavior* (New York: Wiley, 1972).

dimension dominates, alliances emerge among those who share common or complementary issue positions, regardless of other friends or enemies—alliances that are *for something* rather than *against someone*. As new proposals arise, such alliances are fluid and may shift rapidly. The pattern of agreement–disagreement among actors tends to be random with the distribution of agreement–disagreement producing perfect crosscutting (the number of agreements equals disagreements) as the number of separate issues grows larger.*

The distribution and intensity of positive-negative acts are indirectly effected by the issue dimension variable. Such acts are usually directed toward targets that are perceived as respectively aiding or thwarting one's objectives, by either agreeing or disagreeing with one's issue position. In the presence of a stake dimension, those targets tend to vary from issue to issue, indeed even from stake to stake. In contrast, they tend to remain constant where an actor dimension is dominant. Under the latter condition, therefore, positive or negative acts tend to be concentrated upon the same limited number of targets—a condition that contributes to positive and negative spirals, and that reinforces each actor's belief that the behavior of the other is consciously motivated by affect. In practice, actors may derive psychological satisfaction from doing great harm to enemies or favoring friends. In contrast, a stake dimension promotes a wider and more random distribution of positive–negative acts among a variety of targets. In addition, since today's enemy may be tomorrow's friend, it is prudent for actors to moderate the intensity of their acts. Both the intensity and concentration of such acts are functions of the degree of overlap that exists with the issue positions of other actors on the entire agenda of issues; the opportunities for trade-offs; and the strength and nature of resistance that is met when issue positions clash. Figure 7.2 depicts the relationship between crosscutting (agreement-disagreement) and the distribution and intensity of positive-negative acts.

Finally, the issue dimension is related to friendship-hostility (both as a cause and as an effect) through actors' perceptions of potential gains and/or losses. When a stake dimension is dominant, actors aspire to absolute value satisfaction regardless of the consequences for other par-

*This hypothesis follows from the law of large numbers, which states that any distribution consisting of a large number of cases will form a normal curve.

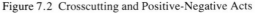

Figure 7.2 Crosscutting and Positive-Negative Acts

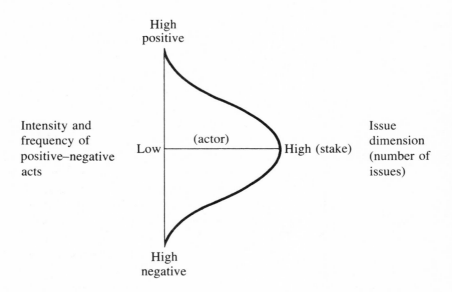

Source: P. Dale Dean, Jr., and John A. Vasquez, "From Power Politics to Issue Politics:
Bipolarity and Multipolarity in Light of a New Paradigm,"
Western Political Quarterly (March 1976), 29(1):24.

ticipants. Value inheres almost entirely in the stakes at issue, so that outcomes which promise mutual as well as individual advantage are acceptable. Movement from a stake dimension to an actor dimension, however, produces perceptions of relative satisfaction and deprivation, so that outcomes are assessed in terms of whether they benefit or harm other participants. With this shift, participants become increasingly oriented toward each other, rather than toward the stakes at issue, and thereby become more sensitive to feelings of friendship or hostility when the prospect of disposition arises. The affect calculus is then employed, so that the very concepts of gain and loss assume a comparative appearance.

In addition to affecting contention in the above manner, the issue dimension also determines the types of stakes that will be raised for contention. Stakes, it will be recalled, are objects to which values are attached. A concrete stake is one the object of which is tangible and divisible, and which would—if disposed of—immediately confer value satisfaction, because the value is inseparable from the object itself. Thus, acquisition of a piece of territory ordinarily provides the acquirer with a finite amount of wealth and security that can be accurately estimated in advance. Indeed, the more difficult it becomes to estimate accurately the value of a stake, the more that stake is infused with symbolic value. For example, prior to the French Revolution, it had been possible for European statesmen and strategists to feel confident that the value of any province was roughly equivalent to its number of inhabitants and amount of territory. This was less possible in the nineteenth century, as Bismarck discovered to his chagrin after Germany annexed the French provinces of Alsace-Lorraine in 1870. In 1914 the French continued to fixate upon these "lost" provinces as symbolic of the *patrie* as a whole, and they remained an immovable obstacle in the path of Franco-German reconciliation. Thus, a symbolic stake is one the object of which is of indeterminate value, because it stands for some other object that has presumably greater intrinsic value to the actor (e.g., Berlin as symbolic of Western Germany or the Free World). However, because it is so intangible, a symbolic stake, unlike a concrete one, loses much of its value if a major contestant declares, "Take it, it doesn't matter!" This was basically the American position toward the offshore Chinese Tachen and Nanchi islands when the United States government assisted Chiang Kai-shek's Nationalists to evacuate them in February 1955. They were not invested with the symbolic quality that was associated with the other offshore islands of Quemoy and Matsu. Finally, a transcendent stake is one whose object is neither tangible nor divisible, and which is virtually equated with the value under contention. Transcendent stakes commonly deal with normative beliefs that guide behavior such as capitalism and communism, or democracy and fascism. They are less concerned with concrete objects than with principles and rules that are intended to govern behavior.

A stake dimension encourages perceptions of stakes as concrete and divisible. The search for arrangements that will permit absolute, rather than relative, satisfaction of values encourages actors to make efforts to keep issues and stakes separated and encapsulated so that actual dispositions can take place swiftly and the scope of competition kept limited. Quiet, even "private," arrangements that limit the number of participants, and the attention of the audience, facilitate the acceptance of proposals that will distribute benefits among a relatively few actors. Only in this fashion is it possible for a few actors to preempt stakes in which others would demand a share if they could. When such a process exists, actors will behave as though they were "special interests"; their ability to expropriate stakes diminishes as the number of participants grows.

In contrast, as an actor dimension becomes more potent, the stakes at issue will be perceived differently, thereby evoking different patterns of behavior. Issues involving common competitors will become increasingly linked as actors become preoccupied with prospects of relative gain or loss, and with depriving or harming a competitor rather than satisfying oneself alone. In the process, concrete states become less salient or are transformed into symbolic or even transcendent stakes, the salience of which reinforces the actor dimension. Even objects with little inherent value may take on symbolic importance if they are regarded as instrumental to other stakes or as indicators of commitment and will, competition for which is vital to assure an actor's credibility. Their acquisition produces psychological victories and defeats. For example, the Soviet government sought for many years to force the West to admit the People's Republic of China to the United Nations, and to recognize de facto the German Democratic Republic, for symbolic reasons that would have psychological consequences. Such symbolic stakes tend to arise as substitutes for conflicts that, for one reason or another, cannot be waged openly or directly. One such reason is the potential for mutual harm implicit when there is status parity.* Overall equality of status generates competition and threat that strengthen the actor dimension. Its presence inhibits the prospects for disposing of individual stakes by making it difficult for any actor to impose a solution unilaterally, and by encouraging the linking of disparate proposals into larger and more complex packages. As the actor dimension continues to intensify, concrete stakes continue to disappear or to be transformed into symbolic ones.

---

* As issues become linked, relative overall status becomes more important than issue-specific strength, owing to the possibility of drawing upon virtually all the instruments of power in order to gain leverage, whether or not they are suitable for acquiring any specific stake.

As symbolic and transcendent stakes begin to play a more central role in competition, strategies fashioned to prevent others from acquiring a share in the stakes (which are seen as difficult to divide) become as, if not more, prominent than those which encourage prompt dispositions. Such "deterrence" objectives, in turn, reduce the incentive to limit the number of participants or the interest of the audience. Instead, each side feels itself compelled to compete for friends and allies, a process which does not reduce the share of the benefits to anyone, since such benefits take the form of satisfaction with depriving a foe. Whereas a stake dimension encourages an atmosphere of opportunity which is conducive to flexibility, a negative actor dimension encourages an atmosphere of threat and suspicion which is conducive to the growth of dogmatism. Consequently, the prospects for actual allocation become increasingly dim unless a way is found to reverse the process, decouple the issues, and eliminate the symbolic and transcendent quality of the stakes, or at least reduce their salience. This is an extremely difficult task because, as social psychologists realize, conflicts that focus on determining " 'who suffers' are more difficult to resolve than those that are perceived in terms of deciding 'who gains'." [12]

Both symbolic and transcendent stakes tend to be perceived by key participants as difficult to divide, because they lack concrete objects of which to dispose. Moreover, actors do not wish to divide them, even were such a prospect to present itself, because to surrender even part of a symbolic stake would represent the surrender of part of the larger stake it symbolizes; and to surrender part of a transcendent stake would mean surrendering the value which is directly equated with it. Indeed, bargaining over a transcendent stake implies compromising the "purity" of the normative beliefs that underlie it, thereby placing the actor upon a slippery slope from which escape is difficult. A Hindu cannot easily compromise his beliefs with a Moslem without becoming less of a Hindu or even no Hindu at all. When ideologies are exclusivist, as are Hinduism and Islam, or communism and capitalism, "there is no way," as Richard Rosecrance declares, "in which there can be a sufficient environmental supply of resources." [13] Perceptions of symbolic and transcendent stakes discourage compromise and bargaining. An actor either acquires the value at stake or does not; it either wins or loses.

Such were the perceptions of American leaders during the Geneva

Conference of 1954, which brought to an end the "first" Indochina war. Both Eisenhower and Dulles viewed Vietnam as symbolic of all of Southeast Asia, the first of the "falling dominoes," and as part of a transcendent issue that pitted the Free World against a communist monolith. Dulles attributed Viet Minh successes to Chinese assistance which was provided on Soviet orders.[14] American adherence to any agreement that ceded part of Vietnam to the communists he regarded as a surrender of principle that would be seen as a weakening of will; to agree to a solution that condemned some Vietnamese to communism was to agree to that form of government, and to the system of ethics and the economic system which it represented. The United States, therefore, would not be "a party to any agreement that makes anybody a slave."[15] Eisenhower declared that he found it difficult to understand British "reliance on the value of negotiations with the Communists," and he bridled at a bargain involving partition "that put great numbers of people under Communist domination."[16] Thus, the United States refused to accept the legitimacy of the Geneva accords and was prepared to continue the struggle, though on a different plane.

As this episode suggests, the type of stake has an important, albeit indirect, influence on the type and sequence of techniques that actors employ in interaction; that is, the pattern of positive-negative acts. Concrete stakes encourage moderate and limited forms of behavior and techniques, because they can be distributed with some ease and are subject to crosscutting pressures that inhibit extreme affect and behavior. Crosscutting also inhibits escalation of techniques. Since concrete stakes have tangible objects with inherent value that are often divisible, trade-offs can be arranged or limited stakes can be seized without creating intensive resistance that may lead to destructive spirals.

In contrast, when an actor dimension produces symbolic and transcendent stakes, the absence of tangible objects with inherent value that encourage bargains and compromises makes it difficult to allocate values. A sophisticated player can even refuse to recognize the value of a symbolic stake, thereby preventing an adversary from enjoying the satisfaction of victory. Even if specific stakes are allocated, issues are rarely resolved and fester for long periods of time, and Pyrrhic victories occur that produce only frustration. The large amounts of value attached to symbolic and transcendent stakes and the sense of frustration associated with a failure to achieve results, may produce escalation both in negative affect and acts as moderate measures fail to resolve the issue. In time, actors may even look toward the destruction of opponents as the only way of achieving true value satisfaction. Complete stalemate or total war are prominent solutions.

Interactions that feature symbolic or transcendent stakes tend to exhibit a certain nonutilitarian quality in contrast to interactions over concrete stakes. Participants tend to perceive stakes as highly salient and to invest large amounts of attention, energy, and material resources in objects of little intrinsic value. During the height of the Cold War, for instance, the United States and Soviet Union were prone to making commitments (which their own friends saw as unjustified by the real value of the stakes under contention) because they were thought to be symbolic or transcendent. Despite the absence of concrete stakes, the superpowers interacted as though there were such stakes, whose acquisition would enhance their overall status in a significant way. In most cases there was no audience that really mattered; and in the end, the fate of most specific stakes was irrelevant to the actual value satisfaction of the central contestants.*

As the preceding discussion implies, perceptions of symbolic and transcendent stakes produce a ''zero-sum'' mentality, in which proposals that offer compromise are rejected as unacceptable, and proposals are made that require the capitulation of an adversary. In this manner, type of stakes condition the final issue-related variable, *nature of issue proposal,* which in turn affects the agreement pattern. Issue dimension indirectly affects proposals through type of stakes. A stake dimension, as noted earlier, encourages resort to a cost-benefit calculus in fashioning proposals. Such proposals in turn focus upon maximizing an actor's benefits while minimizing costs. An actor dimension, by contrast, leads to an affect calculus that results in proposals that emphasize the relative benefits and

* The superpowers also seemed to be oblivious of the possibilities that: (1) an actor may successfully reject certain norms despite its lack of status (e.g., USSR 1917; Cuba 1959; China 1963); (2) force cannot convince but can only destroy; (3) toleration need not reduce the prospects of a favorable value allocation; and (4) even after total war, new transcendent stakes may be placed on the agenda by new opponents, so that permanent acceptance of existing value satisfaction may be impossible to attain. Until such lessons are learned, interaction will tend to result in persistent failure and frustration.

costs of friends and adversaries. An interdependence calculus is produced by an intermingling of the two dimensions.

Proposals based on a cost-benefit calculus aim toward a rapid allocation of stakes, so that benefits can be readily enjoyed. Delay in allocation means investments of resources that produce no return, like loans that produce no interest, and these externalities must be counted either as a reduction in total benefits or an increase in costs. Actors will of course take unilaterally what they can, and such acts may be regarded as negative by other participants; but since such behavior is "opportunistic," it is unlikely to form a pattern of hostility. Moreover, such unilateral acts will generally occur in situations of power preponderance, so that their immediate consequences are small. When resistance is met, however—a condition which will increasingly occur as participants enjoy equal status—actors will be ready to make compromise proposals to acquire what is beyond their own grasp, and will be prepared to permit others to enjoy a share in the stakes, as long as they can do the same. Efforts will be made to avoid stalemates in which benefits are not available to anyone, and to avoid long struggles that are apt to be costly. Proposals which promise variable and even positive-sum solutions are the rule, while those which threaten negative-sum outcomes are avoided. Such proposals tend to produce agreement in time, and limit disagreement to initial issue positions, after which each side gropes to find solutions that offer them maximum payoffs while at least proving acceptable to others. The final distribution of costs and benefits is likely to reflect the perceived status ranking of the participants and to reinforce it, but the process is not likely to degenerate into tests of strength unless these rankings are misperceived in the first place. Consequently, there will be no tendency for positive or negative acts to spiral and change the friendship–hostility pattern. The condition of minimal affect that permitted the stake dimension in the first place will be continued. An interdependence calculus promises a similar process, with the differences that benefits will be made available to different actors in different issues, rather than the same issue, and alliances of expediency among the interdependent are likely to prove costly to third parties.

Proposals arising from an affect calculus are made with an eye to relative costs and benefits of friends and enemies. In the case of positive affect, proposals aim to maximize the benefits and minimize the costs to the friend with less regard for one's own payoffs. In the case of negative affect, proposals are constructed that maximize an adversary's costs, or minimize its benefits, or at least that promise the greatest possible difference between one's own costs and benefits and those of the enemy. Since actors are prepared to bear costs and forgo benefits rather than permit the adversary to enjoy them, preferred proposals may threaten negative-sum outcomes. Proposals based on an affect calculus, therefore, ensure agreement among friends and disagreement among adversaries, and produce clear and consistent patterns of positive-negative acts. In this way, they reinforce the overall patterns of friendship or hostility that originally gave birth to the actor dimension from which they flow.

The preferences and motivations that underlie the different types of proposals which were just described can be depicted as vectors in a two-dimensional space, in the manner suggested by social psychologists.[17] The X, Y, and Z vectors in figure 7.3 express competitive, individual, and cooperative motivations of both a positive and negative sort. The positive (lower right) aspect of the X vector represents proposals that aim to maximize an actor's relative benefits and an adversary's relative costs; that is, pure zero-sum proposals that reflect an intense negative affect calculus of the sort associated with demands for "unconditional surrender" during war. The negative (upper left) aspect of this vector reflect the "martyr's" proposals of self-sacrifice or abject surrender that aim to maximize a partner's benefits while maximizing one's own costs. They would arise from an intense positive affect calculus in which an actor assumes that the survival of a friend can be assured only by the sacrifice of oneself. Robert Jordan's act of self-sacrifice at the end of *For Whom the Bell Tolls* is based on such motivation, though it is obviously rare in global politics, and Machiavelli expressly regarded it as a confusion of private and public morality. The positive side of the Y vector (right hand) reflects proposals that are based on a pure cost-benefit calculus in which the costs and benefits of others are not considered at all. But, since such proposals are rarely feasible except in conditions of absolute dominance, they tend to give way to cooperative proposals that incorporate perceptions of interdependence. The negative side of the Y vector represents proposals that are "masochistic" or "suicidal."[18] Though rare in global

Figure 7.3 Motivational Vectors in a Two-Dimensional Space

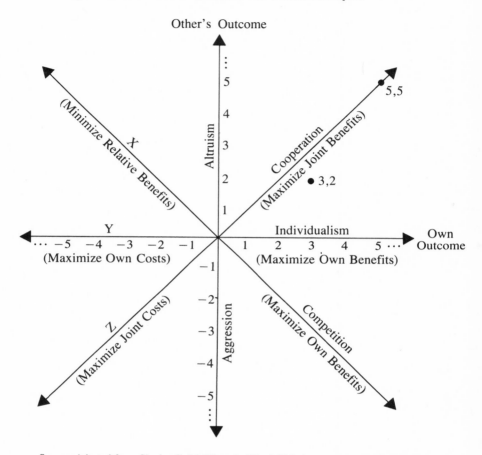

Source: Adapted from Charles G. McClintock, "Social Motivations in Settings of Outcome
Interdependence," in Daniel Druckman, ed., *Negotiations: Social-Psychological
Perspectives* (Beverly Hills, Calif: Sage, 1977), p.58 , by permission of
Sage Publications, Inc.

politics, such proposals occasionally are made in the name of "honor" or
"self-esteem." Whether in the case of small actors which choose to fight
a hopeless battle to retain their independence, or the samurai who chose
to commit suicide rather than surrender, the calculus expresses the con-

viction that it is "better to die like a man than to live like a slave." Finally, the two poles of the Z vector reflect proposals based on strong perceptions of interdependence. The positive side (upper right) constitutes proposals infused with positive affect that offer joint benefits to participants, whereas those in the lower left are strongly colored by negative affect and offer joint loss. Deterrence strategies that aim at assuring credibility implicitly contain such proposals, though the actors obviously hope that adversaries will not "accept" the "offer." [19]

The least amount of subsequent interaction is necessary if the initial proposals of actors are based on the same motivations. Even under such circumstances, proposals may be compatible only under the following conditions:

"Competition" (X)—positive:negative, negative:positive
"Individualism" (Y)—positive:negative, negative:positive
"Cooperation" (Z)—positive:positive, negative:negative

And even in these cases, further interaction is usually necessary to determine precise outcomes and dispositions. Commonly, motivations are not identical and proposals not compatible, and a major result of interaction is ultimately to make them so.

Although issue dimension is the key determinant of type of stake and nature of stake-value, it should not be assumed that there are no other factors that influence these two variables. For the moment, it can be assumed that environmental factors, science and technology, and some of the variables suggested in the agenda model (see chapter 4) are also present. From the point of view of interaction, however, these factors are not directly relevant.

Having described the impact of the issue-related variables upon the three dimensions of interaction, it is now necessary to examine how these three aspects change and feed back upon the issue dimension and themselves over time. The two critical variables here are the success or failure of previous interactions, and the presence of cognitive dissonance or consistency that may arise as a result of previous interactions. Figure 7.4 depicts the relationship, showing that success and failure combine with cognitive dissonance or consistency to affect both the frequency and intensity of agreement–disagreement and positive–negative acts, which in turn condition friendship–hostility which feeds back on the issue dimension. Success/failure describes the extent to which actors' proposals and actions (agreement-disagreement/positive-negative acts) accomplish their tactical and strategic purposes. Cognitive dissonance refers to the extent to which contention involves matching one or more of the cooperative aspects of interaction with one or more of the conflictive aspects. Dissonance is particularly potent when the fundamental attitudinal dimension (friendship–hostility) is incongruent with either or both of the behavioral dimensions.

All other factors being equal, success leads actors to repeat previous actions, whereas failure encourages them to rethink their strategy. Cognitive dissonance tends to be reduced and is thereby a stimulant for change, although to produce change, it must be persistant; cognitive consistency simply reinforces previous behavior and attitudes. Success/failure has a major impact on changing behavior (agreement–disagreement and positive-negative acts), while cognitive dissonance or consistency has more of an effect on attitudes (friendship–hostility). The exact impact of these two variables will depend on how they combine (success with dissonance, success with consistency, failure with dissonance, failure with consistency) for each participant actor. Since the process is fairly complex each of the two new variables will be treated separately.

COGNITIVE DISSONANCE AND THE OPPORTUNITY FOR CHANGE

An actor's map of reality, in addition to providing its leaders with a set of strategies and tactics, informs them of how they can expect to be treated by other actors. Of this map, Leon Festinger writes:

This reality may be physical or social or psychological, but in any case the cognition more or less maps it. This is, of course, not surprising. It would be unlikely that an organism could live and survive if the elements of cognition were not to a large extent a veridical map of reality. Indeed, when someone is "out of touch with reality," it becomes very noticeable.[20]

It is when the elements of cognition are no longer congruent with one another that the second independent variable in the interaction feedback process, cognitive dissonance, arises. "Two elements," declares Fest-

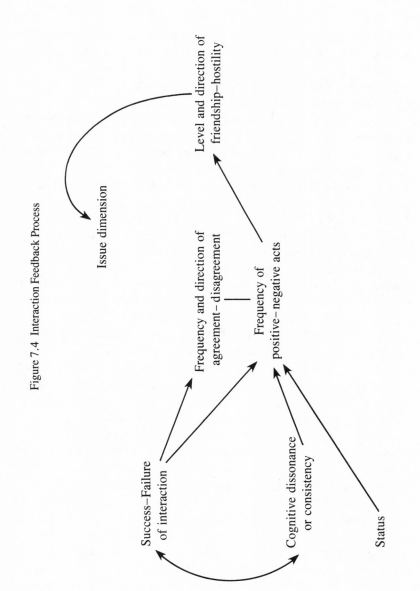

Figure 7.4 Interaction Feedback Process

inger, "are dissonant if, for one reason or another, they do not fit together."[21] Such a condition violates the need for psychological consistency that many psychologists theorize is fundamental for human beings to prevent inner conflict. Inconsistent cognitions, it is hypothesized, generate efforts to make beliefs consistent with behavior.

To maintain consistency between beliefs and behavior, leaders commonly seek to justify the latter by emphasizing, even overstating, the reasons for that behavior and denigrating alternatives that have been rejected. Once a decision has been taken and a course of action adopted, alternatives that were previously considered viable are seen as less so, and new reasons and information are sought to strengthen the alternative that was selected. This process occurs, however, only if the choice among alternatives is perceived to have been a free one, and if it is seen to have had some impact on the situation. If the choice were not free, the absence of a sense of responsibility would eliminate the possibility of psychological conflict; and, if that choice had no impact, it would quickly become irrelevant, thereby also eliminating responsibility.[22] The important relationship between responsibility and dissonance also suggests that decisions which are made, or behavior which is undertaken, as a result either of strong coercion or large rewards will produce less dissonance than where coercion or rewards are minimal or absent. Under the latter conditions, responsibility is much sharper, so that attitudes must be brought in line with decisions and behavior.[23]

This insight is related to what was said earlier about the achievement of success by one party at the expense of another, either through coercion or rewards. Unless an actor's behavior is voluntary, the probability of dissonance—and, therefore, a change in attitudes—is minimal. For this reason, the defeat of one actor by another does *not* alter the former's attitudes but merely intensifies them. A peace which is achieved through voluntary agreement is likely to be more durable than one which is imposed unilaterally as a result of *force majeure*. In the former case, a sense of responsibility exists on the part of both, and those leaders who adhered to the agreement are likely to commit themselves to it and increasingly rationalize its benefits. Where peace is imposed, the leaders of the actor that has been compelled do not alter their attitudes and feel no compulsion to adhere to the agreement. This is, in part, why German officials after World War I had no compunction about taking steps to evade the strictures of the Versailles Treaty, particularly with regard to German rearmament. Finally, this insight helps to explain why leaders tend to believe that they have no alternatives when they take major decisions that are repugnant to them personally, or that they know will entail great costs. Leaders tend to believe that they are acting from necessity while the other side is doing so from choice.[24]

Consistency theory predicts that an actor will become more committed to a course of action once it has been chosen; and that the longer it is pursued, the greater the effort to protect its integrity. While common sense suggests that when a course of action is not achieving its original purpose, or when it is causing unexpected hardships, leaders will seek relief by altering behavior, consistency theory predicts the opposite, suggesting that leaders will continue to pursue unprofitable policies in order to justify the original decision. This results in inertia rather than change and leads to the ignoring of contrary information. The behavior itself signals a commitment to the beliefs that gave rise to it in the first place, so that it is probable that these beliefs will be used again to justify still further behavior. In this way, efforts to reduce dissonance result in a cycle of inertia and repetition. Declares Robert Jervis:

If in reducing the dissonance created by the decision to intervene to prevent revolution in one country, the statesman inflates his estimate of the bad consequences of internal unrest, he will be more likely to try to quell disturbances in other contexts. Or if he reduces dissonance by increasing his faith in the instrument he chose to use, he will be more likely to employ that instrument in later cases.[25]

Thus, American efforts to intervene in Cuba to overthrow Fidel Castro in the early 1960s, and to prevent the spread of Castroism (though they failed), facilitated the decision to intervene in the Dominican Republic in 1965.

As commitment to a chosen course of action deepens, so too does the need to justify that behavior. As the investment of resources grows, admissions of failure or error become more painful, thereby intensifying dissonance. New reasons are sought to justify policy; new goals and objectives are "invented" or "discovered"; concrete stakes are transformed into symbolic and transcendent ones; and ingenious measures of success are used. In addition, costs are underestimated and gains overestimated. World War I and Vietnam both contain apt illustrations of the phenomenon. General Sir Douglas Haig, commander-in-chief of British forces, by 1917 had apparently learned nothing from three futile years of trench warfare. "Haig remained convinced that he could break the German lines and win the war by frontal assault. He refused to be discouraged by the failure in the previous year on the Somme."[26] It was not, he argued, that his strategy was fundamentally wrong, but that the Somme campaign had been fought in the wrong place, before the British Army had been properly trained and bloodied. Instead, he elected to continue the strategy at Ypres, where at the end of July he launched one million British troops against an equal force of well-entrenched and fully alerted Germans:

Failure was obvious at the end of the first day to everyone except Haig and his immediate circle. The greatest advance was less than half a mile. The main German line was nowhere reached. Rain fell heavily. The ground churned up by shellfire, turned to mud. Men, struggling to advance, sank up to their waists. Guns disappeared in the mud. Haig sent in tanks. These also vanished in the mud.[27]

Yet, the offensive ground on into November, by which time the British had suffered some 300,000 casualties and had gained nothing. It was "the blindest slaughter of a blind war."[28] Haig later made up excuses for the offensive, so as to rid himself of responsibility for it—even declaring that Marshal Pétain had pleaded for it, which had not been the case. Undaunted, Haig hoped to renew the offensive in the spring. Similarly, the process of American involvement in Vietnam reveals the effects of commitment combined with efforts to avoid dissonance. Morton Deutsch's assessment of the tragedy, written some years ago, deserves citation at length:

The most direct statement of the reason for our continued involvement is the fact that we are involved: our continued involvement justifies our past involvement. Once involved it is exceedingly difficult to disengage and to admit, thereby, how purposeless and unwitting our past involvement has been. I am stating, in other words, that we are not involved because of any large strategic or moral purpose and that any such purposes we now impute to our involvement are ex post facto rationalizations. . . . As Festinger (1961) has pointed out: "Rats and people come to love the things for which they have suffered." Presumably they do so in order to reduce the dissonance induced by the suffering, and their method of dissonance-reduction is to enhance the attractiveness of the choice which led to their suffering: only if what one chose was really worthwhile would all of the associated suffering be tolerable. Did we not increase what we perceived to be at stake in the Vietnam conflict as it has become more and more costly for us? Were we not told that our national honor, our influence as a World leader, and our national security were in the balance in the conflict over this tragic little land?[29]

Since wars entail greater commitments of resources and greater sacrifices than most other courses of action, they also tend to generate the most intensive efforts to overcome, or to avoid, dissonance. Commonly this takes the form of changing or enlarging the purposes for fighting *during* the conflict by altering the definition of the issues and stakes involved, as Deutsch noted was the case in Vietnam. Such changes provide justification for continued sacrifice and for escalation and enlargement of the conflict. The Prussian military theorist Clausewitz, aware of this tendency, cautioned his readers that "as War is no act of blind passion, but is dominated by the political object, therefore the value of that object determines the measure of the sacrifices by which it is to be purchased."[30] As sacrifice and commitment produce more grandiose justifications, these in turn demand still greater sacrifices, so that a vicious spiral ensues.

Part of the reason for this, no doubt, has to do with maintaining domestic political support as sacrifices grow. Both Rosenau and Lowi argue that, as foreign policy issues command more domestic resources, they are treated more like domestic political issues, meaning that they evoke more attention, participation, and disagreement.[31] To avoid this, Lowi argues that decision makers attempt to make foreign policy issues look like "crises." In doing so, leaders often oversell the threat. This, he argues, was particularly the case with the Cold War.[32] As sacrifices increase in the face of failure, rationalizations become more exaggerated and elaborate to maintain internal support.

While leaders may be affected this way, the public may not. The limited evidence on this question deals with American public support for limited war. John Mueller has shown that, for both Korea and Vietnam, public support declined with an increase in casualties. As casualties increased by a factor of ten (from 10 to 100 to 1,000), public support for the war effort declined by about 15 percentage points in public opinion polls.[33] This demonstrates that large groups may, in fact, be much more "rational" than small elites when it comes to expending large amounts of resources, especially human life.

The failure of American leaders to take account of public discontent during the Vietnam War, or to recognize the fruits of their policy, underlines the importance of Festinger's point that individuals who are resistant to change may intensify their existing attitudes, rather than change them, when they are in high-commitment situations and are faced with clear evidence of failure.[34] Rather than changing their views as a result of negative feedback, they will seek out further reasons to continue doing what they are doing. The results will be a "boomerang effect" or a process of "circular, incremental magnification" that defies common sense.[35] In effect, contrary information and threat may produce a "closed mind" rather than learning.[36]

In the context of the present model, cognitive dissonance exists when there is inconsistency between the overall relationship of actors, as expressed by friendship–hostility, and the issue-specific aspects of interaction; that is, agreement–disagreement and positive–negative acts. Cognitive dissonance exists when generally hostile actors find themselves in agreement on an issue and exchange positive acts, or when generally friendly actors are in disagreement and exchange negative acts. These elements are in dissonant relation because "the obverse of one element would follow from the other;"[37] actors are confronted by attitudes or behavior on the part of others which they do not expect and did not anticipate. Their overall relationship logically predicted different attitudes or behavior.*

Dissonance, according to Festinger, may be reduced:

1. By changing one or more of the elements involved in dissonant relations.
2. By adding new cognitive elements that are consonant with already existing cognition.
3. By decreasing the importance of the elements involved in the dissonant relations.[38]

The first of these, in terms of the model, entails the reduction of dissonance by means of altering either agreement–disagreement and positive–

---

* The level of dissonance can be potentially measured on an ordinal scale, with positive consistency requiring friendship, agreement, and positive acts; and negative consistency entailing hostility, disagreement, and negative acts.

negative acts *or* friendship–hostility. However, *only if dissonance is reduced by means of changing friendship-hostility will a change in issue dimension take place as well,* and this phenomenon occurs only on rare occasions. As Karl Deutsch and Richard Merritt observe, individuals "distort many of their perceptions and deny much of reality, in order to call their prejudiced souls their own."[39] Actors commonly alter agreement–disagreement and/or positive–negative acts, just as the Soviet and American governments manipulated their proposals, so that they were incompatible during the years of the Cold War. A second way to reduce dissonance involves the provision of ad hoc explanations, in order to "explain it away." Adversaries might explain one another's positive acts or agreement as the result of the opponent's "frustration," "weakness," or even as treachery.[40] Or, friends might interpret negative acts or disagreement as the temporary consequences of misunderstanding or misperception. Finally, the dissonance may be overcome by regarding incompatible proposals or actions as minor or insignificant.

To bring about change in perceptions of friendship–hostility, which is the overarching dimension of the relationship of actors, dissonance must persist over time and lead to efforts at reality testing. Dissonance is likely to persist if its magnitude is great; that is, if the difference between the level of agreement–disagreement and the intensity of positive–negative acts is in marked contrast to profound friendship or hostility.[41] Moreover, as Festinger suggests, "the magnitude of total dissonance will also depend on the importance or value of those relevant elements";[42] that is, the salience of the issues on which it arises and the importance of the choices involved. It was recognition of this need for persistence in cognitive dissonance before a change in basic affect is possible that led Charles Osgood to argue that a *repetition* of unilaterally initiated positive acts would be needed before there would be reciprocity, and before a "graduated reduction in tension" (GRIT) could begin.[43]

Both success/failure and cognitive dissonance are manipulative, but the former is less so because of the constraints of status. In contrast, dissonance can be introduced by skillful diplomats. Among the examples of conscious efforts to inject cognitive dissonance into relations were Nikita Khrushchev's efforts to stimulate a "spirit of Geneva" in 1954–55 and Anwar el-Sadat's dramatic journey to Jerusalem in late 1977. Hitler skillfully manipulated cognitive dissonance among his adversaries between

1933 and 1939, mixing positive and negative acts with expressions of agreement and disagreement. The possibilities inherent in this variable invest it with far-reaching policy implications.

SUCCESS AND FAILURE: THE FRUIT OF COGNITIVE MAPS

The concepts of success and failure are relative to leaders' expectations and changing goals and issue definitions. For this reason, a leader's definition of what constitutes one or the other varies as do his perceptions of what is desirable and acceptable. Efforts to restore cognitive consistency may begin a process that will change the criteria for success and failure, so that what might have been considered a failure at t^1 is deemed to be a success at $t^2 \ldots t^n$. This is because leaders may redefine their motives for having embarked upon a course of action as the results of that action are made known, in order to reduce the internal conflict produced by dissonance.

Success/failure can occur at either the tactical or strategic level. Tactical success involves the achievement of short-term objectives that are perceived as creating conditions favorable to an actor's preferred allocation of values, or producing interim dispositions of specific stakes that are incrementally advantageous steps toward a final resolution of the issue. Success at the tactical level, as in war, informs an actor about the success of overall strategy, but the latter is not attained until an issue is resolved and removed from the agenda in a manner that increases value satisfaction or, minimally, avoids value deprivation. The tactics themselves involve the mixing of agreement–disagreement and positive–negative acts with an eye to their effect upon future friendship–hostility, in order to bring about a change in the issue positions of competitors. However, the mixing of these elements in terms of their frequency and intensity is generally limited by the single strategy of which they are a part, and that strategy is in turn limited by the existing pattern of relations among the actors, whether they are enemies, patron–client, topdog–underdog, or friends. In other words, the overall relationship among actors conditions their strategies which, in turn, determine their range of tactics.

Success, ceteris paribus, provides positive feedback and leads to repetition and reinforcement of existing behavior. As tactics achieve their objectives, actors continue to pursue their selected strategy and, if it proves successful in one issue context, the actor will be prone to employ it again in others that involve the same participants, or that share some characteristics with the one in which it was successful. If one "stands up to the Russians" on one occasion and the consequences are satisfactory, one is prone to do so again; or, if a policy of containment has succeeded in one security issue, it will be employed again in the context of other issues that bear some resemblance to it. This tendency is seen in the facile resort to simple analogies that provide substitutes for analyses of individual contexts. It also encourages the employment of instruments that have proved their worth in past situations, without close enquiry as to their suitability for the present. European generals believed in the employment of massed infantry for frontal attack because of its apparent success in the wars of the late nineteenth and early twentieth centuries, and American admirals retain an affection for the aircraft carrier, owing in part to its decisive role in the Pacific war against Japan.

The experience of failure leads either to rationalization, changing criteria for success, and therefore greater effort—or to policy reconsideration and adjustment. As indicated earlier, failure generates painful dissonance for those who are responsible for it. This failure must be overcome, particularly if it persists. The apparent failure may be redefined as success, as occurred after the Tet offensive in Vietnam of January 1968 when General William Westmoreland "'was quick to conclude that 'the enemy's well laid plans went afoul' '' and "dismissed the enemy's tactics as suicidal, and pressed the suggestion that we were witnessing 'a last desperate push,' a final NVN effort to redress a military balance that had been moving inexorably against Hanoi by reason of the great weight of the U.S. effort."[44] Actually, Tet denied previous assurances that the North Vietnamese and the National Liberation Front (N.L.F.) had lost their capacity to fight major battles, and destroyed the pacification and strategic hamlet programs in a single swift blow.*

Apparent failure may also lead to a change in expressed goals and objectives to justify the continuation or intensification of policy, with the

---

* The extent of collective rationalization on the part of the Johnson Administration at the time was remarkable. "'Taking his cue from Saigon and adding his own brand of hyperbole, the President reported to the nation on February 2 that the Viet Cong's offensive had been 'a complete failure' militarily and psychologically"—Townsend Hoopes, *The Limits of Intervention*, (New York: McKay, 1969), p. 140.

only result being a change in tactics. Tactics that fail to achieve objectives may be discarded even while the strategy of which they are a part is continued, since it is likely to embody an array of other tactics and techniques that have not yet been tried. It is partly for this reason that, even as there are specific instances of apparent failure, strategies based upon force or appeasement, for instance, may be escalated for a considerable time rather than show a change in direction. Only if the strategy brings continued and growing failure in its train will there ensue a change in strategic direction. The costs of continuing as before must appear as excessive, regardless of how the issue is defined, or of what types of stakes are at issue. In all probability, this realization is likely to burst first upon those who were not directly responsible for the ongoing course of action, and who therefore do not need to justify themselves. In the case of Vietnam, the election of Richard Nixon in 1968 brought to office individuals who felt less constrained by previous policy than their predecessors.

What leaders regard as successful depend upon their expectations about the effects of their strategy, since these constitute their criteria. This set of expectations can be defined as a cognitive map of the interaction process.[45] Each map provides for leaders a set of beliefs about human and political behavior in general, and about the nature and purposes of the contending actors.* In light of these beliefs and expectations, a cognitive map informs leaders of what they should do to change the issue positions and/or behavior of other actors. If the leaders of an actor believe that another actor would not purposely harm the members of their group, they are likely to react mildly if some harm is done. Or, if harm is done as a consequence of competition for a stake, but if conflict is rarely characteristic of their relations, the reaction will still be mild, even though purpose is ascribed to the competitor. Reaction will be extreme, however, if the leaders of an actor that is harmed expected the competitor to act in such a fashion, and believe that doing harm is the real objective of the adversary. In other words, expectations function to provide past information for the present, as well as projections for the future. They permit leaders to make sense of new information by providing the essential elements out

* An important approach to determining these beliefs and expectations is known as "operational code" analysis. See Alexander L. George, "The 'Operational Code': A Neglected Approach to the Study of Political Leaders and Decision-Makers," *International Studies Quarterly* (June 1969), 13(2):190–222.

of which categories and patterns can be constructed. Among the most important types of expectations in any evoked set is that of affect toward other actors, which is the residue of past interactions, and which will characterize relations at least at the beginning of new interactions. But, regardless of the nature of expectations, they are likely to change only slowly, since evidence that disconfirms them, whether pleasant or unpleasant, will create dissonance.[46]

Cognitive maps, which include expectations, can be exceedingly complex and can contain a variety of tactics and strategies. As leaders make proposals or direct behavior toward a target, their map can inform them of what to do next, depending upon the target's response. Although maps can vary considerably in terms of sophistication, knowledge of them permits an observer (like a chess player) to predict the behavior of actors with greater accuracy than would random guessing. Historians, traditional social scientists, and intelligence operatives have sought to tease out such knowledge and to make predictions on the basis of substantive information about actors. Other social scientists have sought to improve predictions by identifying the structural patterns and resulting logic of cognitive maps, one of which is the upward and downward spirals of cooperation/conflict that is commonly focused upon in studies of arms races, conflict resolution, and crises.[47]

Operationally, success exists if an actor is satisfied with an outcome, while failure is felt if an actor remains dissatisfied. Success can be achieved in either of two ways—through agreement with other participants concerning the disposition of stakes in a voluntary manner and the exchange of positive acts, or through defeat of an adversary by means of superior influence. All things being equal, it is difficult to predict which mode an actor will select. Success through agreement and positive acts promises a minimum of resource expenditure and minimum cost, but success through superior influence promises to limit the sharing of payoffs. Nevertheless, the choice is a significant one. Only in the event of agreement-positive acts can *all participants* succeed (mutual success), since that is the only situation in which all can be satisfied with a decision or outcome.

The voluntaristic nature of the agreement promotes a search for consistency that requires justification of the agreement. This permits the growth of positive attitudes that promote honest communication and mutual trust.

It also encourages further resort to persuasion of the sort that enabled agreement to occur in the first place. If such interaction becomes habitual, it may encourage division of labor among participants that can lead to the creation of new stakes and positive-sum games. This, in turn, promotes the growth of perceptions of similarity, since actors will focus on attributes they have in common, rather than those which separate them. Success through agreement implies what Sawyer and Guetzkow have described as a "process of devising more favorable alternatives and outcomes," a process of " 'creative problem-solving' since it involves innovation rather than mere selection among given possibilities."[48]

In contrast, when a decision is reached through imposition, those that are forced to accept the outcome will regard themselves as having failed, because they are compelled against their will, and such pressure is regarded as an inherently undesirable limitation upon autonomy. It entails the limiting of at least one actor's alternatives. The decision itself will not cause dissonance for weaker participants, since they are not responsible for it; though dissonance will arise if previous relations were based on voluntarism and cooperation. The fact of their capitulation does not mean that weaker participants will cease seeking to reverse it, so that feigned cooperation and resentment will ensue. No stable solution will exist. Morton Deutsch expresses this tendency in the form of the following proposition:*

Conflict that is resolved by a more powerful tendency suppressing or repressing a weaker one, without the extinction of the weaker tendency's underlying motives, leads to the return of the repressed tendency in disguised form whenever the vigilance or defenses of the more powerful tendency are lowered.[49]

It is reasonable to assume, moreover, that the use of coercion and rewards, as opposed to forms of legitimate influence such as expertise, will exaggerate a sense of failure, because legitimate forms of influence are based upon forms of persuasion and produce little alienation.

Mutual or joint failure can be said to occur when no participant is able

---

*The research of Raoul and Freda Naroll in international relations also supports this hypothesis. Studying cases of deterrence from the period of the Greek city-states to the twentieth century, they find that threats of punishment usually led to continuing deterioration of relations among adversaries—Raoul Naroll, "Deterrence in History," in Dean Pruitt and Richard Snyder, eds., *Theory and Research on the Causes of War* (Englewood Cliffs, N.J.: Prentice-Hall, 1969), pp. 150–64.

to achieve value satisfaction—a situation in which the costs of all exceed their gains collectively and individually. Such "negative-sum" games are characterized by persistent efforts on the part of actors to reduce their losses relative to others, as in wars of attrition, trade wars, and tit-for-tat escalatory spirals. In general, mutual failure occurs in the absence of agreement-positive acts and the presence of power parity (as opposed to preponderance) among participants. The former condition precludes mu-

Table 7.1 The Consequences of Success-Failure and Issue Dimension

	Negative Actor Dimension	Positive Actor or Stake Dimension
Mutual success	Cognitive dissonance	Cognitive consistency: escalate agreement, positive acts
Mixed success	Victor: no change Loser: escalate disagree-ment, negative acts, cognitive consistency	Victor: No change Loser: Cognitive dissonance
Mutual failure	Cognitive consistency: escalate disagreement, negative acts	Cognitive dissonance

tual satisfaction, while the latter condition precludes the victory of any single actor.

Success/failure is a critical variable, as it combines with issue dimension to produce either cognitive consistency or dissonance, as depicted in table 7.1. Actors that are initially related on a negative actor dimension will experience dissonance if they attain mutual success (the result of agreement), since such agreement will contradict the expectations that they have formed as a result of hostility. The various agreements that have been reached, for example, by the United States and the Soviet Union—whether SALT, trade, or Helsinki—have produced such mutual dissonance, as they sharply contradict the expectations bred by the Cold War. If, however, actors are initially related on a positive actor or stake dimension, mutual success will lead to cognitive consistency, though it may produce an intensification of cooperation. In this situation, mutual success encourages the continuation or escalation of the level of positive acts and friendship, which, if unabated, may even produce integration of political communities and actor coalescence. The interim disposition of stakes that results from agreement may provide effective positive feedback for an already cooperative strategic pattern. Such outcomes lead to growing acceptance of the logical consequences of stake dimensions and positive actor dimensions—division of the spoils through bargains and issue encapsulation, with the avoidance of symbolic or transcendent stakes.

Mutual failure, the product of disagreement and equal status, will assure cognitive consistency among actors which are initially related on a negative actor dimension. Disagreement is expected, so that dissonance will not occur. The frustration of stalemate, however, may produce amplifying or destructive feedback that will escalate negative acts and hostility in a dangerous upward spiral of conflict. The logical outcome of such a spiral is total war, with each actor seeking to eliminate the putative cause of its frustration. This outcome can be avoided by the intervention of imaginative statesmen, or third parties, who can point out its consequences and, as the issues upon which the actors are divided fester, manipulate cognitive dissonance between them. Dissonance will, of course, be produced quickly if mutual failure occurs in the case of actors that are initially related on a stake dimension or positive actor dimension. Such failure would be incongruent with existing expectations and would likely produce shock, anger, and resentment, such as that which was produced in the series of American-Soviet disagreements and misunderstandings that led to the Cold War or the series of Sino-Soviet conflicts that produced the schism between the communist parties of the Soviet Union and of China.*

Mixed success, which is the consequence of the imposition of superior influence by one of the contenders, produces little dissonance in the "winner," except that which leads to rationalizing the use of power against a "friend." If, however, the contenders are initially related on a

* Such dissonance can, of course, give rise to rationalizations and evasions that permit the retention of initial attitudes. This is, however, less possible if dissonance is mutual than if it characterizes only one actor. Furthermore, shifts from positive to negative attitudes occur more easily than the reverse process. See Morton Deutsch, "Trust and Suspicion," *Journal of Conflict Resolution* (December 1958), 2(4):265–79 and "The Effect of Motivational Orientation Upon Trust and Suspicion," *Human Relations* (1960), 13:123–39.

negative actor dimension, the "loser" will probably escalate its negative acts and hostility. This may assume the form of efforts to accumulate resources in order to achieve influence parity with the adversary (as was the case with the USSR during much of the early Cold War), or it may take the form of opposing the "winner" for some other stake(s), or on some other issue(s), in the hope of gaining revenge. Finally, if the contenders are initially related on a positive actor or stake dimension, the loser is likely to experience dissonance as its "friend" violates expectations of sympathetic treatment and justice. The sense of "betrayal" may prove difficult to contain and, unless aborted or reversed, may spread to relations involving other issues.

Cognitive consistency, then, tends to produce changes in the *level* of cooperation or conflict, whereas cognitive dissonance provides an opportunity for changes to take place in the *direction* of cooperation/conflict; that is, the issue dimension. It must be emphasized that the presence of cognitive dissonance does not assure a change in the direction of cooperation/conflict, as dissonance can be dealt with in several ways that eliminate the need for such change. Such change is most likely to occur so that existing cooperation/conflict spirals are halted, or reversed, when: dissonance persists and recurs; the issue is highly salient to the actors; and the incompatibility between existing affect and subsequent behavior is profound and striking. Dissonance merely acts as a precondition for change in the issue dimension.

Since cognitive dissonance is manipulatable, bold leaders may put an end to friendly relations, or seek to prevent conflict spirals from leading to mutual catastrophe, by manipulating dissonance through positive proposals and acts. Neville Chamberlain's policy of appeasement was designed to produce such dissonance in Hitler and thereby foster more friendly relations. It failed because Hitler remained untouched by it and continued to enjoy numerous successes in the late 1930s. The manipulation of cognitive dissonance by Khrushchev and Kennedy during and after the Cuban missile crisis was considerably more rewarding and was continued by their successors. Such a shift is not self-sustaining, and the termination of one spiral does not assure the onset of one of a different sort. It will be subject to misperception particularly in those instances where only one participant is subject to dissonance, where the participants are subject to differing degrees of dissonance, or where a shift would endanger the cohesion of an actor's membership. This last concern has been of particular importance to leaders of the Soviet Communist Party over the years. They have been fearful lest the improvement of relations with the West be permitted to go so far as to dissipate the siege mentality that was instilled among Russians after 1917 and which serves to justify the Party's continuing iron-fisted rule. This was particularly evident in the years immediately following World War II, when Stalin and Zhdanov reemphasized the themes of capitalist encirclement and international class conflict and declared that the Soviet Union was once more endangered by external attack. The continuation of a siege mentality was apparently seen as a necessary justification for continuing the "dictatorship of the proletariat," which, if undermined, would inevitably weaken its "vanguard" and leaders.

Nevertheless, shifts in the overall relations of actors are possible, and history may interpret the ending of the Cold War as the successful conversion, by Henry Kissinger and Nixon on one side and Leonid Brezhnev on the other, of a situation of persistent mutual failure (punctuated by occasional tactical successes) and dissonance (that had attenuated the negative actor dimension) into a relationship that is increasingly governed by a stake dimension (also interrupted by events like the repression of Soviet dissidents). In the process, a number of stakes in the Cold War (such as Berlin and arms control) were encapsulated into different issues that permitted interim dispositions; the issue-position calculus of the two sides gradually switched from one of negative affect to one of interdependence; and symbolic and transcendent stakes were ritualized and reduced in salience or were converted into concrete stakes. The mutual success enjoyed by the two governments as a result of agreements that produced several interim dispositions of stakes led to growing cooperation in a range of issues and a movement along a stake dimension, a process facilitated by the emergence and recognition of third-party threats to a satisfying status quo.

Whether or not the process of détente or any other shift away from a negative actor dimension proves long term rather than transient depends ultimately upon the growth of trust among the competitors. This is of particular significance since the conditions and leaders that initially permitted mutual success are likely to change more quickly than the underlying attitudes of the collectivities as a whole. The leaders who take chances by concluding agreements with adversaries will tend (according to consistency theories) to seek to justify their decisions and perpetuate their policies; but once they fade from the scene, the process may be aborted, because new leaders will have less stake in, and commitment to, the earlier decisions—unless in the meantime, broader currents of trust have developed. Thus, the Truman and Carter Administrations did not have the same commitment to improving relations with the Soviet Union as did their predecessors and did not feel bound to the decisions which had been made by Roosevelt and Nixon.

Whether trust will develop depends upon a number of factors concerning the issues that arise and the nature of interaction that characterizes them. One factor is the perceived motivation of the other actor. If the latter is seen as having a powerful interest in reaching agreement, trust is facilitated. In the case of the nuclear nonproliferation treaty (NPT), for example, both American and Soviet negotiators saw each other as strongly motivated, because the further development of nuclear weapons by third parties would further undermine their individual and joint influence in world affairs. Such perceptions of strong motivation are strengthened to the extent that each side individually is able to thwart the other but not to obtain the desired benefits by itself. Neither the Soviet nor American governments can prevent the other from providing nuclear information or weapons to third parties, so that neither can retain its privileged position without the other's help. In this case, both are enmeshed in a form of situational interdependence. Trust is additionaly fostered if each side is seeking further benefits on other issues—benefits that are directly controlled by the other side—and is made aware that they are contingent upon agreement about the issue before them. For instance, American anticipation of a new market for exports (the USSR) and the possibility of reductions in military expenditures, and Soviet anticipation of technological and agricultural imports and reductions in military expenditures, provided considerable incentives for reaching arms control agreements in the 1960s. Incentives are even greater if anticipated benefits are equal and available directly from the competitor because (a) the comparative value of the benefits can be easily measured and (b) their provisions do not require trusting third parties.*

The above factors speak to the prospect of trust in single interactions,

---

*This last proposition suggests that trust will be easier if each actor can say to the other, "I will give you X if you will give me Y," than if each can say only, "I will have my friend give you X if you will have your friend give me Y."

rather than to the long-term process of institutionalizing it. In such individual instances, arrangements can be made to "insure" the good faith of participants. These include assuring that the exchange of benefits will be simultaneous, as is commonly the case in American-Soviet exchanges of nationals. Confidence is further instilled by the presence of trusted third parties, which can handle the exchange or act as surrogate hostages. Many of the activities of the Secretary General of the UN and his staff have been of the first sort, while third-party diplomats have resorted to the second procedure in dealing with terrorists (e.g., accompanying them on airplanes out of the country in which an act of terrorism was staged). Finally, the situation may be structured so that penalties automatically ensue in the case of defection or cheating,* as in the exchange of collateral, hostages, or other commitments.[50]

From the perspective of the relationship over time, trust will grow with each succeeding experience of agreement and mutual success. Each individual agreement requires some measure of trust, and each decision to agree commits those who are responsible for it to justifying that decision. As such decisions and subsequent justifications accumulate, the overall commitment to a trusting relationship grows too. The quest for cognitive consistency produces an ever greater commitment on the part of each actor to continue a relationship in which it has invested a great deal. As agreement and the exchange of positive acts continue, a sense of friendship may grow because of an assumption that benefits flow from friendly attitudes. And, once these basic attitudes begin to shift, the background factors of prior pattern of interaction and similarity will contribute to anchoring the relationship. The ongoing cooperation will constitute a positive prior pattern, and successive agreements encourage a mutual focus upon those common attributes of the actors that are sought as explanations for the agreement (e.g., "anticommunism," "economic development," and so forth). Ultimately, the intensity of the positive affect of each actor will be determined by the following factors identified by Morton Deutsch:

a. the strength of the benefit he has received;
b. the frequency of his prior experiences of having been benefited by the other person and the diversity of the settings in which the benefits have occurred;

---

*This arrangement is facilitated once cheating can be clearly verified.

c. the degree of confidence he has that the other person was able to avoid producing the actions that resulted in the benefit—i.e., the knowledge that he was not required or forced to produce these actions;

d. the degree of confidence he has that the other person was aware, before he produced the beneficial action, that it would have a beneficial consequence;

e. the amount of power that the other person has relative to his own, such that the other person had nothing to gain by doing it;

f. the smallness of the gain that others (including the benefit producer) are perceived to have as a result of the beneficial actions in comparison to the gains that the individual himself experiences;

g. the cost that the benefit producer is perceived to have incurred in producing the benefit.[51]

In the aggregate, these factors provide each actor with an explanation for one another's motivation and intentions.

THE MANIPULATION OF DISSONANCE

The above analysis suggests that major changes in the direction and/or intensity of relationships among actors can be brought about by conscious efforts of leaders to manipulate the cognitions of one another. From the close personal ties of eighteenth-century European diplomats and monarchs to the summitry of the present day, individual leaders have sought out such opportunities and used them to engineer shifts in relations that could not easily have been predicted. Often the effects of such manipulation have been transient, failing to outlive the leaders who initiated them, as in the case of Franklin Roosevelt and Stalin, or Napoleon and Tsar Alexander I. In other cases, the effects have been more profound, becoming anchored, accepted, and institutionalized. At this point, it is necessary to address briefly three questions concerning the manipulation of dissonance: *when* can it occur, *who* can initiate it, and *how* can it be carried out. Unfortunately, much of the theory concerning these matters is frankly speculative, especially that associated with personality variables. For that reason, what follows in the final section of this chapter should be treated with care, and should not be considered as central, or even necessary, to the theory that has been presented to this point.

Another way of posing the question of when manipulation of dissonance can occur is to ask under what conditions will it be possible for a leader who is inclined to do so to have a sufficient impact on the formulation and implementation of an actor's policy to outweigh elements like the standard operating procedures of bureaucracy that tend toward inertia. James Rosenau suggests that individual variables, which "include all those aspects of a decision-maker—his values, talents, and prior experiences—that distinguish his foreign policy choices or behavior from those of every other decision-maker,"[52] are likely to be most potent in actors that are small and less developed and in which accountability is low.[53]

Although this suggestion provides guidance as to what type of actor may produce leaders that are relatively free from social and role constraints, it does not indicate the conditions under which such individuals are likely to exhibit idiosyncratic behavior, or when such behavior may be expected from leaders of other types of actors. A more precise stipulation comes from scholars interested in crisis decision making, who contend that social and role constraints will weaken under conditions of time pressure, high threat, and surprise.[54] Such conditions require rapid responses by top officials, who become involved, owing to the high degree of perceived threat, without the benefit of ready plans or large amounts of sifted information. The need for speed reduces the input of the bureaucratic establishments and the society at large; the need for consensus provides greater leeway to leaders to be innovative; and the paucity of information forces leaders to fall back upon their own memories, prejudices, and inclinations in making sense of what is taking place. Something of this last phenomenon, for example, was evident in the response of President Truman and his advisers to North Korea's invasion of South Korea in 1950, when "their minds flew to an axiom—that any armed aggression anywhere constituted a threat to all nations everywhere"—an axiom that was peculiar to those of a specific generation.[55] In this manner "relevant" information is provided by leaders themselves, who then proceed to process it and act upon it.

Even under noncrisis conditions, top political leaders are less constrained by role and other factors than lower level officials.[56] Margaret Hermann summarizes existing research on the conditions in which leaders' "personality characteristics (their views of the world, their motivations, their ways of dealing with other people)" are likely "to influence the decisions which are made."[57] In addition to the impact of crises, Margaret Hermann teases a number of other hypotheses about this question from the literature. One of these is that the impact of leaders' personality characteristics is partly a function of their interest in foreign affairs. A second is that individual characteristics are likely to have a greater impact where leadership has been assumed in dramatic fashion. In such cases (e.g., revolutions, formation of a new actor), role definitions are not fully formed or institutionalized, so that, as sociologist Edward Shils declares, "No framework of action (has been) set for the newcomer by the expectations of those already on the scene."[58] Until role definitions have matured and become anchored, the leader is less likely to profess that "I must do this for my country even though it is against my principles."[59] In this way, both George Washington and Lenin were able to convert their own beliefs into the bases of the roles of President of the United States and First Secretary of the Communist Party of the Soviet Union. This has been the case, too, with many of the charismatic leaders of the host of newly independent governments that emerged in the Third World after World War II (e.g., Nehru, Sukarno, Nkrumah, Mao, Nyerere). Among the other conditions that Hermann identifies are the presence of "charismatic" leaders to whom deference is paid, the presence of leaders to whom considerable authority has been delegated, an absence of differentiation in foreign-policy organization (a condition commonly associated with new or underdeveloped actors), and the presence of an ambiguous external situation (a situation that has not been experienced before, a complex situation, and a situation in which cues are contradictory).[60]

If top leaders occasionally have the opportunity to shape and alter the relations of actions, such is rarely the case for ordinary diplomats, or bureaucratic officials, who are ensnared in a web of role constraints and career obligations. Indeed, this is increasingly the case in contemporary political life, owing to advances in communication and transportation that make it possible for diplomats to remain in constant touch with their superiors. With few exceptions, their decision latitude is severely cramped. Additionally, they are recruited and selected in such a way as to ensure their loyalty to role obligations. "These professionals," as Otomar Bartos reports, "follow their own codes of behavior and nothing we could offer or suggest would change them."[61]

The observation that only leaders are in a position to manipulate dissonance begins to answer the second question that was posed earlier. However, it does not shed any light on what type of leader will have the imagination, self-confidence, and will to initiate the sorts of unexpected actions that might stimulate dissonance on the part of others. Some clues are provided in the social psychology literature.[62] Although little work has been done that is directly relevant to the question, several personality variables are worth exploring: anxiety, dominance, cognitive complexity, tendency toward conciliation, dogmatism, risk-avoidance, self-esteem, and suspiciousness.

Research suggests that anxious individuals tend to be cautious, so that one would expect their choices to be governed by a "maximin" strategy of expecting the worst from competitors.[63] Consequently, it can be hypothesized that the more anxious a leader, the less likely he is to seek to manipulate cognitive dissonance by initiating unexpected behavior. Instead, such leaders will pursue courses of action that are "tried and true," even though their potential rewards are limited.

The second variable, dominance, is apparently related to an individual's propensity to cooperate: the more authoritarian, the less the tendency to cooperate.[64] This leads to the hypothesis that dominance will reduce the propensity to initiate manipulative behavior in conflictful contexts but will stimulate such behavior in cooperative ones. The second part of the hypothesis assumes that a highly dominant leader, such as Stalin, will seek to impose his ideas and proposals unilaterally upon others, including "friends" and would be concerned with proving his "forcefulness."[65]

Cognitive complexity, in contrast to dominance, is seen as positively correlated with a propensity to seek cooperative solutions.[66] Since complex individuals appear to search actively to identify cooperative possibilities, this leads to a hypothesis precisely opposite to that which dealt with dominance.[67] In seeking such possibilities, cognitively complex leaders are likely to make reasonable concessions to adversaries that would facilitate agreement, or to initiate positive acts that would influence an adversary's negative affect (even if by chance rather than calculation). Tendency toward conciliation is related to propensity to seek cooperative solutions in much the same way as is cognitive complexity (though the logic is perhaps more obvious and straightforward).[68] Leaders with a conciliatory bent "urge admitting their own wrongs, and refuse to use threats or belligerent means,"[69] and their tendency to be trusting permits them to initiate boldly cooperative actions, even with adversaries.

The fifth variable, dogmatism, has been found, contrary to common belief, to be positively related to cooperative orientation. One reason that is offered for this result is that such individuals seek approval and support from others.[70] However, this notwithstanding, their tendency to resist change suggests that they are unlikely to initiate a series of unexpected acts that would provoke cognitive dissonance on the part of others. Indeed, the very notion of dogmatism is contrary to traits like imaginativeness and flexibility, which characterize efforts to manipulate dissonance. Interestingly, propensity to avoid risks, like dogmatism, has been found to be related to cooperation.[71] Conflict normally entails greater risks than does cooperation, at least in the short run; and often requires seizing the initiative, a characteristic alien to those who are unwilling to take risks. However, such individuals are unlikely to initiate cooperative behavior unless there is some certainty that they will be treated in similar fashion, so that they may adopt "maximin" type strategies on the basis of "worst case analyses" unless their competitors give them reason to be trusting. Some such reasoning is suggested by Hermann's and Kogan's research on the behavior of dyads in a multitrial prisoner's dilemma game: "Dyads with a high fear of risk showed the lowest rate of initial cooperation, . . . but their rates increased rapidly thereafter."[72] Nevertheless, this does not imply a willingness to initiate novel behavior. Indeed, the greater a leader's propensity to avoid risks, the less likely he is to initiate dissonance-provoking behavior.

In contrast, individuals with high self-esteem, and therefore confidence in themselves, are—it is hypothesized—prepared to act in the sort of dramatic fashion that could encourage dissonance on the part of others. Like Henry Kissinger, they are prepared to take the lead despite the disapproval of peers or the apparent lack of orthodoxy of their ideas. This in no way means that their initiatives will be cooperative. Indeed, the existing literature suggests the opposite.[73] They are quite as liable to seek to manipulate the cognitions of competitors in friendly as in unfriendly contexts; they are as willing to antagonize as to conciliate if such behavior appears to them to be advantageous.

Finally, suspiciousness appears to preclude manipulative initiatives aimed at transforming a conflictive into a cooperative situation, though not the reverse. Leaders who are suspicious will tend to be uncooperative at the outset of an interaction, and to avoid taking the first step toward reducing conflict. Like Stalin, the suspicious leader finds it difficult to take risks that require trust, or to initiate policies that promise large mutual payoffs, when some alternative exists that assures him of a lesser but acceptable and certain payoff. In Stalin's case, virtually all foreign-policy initiatives were the product of a lifetime of suspicion, which was reflected in repeated demands for "vigilance," both within and without the Soviet Union, and by his recurrent purges of foreign and Soviet Communists. That Stalin did not initiate high-level provocations indicates that he was probably prone to avoid risks as well.

The foregoing hypotheses concerning the relationship of individual personality traits to propensity to manipulate cognitive dissonance are summarized in Table 7.2. It suggests that political leaders who are both cog-

Table 7.2 Propensity to Manipulate Cognitive Dissonance

	Conflict-to-Cooperation	Cooperation-to-Conflict
Anxiety	no	no
Dominance	no	yes
Cognitive complexity	yes	no
Dogmatism	no	no
Risk-avoidance	no	no
Self-esteem	yes	yes
Suspiciousness	no	yes

nitively complex and high in self-esteem—but who are low in anxiety, dominance, dogmatism, risk-avoidance, and suspiciousness—will be most likely to initiate the bold and unexpected actions that could terminate a stochastic conflict. In contrast, leaders who are dominant, suspicious, and high in self-esteem are prepared to initiate "illegitimate" behavior that can destroy existing cooperative bonds. Hitler appears to have been such a leader. Neither cautious nor conservative, he had the self-confidence and bitterness to make outrageous proposals and to behave in such a provocative manner that, despite the judgment of his own generals, he alienated Germany from much of the rest of Europe and severed the fragile bonds of cooperation that had begun to replace the antagonisms of 1919.

As to how dissonance can be manipulated, it may be recalled that dissonance can be stimulated by the occurrence of either cooperative or conflictive phenomena when the opposite is anticipated. For example, if in bargaining, one of two friends initiates the process with a "take it or leave it" proposal or an ultimatum, this is likely to shock the other, who had anticipated a constructive process, during which a variety of proposals could be offered from which one that promised mutual benefits would be chosen. Similarly, the willingness of an enemy to agree to a proposal that was not even seriously intended to induce such agreement may produce ripples of dissonance on the part of the first actor.

Turning from tactics to strategy, the best-known suggestion for creating dissonance in a conflictive environment is Charles Osgood's policy of "graduated reciprocation in tension reduction."[74] Osgood's strategy has four components: initiation of unilateral positive acts (though not so as to endanger oneself), increase in the frequency and magnitude of such acts in accordance with the adversary's response, shaping of initiatives so as to invite reciprocation, and continuation of such initiatives for a lengthy period of time so as to give the adversary time to comprehend their intent. According to Hamner and Yukl:

> Osgood implies that his soft-strategy proposal is valid when (1) the two parties have equal power, (2) the parties are stalemated or moving away from a range of acceptable solutions, . . . and (3) the two parties are facing mutually applied high pressure to reach agreement. . . . Osgood's reasoning is that a bargainer will fail to make concessions because he distrusts his opponents. A person who makes unilateral concessions will thereby remove the main obstacle to his opponent's concession-making.[75]

To undertake such a strategy, however, the initiator must be motivated by a desire to reach agreement, rather than either to cause the adversary to lose or to "maximize his personal total profit."[76]

Some experimental evidence tends to confirm the validity of Osgood's assumptions concerning the prospects for achieving agreement using his strategy. Although average payoffs are not as high as would be the case using a "hard" bargaining strategy, the prospects for agreement are improved.[77] Simulation experiments have also provided some support for Osgood's hypotheses, as in the work of Pilisuk and Skolnick on arms races.[78] It has been suggested, moreover, that Osgood's hypotheses were partly supported by a sequence of events that took place between June and November 1963, which began with President Kennedy's American University speech in which he announced a unilateral cessation of atmospheric testing of nuclear weapons. A series of reciprocal concessions ensued, but the process was aborted after the assassination of Kennedy.[79]

Unlike the effort to escape from a hostile environment by producing dissonance, conscious efforts to terminate a friendly situation are difficult to imagine except for tactical purposes. An actor may, of course, choose to employ a harsh bargaining strategy in a friendly context in order to produce maximum benefits for itself, avoid being taken advantage of, or generally focus attention on another problem which is being ignored; and there is experimental evidence that such a strategy—high demands, few and small concessions, and an unyielding posture—will yield higher payoffs if agreement is reached.[80] Nevertheless, the probability of stalemate is increased, and such a strategy will be perceived as conflictive. If it is used frequently in a friendly context, it may lead to a general deterioration of relations, a development that was neither sought nor desired. Indeed, much of the experimental literature on bargaining and negotiating is flawed by lack of attention to the initial context in which interaction takes place, so that conclusions and recommendations have an overly general, ceteris paribus flavor. This leads to the notion that some combination or mix of toughness and conciliation constitutes the best "normal" strategy for any actor in terms of maximizing payoffs and agreement.[81] However, before the strategic role of cognitive dissonance can be fully understood, it is necessary to understand how interactions actually produce allocations of values, the topic of the next chapter.

*To be sure, the idea of theoretical unpredictability can be
cited to discourage further work in explanatory theory of
negotiation. But the notion of theoretical inadequacy
leads one to suspect that current theory is not sufficiently
developed to leave us with theoretical unpredictability as
the last word!*
—*I. William Zartman* [1]

CHAPTER EIGHT

THE COHERENCE OF CONTENTION

THE MODEL presented in the previous chapter provides a general framework with which to understand the elements of interaction and how
they shape the properties of cooperation/conflict. But interaction tends to
be patterned and purposeful, so that it is necessary to investigate how the
goals of these interactions—decision making and subsequent value allocation—are achieved. The purpose of this chapter is to clarify that process and, in doing so, to demonstrate the coherence of contention in
global politics. To this end, the chapter will delineate a new conceptual
framework for comprehending how interactions are transformed into authoritative allocations.

The first section of the chapter defines and explores the concept of
"allocation mechanism" and the logic that lies behind each of them.
Thereafter, the concepts of "interaction and rule-making games" will be
defined and compared, and then employed to illustrate how interaction is
organized in a political arena that lacks formal government. The third
section of the chapter affords a theoretical explanation of the factors that
determine which allocation mechanisms and decision games will be used
for an issue and the variables that lead actors to alter these mechanisms
and games. Finally, one interaction game—war—will be explored in
greater detail to show how the kinds of behavior outlined in the previous

chapter are related to allocation mechanisms and interaction games. In the process, the conditions under which conflict will produce war shall be specified.

FROM ANARCHY TO SOCIETY: ALLOCATION MECHANISMS AND RULES

The previous chapter treated interactions (agreement–disagreement, positive-negative acts, friendship–hostility) as if their meaning and consequences were always the same, regardless of circumstances. This, of course, is not the case. As actors grope toward reaching joint decisions and disposing of the stakes at issue, it is necessary for them to settle upon either tacit or explicit rules for interacting. Such rules are not normative constructs (though such constructs may be accepted as the rules), but are, instead, procedures that are understood by contestants and that eliminate randomness from interaction and provide criteria for determining winning and losing. Only when such criteria exist can decisions be reached. The patterns of interaction that form on the basis of these rules and criteria constitute "decision games" in the absence of which global politics would indeed be random and anarchic.

Boxing is a sport which illustrates what is meant by decision rules and criteria for winning and losing. The contestants are explicitly informed of behavior that is permitted or forbidden in the contest. Kicking is, for example, precluded. However, one or the other boxer may in fact use his feet illegally, in which case (disqualification aside) he may be said to have either changed the rules of the game or to have embarked upon another game not called boxing. Additionally, the sport has criteria to determine winning and losing—number of knockdowns in a single round, failure to answer the bell within a specific time, amount of damage sustained, etc. In the absence of such criteria, physical elimination of the opponent would be the only criterion of decision; the game becomes a true fight. Similarly, in global politics, when there is no agreement about or understanding of decision rules, actors only have recourse to an "elimination game." Obviously, these do occur but are comparatively rare. The rules may permit or even encourage the shedding of blood, yet global politics is generally not characterized by struggles to the death (though, as shall be seen, an actor-destruction strategy may be consciously selected).

In order that anarchy not reign, it is necessary for actors to select, through agreement, coercion, or some mix of the two, a set of rules for making decisions and for implementing them. These rules, no matter how informal or tacit, provide contestants with criteria for solving problems of choice *if allocation were to occur*. Hence, they may be called *allocation mechanisms*. Allocation mechanisms are procedures that are widely regarded as suitable for the apportionment of stakes.* Each general mechanism is characterized by a number of specific techniques that reflect the rules associated with the procedure. These criteria evolve for particular sets of issues by means of discrete and special interaction sequences that produce or identify formal and informal norms on which to base allocations. These include "victory" in the case of war, "capacity to endure pain" in the case of coercive diplomacy, "majoritarianism" in the case of certain voting arrangements, or "equity" in the case of certain principles, but the specific definition of such norms will vary from place to place and era to era.

There are four major allocation mechanisms: (1) force, (2) bargains, (3) votes, and (4) principle.† *Force* is used to dispose of stakes and resolve issues on the basis of superior strength. It may involve the simple seizure of stakes or efforts to apply pressures sufficient to compel other actors to change their issue positions, either to avoid a deteriorating situation or to attain a promised improvement in that situation. In force, the relative strength of the participants is the sole criterion of decision. Though potentially dangerous and costly, force tends to limit the need for coordinated behavior and may facilitate the rapid resolution of issues,

---

* The notion of allocation mechanism is similar to what Oran R. Young calls a "social choice mechanism." See Young, "Anarchy and Social Choice: Reflections on the International Polity," *World Politics* (January 1978), 30(2):246.

† Young identifies three "social choice mechanisms"—bargaining, coercive diplomacy, and organized warfare (p. 250), which he evaluates according to criteria of decisiveness, efficiency, justice, and generation of externalities (p. 249). Warfare and coercive diplomacy, by his definitions, are variants of what is described here as "force," though his notion of coercive diplomacy shades into what is referred to in the text as "bargains." He explicitly denies the significance of principle and votes for global politics and overemphasizes the centrality of coercion.

particularly if it entails the actual elimination of participants or destruction of their means to resist. Among the techniques that employ force are: wars (total and limited, nuclear and conventional), devices that threaten war (like deterrence, balance of power, collective security, and collective defense), coercive diplomacy, revolution, coups, hijackings, and kidnappings. What is unique about the techniques of violence is that they can be applied *unilaterally* and, if continued, will encourage others to respond in kind. In other words, force, more than other allocation mechanisms, is unilateral in application, so that individual actors can always turn to its use. In this sense it is a lowest-common-denominator mechanism.

Bargains, though they may shade into force, aim to dispose of stakes by means of some sort of trade or exchange among contending actors. Some mutually understood "market mechanism" is at work. For this reason, although the decision rule in bargains is in part based on strength, it also incorporates some "trading" norm which serves to encourage reciprocity. For this reason "utility models" may be used to analyze bargains. The addition of a norm to the interaction reduces the total amount of resources that actors must expend in order to dispose of stakes, and limits the centrality of strength in the process; but at the same time, it increases the need for individual actors to gain the collaboration of others. It also reduces the possibility of achieving quick solutions, owing to the need to search for mutually acceptable exchanges among contestants. Various forms of negotiation, hostage exchanges, economic sanctions, bribery, and logrolling techniques entail explicit bargains. However, many of the techniques of force may be infused with bargains if they involve implicit trades. This area of overlap is what Thomas Schelling describes when he writes:

The usual distinction between diplomacy and force is not merely in the instruments, words or bullets, but in the relation between adversaries—in the interplay of motives and the role of communication, understandings, compromise, and restraint. . . . In diplomacy each party somewhat controls what the other wants, and *can get more by compromise, exchange, or collaboration* than by taking things in his own hands and ignoring the other's wishes.[2]

Forceful techniques, then, may be involved in bargaining when it is part of negotiations; that is, "a process in which explicit proposals are put forward ostensibly for the purpose of reaching agreement on an exchange. . . ."[3]

Votes dispose of stakes on the basis of a consent mechanism that specifies which actors have the right to give consent and how much consent is required from the "enfranchised" for a decision to be taken (e.g., veto provisions, two-thirds vote, plurality, majority, and the like). Votes reduce actors' expenditure of resources, augment the role of principle, and reduce the role of strength in determining outcomes, even though strength remains a factor in the disposition. Votes also increase the need for actors to acquire the approval of other participants and to take account of their views, and therefore usually enlarge the audience beyond the size of a bargain. The process may be time consuming if "campaigns" are involved and if a series of separate votes prove necessary to achieve final allocation. Whether voting is more time consuming than bargains depends on a variety of factors, including number of participants, complexity of the issue, and clarity and institutionalization of the procedures entailed. The rule of voting can be seen in the United Nations and other international organizations and regimes, in certain alliances, and in legislative bodies in general.

Finally, *principle* disposes of stakes on the basis of pure consent, derived from some underlying norm that is usually the product of slowly evolving custom or habit. For example, a norm of equality would state that "people should have equal basic rights, that they should begin a contest with equal resources, and that they should divide benefits equally."[4] In contrast, a norm of equity (distributive justice) would claim that benefits should be distributed in proportion to the contribution of each actor to the combined effort.* As with a number of contemporary global economic issues, those who are relatively satisfied are likely to favor equity, whereas those who are relatively deprived are likely to seek the acceptance of an equality norm.

In practice, the operative norm may vary widely, depending on the context in which the allocation mechanism is employed. It may take the form of legal principles (equity), perceptions of legitimacy (Concert of Europe), ethical percepts (utilitarianism), religious beliefs (the Bible in Calvin's Geneva), or ideological doctrine (Marxism-Leninism in a communist utopia). While the specific principle may vary in time and place, it is the product of some notion of justice which makes it the obverse of

---

*This distinction conforms to the Marxian norm of need and the Aristotelian norm of merit.

pure force. Where principle is present, it tends to eliminate the need to expend resources in the traditional power sense, and dispenses with the need for the symbolic equivalent of resources, such as votes. Although resort to principle may entail high costs in terms of decision makers' time and energy, it reduces costs in terms of resource expenditure. In addition, this mechanism inevitably requires joint behavior, since it relies on the existence of an explicit consensus and has no provision for "defeating" those actors who do not agree. However, violation of deeply embedded and widely accepted principles may entail psychological costs for the violator, and may also carry additional penalties if such violation results in the disruption of previously profitable patterns of activity.* Finally, this mechanism seldom encourages rapid solutions, owing to the need to search for the most applicable principle, the necessity of obtaining consensus upon it, and the difficulty in achieving unanimity on how the chosen principle is to apply in specific contexts.†

It is clear from the above that there are several underlying dimensions that hold the four mechanisms together. The first and most important is that, as actors move from force to bargains to votes to principle, power is progressively replaced by some norm as the basis of allocation. Where strength is the key criterion of decision, actors seek to generate influence by manipulating one another's situations. Central to such interactions are resources that are suitable for rewarding or coercing. Where norms constitute the criterion of decision, actors utilize resources that can promote modifications in one another's orientation, and notions of equity, justice, law, and legitimacy are present.‡

---

* Obviously, the assumption that consent has actually been given by all actors is a fiction; this would be possible only if it could be shown that the principle had actually been observed voluntarily by all participants, or that all actors had participated in the establishment of the custom. See Hans Kelson, *Principles of International Law,* 2d ed., revised and edited by Robert W. Tucker (New York: Holt, Rinehart & Winston, 1966), p. 444. In practice, the principle must receive at least the tacit consent of all major participants in an issue, for otherwise their nonobservance of it would constitute a tacit veto.

† Principle may actually provide very rapid solutions if a single norm with an accepted definition is universally held at the outset of interaction. This is, however, rarely the case.

‡ This dimension conforms to Anatol Rapoport's distinction among "fights, games and debates." *Fights, Games, and Debates* (Ann Arbor: University of Michigan Press, 1960). The mechanisms of "force" and "principle" reflect respectively "fights" (by eliminating opponents) and "debates" (by persuading or converting opponents). The mechanisms of "bargains" and "votes" are "gamelike," in the sense that "winning" combines both strength and norms in an effort to outwit and manipulate opponents.

A second dimension is that of unilateral to collective behavior. Some mechanisms permit and even encourage resort to unilateral action and self-help, thereby limiting an individual actor's responsibility to others, and maximizing its flexibility and freedom. Other mechanisms require or encourage joint behavior and collaborative arrangements that reinforce perceptions of interdependence and collective responsibility. A third dimension, though not as clearly a continuous one as the previous two, is that of time. Certain mechanisms are conducive to a rapid disposition of the stakes at issue, whereas others tend to require a slower and more painstaking process before any final allocation of the stakes can be achieved. A final dimension is that of variation in the quantity and quality of resources necessary for the use of each mechanism. The kinds of resources necessary for force are not appropriate for bargains, and games of principle can require unusual resources, like legal reasoning or technological ability.

These underlying dimensions make it clear that certain kinds of behavior are associated with each mechanism. However, the mechanisms, themselves, are pure types that may dominate the interactions of clusters of actors in one or a few issues, but that rarely dominate contention in an unambiguous fashion. Instead, contention usually consists of a mixture of several allocation mechanisms, and to understand behavior it is necessary to appreciate how these pure types are combined. Nevertheless, their presence in the interaction process gives contention a certain coherence and direction, in that it gives behavior a purpose: to reach an agreement to activate one of the allocation mechanisms, thereby making a decision that will resolve an issue or dispose of a stake.

THE SEARCH FOR COHERENCE: INTERACTION AND RULE-MAKING GAMES

When viewed from a long-term perspective, the overall relations of actors are likely to reveal distinctive patterns centered around some mix among allocation mechanisms, based on clusters of specific techniques employed in predictable sequences. Consequently, interaction tends to assume ''gamelike'' qualities with rules and expectations and a high level of tacit communication. These patterns of interaction can be thought of as *interaction games*. On occasion, however, existing patterns of interaction break down as persistent mutual failure reveals the folly of existing rules; as dissenters who are subject to persistent value deprivation refuse to abide by existing rules and defect; or as misunderstanding of the rules arises, so that they are stretched or muddied. Under these conditions, there occurs a search for new rules or an effort to clarify those that exist. Such processes are characterized by *rule-making games.* *

It is through rule-making games that interaction games acquire rules and procedures. Basically, such rule-making games can be either planned and formal or ad hoc. Planned games usually result from a mutual realization among leading actors that prior interaction games promise only continued mutual failure, value deprivation, and frustration. They commonly, though not always, arise after destructive wars have convinced leaders that such interactions are largely futile.† Examples of planned rule-making games, which resulted in the organization of a new interaction game or the revision of an old one, include the Peace of Westphalia (1648), the Congress of Vienna (1814–15), the Versailles Conference (1919), the Yalta and Potsdam Conferences (1945), and the more recent SALT and Helsinki meetings.

Ad hoc rule-making games take place when existing interaction games break down in slow fashion without participants actually realizing it or desiring it, and when defectors persistently violate the rules. Participants must then seek new rules, usually in tacit fashion, by means of probing and testing one another, in other words by trial and error. In this manner they discover what they should expect of one another and are willing to accept. The North Korean invasion of South Korea in 1950, for instance, was one such probe, the result of which was the realization that limited war was possible in a nuclear age, provided that at least one nuclear power was represented by a proxy. The Soviet installation of missiles in Cuba was another such probe, which ended in both sides appreciating the dangers of direct confrontation combined with overt violation of one an-

---

* These interactor patterns have analogues in the relations among members of actors during the processes of coalescence and fragmentation, and the observer may once again distinguish between interaction and rule-making games.

† This is consistent with Singer and Wallace's finding of "a consistently positive correlation between the termination of war and the establishment of new (international) organization"—J. David Singer and Michael Wallace, "Intergovernmental Organization and the Preservation of Peace, 1816–1964: Some Bivariate Relationships," *International Organization* (Summer 1970), 24(3):540.

other's spheres of interest. Ad hoc rule-making games are usually the consequence of defection by individual actors as a result of persistent value deprivation under old rules, or of severe misunderstandings about existing rules. In a sense, it is rule-making from below.*

Owing to the possible mixes of allocation mechanisms and the wide variety of techniques within each, it would be difficult to generate a deductive typology of interaction games. Historians tend to provide names for various games that highlight their unique qualities—"balance of power," "Concert of Europe," "world war," "collective security," "Cold War," and "détente" among others. Once an interaction game has acquired such a name, it can be assumed to have been highly institutionalized, at least for a period of time. However, some games, for example "collective security," prove abortive and are succeeded by an adhoc rule-making game to determine new rules and procedures. The appearance of such games within history reveals that the type of global interactions that can occur will vary considerably, depending on the informal rules that govern them.

In contemporary global politics it is possible to identify a wide variety of interaction games involving different actors and issues. There are a number of détente games which center principally on bargaining, such as SALT and Sino-Japanese economic relations. There are a number of cold wars involving force and bargaining, such as those in the Middle East, South African apartheid, and the Sino-Soviet frontier. There are also conventional wars (internal and external) involving the Horn of Africa, Cambodia-Vietnam, and others, as well as international regulatory regimes that entail bargaining, votes, and principle (e.g., food, pollution, energy, weather, communications, monetary policy, and economic development). Some games even resemble the old balance of power, as on the Indian subcontinent and in Latin America; while others involve unconventional forms of penetration and spheres of influence, as in the case of multinational corporations and Latin America, or the Soviet Communist Party and the international communist community. Finally, there is evidence that some games have become quasi-legislative, with even some of the hierarchical characteristics of government (e.g., the UN General As-

---

* As these examples suggest, specific events may constitute both elements of existing interaction games and ad hoc rule-making games that serve as transitions to new interaction games.

sembly, the European Economic Community, and the Association of Southeast Asian Nations). Additionally, there are ad hoc rule-making games under way, as is the case with many prominent issues that involve both economically developed and Third World actors; and even a few formal rule-making games, such as the Law of the Sea Conference. There is, then, considerable "slack" within contemporary global politics, possibly more than at any time in the past. The choice of games available to an actor as it seeks to dispose of stakes and resolve an issue is not limited as it was in eighteenth-century Europe, or at the height of the Cold War during the early 1950s. Unlike developed sociopolitical systems such as the United States, global society does not have a dominant decision game (government).* Hence, actors contend not only for stakes but over which interaction game (and by implication which allocation mechanisms) shall be employed to reach decisions.

Interaction games are characterized by three key dimensions: institutionalization, hierarchy, and legitimacy. The first of these, institutionalization, describes the extent to which ongoing interactions fulfill existing expectations and are anticipated, in other words, how well the rules are understood. Where institutionalization is high, actors tend to react in expected ways under certain conditions. There are few surprises, uncertainty is minimized, and stability is reinforced. In highly institutionalized games, tacit rules and requirements are sufficiently routinized so that behavior appears to be ritualized. In the eighteenth and nineteenth centuries, for instance, war of a limited sort was regarded virtually as a standard operating procedure to be used when compensations were unavailable, or when one actor threatened to accumulate too much power. As Gulick comments: "The ablest theorists universally accepted the connection and thought of war as one more corollary of the balance of power," and it "was an instrument to be used when other devices failed and to be used relatively deftly and sparely." [5]

The second dimension, hierarchy, refers to the extent to which actors acknowledge the right or ability of one, or some of them, to set and interpret the rules of the game. Nineteenth-century international law entailed such hierarchy, with the British government acting as the equivalent of an executive, legislative, and judicial officer. The existence of

*Even within such societies as the United States there is a wide variety of available games, though many of them are illegitimate.

"government" in its classic sense is hierarchical in that individuals are given the authority to render rule-making and rule-interpretative decisions on behalf of others, which is why many discontented groups seek the imprimatur of sovereignty. As discussed earlier, some hierarchy is necessary for groups to coalesce into actors, though the extent of hierarchy may not reach the actor stage, as in the case of international regimes that are transnational networks providing guidance in various functional areas like food, health, weather, telecommunications, air traffic, and mail.[6] Where hierarchy exists, rules and procedures are likely to be clearer and expectations more firmly anchored. Where hierarchy is absent, games tend to be what Morton Kaplan calls "subsystem dominant,"[7] and there is a heightened probability of misunderstanding over rules and procedures, greater confusion over roles, and a greater temptation for participants to interpret rules idiosyncratically. Generally, hierarchy contributes to institutionalization.

The third dimension, legitimacy, refers to the extent to which the game is accepted by participants as the proper mode of value allocation. Where a game is deemed to be legitimate, disputes will exist over proposals for disposing of stakes but not over the mode of interaction itself. Thus, "procedural challenges," and the degree to which actors are willing to play the same game as one another, indicate the degree of legitimacy that exists. In the era of the classical balance of power, for instance, most actors were prepared to accept limited wars and flexible alliances as proper means to dispose of stakes. Defections from, or challenges to, existing rules and procedures indicate a reduced level of legitimacy for a game. Resort to total war by revolutionary France, and by Napoleon, posed such challenges to the rules of the balance-of-power game. Similarly, Anglo-French support for the independence of Belgium and Greece in the 1830s were defections from the Concert of Europe's understanding about revolution that contributed to the Concert's subsequent decline.[8] After 1919, revisionist governments in Germany, Japan, and Italy increasingly posed challenges to the rules established at Versailles until the rules were no more than memories, and World War II ushered in an entirely new game. In contemporary politics, there are numerous defections from existing rules and procedures. Third World regimes, for instance, refuse to abide by those elements of international law which they did not formulate, and terrorist groups increasingly violate what Fred Iklé calls the "most elementary rule of accommodation," namely, "that the opponent's representatives should not be physically harmed."[9] A game is likely to be accorded legitimacy after it has become institutionalized and has acquired some hierarchy, and a withdrawal of legitimacy (regardless of the reason) may undermine those dimensions as well.

Institutionalization, hierarchy, and legitimacy may be used as measures of the political development of a system. Political development can be defined as the extent to which there are clear and accepted game channels to activate allocation mechanisms; so that, if the rules permit a mix of mechanisms, means exist to specify which channels are used by whom, for what purpose, and under what conditions. Development, therefore, is the product of increasing institutionalization, legitimacy, and hierarchy in games among actors. By contrast, political decay is the movement away from recognized game channels, which features growing confusion, misunderstanding, and lack of clarity concerning rules and procedures; it is the product of declining institutionalization, legitimacy, and hierarchy. Under these conditions, who will use which channels and under what conditions is obscured. As decay sets in and recognized games die, surprises and shocks occur, and instability in the relations among actors is produced.* In highly developed games, the rules provide a map for actors which guides them toward orderly processes for disposing of stakes—a map which is transmitted through time by recruitment to leadership positions and socialization of succeeding generations. The absence of such a map inhibits the disposition of stakes and results in stalemates and "fights."

Even where a game is in the process of decay, efforts will continue to dispose of stakes and to resolve issues, but these will likely be frustrated by the absence of consensus as to how this should be done. As in the periods 1890–1914 and 1933–39, key actors are likely to be playing according to different, often incompatible, sets of rules—a situation that, if unaltered, will stimulate resort to techniques of self-help, and consequently, suspicion and hostility, and a generalized reinforcement of efforts by participants to eliminate "defections" from the rules. This will probably be followed by a planned rule-making game, or new rules will evolve through a process of trial and error (ad hoc rule-making games).

---

* Instability should not be confused with the presence of conflictive characteristics; a stable relationship can be characterized by either cooperation or conflict.

The various characterizations of global politics as "anarchic," "a jungle," or "a state of nature" tend to describe only those periods of political decay. Similar processes of development and decay occur within actors as well. In either sphere, the spread of violence and the introduction of new techniques are reflections of the rejection by actors of existing rules, or of failure to comprehend them.*

In conditions of decay, stakes are present, but there is no way of disposing of them in authoritative fashion, so that actors will seek to seize them by whatever techniques they have at their disposal; self-help will be dominant. Whether war or ad hoc rule-making games are employed to clarify existing rules or develop new ones, the anarchic element will be gradually but inevitably eliminated in almost cyclical fashion. From the perspective of the global system as a whole, the descriptions "development" and "decay" are unlikely to suit all games. Some issues will be orderly and highly developed, whereas others will not. However, "anarchy" is not, and rarely has been in the past the dominant characteristic of global society.

Once it is clear that interaction is not random, and that a variety of patterned interaction games can evolve to reach allocative decisions out of the four major allocation mechanisms, three key theoretical questions arise. First, when more than a single game is in use in an issue system, as is commonly the case, what determines which game will become dominant? Second, why and how do actors switch from one game to another? And, third, how are new games created and integrated into the existing system?

THE POLITICS OF ALLOCATION

A. The Selection of Games

Two key factors condition the choices of actors as to preferred interaction games for any issue. They are the issue-position calculus, which essentially limits perceived alternatives; and the resources or capabilities avail-

---

* Gang rivalry, organized crime wars, and life after the collapse of governments may prove fruitful areas of enquiry in assessing the processes of development and decay. See, for example, Ralph Cassady, Jr., "Taxicab Rate War: Counterpart of International Conflict," *Journal of Conflict Resolution* (1957), 1:364–68; and Muzafer Sherif et. al., *Intergroup Conflict and Cooperation: The Robbers' Cave Experiment* (Norman: University of Oklahoma, Institute of Group Relations, 1961).

able to actors, which pose constraints on what they can do on any occasion. The issue-position calculus for initial and subsequent proposals is determined, it will be recalled, by the existing issue dimension, which describes actors' overall relations with one another and to the stakes at issue. In the presence of a strong actor dimension, an affect calculus will be used, while a cost-benefit calculus will be employed if a stake dimension is dominant. Various interdependence calculi are used for intermediate situations. Each of these calculi encourages resort to certain allocation mechanisms, and discourages the use of others, in specific negotiating sequences. A positive affect calculus encourages resort to principle and votes—those mechanisms which require joint action and trust—but discourages the use of force or bargains that rely on strength, and which would, therefore, alienate friends. In contrast, a negative affect calculus invites the use of force and bargains; and discourages principle and votes, owing to the presence of mistrust and hostility. The interdependence calculus is more permissive; it encourages principle, votes, or bargains, because any of these are suitable for producing trade-offs. Among these mechanisms, bargains are perhaps the most obvious and should occur most commonly, but, if specific norms arise from notions of equity or equality, they too may be used. Force, however, is discouraged because of its unilateral quality and the fact that it usually excludes mutually beneficial outcomes. Finally, the cost-benefit calculus permits the use of any mechanisms, at least initially, because the focus of attention is exclusively upon the stakes themselves and little regard is paid to other participants, one way or the other. When a cost-benefit calculus is employed, the actor's preference among allocation mechanisms is determined by the second key factor, available resources. These effects of issue-position calculi are depicted in table 8.1.

Within the limits set by the issue-position calculus, actors can be expected to try to resolve an issue by recourse to that interaction game that promises them the best possible disposition of stakes. As games are based on a mix of allocation mechanisms, actors will favor those for which their resources are best suited. Actors lacking military and economic capabilities will eschew games based on force or bargains. Instead, they will seek refuge in games that are based on voting schemes, like majoritarianism, as in the UN General Assembly—where each of them "however new, however small, however artificial, has one vote" and

Table 8.1 The Relationship between Issue-Position Calculi and Allocation Mechanisms

Calculus	Mechanisms Encouraged	Mechanisms Discouraged
Positive affect	principle votes	force bargains
Negative affect	force bargains	principle votes
Interdependence	bargains votes principle	force
Cost-benefit	all	none

"they find themselves courted and taken seriously."[10] Actors with ample military or economic resources, even if they are prepared to accept voting arrangements, are apt to demand weighted or veto-based schemes that reflect their capabilities and that minimize obstacles to unilateral behavior. Thus, when the UN was established, the governments of both the United States and the USSR strongly favored a veto arrangement for the Security Council, even though they were at odds over significant aspects of it. Both continue to regard the veto as no more than "the formal parliamentary expression of the real veto" which they possess owing to their capabilities.[11] Its existence permits them to participate in games based on voting for those issues where they would prefer to avoid force, while preserving force as an ultimate option. In addition, the arrangement is such that it provides them with considerable bargaining leverage without resort to threats or coercion.* As for principle, it has already been noted that the poor and weak will favor definitions of justice that emphasize norms of equality and need, while the rich and powerful will more easily accept norms of equity determined by overall status.†

The capabilities that are available to actors will also have a marked impact on the specific game they select, regardless of the dominant mecha-

---

*Other veto arrangements such as those in the European Economic Community (EEC) provide major actors with similar advantages.

†These tendencies are evident in such diverse contexts as developmental issues in the UN and social and economic issues in the United States that touch upon minorities.

nism, because actors will utilize the specific techniques for which their resources are best suited. Thus, if a weak and strong actor become involved in a game based on force (regardless of their preferences for some other mechanism), the weak are likely to make use of unconventional techniques like guerrilla warfare and terrorism, while the strong will opt for conventional war or even the threat of nuclear war. Such was the case with naval warfare in World War I, when Germany resorted to using submarines for sinking commercial vessels without warning. For Germany, the submarine was the only possible response to continued British dominance in surface fleets. The introduction of "unconventional" techniques by one side, regardless of initial objections by the other side, often results in the eventual acceptance of the new techniques. This parallelism may take time, but the unilateral innovations will call forth responses in kind if only in self-defense or for revenge. By World War II, allied submarines also disregarded the restraints on submarine warfare. Likewise, today, those who most strongly decry the use of indiscriminate terrorism are driven to employ "counter-terrorism," which involves many of the same techniques as the terrorists use. A similar tendency towards parallelism exists in the case of broader mechanisms as well as in the case of specific techniques. Once force and bargains (mechanisms that can be employed unilaterally) are used, they almost inevitably drive out those mechanisms that require consent and joint behavior (votes and principle).

But this is only part of the story of what determines the choice of interaction games, and it is necessary to go beyond the issue-position calculus and the distribution of resources to understand why they occur. As the variety of potential games in a system increases, the autonomy of actors is, paradoxically, reduced. This is so, not only because each game has its own rules, but also because additional rules develop about which games are more appropriate and legitimate for different issues and contexts. Such overarching rules must be clearly distinguished from the rules that govern specific games, reflecting as they do more general social conventions about the suitability of different allocation mechanisms in different contexts. The current climate of opinion against the use of naked force by large actors, in contrast to the acceptability of "gunboat diplomacy" in the nineteenth century, illustrates the manner in which such rules operate. These "systemic" rules usually develop slowly in ad hoc fashion and reflect the development of the global political system.* As tacit agreement is reached about rules, they tend to become institutionalized, legitimate, and occasionally even hierarchical. These systemic rules may come into conflict with the "rational" individual calculus of actors based on resources and issue calculus. The game that will be selected by an actor at any given point in time, then, will be a function of the individual preferences of actors within the limitations posed by systemic rules. The more institutionalized, legitimate, and hierarchical these systemic rules, the less potent will be the individual preferences and the more that actors will appear to fulfill roles in global politics. Figure 8.1

Figure 8.1 Determinants of Actor Selection of Interaction Games

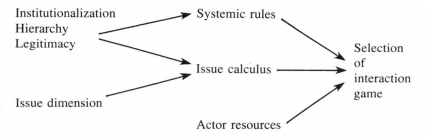

summarizes this process. It can be seen that the levels of institutionalization, hierarchy, and legitimacy are the most important variables, because they determine whether the systemic rules will outweigh the issue-calculus variable. Finally, actor resources serve as a catalyst to actors within the constraints posed by the other two variables.

The reason why systemic rules normally exercise considerable influence over individual preferences—particularly for initial game selection in issues—is that they promise *all* actors as a group more value satisfaction at lesser cost for the entire range of potential issues in a system than would be the case in their absence, or in the face of numerous defections. There are, of course, instances when individual actors can benefit disproportionately by ignoring existing rules, but, in general, the stability of ex-

---

* All political systems exhibit some such rules to a greater or lesser extent. While they are generally stronger in some politically developed societies than in global politics as a whole, it is equally true that a number of less politically developed societies scarcely reflect such rules at all.

pectations they provide, the limitations they place on misunderstanding and miscalculation, and the savings they promise in decision time and expense, constitute important considerations. Since rules that are deemed legitimate appear to have worked in the past, there is a tendency to assume that they will continue to work and to reduce mistakes, so that they produce what are almost "standard operating procedures" for global society and its decision makers.

Recognition of the apparently beneficent impact of systemic rules is produced by the experience of actors that have learned them through difficult and costly ad hoc processes, during which the rules were created or interpreted. Through trial-and-error experimentation with consequent rewards and punishments, actors become accustomed to disposing of certain stakes, and resolving certain types of issues, in a predictable manner. Deviation from such procedures is, at best, apt to be considered illegitimate by others and, at worst, to invite others to enforce the rules through coercion. Therefore, actors tend to follow many systemic rules (even though individual calculation suggests that they are not the best for them) because obedience to them entails less effort and greater certainty of outcome than does challenging them. Expediency, however, is reinforced by the actors' belief that the rules are right (the basis of their legitimacy). Either as a consequence of direct recollection of what the system was like prior to the existence of the rules, or through historical learning, actors come to accept the Burkean assumption that current social relations, while perhaps not the best imaginable, tend in general to provide an acceptable level of value satisfaction, and that to challenge them piecemeal may produce a set of social relations that is not markedly superior and is perhaps worse.

B. The Shifting of Games

Systemic rules not only limit the choice among games for given issues but also inform actors as to when and how they may switch games in the course of interaction. In other words, systemic rules guide actors sequentially into different channels that will facilitate the attainment of acceptable outcomes. To understand this, it is necessary to enquire into how actors adopt a cognitive map. Insight into this question can be found in certain aspects of learning theory.

The impact of learning upon cognitive maps is best explained by the "law of effect" and the "principle of least effort." The law of effect was stipulated by the nineteenth-century psychologist Thorndike and maintains that a bond will develop between stimulus and response which will be strengthened if the response is a reward and weakened if it is a punishment.[12] All learning, he believed, was based upon this process of strengthening and weakening of stimulus-response bonds by reward or punishment. The process consists of a trial-and-error search for responses that produce rewards. Tolman later modified this proposition by suggesting that *insight* as well as trial and error govern this search for rewards. He also suggested that the stimulus-response bond in the law of effect gives rise to *expectations,* so that a given path or channel exists in a cognitive map that directs actors to the attainment of the desired goal (reward). The contribution was later elaborated by O. H. Mowrer, who declared that these expectations guide behavior. Such expectations, according to Mowrer, result "in affective conditions in the organism, that is hope or fear" which are the actual determinants of behavior.[13] If Mowrer is correct, then the fulfillment of expectations of rewards will produce satisfaction, while failure to fulfill them will produce frustration.[14]

The principle of least effort was developed by Tolman, who was primarily responsible for the concept of cognitive maps.[15] Unlike Thorndike, Tolman believed that an organism is able to go beyond trial and error because it possesses a cognitive map of its environment, which is developed and confirmed by prior experience. Such a map includes "knowledge" concerning the various paths that an organism can take to reach its goals. The principle of least effort states that the least difficult and shortest path will always be selected.

If these two propositions have merit, a cognitive map of the political system would be followed by actors because previous experience had "instructed" leaders through a process of reward and punishment. Certain channels, having brought rewards, reduce value deprivation, so that hope is associated with them; other channels, having brought punishment and greater value deprivation, are associated with frustration and anger. Additionally, it would be expected that, from among the channels which offered hope, those which entail the least effort will be selected first. In decision making, the law of effect is applied by reference to both the personal memories of leaders (through analogies and the like) and the organizational memories of bureaucracies, as incorporated in standard operating procedures (though the potency of each will vary in accordance with type of actor and situation). The principle of least effort is translated into the selection of that course of action which keeps costs as low as possible. Its practical application, however, requires considerable sophistication, owing to the variety of possible costs that may be incurred.[16]

This complexity is reduced somewhat by the fact that not all games are equally legitimate for all issues and actors. What is deemed legitimate changes through time and place as systemic rules evolve. At any time, some channels lack legitimacy for certain issues and tend to be closed. Thus, unlimited warfare was seen as illegitimate in Europe during the eighteenth century, just as it is today in a nuclear era. Similarly, revolution as a means of changing leaders was illegitimate in Europe during the first decade after the fall of Napoleon. Currently, a number of functional issues are dealt with by international regimes rather than by games of force, or by international law (a game of principle).

Although perceptions of which games are initially most appropriate for different issues will vary historically, learning theory can assist in explaining why shifts among games will occur, the second question with which this analysis began. One hypothesis is that an actor will not accept a negative outcome regarding the disposition of key stakes in a high salience issue if it perceives that it has resources suitable for another game that promises a more favorable outcome. While this will encourage a shift, systemic rules do not permit the luxury of selecting any game but restricts choice to that game which involves the second least effort; i.e., a game which keeps costs relatively low and is still deemed legitimate. Thus, in the interwar period, once British and French leaders learned that games of principle (e.g., Locarno) would avail them little, they switched to a game based on bargains with Italy and Germany (e.g., Munich). War was not considered a viable alternative until the effort to achieve bargains was exhausted. What this generally means is that "coercion and aggression are 'measures of last resort'."[17] Among equals, such games are avoided because of the potential resource and failure costs implicit in stalemate and/or escalation. Among unequals, such games are generally considered illegitimate (thereby implying a variety of costs) and threaten to draw in third parties as protectors. Movement among games tends to occur when issues are salient and cognitive dissonance is pronounced and sustained. Since such situations are historically rare, systemic rules typically take account of them and permit resort to measures that would otherwise be prohibited. Survival issues, for instance, invite resort to virtually any game, and, regardless of its outcome, history often sanctions it.

C. The Creation of New Games

The key remaining question is how new games are produced and integrated into political life. New games begin to appear as a consequence of ad hoc or formal rule-making games *only* after the cognitive map governed by existing systemic rules fails to facilitate the resolution of an issue, or does so in a sorely disappointing manner, thereby producing mutual dissonance. Something of a crossroad is reached once the sequence of legitimate games has been tried and found wanting, owing to stalemate and/or the expenditure of a prohibitive amount of resources. The United States–Soviet Cold War, for example, which included a variety of specific games, entailed immense expenditures, while failing to resolve the issues it encompassed. Stalemate ensued, and the issues festered until the actors sought out a new game—détente. Similarly, though the two world wars resolved a number of issues, they did so at such cost that, as each ended, efforts were made to develop novel interaction games based upon international organization. In these cases, existing games were tried and found to be disappointing, so that elements in the cognitive maps of key actors were abandoned and a search undertaken for new modes of reaching decisions.

The cognitive map is altered primarily because it does not work; that is, it fails in a highly salient issue to produce value satisfaction. According to the law of effect, the previous bond between the stimulus (following the map) and rewarded response (achieving value satisfaction) is broken, since stalemate and/or high costs are regarded as punishments by all key participants. As in the case of the Capulets and Montagues, "all are punished." Human beings, unlike the rats of the early behavioralists' experiments, have insight, can recognize mutual failure (though not always), and have the capacity to identify shortcomings in their cognitive maps. In such conditions, particularly in the presence of highly salient issues, a search for new games and a revision of old maps are promoted.[18] Failure, as noted in the previous chapter, conditions the behavior of actors and is a key source of cognitive dissonance for leaders. Such dissonance is what promotes, first, the use of alternative tactics within accepted rules, or the stretching of these rules; and, ultimately, if it persists, defections from ongoing games and the search for new and more promising ones.

The failure and recognition of this fact, however, must be general if the search is to produce games that will achieve a final resolution. If only one actor perceives failure and seeks to develop a new interaction game, other actors are likely to regard this as a ''defection'' from existing rules, so that no new agreement regarding suitable modes of interaction is possible. The ''violation'' itself may be seen as a negative act, and existing relationships are apt to become more hostile. A new equilibrium is only possible if a joint search gets under way. Even if all participants undertake such a search—either through formal or informal rule-making games—however, it may prove very difficult to reach agreement as to what new interaction games are suitable.

The search for new maps and games occurs principally through an examination and application of precedents. Actors try to cope with current dilemmas by ransacking the past for analogous situations and drawing ''lessons'' from them. Such lessons can be based either on insight or direct experience, but the latter are, as expected by the law of effect, more potent. Thus, Dean Rusk's opposition to negotiating with the National Liberation Front or the North Vietnamese during his tenure as secretary of state owed much to the analogy he thought existed between the situation he was confronting and the situation in Korea, which he had experienced as assistant secretary of state for Far Eastern Affairs. Like Rusk, many decision makers will tend to behave so as to avoid the mistakes of the past when they are faced with a ''new world'' (e.g., a world which does not operate on their cognitive maps). Harry Truman shaped his cognitive map for dealing with the postwar world to avoid Neville Chamberlain's errors toward Hitler. Of course, Chamberlain himself had been guided in the 1930s by an obsession to avoid the errors which had been made by those of his generation in 1914, and to rectify the excesses of the peacemakers of 1918–19. While such lessons may be properly derived, the emotional setting in which they were originally learned tends to make them appear more generalizable than they actually are, and the passage of time sharpens certain of their characteristics while reducing their original complexity to a few simple axioms. The existence of a new situation encourages actors to repeat behavior which in the past worked, or which they believe would have worked had it been tried. As it is inevitable that the analogy will be flawed owing to differences (some subtle and some not so subtle) between the recalled situation and that which currently exists, it is probable that the lessons drawn from the earlier case, though not obviously incorrect, will be unsuitable to the present.[19] Thus, lessons that teach "firmness in the face of provocation" take on a rather different coloration in the presence of nuclear weapons than in earlier eras.

A more accurate form of experiential learning is the product of ad hoc rule-making games, which occur through a process of mutual probing that brings both rewards and punishments. This probing continues until actors work out in nonverbal fashion an acceptable manner of treating each other, so that a new set of systemic rules and games is created. This is a typical pattern in global politics for revising cognitive maps. At the end of World War II one ad hoc game produced the Cold War and a later one, détente.

Another pattern of learning occurs as the result of conscious and often formal rule-making games. At these conclaves, common efforts are made to apply insight, "reason," and analysis to history in order to identify suitable precedents that will be valuable in developing new social relations. The Congress of Vienna; the Versailles Conference; and the Yalta, Potsdam, San Francisco, and Dumbarton Oaks conferences after World War II; are examples of formal rule-making games, in which efforts were made to engineer a new or revised world order, principally by applying reason to lessons from history in a conscious, formalized fashion. The results of these efforts, however, have often been disappointing, because participants' knowledge of social behavior is extremely limited.[20] In many ways, it is ironic that ad hoc games promise more valuable lessons than formal games in which there is prior agreement to develop new modes of interaction. The failure of conscious schemes like the League of Nations, the Concert of Europe, the Weimar Republic and the UN suggests that most alleged "knowledge" about human relations is really untested theory, resting largely on deductive logic. What both Burke and

---

*There are, of course, exceptions, such as the formation of the EEC by the Treaty of Rome. In this case anticipation of distributive benefits, as much as dissatisfaction with previous deprivation, was an important factor.

Marx (e.g., in Marx's concept of praxis) understood was that true knowledge comes from testing ideas in the laboratory of life, rather than deducing it from ideal frameworks.

As has been suggested, formal rule-making games typically occur after bloody and destructive war. War, itself, is but one interaction game, and the following section will apply the explanation developed to this point to the interaction model presented in the previous chapter in order to delineate the conditions under which one or more of the contending actors selects war as a way of resolving an issue.

WAR, THE ULTIMATE ARBITER OF GLOBAL POLITICS: TOWARD A CAUSAL MODEL

One assumption of this analysis is that war is primarily a way of reaching decisions and that its avoidance requires the creation of some functional equivalent.* An understanding of war requires identification of the conditions under which actors will choose this particular way of making decisions and the various factors connected with that choice. Recent research on war is beginning to identify these patterns.

The most significant contribution to this research is the Correlates of War project directed by J. David Singer.[21] As a result of research connected with the project, a number of old hypotheses may have to be discarded, and a number of nonobvious relationships have been established. For example, war is apparently not associated with the demographic characteristics of societies, as some have argued, nor is it related to type of government, as liberals like Woodrow Wilson believed.[22] Nor does it appear that explanations associated with the debate over "bipolarity" and "multipolarity" afford insights into the causes of war. Both systems are associated with war, the major difference being that bipolarity is associated with infrequent but intense wars, and multipolarity with frequent but less severe wars.[23] With this finding, it is clear that the major difference between the two structures is that multipolarity is simply a way of paying the Grim Reaper on the installment plan.

---

*This assumption implies what Kenneth Waltz calls a "permissive cause," which does not bring about war, but which established conditions that make war more likely in the presence of other causes. *Man, The State and War: A Theoretical Analysis* (New York: Columbia University Press, 1959), pp. 231–34.

Research related to balance-of-power structure has yielded ambiguous results. Brian Healy and Arthur Stein, examining the period of balance of power in late nineteenth-century Europe, found that disruptions in the balance were not associated with predicted changes in conflict.[24] The most definitive study to date, however, is that of Singer, Stuart Bremer, and John Stuckey, who examined the relationship between the *distribution* of power, changes in that distribution, and the onset of war.[25] They found that peace was associated in the nineteenth century with parity of power and change toward parity ($R^2 = .65$), but, in the twentieth century, the inverse was found to be the case. Preponderance of power and the absence of change were found to be moderately associated with peace. ($R^2 = .30$). The inconsistency in the findings for the two centuries needs explanation, since behavior would not be expected to change just because one century ended and another started.

The reason for the change may reside in the fact that the distribution of power and the active effort to balance power are two *different* phenomena. War may be more likely when actors consciously seek to balance each other's power regardless of its overall distribution. If this is the case, then balance of power must be regarded as less of a mechanism for preventing war than as a means of preparing for it. It may actually promote the psychological preconditions of war—high threat and perceptions of insecurity. On the other hand, the findings concerning distribution of power may be spurious if actors in the nineteenth century only sought to balance power in conditions of preponderance, and if actors in the twentieth century sought to maintain a balance once parity emerged.

Explanations of this sort led researchers to ask under what conditions will actors feel insecure, threatened, and seek to balance power. Status-field theory and propositions related to status inconsistency provide some insight into this question. Rummel found that differences in status (measured by distances on various national attributes) were strongly associated with different patterns of behavior in American foreign relations.* This

---

* Factor analysis was employed to delineate six different patterns of U.S. dyadic behavior: Western European (type) cooperation, Anglo-American (type) cooperation, Deterrence, Cold War, Negative Sanctions, and Foreign Aid. Each of these types tended to be associated with different attribute distances, with West European cooperation. Deterrence, and Cold War being predicted most strongly. See R. J. Rummel, "U.S. Foreign Relations: Conflict, Cooperation, and Attribute Distances," in Russett, ed., *Peace, War, and Numbers* (Beverly Hills, Calif.: Sage, 1972) pp. 71–139.

research strongly suggests that differences in status are related to patterns of cooperation and conflict among actors. Are they, however, related to war? The research of Michael Wallace, associated with the Correlates of War project, suggests that they are, but only indirectly.

Analyzing the same data base as Singer, Bremer, and Stuckey, Wallace managed to produce a single theoretical model that holds for both centuries. Following Johan Galtung, Wallace found that status inconsistency has only a moderate direct link with the onset of war but has potent indirect links. His model is depicted in figure 8.2.

The first linkage might be called the path to war. Here status inconsistency in the system is, over time, associated with alliance aggregation (i.e., the attempt to balance power) and this, over time, is associated with arms races, which are highly correlated with the onset of war. The other linkage, which might be called the path to peace, is also interesting from a theoretical perspective. Here status inconsistency is negatively associated with the development and effective functioning of intergovernmental organizations. These, in turn, are negatively related to arms races, which, in turn, are positively correlated with war.[26]

Figure 8.2 Wallace's Status Inconsistency Model

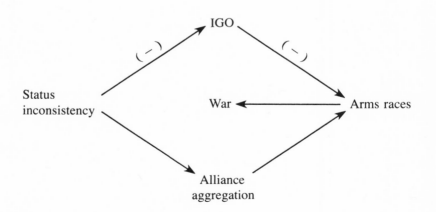

Source: Adapted from Michael Wallace, "Status, Formal Organization, and Arms Levels as Factors Leading to the Onset of War, 1820-1964," in Bruce M. Russett, ed., *Peace, War, and Numbers* (Beverly Hills, Calif: Sage, 1972), p 63, by permission of Sage Publications, Inc.

Wallace's research buttresses the assumption that war is a way of making decisions and suggests the conditions under which this "interaction game" will be selected by contending actors. The negative association of war with intergovernmental organizations (IGO's), and its positive correlation with alliance aggregation, suggest that, when there is little status inconsistency in a system, actors can create functioning international organizations in which interactions occur that can allocate without resort to force and war.* Conversely, when there is high status inconsistency, IGO's seem to be replaced by alliances, almost certainly indicators of the presence of a strong negative actor dimension. These alliances appear unable to dispose of stakes in acceptable fashion, and force or the threat of force become favored allocation mechanisms. In this atmosphere, arms races occur that commonly result, after some time, in the outbreak of war. Recent research by Wallace reveals that of the twenty-eight cases (between 1816 and 1965) in which there were arms races *and* serious disputes, twenty-three erupted in war. Of the seventy-one cases in which there were serious disputes but no arms races, only three resulted in war (Yule's $Q = .96$).[27] Clearly, status inconsistency makes arms races more likely, and this makes it probable that some serious dispute will be resolved by resort to war.

It must be emphasized that Wallace's research is at the system level. He has not demonstrated, nor does he claim that he has demonstrated, that war is actually initiated by those states that are status-inconsistent. If he had made such a claim, on the basis of his tests, he would have been adjudged the victim of an ecological fallacy, inferring individual characteristics from the whole. Despite this inferential gap, Wallace's research on the system level is important, because it helps delineate the characteristics of the system that aid in the development of rules able to resolve disagreements in nonviolent fashion. Nevertheless, if his work is to be taken seriously, then the implication, that status-inconsistent states are the ones engaging in the violence must be tested. It is in this light that the work of Manus Midlarsky is of importance.

Midlarsky examined the behavior of individual nations from 1870 to 1945 to determine if some types engage in war more frequently than others. He found a relationship between high achieved status–low

---

* IGO's are probably simply an indicator of the presence of a variety of interaction games.

ascribed status and the length, frequency, and intensity of war.[28] Various controls on these tests show that inconsistency is much more important in predicting war than are capability or diplomatic status. In other words, power per se, whether achieved or ascribed, is not as important as status inconsistency.

Do Midlarsky's findings mean that Wallace is incorrect in positing several intervening variables between status inconsistency and the onset of war? No. Midlarsky, himself, argued that the reason (rationale) for violence during this period is that status-inconsistent powers were challenging what they regarded as unacceptable institutionalized norms. This is obviously the case in World Wars I and II. In this manner, Midlarsky's analysis overcomes the potential problem of an ecological fallacy, while not undermining the larger theoretical framework implied by Wallace.

The findings of James Lee Ray and Charles Gochman, who also analyze data from the Correlates of War project, are more difficult to reconcile with those of Wallace.[29] Ray found no relationship between status inconsistency at the actor level and war for European powers. Gochman's study clears up somewhat this contradiction with Wallace's analysis by showing that the status-inconsistency model does not fit major European powers very well (especially Britain), but does fit non-European latecomers (U.S., China, Japan) for predicting the threat or use of military force. Although considerably further research in this area is needed, these findings suggest that status inconsistency is too simple an explanation to account for the findings and that changes in the status hierarchy probably produce a number of effects, only some of which are related to war (in a non-spurious manner). Singer implies something like this. He argues in his interpretation of this research that, although status-inconsistent states do not participate in more wars, their presence in the system makes for more wars. In Singer's analogy status-inconsistent states are like individuals who rather than getting heart attacks give them to others.[30] What needs to be done, then, is to offer an explanation of how status changes result in challenges that are resolved by war. It is here that the research on crisis becomes significant.

Studies of the 1914 crisis have suggested that in a crisis, there is a tendency for decision makers to misperceive and to exaggerate threats and hostility—a tendency that can lead to a hostile spiral which can escalate into war. If misperception can be avoided, as it was during the Cuban missile crisis, this hostile spiral may be controlled and war avoided.[31] The large question that remains unanswered by these studies is: What are the conditions that produce crises of the sort that encourage misperception which promotes escalation? Wallace's research provides one possible answer; system-level features may determine the *type* of crises that will occur and whether they can be successfully managed.*

The recent work of Nazli Choucri and Robert North has pursued this line of enquiry. They sought to demonstrate that certain systemic conditions preceded the 1914 crisis, and, presumably, that those conditions generally give rise to the kinds of crises that lead to war. They present a causal model that stipulates that growth in population, need for resources, and high-level technological capability lead actors to expand (i.e., attempt to acquire colonies). These expansionist actors become embroiled in a number of disputes as their expansion begins to intersect. At that point, perceptions of threat grow and spur military expenditure, alliances, and arms races. These disputes, in the presence of alliances and arms races, eventually result in war.[32] The independent variables in Choucri's and North's model (growth in population, resources, and technology) are not conceptually unrelated to status inconsistency, so that the model can be integrated into Wallace's model.

The research on the 1914 crisis makes the linkage between arms races and war more precise theoretically. The linkages between status inconsistency and the outbreak of these crises, alliances, IGOs, and arms races have not, however, been clarified. The models presented in this chapter and in the previous one are of use in elucidating these linkages.

Figure 8.3 integrates Wallace's model into the two models presented in this analysis. The concept of status inconsistency has been divided into two other concepts—similarity and status. Since the relationship of these two concepts to the status literature was explored at length in chapter 6, there is no need to elaborate them here. Suffice it to say that change in the status hierarchy, rather than inconsistency per se, is the key variable. Inconsistency may not be the causal factor as much as it is the psychological effect of a more fundamental cause, status change. Over time, wars are often produced by changes in the status hierarchy, because these

---

* After all, there were a number of dangerous crises prior to 1914 that did not produce war, so that the real question is how long actors can *continue* to provoke crises and still avoid war.

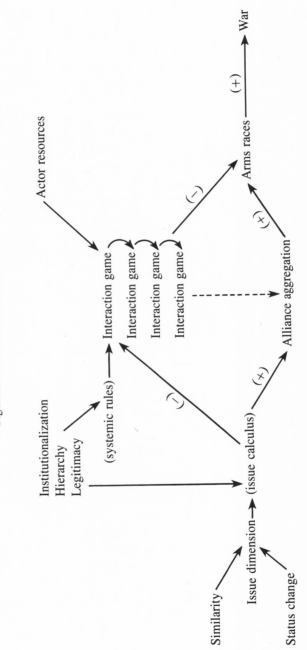

Figure 8.3 Flow Chart of the Onset of War

changes are disruptive of the prior pattern of interaction, and, hence, of the expected pattern of playing the various interaction games. This is, in part, due to the fact that changes in status usually occur after a critical issue has been removed from the agenda, and with it one or more of the losing actors suffer status loss. The latter, of course, occurs because in the global system the removal of a critical issue is often associated with war. But even if the critical issue is not removed from the agenda, a change in the status hierarchy brings new actors to the center of contention, and they may bring new issues to the agenda or redefine existing ones. New issues, in turn, affect alignment patterns, the issue dimension, and the traits regarded as a basis of similarity. Because the status variable has such a profound impact on the issue dimension, changes in status place great stress on the political system, challenging its existing systemic rules and interaction games to resolve the new issue.

The effect of the change in status is gradual, taking at least several years and longer, if the old critical issue is still on the agenda. The result of this is that the systemic rules are followed initially, but the actors that experience changes in status find themselves constrained by the rules, which they usually did not participate in creating, and which support the status quo. As they seek revisions of the status quo by means of existing channels for change (the interaction games), disagreement, negative acts, and hostility begin to occur in the manner outlined in the interaction model.* These evoke a negative actor dimension that sets the stage for prolonged hostile interaction, and that polarizes the political system. The actor dimension is a product of the failure of existing interaction games to resolve in satisfactory fashion the major issue in the system. As losers refuse to abide by interim dispositions or to follow existing rules, shifts take place among existing games. In the face of recurring failure, actors become increasingly hostile and begin to seek unilateral solutions. Initially, games based on principles or votes give way to games based on bargains. But, as the negative actor dimension becomes dominant and stakes assume symbolic and transcendent features, their growing intangibility renders bargaining ineffective as well. Under these conditions, zero-sum perceptions grow, and games involving force or the threat of force begin to dominate contention unless dissonance is somehow imaginatively manipulated.

*See pp. 240 ff.

As mechanisms other than force grow less attractive, polarization occurs in two ways. First, actors reduce transactions like trade and diplomatic intercourse, engaging in what Rummel calls "cold war" behavior.[33] Second, they begin to form exclusive alliances, perhaps the clearest indicator of the use of an affect calculus. The polarization process is correctly seen as threatening, thereby promoting the competitive acquisition of arms and other capabilities. Accompanying interaction games come to feature power politics and coercive diplomacy, and these games heighten the probability of crises—one of which may result in war. Leaders on both sides come to see war as a way to resolve the issue, though it rarely does so unless one competitor is totally destroyed as was Carthage by Rome in 146 B.C. Figure 8.3 depicts this process by the arrows from one interaction game to the next until the process comes to rest at alliance aggregation.

The likelihood that war will erupt is a function partly of the extent to which interaction games exist that can resolve critical issues, and partly of the extent to which such issues can be kept off the agenda. Stable societies may avoid war in both ways. The presence of legitimate governments may resolve issues in an authoritative manner, thereby preventing an unrestrained hostile spiral from engulfing actors and preventing the transformation of concrete stakes into transcendent ones. Thus, war may be avoided both by resolving issues and by keeping "war-prone" issues from emerging.

Three variable clusters—institutional setting, the relational attributes of contending actors, and the characteristics of issues under contention—appear as importantly associated with the occurrence of the sort of intense conflict that produces war. Wars, particularly total wars, tend to be fought over symbolic and transcendent stakes that are intangible and indivisible. These typically arise in connection with critical issues that are highly salient to actors and that are dominated by a strong actor dimension. The actor dimension, it will be recalled, tends to become dominant in the presence of contending actors that are relatively equal in status but dissimilar. Issues dominated by an actor dimension are peculiarly intractable unless there exists an institutional setting (i.e., a series of interaction games) that permits and encourages actors to use methods other than violence to resolve issues. Resolution can occur *only* if "losers" are willing to accept the verdict of interaction games, so that these must be legitimate and institutionalized. Legitimate government may provide a suitable institutional setting. Games of principle have done so as well, on occasion, at a global level. However, in the absence of institutionalized, legitimate, and hierarchical interaction games, there will be resort to self-help techniques. Such techniques, in the context of a critical issue, produce alliances, arms races, and crises of the sort that have been described.

While the above analysis integrates several strands in the theoretical literature, it is incomplete, because it does not present the *reasons* actors seek war (in light of the causal analysis that has been presented). Since war is considered in this model as a way of reaching decisions, a central question becomes: What reasons could compel or encourage rational leaders to select this interaction game? From this perspective, it will be seen that the war model is actually much more complex than it appears, because there are, in fact, different types of wars that can be inferred from the reasons for which they are started. But once started, one type of war may be transformed into another.

THE REASONS FOR WAR

Reasons are not the same as causes. The reason the glass fell was that its holder dropped it, but the cause was the law of gravity. Nevertheless, reasons are related to causes, and an examination of the reasons for war will help elucidate the dynamics of the causal model. Three reasons seem to account for the choice of war:

(1) War is seen as providing a way of obtaining preferred stake dispositions which could otherwise not be attained or at least not attained at such (perceived) low costs.

(2) Frustration-anger and misperception bring leaders and followers to the point where they wish to harm competitors.

(3) Misunderstandings or disputes over existing rules induce resort to war to impose one or another interpretation or to compel the acceptance of new rules.

Each of these reasons has a variety of causal paths associated with it, and each produces its own peculiar form of war. Each emphasizes a different

---

* The fact that such perceptions are often in error when the decision to fight is taken is not germane here.

aspect of conflict and therefore reflects different aims for the violence that is used.

When war is initiated in order to acquire stakes inexpensively, the aspect of conflict from which it arises is disagreement. In other words, the war is waged as a means of altering the situation of an adversary so as to influence it to agree to a proposal which it otherwise would resist. Such wars tend to overlap with "coercive diplomacy" in which political ends are emphasized rather than harm for its own sake. This is the form of war idealized by Karl Maria von Clausewitz:

War belongs not to the province of Arts and Sciences, but to the province of social life. It is a conflict of great interests which is settled by bloodshed, and only in that is it different from others. It would be better, instead of comparing it with any Art, to liken it to business competition, which is also a conflict of human interests and activities; and it is still more like State policy, which again, on its part, may be looked upon as a kind of business competition on a great scale.[34]

It is "an act of violence intended to compel our opponent to fulfill our will,"[35] and "a real political instrument, a continuation of political commerce, a carrying out of the same by other means."[36] Victory per se is not the goal; the achievement of conscious political objectives guides the struggle, and the war itself is only one of a series of acts in the ongoing competition for stakes.

Clausewitz himself recognized the difference between the sort of war just described and war that is fought out of frustration and anger.[37] This second form of war derives most directly from the hostility component of conflict and aims at destroying or harming the enemy for its own sake. Such wars tend to resemble "fights," in which the object is to hurt the adversary, as opposed to "games," in which the object is to outwit and influence the adversary. Strategists like Clausewitz have warned of the tendency to let the first kind of war degenerate into the second as "there arises a sort of reciprocal action, which logically must lead to an extreme."[38] In psychological terms, wars of this ilk appear to reflect a "frustration-aggression" cycle, in which the effort to harm the adversary eclipses whatever the original objectives of the conflict may have been,[39] and it may even reflect "displaced aggression" in which the target (like the Jews in Germany or the Blacks in the American South) is not even the cause of the actor's frustration.[40]

The third reason for initiating war, misunderstanding of interaction rules, has perhaps received the least analysis in the literature. Here war is initiated because competitors are seen to be behaving in ways that are not legitimate and not acceptable according to existing norms. It is fought by one side to end those negative acts and/or by the other to produce acceptance of a new version of the rules. American entry into the Vietnam War was based in part on this reason, notably as an effort to discredit the Chinese notion of ''wars of national liberation.''

In time, most wars come to involve more than any single reason. The Austro-Hungarian ultimatum and declaration of war against Serbia in 1914, for example, were largely the consequence of Serbian nationalist agitation, culminating in the assassination of the Austrian archduke, which threatened the integrity of the Empire. It quickly assumed many of the characteristics of a ''rational'' effort to force adversaries to agree to a resolution of a number of prominent issues (e.g., disposition of colonies and of the Turkish Empire) as other major actors joined in. However, as the war dragged on and became one of bloody attrition, frustration and anger came to occupy a prominent place in the calculi of leaders. Keeping this important point in mind, it may still be useful to separate analytically the reasons for war to understand better its dynamics and internal ''logic.''

A. The ''Rational'' Component of War

Given the overall volume of interaction in global politics, wars actually occur rather infrequently. Those that are most common are of the ''rational'' variety that begin in order to overcome disagreement. That they are relatively rare is because war by its nature entails the commitment of considerable resources and the risking of still more. Even with the most careful planning, the waging of war is fraught with uncertainty, and rationality becomes more difficult as uncertainty increases. Can the objective be attained? Can the war be won? Can it be controlled? Can it be terminated?* ''From the outset,'' writes Clausewitz, ''there is a play of possibilities, probabilities, good and bad luck, which spreads about with all the coarse and fine threads of its web, and makes War of all branches of human activity the most like a gambling game.''[41] This is particularly

---

*For a discussion of possible misperceptions involved in this last question, see Fred C. Iklé, *Every War Must End* (New York: Columbia University Press, 1971).

the case when war is waged among opponents of relatively equal strength, and since it is usually considered as illegitimate against a weaker foe—with the result that third parties may intervene—war tends to be a game of last resort. A necessary condition, then, for the initiation of war is the failure of previous interaction games to produce an acceptable disposition of stakes, although this condition is often not sufficient to produce war by itself.

Actors tend to switch games when previous efforts have been unavailing, and when they believe they possess suitable resources to permit them to achieve a better disposition of stakes than would otherwise be the case. A decision *not* to switch and initiate a war of the first type arises from the actors' belief that they lack sufficient resources to play the war game in a manner that would provide value satisfaction, and/or the predicted expenditure of resources necessary to attain a satisfactory disposition of stakes is incompatible with the marginal benefits that would accrue from the war. In other words, the predicted utility of war—calculated by combining the probability of success with value of the stake(s) at issue—is limited. Mutual loss may be seen as highly probable, as in the case of the contemporary "nuclear stalemate"; or the prospect of victory may be seen as dim, as when Alexander Hamilton argued against joining revolutionary France against Great Britain.

This analysis suggests that the relative status of actors and the estimated worth of the stake(s) are critical variables in deciding whether or not to initiate a war for the first reason. Status, an ascription of an actor's general resource capability, has commonly been operationalized as the ability to play the war game (i.e., military and economic capabilities). An actor which enjoys preponderance over other contenders will find a decision to go to war easier to reach than a weaker actor, particularly if systemic rules do not make such a decision illegitimate. Under such conditions, however, war is usually avoided, because the weak are prone to accept a disposition that is acceptable to the strong. The strong, therefore, while able to wage war with greater impunity than the weak, are generally less in need of doing so. If war does occur in this situation, it often does so because the weak are imprudent; they misperceive the adversary's will and intention, or they overestimate their own capabilities. Some such lack of prudence seems to have played a major role in Japan's decision to attack Pearl Harbor. Indeed, in 1941 General Tojo informed the Japanese

Premier that "he and others in the army believed that there were occasions when success or failure depended on the risk one was prepared to take, and that, for Japan, such an occasion had now arrived."[42] The weak may also become involved in war with the strong if they "play out of their league," refuse to defer, or fail to find a protector. The government of Imre Nagy in Hungary in 1956 fell prey to all three errors of judgment.

The weak may also become involved in war not so much because of a lack of prudence (as when they initiate hostilities), but because their protector failed to deter an aggressor, or because no protector was available against an aggressor.* In addition, the weak may become involved as victims in wars of conquest. These wars are of two varieties—conquest as part of larger military operations (e.g., Hitler's invasion of the Low Countries and Scandinavia) and conquest as part of competitive expansion beyond the confines of the core political system (e.g., European colonization of the New World, Africa, and Asia).

Wars of conquest of the first variety reflect a contagion effect, in which a war already exists among the strong that began for some other reason, and in which the weak become embroiled because they control some intrinsic, but more often some instrumental, stake (usually a strategic location) that is of value to the strong. The weak victims in these cases are true "pawns" that can only avoid invasion with extreme difficulty. Thus, Yugoslavia and Poland were conquered by Hitler as part of his larger effort to prepare for, and then launch, an invasion of the USSR; Denmark, Norway, Holland, Belgium, and Luxembourg were conquered as part of the larger war against Britain and France. Similarly, Finland, Estonia, Lithuania, and Latvia were defeated or conquered by the Soviet Union as part of Stalin's efforts to provide his country with defensible boundaries for the expected war with Germany. In contrast, Sweden, Switzerland, and Spain avoided conquest through a combination of skillful diplomacy, sheer luck, and a capability of offering a potential conqueror advantages that would be lost if they were conquered (e.g., diplomatic "listening

---

* Bruce M. Russett examined 17 cases between 1935 and 1961 when a protector sought to use deterrence on behalf of a "pawn." Of these, 11 were cases of failure, in which either the "pawn" was lost or war was not avoided. However, all 6 cases of success and only 4 failures occurred after 1945, thereby suggesting the important deterrent effects of nuclear weapons—"The Calculus of Deterrence," *Journal of Conflict Resolution* (June 1963), 7(2):97–109.

posts''). Since the demands of the strong on the weak may be severe (the stationing of troops, right of transit, or the provision of goods and services with little compensation) and frequent (a continuing series of small demands), the strong may find it easier and cheaper simply to take over the weak and seize all the stakes needed in a single act, rather than wasting time and energy in playing other decision games that may not obtain compliance. The legitimacy of the act of conquest is not particularly significant in the decision of the strong; nor is the need for additional resources, owing to the existence of a war or the threat of one. Consequently, in major wars, weak actors that stand in the path of the strong tend to be swept aside or confronted with demands for capitulation, such as those made to the island of Melos by the Athenians as recorded by Thucydides.[43] The only protection for the weak are the norms against war, but, since war already exists or is on the horizon, such norms are feeble.

The dilemma of a weak actor in such circumstances is illustrated by the case of Finland in 1939. Fearing that Hitler would violate the Soviet-German Nonaggression Treaty once his war in the West was completed, Stalin demanded that the Finns surrender a buffer zone to the north of Leningrad as well as a naval base on the northern shore of the Gulf of Finland. Leningrad was particularly exposed to the threat of German invasion, as it lay near the western frontiers of postrevolutionary Russia and on the Gulf of Finland, to which access could be gained from the Baltic. Initially, the Finns sought to straddle the fence between Germany and the Soviet Union,[44] but then chose to resist Soviet demands. In the Winter War which ensued, the Finns, though initially successful in their courageous defense, were ultimately crushed by overwhelming Soviet power.*

Wars of conquest of the second variety, competitive expansion beyond the confines of a core political system, were more common in the past than they are at present. A core political system can be stipulated as any set of actors that exhibits regular and intense patterns of interaction. Prior to the twentieth century, barriers to communication and transactions—notably geographic—permitted the coexistence of a number of such systems in virtual isolation from each other.[45] Thus, the Roman world was isolated from the kingdoms of Southeast Asia and the Chinese

* After World War II, the Finns were forced to lease a naval base to the USSR at Porkkala, and the USSR has since played a major role in Finland's internal politics.

Empire and the tribes of Indians in the Americas; the kingdoms and tribes of sub-Saharan Africa remained in isolation from the politics of Europe for many centuries. At the time such isolation is broken, a condition of anarchy can be said to exist between the members of the different systems—owing to the absence of agreement on rules of behavior, normative prohibitions, or legitimized decision games.

In such situations, bargains and force become key allocation mechanisms around which interaction games will develop. As one side is preponderant and sees the other as beyond the pale of what it believes to be civilization, it takes what it believes to be the easiest path to acquiring the stakes it desires. Seizure may be cheaper than trade, but, even if this is not the case, force may be used in order to avoid the complications and commitments inherent in bargains, since games of principle do not exist. The growth of many ancient and modern empires reflects this path to war, and underlines the fact that war can be a rational and profitable means of acquiring exclusive access to valuable stakes. The only protection available to the weaker actor is the existence of a benevolent third party; but in most of the cases of colonial expansion, no protectors were available. Even where one colonial power ousted another, it rarely showed greater consideration for the colonized (e.g., Japan's seizure of Korea from Russia in 1905, and American seizure of the Philippines from Spain in 1898).

The potential profit from war diminishes dramatically when contenders are relatively equal in status, or when the weak are able to punish the strong in a war game, as would be the case if they possessed a minimum or proportional nuclear deterrence system.[46] Under these conditions, the estimated or predicted value of the stake(s) becomes a critical consideration in the cost-benefit determination of whether or not to switch to a war game. The greater and the more equal the military power of rival actors, the less likely it becomes that any concrete stake, or set of stakes, will be worth the costs that would be entailed by war. This is particularly the case in the event the economic pie is growing, a situation which brings with it stakes that are divisible and distributive, and which offers benefits for all participants that would be sacrificed in the event of war.*

---

* One must exercise care in offering such a rationalistic analysis. Norman Angell, a British liberal economist and publicist, "proved" in a book published just prior to World War I that war among the European powers would bring economic dislocation of such magnitude that no one could win. *The Great Illusion* (London: William Heinemann, 1914).

It is this sort of analysis that lies behind the hypothesized relationship of democracy (a decision game based on votes and principle) and social wealth. Democracy, it is claimed,

B. *The Frustration-Anger and Misperception Component of War*

There is an absence of such rationalistic cost-benefit analyses in the case
of the second reason for war—frustration/anger, misperception. War is
produced through frustration/anger when an issue's salience is not reduced as a consequence of failure to achieve disposition, and when actors
seek to justify what they have already expended by redefining the issue in
symbolic and transcendent terms. By their very nature, neither symbolic
nor transcendent stakes can be easily compromised. Symbolic stakes only
lose their value if they are captured by one side, and the other declares
that they no longer matter, or if what they symbolize loses its value.
Transcendent stakes usually entail the imposition of one exclusive set of
beliefs, so that disposition requires a change in actor orientation rather
than situation. Such stakes are neither tangible nor divisible and can only
be disposed of if one or the other adversary alters its norms, or if a third
set of beliefs comes to substitute for the two that are in conflict. Even
physical conquest of one actor by another may not terminate the struggle,
as is evident in the resistance of religious dissenters throughout history to
the imposition of a contrary system of belief. When coupled with a negative actor dimension, the failure to dispose of such stakes intensifies disagreement and negative acts which lead to still greater hostility. If salience remains high (as it almost inevitably does in the case of such
stakes), actors will seek to veto recourse to any game which might result
in loss. Mediation and particularly arbitration are avoided, and institutions like the United Nations or international law are transformed into additional stakes, rather than being used to identify solutions. Instead,
actors will continuously switch games in search of one which is advantageous to them. Such a pattern requires the continuing investment of

can be sustained in wealthy societies because what is at stake are incremental questions
about how much of the benefit members will receive. In the event of recourse to force, joint
benefits would be sacrificed, and everyone would be relatively less well off. By contrast,
where concrete stakes are scarce, as in poor societies, force may be used because an unequal distribution of what there is may be the equivalent of virtually nothing for some individuals. Unequal distribution, indeed even equal distribution if scarcity is great enough,
may entail large-scale value deprivation, involving starvation or perpetual misery. Democracy is not possible because the losers cannot afford to lose.

War is "thinkable" under these conditions because the scarce stakes assume great value
and are worth risking one's life for. Thus, as concrete stakes become very scarce (to the
point of threatening basic survival needs), they acquire sufficient value to make this path to
war possible.

resources whose expenditure requires justification both to leaders and followers—justification which is rarely found in results. The consequence is that frustration, which produces anger, and hostility threaten to become so intense that all that matters is hurting the adversary. The stakes themselves become the instrumental means of self-justification. At such a juncture, each side is searching for any excuse to light the fuse as did Austria-Hungary in 1914. Although frustration and anger are the reasons, war of this sort is not entirely irrational when viewed in its own context, particularly when transcendent stakes are at issue. Logically, disagreement can only be overcome by the destruction or subjugation of the opponent, as the stake necessitates a zero-sum distribution. As a means to an end, the strategy of eliminating the adversary is rational. What may be irrational are actions in the face of the prospect of mutual destruction, and a disregard of the fact that the costs entailed have little reference to any conceptualization of gain.

War through misperception often occurs because one or more of the contenders mistakenly believe that the other side has opted for an actor-destruction strategy, a belief that stimulates arms races, as well as preemptive and preventive wars. Here, fear and insecurity, rather than frustration and anger per se, play key roles in the conflict helix. In such an atmosphere, "decision-makers . . . worry about the most implausible threats," and their efforts to achieve security avail them little because "most means of self-protection simultaneously menace others."[47] Security under these conditions is inevitably a relative value, since it must be assessed in terms of someone else; one actor's security is another actor's insecurity. Leaders tend to assume the worst of their opponents and to focus upon capabilities (rather than intentions), which are generally subject to overestimation. In this manner, actors become prisoners of the "security dilemma," in which, fearing for their own safety, "they are driven to acquire more and more power in order to escape the impact of the power of others."

This, in turn, renders the others more insecure and compels them to prepare for the worse. Since none can ever feel entirely secure in such a world of competing units, power competition ensues, and the vicious circle of security and power accumulation is on.[48]

None of the actors may actually wish war or, at least, total war, but their fear of one another leads to overreaction in crises, in the manner depicted by the 1914 studies. As tension generates stress and channels of information become blocked, only input that supports the "worst case analysis" is sifted and analyzed, thereby reinforcing the original pessimistic expectations. This, in turn, encourages additional overreaction.

Overreaction, which consists of negative acts, further intensifies hostility and leads to more overreaction, "unshakable" commitments, and tests of will until war finally erupts. The perceptual problem is illustrated by an example provided by Thomas Schelling:

> If I go downstairs to investigate a noise at night, with a gun in my hand, and find myself face to face with a burglar who has a gun in his hand, there is a danger of an outcome that neither of us desires. Even if he prefers just to leave quietly, and I wish him to, there is a danger that he may *think* I want to shoot, and shoot first. Worse, there is a danger that he may think that *I* think *he* wants to shoot. Or he may think that *I* think *he* thinks *I* want to shoot. And so on. "Self-defense" is ambiguous, when one is only trying to preclude being shot in self-defense.[49]

Misperception, then, assumes two guises—misperception of the original threat, and misperception of the specific behavior of the competitor in a crisis. The second follows logically from the first in the absence of contrary information—which, in fact, is filtered out—and both combine to produce a positive feedback spiral that, in the absence of correction, forces actors into an unwilling confrontation that might have been defused. This result is, of course, not inevitable if unorthodox channels of information can be introduced and utilized, as was the case during the Cuban missile crisis. Where the elements of this situation exist, pugnacious behavior merely intensifies existing illusions and misperceptions. Each actor believes that its behavior is pacific and necessitated by the aggressive acts of the other, so that the cycle promotes self-fulfilling prophecies through amplifying feedback; the illusions are ultimately borne out. Indeed, even small efforts to induce conciliation are thought to promote an image of weakness that must be avoided.*

The obvious prescription for lessening misperception based on expectations of an actor-destruction strategy is somehow to induce one party to cease overreacting, and to avoid hasty commitments, in order to permit a dampening process to begin. Unfortunately, this prescription may fall

---

*This is one of the major findings of Glenn H. Snyder and Paul Diesing, *Conflict Among Nations* (Princeton, N.J.: Princeton University Press, 1977, pp. 185–189, 488–493. For an excellent analysis of a "spiral" situation, see Jervis, pp. 58–113.

prey to yet another source of misperception of the sort feared by deterrence theorists. Conciliatory behavior by one actor may indeed be seen as weakness, or even trickery, in an atmosphere governed by hostility, and the result may be optimistic miscalculation. The appearance of weakness may be seized upon as evidence that the issue can be successfully forced without recourse to major war. In this fashion, one actor may fail to appreciate the resources necessary to win or the costs that will be entailed by persisting in its present course. Thus, the ambiguity of the British commitment to France in 1914 apparently emboldened German leaders to believe that an invasion of the Low Countries would not meet with British intervention, and the Anglo-French strategy of appeasing Hitler in the 1930s may have encouraged further Nazi adventures. A suitable strategy requires navigating between the Scylla of provocative commitments and the Charybdis of weakness. Both dangers reflect failures of accurate communication. In the case of avoiding hasty commitments, the error is initiated by the ambiguous deterrer and is compounded by the failure of the other party to interpret accurately the motivation behind the apparent restraint.

Communications difficulties are exacerabated by two conditions. The first, and usually more potent, is division within an actor, and the second is the very complexity of the crisis leading to war. The two conditions are related in the sense that during crisis each side tends to select information that suits its preconceptions, and so will focus upon those leaders and groups within the opposition that are expressing views that fit these preconceptions. In 1914, German leaders heeded the views of members of the British Cabinet that opposed an alliance with France or intervention on the continent. The conflicts within the Cabinet mirrored larger conflicts within the Conservative Party and Parliament, and provided the raw material for German miscalculation. In the 1930s Hitler underestimated the influence of the critics of Chamberlain's policy of appeasement. Churchill, he believed, was a has-been who had lost all opportunity to attain higher office; when Churchill succeeded Chamberlain it proved a shock to Berlin.

The selection of information that supports preconceptions, and the sifting out of contrary data, stem directly from the complexity of decision making in crisis conditions. As stress mounts, it is seen as safer to assume the worst and calculate solely on the basis of capabilities, rather than trying to weigh the strength of the adversary's various motivations, for which little concrete intelligence is available, anyway. It is also simpler to regard the conflict as involving only two sides, even if additional actors are present. Thus, the German government was caught by surprise in 1914 when Italy declared its neutrality. Information overload is a real problem when decision time is short, the total amount of information is increasing, and the bureaucracies are either kept out of the process (for reasons of secrecy) or are still operating under "normal" conditions. In such conditions, leaders are apt to fall back upon simple personal memories or analogies of the sort which gave rise to their preconceptions in the first place.*

Only in the presence of these kinds of tensions is "war though accident," as a consequence of inability to maintain command and control over the technology of destruction, or over subordinates (e.g., Manchuria 1931), ever possible. The danger of such accidents grows as the technology of warfare becomes more complex, and it is a particular hazard when retaliatory systems are vulnerable to preemptive or preventive attack. In these circumstances, military commanders find themselves under pressure to launch their own weapons when confronted with ambivalent or ambiguous circumstances, such as the presence of unidentified objects on radar screens. Under conditions of vulnerability, retaliatory systems must be kept on alert and provided with "hair-trigger" mechanisms, lest they be eliminated by a surprise strike that would render the defender powerless. In addition, a necessary condition for effective deterrence is the certainty that a deterrent threat can be carried out. These requirements may lead to devices that permit instantaneous retaliation, such as the maintaining of bombers in the air along a potential enemy's frontier, or the dispersion of weapons of mass destruction to local field commanders. Under conditions of alert, there are two dangers—the danger of a technological accident, such as the accidental launching of a missile, or crash of a bomber, and the danger of erratic behavior by individual commanders.

As the discussion implies, the threat of "accidental" war is greatest at

* Kenneth Waltz's argument concerning the superiority of a dyadic situation (bipolarity) in these conditions certainly has some merit—Waltz, "The Stability of a Bipolar World," *Daedalus* (Summer 1964), 93:881–909. The presence of only two actors (assuming a prior history of interaction) gives rise to less misperception, because the leaders of each can pay more attention to the other, particularly to its motivations. Calculations of capabilities are likely to be better as well, since the question of third-party intervention does not arise.

the nuclear level, particularly in periods when second-strike systems are insecure. Technology makes it inevitable that such periods will arise from time to time, as in the early 1960s when bombers were rendered vulnerable to first-generation missiles, or as may be the case in the early 1980s as missile accuracies are improved and new antisubmarine and laser techniques are perfected. However, the problem may also be relevant under non-nuclear conditions when offensive technology attains, or is believed to have attained, significant advantages over defensive technology—as in 1914, when it was thought that mobilization could provide an aggressor with such significant advantages as to make victory almost certain in a *guerre à outrance.*

Whether technology is nuclear or conventional, war by "accident" is rarely a danger except in conditions of stress produced by the reciprocal cycle of hostility and fear, when actors perceive one another as following an actor-destruction strategy. Without such hostility and fear, even severe accidents such as the crash of a nuclear-armed bomber or the destruction of a single city by the accidental launching of a missile, would not necessarily lead to war. War only becomes inevitable when potential victims are not likely to believe that the incident is accidental (even if it is).

In summary, the factors of frustration-anger and misperception are related to one another and tend to co-occur. World War I is perhaps a model of how such factors can appear jointly and feed upon each other. It was a war no leader wished, yet for which all leaders had been preparing. In many respects, the war was "overcaused," so that the combination of frustration, misperception, and even "accident" made leaders feel helpless to avert the catastrophe which they could see was approaching. A sense of resignation dominated Europe, as each actor increasingly believed that only some other actor had the ability to interrupt the chain of events; every leader saw responsibility as residing elsewhere.*

C. The Rule-Making Component of War

The third major reason why war is chosen as a decision game in global politics is to impose a particular version, or interpretation, of the rules of interaction upon other actors that are seen to be behaving in an illegitimate fashion. The other side of this is the initiation of war in order to

---

*For a similar attempt to relate causes and accident see Bruce M. Russett, "Cause, Surprise, and No Escape," *Journal of Politics* (Feb. 1962) 24(1):3–22.

overthrow an existing set of rules that is viewed as governing interaction to the advantage of status quo actors, and therefore perpetuating the relative value deprivation of others. Such wars are closely related to those which have been described, in that the decision is based on a calculation of relative costs and benefits, as in wars to obtain preferred stake dispositions; and such decisions are often taken under conditions of frustration and anger, when it appears that no other game can convince adversaries of the error of their ways. However, when the third reason is involved, wars have a distinctive character as well; their aim is to impose acceptance of rules that promise preferred stake dispositions, rather than to obtain specific stakes, and their aim is not necessarily to eliminate or harm competitors if they can be brought to accept such rules. Since such wars commonly are initiated to overthrow particular regimes or leaders, rather than to seize something concrete, or to destroy or harm the actor as a whole, they are identifiable.

Specifically, wars that arise owing to differing interpretations of the rules may assume three distinct, though related, forms. The first of these may be termed "wars of revolution" and involve purposeful efforts by particular dissatisfied actors to overthrow an existing structure that perpetuates relative value deprivation and the rules that underlie it. Marxist revolutionary theory, for instance, explicitly advocates such behavior to eliminate both national and global capitalist systems that Marxists see as perpetuating economic and social exploitation of one class by another. As in the case of the Marxists, some defectors may seek the overthrow of local systems and their rules as manifested by national revolutions. Others, however, may seek to do away with global structures as a whole. Thus, following the French Revolution, French armies swept across Europe in an effort to force the continent to accept "liberty, equality, and fraternity" as the new bases of social relations; the "blessings" of the Revolution were exported with bayonets. Similarly, Hitler's fundamental foreign-policy objective was to sweep away the European system that had been established at Versailles. In 1941, he recalled:

My programme was to abolish the Treaty of Versailles. It is nonsense for the rest of the world to pretend today that I did not reveal this programme until 1933, or 1935, or 1937. Instead of listening to the foolish chatter of émigrés, these gentlemen would have been wiser to read what I have written and rewritten thousands of times. No human being has declared or recorded what he wanted more often than I. Again and again I wrote these words—the Abolition of the Treaty of Versailles.[50]

The response of actors whose interests are threatened by such efforts to overthrow the existing rules is generally fierce resistance and collaboration, as in the Holy Alliance of a Europe confronted by Napoleon.

The two other species of wars concerning differing interpretations of the rules are closely related to wars of frustration and anger, and can be labelled "wars of cognitive miscalculation" and "wars of cognitive misperception." The former type involves actors with such radically different cognitive maps that it is difficult for them to identify common games, short of war, upon which they can agree. Their cognitive differences may lead them to employ existing games in different sequences (so that they are unable to synchronize their behavior), or it may encourage them to play entirely different games for the same stakes. In either case, the failure of some actors to respond as others expect creates impressions of defection, heightens suspicion, and ultimately leads to hostility and frustration. Such starkly different maps tend to arise in periods of rule ambiguity, during which ad hoc rule-making games fail to identify rules deemed legitimate by all key actors.

The second species of war grows out of differing definitions of the relationship (rather than rule ambiguity), in which some actors perceive an issue in terms of a stake dimension, whereas others perceive it in terms of an actor dimension. As noted earlier, issue dimension is partly responsible for determining the choice by actors of allocation mechanisms. Reliance by selected actors upon variants of force or harsh bargaining violates the expectations of those actors which were prepared to employ games based on principle or votes. Since the former mechanisms can be imposed unilaterally, they will come to dominate the situation in an atmosphere of acute mistrust and hostility, exacerbated by perceptions of "betrayal."

Wars involving rule interpretation have received relatively little attention by scholars or are viewed incorrectly as explicable entirely in terms of rational choice or frustration/anger, even though such explanations focus largely on immediate causes. In general, rules become muddied after actors have experienced mutual failure and/or when some are engaged in efforts to manipulate the cognitive dissonance of others in order to alter basic relationships. They, therefore, may reflect the failure of such efforts.

The failure, periodically, of the global political system to maintain interaction games that can allocate values embedded in critical issues provides an important explanation of war—not just globally, but domestically as well. With this explanation, the major theoretical questions with which this study began have been addressed—from the raising of issues to the political agenda to their resolution by the allocation of values. The questions, however, have only been addressed; the theoretical answers that have been given must be considered preliminary and tentative until tested systematically. Such tests, as well as conceptual criticism, will no doubt bring about many changes in what has been hypothesized here. And that is as it should be. The paradigm presented here has not provided definitive answers, but only the *promise* of such answers if it is taken as a guide to future research and theory construction.

Whenever such a broad, sweeping theory is offered, however, it is easy to misinterpret or oversimplify the authors' intent and meaning. More importantly, it is often possible for the authors themselves to distort history.* One way to avoid such pitfalls, and to demonstrate the plausibility of the paradigm, is to try to interpret well-known events and to see if the paradigm can account for them without straining the evidence. If, in addition, the paradigm can bring new insight and understanding to these events, then its explanatory power will be enhanced. The last section of this work will examine some of the major events of modern global history, in particular the last major critical issue in global history, the Cold War, as a way of accomplishing the above goals. It should be emphasized, however, that this section is by no means a test of the theory or offered as corroboration of the theory. Such outmoded "traditional" procedures are fraught with logical flaws and are unscientific. Rather, the intention is to clarify, through systematic example, the various meanings of selected propositions; and in doing so, to demonstrate that the paradigm and its theory are worthy of systematic testing.

* For an analysis of the possibilities of rigorous and systematic use of history in the social sciences, see J. David Singer, "The Historical Experiment as a Research Strategy in the Study of World Politics," *Social Science History,* (Fall 1977), 2(1):1–22; and "The Behavioral Approach to Diplomatic History," in Alexander DeConde, ed., *Encyclopedia of American Foreign Policy, Studies of the Principal Movements and Ideas,* vol. 1 (New York: Scribner's, 1978), pp. 66–77.

PART THREE

PRACTICE

These records of wars, intrigues, factions, and revolutions, are so many collections of experiments, by which the politician or moral philosopher fixes the principles of his science, in the same manner as the physician or natural philosopher becomes acquainted with the nature of plants, minerals, and other external objects, by the experiments he forms concerning them.
—David Hume [1]

CHAPTER NINE

REASSESSING THE PAST: GLOBAL HISTORY FROM A CHANGED PERSPECTIVE

HISTORY, AS Hume understood, constitutes the single greatest source of data for constructing a science of politics. But history does not surrender its lessons easily; patterns of behavior are not an inherent characteristic of history. If they exist, they are nonobvious and are "imposed" by scholars, who must identify them if history is to provide a basis for predictive or explanatory theory. At best, "what we obtain is a wager; and it is the best wager we can lay because it corresponds to a procedure the applicability of which is the necessary condition of the possibility of predictions."[2] The patterns that emerge and the quality of the wager are determined by the framework that guides the observer in his effort. Those guided by realist assumptions seek different phenomena and so weave the facts of history together in different fashion than does an observer who proposes to look at the data with fresh assumptions.

This chapter is neither an effort to rewrite history nor to provide a comprehensive historical narrative. Rather, it is a brief examination of several key epochs in light of selected variables and processes that have been discussed to this point in abstract form.[3] The chapter applies several aspects of the new paradigm to problems that have received insufficient attention, because previous analyses have seen global history as the unending repetition of a great game, in which unitary nation-states pursue their national interests, defined in terms of power.

The chapter covers the period from 1648 to the outbreak of World War II and is divided into periods conventionally recognized as distinctive by historians. Critical issues are identified and described, and changes in those issues and in major participant actors are delineated. Patterns of interaction relating to those issues, and the characteristics of interaction games—as well as the impact of various rule-making games—are briefly assessed in terms of some of the theory that was discussed previously. The events that are emphasized are those from which contemporary global politics has emerged, the raw material which the dominant paradigm sought to shape and to which it tried to give meaning.

THE HALCYON ERA OF LIMITED AFFECT AND CONCRETE STAKES

Commonly known as the era of the "classical balance of power," this period of global history, which stretches roughly from 1648 to 1789, is the source of much realist "wisdom" and remains the object of wistful admiration on the part of these same scholars. It began with the Peace of Westphalia, one of the major rule-making games of modern history. Westphalia brought to a close an era of civil strife, dominated by transcendent stakes, a particular mode of political organization and religious faith, in which the only stability had been that of interminable war. Although the Thirty Years War had witnessed innumerable dispositions and redispositions of specific stakes, the logic of interaction was that a final resolution of the great issues of the time could be achieved only through the extermination of adversaries. This proved to be impossible, despite the virtual depopulation of Germany which took place, resulting in a bloody and frustrating stalemate. Each succeeding episode in the war increased conflict along all its dimensions until finally exhaustion forced the foes to bring the war to a close.

Talks leading to the Peace of Westphalia began in 1644. In the words of one historian:

The German states were crying for peace, for a final religious settlement, and for "reform" of the Holy Roman Empire. . . . To Westphalia . . . hundreds of diplomats and negotiators now repaired. . . . There had been no such European congress since the Council of Constance (1415).[4]

The Peace resolved the two great transcendent issues in a manner that provided rules that would govern the behavior of major European actors for almost a century and a half. Of greatest importance was recognition of the territorial sovereignty (*Landeshoheit*) of the states of the Holy Roman Empire, thereby effectively legislating in authoritative fashion the principles of sovereignty—legal equality, non-intervention into internal affairs, and the need for consent in international law—that formed the fabric of the classical balance of power (and of the dominant paradigm of global politics that began to take form at this time). Also of importance was the fact that the Peace, in effect, declared the religious issue to be outside the boundary of political discourse. The Counter Reformation was halted, and Calvinism was accepted alongside of Lutheranism and Catholicism. In other words, limited religious tolerance (among, though not within, states) was decreed as part of the decision to eliminate transcendent stakes from political life. The Peace therefore represents a conscious reaction against, and rejection of, unlimited war as a legitimate decision game and transcendent stakes as legitimate objects of contention.

The Thirty Years War was remarkable for the way in which *two* critical issues—Protestantism and national sovereignty—shared the top of the agenda. Although their simultaneous existence permitted some crosscutting, by and large they tended to reinforce a single great cleavage that rent European society. The virtual elimination of medieval political structures in the war resolved the sovereignty issue; the dominance of Catholicism and Protestantism within different sovereign states, however, meant that the religious issue remained stalemated, thereby requiring agreement for resolution.

Global politics during the subsequent "balance-of-power" era was truly "international" politics, as the key actors were territorial states—the patrimonies of the great European dynasties—which were governed by monarchs and statesmen who proclaimed "the priority of order and the status quo over movement."[5] Issues during this period consisted of concrete stakes that were linked along a stake dimension. The names associated with them reflect their tangible nature, notably their territorial aspect—"Spanish Netherlands," "Spanish succession," "Polish succession,'' and ''Austrian succession.'' Issue positions of major participants tended to be based on a mix of cost-benefit and interdependence calculi. The existence of numerous individual issues consisting of concrete stakes encouraged crosscutting cleavages, short-term temporary alliances, and a limiting of conflict to dimensions of disagreement and negative acts without the addition of fundamental hostility. Although issues of dynastic succession were sources of continual controversy, these did not lead to problems of actor coalescence or fragmentation, problems of the sort which had played so central a role in the years prior to 1648 and would do so again by the end of the eighteenth century. But during the intervening years, the rules of Westphalia were for the most part obeyed. Since there were few challenges to the rules, ad hoc rule-making games were absent.

Indeed, legitimate behavior became so institutionalized (and predictable) that contemporary writers like Lord Brougham, Friedrich von Gentz, Emmerich de Vattel, David Hume, Edmund Burke, and even Jean-Jacques Rousseau elevated the balance-of-power game to the status of an eternal principle and the basis of an alleged law of nations. The ''balance-of-power'' game in practice consisted of a mix of principle, bargains, and force. Principle was manifest in the norms that related to power equilibrium and compensation, the requirement for flexible alliances, the prohibition of internal influence and efforts to create supranational political units, and the solidarity of monarchs (the legitimacy principle).* Underlying these principles were the values of independence and security which came to be spoken of as the ''liberties of Europe.''† The nine ''means'' that Edward Vose Gulick identifies as characteristic of the balance of power may be regarded as the principles from which behavior flowed—vigilance, the alliance, intervention (in extreme cases), holding the balance, mobility of action, reciprocal compensation, preservation of components, moderation, the (preponderant) coalition, and (limited) war.[6]

Bargains, too, were present and were prescribed by the norms them-

* Several of the ''essential rules'' that Morton A. Kaplan identifies with the balance-of-power system reflect such norms. See his *System and Process in International Politics* (New York: Wiley, 1957), p. 23.

† To appreciate the extent to which principle was at the hub of balance of power, see the citation from *Europe's Catechism* in Edward Vose Gulick, *Europe's Classical Balance of Power* (New York: Norton, 1967), p. 2.

selves, which demanded the maintenance of equilibrium among major actors by means of trade-offs and compensations. In fact, the colonial expansion of Britain, France, and Holland into the Americas and Asia, although a source of disagreement, expanded available stakes and provided ever greater opportunities for compromises and dispositions based on perceptions of interdependence. Finally, force, though used episodically, was integral to the game and was reflected in the numerous wars, limited as they might be. For this reason, Gulick declares that "peace was not germane" and "was no more essential to equilibrist theory than the barnacle to the boat."[7] Military alliances were formed and reformed and limited wars fought for provinces, trading rights, and other concrete political goods. Force also existed in the form of the tacit (deterrent) threat of a preponderant alliance and major war in case one or more of the participants were to flaunt the rules and so endanger the arrangements which were believed to be the source of happiness and prosperity.*

In the balance-of-power game, actors commonly adopted issue positions from an interdependence calculus, fostered by a sense that the system as a whole provided value satisfaction to the monarchical rulers of the time. This was combined with a conscious interest in all major issues on the agenda. Decisions were based on a unique combination of strength and norms—strength in the sense that only "great powers" merited consideration; and norms in the sense that among those powers there must exist equality in law and equity in fact. The entire arrangement was reinforced by painful memories of pre-1648 Europe that combined with a growing pattern of agreement after 1648. Relative equality of capabilities produced a pattern of vigorous competition that was tempered by the great similarity among elites that fostered trust, identity, and empathy. Royal houses were bound by intermarriage, a common language, and a common set of historical referents. Cosmopolitan diplomats, tied by a fiduciary interest in those they served, pursued concrete stakes and eschewed transcendent aims. Like Sir Harold Nicolson, they believed that

---

*The peculiar combination of force and principle called "balance of power" was of course not unique to eighteenth- and nineteenth-century Europe, though it reached its zenith there. Historically, similar games can be identified in ancient India, China, Renaissance Italy, and elsewhere and can be discerned within actors as well as among them. For the deterrent quality in balance of power, see Alexander L. George and Richard Smoke, *Deterrence in American Foreign Policy: Theory and Practice* (New York: Columbia University Press, 1974), pp. 13–14.

"the worst kind of diplomatists are missionaries, fanatics and lawyers; the best kind are the reasonable and humane sceptics."[8]

THE COLLAPSE OF THE BALANCE OF POWER

The balance of power of the eighteenth century ended suddenly and brutally with the defection of revolutionary France and the efforts of the revolutionary regime there to export its ideology abroad and overthrow the *anciens régimes* of its neighbors. Political liberalism and the "Rights of Man" emerged as a genuine critical issue, one which was not fully resolved by the defeat of France and Napoleon. Prior to the Revolution, France had become a model unitary actor, owing to the triumph of absolutism in that country under Louis XIV. Under Louis (1643–1715) and his chief minister, Cardinal Mazarin, major groups and institutions that had survived the feudal period and that were potential actors—or that could foster transnational ties—were crushed, thereby bringing the doctrine of sovereign power in line with political reality. The first victims were the *parlements* (courts of law) and rebellious nobility who sought in the Fronde of 1648 to resist the monarchical power. The nobles sought Spanish assistance, thereby linking France's internal politics to its external relations, since France was at war with Spain at the time. In other words, dissident members sought the fragmentation of the existing actor in alliance with another formidable actor. But the rebellion ended in failure.* Other dissidents suffered a similar fate. Jansenism was repressed, and in 1685 the monarchy revoked the Edict of Nantes, which had guaranteed French Huguenots (Protestants) a measure of independence and security. Under Louis XIV, French industry was subsidized and brought under state administration; and the army, which had previously been largely the responsibility of local nobles—who employed mercenaries—was thoroughly nationalized. Gradually, all the strands of policy and administration were woven together at Versailles, where the King had himself built an establishment worthy of his stature. By the end of his reign, there was considerable basis for his apocryphal "L'état, c'est moi." His theorist was Bishop Bossuet, who argued that all power flows

---

* Louis himself in later years was prepared to assist, even sponsor, the exiled Jacobite court of the Stuarts in its effort to overthrow the Hanovarian monarchs of Great Britain.

from God and that the monarch was responsible only to God for his actions. In the words of one observer:

King and subjects, these according to Louis should be the only two classes in the state. The *noblesse* is thrust aside and its place taken by *bourgeois viziers* whom the King has raised from nothing, and can dismiss to their original nothingness at a wave of his hand. Thus he endeavours to create a world in which he only shall stand out above the dead level of twenty million subjects.[9]

In 1789, the centralized system which Louis XIV had nurtured and built collapsed. Sapped by continual wars and financial crises and led by the weak successors of the "Sun King," the Old Regime crumbled, and the country began to come apart. The fact that these events occurred in the most powerful and wealthiest centralized state in Europe could not but have profound repercussions for other major actors in global politics. Although internal strife continued to plague the country, the principles of the new regime—equality before the law, collective sovereignty of citizens of *la patrie* (nationalism), and the rule of law—published on August 26, 1789 as the Declaration of the Rights of Man and Citizen, immediately created ferment beyond the frontiers of France. In pronouncing these principles fit for all the world, the new regime rejected the rules of the game, defected from the legitimacy principle (the primacy of inherited monarchy), and set itself against the remainder of Europe. Open intervention in the internal affairs of other sovereign powers was deemed an obligation, and a transcendent stake of profound importance was injected into political life once again. Its effects were not long delayed as deprived elements in Belgium, Germany, Poland, Ireland, and elsewhere were galvanized to action and as divisions appeared within Europe's previously homogeneous elites between those who were infected by the "revolutionary disease" and those who sought to perpetuate the status quo. If for the poet Wordsworth

Bliss was it in that dawn to be alive,
But to be young was very heaven![10]

for Edmund Burke the Revolution "doubled the licence, of a ferocious dissoluteness in manners, and of an insolent irreligion in opinions and practices," "utterly disgraced the tone of lenient council in the cabinets of princes," "sanctified the dark suspicious maxims of tyrannous distrust,'' and authorized "treasons, robberies, rapes, assassinations, slaughters, and burnings throughout their harrassed land.''[11] Even in the United States, political divisions centering around attitudes toward the French Revolution surfaced as the followers of Jefferson and Thomas Paine were pro-Jacobin, in contrast to the supporters of Alexander Hamilton.

The explosive combination of internal nationalism and fragmentation in France, the growing links between supporters and opponents of revolutionary principles throughout Europe, and the replacement of issues based on concrete stakes by those with a symbolic and transcendent quality, gradually reintroduced actors to the game of "total war.'' As had been the case during the Thirty Years War and would again occur in 1914–18 and 1939–45, the game was dominated almost entirely by extremes of force in which strength alone was the mode of allocation, and issue positions were determined primarily by affect. Even in total war, there remains some limited room for bargains among enemies, but bargains notwithstanding, the rules of total war encourage the destruction of actors and/or the replacement of defeated actors' decision makers by new leaders approved by the victors. Thus, in 1815, Napoleon was deposed and replaced by Louis XVIII; in 1918, Kaiser Wilhelm II was forced to abdicate and seek refuge in Holland, and the Empire was replaced by the Weimar Republic; and in 1945, the Nazi regime and all of its laws were effectively extirpated and replaced by direct military rule during a period of "denazification.'' The very term "game'' seems somehow out of place during such conflagrations, as they usually entail a rejection of almost all former rules of behavior and are fueled by disagreement about what future rules shall be. Yet the logic behind such wars that arise out of widespread defection from prior rules and growing resort to a lowest-common-denominator allocation mechanism that can be used unilaterally is rarely understood or perceived at the time of its occurrence. This was the case as the old balance-of-power game crumbled, and Europe descended once more into a period of virtual anarchy.

Initially, conflict over the French Revolution was limited to fiery rhetoric. Britain's prime minister, William Pitt, resisted calls for war by Burke and his partisans, claiming that France's domestic politics were of little concern to England. But matters were more complicated for the Austrian emperor, Leopold II, the brother of the French queen Marie Antoinette.

He was besieged by pleas from the numerous French royalist emigrés who had gathered at the Habsburg court and were busily engaged in promoting a transnational network of counterrevolutionaries in Europe and America. The new French regime, in addition to spreading propaganda openly, did little to calm the rising fears as it unilaterally annexed Avignon without the consent of the pope—the city's sovereign—and abolished feudal practices in Alsace, even though the province was under a German as well as French authority. German princes whose rights in Alsace had been abrogated, already uneasy for their thrones, appealed to the Holy Roman Emperor. After June 1791 anti-French agitation reached a crescendo with the arrest of Louis XVI after his abortive attempt to flee the country. Still procrastinating, the Austrian emperor met with the king of Prussia at Pillnitz and declared that he would intervene if the other major powers joined with him (an unlikely prospect at the time).

Although the implied threat was not serious, the gleeful reaction of the emigrés to the Declaration of Pillnitz, and their continued plotting and subversion, enraged the more radical among the French revolutionaries and added to the support for those within the dominant revolutionary club, the Jacobins, who believed that the French Revolution would never be secure until it had spread abroad. The outbreak of war in Europe followed the defection by French leaders from established systemic rules, thereby establishing a strong negative actor dimension. This dimension was reinforced by the erosion of perceptions of similarity among leaders and a rapid change in Europe's status hierarchy as nationalism added to French capabilities and raised to the top elements of the previously despised middle classes. Virtually all the factors associated with war (as in figure 8.3) were taking effect. Moreover, the dominant reasons for the wars which followed were frustration/anger and disputes over rules, not cost-benefit calculations, as had been the case with wars of the previous century. Intensification of hostility and exchange of negative acts rather than simple disagreement were the bases of conflict.

In April 1792 France declared war on Austria—the "War of the First Coalition"—during which French revolutionary armies suffered a number of setbacks that served only to inflame revolutionary and class passions at home, culminating in the storming of the Tuileries and the imprisonment of the king. In August the legislative assembly was virtually stripped of its authority by the revolutionary government of Paris, and the Parisian mob began arresting and summarily executing alleged counterrevolutionaries, initiating a three-year period in France known as the "terror."

The explosion of the "second revolution" at home was matched by the energetic prosecution of war abroad. In September the Prussian advance on Paris was halted by the symbolic battle of Valmy, and French armies rapidly moved into Belgium and the left bank of the Rhine. As the National Convention offered aid to those who believed themselves oppressed and ordered its armies to act against "counterrevolutionaries" abroad, Europe began to feel the weight of the great energizing forces of nationalism and popular participation, which the French Revolution was unleashing. Armed clashes were no longer to be limited engagements among relatively small numbers of mercenary soldiers. The system was to be replaced by the nation at war, a transformation symbolized by the decree of the *levée en masse* of 1793.[12]

As French armies annexed Savoy and Nice, occupied Belgium and the Rhineland, and declared war on Britain and Holland, the prospects for resolving the critical issue were all but eliminated by the trial and execution of Louis XVI in January 1793 and the ensuing "reign of terror" at home. Between 1792 and 1799, general war engulfed Europe. Within France, chaos continued as the National Convention was replaced by the Directory (1795–99), the terror ebbed and flowed, rebellions erupted and were brutally repressed, and society and law were turned upside down.

In 1799 the French Revolution came to an end at home, though not abroad, as the Directory was overthrown by General Bonaparte's coup d'état and replaced by the Consulate with Napoleon as First Consul; Napoleon Bonaparte was now dictator of France. Napoleon continued the reform of French society and government that had begun during the Revolution; he also successfully eliminated dissension at home, so that France once more could face the world as a unitary actor. Abroad the continental struggle continued as the map of Europe was redrawn. From 1800 to 1812 Napoleon waged war against the sovereigns of Europe, defeating all of them at one time or another with the exception of Great Britain.* By 1811 the Grand Empire was at its apogee, from the Atlantic to the frontiers of Russia. Napoleon reorganized the continent both economi-

---

* War was not continuous as Napoleon skillfully played allies off against one another, concluding treaties with first one and then the other.

cally and politically. Under the Continental System, Europe was forbidden to trade with Great Britain. Belgium, Holland, the left bank of the Rhine, the German and Italian coasts were all incorporated in the Empire, buttressed by a string of dependent states in Germany (Confederation of the Rhine), Poland (the Grand Duchy of Warsaw) and the Swiss federation. For them, the sovereignty principle of the eighteenth century was negated. In the cases of Austria, Prussia, and Russia, all were unwillingly wedded to the French Empire by alliance and agreement. And, wherever French arms appeared, revolutionary reforms followed in their train. These included the elimination of feudal obligations, the weakening of the church, and the elaboration of liberal, republican constitutions.

Unwittingly, however, Napoleon by his conquest of Europe produced the very forces of nationalism and mass participation in politics that had energized the expansion of France in the first place. Such "reactive" nationalism drew its inspiration from the very forces which it opposed. For as the Prussian military reformer Gneisenau wrote in 1807:

The Revolution has set in action the national energy of the entire French people, putting the different classes on an equal social and fiscal basis. . . . If the other states wish to establish the former balance of power, they must open up and use these same resources. They must take over the results of the Revolution, and so gain the double advantage of being able to place their entire national energies in opposition to the enemy and of escaping from the dangers of a revolution.[13]

The greatest importance of this phenomenon was the linking of the ideas of nation and state, the emergence of the concept of popular sovereignty, and a growing belief that the nation-state must be the core actor in global politics.

By 1811 the Napoleonic dream was near fulfillment, yet in a year it lay shattered in the wastes of Russia. Overcoming their suspicions of one another in order to rid Europe of Bonaparte, Austria, Britain, Prussia, and Russia, in March 1814, concluded the Treaty of Chaumont and bound themselves to a Quadruple Alliance against France.* At the end of March the allied armies entered Paris, and on April 11 Napoleon abdicated and was exiled to Elba.

With the elimination of Napoleon, his adversaries set out to resolve once and for all the critical issue of political liberalism. Despite their ef-

* So utterly had the balance of power failed to operate that this was the first solidly preponderant alliance that had been formed against France since the Revolution.

forts, they failed to do so, and global politics during much of the nineteenth century was preoccupied with it and with a second critical issue
(with which it vied for preeminence), national self-determination—
another product of the Revolutionary and Napoleonic wars.

THE CONGRESS OF VIENNA: THE GREAT RULE-
MAKING GAME

The choice of a successor to Napoleon fell to Louis XVIII, thereby re-
storing the Bourbon dynasty. The choice, though obvious, was not inevitable and was assured only after Talleyrand was able to persuade the tsar
of its naturalness:

Neither you, sire, nor I . . . could impose a king upon France. France is a
conquered country, and you are its conqueror; even so, you have not that power.
. . . In order to establish a durable state of affairs, one which can be accepted
without protest, one must act upon a principle. . . . And there is only one principle. Louis XVIII is that principle. He is the legitimate King of France.[14]

In this Talleyrand revealed, and the allies accepted, what would serve as
a key principle in the "Concert of Europe" that would be legislated by
the Congress of Vienna, namely, the "legitimacy principle."

At the end of May 1814, in their effort to bolster the restored Bourbons
and in conformity with the balance-of-power rule of reintegrating defeated actors into the system, the allies concluded the first Treaty of
Paris. It permitted France to retain its 1792 boundaries, including Avignon, parts of Savoy, Germany, and Belgium—none of which had been
French prior to 1789. Other lands conquered by Napoleon were restored
to independence, and certain colonial concessions were made to the British. These, combined with Britain's naval predominance and the advent
of the industrial revolution, were to ensure British colonial domination
for another century.

The complexity of the issues confronting the allies, and the fissures
among them—which rapidly emerged once their opponent had vanished—required the summoning of a major conference, which opened in
Vienna in September 1814. Disagreements among the participants, as
well as remembered negative acts, made cooperation difficult. Their prior
pattern of disagreement until the Treaty of Chaumont and their relative

equality of status generated considerable mistrust, which was exacerbated by the imperious behavior of individual leaders, notably the tsar. Thus, as the assembly of luminaries gathered in Vienna, numerous disagreements remained to be ironed out, and there existed consensus on only two points: "the condemnation of the revolutionary principle . . . and the necessity of checking French power."[15] The difficulty stemmed in part from the fact that, although stakes were seen as concrete and discussed as though they were discrete issues, several of the leading statesmen continued to perceive them as symbolic of still larger issues. Prince Metternich of Austria, for instance, formed issue positions to conform with his belief that all decisions must foster the existing, conservative social order; the primacy of absolute monarchy; and the repression of participant politics. Britain's Castlereagh was less preoccupied with such abstractions than with the principle of the balance of power itself. Finally, Tsar Alexander was inspired by a vague ideological belief in the moral oneness of Europe, governed by Christian goodwill. This belief, which took the form of the innocuous Treaty of the Holy Alliance (September 1815) and which echoed earlier ideas of the Abbé de Saint Pierre, was described by Castlereagh as "a piece of sublime mysticism and nonsense."[16]

Before the Congress of Vienna could complete its task, Napoleon escaped from Elba, landed in France, and entered Paris, beginning the so-called Hundred Days. The adventure, however, was quickly and finally brought to an end by the battle of Waterloo and the subsequent exile of Napoleon to the island of St. Helena in the South Atlantic. Shaken by the episode, the allies agreed that no Bonaparte should ever again govern France and returned to their labors in Vienna.

Despite the wrangling which ensued on such matters as the disposition of Poland and Saxony, the Congress did serve as a true rule-making body, laying down the law of Europe and constructing what came to be known as the Congress System. Its results were "attempts at giving institutionalized direction to these moral and intellectual forces which had been the lifeblood of the balance of power,"[17] from which "certain assumptions and procedures became customary and prescriptive through application" owing to "the common realization of European statesmen of the Napoleonic era that something new and different must be devised to mitigate the increasingly chaotic and warlike balance-of-power system of the previous century."[18] The final settlement was deemed the law of

Europe in the name and for the benefit of Europe as a whole. In the words of Metternich's advisor, Friedrich von Gentz:

The system which has been established in Europe since 1814 and 1815 is a phenomenon unheard-of in the history of the world. The principle of equilibrium . . . has been superseded by a principle of a general union, uniting the sum total of states in a federation under the direction of the major powers. . . . And Europe seems to form finally a great political family, united under the auspices of an areopagus of its own creation.[19]

The Treaty of Vienna, which summarized the efforts of the Congress, formed "the nucleus of an international public code to which additions were to be made as occasion served."[20]

THE CONCERT OF EUROPE

The interaction game established by the Congress of Vienna came to be known as the Concert of Europe and is regarded as an early effort to establish an international organization, albeit an informal one. The new game retained some of the characteristics of balance of power in that it was based once again on a mix of principle and force, what Talleyrand called "the principle of solidarity and of the balance of power between states."[21] Legitimized by the Treaty of Chaumont, the Quadruple Alliance, the Treaty of the Holy Alliance, and the Treaty of Vienna, the "congress system" was more hierarchical than the balance had been, since responsibility for its maintenance was consciously vested in the governments of the four victors, with the addition of France in 1818. However, the Concert of Europe was never as fully institutionalized as had been the balance system, nor did it acquire the same degree of legitimacy. In its pure form, it failed to survive a decade as major actors violated its rules and defected, and the game was altered by a series of ad hoc rule-making games. What ensued, Richard Rosecrance calls "the truncated concert," "the shattered concert," and "the Bismarckian concert."[22]

During its heyday, however, global politics was based on a set of widely understood and obeyed rules, a classic game of principle. The key technique of the game was diplomacy by conference, to which end Article VI of the Quadruple Alliance required periodic meetings.[23] In practice, these meetings were to be summoned when issues arose that required mediation and bargaining in order to prevent war, and they were preceded by considerable bilateral and multilateral diplomacy among lesser officials. In addition to bargains and principle, the conferences accorded at least an implicit role for votes in requiring unanimity among the great powers to effect changes in Europe's status quo.

Four key rules directed behavior under the Concert system. The first was to dispense with the principle of equality, although secondary actors might be consulted. None of the great powers, however, was to act unilaterally, so that the privilege of power was tempered by the responsibility of collective behavior in the name of Europe. A second rule was that territorial alterations in Europe must be agreed to by the great powers. In this sense, the rule also expressed the underlying principle of the status quo (as defined in 1815). It was, however, confusion over the meaning of this principle that was partly responsible for the decay of the Concert system.[25] For Britain, the status quo meant only preservation of the European balance of power as it applied to France after the defeat of Napoleon. For the other powers, notably Russia and Austria, the meaning of the status quo was the maintenance of existing (internal) constitutional and social arrangements as well as territorial boundaries. This implied the existence of an obligation to intervene if necessary in the internal affairs of European actors to prevent revolutionary change.

The third key rule of the system was that great powers with responsibility for the Concert mechanism and their interests must be protected, a rule very similar to that which had existed under the classical balance of power. The rule also applied to lesser actors which occupied strategic positions in the post-Napoleonic structure. The final rule, closely related to the third, was that the great powers not be exposed to the sort of humiliation that creates rigidity in behavior and promotes escalation of conflict. "They must not be challenged," declares Elrod, "either in their vital interests or in their prestige and honor."[26] Both of these rules implied a recognition of the danger inherent in equal status. Since any one of the great powers *could* harm another, the conditions for mutual fear and suspicion existed. To avoid this, it was seen as necessary that the relative influence distribution remain unchanged and that each actor be permitted to "save face" in the event of disagreement. In this way, disagreement or negative acts, it was hoped, would not degenerate into ill will and hostility.

The Concert-of-Europe game functioned as planned only until 1822, during which time four major European conferences were summoned. Although the game began to disintegrate in the following years, it reflected, while it lasted, the important role that principle could play in global interactions. As in the case of balance of power, it sought to preclude the emergence of symbolic and transcendent stakes, since only concrete stakes could be subjected easily to bargains and quick dispositions. In this way, also, an interdependence calculus could be consistently applies in assuming issue positions and making proposals.

The first of the great European conclaves was the Congress of Aix-la-Chapelle (Aachen) in 1818. Its main theme was the reintegration of France into Europe and the termination of the onerous obligations that had been placed upon that country in the form of indemnities and occupation after Napoleon's return.* To strengthen the Bourbon regime, occupation forces were withdrawn, and the reparations debt was turned over to private bankers. In addition, it was agreed that both the Atlantic slave trade and the Barbary priates should be suppressed (though little was done in either of these areas, owing to a hesitance to give the British navy *carte blanche*). At the congress, Tsar Alexander even proposed the formation of an international army and a permanent European federation, but these proposals were turned down as they went beyond the aims of the allies. Nevertheless, Aix-la-Chapelle closed on an optimistic note, suggesting that the prospects for institutionalizing the congress machinery were excellent. Castlereagh was so enthused that he wrote:

At all events, it is satisfactory to observe how little embarrassment and how much solid good grow out of these reunions. . . . It really appears to me to be a new discovery in the European Government, at once extinguishing the cobwebs into which diplomacy obscures the horizon, bringing the whole bearing of the system into its true light, and giving to the great Powers the efficiency and almost the simplicity of a single state.[27]

The pattern of agreement, it seemed, was itself generating bonds of amity.

The next two meetings, the Congresses of Troppau and Laibach (1820–21), were summoned to deal with revolutionary outbursts in Spain and the Kingdom of the Two Sicilies, and it was in the course of these

---

*The importance of the congress and its effects may be seen by contrasting it with the failure of Europe to revise the Versailles settlement after 1919.

conferences that the first fractures in the Concert system became apparent as a result of differing interpretations of the rules of the game. In both Spain and Naples, ruling governments collapsed with ease, events that profoundly disturbed Metternich. The latter, therefore, summoned a congress at Troppau in order to obtain its authority to put down the revolution in Naples, an area which Austrian officials viewed with particular sensitivity. Neither France nor Britain were, however, inclined to confer collective legitimacy upon such clear violations of the sovereignty principle, though Castlereagh was grudgingly prepared to permit Austria to intervene in Italy unilaterally, granting that the latter was of special concern to the former. As France and Britain sent only observers to the congresses, neither meeting truly voiced the opinions of a united Europe. At Troppau and later at Laibach, Metternich was able to persuade the tsar of the perniciousness of revolution, a view to which Prussia adhered. Metternich's interpretation of the rules of the game, as well as his influence with Alexander, was reflected in the preliminary protocol of Troppau:

States which have undergone a change of Government due to revolution, the results of which threaten other states, *ipso facto* cease to be members of the European Alliance, and remain excluded from it until their situation gives guarantees for legal order and stability. If, owing to such situations, immediate danger threatens other states, the Powers bind themselves, by peaceful means, or if need be by arms, to bring back the guilty state into the bosom of the Great Alliance.[28]

This genuinely counterrevolutionary document reveals the extent to which Metternich had come to see revolution in symbolic terms. His attitude severely tested the existing rules precisely because he was prepared unilaterally to extend them beyond the meaning which the British government, increasingly under the influence of liberal and reformist public opinion at home, was willing to accept. His linking of events in Spain and Italy proved a major step in returning the issue of political liberalism to the crisis stage in 1848. And, it was these very questions which continued to bedevil European statesmen at the fourth and final congress, the Congress of Verona (1822).

The situations in Spain and Greece were the key topics at Verona. Spain remained in ferment, and the Spanish colonies in Spanish America had seized the opportunity to free themselves of European rule. The Spanish monarch was determined to repress rebellion both at home and abroad. In addition, in 1821, Greece arose in revolt against rule by the

Ottoman Turks in an affair that was in part the work of a Greek adventurer who had lived in Russia and who had hoped to rally the tsar to the support of the Greek Christians. At Verona, the Greek case never recieved a hearing, since Tsar Alexander remained in sympathy with Metternich's position, and the rule of the Sultan was quickly restored. The Spanish case was considered, and it was on this issue that the Concert of Europe began to unravel. True to the principle of intervention, Alexander tried to persuade his colleagues to mediate between Spain and its colonies with the clear possibility of military intervention. This suggestion met with the blanket refusal of British foreign minister George Canning (Castlereagh had committed suicide some months before) who, like his predecessor, saw the Concert system merely as a means of maintaining a European balance of power.*

The strong British issue position removed the "wraps" from the emerging disagreement that had begun at Troppau-Laibach. But British behavior was still more ominous, since Canning's issue position was determined less by an interdependence calculus than a cost-benefit calculus, and was based on an increasing willingness to act alone. For some time, British commerce and industry had penetrated the Latin American market. British trade with Europe had been markedly reduced during the Napoleonic era, and the pressure to secure new markets, combined with British sea power, produced growing trade with Latin America. Moreover, the industrial revolution in Great Britain, particularly in the production of cotton goods, created added pressure for export markets (as well as secure imports of cotton from the United States). Canning, therefore, sought to exclude continental politico-military or economic intrusion into a highly valued sphere of interest which Britain would share with the United States.† Technology and industry were creating new stakes and making old ones obsolete, while a combination of internal political changes (particularly in Britain), and the growing sense of political efficacy on the part of a broader spectrum of the British public, was setting

---

* The British feared French intervention in Spain, which would upset the balance precisely in the manner they had hoped to avoid by the Concert of Europe. Although the French did intervene, its consequences were limited.

† Canning was instrumental in persuading the U.S. government to issue the Monroe Doctrine in 1823. He boasted that he had "called the New World into existence to redress the balance of the Old," a boast made plausible by the British navy.

in motion a train of events that would at once undermine the Concert of Europe and fuel overseas imperialism.

By 1822, the Concert of Europe was in decay as the conditions which had brought about its creation waned and the leaders who were responsible for it faded from the scene. After that date, the forces of reaction which the Concert represented were besieged both within and without. Nationalism, industrialization, the emergence of new actors in Europe and abroad, and the reorganization of old ones, were phenomena with which Concert statesmen were ill-prepared to deal. The continuing linkage between intra- and inter-actor politics, which they had tried to sever, remained a puzzle to them. After 1822 the "edifice of the coalition, so difficult to build and so hard to maintain, was soon torn down by the rush of new circumstances."[29] Canning himself understood this when he enthused: "Things are getting back to a wholesome state again. Every nation for itself and God for us all!"[30]

AN ERA OF AD HOC RULE MAKING

With the demise of the Concert owing to disagreements about rules, global politics entered a period of ad hoc rule-making games which culminated in the revolutions of 1848. Although conference diplomacy and many of the features of the old balance of power persisted outwardly, the role of principle declined precipitously as repeated clashes took place over competing ideologies—nationalism, liberalism, conservatism, and finally socialism. The role of force grew, a fact highlighted by the Crimean War, and the interdependence calculi of the previous epoch were infected by strong positive and negative affect. Although concrete stakes remained, they were gradually pushed aside by symbolic and transcendent stakes that had the effect of reducing flexibility and maneuverability. As had been the case during the years prior to 1815, the critical issues of political liberalism and national self-determination dominated the agenda, to be joined after 1848 by the issue of socialism. Until 1848, a watershed year, the first two reinforced European cleavages as liberalism and nationalism were believed to go hand in hand. What is most conspicuous about the period is that the key struggles and the search for rules were waged largely *within* actors rather than between them; once again internal politics shaped external politics. One of the major consequences of these events was to undermine the previous status quo, and to create significant status inconsistencies, the results of which were hidden, but not eliminated, by the later period of Bismarckian hegemony.

As had been the case in 1789, it was in France that internal reform and change had the most profound consequences. Between 1824 and 1830, reactionary measures were enacted that predicted a return to prerevolutionary days. When, in March 1830, the Chamber of Deputies resolved "no confidence" in the government of King Charles X, and the electorate thereafter refused to produce a legislative majority in favor of the monarch's policies, the government issued the "July Ordinances," which dissolved the chamber, altered the electoral system to ensure control by reactionaries, and established controls on the press. These actions precipitated the July Revolution, which quickly overthrew Charles X. As a compromise between republican and moderate monarchical sentiment, the Duke of Orleans was selected to assume the throne as Louis Philippe (1830–48). Though prepared to accept the limitations imposed by constitutional monarchy, Louis Philippe proved less of a reforming radical than many had hoped, and the next six years featured repeated uprisings (Lyons, 1831; Paris and Lyons, 1834), followed by bloody repression.

The Paris revolution of 1830 had immediate consequences elsewhere, notably in the Belgian revolt against Dutch dominance. Belgian independence was the first major territorial change on the continent since the Congress of Vienna. Unified action by the great powers proved elusive. Louis Philippe refused to intervene as long as others abstained, and this position was supported by the British government. Only Tsar Nicholas I seemed anxious to send troops, but he was confronted with revolution in Poland. This he repressed vigorously, and "Congress" Poland was absorbed into the Russian empire.* At a conference summoned in London during the final months of 1830, Belgian independence and neutrality were legitimized, thereby revising the 1815 settlement and endorsing "permanent" Belgian neutrality as a new rule of Europe.

Agitation on the continent, and particularly in France, had direct repercussions in Britain, where the winds of reform blew strongly enough for there to occur a second "bloodless" revolution, which would alter British political and social life, and which would create a gulf between

---

* Nicholas, who had succeeded Alexander in 1825, was himself faced with domestic agitation that climaxed in the abortive Decembrist revolt.

the British government and its former authoritarian allies on the continent. Prior to 1830, the dominant Tories had already begun to adopt liberal measures. However, until the Whigs took power in 1830, reformers had little success in seeking to revise an obsolete parliamentary system that ensured the overrepresentation of country gentry and the underrepresentation or nonrepresentation of large numbers of the new urban working and business classes. Shortly after the revolution in Paris, the Whigs introduced a reform bill, which was initially rejected by the Commons. Only after agitation had swept the country was electoral reform achieved in 1832. The Reform Bill revealed the growing political consciousness of the industrial and commercial classes and fundamentally altered the nature of "membership" in the British actor.

Most of the reforms were of benefit to the industrial bourgeoisie at the expense of the aristocratic landholding class. The bourgeoisie's greatest victory did not occur until 1846, with the repeal of the Corn Laws, which climaxed a movement which had begun with the formation of the Anti-Corn Law League in 1838. The significance of this action was that it strengthened the newly emerging industrialists by removing the high tariffs which had existed on imported food and by encouraging the export of manufactured goods. This triumph of the "liberalism" of Richard Cobden and John Bright was a victory for free trade, which, it was believed, would ensure inexpensive food and higher wages for the British worker and cheap raw materials and vast overseas markets for the British industrialist.

Far from satisfying the British proletariat, the reforms which benefited their employers merely encouraged the spread of socialist doctrines from the continent. Influenced by the ideas of French socialists, the proletarian organization called the "Chartists" made its appearance in 1838. Between 1839 and 1842, violent agitation rocked Britain and was met by the government with violence. In 1842 and again in 1848, Chartist agitation threatened revolution, a menace which was met by the government with a combination of force and timely reforms. Chartism represented an early phase in the growth of a new critical issue, socialism, which, unlike nationalism, was no respecter of state frontiers. Indeed, as events between 1815 and 1848 revealed, linkages between the internal and external political spheres were of increasing importance, rendering obsolete the ideas inherited from both the balance-of-power and Concert of Europe systems. Key issues were of consequence for both "domestic" and "international" life—just as the writings of Marx and Engels, begun at this time, would profoundly affect political life in all arenas.

If the 1830s undermined the vestiges of the Concert of Europe and initiated a period of intensive internal change in the major states of Europe, conditioning political behavior among leading actors; then 1848 witnessed a veritable explosion of transcendent "isms," which showed the very real limitations of the doctrine of sovereignty. The spread of powerful ideas that reflected rapid socioeconomic changes paid little heed to political boundaries, and internal fragmentation and reorganization once more profoundly conditioned global politics. In the presence of these "isms," stakes assumed an increasingly symbolic and transcendent character, and an actor dimension characterized the leading issues of the time. Once more, political life lost its moderate character as decisions were made on the basis of an affect calculus and the three elements of conflict reinforced one another.

As in 1830, the spark was ignited once again in Paris, where dissatisfaction with the July Monarchy continued to seethe despite efforts to repress it. In late February, 1848, street demonstrations erupted in Paris. Large-scale rioting and violence ensued, and on February 24 Louis Philippe abdicated and a republic was declared. Although including the socialist Louis Blanc, the new government was mostly bourgeois republican in its composition. Blanc was given the opportunity to try out his scheme of "national workshops" in Paris, and these, though given little authority, became centers of radical socialist agitation. France found itself increasingly divided between urban radical and rural conservative. The former—living in some of the worst conditions in industrial Europe—demanded the completion of a social revolution, which terrified the latter, who saw the demands as nothing less than "communism." Parisian workers unsuccessfully sought to dissolve the nationally elected Constituent Assembly, and the Assembly then sought to dissolve the national workshops and so eliminate the threat of socialism, to which the Parisian proletariat reacted violently. Between June 23 and June 26, Paris witnessed the bloodiest street-fighting in European history, resulting in the imposition of a military dictatorship. What had occurred in Paris was class war, and its effect was to frighten the bourgeoisie throughout Europe. Thus, when Chartism revived in Great Britain that year—encouraged partly by events in France—official reaction was swift and vigorous, climaxing in the arrest of the movement's leadership. In France a new constitution was drafted, based on a strong presidency; and in December, Prince Louis Napoleon Bonaparte, nephew of Napoleon Bonaparte, was overwhelmingly elected. By skillfully combining plebiscitary and demagogic techniques and by posing as an ally of radical nationalism, Louis Napoleon, in December, 1851, was able to institute a dictatorship by coup d'état. The following year he proclaimed himself Napoleon III, Emperor of the French.

THE UNLINKING OF LIBERALISM AND NATIONALISM: NEW CROSSCUTTING ALIGNMENTS

Events in Britain and France revealed that liberalism and socialism, on the one hand, and nationalism, on the other, were not necessarily compatible. The enemies of the French Revolution and Napoleon had stimulated nationalism to save themselves and to stem the radical tide. But it was not until after 1848 that they key critical issues assumed new faces. Since these issues (as well as socialism) involved different friends and foes, rulers came to understand that the adroit manipulation of one could generate the sort of crosscutting effect that would vitiate the intensity of the other. In particular, by manipulating nationalism, they discovered that it was possible to create cognitive dissonance on the part of adversaries that could produce indecision and/or moderation. The fact that "flag" and "class" involved overlapping, but not reinforcing, cleavages was implicitly comprehended in 1848; it was also keenly appreciated by Bismarck in Germany, and even served to wean the socialists of Europe from their principles in 1914.[31]

The year 1848 marked a turning point in European history. Ad hoc efforts to achieve a new consensus on the rules of the game after the Concert of Europe had begun to erode had not revealed any satisfactory solution. Individually and jointly, ruling elites, particularly in Central and Eastern Europe, proved unable to move beyond blind resistance to the growing clamor for value satisfaction that found expression in the issues of political liberalism, socialism, and nationalism. In the Austrian empire, Metternich, representing the interests of the Habsburg dynasty, took the lead in adamantly opposing both liberalism and nationalism. In 1819, parallel to his efforts in the Concert, he had summoned a conference of the principal states of Germany, which jointly issued the Carlsbad Decrees for the suppression of liberal-national sentiment at German universities. The Habsburg Empire itself consisted of numerous national groupings, including Italians, Germans, Czechs, Hungarians, Poles, Slovaks, and Serbs. Within the Empire, the privileged elite—like the ruling house itself—was Austrian (Germanic), so that both doctrines appeared to Metternich as deadly threats to the political and economic status quo. By this perception and policies designed to uphold that status quo, Metternich unwittingly linked the two transcendent issues and thrust together both liberals and nationalists in an uncomfortable coalition, the sole common bond of which was opposition to him and his supporters.

Repression of nationalist sentiment and demands for constitutional and economic reform set the stage for the explosions of 1848. The former was particularly strong in Hungary, where nationalists sought Hungarian autonomy; while demands for liberalization were potent in Austria, where industrialization had created a large urban working class. The spark was provided by news of the successful revolution in Paris in February. A rising of workers and students in Vienna shook the Habsburg throne, forcing Metternich to resign and to flee to Britain in disguise. Rioting also swept Berlin, forcing the king of Prussia to promise a constitution. Rapidly, the ruling houses of Austria and Prussia were forced to concede one demand after another, and Hungarian and Bohemian autonomy were recognized. Austria's Italian provinces, too, burst into flames, and the king of Sardinia (Piedmont), hoping to form the kernel of an independent Italy, declared war on Austria. April and May proved to be the highwater mark of revolution as adherents of liberalism and nationalism throughout Germany, Italy, and Austria's Slavic provinces saw the opportunity to create national states based on liberal principles.

The tide began to turn in June, in part because the alliance between liberals and nationalists was, in fact, artificial. Bourgeois nationalists and proletarian and peasant reformers were deeply suspicious of each other. The nationalists themselves had little in common, so that when an all-German national assembly was convoked in Frankfurt-on-the-Main to author a German constitution, it had little contact with a parallel Pan-Slav congress that met in Prague. As debate continued in both assemblies, the forces of order reorganized and assumed the offensive. Prague was bombarded by a Habsburg army, and the Pan-Slav congress dispersed. A week later, a second Austrian army crushed the Piedmontese-Italian forces and resumed control of Lombardy. In September and October military control was successfully reimposed upon Hungary and Austria.

German nationalism fared little better. By the end of 1848, the Prussian monarchy had crushed revolution by military means though the Frankfurt assembly continued to meet. However, its impact was limited from the outset since, as bourgeois nationalists, its members were alienated from both radical reformers and landholding aristocrats. Enjoying only a narrow base of political support, the assembly was further divided over the definition of a united Germany—Should Austria be included or not? After prolonged debate on this question, a de facto answer was provided by Habsburg refusal to consider joining such a federation.

The Frankfurt assembly sought to forge a united Germany by means of a combination of principle and votes and was met by force and bargains. Austrian, Hungarian, Slavic, and Italian patriots and reformers sought to resolve the issues of liberalism and nationalism by force and were crushed by force. Indeed, one of the key effects of the revolutions of 1848 was to invite strong reaction, both internally in the states directly effected, and externally toward the sources of liberal and nationalist doctrines. Within Austria, Prussia, and Russia reform was aborted, while externally the three states were joined in a front opposed to those governments in the West that to a greater degree reflected liberal norms. Perhaps, the strongest expression of reaction emerged from Rome where, in 1864, Pope Pius IX (who had initially been known as the "pope of progress") released his encyclical *Quanta cura,* with its appended *Syllabus errorum,* in which were denounced such errors as nationalism, socialism, and communism. "It is an error," the pope declared, "to believe that the Roman Pontiff can and ought to reconcile himself to, and agree with, progress, liberalism, and contemporary civilization."[32] Almost a pronouncement of "cold war," the papal encyclical reflected the degree to which issue positions had become rigid and the issues transcendent and tightly linked by an actor dimension.

Despite the easy defeat of revolution in 1848, it became clear that the liberal–conservative struggle, at least externally, defied final resolution short of major war. That such a war was not fought owes much to the realization by major statesmen, like Palmerston and Disraeli in Britain, and

Bismarck in Germany, that it could not be won, and that while failing to eradicate the "pernicious" doctrines of the adversaries, its costs would be enormous, even threatening the survival of governments that chose to wage it. The dispersion of power in Europe ensured mutual failure, at least in terms of this issue, and, though it produced intensive conflict for a time, manipulation of cognitive dissonance by key leaders eventually led to its being tacitly shelved.

THE TRIUMPH OF REALPOLITIK AND THE DORMANCY OF CRITICAL ISSUES

In ad hoc fashion, major actors began to focus on a revised set of rules that helped restore a measure of stability to global politics after the outbursts of 1848. The external and internal realms of politics were again rigidly separated. Internally, governments were free to cope with the issues of liberalism and nationalism as best they could, and they did so by resort to a cost-benefit calculus that encouraged them to take advantage of one issue (nationalism) to deal with the other (liberalism). Externally, the game of realpolitik was introduced as part of a general reaction to romanticism and idealism. The struggle for transcendent and symbolic stakes was abandoned, and the intensive pursuit of concrete stakes was resumed. The underlying mechanisms of the game were bargains and force. The former were evident in the numerous dispositions of colonies in Africa, the Near East, and Asia; and these were related to the ubiquitous alliances which, during the Bismarck era, came to augment the conference mechanism of the Concert. So important was the role of alliances that Bismarck was moved to declare, "All politics reduce themselves to this formula: Try to be *à trois* in a world governed by five Powers."[33] Only after 1890 did the alliances become rigid, thereby revealing the renewed dominance of an actor dimension after a period in which issues had been linked by a stake dimension. Bargains were also carried out at the numerous international conferences of the time.* The list of conferences and congresses during the period is also impressive and includes such conclaves as the

* The list of alliances concluded between 1850 and 1890 is impressive. Singer and Small identify some twenty-three. "Alliance Aggregation and the Onset of War," in J. David Singer, ed., *Quantitative International Politics* (New York: Free Press, 1968), pp. 268–69, table 3.

Vienna conference of 1854, the Congress of Paris in 1856, the Zurich conference of 1859, the conferences of Paris of 1866 and 1869, the London conferences of 1867 and 1871, and the Congresses of Berlin of 1878 and 1885.

Force was manifested in the numerous wars that erupted between 1850 and 1890, most of which were modest in scope and took place outside of Europe itself.* The most important of these were the three waged by Bismarck to unify Germany (Schleswig-Holstein, 1864; Austro-Prussian War, 1866; Franco-Prussian War, 1870). After 1870, until Bismarck's ouster in 1890, war in Europe was avoided by bargains buttressed by Bismarck's policies of deterrence and manipulation of alliances. Gradually, affect calculi came to be replaced by interdependence and cost-benefit calculi, although the role of affect remained greater than at the height of the balance of power.†

After 1848, then, the critical issues of liberalism, nationalism, and socialism remained alive but, with the exception of nationalism until 1870, were at the periphery of the agenda, and were for the most part contained *within* national polities and prevented from infecting the relations of major actors. In the case of liberalism and socialism, skillful leaders, notably Bismarck, successfully blunted them by turning the one against the other and then turning nationalism against them both.‡ Bismarck became minister-president of Prussia in 1862 and German chancellor after unification, and remained the leading figure in German politics until his dismissal. As a conservative member of the *Junker* class, he abhorred both liberalism and socialism and was personally not even sympathetic to German nationalism. He undermined the parliamentary reforms of 1850, enlarged the army, and generally strengthened the monarchy which he served. Nevertheless, he was sufficiently flexible to undercut the growing influence of socialism, by playing on the fears of the liberal and nationalist bourgeoisie, passing antisocialist legislation between 1878 and 1890,

---

*Singer and Small list sixteen wars. *Ibid.,* pp. 262–63, table 2. Also see George and Smoke, pp. 15–18.

†Franco-German relations after 1870, for instance, continued to be governed by negative affect owing to French *revanchism* following the German seizure of Alsace-Lorraine in the Franco-Prussian War. None of Bismarck's efforts to alter this condition sufficed to do so.

‡There were those who were prepared to "globalize" these issues, such as Marx and Engels in the case of socialism, and William Gladstone in the case of liberalism in the 1870s, but these efforts were generally abortive.

initiating his own program of social reforms in the 1880s, and wooing the German proletariat with the attraction of national unity and expansion. Although not a passionate nationalist, Bismarck was prepared to unleash the forces of nationalism to settle accounts at home, as he did in 1871 by initiating the *Kulturkampf* against the Catholic Center party, which supported the new doctrine of papal infallibility and which he pictured as a threat to the loyalty of German Catholics. In this he was supported by German liberals who were opposed to clerical influence. In 1879, he abruptly turned on his liberal friends by abandoning free trade. In this *volte face* he was joined by his former Catholic adversaries and by conservative industrial and landholding interests. In brief, Bismarck's policies produced a Germany characterized by unprecendented industrial and population growth, a docile proletariat, and a centralized political and administrative system.

Bismarck's cultivation of German nationalism was manifested by the three rapid wars waged against Denmark, Austria, and France. For the most part, they were provoked by Bismarck's effort to impose new rules on the system with himself as arbiter of those rules. They were also encouraged by the rapid growth in German power, the result of industrialization and military modernization, combined with a desire to have this new status recognized. The immediate reason for the wars was Bismarck's desire to acquire quickly and inexpensively the stakes which represented national unification. Thus, the chancellor will be remembered for a speech delivered to the Prussian parliament in 1886, in which he recalled his policy:

Place in the hands of the King of Prussia the strongest possible military power, then he will be able to carry out the policy you wish; this policy cannot succeed through speeches, and shooting-matches, and songs; it can only be carried out through blood and iron.

A secondary reason for the wars was the desire to impose unilaterally Bismarck's interpretation of the rules of the system and thereby enable Germany to carry out Bismarck's policy of maintaining a conservative status quo by the adroit use of bargains (particularly in the colonial sphere) and the threat of force. Throughout his tenure, Bismarck remained aware of the close connection between the internal and external realms of policy. Unrequited nationalism and alleged threats to security provided persuasive arguments for centralization of control at home, while such control was necessary to carry out foreign policy effectively.

The other great manifestation of the nationalism issue was in Italy, where Bismarck's policy also left its mark. In general, the failures of 1848–49 revealed that the liberal republicanism of Mazzini only frightened the other powers and was a liability to the cause of Italian unification. Thereafter, the core of the movement was in Piedmont, under its premier, Count Camillo Benso di Cavour. Piedmont's participation in the Crimean War created a favorable impression upon leaders of Britain and France, and in 1858 Napoleon III was persuaded to succor the Italian cause. In 1859 France and Piedmont went to war against Austria, winning two key victories. But at the moment of decision, Napoleon III backed away from the venture as a result of pressure from Prussia, opposition from Catholics both at home and abroad, and personal revulsion at the revolutionary excesses that took place throughout Italy. In a fury, Cavour resigned. Nevertheless, Parma, Modena, Tuscany, and Romagna all petitioned for union with Piedmont, an action of which Napoleon approved only after Nice and Savoy had been ceded to France. In the following year, Giuseppe Garibaldi landed with his "Red Shirts" in Sicily, crossed over to the mainland, and was greeted with popular acclaim. To temper the revolutionary spirit thus roused and to avoid raising the suspicion of the pope and the French, Cavour proceeded southward, where he joined up with Garibaldi and adroitly wrested control of the movement in the name of Piedmont's King Victor Emmanuel. A Kingdom of Italy was formally proclaimed in 1861, thereby unifying the entire peninsula except for Venetia and Rome. The former was ceded to Italy five years later by Bismarck, as a reward for Italian assistance in his war against Austria. The disposition of Rome, however, was delayed an additional four years as papal forces aided by French troops resisted the efforts of Garibaldi. With the outbreak of the Franco-Prussian War of 1870, these troops were withdrawn, and shortly thereafter Rome was added to Italy.

With the completion of German and Italian unification, nationalism, as a critical issue, entered a dormant stage, in which it remained until after the ouster of Bismarck. The stakes associated with national self-determination had been divided in such a way as to satisfy the deepest grievances, at least in Western Europe. In Eastern Europe and in the Balkans, however, national aspirations remained unfulfilled, but, for the time, the dissatisfied were unable to return the issue to the top of the agenda. The Bismarckian hegemony also shifted liberalism and socialism to the periphery of the agenda, and with them went the symbolic and transcendent stakes with which they were associated. The former did not return to the top of the agenda until the final years of World War I, and the latter did not return until after the 1917 revolution in Russia. The immediate consequences of Bismarck's wars and the two unifications were seen in the substitution of concrete, particularly economic, stakes for symbolic and transcendent stakes. However, the results of the immense shift in the status hierarchy, notably in the rise of Germany and decline of Austria, Russia, and Turkey, would make themselves felt by 1900, initially in the form of rigid alliances and arms races, and ultimately in war.

The growing pool of concrete stakes after 1870 was reflected by the rapid upsurge of European expansion into Africa and Asia (which created the basis for the later issue of colonialism, the successor to that of national self-determination). Set against a background of unprecedented industrial growth, technological innovation, urbanization, population growth, and political reform, the energy of Europe's expansion outward assumed two forms. The first was the emigration from Europe to the United States, Canada, Latin America, and Australia of some sixty millions between 1846 and 1932.[34] The participants in this vast movement were primarily the least privileged and most deprived members of European society, coming from the least prosperous areas of the continent. This wholesale exodus was in no small measure responsible for the rapid development of economic power in areas outside Europe. The second form of expansion manifested itself in a new imperialism.

Numerous explanations have been given for the great wave of imperialism which took place after 1870. The need for raw materials to fuel industrial growth, the desire for protected markets abroad for finished goods, the search for profitable investment opportunities, and the desire of missionaries to spread Christian enlightenment are among the plausible motivations. What is clear is that the technological and industrial development of Europe, translated into military power, permitted the easy penetration and conquest of non-European regions. Although this expansion created new opportunities for friction and disagreement among the major European actors, it initially provided an infusion of new stakes that promised wealth and status. In this manner, the scarcity of these values was at least temporarily relieved. "There was still much unpreempted space in the world—Africa, for example, was predominantly *terra incognita* in 1870—hence ample room for all."[35] Even when disagreements occurred over imperial claims, it proved relatively easy to adjust them by means of bargains that took advantage of their tangible and divisible nature.

Among the best illustrations of bargains in this context was the Congress of Berlin, which was summoned by the French and German governments in the autumn of 1884 and which met until February 1885. The Congress was called to prevent the growth of friction among the major actors, which seemed destined to occur if expansion in central Africa continued in unregulated fashion. The ostensible reason for the conclave was to legitimize Belgian control of the Congo. However, as France was extending its influence north of the Congo River from Gabon, and Britain and Portugal were doing the same to the south of the river, fears existed that misunderstanding might arise. In the meantime, German penetration of East Africa, and British movement up the Nile, also forecast stormy weather. The representatives of some fourteen governments—including the United States—meeting in Berlin, agreed to seek suppression of the slave trade and declared freedom of trade in the Congo basin and freedom of navigation upon the Congo and Niger Rivers. "Effective occupation" of territory was agreed to as a suitable standard for laying claim to territory. These agreements represented the articulation of joint principles to regulate the imperialist venture. As René Albrecht-Carrié notes: "The tone of the gathering reflected the acceptance of the equally legitimate right of all to imperial activity, both trade and territorial acquisitions."[36]

In this way, the game of imperialism acquired its own special rules, and conflicting claims were threafter largely resolved by principle and bargains. These mechanisms served well in the adjustment of Anglo-French differences over Egypt and Morocco in 1904 and Anglo-Russian differences in 1907. Indeed, straightforward territorial swaps served to prevent the explosion of crises, for instance, in 1911, when in return for German assent to French penetration of Morocco and a small area near Lake Chad, France ceded to Germany some 100,000 square miles of the French Congo.

Yet, if the rules governing imperialism were reasonably clear and legitimate, those governing the relations among major powers in Europe never achieved clarity or legitimacy and consequently were not institutionalized. What rules existed were articulated primarily by Bismarck himself and enforced by his skillful manipulation of alliances and conferences and cautious application of coercive diplomacy. Under these conditions, arrangements which had been reached by ad hoc means never became more than ad hoc. When the architect of German policy, Bismarck, was relieved of office by Kaiser Wilhelm II in 1890, he was succeeded by "epigones" who "inherited neither his chart nor his compass."[37]

THE SEARCH FOR VIABLE RULES AND THE DESCENT TO GLOBAL WAR

Bismarck understood what his successors did not—that a united and nationalist Germany could easily be perceived as a mortal threat to its neighbors, and that in geographical terms it was among the most vulnerable of actors. To Bismarck, alliances represented a means of mixing coercion and principle in a flexible and imaginative manner, so as to prevent the development of anti-German feeling, cleavages that would force Germany to take sides and contribute to tension that would highlight Germany's peculiar vulnerability. "The effects of this vulnerability," declare two observers, "are seen in later German history: a stress on military preparedness and first-strike capability, an over-emphasis on internal political cohesion leading to a neurotic preoccupation with politico-economic scapegoats such as the Jews and the Communists, and a diplomatic mesh of agreements which was often as comprehensive as it was inconsistent."[38]

Indeed, "inconsistency" was the hallmark of the ad hoc arrangements which Bismarck engineered, a characteristic which he saw as inherently necessary to keep his own allies from each other's throats as well as from Germany's. Although disagreements were inevitable, flexibility, he believed, was the one way to prevent negative acts and hostility from hardening, so that concrete stakes would become linked into larger issues by an actor dimension. His policy aimed at conscious manipulation of crosscutting issues in order to encourage the use of interdependence calculi. The critical problem was to prevent major actors from throwing in their lot with France, which could not be swayed from the attitude of enmity towards Germany that it adopted after 1870. To achieve this meant keeping Austro-Hungarian and Russian relations from deteriorating over the issue of the disposition of the Balkans.

This last problem became increasingly vexatious as Turkish authority and influence in the region continued to wane in the last half of the nineteenth century, thereby making available the Balkan stakes for competition. They were particularly tempting to the imperial regimes of Austria-Hungary and Russia, in part because of their strategic location, which promoted their perceived association with security values, and in part because of their connection with the process of decay in both empires. For the Habsburgs, this meant bringing under control the growing unrest of South Slav inhabitants of the empire, who viewed their interests as connected to those of Balkan Slavs in Serbia and elsewhere, threatening to push Austro-Hungarian fragmentation from the stage of "factions" across the threshold of "competing actors." The Romanovs viewed the prospect of growing influence in the Balkans as the means of encouraging the growth of the transcendent issue of "Pan-Slavism" that might stimulate nationalism and slake the growing thirst at home for reform and socialism. After Russia's 1905 defeat in war with Japan and subsequent revolution at home, this prospect became a matter of some urgency. Thus, for these two principal actors, the Balkans became an issue of very high salience, involving survival values, transcendent stakes, and a joint fear of relative loss.

The Balkans, to Bismarck, were not worth "the healthy bones of a single Pomeranian grenadier," and to keep the potential adversaries apart meant the weaving of an alliance network which contained significant inconsistencies. In October 1879, Germany and Austria-Hungary reached a secret military agreement that essentially guaranteed the latter in the event of Russian attack. Yet only two years later Bismarck drew both Austria and Russia into the first *Dreikaiserbund* (Three Emperors' League) which resembled "the non-aggression pacts so popular in the period between the two world wars and now again in the late 1960s and early 1970s *détente* between East and West."[39] This alliance represented Bismarck's effort to refocus Austrian and Russian attention from each other and upon Great Britain. After the strategy collapsed in the wake of the Balkan crises of 1885–86, Bismarck, with characteristic flexibility, sought to tie each of the two Balkan adversaries to Germany separately. While retaining the

Austrian alliance, he concluded the secret Reinsurance Treaty with Russia in June 1887, under which Germany and Russia would remain neutral unless Germany attacked France or Russia attacked Austria-Hungary. Though the two treaties were technically consistent with each other, their spirit was clearly in contradiction, and only a diplomatic tour de force could have concealed this fact.

If it is possible for imaginative statesmen to manipulate cognitive dissonance to break out of a conflict cycle, it is perhaps easier for conventional and unimaginative leaders to produce unwittingly the dissonance that gives rise to a conflict cycle. This was precisely what occurred after the dismissal of Bismarck in 1890, as his successors defected from the game Bismarck had played and unilaterally sought to impose their own rules. By their words and deeds, they provoked a diplomatic revolution in Europe that left Germany isolated. While the issue positions which they assumed were often legally sound (as in the 1906 Moroccan crisis), the harsh techniques adopted to promote them alienated and frightened other major actors and gave rise "to the complaint that Germany always wanted to negotiate with a pistol on the table."[40]

Seeking to iron out prior inconsistencies in policy and to achieve status consistency, their diplomacy reflected a narrow rigidity which transformed concrete stakes into symbolic ones, and linked them into larger issues through an actor dimension. Efforts to make Germany a naval and colonial power, for instance, were logical steps to end status inconsistency but provoked the birth of a new issue, "Prussian militarism," through which prism proposals concerning such disparate stakes as the Berlin–Baghdad Railway and Morocco were formulated. After 1890, a game emerged with characteristics not unlike those of the later Cold War. Principle disappeared as an important mechanism; bargains became less central; and force and the threat of force assumed a more dominant role. This combination was reflected in the increasing resort—first by Germany and then by others—to techniques of coercive diplomacy, in which military force was used just short of war in the effort to press adversaries to capitulate rather than agree freely. Coercive diplomacy was characteristic of the string of crises that terminated just short of war in the years prior to 1914—Morocco (1906), Bosnia (1908), Morocco (1911). Although institutionalized, this game never came to be regarded as legitimate by all participants, some of which still believed they were subject to the rules of a Concert-of-Europe game. The last crisis ended abruptly as Austria-Hungary's effort to employ coercive diplomacy against Serbia provoked world war.

In the name of consistency, Kaiser Wilhelm II and his advisors abandoned the Reinsurance Treaty with Russia in 1890, thereby isolating Russia and creating the conditions for a Franco-Russian rapprochement. In the ensuing years, German behavior alienated Great Britain and so promoted the conditions for the formation of the Triple Entente. In the case of Russia, Germany's insensitivity and blind support of Austria-Hungary, which culminated in the provision of a "blank check" to Austrian officials in 1914, served to promote cognitive dissonance on the part of Russian leaders, who saw the Dual Alliance as frustrating their ambitions at every turn. Then, once a negative actor dimension had been created, German actions produced the sort of cognitive consistency on the part of the Russians that escalated conflict. The latter was illustrated in the Bosnian crisis of 1908 that grew out of a misunderstanding between Austrian foreign minister Aerenthal and Russian foreign minister Isvolsky. The two had apparently agreed to a bargain in the Balkans that would have permitted the opening of the Straits at Constantinople to Russian warships in return for Austrian annexation of Bosnia and Herzegovina. However, while Austria-Hungary proceeded to annex the Turkish provinces in October, 1908, Isvolsky was unable to persuade the major European actors, notably the British government, to go along with his Straits proposal. Furious, the Russian foreign minister denounced Aerenthal and demanded an international conference. Germany need not have been involved but for a Russian request that Berlin use its "good offices" in Vienna. Instead of acceding to the Russian request, the German government took the opportunity to express its full backing of Austria and in March, 1909 proposed in a peremptory note to Russia that the Tsarist government surrender its support of Serbia and recognize the Austrian annexation. The Russians were told to answer yes or no, and in the event of the latter, to accept the consequences—a clear threat of war. Owing to its recent defeat at the hands of Japan and the incomplete nature of military reforms begun with French loans, Russia was in no position to accept the challenge and was forced to surrender in humiliating fashion. Thus, Germany leaders had chosen to deal with the Bosnian stake as though it were symbolic of the Austro-German alliance, and Russia, while suffering defeat, resolved to be better prepared for the next round.

In the case of Britain, German leaders recklessly sacrificed an amicable relationship in the Kaiser's quest for "a place in the sun" for his country and in pursuit of *Weltpolitik*. Prior to 1895 Germany and Britain, particularly under Bismarck and Disraeli, had enjoyed a pattern of agreement that was reinforced by close financial, social, and familial ties between elites in the two countries. Although two decades of industrial and military growth had created conditions of parity between the two, the nature of their relative power was not threatening. German commerce and trade was directed mostly to Europe, while Britain's commercial connections were increasingly directed outward to the United States and the Empire. Germany's military strength tended to be in the form of a land army, whereas Britain's was concentrated in naval supremacy.

It may be that German officials believed that a rapprochement between Britain, on the one hand, and France and Russia, on the other, was out of the question. If so, they behaved so as to make it a reality. German insensitivity to issues of salience in Britain transformed positive into negative affect. As early as 1895, by rejecting out of hand all of Prime Minister Salisbury's proposals for partitioning the Ottoman Empire as a brash effort to embroil Germany in Near Eastern issues, the Kaiser alienated the formerly pro-German Salisbury. The following year, as British relations with the Boers of the Transvaal were worsening (a process which culminated in the outbreak of the Boer War in 1899), the Kaiser impetuously sent a telegram to President Paul Kruger of the South African Republic, congratulating him on the repulse of a raid led by Dr. Leander Jameson, a close friend of Cecil Rhodes and administrator of the territories of the British-owned South Africa Company. German officials reasoned that their support of the Boers would convince Britain of its need for German friendship. Instead, the Kruger telegram roused a storm of indignation in Britain and fed the growing belief that Germany wished to challenge British colonial dominance in Africa. This belief was further fueled by the passage in the German Reichstag in 1898 of the first naval law which called for the construction of a large German high-seas battle fleet, needed to protect colonies and commerce and to permit the exercise of

German influence beyond Europe. This effort was viewed as a mortal threat by British officials and the subsequent naval arms race was seen in Britain as symbolic of British security. "Britain was so identified with the concept that its strength, and even its very existence, lay in being the major naval power, that fears and resentment were bound to come once Germany began to develop a navy."[41] Advances in technology exacerbated the rivalry, when, in 1905, the deployment of the new Dreadnought-class battleship negated the advantages of Britain's numerical superiority in older vessals. Bargains to adjust Anglo-German differences over colonial and naval policies were unavailable because "Germany lacked suitable material to exchange."[42]

Between 1890 and 1914, then, German leaders sacrificed the opportunity to promote the atmosphere of Anglo-German interdependence which Bismarck had taken pains to cultivate. Ironically, German leaders tended to behave as they did in order to persuade the British of the need for German friendship but instead ended up taking advantage of British difficulties. Disagreements and negative acts transformed prior amity into enmity and gradually intensified mutual suspicion. The growth of disagreement made the existence of military parity appear to both actors a dangerous condition. Almost every German proposal and issue position seemed only to sour Anglo-German relations further. In the midst of British difficulties during the Boer War, for instance, Germany pressed Britain into an unfavorable agreement regarding the disposition of the Samoan Islands and took the opportunity to obtain a concession to construct the Baghdad Railway. The hostility of the German press to Britain's prosecution of the Boer War, and the halting of German vessels by the British navy on suspicion that they carried contraband, left further deposits of ill will. British efforts to cultivate support for the Boer War were greeted by Germany's heavy-handed demands for a formal alliance, and mutual hostility was exacerbated by verbal blunders on the part of leaders in both countries. Thus, in seeking to defend British tactics in the Boer War, Joseph Chamberlain suggested that British behavior was no more "barbarous" than had been German behavior in the Franco-Prussian War, a comment regarded in Berlin as an insult to the German army. Not to be outdone, the Kaiser in 1908 granted an interview to the British *Daily Telegraph* which emerged as "an emotional, aggrieved plea for English friendship, naively voicing the bewilderment which most Germans genuinely felt at English resentment against the German navy and German world policy.''[43]

Gradually concrete stakes that were at issue between the two actors assumed symbolic significance and encouraged escalation of negative affect. Crude German efforts to use the Moroccan crisis of 1906 as a lever to pry Britain and France apart merely served to cement the *entente cordiale,* with Morocco as a symbol of it. In the midst of the crisis, the two allies initiated secret military and naval conversations. Again, the German dispatch of a gunboat to Agadir at the outset of the second Moroccan crisis in 1911 prompted a threatening speech by David Lloyd George, chancellor of the exchequer, in which he declared that if Britain were treated ''as if she were of no account in the Cabinet of Nations, then I say emphatically that peace at that price would be a humiliation intolerable for a great country like ours to endure.''[44]

Although the actual outbreak of war in 1914 was the product of yet another confrontation in the Balkans between Russia and Austria-Hungary, it was a logical consequence of the transformation of global politics after 1890. German behavior had given rise to two competitive alliance systems, which after 1907 became two armed camps. Concrete stakes had increasingly become linked to each other by negative affect. Increasingly, these stakes were seen as symbolic of alliance solidarity and national security, rather than as independent stakes of limited value. The crisis brought on by the assassination of the Austrian archduke was merely the final ''test of strength.'' In the light of technological changes that seemed to place a premium on rapid military mobilization and *guerre à outrance,* the flexibility of negotiators was limited, and this combination of military strategy and its association with alliances made it difficult to localize war when it erupted. At a deeper level, reliance on force as the dominant allocation mechanism, a reliance reflected in arms races, intra-alliance collaboration, resort to coercive diplomacy, and limited outbreaks of war (e.g., the Italian-Turkish War of 1911 and the Balkan Wars of 1912–13) reflected what Colonel House described as ''militarism run stark mad.''[45] It reflected, too, the failure of leading actors in earlier encounters to fashion an agreed-upon set of rules to replace those which had fallen into disuse. Principle and votes had largely disappeared with the decay of the conference system, and bargains became increasingly difficult to arrange as concrete stakes disappeared (illustrated by the Fashoda crisis of 1898) and symbolic and transcendent ones came to take their place. The abandonment of earlier rules, and the dramatic revisions in the status hierarchy of Europe during the period after 1870, had promoted a potent actor dimension, which was reflected in the rigidification of alliances and the movement from one to another interaction game until force, a unilateral mechanism, seemed all that was available. Finally, the egregious misperceptions of leaders under stress during the last crisis— and their resulting overreaction to, and distortion of, the initiatives of adversaries—were the products of the previous spiral of disagreement, negative acts, and intensifying hostility that strengthened the underlying actor dimension. In the words of one eminent historian:

The Old World had degenerated into a powder magazine, in which the dropping of a lighted match, whether by accident or design, was almost certain to produce a conflagration. . . . It is a mistake to imagine that the conflict of 1914 took Europe unawares, for the statesmen and soldiers had been expecting it and preparing for it for many years.[46]

When Austria-Hungary declared war on Serbia, its ostensible reason was to solve internal problems at minimal cost, but the frustration of its leaders was so great that it sought to destroy Serbia as well. Others joined in, for the most part, out of a combination of misperception and misunderstanding of existing rules, but in time frustration-anger became their reason for fighting as well. In the end, four great empires disappeared, and the "victors" were so exhausted by the contest that the ensuing status hierarchy was changed almost beyond recognition.

VERSAILLES: FORMAL RULE MAKING TO REMAKE THE WORLD

World War I ground on until 1918, eventually drawing in all major actors, including the United States and Japan. Whatever issues gave rise to the conflagration were forgotten in a joint frenzy of annihilation. As the years wore on and the war became a struggle of attrition, leaders found it difficult to bargain, as they felt it necessary to justify the immense costs of blood and wealth that were involved. The "absolute war" that Clausewitz had foreseen as a logical possibility in the early nineteenth century became a reality, and politics itself was forced to take a back seat to military exigencies. If the German invasion of Belgium in 1914 tore up the last vestiges of the rules laid down by the Concert of Europe, the virtual dictatorship of German Supreme Headquarters under Hindenburg and Ludendorff after 1917 assured that military considerations would dictate political objectives, a fact made manifest by Germany's initiation of a compaign of unrestricted submarine warfare.

Although Germany was the first to sue for peace, all the major participants were really losers. The war toppled the empires of Central and Eastern Europe, bled France and Britain beyond easy recovery, and set in motion the forces that ultimately toppled their global empires. As in the case of Europe in 1815, the great catastrophe proved a singular learning experience, which brought the rules of realpolitik into disrepute. In an effort to restructure global politics and legislate new rules of interaction, the Versailles Conference formally opened in January 1919. At least one major participant, President Woodrow Wilson, representing the most economically powerful actor to emerge from the war, was determined to turn away from prior rules and impose a revolutionary set of rules and procedures upon the assemblage. Later described by realists as an "idealist" and a "utopian," Wilson "transplanted the nineteenth-century rationalist faith to the almost virgin soil of international politics and, bringing it back with him to Europe, gave it a new lease of life."[47] He regarded the balance of power as "the great game, now forever discredited," and he declared that World War I had been "fought to do away with an old order and to establish a new one, and the center and characteristic of the old order was that unstable thing which we used to call the 'balance of power'. . . ."[48] In its stead, he proposed to substitute the game of "collective security," which would be established first and foremost upon a foundation of principle.* The norms which Wilson advocated were those of domestic liberalism applied worldwide, including self-determination, political democracy, and equality. These were incorporated into Wilson's Fourteen Points and were the basis of Germany's willingness to sue for an armistice in November 1918. Aggression was to be prohibited and peace regarded as indivisible, norms to be enforced by public opinion oper-

---

* For the intellectual roots of collective security, see Martin David Dubin, "Toward the Concept of Collective Security: The Bryce Group's 'Proposals for the Avoidance of War,' 1914–1917," *International Organization* (Spring 1970), 24(2):288–318.

ating through a league of nations. Wilson would have no truck with bargains as a mechanism, but he was prepared to provide a role for votes within the League. Force, instead of playing a major role in the new game, was to be relegated to a secondary status. It would be present in the threat of economic sanctions and, if these failed, armed forces would be used against defectors.[49] In other words, Wilson advocated a rudimentary form of deterrence with the possibility of world war to halt violations of the League Covenant. Principle and force were to be mixed in approximately opposite proportions than they had been in balance of power. In this way, Wilson sought to return the issues of liberalism and national self-determination to the center of the global agenda.

It was surely "a time for angels" when the representatives of the victorious powers assembled in Paris.[50] Germany lay impotent; Austria-Hungary had fragmented into a number of quarrelsome national units which were already at odds with one another; Russia, too, had fragmented and was still in the throes of revolution; and all of Europe was in economic disarray. Britain and France, moreover, were in no mood to accept the Fourteen Points, either as a basis for the armistice or the subsequent peace, for they believed that the manifesto deprived them of an ability to negotiate effectively or to recoup national losses at the expense of Germany.

Although a treaty with Germany was finally imposed at the end of June 1919, its terms constituted an unhappy compromise that satisfied none of the participants fully. Unlike the statesmen of 1815, the leaders of 1919 held widely different conceptions of global politics; and Wilson, whose scheme for peace had no place for bargains, was forced to bargain long and hard with Lloyd George and Clemenceau. To achieve agreement on a League Covenant to be included in the treaty, Wilson had to surrender many of his most cherished issue positions. His opposition notwithstanding, Germany was required to pay for all civilian damage sustained during the fighting and to agree to accept guilt for the war. To the extent that the Fourteen Points found expression at all, they were at the expense of Germany. *Only* Germany was forced to surrender its overseas colonies; *only* Germany was forced to disarm; and *only* Germany was not granted frontiers in accordance with the nationality principle. Under additional stipulations, Alsace-Lorraine was to be returned to France; several frontier areas to Belgium; and the Saar was to be under international administration for fifteen years. Also, Germany was to surrender part of West Prussia to Poland, and plebiscites were to be held in parts of East Prussia and in Silesia. Finally, Germany was required to surrender its merchant fleet, and the allies were to occupy the Rhineland for fifteen years (or longer if necessary), while a belt on the right bank of the Rhine was to remain demilitarized. To the young economist John Maynard Keynes, the Versailles Treaty was sheer lunacy, an invitation to yet another war. "The spokesmen of the French and British peoples," he wrote, "have run the risk of completing the ruin, which Germany began, by a Peace which, if it is carried into effect, must impair yet further, when it might have restored, the delicate, complicated organization, already shaken and broken by war, through which alone the European peoples can employ themselves and live."[51]

The "collective security" game was stillborn. Although the League was established, its founders were never in agreement over what the institution was meant to represent. Wilson believed it to be a means by which collective security could be carried out, a forum of democratic public opinion which would raise a "hue and cry" in the event of aggression. Wilson's Secretary of the Navy, Josephus Daniels, declared enthusiastically that "the draft of the League of Peace is almost as simple as one of the Parables of Jesus and almost as illuminating and uplifting."[52] But, the Treaty of Versailles, of which the League Covenant was part, was never ratified by the United States Senate. On the one side were the Wilsonian liberals who believed that the President had compromised himself and his principles in Paris. On the other were "the giants of the Republican party, tuned to the isolationism of middle America, leaders of the 'irreconcilables,' the bitter end foes of any League,"[53] and nationalists like Senator Henry Cabot Lodge, who sought to amend a document which they believed violated American sovereignty and committed the United States to intervening overseas regardless of the dictates of national interest. In the partisan battle which ensued, Wilson was defeated, despite taking his case to the country, and the Republican Party was swept to power in 1920.

The European victors viewed the defeat of the League in the United States with mixed feelings. On the one hand, just as they "had been unwilling to accept the Fourteen Points as a yardstick for every European problem, so they did not regard the text of the League covenant as a criminal code which must be enforced by the total military and economic force of every state.''[54] But what was alarming, particularly to French officials, was the refusal of the United States government to ratify an Anglo-American treaty of guarantee to France, which had been for Clemenceau a quid pro quo for French willingness to go along with the League and surrender their demand for occupation of the Rhineland.* "Where then," declared Winston Churchill, "was that SECURITY without which all that had been gained seemed valueless, and life itself, even amid the rejoicings of victory, was almost unendurable?"[55] With empty hands, the French hoped the League would be an instrument of the victors to perpetuate their dominance over Germany. French leaders looked to a game which would be dominated by the threat of force. Even at Versailles, Clemenceau had been assailed by those like President Poincaré and Marshal Foch who believed he was surrendering French security in order to preserve allied unity. French policy for the next twenty years was dominated by the quest for this elusive but salient value.

In contrast to the French and Americans, the British government hoped that the League would become a twentieth-century version of the old Concert mechanism, a permanent and institutionalized conference that would encourage bargains and reaffirm past principles. Indeed, British leaders were not entirely displeased at American rejection of the Anglo-American treaty of guarantee because it relieved them of similar obligations at a time when attention was focused on the Empire, which, at least momentarily, looked to be secure.

Incompatible interpretations of the rules by the victors and the American defection boded ill for the League from the outset, and as Inis Claude declares, "The framers of the Covenant were neither the first nor the last statesmen who proclaimed their adherence to a principle and then failed to grasp—or shied away from—the implications of their position."[56] Even more ominous was the fact that several key actors—including the governments of Germany, Japan, and Italy—left Paris so dissatisfied with the peace settlement that, from the outset, they regarded the League and

---

* The consequences of French perceptions of insecurity became evident shortly afterwards in Anglo-French disagreements concerning joint policy to prevent German revival. British leaders sought the reintegration of Germany into Europe and financial control over the German economy by means of Anglo-American loans. The French sought military dominance by severing the Rhineland from Germany.

the rules it embodied with either suspicion or unconcealed rancor. Either unconsulted or harboring resentments, they were determined to design new rules of their own making.

Finally, at least one major actor—the Bolsheviks—was excluded from the Versailles conference and proposed to live by its own set of rules, as revolutionary as those proposed by Wilson, but incompatible with the norms of other central actors. As expounded by Lenin and Trotsky, initial Bolshevik rules entailed the encouragement of revolution and the abolishment of the sovereign nation-state as actor. To them global politics consisted of a single critical issue, socialism vs. capitalism, and they sought to base interaction upon a combination of force and principle, the key norm being proletarian internationalism.* The techniques of force they proposed to use differed dramatically from Wilsonian notions of collective war and economic sanctions. "War," thundered Trotsky, "is the method by which capitalism, at the climax of its development, seeks to solve its insoluble contradictions. To this method the proletariat must oppose its *own* method, the method of the Social Revolution."[57] What was unique about this formula was that no dichotomy was seen between the internal and external realms of politics. The Bolsheviks set about to attract and join with members of other collectivities and thereby encourage their fragmentation and dissolution. Thus, upon becoming people's commissar for foreign affairs, Trotsky confidently declared: "I will issue some revolutionary proclamations to the peoples and then close up the joint."[58]

The contradictions and inconsistencies in the new game that was legislated at Versailles did not immediately become apparent, owing to the postwar impotence of several major actors, the preoccupation with internal economic and political problems, and the universal exhaustion that followed World War I. On the surface, global politics appeared calm, and the League enjoyed a number of modest successes—the Albanian-Yugoslav frontiers dispute (1921), the Upper Silesia plebiscite (1922),

---

* Though the Bolshevik issue position and vision of global politics were quickly modified by circumstances, proletarian internationalism remained a central tenet, appearing especially in the context of the Comintern and later the Cominform. After the defeat of Trotsky, however, and the adoption by Stalin of "socialism in one country," a realist conception of global politics once again came to dominate Soviet thinking. See Richard W. Mansbach and Thomas Oleszczuk, "En Passant: Soviet-American Approaches to International Politics," paper delivered at the 1979 annual meeting of the International Studies Association.

the Aaland Islands convention (1922), and the Greco-Bulgarian dispute of 1925. However, none of these represented a challenge to the settlement by a major actor. In fact, even in this period, the League was notable by its absence or ineffectiveness in flare-ups in which a major actor took sides either directly or indirectly—the Vilna dispute (1919–22), the Russo-Polish War (1919–20), and the Italian shelling of Corfu (1923). Moreover, violent conflict continued to erupt on the peripheries of Europe and beyond: as Poles, Estonians, and Latvians fought the Soviet Union, Lithuania became a battlefield; Turks fought Greeks; Chinese in Shantung opposed Japanese penetration; Poles and Czechs fought over Teschen; Italians and Yugoslavs fought over Fiume; Japanese troops occupied the Russian maritime provinces; and civil strife engulfed Hungary, Germany, and Russia.

Thus, World War I and the Versailles conference had only partly resolved the critical issues of their time. Prussian militarism had been crushed; but the capacity of Germany to rebuild its power, and the inequities imposed upon it, virtually assured that the postwar years would be merely a respite between wars. The result was the worst of all worlds. The war and the treaty were sufficiently harsh to scar an entire generation of Germans and make them easy prey for Nazi demagoguery once the brief era of economic prosperity of the late 1920s disappeared. Yet prewar Germany remained intact. Marshal Foch had been singularly prescient when he noted upon hearing of the terms of Versailles: "This is not Peace. It is an Armistice for twenty years."[59]

THE CRITICAL ISSUE OF FASCISM

Since collective-security rules proved unacceptable, global politics was characterized by another series of ad hoc rule-making games. Rarely had leading statesmen seemed so at sea about rules as in the 1920s and early 1930s. They fluctuated wildly between extremes of principle (as reflected in the Locarno Treaty; the Kellogg-Briand Pact, or Pact of Paris which "outlawed" war; and the Stimson Doctrine of Nonrecognition) and unilateral resort to force (as in the French occupations of Dusseldorf, Duisburg, and Ruhrort in 1921 and the Ruhr in 1923). Bargains, too, became an increasingly significant mechanism in the 1920s and 1930s—from the Washington and Genoa conferences of 1922, and the Dawes Plan on German reparations in 1924, to the final acts of appeasement. Only the fascists after coming to power seemed to have any coherent sense of what the rules of the new game should be, and these rules proved both shocking and unacceptable to other major actors. A. J. P. Taylor describes this conundrum well:

Hitler and Mussolini boasted of their freedom from accepted standards. They made promises without any intention of keeping them. . . . The statesmen of other countries were baffled by this disregard of accepted standards, yet could think of no alternative.[60]

The one rule on which the victors at Versailles seemed to agree was that of nonintervention in internal affairs and the rigid demarcation of the internal and external realms of politics. By resort to ambassadors' conferences along with negotiations in the League in the 1920s, they sought to reconstruct at least some of the elements of the old Concert game while permitting explosive internal events to run their course, as in the cases of the triumph of fascism in Italy, Germany, and Spain.

However, their own inconsistency on this question undermined the rules from the outset. Wilson's emphasis on national self-determination, and his emphasis on democracy, for instance, were clear intrusions into matters of internal political organization and administration, which had their most deleterious effects in the emergence of politically, socially, and economically nonviable nation-states in Eastern and Central Europe. Allied interventions in the Soviet Union had set an unfortunate precedent, which France continued throughout the 1920s in an effort to force German obedience to the letter of the Versailles Treaty and maintain French dominance in Western Europe.

Paradoxically, Lenin and Trotsky, though unsuccessful in their efforts to spread revolution, had correctly seen the futility of trying to maintain the distinction between internal and external rules of conduct. Thus, the great issues of the 1920s and early 1930s, originally consisting of separated concrete stakes of government control in several countries and later linked into the single issue of fascism, arose from internal contexts.

In China, civil war, climaxing in the triumph of the Kuomintang and unification of the country under Chiang Kai-shek in 1928, generated opposition to "unequal treaties" and foreign penetration that, in turn, provoked acute anxiety in Japan about that country's economic and political position in China. Since Japan had been "opened" in 1854, that country had undergone rapid industrial and technological change, guided by gigantic family trusts.

Japan had also witnessed rapid population growth and the imposition of a veneer of Western social and constitutional reforms upon an essentially feudal sociopolitical structure. Resentful of corruption in high places and continued European influence in Asia, and fearful of communism and the growth of nationalism in China, young nationalists demanded the militarization of Japanese society and government to cope with problems of modernization, preferably by means of external expansion. By the late 1920s military influence was institutionalized in the Japanese government. Confronted by economic difficulties at home and growing Chinese resentment abroad, Japanese military officers saw a future in Manchuria. This region, declares John Toland, "could be transformed from a wilderness into a civilized, prosperous area, alleviating unemployment at home and providing an outlet for the overpopulated homeland, where more than two thirds of all farms were smaller than two and a quarter acres. Manchuria could also supply Japan with what she so desperately needed to remain an industrial state—a guaranteed source of raw materials and a market for finished goods."[61] On September 18, 1931, the Japanese Kanto Army staged the "Mukden incident" and began the occupation of Manchuria despite the opposition of liberal politicians in Tokyo.[62] In February 1932 the puppet state of Manchukuo was declared, and even the supine report of Lord Lytton to the League was angrily rejected by the Japanese, who withdrew from the organization. League adoption of the declaration of American Secretary of State Henry L. Stimson that no conquests by force which violated international treaties (the Nine-Power Treaty of 1922) would be recognized was treated with similar disdain. The clash between principle and force left the latter a clear winner. In June 1932, 70,000 Japanese troops occupied Shanghai to compel China to end its boycott of Japanese goods, and in 1937 Japan's invasion of China began in earnest.

If the Japanese nationalists and militarists showed their scorn of principle, votes, and bargains by resort to assassination at home and war abroad, as well as by a propensity to perceive issues in terms of a negative actor dimension, events in Italy were just as ominous. In that country, dissatisfied with the peace settlement which had deprived it of colonial and territorial rewards promised in secret treaties made with Britain and France during World War I and burdened by wartime debt and post-war unemployment and depression, Benito Mussolini established the first *Fascio di Combattimento* in March 1919. Mussolini's doctrine, which was to give its name to the great issue of the 1930s and 1940s, combined radical nationalism with an organic conception of the nation-state inherited from the German Hegelians of the nineteenth century, and entailed a fervent rejection of socialism (with its emphasis on classes), democracy (with its emphasis on parties and majorities), and liberalism (with its emphasis on materialism and constitutional guarantees). Implicitly, it involved a rejection of votes, bargains, and principle and the enshrinement of force as the ultimate adjudicator:

War alone brings up to their highest tension all human energies and puts the stamp of nobility upon the peoples who have the courage to meet it. All other trials are substitutes, which never really put a man in front of himself in the alternative of life and death. . . .[63]

In February 1921 communist and fascist riots erupted in Florence as a pattern of civil disorder began that would repeat itself some years later in Germany. In March 1922 the fascists executed a coup in the disputed city of Fiume, which was then occupied by Italian troops. Two months later, fascists overthrew the communist city government of Bologna and later that summer seized the Milan city government. On October 28 Mussolini began the "march on Rome," and the Italian government crumbled. Within a month, king and parliament granted Mussolini dictatorial powers, which he proceeded to institutionalize by virtue of the fascist *squadristi,* assassination, and internment.

The external side of fascism was revealed in the Italian invasion of Ethiopia, which began in October 1935. The invasion, which featured the Italian use of air power and poison gas, culminated in the occupation of Addis Ababa in May 1936, the flight of Emperor Haile Selassie, and the annexation of the country by Italy. The response of major actors to the Italian action was instructive, because it revealed the extent to which they failed to apprehend the logic of fascism and could not come to grips with the rules of the game the fascists proposed to play. The British government was the key both as the strongest member of the League and as the only actor capable of imposing the painful sanctions that might have aborted the Italian invasion. But following a balance-of-power strategy, neither the British nor French governments were prepared to antagonize Mussolini to the point where Italian support against a resurgent Germany would be sacrificed.* The British Cabinet would not employ the threat of force that was fundamental to an effective balance of power. Domestic political opinion (reflected by the strong prodisarmament sentiment expressed in the unofficial "Peace Ballot" of 1935 and the 1933 Joad Resolution of Oxford undergraduates that they would not "fight for king and country") dissuaded the government of Stanley Baldwin from considering the use of force. Instead, the French and British tried unsuccessfully to bargain with Mussolini, a strategy that was too feeble to halt him but was sufficiently punitive to alienate him. Meeting in Paris in December 1935, the British and French foreign ministers—Sir Samuel Hoare and Pierre Laval—agreed to cede to Mussolini large areas of Ethiopia and to designate much of the remainder an Italian sphere of influence, with Ethiopia to receive in return a narrow corridor to the sea. The "Hoare-Laval deal" was consistent with French efforts earlier in the year to tempt Mussolini into a solid front against Germany while quietly giving him a free hand in Ethiopia. The deal, however, crumbled in the face of indignant public reaction in Britain against its open cynicism and blatant disregard for League principles.† Winston Churchill succinctly summarized Baldwin's dilemma:

The Prime Minister had declared that sanctions meant war; secondly, he was resolved there must be no war; and thirdly, he decided upon sanctions. It was evidently impossible to reconcile these three conditions.[64]

It was within Germany, however, that the process of actor fragmentation and coalescence was to have its most profound and shattering consequences for global politics. From the outset, Germans of all classes and stations harbored deep resentment toward the inequities imposed by the peace settlement of 1919. Denied an army and navy, deprived of colonies and of the opportunity for national self-determination and unification, and burdened with onerous reparations, most politically conscious Germans

---

*Only the British navy could have enforced an oil embargo upon Italy by closing the Suez Canal to Italian shipping.

†The British Cabinet was surely not above such bargains, as it showed by concluding an Anglo-German naval treaty in June 1935 that effectively legitimized Hitler's naval rearmament in violation of the Versailles Treaty. The agreement infuriated France.

were resolved to evade or overthrow the settlement that had been imposed upon them. Assailed by militant groups on both the left and the right, the Weimar Republic was viewed as a "regime of surrender." As early as 1918–19 civil strife initiated from the left erupted in Munich, Berlin, and the Ruhr. Some months later, the new republic was battered from the right as semisovereign bands of patriotic and disgruntled veterans staged the Kapp putsch in Berlin, a coup which failed not because of government action but because of a general strike by the trade unions. Then, in November 1923, following the French occupation of the Ruhr, a putsch was attempted in Munich by Adolf Hitler and General Erich Ludendorff on behalf of the National Socialist Party, a minor nationalist organization which had been founded by Anton Drexler in 1918 as the German Workers' Party. Hitler's attempted coup, a pale replica of Mussolini's march on Rome, was crushed, and he himself was imprisoned for a year, during which he wrote *Mein Kampf*.

To the ideas of fascism, Hitler wedded his own peculiar philosophy of race supremacy, which had been part of the intellectual baggage of his youth in Vienna. Like Mussolini, but unlike his adversaries both at home and later abroad, Hitler was quite clear about the nature of the game which he was prepared to play. It was force, not principle, bargains, or votes, which counted as far as he was concerned, though he was prepared to use any and all of these tactically in order to confuse his enemies and achieve his ends. Thus, in *Mein Kampf* he wrote: "It is only in the struggle between *Weltanschauungen* that physical force, consistently and ruthlessly applied, will eventually turn the scale in its own favor."[65] In time, Hitler managed to identify his own grievances with those of unemployed and disgruntled veterans and middle-class opportunists to forge the Nazi party. By resort to demagoguery, ruse, and force, he identified the grievances articulated by his party with those of Germany as a whole, and these in turn were unleashed upon the outside world as the collective grievances of the German *Volk*. Unwilling to suppress dissatisfaction in Germany when it might have been possible to do so in the early 1930s, the other major European actors, vainly seeking to play by a different set of rules, were forced into still another world war with Germany, which they almost lost.

Between 1924 and 1929, however, Nazi fortunes remained at a low ebb, and global politics assumed a relatively moderate tone, owing to a combination of factors—the withdrawal of the French from the Ruhr, currency reforms, loans from America, and the "policy of fulfillment" of German Chancellor Gustav Stresemann. Stresemann was willing to collaborate with the efforts of the victors to eliminate symbolic and transcendent stakes and to pursue concrete ones, using an interdependence calculus, in return for the gradual reduction of German obligations under the Versailles Treaty. Yet, even Stresemann was secretly at work undermining the settlement by evading the Versailles strictures against German rearmament. Nevertheless, Germany's public posture—acceptance of the Dawes Plan, ratification of the Locarno treaties, negotiation of friendship treaties with Russia and others, application for admission to the League, and participation in the Kellogg-Briand Treaty—all functioned to bring an end to Germany's status as a pariah.

The Great Depression, which began in 1929, changed everything as Germany suffered an economic collapse even more complete than that which occurred elsewhere. Foreign loans dried up, and unemployment grew to six million. The popularity of communism grew dramatically, and the German middle class flocked to the ranks of the Nazis as a viable alternative. Hitler now publicly united the alleged internal and external sources of Germany's woes in denouncing Versailles, Weimar democracy, Bolshevism, and the Jews into a single transcendent issue. In the Reichstag elections of 1930, the National Socialists emerged as a major political party, and the Nazis increasingly took to the streets to do battle with communists. Though Hitler experienced a setback in the 1932 presidential election, which he lost to the aged Marshal Hindenburg, he came to be perceived by German industrialists, landowners, and military officers as a possible ally to rally the forces of authoritarianism and nationalism against the growing peril of communism. In this manner, Hitler and the Nazis were accorded the legitimacy which had been denied them earlier, and, as successive governments undertook to rule by presidential decree, Hitler began to be viewed as a popular "front man" by traditional conservatives like Hindenburg, Franz von Papen, Alfred Hugenberg, and General Kurt von Schleicher. Unable to form a majority in the Reichstag, the right finally turned to Hitler on January 30, 1933. In the words of Alan Bullock, "The improbable had happened: Adolf Hitler, the petty official's son from Austria, the down-and-out of the Home for Men, the *Meldegänger* of the List Regiment, had become Chancellor of the German Reich.''[66]

The new government was still a coalition, and Hindenburg remained president. Thus, Hitler proceeded to employ an artful combination of coercion and bargains to acquire the complete power after which he quested. With the threat of violence hanging over it, the Reichstag was compelled to pass an enabling act in March which gave the government dictatorial power. In the previous month, the Reichstag building had been burned under suspicious circumstances, an incident that the Nazis used to persuade Hindenburg to suspend constitutional guaranties and outlaw the Communist party. In June 1934 Hitler won over his last potentially powerful adversary, the German army, by launching a blood purge against some of his own most rabid followers, particularly Ernst Roehm and Gregor Strasser, who had advocated social revolutionary changes in German society and the incorporation of the Nazi storm troopers (S.A.) into the smaller regular army. This bargain ensured Hitler of military support after the death of Hindenburg, a month later, and the combining of the presidency and chancellorship in his own person.

Having disposed of potential political foes at home, Hitler and the Nazis now proceeded to unleash a fundamental revolution in Germany. It affected all realms of life. The federal system was ended, and regional government was placed in the hands of local party organizations, governed from Berlin. The existing legal system was dispensed with and replaced by one which set up the welfare of the Nazi regime as the sole criterion of justice. Toward this end, summary execution of opponents of the regime became common, and concentration camps were erected. All political parties except the Nazis were liquidated. All non-Aryan officials were dismissed, and persecution of the Jews was legitimized by the Nuremberg Laws of September 1935. In the economic sphere, strikes were forbidden, and unions replaced by the Nazi Labor Front. By means of forced internal loans, government regulation of industry, rapid rearmament, and compulsory universal military service, Germany embarked upon a policy of autarky and managed with breathtaking speed to end unemployment and boost productivity. In its sheer breadth, the revolution in Germany was unparalleled and quickly created status disequilibrium in Europe.

The game which Hitler proposed to play globally was similar in most respects to the game he imposed upon Germany. He did not regard "domestic" and "foreign" affairs as subject to different rules or prescriptions; and upon conquering a foreign territory, he applied the same techniques that had been used at home. Indeed, one historian argues that Hitler's foreign policy was little more than an extension of domestic policy, and that the latter was what aroused such antipathy outside Germany:

Hitler's protectorate brought tyranny to Bohemia—secret police, the S.S., the concentration camps; but no more than in Germany itself. It was this which roused public opinion in Great Britain. Hitler's domestic behavior, not his foreign policy, was the real crime which ultimately brought him—and Germany—to the ground.[67]

The techniques of coercive diplomacy and open force which Hitler employed violated whatever rules other statesmen thought to exist, and reflected externally the lessons learned during the years in which the Nazis were struggling for power within Germany. These techniques included what Andrew Scott calls "informal penetration," including "information and propaganda activities, the use of front groups, financial subsidy of various organizations, the use of economic warfare techniques, organization of guerrilla warfare, sabotage, strikes and riots, establishment of military party formations, and the organization of *coups d'état.*"[68]

From 1933 to 1939, Hitler and his opponents played according to different conceptualizations of the rules, so that one ad hoc confrontation succeeded another. For the most part, Hitler's issue positions were determined by an affect calculus. His opponents, with one eye on the inequitable provisions of the Versailles Treaty, believed that his calculus was cost-benefit or interdependence—a belief they sustained until Hitler's annexation of "rump" Czechoslovakia in March 1939 dispelled their assumption that he wished only to reunite all ethnic Germans in the Reich.[69] To that time, the British government under Baldwin—and then Neville Chamberlain—regarded each successive stake as concrete and hoped that by satisfying Hitler's "just" grievances it could gradually move him to an interdependence calculus. If Hitler regarded each stake as symbolic and linked them together by an actor dimension, British and French leaders hoped in vain that they were linked by a stake dimension consisting of the values of "national autonomy" and "political equality." In this manner, the British and French sought to appease Hitler's demands by proffering attractive bargains, or by abstaining from and avoiding resort to force, which, they believed, would only escalate negative affect.

In October 1934 Germany withdrew from the disarmament conference and League of Nations, thereby indicating its intention to follow an independent course. In March 1935 Hitler unilaterally denounced the disarmament provisions of the Versailles Treaty (already violated in fact); the Western allies vainly protested. A year later, Hitler denounced the Locarno pacts of 1925 and boldly reoccupied the Rhineland, a move which the allies protested but quickly accepted. By "salami tactics," Hitler was inexorably tearing down the postwar settlement. In October 1936 the formation of the Berlin–Rome Axis indicated a growing division of Europe into two camps and the recognition of the transcendent issue of fascism. In the following month, Japan joined the Axis. In November 1936 the German government recognized the fascist government of General Francisco Franco in Spain, while Britain, France, and the United States agreed to "nonintervention" and "neutrality" in the Spanish Civil War. In March 1938 Germany invaded and annexed Austria. Finally, from September 12 to September 29, the Anglo-French policy of appeasement reached a climax during the Czechoslovak crisis, which resulted in Germany's annexation of the Sudetenland *with* the assistance of the French and British governments. As a result of appeasement at Munich, the French alliance system in Eastern Europe collapsed, and British aspirations to restore a balance of power were thwarted. Munich is, in the words of one observer, "a case-history in the disease of political myopia which afflicted the leaders and the peoples of the world in the years between the wars."[70]

In sum, the 1930s ushered in a period in which inconsistencies in relations between Germany and the Western democracies were eliminated. The inequities of the past were sufficient to constitute a prior pattern of negative relations. The triumph of the Nazis and the imposition of a brutal dictatorship in Germany was the main factor in promoting perceptions of dissimilarity, to which was added fear once the rapid rearmament and economic recovery of Germany under Hitler restored parity. The impact of the last factor was particularly evident when Hitler casually announced to British Foreign Secretary Sir John Simon on March 25, 1935, that Germany had achieved "parity" with Britain with regard to air power.[71] With this comment, British optimism was shattered, and what had been distaste for the Nazis turned quickly to fear. Churchill recalled his own reaction:

A disaster of the first magnitude had fallen upon us. Hitler had already obtained parity with Great Britain. Henceforward he had merely to drive his factories and training-schools at full speed, not only to keep his lead in the air, but steadily to improve it. Henceforward all the unknown, immeasurable threats which overhung London from air attack would be a definite and compelling factor in all our decisions.[72]

Thereafter, a negative actor dimension governed Anglo-German relations, and concrete stakes increasingly assumed symbolic features and were wedded together in the single critical issue of fascism.

In the presence of this negative actor dimension, rigid alliances were forged on both sides. (Since France had never ceased to view Germany as a mortal threat, successive French governments had sought with varying success to forge anti-German alliances since 1919, and this effort had been the basis of all French policy in Europe.) German rearmament and the formation of alliances had the predictable effect of stimulating an arms race, which was further promoted by German defection from Anglo-French perceptions of systemic rules. Successive crises in the 1930s reflected Anglo-French efforts to find interaction games that would satisfy Hitler and Mussolini. While seeking to persuade his adversaries that he would accept these, Hitler repeatedly had recourse to force or the threat of force (even against the advice of his generals). Principle and votes were abandoned early, with the Nazi withdrawal from the disarmament conference and the League. However, in at least four major crises— Ethiopia, the Rhineland, Austria, and Czechoslovakia—British and French leaders showed a willingness to bargain as though Hitler and Mussolini were prepared to adopt an interdependence calculus. In the case of Mussolini, they hoped to trade support of his imperial pretensions for support against Germany, an illusion which they retained almost to the end. In the case of Hitler, they expected to achieve peace in return for elimination of the strictures of Versailles and support for German national self-determination.

The annexation of what remained of Czechoslovakia finally clarified the nature of Hitler's rules for Britain and France, and two weeks later they unilaterally pledged themselves to the defense of Poland. Poland, though militarily indefensible and governed by an authoritarian regime with which neither British nor French officials were in sympathy, was nevertheless seen as symbolic of Nazi expansion. Once the French and British governments had determined to play Hitler's game, world war once again became probable, as there was little choice but to meet a unilateral resort to war except by force. On September 1, 1939, following the conclusion of a nonaggression treaty with the USSR, Nazi Germany invaded Poland (ostensibly over the disposition of the city of Danzig), and two days later Britain and France declared war on Germany. Once again, in the absence of interaction rules, global politics assumed the aspect of a "fight" in which the destruction of adversaries became the logical consequence.

In a sense, World War II, like World War I, was "overcaused." All possible reasons for war existed—disagreement, negative acts, intense hostility, and nonexistence of viable systemic rules. The dominance of transcendent stakes in the single "superissue" of fascism heightened the probability that, in time, other major actors, including Japan, the United States, and the Soviet Union, would enter the war. Ensuing realignments, particularly the formation of the "Grand Alliance" and the United Nations, made it possible that, once the war was over, the victors would jointly work out a system of rules acceptable to them all. The ferocity of the war itself provided sufficient incentive for them to do so.

CONCLUSION AND SUMMARY

The preceding pages represent an effort to illustrate the descriptive and explanatory utility of certain aspects of the new paradigm when applied to the grand sweep of history. Thus, identifying planned and ad hoc rulemaking games, and pointing out the explicit and implicit system rules which existed during major historical epochs, help to clarify the underlying logic of events and the sequences in which they occur. Identification of critical issues and the stages through which they passed lends coherence to the historical narrative and, for the most part, reinforces the distinctions that have been made among eras by conventional historians. In other words, history can be seen as propelled by recurrent shifts among issues, accompanied by the rise and demise of key actors in conjunction with issue change.

Knowledge about the nature of the issue, including the linkages among stakes, the salience of those stakes, and the type of stakes, provides additional coherence to the interaction patterns that characterized the various eras. Indeed, war itself, as one of several mechanisms, is seen to occur in logical and explicable sequence, and its underlying relationship to the evolution of issues, the search for rules of interaction, and the changing patterns of affect and behavior provide the bases for predicting and explaining its outbreak.

If the elements of the theory presented in this book help to provide coherence for the long period during which the dominant paradigm itself emerged and took shape, it should assist us to comprehend more deeply the postwar era as well. It should indicate how a world of hot war became a world of cold war, and how that in turn eroded and was transformed into the contemporary global system.

I had hoped that the Russians would return favor for favor, but almost from the time I became President I found them acting without regard for their neighboring nations and in direct violation of the obligations they had assumed at Yalta. The first Russian leader I had had an opportunity to talk to was Molotov, and it had been necessary, even then, for me to speak bluntly and plainly. I was sure that Russia would understand firm, decisive language and action much better than diplomatic pleasantries.
—Harry S. Truman [1]

CHAPTER TEN

THE COLD WAR

THE ULTIMATE test of the relevance of a paradigm is its value in making sense of, and explaining, contemporary history. To apprehend why the Cold War occurred, and grasp the causal dynamics that might rekindle it, are pressing goals for those who are concerned with the possibility of nuclear war. The issue paradigm promises a deeper understanding of, not only why cold wars occur, but also how periods of détente can be produced by the manipulation of key variables. This chapter provides an account of the Cold War from the perspective of this paradigm and its theory. It reveals how the three backround variables—prior pattern of interaction, status, and similarity—conspired to set the stage for a confrontation between the United States and USSR. It traces how the interdependence of the wartime associates gave way to a negative actor dimension that led to a series of spiraling conflict interactions that gave birth to a new critical issue—communism–capitalism. Some observers even see realism itself as having fostered the intellectual climate which encouraged the transition from hot to cold war. [2] These interactions and this climate converted the postwar concrete stakes into symbolic ones; and, as domestic support in each society for the Cold War was cultivated, the struggle assumed a transcendent quality. The early stages of the critical issue—crisis and ritualization—are detailed with attention paid to resulting interaction games. The process by which these stages were replaced by détente is explained theoretically with special attention to the dynamics of defusing explosive critical issues. Finally, the chapter provides an assessment of the model from the evidence provided by the case of the Cold War—and a concluding note on the historical debate between revisionists and traditionalists over the origins of the Cold War.

THE PRIOR PATTERN OF INTERACTION

Implicit in the theory presented in this book is the idea that political change proceeds in part by means of a struggle for precedence among issues on a global agenda. New issues characteristically grow out of issues internal to specific actors that spill over into the global arena. Not only has the distinction between domestic and global politics been blurred, a fact emphasized in the previous chapter, but actions in one arena have commonly been initiated because of disturbances in the other. This was the case in 1789 and again in 1917.

The dominant issue in 1917 was World War I itself, which—though it had come to involve a struggle for territory, wealth, and status—had been partly sparked by incompatibility among leading actors' views about suitable decision-making rules. Once the war began, domestic questions had little to do with the manner in which it was waged, except for propaganda purposes, until Woodrow Wilson took seriously the matter of Prussian autocracy. Wilson's views notwithstanding, during three years of war domestic issues had been salient to combatants only to the extent that they interfered with the war effort. Ideological differences, moreover, were secondary to winning the stakes directly on the field of battle. The conditions of a war of attrition had encouraged a sturdy negative actor dimension among adversaries and a strong positive actor dimension among allies. Differences among allies about *other* issues mattered little. Perceptions of mutual military need—Anglo-French economic, financial, and military assistance; and Russian troops—produced a bond of interdependence that overshadowed prior differences and minimized doubts about the compatibility of Tsarist autocracy and Western liberalism. The February Revolution in Russia did little to alter these perceptions, so long as the Kerensky government, or some other Russian regime, carried on the war effort.

Officials of imperial Germany were prepared to bargain with any individual or regime that promised either to undermine the Russian war effort or take Russia out of the war, regardless of ideological differences—a willingness that became manifest after the Provisional Government rebuffed informal German offers for a separate peace.[3] In the words of General Hoffmann, chief of the German General Staff on the Eastern Front:

We naturally tried, by means of propaganda, to increase the disintegration that the Russian Revolution had introduced into the Army. Some man at home who had connexions with the Russian revolutionaries exiled in Switzerland came upon the idea of employing some of them in order to hasten the undermining and poisoning of the morale of the Russian Army.[4]

In such a situation, a bold man, willing to play the opportunist for a higher cause, could bargain effectively. Willing to betray his country in time of war for a transcendent stake which was as salient to him as the war was to the "bourgeoisie," Lenin believed that his followers in St. Petersburg were incapable of taking advantage of events, and that the Provisional Government could not give the Russian people what they wanted. Argues Edmund Wilson:

It could not give them peace because it depended on the subsidy of France and England and was committed to carrying on their war. . . . It could not give them bread, because the only way to give them bread would be by violating the sanctities of both capital and landlordship, and the bourgeoisie by definition were bound to protect the principle of property. It would not give them freedom, because it was the government of those landlords and capitalists who had always shown themselves afraid of the people.[5]

In April 1917, Lenin was given safe passage through Germany in a sealed train, arriving at the Finland Station in St. Petersburg on April 16, where he reasserted his leadership of the Bolsheviks. Within months, the Kerensky government was overthrown, having isolated itself by a stubborn unwillingness to abandon its commitment to keep Russia in the war. Kerensky was pressed in this direction by Russia's allies which, in the words of one contemporary observer,

were blinded in their desire to prolong the military collaboration of Russia at all costs. They entirely failed to see what was possible and what was not. Thus they were simply playing into Lenin's hands and estranging Kerensky from the people.[6]

The issue of bolshevism or communism was, at the time, not salient to the allies, whose primary concern remained Russia's prosecution of the war and the question of a separate peace. And so the allies intervened in Russia to support those who supported the war effort. For their part, the Bolsheviks under Trotsky opened negotiations with Germany and responded to German demands for economic and territorial concessions with rhetoric and a refusal to fight or conclude peace. Frustrated by the failure to reach agreement, and irritated by the unorthodox negotiating tactics of the Bolsheviks, the German army simply continued its virtually unopposed advance, until on March 3, 1918, the Bolsheviks capitulated and signed the Treaty of Brest-Litovsk, by the terms of which the old Russian empire was for all intents and purposes dismembered.

This capitulation, in turn, egged Russia's former allies on to fury and focused attention on the dissimilarity between Bolshevik ideology and that of the capitalist West. This was particularly the case in the United States, where Wilson had originally greeted the overthrow of tsardom enthusiastically, declaring that "the great, generous Russian people have been added in all their naive majesty and might to the forces that are fighting for freedom in the world, for justice, and for peace."[7] Brest-Litovsk changed all this and encouraged the perception of a linkage between bolshevism and the war, a link expressed in these words by one prominent American journal in June 1918: "The Russian people in large numbers . . . know that the rule of the Bolsheviki is not an extension of democracy, but a class absolutism. . . . Today Russia is under German bonds."[8] In the spring of 1918, the British, French, and Japanese governments offered assistance to the internal enemies of the Bolsheviks, and in August the Wilson Administration dispatched American forces to join British and Japanese forces in eastern Siberia and northern Russia.*

The defeat of Germany and the imposition of the Weimar Republic there, and the debate in left-wing circles as to whether communist revolutions would erupt elsewhere, resurrected the old concerns of 1848 sufficiently, so that in the West, Soviet Russia was viewed as markedly dissimilar on an important trait relevant to a salient issue. However, Russia's momentary weakness and internal fragmentation allowed ob-

---

*This action was ostensibly taken to protect Western supplies from falling into German hands, and to assist Czech units in Russia that were seeking to escape the country and were resisting Soviet demands that they disarm themselves.

servers to discount the threat it posed. Nor did it seem that Europe was ripe for revolution, or that European leaders were prepared so soon after World War I to commit the resources necessary for serious contention over internal stakes in Russia. Although prominent individuals, like Marshal Ferdinand Foch, advocated a crusade against bolshevism, the issue of communism, though on the global agenda, was of only moderate salience. Its significance was not in how it affected global decision making (as the Bolsheviks were not even represented at Versailles), but how it affected the way others treated the new regime and how Soviet leaders reacted to the world around them—how it established a pattern of interaction—of disagreement, negative acts, and animosity that shaped later behavior and perceptions, which, in turn, reinforced the intensity of conflict.

The pattern of disagreement became well-established shortly after the war as the West interpreted the major thrust of Lenin's foreign policy as an effort to export revolution overseas through the agency of the Third International (Comintern), which was tightly controlled by Moscow, and whose member parties were subject to Leninist discipline in the form of the "Twenty-One Conditions."* If the Bolsheviks were outraged by the futile interventions, Western leaders were incensed by the verbal abuse of Soviet officials and the behavior of Soviet representatives, which violated the customs, usages, and laws that had constituted the basis of "normal" relations among sovereigns for hundreds of years. The first Soviet ambassador to Germany—Adolf Joffe—for instance, was a professional revolutionary who abused his privileges by passing out subversive literature and inciting revolutionary acts in the country, which the Bolsheviks believed was ripe for revolution and in which they believed that revolution was necessary for socialism to survive. The behavior of Joffe points up the tension that came to exist between the two "levels" of Soviet foreign policy—one of which recognized the world as state-centric; and the other, which ignored established usages. Declares Theodore von Laue:

After the formation of the Comintern and the end of the civil war, the separation of the two spheres of Soviet foreign relations proceeded apace. If the Soviet government wanted to deal with capitalist governments it had to conform to their standards of diplomacy. The issue of revolutionary propaganda cropped up at

*These refer to Lenin's strict conditions of membership which subjected member parties to Bolshevik governance and discipline.

once as an almost insurmountable obstacle to diplomatic recognition and even to the resumption of trade relations. The result was a strict outward separation of the two spheres.[9]

The Leninists further isolated themselves by their hostility toward moderate Western socialists. The Comintern served to divide the world socialist movement and split into warring factions the socialist parties of Europe and elsewhere. Even after the fall of the Hohenzollerns in Germany and the formation of a government of moderate socialists, the communists continued to behave in sectarian fashion and sought to overthrow the regime. In January 1919, the *Spartakusbund* of Karl Liebknecht and Rosa Luxemburg (themselves opposed to many aspects of Leninism), encouraged and advised by Moscow's representative Karl Radek, rose up in Berlin against the government of socialist President Friedrich Ebert. Ominously, their action so frightened the German government that it called upon right-wing elements that would later form the kernel of the Nazi movement to crush the rising. In March a communist government seized power in Hungary under Bela Kun, until it was ousted by Rumanian intervention (supported by the Western allies), and in the following month an abortive revolution took place in Bavaria, to be crushed also by German nationalists.

Although hindsight reveals that these revolutionary stirrings were neither so serious nor so coordinated as they seemed at the time, they had the effect of frightening "respectable" Western opinion, and Western governments reacted by trying to quarantine the source of the "pestilence." In the United States, the reaction assumed the form of a hysteria known as the "Red Scare" in 1919–20 when some 5,000 alleged communist aliens were arrested at the behest of Attorney General A. Mitchell Palmer. Even after the "Red Scare" and Western intervention ended, relations between the United States and the Soviet Union remained frosty, as the American government refused to extend recognition to the Soviet regime, because, in Secretary of State Bainbridge Colby's words:

The existing regime in Russia is based upon the negation of every principle of honor and good faith, and every usage and convention, underlying the whole structure of international law; the negation, in short, of every principle upon which it is possible to base harmonious and trustful relations, whether of nations or of individuals.[10]

For its part, the Soviet regime refused to acknowledge debts of the Provisional Government, provide compensation for Americans whose property in Russia had been seized, or abate its revolutionary rhetoric. Strong pressures in the United States against recognition came from church groups opposed to the suppression of religion in Russia, and from American labor, particularly Samuel Gompers, head of the AFL.[11] It was not until 1933 that American recognition was forthcoming.

Soviet belief in Western hostility was deepended by incidents like French assistance to Poland during the Russo-Polish War of 1920 and the "Zinoviev letter" of 1924. The latter involved the publication in Britain of a forged letter allegedly sent by G. E. Zinoviev, then head of the Comintern, to a British communist, containing instructions for subversion. The letter was published during an election campaign which ended in the triumph of the British Conservatives and the fall of Britain's first Labour government. The effect of the letter, which became known as a forgery almost immediately, was to embarrass Ramsey MacDonald's policy of seeking a normalization of relations with the USSR and to poison Soviet-British relations. Three years later these relations were severed as a consequence of a British government raid on the Soviet trade delegation in London (the "Arcos raid") in which subversive materials were allegedly uncovered; relations were not restored until 1930.

At an interstate level, matters were exacerbated by Soviet efforts to wean Germany from the West, and to undermine French efforts to isolate Germany and enforce the Versailles Treaty to the letter. Soviet leaders secretly connived to provide facilities for the training of the German army in return for German military advising. In addition, the conclusion of the Russo-German Treaty of Rapallo in 1922, concerning financial and trade arrangements, enraged London and Paris because it appeared to provide Germany with an alternative to dependence upon them. The long-term implication of Rapallo was probably more important than its immediate effect, however. Years later the possibility of a Soviet-German connection was not lost on Stalin, when he contemplated the prospect of a nonaggression treaty with Hitler.

Neither American recognition of the Soviet regime in 1933, nor the rise of fascism and nazism in Italy and Germany, substantially contributed to a reduction of Soviet-Western tensions and misgivings. Among the few liberals in the United States, who, like Eugene Lyons and Max

Eastman, sympathized with the aspirations of the Bolshevik Revolution and with Soviet efforts to transform Russian society during the years of industrialization and collectivization, there was disillusionment with the brutality of these efforts, the imposition of Stalin's cynical dictatorship, and finally the blood purges of the 1930s, during which the last traces of idealism were eliminated from the Soviet Communist party.

Even as the threat of fascism spread—in Ethiopia, Spain, Austria, and finally Czechoslovakia—efforts to find common ground between Western and Soviet leaders proved elusive, and prior suspicions and animosities lingered. The USSR joined the League of Nations in 1934, and through its spokesman, Maxim Litvinov, became a leading exponent of "collective security" in Europe—but only after it had encouraged the German Communist Party to do everything in its power to bring down the Weimar Republic. Stalin, too, had good reason to suspect Western willingness to confront Hitler. The United States was unwilling to act on the occasion of Japan's thrust into Manchuria in 1931. Japan's expansion into China ended in the ousting of Soviet influence from Manchuria and the imposition of pressure upon the USSR's eastern frontier from Siberia to Outer Mongolia. France and Britain did nothing to resist Germany's reoccupation of the Rhineland, avowedly Hitler's "last claim" in Western Europe (though many more claims remained to be settled in Eastern Europe). Fascist intervention in the Spanish Civil War was met by a timid Western policy of "nonintervention," and only the Soviet Union made an effort to save the Republic.* Even France's treaty of defense with the USSR, concluded in 1935, was ratified in Paris only with difficulty, and its terms were hedged in such a way as to make Franco-Soviet collaboration against Hitler an unlikely eventuality.† Publicly, Litvinov con-

---

* Stalin's ardor for Spain quickly cooled, and he took pains to reduce the Soviet commitment to the point where it served to eliminate left-wing rivals to the communists within the Republic, and to keep the Civil War going, but not to defeat the forces of Franco. During the purges, he took steps to eliminate all those communists who had been involved in the Civil War, lest the idealism of that conflict infect the Soviet party itself.

† The prospects for Soviet assistance to Czechoslovakia at the time of the Munich agreement were complicated by the facts that the Franco-Soviet Treaty required Soviet action only *after* France had acted, and that it would have been difficult for the USSR to obtain a right of passage for its troops through either Poland or Rumania, owing to the hostility of the regimes in these countries to the USSR. In addition, France's defensive military strategy, symbolized by the Maginot fortifications, implied that a French offensive to link up with Soviet troops was improbable.

tinued to berate the West for its timidity in the face of Hitler and Mussolini, and these attacks took a further toll on whatever goodwill existed.
As John Wheeler-Bennett surmises:

The result of these tactics was to render hostility toward Moscow in London and
Paris almost as acute as in Berlin and Rome, and the pressing issue of resistance
to German aggression became obscured in the floating vapours of suspicion. Britain and France suspected the U.S.S.R. of wishing to precipitate a general European conflict to the greater glory and advancement of the Dictatorship of the Proletariat. The Soviet Union, for its part, believed the Western Powers guilty of a
desire to embroil Germany and Russia for the advantage and preservation of
bourgeois-capitalism.[12]

Given the simplification of that which is unfamiliar, it is probably the
case that both sides were correct, in part, but neither had the patience or
skill to unravel the complex motivations of the other that were embedded
in the complexities of internal politics, individual fears, and differences
in tradition and historical experience.

Unilateral Western appeasement of Hitler at Munich in 1938 probably
made Stalin think seriously about the possibility of a quid pro quo with
Hitler, though he may have given it thought as early as 1936, after the
German reoccupation of the Rhineland. Stalin's purge of his generals two
years later suggests he was giving no serious consideration to military
collaboration against Hitler at this time. In addition, the USSR was already engaged in serious (albeit undeclared) military hostilities with
Japan along the Siberian frontier. "To be cautious and not allow Soviet
Russia to be drawn into conflicts by warmongers who are accustomed to
have others pull chestnuts out of the fire" was, Stalin declared, the basis
of Soviet policy.[13] Stalin offered Hitler another clue in the spring of 1939
when he replaced Litvinov, a Jew, by Molotov as foreign minister.

Similarly, the prejudices of Western leaders augured poorly for effective collaboration with Soviet Russia even after the fall of Czechoslovakia. British Prime Minister Neville Chamberlain confessed "to the most
profound distrust of Russia" without belief "whatever in her ability to
maintain an effective offensive, even if she wanted to."[14] As for Soviet
motives: "I can't believe that she has the same aims and objectives as we
have, or any sympathy with democracy as such. She is afraid of Germany
and Japan, and would be delighted to see other people fight them."[15]
Clouded by these suspicions, the leisurely negotiations between the repre-

sentatives of Britain and France and the Soviet Union for collaboration against the Nazis in 1939 bore no fruit.

Agreement proved no more possible in the face of a common threat than it had earlier. Instead, on August 23, 1939, Nazi Foreign Minister Joachim Ribbentrop flew to Moscow to conclude a nonaggression treaty with Stalin, a cynical agreement which doomed Poland to partition and ensured that war would commence in a matter of days. Soviet willingness to blind themselves to Hitler's motives in this case was another instance of a failure to distinguish between the Nazis and "other" capitalists, who were regarded with loathing not because of what they did, but simply because they were capitalists. The treaty and subsequent events proved in addition that Western policies toward the Soviet Union (and Germany) had been ill-conceived from the outset. George Kennan cogently summarizes these errors:

In 1917, the Western powers, in their determination to inflict total defeat on a Germany far less dangerous to them than that of Hitler, had pressed so unwisely for the continuation of Russia's help that they had consigned her to the arms of the Communists. Now, in 1939, they were paying the price for this folly.

In 1917, they had cultivated an image of the German Kaiser that was indistinguishable from the reality of the future Hitler. Now they had a real Hitler before them.

In 1917, they convinced themselves that Russia's help was essential to their victory, though this was not really true. Now, they had a situation in which Russia's help was indeed essential but the Russia they needed was not there.[16]

It cannot be emphasized too strongly that Soviet-Western agreement concerning the Nazi threat, when it was finally achieved, was not an agreement on principles or ideas and was not based on trust, but instead was thoroughly limited and expediential in nature and was forced upon them by Hitler. Indeed, during the two years of the Nazi-Soviet Nonaggression Treaty, the relations of Britain and France with the USSR reached their nadir. The Soviet government carried out its part of the bargain with Hitler by occupying eastern Poland and absorbing the Baltic territories that had formerly been part of the Russian empire. When, however, the Soviet Union invaded Finland in late 1939 to secure for itself additional defenses for Leningrad, the Western governments protested vigorously, even considering the dispatch of an expeditionary force to aid the Finns, plans which were aborted by Hitler's seizure of Denmark and

Norway. These plans, drawn up during the "phony war," at the moment when the Nazi threat to Western Europe was at its zenith, were a final reflection of boundless illusion. And, for the League of Nations, the Finnish episode was "one last political fling."[17] The fall of France in 1940 was an unpleasant shock to Soviet leaders, who had expected Nazi military strength to be dissipated on the western front, thereby providing the USSR with time for rearmament and military reorganization. Instead, by June 1941, Hitler was prepared to set out on the road taken by Napoleon over a century before. Thus, until collaboration was forced upon them by the exigencies of war, the democracies and Bolsheviks rarely found themselves in agreement, and mutual suspicion even prevented the achievement of a common outlook between them in the days immediately prior to the German invasion of Poland.

With the invasion of the Soviet Union in 1941 and American entry into the war, the overriding threat to survival posed by the Axis powers brought West and East together. In the darkest days of the war, Axis victories effectively removed all other issues from the agenda, and all other concerns became tangential to the struggle against Hitler. Soviet resistance was lauded in the West, and the extension of massive American lend-lease aid to the USSR made its war effort feasible. Nevertheless, the prior hostile pattern still left suspicions, particularly on the part of Stalin and Churchill. Stalin was extremely suspicious about Western tardiness in opening a second front and about a possible separate peace. These concerns were, in fact, partly due to Roosevelt's repeated promises to open a second front, which was an honest effort to stiffen his ally's resolve. But such promises may have created overly optimistic expectations in Stalin, whose own view of the West had, after all, been shaped by the prior pattern of conflict.[18] Neither leader saw that differing strategies for victory, based on unique national conditions, contributed to "second front confusion." As John L. Gaddis notes:

Roosevelt failed to see . . . how this strategy for winning the war might undermine his effort to build trust between Washington and Moscow. F.D.R. sought to defeat the Axis through the maximum possible use of American industrial power, but with the minimum possible expenditure of American lives. Such a policy precluded launching military operations when chances for success were not high. Yet to the Russians, who did not enjoy the luxury of deciding where and how they would fight Germany, a "blood sacrifice" in the form of an early second front seemed the acid test of Anglo-American intentions.[19]

That such suspicions were not entirely unfounded is even more clearly evident when Churchill's view on the second front is recalled. He opposed a landing in France, but instead sought an invasion in southern Europe, through Italy and then Greece, coming through Eastern Europe— a plan whose only main advantage would be keeping Soviet influence in Eastern Europe at a minimum after the war. When F.D.R. rejected this plan and sided with Stalin, there was a visible change in Soviet affect toward the U.S., particularly after D-Day.[20] The common war effort eventually did much to allay negative affect and even germinated, between the U.S. and the USSR, a foundation of trust that could be built upon. This was especially true for the American public for whom the Red Army was pictured as heroic and Stalin was affectionately called "Uncle Joe."

THE INITIAL CAUSES OF THE COLD WAR

The emergence and ascendancy of the Cold War after World War II provides an intriguing test of the extent to which the background variables of similarity and status elicit selected perceptions and predispositions, which may be reinforced or diluted by subsequent interaction among contenders. It provides such a test, because the period between 1944 and 1947 witnessed a deterioration of the prior pattern of relative trust between the United States and Soviet governments in an interdependent military alliance, first to mistrust, and then to the chronic enmity characteristic of combatants in war. This shift has been chronicled by numerous scholars and will not be repeated here.* Instead, the focus will be on why, in a

---

* Standard interpretations of the sort accepted by many American academicians and leaders during the Cold War include John W. Spanier, *American Foreign Policy Since World War II,* 7th ed. (New York: Praeger, 1977); Arthur M. Schlesinger, Jr., "The Origins of the Cold War," *Foreign Affairs* (October 1967), 46(1):23–52; Herbert Feis, *From Trust to Terror: The Onset of the Cold War, 1945–1950* (New York: Norton, 1970); and Adam B. Ulam, *Expansion and Coexistence: Soviet Foreign Policy 1917–1973,* rev. ed. (New York: Praeger, 1974). Revisionist interpretations include D. F. Fleming, *The Cold War and Its Origins,* 2 vols. (Garden City, N.Y.: Doubleday, 1961); Gar Alperowitz, *Atomic Diplomacy: Hiroshima and Potsdam* (New York: Vintage, 1967); Diane Clemens, *Yalta* (New York: Oxford University Press, 1970); William A. Williams, *The Tragedy of American Diplomacy,* rev. ed. (New York: World Publishing, 1962); Lloyd Gardner, *Architects of Illusion* (Chicago: Quadrangle, 1970); and Gabriel Kolko, *The Politics of War* (New York: Random House, 1968). For an effort to integrate these perspectives, but one which

theoretical sense, this shift took place—a question that has received limited treatment.

The three background variables—prior interaction, similarity, and status—pushed the actors in different directions. Changes in status generated competition and so enhanced perceptions of threat. Prewar interaction had produced an atmosphere of mistrust, but the wartime coalition and the identification it engendered through mutual suffering softened that suspicion, while the personal diplomacy of F.D.R. mitigated it still more. Similarity was the key. If the actors could come to view one another as similar, the competition produced by changes in status might be negated by the trust produced by perceived similarity. However, if perceptions of dissimilarity were heightened, competition would be coupled with mistrust. Perceptions of similarity depended, in part, upon which issue(s) dominated the postwar agenda and how decision makers defined them.

A. The Effect of Agenda Content on Perceptions of Similarity

To understand how it was that postwar efforts to fashion an acceptable interaction game were transformed into Cold War, it is necessary to recall the global agenda in the last years of World War II and the initial issue positions of major actors and the relative importance they accorded to outstanding issues. Only after the Battle of Stalingrad in 1942 did the likelihood of allied defeat wane sufficiently for it to become possible once more to turn an eye to issues other than the war itself. The first major issue to surface was the nature of the postwar world, a classic division-of-the-spoils question which was the subject of the wartime conferences at Cairo, Teheran, Yalta, and Potsdam. The second overarching issue to emerge, closely linked to division of the spoils and partly a product of it, was that of the place of communism—and its relationship to capitalism—in the postwar world. A final key issue was the future of colonialism, especially in Asia, itself something of a division-of-the-spoils issue. Of these three, the first was the most salient to all contenders during the final phases of the war, growing increasingly salient as fascism-nazism ebbed.

The respective level of salience, and the relative prominence of each of

still sees the United States as less responsible for the Cold War than the USSR, see William L. Gaddis, *The United States and the Origins of the Cold War, 1941–1947* (New York: Columbia University Press, 1972).

these issues on the agenda, affected the similarity variable. As long as fascism-nazism remained the dominant issue to be resolved by total war and "unconditional surrender," an emotional bond and a sense of "we-ness" among the allies was reinforced, and perceptions of dissimilarity were brushed aside. Indeed, Roosevelt's insistence upon "unconditional surrender" was influenced, in part, by a desire for cooperation with the USSR, because it offered a means of postponing a discussion of other issues.* The perceived common trait of the allies was essentially the negative quality of antinazism, which could produce little more than a coalition of expediency. The injection of a division-of-the-spoils issue tended to dissolve the bond of similarity as each member of the coalition sought to maximize its winnings. Nevertheless, a residual sense of interdependence and the concrete nature of the stakes encouraged resort to cost-benefit and interdependence calculi until the issue of communism, with its emphases on "correct" economic and political systems, intruded. For a time, at least, the issue of colonialism (though initially of minor importance to the United States and the Soviet Union) provided a bond of similarity between Soviet and American leaders, who perceived themselves as different from British and French leaders.

This mix of issues contributed to a volatile level of trust among the victorious allies as the war ended. The issue of communism, in particular, encouraged Stalin to perceive his allies as different and was mirrored in Winston Churchill's suspicion of bolshevism, a suspicion with roots dating back to 1917. Ultimately, Stalin's viewpoint became consistent, whether justified by the facts or not: the Western powers had done nothing to prevent Hitler's rise to power and prewar expansionism in the hope that the dictators would bleed one another to death; they had looked gleefully upon Hitler's annihilation of the German Communist Party and saw him as a bulwark against communism; they had spurned Soviet efforts to enforce collective security and had then criticized his efforts to gain time through the Nazi-Soviet Nonaggression Treaty; and they had procrastinated in opening a second front while the Soviet people were bearing the brunt of the war effort. They had even sought a separate peace with Hitlerite Germany, which had been prevented only by Soviet vigilance.[21]

* It was also influenced by the myth propagated in Germany after World War I that Germany had not really been defeated but had been "stabbed in the back."

Stalin's suspicions were reinforced by Churchill's attitude toward the Soviet Union—an attitude that, during the last years of the war, was probably less a function of the communism issue than of the other two. For Churchill, the return to a prewar status hierarchy and the maintenance of the British empire were dominant considerations. He sought to postpone an early invasion of Western Europe, because it would have required at that date a preponderance of British rather than American troops—troops he believed were necessary to safeguard the imperial bastions of Egypt and India. In an effort to limit relative postwar Soviet influence, he recommended that Germany be defeated by means of an invasion through Italy and the Balkans, a plan that was to deny the Red Army undisputed supremacy in Eastern Europe after the war. This scheme was aborted by F.D.R.'s refusal to consider issues not germane to the central problem of military strategy.[22] Thus, at Teheran, Roosevelt and Stalin agreed that the second front must proceed through France. For F.D.R., the war itself remained the most salient issue, and his military advisers corroborated the obvious fact that the fastest way to defeat the German armies and arrive at Germany's heartland was the direct path from Great Britain through France.

F.D.R.'s willingness to side with Stalin on this question made it possible for the Soviet leader to see differences between the "two capitalist states." In fact, the American position was a source of some confusion to both allies, because American issue positions cut across theirs on both communism and colonialism, agreeing with Britain on the former and the Soviet Union on the latter. Since both of these issues remained of less salience to the United States than did fascism-nazism until the death of Roosevelt, neither ally could be certain as to which side the United States would tilt after the war, particularly since it was not known which issue would dominate the global agenda. Roosevelt himself went to great lengths to convince Soviet leaders that he and they shared a common issue position, as well as similar traits relevant to the colonial issue. During his initial meeting with Molotov, F.D.R. took pains to talk about the need to eliminate colonialism, and suggested that former European colonies which had been seized by Japan should be placed under international trusteeship after the war until they were prepared for independence. He even declared his suspicion about the possibility that Great Britain might seek to expand its empire after the war. Similar views were expressed directly to Stalin.[23]

On the issue of communism, Roosevelt seemed a moderate in comparison to Churchill and Stalin. Though anticommunist, he was referred to as a socialist, and even a communist, by Republican foes at home; and he was particularly galled by Wendell Wilkie's quoting of Churchill's "criticisms, made in 1937 and 1938, of Roosevelt's 'ruthless' war on private enterprise" during the 1940 presidential campaign.[24]

In the structure of a three-actor game, Roosevelt's varying attitudes concerning the several issues made him appear an ideal candidate to mediate between Churchill and Stalin. Sharing traits with each of them, he could generate a degree of trust with each, and perhaps get each to trust the other through him. That he succeeded in gaining considerable respect and trust from the Russians became clear after his death. According to Gaddis:

> The Soviets knew Roosevelt, Stalin had told Harriman in 1944, and could communicate with him. With Roosevelt alive, Molotov explained to (Joseph E.) Davies, the Soviet government had always had "full confidence" that differences could be worked out.[25]

Had Roosevelt succeeded in building a "bridge of trust" the wartime alliance might have acquired the emotional bond necessary to transform it into something more profound than a coalition of expediency. This, of course, was precisely what Roosevelt hoped would occur, so that after the war the alliance against Germany might be institutionalized. The new international organization would take its name from the name of the alliance itself, the United Nations; and the three allies, along with China and France, would serve as the Five Policemen of the world (their continuing unity a precondition of peace).[26]

The four concurrent issues—fascism, division of spoils, communism, colonialism—provided sufficient elasticity in the similarity variable to permit leaders considerable latitude in shaping their relationships by conscious manipulation of policy. Cooperation could be encouraged by emphasizing the fascism issue, with its high threat and transcendent stake uniting the allies. Moderation and compromise in the postwar world could be abetted by keeping the communist and colonial issues at equal salience levels, preferably low. In this fashion there would be sufficient crosscutting pressures to prevent contamination by negative affect and the emergence of a negative actor dimension based on a new transcendent stake. Finally, perceptions of interdependence could be maintained by treating the division-of-the-spoils issue as consisting of concrete stakes. A stable stake dimension would be assured by effectively eliminating or downplaying issues with symbolic and transcendent qualities, that is, communism and colonialism.

B. The Effect of Status Change

While the similarity variable was manipulatable, the status variable was not, and the profound changes in the status hierarchy created a power vacuum in which only the U.S. and USSR were in any position to threaten one another. Revision of the status hierarchy was inevitable once it became clear that the fascists would be defeated. The profound changes in the balance of forces precipitated by the war left little room for maneuver. The extent to which the status hierarchy was altered can be judged by examining it in terms of the defeated Axis powers, the decline of major allied powers, and the rise of two superpowers.

By 1945 the prospective destruction and transformation of the German and Japanese societies were manifest. Yet the extent of this was in some measure a function of variation in the degree of threat the enemies had posed. That threat itself was largely a function of their relative strength and their relative capacity in competing for highly salient stakes. Germany, which had the highest status within the Axis prior to the war, and which competed for higher stakes than either Japan or Italy, was the focus of allied attention and was made to pay the highest price. Hitler introduced a number of transcendent stakes, including militarism and racism, that challenged the ethical foundations of Western civilization. In contrast, Japan's aggression was partly an effort to emulate Western imperialism (in China) and partly a response to negative American actions (such as the embargo on raw materials) that threatened Japanese independence. Germany's attack on the USSR, France, and Britain sought conquest and entailed national survival. Japan's attacks on Pearl Harbor and on Europe's colonial possessions in Asia were part of an effort to create a "Greater East Asia Co-Prosperity Sphere" or empire in the nineteenth-century sense of the term. Indeed, the Japanese attack on the U.S. Navy was based on an assumption that "if Japan took decisive action at once . . . the Japanese Navy could win a decisive fleet encounter while it still had a lead over the scattered forces of its enemies"[27] and so eliminate opposition to Japan's imperial designs. But it was not part of a plan to attack California or impose a new global order. Japanese leaders were under no illusion that in the long run they would prevail. Instead, they hoped to negotiate a peace with the United States that would permit them to retain their conquests in the Pacific. Finally, Germany had posed a similar threat in the past and must, it was believed, be taught a lesson once and for all, whereas Japan had actually been an ally in World War I.

Germany, therefore, became the principal target of allied military operations during World War II; and even as late as 1942, when Roosevelt's senior military advisers advocated a shift in priorities owing to pique with Great Britain, Roosevelt refused to sanction such a change.[28] Germany was also treated more harshly than either of its allies after the surrender. It was forced to cede one-quarter of its pre-1938 territory and was divided. Each superpower then created a new Germany in its own "image" upon which it imposed a client relationship. Throughout the Cold War, both West and East Germany were severely limited in their military and foreign-policy autonomy, and each continues to host foreign troops (originally there as conquerors, then as occupiers, and finally as allies). Soviet and American policy toward Germany cannot be explained only by the growth of the Cold War. At the outset at least, their policies were conditioned by a desire to punish Germany and their fear of yet another German resurgence.

By contrast, Italy, always viewed as the least dangerous of the Axis partners, was accepted as an ally after 1943. Similarly, Japan's territorial losses were limited to southern Sakhalin and the Kuril Islands, as well as its colonial territories (much as in the case of Germany in 1919). Japan, though occupied, was permitted to retain its own government and emperor, while Germany was subjected to direct rule by the victorious allies. In any event, the major Axis powers were reduced to the lowest rungs of the status hierarchy at the end of the war.

The process of the war itself meant that little could be done to prevent changes in the status hierarchy at the end of the war. The formerly great powers, Britain and France, were in the twilight of their ascendance. Harold Macmillan sensed this during the war, declaring to a close friend:

We . . . are Greeks in this American Empire. You will find the Americans much as the Greeks found the Romans—great big, vulgar, bustling people, more vigorous than we are and also more idle, with more unspoilt virtues but also more corrupt. We must run the AFHQ as the Greek slaves ran the operations of the Emperor Claudius.[29]

France's rapid capitulation in 1940 revealed that its energy, manpower, and will had been sapped by World War I. Thus, Stalin was contemptu-

ous of the French wartime contribution and resisted giving Charles de
Gaulle a share of the spoils; France was made a member of the UN Security Council only at Churchill's insistence. France's reduced status became quickly visible with the ending of the war, and French representatives did not even participate in the major conferences that created the
postwar order (much to de Gaulle's displeasure). Lacking a "special relationship" with the United States, France was not provided with the information about nuclear energy that was given to Britain and was excluded
from a number of key postwar decisions. Britain and France were no
longer dominant actors, but the French decline was more precipitous and
palpable. Unable to accept its new status gracefully, the Fourth Republic
became embroiled in two protracted colonial struggles, the second of
which prompted the fall of the republic and the reentry of Charles de
Gaulle into political life in 1958. A final effort to bestride the global stage
(with Britain) independently of the United States ended in humiliation in
1956 with an enforced withdrawal from Suez.

Great Britain, too, was called upon to pay the piper after 1945 for
losses suffered in the first world war and for the further exhaustion of the
second. Financially bankrupt (so that only a massive infusion of American loans in 1946 kept the British economy afloat), Britain was in some
respects defeated in the flush of victory. Instead of occupying the roles of
"balancer," ruler of the seas, banker of the world, and center of world
empire, Britain had to adapt quickly to a lesser status. "It was obvious,"
writes Joseph Frankel, "that Britain could not play a decisive part in determining the postwar settlement."[30] Although the denouement came in
stages, it was inevitable. Led by the Labour Party, the British Empire
was gradually and voluntarily dismantled, with India achieving independence in 1947 and much of Africa in the late 1950s.* Unable to carry out
commitments to Greece and Turkey in the face of Soviet pressure, the
British government handed over the torch to the United States, informing
Washington that economic exigencies required withdrawal from these
areas by the end of March 1947.† But even limited involvement proved
too costly, so that British troops were withdrawn from Egypt in 1954,
and British participation in the 1956 Suez adventure was stymied by the

* Churchill himself had been unwilling to consider such a course of action, but he was replaced as prime minister by Labour leader Clement Attlee in 1945.

† The British telegram triggered a series of events that culminated in the Truman Doctrine
and the Marshall Plan. See Joseph M. Jones, *The Fifteen Weeks* (New York: Viking, 1955),
pp. 5–8.

refusal of the Eisenhower Administration to extend the loan necessary to underwrite it. At the end of 1971 Britain cancelled its remaining commitments east of Suez, opting instead for a limited role in a uniting Europe: "Britain's crucial sterling policies became inextricably linked with the maintenance of her world role in general and, specifically, east of Suez. . . ."[31] British entry into the European Economic Community in January 1973 represented a final step in the retreat from an independent global role.

The defeat of the Axis and the exhaustion of the colonial powers coincided with the emergence of the United States and Soviet Union atop the status pyramid. Similar in a number of physical features and historical characteristics, these two "latercomers" came of age as Alexis de Tocqueville had predicted, owing to the sheer size of their resource bases, populations, industrial capabilities, and armed might. It was agreed at Teheran in 1943 that their soldiers would meet in the heartland of Germany and so they did, powerful symbols of the new status hierarchy. This meant that these two actors, the strongest in the system, but both relatively inexperienced in global politics, would determine the division of the wartime spoils.

Relatively equal status produces competiton and is threatening; and rapid change in relative status is destabilizing. But the movement of two actors to the top, two to the middle, and three to the bottom was dramatic indeed. Anticipating and coping with resulting strains posed a major problem during the 1945–47 period. The absence of predictability increased the probability that conflict would grow out of competition. These status changes, coupled with the pre-1941 interaction pattern, meant that the only hope for salvaging the U.S.–USSR coalition was the manipulation of issues, so that those that emphasized dissimilarity would be kept off the agenda, and the others would be seen in terms of concrete stakes that could be divided through compromises. In the last days of Roosevelt's tenure, it almost seemed that this might just happen.

FROM INTERDEPENDENCE TO ENMITY

A. *The Possibility for Compromise*

Roosevelt believed that he would have to play a major role among the Big Three if unity and peace were to be maintained after the war. American economic dominance would provide him with leverage to act as mediator; and in so doing, he could encourage Anglo-Soviet trust. The first item of business was to establish a new set of rules for making decisions, and therefore a new interaction game. This was the task of the conferences at Yalta and Potsdam. In the course of these rule-making conferences, the participants sought to give scope to all four allocation mechanisms. Although the resulting game proved abortive, as had collective security, some of its elements can be identified. The mechanism of principle was revealed in the norms of the Charter of the United Nations, an institution of great importance to F.D.R.,[32] but confusion persisted over the interpretation to be given them and the weight accorded to them, a fact reflected by misunderstandings over the meaning of "self-determination," "democracy," and "friendly regimes" in the context of Eastern Europe. As in the Concert of Europe, principle and force were merged in the norms of unanimity and equality as reflected in the Security Council's task of maintaining world order, by military means if necessary.

Perhaps the most significant mechanism in the abortive postwar game was to be bargains, a fact highlighted by the informal October 1944 agreement reached between Stalin and Churchill under which the USSR was to enjoy predominance in Rumania and Bulgaria, Britain was to be preeminent in Greece, and "influence" would be shared in Yugoslavia and Hungary.[33] But such bargains were incompatible with the Atlantic Charter and traditional American practices. Consequently, even though Roosevelt may have been sympathetic to some form of bargains,* a major share of the blame for the failure of the game rests with the U.S. government which saw trade-offs as contradictory to the norm of self-determination and as potentially destructive of the foreign-policy consensus which existed at home. As early as December 1944, *Life* magazine, recalling Cordell Hull's promise that there would no longer be need of spheres of interest, asked rhetorically: "But who believes that?"[34] Although the United States did not definitively turn its back on bargains until Truman assumed office, the tension between them and American public opinion—and the fear of what this might bring—prompted George Kennan in Moscow to pen a memo to Ambassador Averell Harriman, which read in part:

* For example, "by the end of 1943, the President had cautiously indicated to the Russians that they could count on a free hand in Eastern Europe"—Gaddis, *Origins of the Cold War*, p. 134.

We should realize clearly what we are faced with. It is this—that as far as border states are concerned the Soviet government has never ceased to think in terms of spheres of interest. They expect us to support them in whatever actions they wish to take in those regions, regardless of whether that action seems to us or to the rest of the world to be right or wrong. . . . I have no doubt that this position is honestly maintained on their part, and that they would be equally prepared to reserve moral judgment on any actions which we might wish to carry out, i.e., in the Caribbean area. . . . We are now faced with the prospect of having our people disabused of this illusion. This involves the danger that bitter things may be said at home . . . which will offend Moscow's abnormal sensibilities and cause violent repercussions on our relations.[35]

Roosevelt's plan for a UN was an effort to institutionalize and generalize the conference procedure among the victors in which he participated at Yalta. He thought in terms of a world governed by the victors, an elite group making decisions by means of an interdependence calculus. In this he was opposed by a number of his own advisers who found his ideas undemocratic and who advocated a voice for small actors as well.[36] The UN was something of a compromise between these ideas, with a powerful Security Council composed of the five victors armed with a veto and other elected representatives from the universalistic General Assembly. More important than the Council's structure was the effort it represented to institutionalize a new order of decision making and a new status hierarchy. This is why France and China were given the veto. But the UN was not to be a world government, despite the claims of postwar idealists.

Both Stalin and Churchill were aware of Roosevelt's feelings about the UN, and Stalin was prepared to compromise on specific differences concerning the institution at Yalta in order to cultivate the President's support against Churchill in other matters. Thus, Stalin agreed that the great power veto would not be used by a party to a dispute and would not apply to procedural matters. Stalin also reduced his original demand that all sixteen Soviet republics be admitted to the General Assembly to a demand for the admission of Byelorussia and the Ukraine. Finally, the three leaders agreed that initial membership would be restricted to those states which had declared war on Germany by March 1, 1945.*

At Yalta, it was also agreed that the great powers would host a special

---

*These compromises settled the major disputes which had arisen in the course of the revolving conferences held at Dumbarton Oaks outside of Washington among representatives of the United States, Britain, the USSR and China from August to October 1944.

conference at San Francisco to create the UN, a true rule-making conference to establish officially the rules of the postwar game. That conference
opened on April 25, 1945, attended by representatives of forty-six governments, and, although a number of disputes arose concerning the rights
of small actors in particular, the charter was signed on June 26. Nevertheless, the conference failed to institutionalize the interaction pattern that
had characterized relations among the Big Three during the war. Instead,
it ushered in a period of change in relations among the victors, characterized by a series of ad hoc games that gradually eroded the goodwill that
had existed within the alliance. That erosion was complete by 1947. The
ad hoc games were based on resort to an interdependence calculus which
failed to dispose of "the spoils of war." In this regard, the origins of the
Cold War must be seen as an incremental process and not as a conspiracy
by any side. Stalin was not so Machiavellian, or F.D.R. so naïve, as
some commentators have claimed.[37]

Initially, all three victors were prepared to make decisions on the basis
of interdependence—a willingness reflected in the Stalin-Churchill "percentages" agreement, and in the inclination of F.D.R. and a reluctant
Churchill to concede to Stalin at Yalta much of what he demanded in
Poland. That country was to be governed by a provisional regime consisting of representatives of the Polish government-in-exile (from London)
and the communist "Lublin Poles." The new Poland, which was to be
"friendly" to the Soviet Union, would receive large amounts of territory
from defeated Germany, while parts of eastern Poland would become
Russian. The inclusion of some noncommunist Poles and the provision
for holding "free and unfettered elections as soon as possible" were
mostly face-saving concessions to the West, partly to placate potential
objections by the Polish population in the United States.*

Those who point to the agreement on Poland (which was already occupied by the Red Army), and the provisions for Soviet control of Manchuria and the Japanese islands, as "appeasement" or "sellout" disregard the importance to F.D.R. of the UN and of Soviet entry into the war

---

* The Yalta agreement concerning Poland remains a source of controversy. The best
recent scholarship is that of Diane Shaver Clemens, *Yalta*. For a critical review, see Robert
James Maddox, *The New Left and The Origins of the Cold War* (Princeton, N.J.: Princeton
University Press, 1973), ch. 6. An early summary of the divergent views about Yalta can be
found in Richard F. Fenno, Jr., ed., *The Yalta Conference* (Boston: Health, 1955).

against Japan (which was believed to be able to fight on for a considerable period in China as well as at home). Whether F.D.R. was "duped" by Stalin or whether Stalin viewed the elements of the Yalta agreement as a genuine quid pro quo, it is clear that F.D.R. was moved by an interdependence calculus. Though the evidence concerning Stalin remains clouded, it is likely that at this time he, too, was employing an interdependence calculus and was more interested in defeating Germany completely, and then dividing the spoils amicably, than in spreading communism. As the advocate of "socialism in one country," Stalin, it may be argued, was concerned with assuring Soviet security against Germany and sought to reacquire territories of the former tsarist empire which had been lost at Brest-Litovsk.

Careful analysis of postwar Soviet behavior tends to confirm that Soviet leaders, though tough bargainers, were moved by national rather than ideological motives. Stalin, in particular, restricted much of his activity to areas immediately adjacent to the USSR and offered little encouragement or assistance to foreign communists, including Mao Zedong and Marshal Tito. It is even possible that Stalin feared "autonomous" communists elsewhere as a threat to Russian interests and his own personal power. This supposition conforms, too, to Stalin's prewar behavior—the purges of the international communist movement and of "adventurers" within the CPSU after the defeat of the Chinese Communists in 1927.

Stalinism was based on a profoundly nationalistic attitude, and Stalin's rise to power, closely associated with the defeat of Trotsky's internationalism, was based on efforts to develop and consolidate Soviet State power. It was bound up with the substitution of the idea of world revolution by considerations of Soviet national security and defense.[38]

Furthermore, empirical analysis of Soviet behavior in crises between 1945 and 1963 reveals it to have been "conservative rather than radical, cautious rather than reckless, deliberate rather than impulsive, and rational (not willing to lose) rather than nonrational"[39]

Stalin's postwar actions, too, tend to support this interpretation. Only when it became clear that relations among the victors had deteriorated did the Soviet government begin to abandon the commitments it had made at the end of the war. Thus, almost immediately after the October 1944 agreement on spheres of interest with Churchill, Stalin refused to support the Greek communist rebellion against the British and their Greek partners. The communist movement in that country was decimated with little protest from Stalin. But in Rumania and Bulgaria, where Churchill had agreed to grant the USSR 90 percent and 75 percent of local influence respectively, the Soviet Union moved quickly to assert its will.[40] In Rumania, the Red Army actively pressed King Michael in 1945 to appoint a procommunist government under Petro Groza; and, in Bulgaria, Soviet pressure led to the demise of the Agrarian League and a communist electoral victory in October 1946. Yet, in Hungary, and Yugoslavia, where the agreed division of influence was 50–50, Soviet interference was muted. In Hungary, elections were held, which one Western historian characterized as the "only free election in the history of that nation."[41] In the case of Yugoslavia, Stalin called upon Tito to cooperate with noncommunist elements in a coalition government.[42] To Tito, such demands seemed designed to further Soviet, rather than communist, interests and so fostered suspicions that contributed to the 1948 rift. Finally, in Czechoslovakia, about which Western leaders felt a particular sense of guilt and shame owing to Munich, an agreement was worked out for President Eduard Beneš to form a popular government, with the communist Klement Gottwald as premier and the respected Jan Masaryk as foreign minister. Though limits were placed on capitalism, individual liberties were maintained.

What accounts for these variations in Soviet policy toward Eastern Europe? Perhaps the most important factors were the differences in value and salience to Stalin of the various stakes clustered along the perimeter of the USSR. Poland was the most salient of these stakes, because it was the land bridge between the Soviet Union and Germany that had twice served as an invasion corridor from Germany. On the second occasion, this had led to the death of from 20 to 24 million Russians.[43] The significance of Poland for Soviet security was reflected in the scope of population and territorial transfers which Stalin unilaterally carried out there. In light of the sacrifices made by the Russians in the course of the two wars, it was probably naïve to expect Stalin to accept the existence of any Polish regime that was not a Soviet client. Even the limited Soviet concessions regarding elections and noncommunist participation in the Polish government must be regarded as efforts at accommodation. This spirit was even more pronounced in Hungary, Czechoslovakia, and Yugoslavia, where the stakes were less salient to Stalin for reasons of history and geography.* Finally, the Soviet Union showed the least restraint in the cases of Bulgaria and Rumania, because it had been given a virtually free hand there, and because those two countries had served as German allies during World War II.

The logic of this analysis suggests that, in the absence of the Cold War atmosphere which later became ascendant, Stalin *might* not have moved to establish a communist dictatorship in Hungary or Czechoslovakia so long as the coalition regimes in those countries had remained friendly to the USSR (as in Finland). In fact, the two regimes remained relatively unmolested until May 1947 and February 1948, respectively, before which time the Truman Doctrine was proclaimed (March 1947) and the Cold War began. Thereafter, there seemed little reason to forgo spoils that could be had unilaterally, and that could offer additional security. Where restraint was the outcome of an interdependence calculus, that restraint disappeared once a simple cost-benefit calculus was substituted for it in the case of Eastern Europe

The Soviet use of an interdependence calculus on the division-of-the-spoils issue prior to 1947 can also be seen outside of Eastern Europe. Soviet behavior in Germany and Austria may have been governed principally by a concern to limit the prospect of German recovery and to seize whatever resources were available to assist Soviet reconstruction. The communist issue took second place in both cases, as well as in Manchuria. Only the failure of the victors to arrive at a satisfactory formula for German unification, accompanied by unilateral Western moves to promote German economic recovery, induced Soviet leaders to move quickly to communize the Eastern zone. The foreign ministers' conferences of 1947 paradoxically indicated that both sides sought a united Germany—but for fundamentally incompatible reasons. Stalin sought a Germany that would never again pose a threat to Soviet security, while by this time the West sought an economically robust Germany that would no longer depend upon Anglo-American largesse and could contribute to economic recovery in Western Europe. Disagreement was, therefore, related to the relative salience of the several values associated with the German stake. Neither party was prepared to accept the honesty of the

---

* Contrast these limited Soviet concessions in Eastern Europe with American refusal to permit more than token Soviet participation in the postwar administration of Japan and Italy.

other's professions concerning the value that was uppermost in its thoughts. That the two sides were talking past each other is revealed in a dialogue between Molotov and British Foreign Minister Ernest Bevin as recounted by Harold Nicolson:

Bevin: What do you want?

Molotov: I want a unified Germany.

Bevin: Why do you want that? Do you really believe a unified Germany would go Communist? They might pretend to. They would say all the right things and repeat all the correct formulas. But in their hearts they would be longing for the day when they could revenge their defeat at Stalingrad. You know that as well as I do.

Molotov: Yes, I know that. But I want a unified Germany.[44]

In the case of China, Stalin acceded to an American plan to revive the country under Chiang Kai-shek as a balancer of Japan. Stalin sought to persuade Mao that he should enter a coalition and that the time was not ripe for a communist revolution. In view of Stalin's earlier "nationalist" policy toward China, it is not surprising that Mao found this advice disingenuous. Once again, Stalin's effort to accommodate the West planted the seeds for a later rift among communist leaders.[45]

Finally, a number of Stalin's probes that stimulated Western counterpressure can be interpreted as the results of an interdependence calculus. The employment of such a calculus does *not* connote unselfish behavior. An actor seeks to maximize its own share of the stakes and retreats either when the costs are too high, or when such behavior imperils its share of other, more salient, stakes. Soviet demands for a trusteeship in Libya, a share of the Ruhr, a vote for the sixteen Soviet republics in the UN, continued occupation of northern Iran, and control of the Dardanelles can be viewed in this light. All involved tentative probes that were called off when met by resistance. If they were viewed as symbolic stakes by Western leaders, they were still probably seen as concrete stakes by Stalin, who was willing to use them as items to barter.

The Cold War, then, emerged in part because each side came to perceive the other as maliciously standing in the way of its acquisition of the fruits of victory. Perhaps vigorous bargaining might have prevented contention over division of the spoils from deteriorating in this fashion had not the issue of communism intruded and so sensitized each side to the alleged threat posed by the other. It was through this issue that previously concrete stakes began to assume the clothing of symbolic ones. Stalin's speech of February 1946 provided indications of the changing atmosphere, with its stress on Marxist doctrine. Interestingly, the Soviet leader took this opportunity to declare his support for anticolonial movements in India, Palestine, Syria, Lebanon, Indonesia, Greece, and Egypt, thereby linking the colonial and communist issues. In his mind, the colonial territories constituted an internal contradiction within the capitalist system. The following month, Winston Churchill, though occupying no official position at the time, provided a picture of emerging Western perceptions, when he declared at Fulton, Missouri:

From Stettin in the Baltic to Trieste in the Adriatic, an iron curtain has descended across the Continent. Behind that line lie all the capitals of the ancient states of Central and Eastern Europe. Warsaw, Berlin, Prague, Vienna, Budapest, Belgrade, Bucharest, and Sofia, all these famous cities, and the populations around them lie in what I must call the Soviet Sphere.[46]

The process was largely completed for the West by the time Truman called upon Americans on March 12, 1947 to assist "free peoples" everywhere who "must choose between alternative ways of life," one "based upon the will of the majority" and the other "based upon the will of a minority forcibly imposed upon the majority." It was completed for the East when representatives of the Soviet, Eastern European, French, and Italian Communist Parties met at Szklarska Poreba in late September to form the Cominform and hear Andrei Zhdanov, then second only to Stalin in the Soviet Politburo, call upon communists to struggle against American and British imperialism. Gradually, Stalin's fears of capitalist encirclement and Western fears of communist expansionism had fed upon each in a viciously expanding cycle of mistrust, negative acts, and hostility.

Stalin must have reasoned that the Anglo-Americans were seeking to deny him Eastern Europe, which Soviet troops already occupied, and which had cost so much Russian blood. By what right, he might have wondered, do they meddle in this region? Meanwhile, President Truman tried to fathom where Soviet aggression would end. The large and belligerent communist parties of Italy and France, for instance, posed threats in countries that could hardly be viewed as traditional Russian spheres of influence. By 1947, every slice of territory and every sentence in the World

War II agreements became symbolic of the strength and aggressiveness of the opposing camp. This was implicit in Truman's attempt to "contain" the Soviet Union and communism.* Both sides drew a line the crossing of which by the other was tantamount to an act of war. How did this transformation in perceptions take place? How did a stake dimension become converted to an actor dimension? The process is illustrated by the interaction among the victors over Germany, the greatest of the postwar prizes.

B. The Emergence of Negative Affect: An Illustration

The zonal division of Germany was agreed to well before the end of the war, with Berlin to be the headquarters of the Allied Control Authority. In 1945, F.D.R. and the allied high command agreed that the Red Army be permitted to take Berlin in recognition of its enormous sacrifices. At Potsdam, agreement was reached that Germany be stripped of much of its prewar territory, divided into three zones of occupation, subjected to "denazification," and made to pay heavy reparations. The latter, however, proved a difficult topic to resolve, as Stalin demanded an unconditional German obligation to pay reparations amounting to twenty billion dollars, of which half would go to the USSR. This last demand was refused, and no exact sum was settled upon. However, the principle of reparations was agreed to, with provision for the removal of industrial equipment and other goods from the Soviet and Western zone, confiscation of Germany's foreign assets, and surrender of a percentage of current production from the British and American zones—so long as Germany could maintain a modest peacetime standard of living.[47] This last provision proved later to be a major bone of contention,† as German industrial production was to be reduced to a level compatible with the prevention of "disease and unrest" and sufficient for the payment of essential imports.[48] Finally, Germany was to be governed as a *single* economic and political unit; the zones were to be merely lines of demarcation, not sepa-

---

* Truman's policy is often seen as a broadening of the concept of containment put forward by George Kennan in "X" (Kennan), "The Sources of Soviet Conduct," *Foreign Affairs* (July 1947), 25(4):566–82, a suggestion Truman resented. Kennan later expressed regret that his original article had "lent itself to misinterpretation"—Kennan, *Memoirs, 1925–1950*, (Boston: Little, Brown, 1967), p. 359.

† Western leaders were sensitive to the effects of the onerous reparations which had been imposed upon Germany after World War I.

rate entities. Whether these arrangements were workable or not, the fact is that agreement was at best superficial. As Herbert Feis declares:

The negotiators, in their wish to reach an accord rather than separate in anger, had fooled themselves and the world; they had obscured or evaded the antithesis by three devices of diplomacy. One was by recourse to ambiguous language. Another was by adopting countervailing provisions. The third was by relegating some of its most disputed and unsettled questions to the Four-Power Control Council which they were creating, to exercise joint control over Germany.[49]

The Potsdam agreements were to guide administration in Germany until a peace treaty could be concluded between Germany and the victors. But that treaty was never signed because the original agreements came apart. The first collision was over Soviet reparations. Almost immediately, Soviet officials began to strip their zone of anything of value, failing to inform their allies of what was being seized. This appeared to violate the understanding that a bare minimum of productive capacity was to remain. However justified this behavior may have seemed in Soviet eyes, its consequence was that the Western allies had to pay for Germany's imports out of their own pockets, a particularly onerous burden for Great Britain. The anger generated by what Western officials viewed as a unilateral Soviet action was intensified in the spring of 1946, when the Soviet Union ceased food shipments from its zone to the Western zones. In May the American commander, General Lucius Clay, announced the suspension of reparations payments from the American zone, claiming that Germany was not being treated as an economic unit, in violation of the Potsdam agreements, and that the United States was being forced to underwrite the German economy.

As the original agreement to treat Germany as a single economic unit was undermined, American and British officials, in late 1946, moved to consolidate their zones into a separate economic unit which would increase industrial production above the bare minimum. On September 6th, Secretary of State Byrnes declared in Stuttgart that although the United States continued to support the Potsdam agreements, it would seek "maximum possible unification" of Germany's economy in the absence of complete unification. German industrial production, he noted, was necessary for European recovery in general and must not be hindered.[50] In January 1947 the British and American zones were unified as "Bizonia," and the two allies proceded to introduce measures to revitalize the German economy. To both the French and the Russians, these efforts were anathema.

While Anglo-American decisions at this time were no doubt influenced by the hope of winning Germany to their side, Bizonia was more a reaction to the problem of making the zones of occupation economically self-sufficient and a riposte to what was seen as Soviet efforts to impose communism on—if not all of Germany—certainly its zone of occupation. In the spring of 1946, the Russians had compelled the smaller socialist party in its zone to merge with the communist party, forming the Socialist Unity Party (SED). Under these conditions, German political unity appeared less attractive to the British and Americans, though advocacy of such unity was resumed once it became clear that the SED could not generate much political support in the Western zones. In effect, both sides switched positions, with the West favoring a unified democratic Germany and the Soviet Union resisting such a development. What emerged from the struggle over the future of Germany was a marked change in the attitudes of the allies toward each other and a redefinition of the stake. By the end of 1946 Germany was no longer viewed as a common threat to be suppressed but as a prize to be won in the battle of communism versus capitalism.

The creation of Bizonia led to the failure of efforts to conclude a German peace treaty by the foreign ministers in Moscow in March 1947. The deteriorating situation in Greece and Turkey further complicated the search for a way out of the impasse. Instead, disagreement was reinforced by negative acts and intensified hostility. In May the Western allies established an economic council to run Bizonia and took steps to institute a form of democratic self-rule in their zones. They also introduced a plan to internationalize the Ruhr, in order to calm those—notably the French—who feared the prospect of German sovereignty. In June the two allies devalued the German currency, despite Soviet opposition to this violation of the principle of economic unity. A last, futile effort to come to terms on Germany in accordance with the Potsdam agreements was made at a meeting of the foreign ministers in London in November 1947.

With disagreement over Germany having become an open rupture, and with initial steps having been taken the previous June toward the economic recovery and unification of Western Europe through the Marshall

Plan, the British government took the first step in January 1948 toward concluding a defense treaty with France and the Benelux countries. Soviet representatives had remained on the Control Council, probably in order to use their veto power to prevent further Western actions in Bizonia. But this proved futile as the American and British governments moved ahead at the beginning of February to proclaim the establishment of a provisional German government in their zones. Further reforms ensued, including a reorganization of German administration and the inclusion of the Western zones in the Marshall Plan. Perhaps in response to unilateral Western moves in Germany, and perhaps as a move to consolidate its own position in Eastern Europe, the Soviet Union in February 1948 terminated Czechoslovakia's independent status. In a coup, apparently directed by Soviet Ambassador Valerian Zorin, the coalition government in Prague was dissolved, and the Czechoslovak Communist Party swiftly seized power. In a matter of weeks, Jan Masaryk was dead, probably the victim of murder, and rigged elections gave the communists control of the National Assembly.

The Czech affair, more than any other event, encouraged the French government to alter its position toward Germany and unify its zone with Bizonia. Fearful anticipation dominated Western councils, and General Clay claimed to sense "a change in the Soviet position which I was certain portended some Soviet action in Germany."[51] Even the possibility of war was discussed in Washington. On March 17 Britain, France, and the Benelux countries formally signed the Brussels Pact of mutual defense, and Truman requested that Congress reinstitute conscription. Three days later, the Soviet representative, Marshal Sokolovsky, stormed out of the Control Council, never to return.

At the end of March, the first Soviet harassment of free movement into and out of Berlin began, partly as a response to the creation of a Western zone in Germany and partly to consolidate the Eastern zone. The symbolic nature of the stake was already apparent when General Clay came out strongly against the evacuation of American dependents from Berlin: "Evacuation in the face of the Italian elections and European situation is to me almost unthinkable."[52] In the meantime, further steps were taken toward the genesis of an anti-Soviet coalition in the West. On April 3, 1948, Truman signed the European Recovery Act, by which the United

States undertook to finance the Marshall Plan. Negotiations also began for an extension of the Brussels Pact to include North America, and Senator Arthur Vandenberg, the leading Republican member of the Foreign Relations Committee, undertook to introduce a resolution endorsing the idea.[53] Meanwhile, a Six-Nation Conference on Germany in London had laid the groundwork for the creation of a West German government, including a plan for the administration of the Ruhr that excluded the USSR.

It was in the context of these events that on June 11, 1948 the Red Army halted rail traffic to Berlin for one day. The Western position was that any interference with free movement was a violation of the stipulation that Germany be treated as an economic unit, whereas the Soviet position was that the breakup of the Control Council, as well as of the Four-Power Kommandatura in Berlin, also meant the end of Western "privileges" in the city. The ostensible Soviet motive for imposing a full-scale blockage on Berlin was the introduction by the West of a currency reform in their zones (later extended to West Berlin). In fact, it was probably the London Conference which was the trigger, because it signified to Stalin Western determination to move ahead in the creation of an autonomous German government. Although the Soviet action was crude, it represented less an act of blatant aggression than the breakdown of a vague agreement in conditions of intense hostility.[54] In retrospect, the blockage seems an obvious countermove to Western consolidation of its zones, and to the termination of four-power control in Germany and Berlin. But, if Soviet leaders viewed their actions as defensive, Western leaders saw them as part of a Soviet effort to exert control over all of Germany. Berlin had become a symbol of the prize that neither side had the strength to win—a united Germany.

Berlin was only the most prominent of the concrete stakes in Europe that were imbued with symbolic qualities when the division-of-the-spoils issue was swallowed up by the communist issue. By the time the first Berlin crisis ended in May 1949, the Soviet Union had been the target of several other significant negative actions. On April 4, 1949, the North Atlantic Treaty Organization (NATO) was born. Five months later, the Federal Republic of Germany was created, with the Christian Democrat Konrad Adenauer as its first chancellor. By this time, it was clear that the United States and Britain had secured most of Germany as an anticommunist bulwark, while even West Berlin, deep inside the Soviet occupation zone, remained beyond Stalin's grasp.*

C. Conclusion: From Partnership to Cold War

In light of their prior pattern of disagreement, dissimilarity, and rapid rise to the first and second ranks in the status hierarchy, it may have been inevitable that the United States and the Soviet Union would drift apart after the defeat of Hitler. So it appeared to Herbert Feis when he wrote:

History . . . might well have asked the winds of time: "Can these countries with such different visions and opinions as I have allowed to shape in their hearts and minds, really settle their respective claims, adjust their respective visions, and maintain a lasting friendship?"[55]

But, as though to show that he was not certain that the transformation was inevitable, Feis added: "To make this the more unlikely, on one lovely day in April 1945 he [history] broke with the tip of his finger an artery in Franklin Roosevelt's brain."[56] Clearly, the perceptions of leading decision makers, notably Truman's, were important, but how important?†

According to the interpretation presented here, unfavorable background factors heightened the probability of conflict. But it was not inevitable for that conflict to have intensified into a Cold War over transcendent stakes. The American government's rejection of the role of bargains, for instance, must be seen as a critical withdrawal of legitimacy from a game which never became institutionalized. "It seems likely," as Gaddis argues, "that Washington policy-makers mistook Stalin's determination to ensure Russian security through spheres of influence for a renewed effort to spread communism outside the borders of the Soviet Union."[57] As Kennan's memo indicated, the Soviet Union was behaving primarily on a stake dimension, which *may* have persisted had the Truman Administration remained more tolerant in late 1945 and early 1946. Truman did not so much cause the Cold War as fail to prevent it or temper it; he was carried along by events rather than manipulating those events, as

---

*The Eastern counterpart of the Federal Republic, the German Democratic Republic (GDR) was not officially established until 1955.

†Some American revisionist historians have emphasized the change in American leadership during a critical transition period as a major step in the origin of the Cold War. See, for instance, David Horowitz, *The Free World Colossus* (New York: Hill and Wang, 1965).

F.D.R. had sought to do in mediating between Stalin and Churchill. Thus, Truman's first meeting with Molotov—a few days before the San Francisco Conference—was something of a harbinger, as he used "blunt language" to "scold" the Soviet foreign minister, who complained: "I have never been talked to like that in my life."[58] Such tactics did little to de-escalate a hostile spiral. Truman also saw the communist issue as more salient than colonialism, thereby reinforcing the positive prior pattern of Anglo-American interaction but eliminating the prospect for American mediation.

THE EMERGENCE OF THE TRANSCENDENT STRUGGLE

The genesis of the Cold War took place in 1947, but the process was one of evolution and did not represent the sharp break often depicted by historians. The stakes under contention were being defined in two distinct frameworks—the loosely knit division-of-the-spoils issue and the tightly fused communism issue. It can be argued that the period after 1947 represented an effort to divide the spoils by resort to ad hoc games of coercion. Indeed, with the rejection of bargains, continuing controversy over principle, and the development of bloc voting in the UN and other forums, a new interaction game began to take shape, based largely on force alone.*

As the game evolved, it was accompanied by changing perceptions of stakes. The infusion of a transcendent quality marked the final ascendancy of the communist issue over the division-of-spoils issue as each side remained dissatisfied with the interim disposition of stakes, stood in the way of the other's altering that disposition, and sought to weaken the other. This transition was closely linked on both sides to internal politics and membership cohesion.

For Stalin, the emergence of the Cold War and the growing hostility between East and West served as a convenient rationale for the consolidation of his rule at home and for the reimposition of the strong ideological and coercive bonds that had been loosened during World War II.

---

* By 1946, voting in the General Assembly had become tests of strength and a means by which the United States could exert pressure upon the Soviet Union. The implications of American dominance in the UN became clear at the time of the Korean War and the passage of the "Uniting for Peace Resolution."

Alleged capitalist encirclement produced calls for "vigilance" at home and provided an excuse for a thorough purge of the CPSU of "liberal" elements and of "careerists" who had gained entry during the years of "patriotism." Even returning soldiers and prisoners-of-war who had been exposed to Western Europe found themselves in prison camps as Stalin sought once more to draw all the strands of power into his own hands. During his final years, the Stalinist dictatorship and "cult of personality" were at their apogee, climaxing in the so-called "doctors' plot" of 1952 and the planning of yet another purge of his own Presidium.

The communist issue served the Truman administration in three ways. Anticommunist sentiment was of value in eliminating, once and for all, isolationist sentiment on the right and severing the Henry Wallace wing of the Democratic Party on the left. The issue also provided ideological legitimacy for assuming the extensive foreign-policy burdens implied by foreign assistance, the peacetime draft, permanent peacetime military alliances, a vastly enlarged defense budget, and the general assumption of world leadership in economic and political affairs. To rally public and bipartisan support for these programs, Truman engaged in rhetorical "oversell," particularly to the Congress, where isolationist sentiment remained strong.[59] In effect, oversell reawakened prewar fears and brought an end to pro-Soviet sentiment that had grown in the country—first during the Great Depression and then more broadly during the war, when Stalin was referred to as "Uncle Joe." Finally, the communist issue proved a powerful rationale for a strong presidency at a time when the office was occupied by a relatively uncharismatic figure, who was not popularly elected until 1948, and then only by a hair.

The communist issue also served the needs of the Republican Party, which had been exiled in the political wilderness since 1932. It provided a weapon to criticize Roosevelt's New Dealers, who had long been viewed by many Republicans as "socialist." More importantly, it became a means of rallying opposition to Truman and Secretary of State Dean Acheson after Dewey's defeat in 1948. Since the Republican Party had been unable to defeat the Democrats in a straight battle of economic philosophies, the addition of a new issue which crosscut the old 1932 issue could serve to weaken Roosevelt's urban-ethnic coalition.* The

* For an analysis of anticommunism as a realigning issue, see James Sundquist, *Dynamics of the Party System* (Washington, D.C.: Brookings, 1973), pp. 310–314.

"fall of China," the "no-win" policy in Korea, and the frustrations of containment all became lightning rods for accumulated discontent with the Truman Administration.

Since leaders of both major political parties found the communist issue to be of use, they were encouraged to outdo each other, thereby transforming the longtime popular suspicion of communism into public "hysteria."[60] This hysteria was shrewdly cultivated by Joseph McCarthy, the Republican senator from Wisconsin, who used it to thrust himself to national prominence in the early 1950s. During this period, he conducted a virtual purge of liberal and quasi-leftist circles in both parties, whose loyalty had been unquestioned during the depression and war years. Those who refused to adopt a less-than-transcendent line toward U.S.-Soviet relations were removed or smeared, because they were not prepared to see all internal and external issues in the light of the communist issue.* One of the major consequences of the McCarthy era was to produce a narrow foreign-policy elite, which was intolerant of dissent. The resulting ideological conformity reinforced the subsequent misperception of events, because no voice remained to interpret Soviet behavior in a nonconsensual fashion. This closed-mindedness was aggravated by an atmosphere of fear and suspicion that reigned within the public at large, and which claimed victims in virtually all walks of life. Advocates of foreign policy flexibility could expect to be criticized as "soft on communism," a charge as ruinous as "waving the red shirt" after the Civil War.

In effect, Truman's manipulation of the communism issue came to haunt the Democratic Party and was in part responsible for the victory of Eisenhower in 1952. Truman had sought to use the issue to silence domestic critics of his foreign policy of "get-tough-with-the-Russians," but Republicans seized the issue for themselves to flay Roosevelt's New Dealers and criticize Truman's containment policy as defeatist and insufficiently assertive. Eventually, the leadership of both parties lost control of the issue to the irresponsible elements around McCarthy, particularly as communism appeared poised to engulf Asia.†

---

*Interestingly, McCarthy drew strong support from neo-isolationist elements in the country who had found themselves political outsiders after the advent of World War II.

†For background on the tenor of the times, see Herbert Feis, *The China Tangle* (Princeton, N.J.: Princeton University Press, 1953), and Tang Tsou, *America's Failure in China, 1941–1950* (Chicago: University of Chicago Press, 1963).

If by 1947 issues in Western Europe had become fused in the Cold War, stakes in Asia were still separated from this emerging critical issue and isolated from each other until 1949. The colonialism issue was linked only loosely and faded from political consciousness in the United States as the Cold War in Europe grew more salient. Prior to 1949, the Truman Administration managed to pursue a reasonably sophisticated set of discrete policies toward the various stakes at issue. Although generally tilting toward Chiang Kai-shek in the Chinese civil war, several missions were dispatched, including one led by General Marshall, to try to find a coalition solution. Initially, Mao was regarded as a nationalist as well as a communist, who might be encouraged to do as Tito had done in Yugoslavia in 1948. As the end of the Kuomintang drew near in China, the Truman Administration resisted the temptation to pour massive amounts of military and economic assistance into this theater. Instead, a number of symbolic gestures were made as concessions to the rabid Republican supporters of Chiang Kai-shek, like Senator Knowland and Congressman Judd, who threatened to torpedo the President's proposals for Europe. They claimed that communism was more of a threat in Asia than in Europe and that Truman seemed unable to see the parallel between events in Eastern Europe and in China.*

Revolution and change in Asia were not officially linked to Soviet expansion in the West until after the outbreak of the Korean War in June 1950. In fact, shortly before that war, Acheson publicly indicated that neither Korea nor Taiwan were part of the American defense perimeter in Asia.[61] Plans were even readied for an early recognition of the newly established People's Republic of China. This policy was, however, not consummated, and Truman and Acheson were severely criticized as responsible for "losing China," a phrase which reflects the degree to which an actor dimension came to characterize the communism issue. The "loss of China" only made sense if international communism were monolithic and if communism constituted the sole issue on the global agenda. Some American critics of Truman's Asia policy believed China to be such a valuable stake that only the presence of traitors in high places, like the

*Many of these same individuals had argued during the war that the principal American military effort be directed against Japan rather than Germany, and they were to become the sponsors of the "Committee of One-Million," which so successfully lobbied for years against recognizing the Maoist regime.

State Department, could explain its advocacy by the administration.*
Later charges by Richard M. Nixon against Alger Hiss, and by Mc-
Carthy, were effective in part because of the atmosphere produced by the
China question, and experts on China like John Carter Vincent, John Service, and Owen Lattimore were purged from the foreign-policy establishment.† At the height of what Dean Acheson called the "shameful and ni-
hilistic orgy," Acheson and General George Marshall were accused of
procommunism.[62] Even John F. Kennedy was caught up in the atmosphere of the time. Speaking in the House of Representatives, he argued:

So concerned were our diplomats and their advisors, the Lattimores and Fair-
banks, with the imperfection of the democratic system in China after twenty years
of war and the tales of corruption in high places that they lost sight of our tremendous stake in a non-Communist China. . . . This House must now assume the
responsibility of preventing the onrushing tide of Communism from engulfing all
of Asia.[63]

Criticism of this sort frustrated Truman's Asia policy and intensified
after the invasion of South Korea. Truman himself reacted vigorously to
the North Korean attack, viewing it as a prelude to a Soviet challenge in
Europe, and as a challenge to the West not unlike that which Hitler had
posed in 1938 at Munich.[64] Not only was Korea immediately linked to
the communist issue but Taiwan also, as the Seventh Fleet was deployed
to protect Chiang's island bastion and so intervened in the Chinese civil
war. Similarly, the French effort against Ho Chi Minh in Indochina,
previously regarded as an element of the colonial issue, was now redefined as part of the communist issue. Even the Huk insurgency in the
Philippines was viewed as part of the larger communist threat, and Edward Lansdale was dispatched to develop a counterstrategy, later to become the doctrine of counterinsurgency. Malaya, where the British confronted a communist insurgency, was seen in the same light.

Korea was for Truman and Acheson a test of strength and perhaps even
a prelude to general war. At minimum, it reflected Soviet efforts to probe
for "soft spots" in the Free World, having been rebuffed by containment

---

* This suspicion was also voiced in connection with the surprising explosion of a nuclear
device by the Soviet Union in August 1949.

† Apparently, the major "sin" of the China experts was predicting that Chiang Kai-shek
would almost certainly lose the civil war.

in Western Europe. In the words of a leading exponent of the standard American interpretation of the Cold War:

So they [the Soviets] turned their attention to the Far East. Here was a much more attractive field for political and military exploitation. Most countries in this area had only recently emerged from Western colonialism and their nationalist and anti-Western feelings were very strong.[65]

The possibility that any of these events—in China, Malaya, Indochina, the Philippines, or Korea—might have stemmed from local conditions, or that Stalin might have been unaware of or unable to guide them, was hardly considered. Korea was no longer a concrete stake but rather was symbolic of Japan and all of Asia. Truman reacted firmly, but not sufficiently firmly to satisfy his critics.

To his critics on the right, Truman had failed to correct Roosevelt's "surrender" of Eastern Europe and had himself lost China. Containment, they believed, was fundamentally defensive and included no provision for liberating those who had fallen under communist rule. So thought General Douglas MacArthur, commander of UN forces in Korea, who persuaded Truman to permit his armies to sweep north of the 38th parallel in order to unify Korea under the "democratic" regime of President Syngman Rhee.[66] MacArthur miscalculated China's willingness and capacity to intervene as he moved toward the Yalu River,[67] but was not deterred by the prospect, which he believed would provide him with the opportunity to liberate China as well. MacArthur's open disobedience and willingness to escalate the war forced Truman to dismiss him, an event which precipitated an outcry among Truman's critics. The general returned home to a hero's welcome and talk of his being nominated for the presidency by the Republican Party.

Advocacy of liberation in Europe, which had been briefly publicized by General George Patton at the end of the war, also became a popular theme of the Republican Party as the 1952 election drew near. Taking advantage of popular frustration with limited war in Korea and the stalemate in Europe, Dwight Eisenhower was overwhelmingly elected in 1952. Eisenhower was able to bring an end to the war, partly owing to a threat to use nuclear weapons,[68] and partly owing to the death of Stalin in March 1953. In the presidential campaign, Eisenhower's nominee as secretary of state, John Foster Dulles, began to describe an alternative to containment for Europe—liberation. Ultimately, the administration's passivity during the 1953 rising in East Berlin, and the 1956 Hungarian revolution, proved that the new doctrine was empty rhetoric.

If domestic actors and processes played a major role in producing a frenzied atmosphere of anticommunism in the United States, domestic processes and internal struggles for power appear to have had a profound impact upon Soviet foreign policy as well. Thus, one major difference between Stalin and Trotsky after Lenin's death was the question of socialism in one country versus international revolution. Stalin himself found the Cold War to be valuable in reasserting personal control over Soviet society after World War II. Clearly, the atmosphere of tension in global politics provided a rationale for growing military expenditures and continued emphasis upon heavy industry in economic planning. At the Nineteenth Party Congress in October 1952, Stalin took a hard line in foreign policy and spoke of the inevitability of war.[69] At the time of the Congress, two party factions had developed—one around Georgi Malenkov, Stalin's heir apparent, and the other around Nikita Khrushchev. Stalin's speech seemed a slap at Malenkov, who was associated with a more conciliatory foreign-policy approach toward the German question that would permit something of a shift to the production of consumer goods in the USSR.

In January 1953 the equivalent of McCarthyism erupted in the Soviet Union when a group of Jewish physicians were accused of having poisoned Andrei Zhdanov—the previous heir apparent, who had died in mysterious circumstances in 1948—and of having served the American and British intelligence agencies.* If the U.S. State Department was plagued by communists in high places, the Kremlin was allegedly riddled with assassins in the pay of the West.† Apparently, Stalin was on the verge of initiating another major blood purge when he died. Whether he was assassinated remains a moot point, but Malenkov succeeded him and brought talk of the "doctors' plot" to an end.[70]

Malenkov quickly sought to reverse Soviet policy, arguing that there

---

* It is likely that Zhdanov was involved in a vicious struggle with Malenkov in 1948. Whatever the cause of his death, his followers were purged afterwards in the "Leningrad Affair" and replaced by supporters of Malenkov.

† Similar charges had been made against prominent Eastern European leaders such as Rajk in Hungary and Kostov in Bulgaria after 1948 during Stalin's campaign against Tito and "Titoism."

was "no disputed or unresolved question that cannot be settled peacefully,"[71] and he tried to hasten negotiations on Korea and Germany. His efforts, however, were undermined by the opposition of Khrushchev at home and the continued ascendancy of McCarthyism in the United States. Eisenhower's response came in April 1953 and was tantamount to a call for Soviet surrender—"free elections in a united Korea," "a free and united Germany," and "free choice" for the peoples of Eastern Europe.[72]

For the next two years, an intraparty struggle ensued until Khrushchev finally prevailed with the assistance of the Red Army.* This outcome was viewed with trepidation in the West owing to Khrushchev's association with a hard-line position, a fact that reinforced Dulles' own hard line in Washington. However, once Khrushchev consolidated his position, he denounced Stalinism at the Twentieth Party Congress in 1956, embraced "peaceful coexistence," and rejected the old Stalinist line of Molotov, whose support he had previously wooed. But Khrushchev had succeeded in winning power for himself by demanding sacrifice at home and vigilance abroad, and this lesson was not lost upon other members of the CPSU hierarchy. By 1964 he himself was vulnerable to the same attack, when he supported a cut in military expenditures and economic reforms at home that would be possible only by an easing of world tensions. He was also vulnerable because he had failed to bring Mao Zedong to heel, and had been forced to retreat ignominiously before American threats in the Cuban missile crisis of 1962, clearly one of the "harebrained schemes" of which he was accused at the time of his ouster. He was suddenly replaced by Leonid Brezhnev and Alexei Kosygin, old Stalinists who now had the military on their side. In the Soviet Union, as in the United States, advocacy of the Cold War proved a convenient route to political power.

The critical role of internal pressures in promoting a hostile spiral and encouraging misperception suggests that the Cold War is amenable to explanation by the mediated stimulus-response model used in the 1914 (Stanford) studies. Each side was prone to perceive and overestimate a growing threat from the other (disagreement and negative actions) but

---

* In 1957 when Malenkov and others were denounced as an "antiparty" group, Khrushchev was rendered decisive assistance by Marshal Georgi Zhukov. A year later Zhukov himself was humbled by Khrushchev.

failed to perceive the threatening nature of its own actions and reactions. Each perception of threat triggered negative actions, which confirmed the opponent's initial perception of threat, thereby triggering similar acts. Since each perceived the acts of its opponent as more hostile than its own initiatives, the sequence of action and reaction escalated and lacked reciprocity. In time, what Urie Bronfenbrenner described as a "mirror image" engulfed elites and general publics on both sides.[73] Each side came to believe that the adversary's goal was expansionism (at the expense of its values), while it sought merely consolidation and security, a fact that was known to the enemy. In a word, each side saw itself as unjustly "wronged."[74]

CRISIS AND RITUALIZATION

The hostile spiral of the Cold War was born in a redefinition of the relationship among the former allies and the emergence of two actors as *primi inter pares,* each with its own bloc of friends and clients. This "bipolarity" flowed from the ascendance of the communism issue, and the eclipse of other issues, during the 1947–50 period. The growing salience of this issue overwhelmed the wartime pattern of behavior among the victors and ultimately reordered their relationship to the defeated Axis. The failure to institutionalize a new set of interaction rules after San Francisco set in motion a sequence of ad hoc games necessary to define mutual expectations and rules.

Theoretically, such a period should be fraught with crises, as was 1947 to 1950. The Truman Doctrine itself was a response to crisis in Greece and Turkey, and was followed by a series of measures and countermeasures in Germany that culminated in the Berlin blockade and airlift. Then, in rapid succession, ensued the coup in Prague, Mao's victory in China, and the invasion of South Korea—events which dramatically enlarged the arena of confrontation. Furthermore, the period was punctuated by recurring probes to obtain favorable dispositions of stakes and to discover the opponent's perception of rules; for example, in Iran, Vienna, Trieste, and Yugoslavia.

In retrospect, these crises and probes served to dispose of a number of stakes in interim fashion, and to establish and institutionalize certain patterns of interaction, thereby fostering the growth of stable—though negative—mutual expectations. The rewards or punishments that resulted from each crisis and probe operated to inform each side of the wisdom of certain patterns of behavior and the folly of others, thereby permitting each to calculate how to minimize the gains of the adversary at limited cost. Through tacit bargaining, which revealed respective levels of salience, both sides identified "legitimate" techniques of competition and permissible stakes for which to compete. The use of proxies instead of direct military confrontation; the arms race; and resort to propaganda, political agitation, and overt and covert economic and political assistance— all became accepted practices.

What emerged was a new interaction game which bore many resemblances to the game which had been played just prior to 1914. Once again rigid alliances based on deterrence came to characterize global politics. Only now they were organized and elaborated to an unprecedented degree. Crises again came to substitute for hot war between the major blocs, though limited wars did occur among clients of the leading powers. Efforts were made by both the USSR and United States to mobilize lesser actors, and dissent was dealt with unhesitatingly as defectors were punished. Episodes of this nature include Soviet repression of the Hungarian revolution in 1956 and Czechoslovak disloyalty in 1968; and the American-assisted overthrow of "disloyal" regimes in Guatemala (1954) and Iran (1953), and invasion of the Dominican Republic in 1965. Alleged disloyalty within the Soviet Union and United States was dealt with in similar fashion as the Stalinist terror once more took root and the McCarthy years took their toll.

Among the key techniques of force used in the game, variants of coercive diplomacy were common, as reflected in crises over Berlin, the Formosa Straits, and Cuba. Concepts of "calculated control," "penetration," and "intervention" were elaborated and systematically analyzed to describe the numerous new and subtle techniques of force which the leading contenders and their proxies ritually came to use against each other.[75] Covert operations were undertaken which tended to follow informal rules and procedures that came to be well understood by adversaries.[76]

In time, the game came to feature certain important rules that both sides observed. Each side, while continuing to build up enormous stockpiles of conventional and nuclear armaments, avoided direct military confrontations with the other while making use of other techniques short of war, including espionage, propaganda, covert operations, bribery, and coercive diplomacy. Each side, while challenging stakes that were weakly held by the other or were ambiguous—such as Berlin, Laos, Korea, Yugoslavia, and the Middle East—was prepared to respect the other's strong control of key stakes. Such rules were articulated in and legitimized by a series of summit meetings between American and Soviet leaders from 1953 to 1966. It was Nikita Khrushchev who provided some of the clearest descriptions of the rules that were evolving. In February 1956, for instance, he declared before the Twentieth Congress of the Soviet Communist Party:

The Leninist principle of peaceful coexistence of states with different social systems has always been and remains the general line of our country's foreign policy. . . . When we say that the socialist system will win in the competition between the two systems . . . this by no means signifies that its victory will be achieved through armed interference by the socialist countries in the internal affairs of capitalist countries. Our certainty of the victory of communism is based on the fact that the socialist mode of production possesses decisive superiority over the capitalist mode of production. . . . As long as imperialism exists, the economic base giving rise to wars will also remain. . . . But war is not a fatalistic inevitability.[77]

In Europe, the original arena of the Cold War, the Iron Curtain came to represent a line of demarcation across which informal penetration, but not high level provocation, was legitimate. Thus, American propaganda played a role in provoking riots in East Berlin in 1953, unrest in Poland in 1956, and revolution in Hungary the same year, but the Eisenhower Administration recoiled in trepidation at the results of its policy and stood by passively while the Soviet Union reimposed order on its sphere. Stable expectations were also reinforced by Western passivity in the face of the erection of the Berlin Wall in 1961 and the Soviet invasion of Czechoslovakia in 1968, both of which reaffirmed the tacit lines of demarcation. In the same fashion, the Soviet Union largely limited itself to verbal abuse in the face of the rearmament of West Germany and its incorporation into NATO, and gave little encouragement to the communist parties of Western Europe. Only Berlin remained an anomaly because of its location within East Germany and its symbolic importance to both sides—a dangerous combination which produced a series of crises in the 1950s and early 1960s. In effect, both sides recognized the interim disposition of

European stakes produced by World War II as necessary, if not legitimate, so that stable expectations were produced except in those rare cases where internal changes seemed to place stakes unexpectedly up for grabs. Tito's defection from the Soviet bloc and the Cuban revolution in the late 1950s were examples of these.

One characteristic of ritualization in Europe was the severing of transactions and other routine ties—a process which began with the Soviet refusal to participate in the Marshall Plan, and the imposition on Eastern Europe of enforced economic dependence on Moscow. The latter was initially done by the conclusion of bilateral trade agreements between the Eastern European and Soviet governments, but was modified in the mid-1950s by the activation of the Council for Mutual Economic Assistance (COMECON) as a device to integrate the economies of the Soviet bloc. The Soviet Union refused to participate in the economic institutions created by the Western allies at Bretton Woods—the World Bank and the IMF—and declined to participate in a number of UN specialized agencies, such as FAO, which it viewed as instruments of American foreign policy. For its part, the United States government refused to extend recognition to the Ulbricht or Mao regimes and encouraged the creation of an isolated but integrated economic community in Western Europe. American economic dominance, moreover, enabled the enforcement of congressional legislation to prevent trade with the Soviet bloc either by American or Western European actors.

This severance and "freezing" of relations was both a means of punishing the adversary and of preventing the injection of unexpected but destabilizing factors into the relationship, in the same manner that individuals may refuse to interact with one another after a quarrel. R. J. Rummel in his analysis of American foreign policy found this pattern to be one of the two (the other being deterrence) typical of American behavior toward the Soviet bloc in the Cold War.[78]

Outside of Europe, particularly in the Far East, a similar, but less successful attempt was made to establish a demarcation line. First, the Korean War, and then the Indochinese wars, showed that here, at the periphery, the struggle would not be nonviolent, and that each side could find itself miscalculating the willingness of the other to resort to force. Certainly, prior to the war, the United States had not made a clear commitment to South Korea, nor did the United States understand China's determination to defend North Korea. In Vietnam, the U.S. government fundamentally misunderstood the nature of Ho Chi Minh's struggle. This spread of the Cold War outward from Europe, and the subsequent globalization of the East-West conflict, served in part as a substitute for direct collision in the high salience arena of Europe. Consequently, both sides tended to imbue the peripheral struggles with greater significance than they really had. Thus John Foster Dulles in 1956 declared that neutralism had "increasingly become an obsolete conception and, except under very exceptional circumstances, it is an immoral and shortsighted conception."[79] In a similar vein, Khrushchev's 1956 proclamation of peaceful coexistence made struggle in the Third World a decisive arena of East-West competition. Subsequent events reflected the extent to which an actor dimension was operating to spread the communism issue and to fuse stakes that previously had been unrelated by investing them with a symbolic value they had previously lacked.

The competition to "win" the Cold War in the Third World produced in time an acceptable, though subtle, interaction game based on limited force and bargains. The key rule was to avoid direct Soviet-American confrontation, and thus restrict the probability of nuclear war—a rule that seemed to be in imminent danger only during the missile crisis in Cuba in 1962. Otherwise, a broader range of permissible techniques were employed by both sides, in part because demarcation lines were less clear than in Europe, and in part because deterrence proved a much less effective strategy in the Third World than in Europe (as Dulles discovered shortly after enunciating the massive retaliation doctrine). Foreign aid—both military and economic—became a standard technique for wooing the uncommitted and reinforcing clients, but rather than producing gratitude, it tended to intensify suspicions of intervention and was no insurance against local anger, as the United States discovered in the cases of India and Iran, and the Soviet Union learned in the cases of Egypt and Somalia.

Foreign aid was part of a larger game, in which each side sought to penetrate local governments and societies in the Third World. Members of the CIA and KGB became the real soldiers of the Cold War. Among the more celebrated feats of the CIA, for instance, were the overthrow of the Mossadegh government in Iran in 1953, that of Arbenz in Guatemala in 1954, Lumumba in the Congo (Zaïre) in 1960, perhaps Sukarno in Indonesia in 1965, and Allende in Chile in 1973. The CIA also was active in the elections of a number of Western European countries, such as Italy and Greece. It was responsible for large-scale military operations in Central America, Cuba (the Bay of Pigs), China, Laos, Cambodia, and North Vietnam. In addition, the agency provided assistance and advice to various political factions in Latin America and Africa (as in the case of Angola).[80]

The reliance on coercive techniques emphasizes that the Cold War was neither a debate where two competitors seek to persuade objective observers of their cause, nor—owing to the incubus of nuclear weapons—a fight where the competitors seek to obliterate each other. Rather, it was a game in which each side sought to outwit and weaken the other. Though the game was on occasion quite violent, one of its cardinal rules was the avoidance of direct military confrontation, even in the event of occasional loss. Wars, if fought, required proxies and various tacit limitations to prevent the eruption of total war.

Weapons of mass destruction, rather than being used to win a war, became the basis of the strategy of deterrence that was to deprive the adversary of access to, or control of, disputed stakes. Until the achievement of strategic parity between the United States and the Soviet Union in the late 1960s, the United States succeeded in employing nuclear weapons as part of a strategy of coercive diplomacy. Thus, in May 1953, Eisenhower alluded to the possible use of nuclear weapons in the absence of agreement in Korea, and in 1958 he ordered the deployment of eight-inch howitzers capable of firing tactical atomic weapons to persuade China to cease shelling Quemoy and Matsu.[81] Similarly, in 1956, the Soviet Union threatened the use of "atomic rockets" if Britain and France refused to withdraw from the Suez Canal.

However, the credibility of nuclear deterrence declines in proportion to the declining salience of the stake. This fact became highly significant with the development of elaborate nuclear deterrent systems by both sides. While American threats to retaliate in event of a Soviet first-strike upon the homeland remained credible, willingness to employ such weapons in the event of conventional aggression elsewhere became less believable as the Soviet nuclear arsenal grew increasingly sophisticated after 1958. In the case of Berlin, for instance, President Kennedy's public commitment in 1963 ("Ich bin ein Berliner!") was reinforced by the presence of American troops who served as "hostages" (a "trip wire") to convince the USSR of American willingness to retaliate at the nuclear level.

The fear of nuclear war through error or escalation was mutual and was manifest in the recurring crises over Berlin and the Straits of Taiwan, where contenders carefully prevented hostile spirals from getting out of hand. Attempts to settle the crises seemed to correspond in each case to growing recognition of the danger of nuclear war. Each side pushed the other to the brink or just short of it in the manner of a game of "Chicken," where there is a winner only if one side compels the other to swerve by maneuvering itself into a position with little opportunity to back off—in other words, eliminating alternatives other than resort to nuclear weapons.[82] Successive American and Soviet leaders seemed content with this aspect of the game until the Cuban missile crisis brought home to them in October 1962 a frightening awareness of the realities of the nuclear age.

By the early 1960s, crisis diplomacy and brinksmanship had become central characteristics of the Cold War game in those cases where direct Soviet-American interaction proved unavoidable. Informal penetration characterized the efforts of the leading adversaries to control clients and influence friends and compete for additional clients in the Third World. Behind these procedures were crucial perceptions of the overall military balance and status hierarchy, as hosts of planners and strategists on each side searched for evidence of even minute shifts to discern whether the relative position of either had improved or slipped.*

One consequence of this preoccupation was an intensive arms race, with perceptions of changing capabilities a major determinant of caution or boldness in utilizing crisis diplomacy and penetration. The arms race and the state of technology remained critical factors throughout the Cold War for at least three reasons. The first is that a dramatic shift in the military balance might encourage rash behavior and even military victory. The second is that a change in the balance might produce a change in the status hierarchy, in which the rising power would expect an increase in rewards and influence commensurate with its new capabilities. In this sense, the Soviet achievement of parity was viewed as a threat by Ameri-

---

* The almost panic reaction in the United States after the discovery of an alleged "missile gap" in 1958 is instructive in this regard. In many ways it resembled the panic that overtook the British public in 1909 regarding the relative naval balance with Germany.

can leaders, who after 1945 had been alone at the top of the hierarchy. Finally, the mere fact of change is destabilizing, because it has unpredictable effects upon the behavior of the emerging power. That actor would either grow more cautious, owing to a greater sense of security and the internalization of status quo attitudes—or bolder, owing to a belief in its capacity to demand a larger share of the stakes. This would pose a dilemma for the relatively declining actor. If it were accommodative, it might convey an image of weakness that would tempt the adversary to make greater demands. Conversely, if it resisted or challenged the adversary too vigorously, it might anger and frustrate the latter and heighten the likelihood of violent confrontation.

What is remarkable about the Cold War is that despite marked shifts in the military balance, which produced changes in the behavior of the key rivals, central war was avoided. The advent of nuclear weapons, ironically, may have prevented the sort of deterioration in relations that led to two world wars, but a disaster almost occurred in 1962.

October 1962 was by many estimates a turning point in the Cold War. The affair was typical of Cold War crises in that it was primarily a symbolic test of strength and will rather than a conflict over a concrete stake. The crisis proved to be the most dangerous "Chicken" game of the Cold War. In the end, in Dean Rusk's words, both sides were "eyeball to eyeball" and the Soviet Union "blinked" first.[83] The proximity of the abyss had a cathartic effect on Kennedy and Khrushchev and revealed the existence of a common interest in avoiding nuclear disaster. Continued games of "Chicken" in the tradition of brinksmanship held the horrifying prospect of the one occasion when neither would yield.* On February 27, 1963, Khrushchev declared that he had saved the world from nuclear war by withdrawing Soviet missiles from Cuba, and his speech set the stage for an end to his probes of Kennedy and a renewed effort to impose the rules of peaceful coexistence. Only a few months later, in his speech at American University on June 10, Kennedy urged an end to the Cold War mentality and a search for peace as the only "rational end of rational men."[84] With a growing appreciation of the fact that the transcendent stake of communism was not worth nuclear war, conditions became

---

* Snyder and Diesing interpret the missile crisis as a game of "Called Bluff," in which one side (U.S.) was playing "Prisoner's Dilemma" and the other (USSR) was playing "Chicken." *Conflict Among Nations,* pp. 114–116, 506–507.

amenable to the stage of issue dormancy and the onset of détente between the United States and the Soviet Union.

DORMANCY AND DECISION MAKING: THE RISE OF DÉTENTE

Issue dormancy occurs when mutual frustration arises without any realistic alternatives available to key actors. Crisis diplomacy in conditions of nuclear parity, and the struggle for symbolic stakes in the Third World, produced a mutual failure to allocate the values being sought. The Cuban missile crisis brought home the fact that the arms race had produced little security for either of the major participants. Mutual deterrence did not produce an allocation of stakes and could not, because it was principally a strategy to prevent any further serious deprivation. It served to preserve many of the interim dispositions of stakes that had come about at the end of World War II, particularly in Europe, but in the long run it proved frustrating, because of the absence of authoritative decisions that would legitimize those dispositions and resolve the issues in final fashion. This was particularly so in the case of those stakes which had been part of the old division-of-the-spoils issue in Europe.

The existence of nuclear weapons accomplished what the balance-of-power game had failed to do: it made the principal actors aware that they would lose a war if one were fought, thereby eliminating the desire for war. As sophisticated realists knew, the balance of power never prevented war in the long run and probably was not intended to do so.[85] War can only be prevented by a preponderance of power, as Woodrow Wilson understood in his effort to introduce collective security, and only then if principal leaders perceive the preponderance and are sufficiently rational to assess the probable costs and benefits of waging war under such conditions. A rational actor will eschew war if assured of defeat, and a balance cannot provide such assurance. Indeed, the more equal the distribution of military capabilities, the more difficult it becomes to predict which actor will win. This is why balance-of-power advocates commonly call for a "balancer"—an actor able to enter a war at a critical moment and so tilt matters in favor of the defenders.

In the presence of an actor dimension, no actor can feel secure unless it holds a preponderance of military power over its enemies. But, what then prevents it from initiating a war of conquest? Nothing does, though such a war is probably unnecessary, owing to its relative satisfaction with the status quo and its ability to secure desired dispositions of stakes by means short of war. War only appears irrational either when relative satisfaction is widespread or when conditions conspire to produce clear assurances of mutual defeat. It was appreciation of this last fact after 1962 which made avoidance of central war not only appear more valuable than transcendent stakes but a transcendent stake itself.*

With nuclear weapons having eliminated the possibility of central war as a decision game to allocate transcendent stakes—except as a last re-sort—between the United States and the Soviet Union, the battleground shifted to symbolic stakes, particularly in the Third World. Techniques of penetration and limited war could produce interim stake dispositions and serve as substitutes for central war. But such dispositions in most cases had little impact upon the central Soviet-American contest despite the costs associated with them. The two key actors found themselves unable to translate their enormous efforts into palpable successes, and acute frus-tration grew as the Soviet Union was unable to raise the standard of living for its citizens—and the United States became bogged down in Vietnam, while its economy floundered as global inflation and the decline of the dollar eroded domestic satisfaction. Behind the expensive competition in the Third World lurked an unexamined belief that transcendent stakes could be ultimately won by isolating the adversary to the point of political and economic collapse.

Paradoxically, Soviet-American competition in the Third World en-hanced the alternative of nonalignment, because it encouraged actors to play one adversary off against the other. The cases of Egypt and India are instructive in this regard. In the mid-1950s, President Nasser of Egypt wooed Soviet support against British colonial interests. When Dulles reneged on a commitment to finance construction of the Aswan Dam, Nasser seized the Suez Canal and, with Soviet assistance, survived the Anglo-French invasion of 1956. The zenith of Soviet influence in Egypt was reached during the 1973 Yom Kippur war, which had been en-couraged by Soviet advisers. Successful prosecution of the war was made possible by the presence of Soviet personnel to operate Soviet military

* Such slogans as "Better Dead than Red" were rhetorical flights of fancy that aimed to deny this fact.

hardware, and the threat of Soviet intervention was instrumental in aborting the successful Israeli counteroffensive.* However, Soviet influence in Egypt became too great and Henry Kissinger's offers of rewards too tempting, so that President Anwar Sadat turned out the Russians and invited Kissinger to try to impose a settlement in the area. A major Soviet prize had turned to ashes.

In India, the United States, in the 1950s, provided large amounts of economic assistance to build a "democratic showcase" that could compete with the Chinese communist model of development. Although the Soviet Union also sought to woo India, its efforts were initially thwarted by the dissatisfaction of its own ally, China. Ironically, Soviet efforts only began to bear fruit as the Americans "tilted" too conspicuously toward its ally (and India's enemy) Pakistan—a tilt which began with Pakistan's entry into the Southeast Asia Treaty Organization (SEATO) and climaxed with the dispatch of U.S. naval units towards India in 1971 to prevent the partition of Pakistan. American behavior at this time was not only pro-Pakistani but pro-Chinese as well, since the Sino-Soviet split had become complete and China was supporting Pakistan. With the signature of a Soviet-Indian treaty of friendship by India's Prime Minister Indira Gandhi, it appeared that an American prize had also turned to ashes (although another shift became manifest a few years later with the ouster of Mrs. Gandhi and the electoral victory of the Janata party in India).

The limited wars in Asia demonstrated even more conclusively how elusive was influence in the Third World. The Korean War ended in the division of the peninsula, a situation which had prevailed at the outset. Although the United States lost the war in Vietnam, the result had little effect on Cold War competition. The Chinese "challenge" had become irrelevant, and the expectations of the domino theory proved to be false as noncommunist Southeast Asia thrived and communist Cambodia and Vietnam became quickly embroiled in a dispute with all the aspects of a proxy war between the USSR and China. Chinese merchants in Vietnam found a protector and refuge in China. American oil corporations secured rights to Vietnamese offshore oil, and Vietnam expressed its willingness to normalize relations with the United States. What had the United States

---

* This threat produced a major Soviet-American crisis as President Nixon ordered American forces to an alert status.

gained or lost after its vast expenditure of blood and treasure? Vietnam had been a symbol and—like other symbolic stakes—its disposition did not allocate the values that were at issue in the Cold War. Nor did the arena provide an escape from the frustration of nuclear parity.

In the face of mutual failure and frustration, the United States and the USSR gradually began to work out the elements of a *modus vivendi*. Through trial and error, each began to revise its expectations about the other and—through probes and counter-probes, and punishment and reward—a tacit set of rules began to evolve, concerning what behavior is permitted and what is not; what can be achieved and at what cost; and what is beyond the reach of either.* The gradual revision of cognitive maps, combined with the fear and caution produced by the missile crisis, prepared both sides to formalize what was being institutionalized by ad hoc games. Although the process was slowed by the sudden disappearance of both Kennedy and Khrushchev from the scene (and with them their efforts to manipulate dissonance), followed by the escalation of the Vietnam War, recognition of a common interest in avoiding nuclear war was sufficiently widespread among elites on both sides to prevent the process from coming to a full halt.

Unlike previous efforts to manipulate cognitive dissonance, the Kennedy-Khrushchev dialogue set in motion a train of events that slowly produced changes in behavior. Previously, dissonance, even when encouraged by one side, was overcome by leaders of the other, who interpreted positive acts as either trickery or signs of weakness.† The strength of domestic critics in both countries further complicated Soviet-American relations. A negative American response merely supported the views of those in the Kremlin who desired more aggressive initiatives, and evidence of "neo-Stalinism" served as fodder for American "cold warriors." In this fashion, several opportunities to alter relations were lost including Malenkov's overtures in 1953, Eisenhower's "open skies"

---

* For an interesting analysis of this point with reference to containment, see Carl Oglesby, "Vietnamese Crucible," in Carl Oglesby and Richard Shaull, *Containment and Change* (London: Collier-Macmillan, 1967), pp. 18–31.

† Ole Holsti has demonstrated that John Foster Dulles consistently viewed conciliatory gestures by the USSR as tricks to conceal weakness, while viewing Soviet truculence as a sign of strength. The correlation was .94 for the period of a year—David J. Finlay, Ole R. Holsti, and Richard R. Fagen, *Enemies in Politics* (Chicago: Rand McNally, 1967), p. 63, table II-5.

disarmament proposal, Khrushchev's speech at the Twentieth Party Congress, and the Eisenhower-Khrushchev summit at Camp David.

Several reasons explain why the process was not similarly aborted in the 1960s, including the *mutuality* of leaders' perceptions, their command of prospective domestic critics—particularly important in the case of the former cold warrior, Richard Nixon—and the development and recognition of nuclear parity. However, the most important factor was the overwhelming sense that the existing interaction games were failing to allocate important values, while risking the very survival of civilization. Consequently, leaders on both sides, starting with Kennedy and Khrushchev, permitted a number of salient symbolic stakes—notably Laos (for a brief time), Cuba, Berlin, and Quemoy-Matsu—to become dormant, and actively sought to identify stakes upon which they could find agreement. Concurrent structural changes reinforced these efforts. New issues began to emerge which seemed to be only tangentially associated with the Cold War, and these animated a range of actors which were determined to set their own rules. The defection of major actors from the two main blocs—de Gaulle's France and Mao's China—made it difficult for the United States and the Soviet Union to enforce their interpretation of the overarching game. Additionally, the growing dispersion of significant global resources began to have an impact on the status hierarchy, thereby reducing the polar attraction of Washington and Moscow for other actors and sapping the bases of patron–client relationships. New centers of influence emerged, determined by different types of resources: Japan's economic efficiency and modernized productive capacity assured it of leverage in global economic and trade issues; increasing dependence on a narrow range of energy sources provided OPEC with unprecedented influence in a range of issues; a vast population, an attractive ideology, and a charismatic leader provided the People's Republic of China with great influence; and technological sophistication and organizational capacity gave multinational corporations and certain specialized international organizations strategic positions in selected issues.

Instead of a single global issue called the "Cold War," a host of new issues with functional or regional appellations began to appear, both as a result of the decomposition of the Cold War itself and the emergence of new stakes from the environment, and from newly energized actors. And, on some of these issues, like that of large-scale multilateral economic aid to the Third World, the Soviet and American governments began to find themselves in agreement. The combination of persistent mutual failure and frustration, decreasing global control, and random crosscutting agreement provided incentives to reach other agreements to reverse the hostile spiral. The most important were the adoption of measures to avoid nuclear war—the "hot line;" banning nuclear weapons in Antarctica, the seabed and outer space; and the Nuclear Nonproliferation Treaty. By the end of the Nixon Administration, the list of issues in which the two sides had discovered common interests included space exploration; environmental protection; and limitations on climate modification as a weapon, and on the production or use of chemical and bacteriological weapons.[86]

The most salient issues, however, were control of the arms race to assure strategic stability, the maintenance of nuclear parity at bearable cost, and the old division-of-the-spoils issues in Europe. What came to be called "détente" was the achievement of substantial progress on these issues by Nixon and Brezhnev. Having both been hard-liners in foreign policy, they were more able than their predecessors to acccommodate one another without sacrificing domestic support. Détente coincided with a reduction in the potency of the actor dimension and movement toward a stake dimension, as a result of which both actors began to view the key issues as separately negotiable. Encapsulation heightened the possibility of their resolution or of at least their substantial interim disposition. These issues remained linked, but the linkages arose out of common values like security and survival. The movement toward encapsulation and the weakening of the negative actor dimension were explicitly recognized by Secretary of State Kissinger in testimony before the U.S. Senate Committee on Foreign Relations on September 19, 1974:

We did not invent the interrelationship between issues expressed in the so-called linkage concept; it was a reality because of the range of problems and areas in which the interests of the United States and the Soviet Union impinge on each other. We have looked for progress in a series of agreements settling specific political issues, and we have sought to relate these to a new standard of international conduct appropriate to the dangers of the nuclear age.[87]

The Strategic Arms Limitation Treaty (SALT) agreements, in particular, were important efforts to articulate an agreed-upon set of rules for détente, including the partial substitution of principle for the implicit force involved in the arms race.

But what were these new rules? "Détente," writes Simon Serfaty, "did not mean global reconciliation with the Soviet Union. . . . Instead, détente implied the selective continuation of containment by economic and political inducement and at the price of accommodation through concessions that were more or less balanced."[88] As revealed in key documents like that of "Basic Principles of Relations between the United States of America and the Union of Soviet Socialist Republics" of May 19, 1972 and the "Agreement between the United States of America and the Union of Soviet Socialist Republics on the Prevention of Nuclear War" of June 22, 1973,[89] détente would feature a smaller role for force and a considerably greater role for bargains and principle than the Cold War. Principle, in particular, became a key focus as indicated by Leonid Brezhnev, General Secretary of the CPSU, when, in his report to the Twenty-Fifth Congress of the CPSU on February 24, 1976, he described the significance of the key documents mentioned above as having "laid a solid political and juridical foundation for greater mutually beneficial cooperation between the USSR and U.S. in line with the principles of peaceful coexistence."[90] According to Kissinger, the norms which were articulated include: "(1) the necessity of avoiding confrontation; (2) the imperative of mutual restraint; (3) the rejection of attempts to exploit tensions to gain unilateral advantages; (4) the renunciation of claims of special influence in the world; and (5) the willingness, on this new basis, to coexist peacefully and build a firm long-term relationship."[91] Accitionally, if a risk of nuclear war were to arise, the two governments were obligated to consult with one another immediately.

Efforts to end the arms race and institutionalize a new set of rules were not easy tasks, because they aroused the opposition of those who wished to continue the Cold War, even if it could not be won, as well as those with vested bureaucratic and/or economic interests in the continuation of the arms race. Still, SALT was important because it represented a willingness of elites on both sides to forgo efforts toward a technological breakthrough to achieve a first-strike capability. In addition, SALT reflected mutual recognition that agreements reached must not be challenged, because, under conditions of nuclear parity, no further allocations are possible without future agreement. For this reason, it was natural that negotiations on SALT be accompanied by negotiations to resolve the division-of-the-spoils issue.

Finding precedent in the West German *Ostpolitik* and the French "opening to the East," a series of Soviet-American conferences were held, including those on Mutual and Balanced Force Reductions (MBFR) and European Security and Cooperation (Helsinki). Although the specific rules which leaders had in mind remained obscure (and were probably unclear to them), they almost certainly involved avoidance of superpower military confrontation; maintenance of prevailing superpower roles in different regions, and of existing intraregional balances of power; prevention of the spread of local or regional crises; and efforts to promote a suitable foreign-policy consensus at home.[92] Encapsulation permitted a number of specific agreements to be reached, including one on Berlin in 1971, one on the frontiers of Central Europe (Helsinki) in 1975, and several in the areas of cultural exchange and scientific cooperation. Issue positions increasingly reflected perceptions of interdependence rather than negative affect, as rules evolved by fits and starts.

The Helsinki agreement was effectively a peace treaty ending World War II. This had been a major goal of the USSR during the entire period and became one of even greater urgency with the deepening of Sino-Soviet hostility. Helsinki was also an agreement to allocate a number of Cold War stakes in final fashion. First, the territorial changes of 1945 were recognized as legitimate. Second, the development of communist Eastern Europe was also recognized as more or less legitimate. Third, the question of human rights was accorded at least minimal treatment. Overall, the Helsinki accord entailed mutual recognition of the division of Europe, accompanied by a tacit understanding that neither side would intervene to overturn the order of things on the other side. This entailed the transformation of a de facto into a de jure situation. The West, after all, had time and again remained passive in the face of Soviet efforts to prop up friendly regimes in its sphere, having even accepted in tacit fashion the "Brezhnev Doctrine" of 1968, a unilateral declaration of the Soviet Union's right to intervene to preserve communism in the Eastern bloc. Similarly, ties between the Soviet Union and the communist parties of Western Europe had loosened to the point where the term "Eurocommunism" had become fashionable to describe the independent, often non-Marxist, behavior of several of them, including those of Italy, Spain, and Portugal. By the early 1970s, a point was reached where the Italian Communist Party could quietly cooperate with the dominant Christian Democrats in that country to try to overcome their country's economic problems, including labor union indiscipline; and where the French Communist Party could enter into a formal electoral alliance with the French Socialist Party in an unsuccessful effort to overcome the dominant coalition of Gaullists and Independent Republicans.

The détente game has not proceeded smoothly or easily since its inception, particularly since the Soviet invasion of Afghanistan and the failure to ratify SALT II quickly. The U.S. and Soviet governments have sought to "test" the new rules to see just how far they might be stretched— Soviet interference in Angola and the Horn of Africa, and the Carter Administration's support of Soviet dissidents under the rubric of human rights, and unilateral defense of the Persian Gulf represent such probes. The norms which underlie the new relationship have been subject to differing interpretations that are conducive to acute misunderstanding, as was the case during the 1973 Middle East crisis, the 1977 Carter-Vance SALT proposals, and the Helsinki review conference. Soviet leaders continue to worry about Western overtures to recalcitrant members of the bloc, particularly Rumania, while the United States remains concerned about the activities of Cuba, particularly in Africa and Central America. Finally, the domestic opponents of détente remain formidable, a fact reflected in the Jackson-Vanik amendment, which linked the granting of "most-favored-nation" trading status to the Soviet Union to the right of Soviet Jews to emigrate; and the ensuing Stevenson amendment, which limited the authority of the Export-Import Bank to grant credits to the Soviet Union to finance large-scale Soviet-American trade.[93] Thus, détente is a process that requires consistent manipulation. Both Brezhnev and Nixon were concerned lest successors failed to observe the rules they had worked out or lest the process be wrecked on the shoals of bureaucratic inertia or domestic reaction. For this reason they sponsored dramatic "happenings" like the Soyuz-Apollo mission to symbolize cooperation.

For the Soviet Union, SALT and Helsinki represented the settling of the Cold War in Europe and a means of coping with the threat of China in the East. The Cold War issue was even more complex for American leaders because of China. For the Cold War to end, China, too, had to be dealt with, and this could not be accomplished through the Soviet Union, owing to the Sino-Soviet rift. Overtures to China, moreover, represented a means of encouraging Soviet willingness to bargain in the West. However, the Nixon Administration faced two problems in dealing with China. First, unlike prior relations with the USSR, prior U.S.-Chinese interaction had not established a tacit modus vivendi that could be institutionalized and legitimized. Indeed, the United States had not even accorded the Maoist regime formal recognition, had fought one war with it, had intervened in a second to counter a perceived threat from China, and had communicated with it directly only at occasional meetings held in Warsaw. Second, the process of détente with the Soviet Union meant that China had to be treated delicately. Though the Sino-Soviet split encouraged an American opening to China (by putting to rest any notion that the communist bloc was monolithic) and made China a source of potential leverage with the USSR, American overtures were bound to excite Soviet anxieties, particularly after the outbreak of open hostilities along the Sino-Soviet frontier in 1969.

The change in Sino-American relations was encouraged in the late 1960s and the early 1970s by the existence of mutual failure and frustration. It was clear to China's leaders that in the face of American hostility and the rift with Moscow, little could be accomplished toward regaining Taiwan, or toward achieving rapid economic and technological development at home. Moreover, the Soviet Union was viewed as a more dangerous—and proximate—rival than the United States had been, even during the height of the earlier Taiwan crises. For the United States, Vietnam was the focus of failure and frustration. The Chinese took the initial public step by inviting an American ping-pong team to participate in a Chinese tournament. Despite a warm American response to "ping-pong diplomacy," the issue of Taiwan remained intractable, because normalization of Sino-American relations required the United States government to undercut its long-time Taiwanese ally, and in so doing, risk considerable domestic opposition. Since the Chinese leadership had tied normalization to the disposition of Taiwan, the only way around the problem was to render the issue dormant for the time being. This was the route followed as first Henry Kissinger secretly visited Peking from Pakistan, and then Nixon dramatically called upon Mao Zedong and Zhou Enlai during which time neither side raised the Taiwan issue publicly except in oblique fashion. The Kissinger-Nixon visits and the later journey of President Gerald Ford effectively constituted de facto recognition of the communist regime, which was accompanied by the setting up of an

American "mission" in China and an understanding to proceed slowly toward full normalization.

Owing to the absence of formal negotiations on salient issues, and the relatively limited sphere of high-level contacts, the ensuing phase in Sino-American relations was one of transition, rapprochement rather than détente. The principal change was in affect, accompanied by agreement that the rules of the game *ought* to be changed. In this sense, the phase resembled that of the Kennedy-Khrushchev dialogue after Cuba rather than the SALT-Helsinki period. As the old leadership in China passed from the scene with the deaths of Mao and Zhou, however, leaders on both sides determined to pursue the opportunity more vigorously lest it be lost. In China, the defeat of the so-called "gang of four," and the triumph of a pragmatic leadership determined to modernize China by the import of technology, created an environment even more conducive to normalization. In December 1978, President Carter announced his government's decision to recognize the People's Republic of China on January 1, 1979 and to sever formal relations with Taiwan. Although the logjam had been broken, the public announcements merely reaffirmed the earlier decision to make the Taiwan issue dormant, rather than to seek to resolve it definitively. American commercial and cultural transactions with Taiwan would continue (in accordance with a model developed earlier by Western Europe and Japan) though the U.S.-Taiwan mutual security treaty would be abrogated, and China would seek to open a dialogue with Taiwan's leaders.

The era of détente-rapprochement involved a set of changed relationships, based on the legitimization of earlier interim dispositions and the agreement to leave dormant, or paper over, other issues. In the case of China, it left open the questions of Taiwan and American support of China in the event of a further deterioration of Sino-Soviet relations (though Vice-President Walter Mondale declared while in Peking in August 1979 that Chinese independence was a significant American interest). With the Soviet Union, the domain of the new game was not fully elaborated. Did it apply to the Third World or just Europe? Was the human rights clause of Helsinki merely a face-saving device, or did it have broader applicability? Such unanswered questions can be worked out only in the manner that the earlier *modus vivendi* was reached, through trial and error—but this time there is a set of formalized rules to which each side can appeal.

From the preceding analysis, it is clear that a hostile interaction pattern is difficult to shift, because it encourages misperception and sensitivity, which lead rivals to reject conciliatory overtures and not to respond positively to opportunities provided by periods of cognitive dissonance. The latter is partly a product of resistance by domestic actors within each rival, who cannot overcome old prejudices and who find the persistence of external tension of value to them in maintaining group cohesion and in obtaining a satisfactory share of salient stakes, like contracts, budgetary allocations, and political recognition and influence. The failure of actors to seize opportunities in turn legitimizes the animosity of the opposing side.

Hostile interaction is also difficult to reverse because misperception is only *partial* but is constantly being reinforced. Soviet and American perceptions that the adversary would overthrow its socioeconomic system if the opportunity arose are quite *valid* and are *not* the consequences of misperception. What generally constitutes misperception is the belief that the adversary is actively and constantly working toward this end. Though a logical conclusion, it overestimates the consistency of the opponent in the effort to be consistent oneself. This is especially difficult to discern, because there do indeed exist individuals and groups within both actors that do, or would, behave according to this logic, and the possibility that they might find their way to power (as did Hitler in Germany) provides an incentive to assume the worst. The existence of competing ideologies forms the basis for placing the most extreme interpretations upon random disagreements and negative actions. These interpretations reinforce hostility, which, in turn, eliminates randomness from the pattern of disagreement and hostile interaction. Misperception and false precedent are elements—but only elements—in the cycle.

THE MODEL: INSIGHTS AND EVIDENCE

The hostile Cold War cycle began with the decline of the unifying wartime issue of fascism and the dramatic changes in the status of key actors. In the absence of a long-term prior pattern of agreement, changes in status made the U.S. and Soviet governments sensitive to possible threats each might pose to the other. The shape of the issue agenda proved critical for the onset of the hostile cycle, because it was largely responsible for conditioning the similarity variable and, therefore, influencing whether trust or mistrust would characterize the relationship. Intimate Anglo-American relations and the death of F.D.R. prevented the colonialism issue from becoming salient, thereby leaving only two key issues—division-of-the-spoils and communism—dividing the United States and the Soviet Union.

The division-of-the-spoils issue, initially linking concrete stakes by a stake dimension, gradually acquired symbolic stakes linked by an actor dimension. This occurred in part because of the presence of the communist issue, even though it did not become the most salient of the three main issues until 1947. It functioned to promote mutual suspicion and mistrust. It had been potent, though dormant, even during the war, during which time it repeatedly heightened suspicion among allies. The disappearance of F.D.R. and the ending of the wartime threat renewed its potency after 1945, thereby encouraging perceptions of dissimilarity. Resulting mistrust was aggravated by the anticommunist predispositions of individuals like Truman, Byrnes, and Churchill.

The inheritance of mistrust was activated by the widespread disagreement that surrounded the division-of-the-spoils issue. Some disagreement was almost inevitable, owing to the sudden availability of a multitude of important stakes and allied failure to look ahead toward their disposition while the war was being fought. It was intensified because the dramatic changes in status led the second-ranking of the two principals to seek a protective buffer along its western frontier, while the first-ranking actor sought to impose a new world order and a new set of rules. It was easy for the former to view the latter as seeking to prevent it from asserting its rightful position of eminence, and for the latter to see the former as endeavoring to catch up through expansion.

In itself, disagreement does not necessarily lead to negative actions, and the two need not deteriorate into a consistently hostile pattern of interaction. That they did after 1945 requires analysis of what actually took place. After 1945, the change in status (which created the possibility of competition), the actualization of that competition in the presence of numerous new and major stakes, and the mistrust aroused by perceptions of dissimilarity predisposed both sides to use a negative affect calculus in determining issue positions. This did not occur overnight. With growing hostility, each saw the other as pressing too hard and breaking wartime agreements. Thus, both became prone to overreact in an interaction that had begun as a vigorous bargaining process on the basis of cost-benefit calculi.

Stalin's public declaration of "two camps" and Truman's pronouncement of the Truman Doctrine amounted to the joint proclamation of a negative actor dimension and the virtual abandonment of any mechanism other than force to dispose of the division-of-the-spoils issue. The ensuing transformation of concrete stakes into symbolic ones, as in the case of Berlin, encouraged the merger of the division-of-the-spoils and communism issues. Issue proposals assumed the character of efforts to embarrass the adversary and highlight disagreement, rather than sincere efforts to bargain and reach accommodation. This tendency was most evident in the United Nations, particularly when admissions or disarmament questions arose. Indeed, most of these proposals were framed to ensure nonacceptance by the adversary by offering an asymmetrical distribution of costs and benefits. The predictable and inflammatory sequence of proposals and rejections provided the fuel for moralistic justifications of the behavior of each that were necessary to preserve cognitive consistency in the face of rising costs, accompanied by few tangible benefits. The clear implication that the adversary was immoral in accompanying discourse ("atheists," "running dogs," and the like) provided each with the moral fervor that promoted the ascendancy of ideological competition in the communist issue and the perception of a transcendent stake.

If the process was initiated largely by structural factors, it was intensified by the manipulation of dissonance on the part of "true believers" on both sides and leaders who sought to justify their policies, and thereby retain political popularity, while convincing their publics of the need for greater sacrifice.* With the outbreak of the Korean War, it became increasingly necessary to oversell the Cold War at home in order to justify sacrifices and prevent domestic alienation. Consequently, within both actors advocacy of greater vigilance and effort became *de rigeur* for poli-

---

*This is not an uncommon characteristic of leaders during periods of intense hostility. It characterized the behavior of leaders of almost all belligerents during World War I, and was manifest in the changing nature of war aims.

ticians seeking power. Within both societies, this situation was power-
fully abetted by bureaucratic and economic interests, whose roles had
become closely associated with pursuit of the Cold War.* These interests
found the arms race in particular a profitable undertaking but one which
made sense only in conditions of tension. The domestic political climate
within both actors reduced the capacity of officials to suggest or implement innovative ideas and made it difficult for them to accept the authen-
ticity of conciliatory gestures by the adversary.

Under such conditions, major dispositions of stakes were possible only
through war, and only the destruction of the adversary opened the prospect for a final resolution of the critical issue. Since the presence of
nuclear weapons denied this possibility, both sides sought to outwit one
another in crisis diplomacy, and to isolate one another through penetration of the Third World. The consequences of immense energy and expenditure were mutual frustration and the prospect of nuclear war in the
course of the Cuban missile crisis. This last event produced a *simultaneous* comprehension of the risks that were being run in the name of
ideological competition and recognition that avoidance of nuclear war
was itself a transcendent issue.

Each stood away from the abyss, aware of the compulsive need for tolerance and compromise, but had to settle, for the time being, for letting
explosive issues lie dormant. Gradually and erratically, leaders sought to
generate new issues upon which they could agree, and so light a spark of
goodwill in the hostile darkness. It was agreement for its own sake that
was sought, even though the stakes at issue were relatively minor and
even artificial. Behind the elaborate hosting of conferences and summit
meetings lay the quest for a pattern of agreement that might produce
habits of agreement and a minimum of trust. Agreement itself might generate positive acts to lay the foundation for friendly attitudes. In this manner, the hostile cycle was broken.

Ultimately, a reverse cycle, though very tentative and delicate, became
apparent. Agreements were produced concerning key aspects of the arms
race, starting with the partial test ban and moving to SALT. Mutual satisfaction with nuclear parity represented the allocation of a major stake to

---

*In the United States, for instance, the massive reorganization of the foreign-policy bu-
reaucracies after 1947, including the founding of the CIA and the centralization and proliferation of military agencies, was justified to assure a more efficient waging of the conflict.

replace the constantly changing dispositions arrived at through competitive research and development. Détente then assumed a more formal character as a limited but highly significant set of interaction rules were agreed to, even while the communism issue remained. In the presence of these rules, the old division-of-the-spoils issue was largely resolved as European stakes were uncoupled from stakes in Asia (e.g., Vietnam) and the rest of the Third World.

A CONCLUDING NOTE ON THE "DEBATE" OVER THE ORIGINS OF THE COLD WAR

Recent historical scholarship on the Cold War has entailed a debate between those who subscribe to a standard American interpretation and revisionists of that interpretation. The central question in this debate is who is to "blame" for starting the Cold War. While this is an important question and the analysis presented here is relevant to it, it is, on the whole, impossible to answer objectively, given limited access to classified documents in the United States and the Soviet Union. The analysis to this point has largely addressed other questions, which in the long run are not only more important but more relevant as well; that is, why did the Cold War occur in the first place and why did détente, rather than hot war, follow it? A model that helps answer such questions, however, cannot but have implications for the debate over blame.

A singular attempt to assess the various positions in the debate is the work of William Gamson and André Modigliani, who provide the only systematic and falsifiable test of the several positions.[94] They tested conflicting theories of the Cold War by classifying them according to what each side thought to be its goal (destruction of the enemy, expansion of self, or consolidation), whether the other side believed that that was its goal, and what the other side's goal was thought to be. Thus, the standard American interpretation views the American goal as one of consolidation, a goal of which Soviet leaders were fully aware, and sees the Soviet goal as one of expansion. This combination can be expressed in notational form as CCE, where the first letter represents the United States' view of its own goal, the second letter the United States' view of how the USSR perceived the United States' goal, and the third letter as the United States' view of the goal pursued by the USSR. The Soviet belief system can be designated in similar fashion. According to the standard American interpretation, the Soviet goal was expansion; the USSR was aware that American leaders knew this; and Soviet leaders knew that the American goal was one of consolidation. This can be abbreviated as EEC. By combining the belief systems of both sides in the dyad, an overall interpretation of the Cold War emerges. Thus, standard American interpretations see the United States as CCE and the Soviet Union as EEC. Gamson and Modigliani sought to evaluate empirically the relative accuracy of competing interpretations.

Gamson and Modigliani argue that if an actor manifests a belief system, it will behave in predictable fashion. For example, if the United States were CCE and the Soviet Union EEC, and if the Soviet Union behaved uncooperatively, then the United States would react with conflict (assuming rationality and a dyadic relationship that is mutually contingent and hostile). The reason for this is that a combative response from an actor seeking consolidation to the truculent behavior of an expansionist actor will be understood by the latter as resistance and be taken as a sign of strength. Conversely, compliance or deference would be taken as a sign of weakness and encourage further expansionism. Differing interpretations of the Cold War were tested by comparing their predictions for each model with actual patterns of interaction.*

The tests performed by Gamson and Modigliani produced some interesting and provocative results. They found that the CCE model accurately predicted Soviet behavior in 73 percent of the cases, (n = 45) while the ECE model was a successful predictor in 69 percent of the cases.† According to the data, the Soviet Union pursued either the goal of consolidation (CCE) or expansion (ECE), believed the United States perceived it as consolidationist, and viewed the United States as expansionist. The two models disagree only about what goal the Soviet Union actually pursued, and not about how Soviet leaders thought they were perceived by American leaders, or how they interpreted the American goal. The standard American interpretation (EEC) was a poor predictor, as six alternative models performed better—a finding which provoked the authors to

---

* See William Gamson and André Modigliani, *Untangling the Cold War* (Boston: Little, Brown, 1971), Appendix C, for the various predictions of each model.

† The probability of either result being random is .001 and .005 respectively. All other models did less well. See *ibid.*, Tables 5.2 and 5.3, pp. 76–77.

quip that the United States could have predicted Soviet actions just as well by flipping a coin and could, therefore, have saved vast amounts of money by replacing its entire foreign-policy establishment with a shiny new quarter!*

Gamson and Modigliani then conducted several tests to determine which of the two best models, CCE or ECE, is superior. Though none of these was definitive, one test suggested to them the superiority of CCE.†
They found that the two models differed only in their capacity to predict accommodative behavior—CCE 88 percent and ECE 62 percent. But the percentage difference is misleading, since only eight cases were involved, so that CCE merely predicted two more than ECE. Although such a minor difference does not provide decisive evidence one way or the other, Gamson and Modigliani indicated their overall preference for CCE. A more cautious interpretation would be to conclude that the results were mixed and then try to account for this unexpected finding.

The findings for Western patterns of behavior were similar. The CCE model proved most accurate, predicting 82 percent (n = 57) of the cases, with the probability of this being random less than .001. But, the ECE model also did well, predicting 78 percent of the cases (n = 55, probability less than .001). The CCE model proved to be somewhat better than the ECE model in predicting patterns of interaction rather than just single events, but this involved a difference of only three predictions.‡ Further efforts to test the differences between the two models were somewhat unfruitful, as both predicted accommodative behavior less well than they had in the case of Soviet behavior.§

Gamson and Modigliani concluded that Western behavior was in fact consolidationist and that, in view of this conclusion, the "mirror image" hypothesis is confirmed by their findings.[95] There was a strong tendency to accept this conclusion, because the mixed results, on the whole, fit that hypothesis better than any other. But, the tendency should be resisted,

---

Ibid., p. 77. The EEC model was able to predict only 36 percent of 58 cases, and this had a .97 probability of being random.

† Since the difference between the two models is only the first variable, the number of cases available in the data was limited.

‡*Ibid.*, Tables 5.8 and 5.9, p. 86.

§ The CCE model predicted successfully in 69 percent of the cases (n = 13), and the ECE model was accurate 45 percent of the time (n = 11), an absolute difference of only four cases.

because it leaves unexplained the striking performance of the ECE model in predicting both Soviet and Western behavior. In seeking to explain the anomalous ECE findings, it becomes clear that the mirror image hypothesis is incomplete.

To assess the utility of the two models for developing a theory of the Cold War that is dyadic, it is necessary to examine the possible combinations that arise by combining them, as depicted in table 10.1. Cell *a* represents the mirror image hypothesis as it is typically portrayed. Cells *b* and *c* appear to be somewhat implausible, because they require that one side be consistently able to deceive the other. Finally, the combination

Table 10.1 Combining the CCE and ECE Models of William Gamson and André Modigliani Dyadically

		East	
		CCE	ECE
West	CCE	*a*	*b*
	ECE	*c*	*d*

represented by cell *d* entails mutual self-delusion, obviously a possibility. Any effort to choose one of the four possibilities requires more than the data can support. Indeed, the data suggest that East and West were both consolidationist *and* expansionist. In other words, both sides behaved on occasion in one fashion, and on others, in the other fashion. At any point in time, Cold War behavior might have fallen into any of the cells. There is no need to discard the findings concerning the ECE model as anomalous.*

This interpretation enriches the mirror image hypothesis in a manner compatible with psychological insight, and in a fashion that accounts more completely for historical facts. The fact that both principal actors actually probed and prodded one another at different times suggests that they were entertaining goals of consolidation and expansion simultaneously, between which they shifted by issue and in time. Truman and

* In chapter 6, Gamson and Modigliani ask if the models change during different periods and conclude that they do not. The hypothesis being offered here is not that one or another model is more relevant for different periods, but that both models simultaneously reflect behavior and perceptions accurately.

Churchill made demands upon Stalin concerning Eastern Europe that would have entailed an enlargement of their sphere of influence and were beyond their strength to impose. A number of American actions in Iran, Greece, Germany, and Yugoslavia can hardly be described as consolidationist. MacArthur's thrust north of the 38th parallel in Korea was a clearer case of expansion, and the covert behavior of the CIA in the Third World can be treated in similar fashion. Nor is there any question that Soviet interference in Hungary and Czechoslovakia prior to 1950 was expansionist. So, too, were Khrushchev's probes of Kennedy in Berlin and Cuba, as were many of the activities of the KGB in the Third World.

Each side probed and expanded its influence when not confronted by the other's resistance. It was the threat of war—and, increasingly, the threat of nuclear holocaust—that precluded any consistent pattern of expansion and promoted consolidationist behavior. Whatever political leaders like Khrushchev or Dulles might have hoped in their hearts to accomplish was tempered by realities which they knew in their heads. In the face of these realities, rhetoric was often a substitute for action, often covering a retreat in crises. Rhetoric also proved a means by which leaders could protect themselves from domestic criticism, even while it had the unfortunate effect of convincing adversaries that expansionism was indeed the goal. Thus, the hawks on both sides encouraged a rhetoric of expansion.

The hawks, moreover, tended to have the ear of specialized bureaucracies within each actor, particularly the military establishment, defense industries, and elements of the Congress in the United States. Such institutions not only believed in the threat posed by the other side, thereby attracting individuals with this mental set, but also had a tangible interest in the continuation of tension. This predisposed them psychologically to accept evidence that conformed to their belief system and reject evidence that was in conflict with it. In addition, these bureaucracies, as Graham Allison and Morton Halperin show, tended to behave in ways that reflected their mind set, whatever the aims of central decision makers.[96] No conspiracy theory is necessary to explain how bureaucrats retain considerable leeway in implementing policy decisions in a manner compatible with their psychological predispositions and interests.

In the end, the hypothesis that both sides tended to move back and forth among goals fits the facts well and conforms to psychological theories that might explain the mirror image hypothesis. It suggests, for instance, that misperception was partial, not complete. It conforms also to the psychological proposition that intermittent rewards reinforce behavior more strongly than consistent rewards, a hypothesis that can be applied to belief systems as well. The tendency to focus attention on evidence that conforms to one's mind set means that the periodic expansionist sorties of each side were clearly recognized by the other, whereas efforts toward consolidation and accommodation were ignored, discounted, or misperceived.

The so-called anomalous finding of Gamson and Modigliani enriches the mirror image hypothesis, adding a dynamic aspect to it. The model presented here helps to explain more fully both the Cold War and the findings of Gamson and Modigliani. Notions of misperception, learning, multiple aspects of conflict and cooperation, issue salience, manipulation of dissonance, and the absence of unitary actors must be systematically organized, and brought to bear on the question of the Cold War, to assess and interpret the findings of scholars like Gamson and Modigliani in a sophisticated manner. But, if the theory that has been described here can account for existing empirical analysis, as well as apparent anomalies in those analyses, and can shed light on differing historical interpretations, it remains necessary to see whether it can provide assistance in prescribing policy that might guide analysts and decision makers.

The truth of the nuclear age is that the United States and the Soviet Union must live in peace or we may not live at all. From the beginning of history, the fortunes of men and nations were made and unmade in unending cycles of war and peace. Combat was often the measure of human courage. Willingness to risk war was a mark of statecraft. My fellow Americans, that pattern of war must now be broken forever.
—*Jimmy Carter* [1]

CHAPTER ELEVEN

THE FUTURE

W HILE AN empirical theory is not logically linked to any specific normative or prescriptive analysis, the gap between facts and values is not so unbridgeable as early logical positivists believed. [2] Science has implications for policy prescription, because science has consequences, and a finding that denies the claims of an ideology (such as the failure of the proletariat to revolt) may cast doubt on the entire ideology. If, for instance, research established that selected minorities had generally lower IQ's than the broad majority in a population, this finding would support an important aspect of the empirical portion of racist ideology. But, this does not mean, as Charles Taylor argues, that social science cannot be objective. [3] Even *if* those minorities were less capable of performing certain tasks, this would not logically entail that they be stripped of equal protection under the law, or the right to vote, or that they be subjected to discrimination. Moreover, such a finding, no matter how strongly established, does not logically entail the enactment of racist proposals as policy. Indeed, there is no reason why such a finding could not be used to combat racism by determining the cause of the deficiency and undertaking remedial efforts to alleviate it. In the final analysis, science and policy are neither as separate as early logical positivists claimed nor so enmeshed that objective science is impossible.

The theoretical insights presented in this book have implications for policy. Applying them to explain the Cold War provided support for certain interpretations and not for others. This does not mean that a single policy preference is inherent in the theory, but it does suggest that every policy prescription is not as easily justified as any other. The theory is intended to be a guide to reality, and if it is a good guide, it will suggest policies and techniques for approaching desired goals. The goals themselves are, of course, not determined by the theory.

The following pages entail an application of the theory to the two dominant issues on the recent global agenda—the declining Cold War and the surging North–South dispute—for prescriptive purposes. Prescriptions will reflect the authors' goals, but the strategies will be derived from insights provided by the theory itself. Others are free to employ these insights in aid of their goals. The aim of the authors is simply to demonstrate that the approach outlined in the previous chapters is capable of giving rise to prescriptions as significant and nonobvious as those generated by the realist paradigm.

DÉTENTE: A THEORETICAL JUSTIFICATION

The origins of détente as an emerging game in global politics have been outlined, yet the theory presented here also serves to provide a sophisticated rationale for the policies underlying this game, as well as to point up some of their potential pitfalls. Policies that reinforce and anchor détente are, from the perspective of this analysis, the bases of a sound foreign policy for American leaders if peace is their main goal. Policies that rekindle the Cold War or that press Soviet leaders too hard by demanding major concessions are not only less sound but highly dangerous for the world as a whole.

Policies that reinforce détente buttress peace, because they offer the prospect of institutionalizing a new foundation for Soviet-American relations free from a hostile interaction spiral—and a new way of making global decisions. Such policies would stress the interdependence of Soviet and American interests in stakes at a time of relatively equal status while leaders may still recall vividly the costs of mutual failure. A commonly overlooked aspect of the process of détente is that it involves a *conscious* search for new decision-making rules, based on renewed reliance upon the mechanisms of principle and bargains. In order to move decisively to a new decision game, the hostility that provided the glue for the Cold War issue must be scraped away. To accomplish this, the negative actor dimension must cease to serve as the perceptual lens through which individual stakes are seen to be linked; and this in turn requires mutual reinterpretation of the type of stakes around which contention revolves. In a word, transcendent and symbolic stakes must be abandoned in favor of, or transmuted into, concrete stakes.

Only in this fashion can the Cold War be resolved, rather than being left in a state of dormancy in the hope that it will simply disappear in time. Dormancy, through a valuable precondition for change, is ultimately unacceptable, because it holds out the dangerous possibility that some future demagogue or third party might reactivate the issue at a propitious moment. A resolution of the Cold War requires that a decision be made about the transcendent stake (capitalism vs. communism), and the only possible decision is acceptance of both systems. So long as any major actor seeks to overthrow or eliminate either system, final resolution of the issue will be impossible. This requires toleration of differing ideological practices and beliefs; the Cold War can be ended, but not with a victory for either contestant.

For some individuals and groups in both the United States and the Soviet Union, this price seems too high. For them, no compromise can be made with the devil; the opposing ideology is seen less as a rival "ideal type" than as an immoral and degrading philosophy. And, even if each side exaggerates or concentrates upon past excesses of the other side (e.g., Stalinist labor camps or American sweatshops), the dispute is real, not the result of misperception or miscommunication. There exists a real and profound difference of opinion about how to live; and neither side wishes to have the other's ideology imposed upon it, regardless of costs or benefits. Since this is the case, resolution of the Cold War requires that each side surrender pretensions to impose its system upon the other, and not that either side concede the superiority of the other. The surrender of such pretensions would remove the transcendent issue even while leaving existing beliefs intact. There is a difference in declaring the importance of not losing as opposed to the importance of winning. And, while such a position may seem to entail acceptance of "immorality," it at least precludes the imposition of one party's will upon the other.

When this obvious distinction is not conveniently forgotten, the battle over the transcendent stake appears less dramatic than it has been painted. Couple this with the fact that the Soviet regime has eliminated some of the worst aspects of its behavior toward dissent and political opposition within the communist party, and that the United States government has increased the scope and quality of its welfare policies, then the difference between regimes becomes one of emphasis and relative hardships that must be borne.* Finally, there is the question of jurisdiction and effectiveness. To what extent is the struggle of the Soviet or American dissenter his own battle, rather than that of the opposing government? What can either side do other than give aid and comfort to the other's dissenters, and what risks and costs ought it be willing to bear to do so? No matter how genuinely sympathetic either side is to the efforts of such dissenters, a minimal obligation would be to avoid succoring them *for the purpose of achieving a competitive advantage.*

When the transcendent stake is seen in this light, it loses its millennial quality, and tolerance is easier. Since sweeping condemnations of the opposing system carry an implicit vision of the perfection of one's own system, little more is necessary than intellectual humility. If neither system is perfect, neither is utterly imperfect. Each encourages or perpetuates certain injustices, even while both experience reform in almost dialectical fashion. There are, moreover, in the world today a number of additional social experiments associated with particular regimes that fit comfortably in neither of the dominant models of socialism and capitalism. Indeed, even the Soviet Union has for some years accepted the legitimacy of "many roads to socialism" (though the limits of this acceptance have on occasion been rigid). There seems to be no need for everyone to travel the same path or even seek the same destination. And, while each path inevitably encourages different injustices, remedying them must remain primarily in the hands of those who are directly affected by them. The extent to which outsiders do get involved should depend not only on the severity of the injustice and the amount of opposition it generates, but also upon the costs of intervention, its probable effectiveness, and the expected long-term consequences of meddling.

---

*This does not imply acceptance of the "convergence thesis." See Zbigniew K. Brzezinski and Samuel P. Huntington, *Political Power: USA/USSR* (New York: Viking, 1965).

Extremists on both sides often fail to consider these questions. How did the Cold War aid Soviet dissenters or American radicals? Indeed, external intervention largely promoted renewed internal repression. Both the Cold War and détente can only produce stalemate, as far as the transcendent stake is concerned, with the key difference being that in the former the decision is not accepted, so that there ensues a hostile pattern of interaction with risks of nuclear disaster. But even if there is mutual willingness to avoid these risks, there remains the problem of how each side is to convince the other of its sincerity. At minimum this requires cessation of mutual criticism, so that the rhetoric of threat is not confused with the reality of threat. Such restraint seems an obvious step, yet "hawks" on both sides will periodically try to undermine détente by vociferously raising the transcendent stake and trying to ride to political power upon it. Unfortunately, elites on these occasions typically tend to pull back from exposed conciliatory positions, thereby raising doubts about the sincerity and stability of policy and encouraging the other side's "hawks." Paradoxically, Soviet and American "hawks" are one another's allies, while leaders on both sides share a common interest in the success of détente.

It is because of this dynamic, and the resiliency of the hostile interaction pattern, that the issues of human rights and Jewish emigration from the Soviet Union are dangerous. Although they have a reformist tone in comparison to the rhetoric of John Foster Dulles' liberation doctrine, they touch upon the transcendent stake. Do citizens have a right to emigrate from one nation in unlimited numbers, and to provide assistance to another which is fighting against an ally of the USSR? That is the way one might pose the question of Jewish emigration from a Soviet perspective. Since the right of emigration is related to other rights, it is logical for Soviet leaders to ask to what extent this issue is a "cover" for demands that Soviet society become more democratic in the Western sense. If the USSR is more lenient with dissenters and permits greater freedom of artistic expression and religious practice, must it also permit more freedom of speech for political purposes? Would this be followed by demands to permit political groups outside the communist party to organize? Taken together, such "salami tactics" would seem to constitute a demand for Soviet surrender on the transcendent issue. To raise the issue of human rights, as Jimmy Carter did when he first entered office is to pose the transcendent stake and make détente more difficult by encouraging American hawks to press demands, and by providing Soviet hawks with evidence of American belligerence.

This was an egregious move for Carter, because he was a new and unknown quantity, and had seized a position to the right of Ford and Kissinger during the campaign, thereby reconfirming the Cold War "truth" that a sure way to power is to be more hawkish than the current leadership. In particular, Carter's foreign-policy debate with Ford, while winning a number of votes from Americans of Eastern European ancestry, came painfully close to Dulles' position of not recognizing Soviet hegemony in Eastern Europe and the fact that it would remain communist. It therefore seemed a retreat from the so-called Sonnenfeldt doctrine. The cool reception Carter received from Soviet leaders should have come as no surprise. Regardless of the Soviet domestic situation, Soviet leaders had little choice but to rebuff Carter's interference publicly. To have done otherwise would only have encouraged him to step up his demands. Both globally and domestically, human rights and Jewish emigration are code words for the transcendent stake, and so risk rekindling the Cold War.*

The transcendent stake is only one obstacle that must be overcome. Symbolic stakes pose additional obstacles. If overcoming the transcendent stake involves accepting the right of the other major contender to adopt and practice an alien ideology, coping with symbolic stakes requires learning that it does not really matter if third parties adopt the preferred ideology, nor if the adversary gains influence with them. Such influence is ephemeral. The Soviet Union, for instance, has discovered that another communist regime can pose as great a threat as a capitalist regime when it comes to traditional political competition; and an even greater ideological threat, because it can offer an alternative model of socialism and a challenge to Soviet aspirations to socialist leadership. The Sino-Soviet dispute has dispelled the Marxian illusion that rulers of the same class will not engage in conflict. There is no reason to believe that a communist world would reduce competition for scarce stakes and be any

---

* If American domestic groups insist on raising these questions, it would be best to meet them directly. This would probably lead to the defeat of the "hawks," since détente is popular among the public at large. In addition, it would strengthen the position of those in the USSR who are in favor of détente. Nevertheless, the 1980 presidential campaign of Ronald Reagan again showed the attractiveness of "hawkishness" to political challengers.

safer or more secure than either a capitalist world or a world of mixed ideologies. However one might describe contemporary Chinese doctrine and practice, they bear little resemblance to the Soviet brand of socialism. American recognition of the Chinese communist regime, the conclusion of a Sino-Japanese peace treaty, Chinese resistance to Vietnamese conquest of Cambodia, and Chinese intrusion in both Eastern and Western Europe, provide recent evidence that the spread of communism to the most populous society in the world did not, in the long run, bring dividends to the USSR. It is, moreover, unclear that the victory of socialism in one or another of the societies of Western Europe would be a boon for the Soviet leaders. It might merely produce yet another challenger to Moscow's ideological hegemony in Eastern Europe, if not to its economic and political hegemony as well.

If Soviet leaders have learned that a communist actor is not necessarily an ally, American leaders must still learn that an actor which professes to be socialist need not be a threat. If Presidents Nixon and Ford were prepared to accept the fact that détente meant accepting the status quo in Europe and China, they also thought it meant that Soviet leaders would accept the status quo in the rest of the world, *and that the rest of the world would accept it as well.* Any further expansion of communism was, thus, a violation of détente. Consequently, among the ironies of history were that as Nixon was toasting Zhou Enlai American troops were fighting in Vietnam; and that while Ford and Kissinger were trying to institutionalize détente, Washington was busily fighting communism in Angola, Chile, Portugal, Italy, and France, and was claiming in each instance (with the exception of Chile) that Soviet aid and encouragement to communists in these countries constituted violations of détente. Such claims implicitly interpret détente as an abandonment of Dulles' rollback policy *in return for* Soviet acceptance of containment. The Soviet regime is, of course, not prepared to accept that definition, and, even if it were, revolutionary movements would not. If détente is to prove durable, there must be room for social change, even upheaval, in the Third World.

There is no prima facie reason why American leaders should find the creation of socialist or communist regimes to be a major threat. The success of the Movimento Popular de Libertaçao de Angola (MPLA) of Dr. Antonio Agostinho Neto, who favored "state control over the means of production and close ties with the Soviet Union,"[4] did not produce the catastrophe that was feared by Ford-Kissinger or even Carter-Brzezinski. Neto, for example, employed Cuban troops to protect Gulf Oil's installations from rebels in Cabinda. Indeed, it is difficult to see what Marxism can possibly mean in rural, tribal-dominated settings like those of Angola or Afghanistan. Its primary function seems to be ideational, rather than actually producing a system similar to that of the USSR or even China.

And, what of the much-feared communization of Indochina? Instead of ousting American influence from all of Southeast Asia, the development stimulated the strengthening of the Association of Southeast Asian Nations (ASEAN) and triggered a nasty war between Vietnam and Cambodia, with the former ousting the murderous Pol Pot regime from the latter. Ironically, the USSR and China became involved as the two combatants symbolized their own cold war! Rather than a single strategy for world conquest, as it was once thought to be, Marxism-Leninism has turned out to be a rhetorical weapon available to any actor to rationalize its political interests. To take labels seriously under such conditions means missed opportunities and unnecessary conflict.

This last point is dramatically illustrated by Vietnamese negotiations with American oil companies for offshore drilling rights. Despite years of slaughter, the Vietnamese are prepared to permit their most valuable natural resource to be developed by American corporations simply because the multinational corporations possess suitable technology. Even if a noncommunist Vietnam would have given the corporations more extensive property rights, such a marginal advantage is scarcely worth the use of force. If the sole difference between communist and noncommunist regimes is not even whether they permit investment and trade but the terms of transactions, then the stakes at issue are not symbolic at all but are concrete. As the growing competition between American, European, and Japanese firms for trade with the USSR and China reflects, the Vietnamese case is not the exception. Few stakes could be more concrete than exclusive rights to bottle cola in the USSR and China!

Third parties, then, have become less potent ideological symbols to the United States and the Soviet Union. Nevertheless, preoccupation with third parties as symbols of "influence" remains, much in the tradition of power politics. Perceptions of relative status account for much of American concern with Soviet-Cuban influence in Africa; and in such contexts, an actor dimension remains potent, largely because the Soviet Union and the United States remain at the apex of the global status hierarchy.

Like ideological battles, struggles for "influence" involve a number of illusions. First, influence, as perceived in terms of the general orientations of specific regimes, is ephemeral and is important only insofar as it can be converted into value satisfaction. Second, influence of this sort is not necessarily zero-sum as a negative actor dimension implies. Thus, the unrest in Iran directed against the regime of the Shah in late 1978 and early 1979 was perceived as a weakening of American influence and an opportunity for the further spread of Soviet influence. What is, however, really at stake for the United States in Iran is access to oil, a concrete stake. With the advent of an Islamic republic in Iran, the key problem for American leaders is to ensure the continued flow of oil at reasonable terms. Yet such a regime also poses problems for Soviet leaders, principally because of its attraction to the large Muslim minority within the USSR that is located along the Turkish and Iranian frontiers. Thus, the overthrow of the Shah in Iran is not automatically a gain or opportunity for the Soviet Union.

The key test in unraveling symbolic stakes is coming in Afghanistan and the Persian Gulf. While there is much discussion of these events reactivating the Cold War, this is only part of the story, since other issues like defining détente and the post-Cold War global order, the Sino-Soviet dispute, and oil and resources are at stake. At this writing it is too early to discern clearly all the Soviet motivations in invading Afghanistan, but it does seem clear that to regard this as a symbolic first step to the Persian Gulf is an exaggeration of what has been an historic Russian concern with its periphery. The mistake on the part of the Carter Administration is not in resisting the invasion, but in exaggerating the threat and linking it to other issues. Failure to protest the invasion would have accepted by acquiescence the right of the USSR under détente to "prop up" friendly regimes on its borders outside Eastern Europe, as well as encouraging hard-liners in the USSR. But to exaggerate the invasion and link it to other issues encourages hard-liners in both the US and USSR, drives the US to support reactionary regimes like those in Pakistan and Oman that are very unstable, and threatens a new cycle in the arms race.

These consequences are potentially more dangerous than Afghanistan, which is a symbolic stake. Even if Afghanistan should become a satellite of the USSR, a proposition which is dubious, that hardly threatens the interests of the United States. Unlike England the United States need not protect India! The only interest the United States has in the Persian Gulf area is oil, and the United States should confine its threats to the USSR to the question of access to mid-Eastern oil. For the short term that is a vital concrete stake; the rest is negotiable. Commitments to Afghan rebels, Pakistan, Oman, or a hostile Iran are unnecessary symbolic burdens. The fact that Washington, out of misperception and/or domestic politics, has raised the symbolic quality of this issue and that Moscow has not done so leaves hope that Afghanistan and the Persian Gulf will only be temporary setbacks; likewise, the resistance Moscow faces from Afghan rebels may lessen her appetite for further expansion. The key for both sides is learning the ephemeral nature of influence in symbolic stakes.

The case of Soviet-Cuban influence in Africa illustrates this point. The shift in Soviet allegiance from Somalia to Ethiopia cost the Soviet Union an important naval base for the prospect of a better one; it also involved the sacrifice of considerable pro-Soviet sympathy in the Islamic world. For its part, revolution in Ethiopia severed close American links to the Ethiopian government, even while American relations improved with such proximate Muslim countries as the Sudan, Egypt, and Somalia. In the end, what were the net results? And, were the marginal changes worth the costs and risks involved? How long can Cuban troops remain deeply committed to adventures in Angola and the Horn of Africa before costs generate domestic discontent? How often and how long can the Soviet Union prop up transient African regimes before it blunders into its own African Vietnam? And, what happened to the bright prospects the USSR seemed to enjoy in Africa in the past—in Ghana, Guinea, Nigeria, the Congo? Africa's very instability suggests that influence is easily bought (at the right price) but can evaporate just as quickly. Concrete stakes in Africa are comparatively scarce, and abrupt shifts in relative Soviet-American influence there are not likely to affect their relative ranking in the status hierarchy in any profound fashion.

Efforts to acquire allies and clients are only one manifestation of Soviet-American competition for status. An even more important arena is the competitive acquisition and improvement of armaments. However, the arms race does not only involve symbolic competition; it also entails the acquisition of capabilities that enable unilateral action in the case of hostility. For this reason, despite its symbolic quality, the arms race cannot be resolved by merely forgetting it. Instead, it must be regulated; and agreement must be reached about relative status, with a set of rules about how to run the race itself. The most obvious basis for such agreement would be general parity (despite the difficulties in comparing different weapons systems and in monitoring adherence to technological limitations). Such agreement would not end the arms race—a virtually impossible task because of its links to domestic interests and rivalries, and its connection to issues other than the Cold War—but it might regulate the process. It would not only institutionalize the notion of mutual assured destruction but provide the only feasible, and the most prominent, solution, given the continued autonomy of the rivals. If either side seeks preponderance, the resulting competition will prove dangerous, because such preponderance can only be attained by a technological breakthrough that would eliminate the second-strike capability of the opponent—a prospect that heightens the probability of preventive or preemptive war. It is the purpose of SALT to negotiate agreements that will regulate the race to maintain approximate parity and to avoid seeking preponderance. "Legitimate espionage," notably through mutual tolerance of spy satellites, provides one means to limit mutual suspicion.

SALT, however, has powerful critics in both the United States and the Soviet Union. Critics of SALT in the United States are particularly disturbed by the rapid Soviet strategic buildup that continued even after the conclusion of SALT I, combined with the modernization of Soviet conventional forces and apparent truculence in Africa and Vietnam. "There is every prospect," declared Paul Nitze, "that under the terms of the SALT agreements the Soviet Union will continue to pursue a nuclear superiority that is not merely quantitative but designed to produce a theoretical war-winning capability" and that "the trends in relative military strength are such that, unless we move promptly to reverse them, the United States is moving toward a posture of minimum deterrence in which we would be conceding to the Soviet Union the potential for a military and political victory if deterrence failed."[5] In effect, these critics suggest that the USSR is moving towards a posture of strategic superiority that would permit a successful counterforce attack against America's land-based retaliatory forces. Pointing to Soviet installation of MIRVs,

Soviet advantages in "large" missiles, the development of the "Backfire" bomber, the ambitious Soviet program in civil defense, and the Soviet deployment of a "blue seas" fleet, they contend that the USSR may be seeking a "war-winning" capability to which they attach the most negative possible intentions.

The attempt to measure relative strategic capabilities is admittedly complex and difficult. Soviet advantage in throw-weight—the total weight of missile warheads that could be delivered—is emphasized by critics who view this as providing the USSR with a potential first-strike.* This preoccupation ignores Soviet apprehension over China and the fact that the USSR views itself as confronted on three "fronts"—the United States, Western Europe, and China. When this is included in the equation, a somewhat different picture emerges. The "Backfire" bomber, for instance, is unlikely to prove effective against the United States, though it does constitute a considerable threat to China.

The emphasis on throw-weight, with its potential for destroying existing American land-based missiles, omits American advantages in missile accuracy, numbers of warheads, long-range bombers (soon to be equipped with cruise missiles), and Submarine-Launched Ballistic Missiles (SLBMs) (soon to be reinforced by the introduction of Trident). Although the USSR may by the mid-1980's be able to destroy much of America's land-based ICBM force (barring the introduction of American mobile missiles), "even in the worst case, 5,000 to 6,000 nuclear weapons on alert bombers and submarines at sea would survive a surprise attack," and by that time "the United States will have the capability to respond to a Soviet counterforce attack with a counterforce response of its own" owing to the deployment of 2,000 to 3,000 cruise missiles on bombers and an additional 3,000 weapons aboard submarines.[6] Finally, the assumption of a "worst possible case analysis" by the critics fails to recognize that Soviet development of large missiles was begun several years prior to SALT I in an atmosphere of uncertainty, and may even have taken the form it did precisely because of relative Soviet backwardness in missile accuracy and warhead miniaturization.

---

* It is unclear that the Soviet advantage in throw-weight will provide any edge at all, since "there is only a very narrow range of accuracies in which throw-weight is important to a hard-target counterforce capability." Jan. M. Lodal, "Assuring Strategic Stability: An Alternative View," *Foreign Affairs* (April 1976), 54(3):465.

Ultimately, comparative assessments of strategic weapons systems cannot be very precise because of the variety and numbers of weapons involved. Additionally, perfect parity is probably unnecessary because what is really needed is confidence in a mutual second-strike capability. Quantitative additions to existing systems through larger numbers of launchers and greater throw-weight are unlikely to alter that capability except at the margins, so that much of the debate about SALT is irrelevant. Perhaps, the real reason for unhappiness with SALT in the United States is that it was oversold in the first place, and that expectations about its impact on Soviet-American relations, or on the American defense budget, were simply too high. Only a technological breakthrough (most likely a defensive weapon like a laser shield) could alter dramatically the strategic equation, and the prevention or regulation of just such a contingency is the major objective of SALT. The aims of SALT are fairly modest, but the process "can serve to restrain the flow of the strategic arms competition, deflecting its path periodically and warning the participants away from especially hazardous waters."[7] In large measure, both sides have observed the rules of the game that were established in 1972, and the existence of the Standing Consultative Committee, established at that time, serves the highly valuable purpose of providing "a process by which the two superpowers define illegitimate behavior."[8] The arms race arouses the most dangerous elements of the Cold War mentality, and without minimal agreement on nuclear weapons, détente will unravel. Yet in no other area do Soviet and American leaders have a greater common interest.

In order to institutionalize the détente game, Jimmy Carter and Leonid Brezhnev (and their successors) must pursue policies that will accomplish three tasks: (1) remove the transcendent stake from the global agenda (and avoid letting it slip back as Carter did by introducing "human rights" in provocative fashion); (2) de-mythologize symbolic stakes (the major task that Henry Kissinger failed to foresee, and the one which provides the Carter Administration with its greatest opportunity to make a contribution to world history as profound as Kissinger's "grand design"); and (3) develop standard operating procedures to regulate the arms race, particularly at the level of research and development (where there exists perhaps the greatest threat to détente and world peace). These tasks can only be accomplished if domestic opposition to détente in the USSR and the United States is successfully curbed.

In the case of the Soviet Union, the main danger lies in the disappearance of current Soviet leaders and a renewed struggle for succession, in which candidates are tempted to seek allies in the party, or the military, by advocating hard-line policies toward the United States and/or China. In the case of the United States, the danger lies with a loosely tied anti-Soviet opposition, consisting of the military, defense-related industries, traditional conservatives, the pro-Israel lobby, and Eastern European ethnic communities. Each of these fairly narrow groups, for their own reasons, are skeptical of détente and have strong allies abroad and in Congress, who can act as a restraint on a president—particularly in the Senate, where a two-thirds majority is needed to ratify treaties. In addition, they pose a potential electoral threat to Carter, particularly if the ethnic groups can be attracted away from the Democratic Party. As in the 1950s, these groups offer the prospect for hawks of providing sufficient additional votes to sweep them to power. To prevent a hardening of the antidétente forces and preclude détente itself from becoming a critical issue within the United States, it is necessary to approach separately the various concrete and symbolic stakes that animate the critics of détente and to build a counter-coalition from among business, labor, and agriculture that can profit economically from an end to the Cold War. The best way to do this is to make détente work.

The extent to which détente is successful can be measured by the degree to which: (1) it actually establishes a legitimate set of rules for the making of decisions (viz. allocating values authoritatively); (2) such decisions produce a better net mix of costs and benefits to American groups than did the Cold War; and (3) there is no feasible alternative game that could produce more satisfactory allocations. All of these criteria have already been partially satisfied. Minimally, détente promises a number of benefits to American groups, including the disposition of stakes that formerly could not be allocated owing to their symbolic quality, including those associated with the old division-of-the-spoils issue in Europe.

Détente will also enhance the prospects for Soviet-American cooperation in issues of joint concern like population control, technology transfers, food, and energy that will not disappear in the near future. Additionally, it will lower a number of costs, psychological and otherwise, that have burdened Soviet and American actors throughout the Cold War, notably the omnipresent peril of nuclear exchange, the fear of conquest by an alien ideology, and the wasteful expenditure on increasingly expensive armaments. The arms race has been partly stabilized, and with the exception of the 1973 Middle East alert, brinksmanship has been largely avoided. These are benefits which SALT and détente can provide but which the old deterrence strategy cannot.* More importantly, the continuation of détente and SALT improve the prospects of furthering stability in, and eventually diminishing, the arms race. In the end, the strongest argument for détente is that the only alternative, the Cold War, is not only too dangerous, but is irrelevant to the real needs and interests of Americans. Détente at least promises the *possibility* of a new world order.

The dilution or elimination of the Cold War will, of course, not lead to a world of concrete stakes, as a number of major issues will continue to be dominated by symbolic or transcendent concerns. Indeed, a major question for détente is how the United States and Soviet governments will treat key issues in the rest of the world. The Sino–Soviet dispute, the North–South confrontation, regional disputes such as Afghanistan, the Middle East and southern Africa, international monetary instability, nuclear proliferation, and the general specter of a neo-Malthusian collapse, are examples of issues that have assumed or could assume symbolic and/or transcendent qualities for participants, even as the Cold War grows less salient. Indeed, these issues could even revive the Cold War, much as other issues were responsible for its introduction after 1945. The temptation, for instance, for American leaders to play the "China card" vigorously or for Soviet leaders to eliminate the threat posed by China illustrate ways in which the Cold War could again be mounted. Since peace and stability are partly determined by the nature of the issues on the global agenda, the regulation of that agenda and the manner in which those issues are treated pose major problems for world order. Détente itself is entirely too narrow a decision game to cope with such issues.

One possibility for the United States and Soviet Union is the transformation of détente to entente—and even to a new concert of power not unlike that which Roosevelt envisioned before his death. This would en-

---

*This is the key error in Theodore Draper's argument that deterrence can provide the same benefits as détente but without its attendant risks. See his "Appeasement and Détente," in Steven L. Spiegel, ed., *At Issue: Politics in the World Arena,* 2d ed. (New York: St. Martin's Press, 1977), pp. 182–203.

tail the introduction of a duopoly to determine informally how major global issues might be resolved, and then the implementation of necessary measures to enforce and administer such decisions. For such a system to evolve, a number of ad hoc games would be necessary, in the course of which the scope and domain of the concert would expand. The concert's primary responsibility would be to assist participants to reach decisions about controversial stakes and try to prevent their being infused with symbolic or transcendent qualities. The rules for such decisions could only emerge from praxis, but initially would surely entail bargains backed by the possibility of coercion. The prospect for such a transformation is not bright, and it would confront resistance by opponents of "hegemony," many of which have access to major capabilities and are acquiring greater status. Paradoxically, this would run the very great risk of generating yet a new disturbing issue of the sort which emerged in Europe during the days of the old Concert. Ultimately, the success of a new concert would depend heavily on the nature of the issues with which it would have to deal and on its ability to control actors that are rising in status.

THE EMERGING POLITICAL ORDER

The political order of any system, global or domestic, is determined by the issues that dominate the agenda, particularly the critical issue, and the actors that dominate contention over those issues. The nature of the critical issue is important, because it determines how fused the various stakes will become and hence whether the issue will be formed by an actor or stake dimension. The nature of the actors is even more important, because their relative status and similarity will determine whether existing issues are likely to be linked and treated as part of an actor dimension or are to be kept separate.

The current period of history is not unlike 1945–47 in that the present critical issue has not been fully resolved but has been sufficiently reduced in salience so that older issues, like anticolonialism, have been raised in salience, and newer issues, like energy, have come to the fore. All these issues are clamoring for attention and, in a sense, struggling to become the new critical issue. This change in issues is also accompanied by a change in the status hierarchy and an influx of new actors. Although the shifts are not as drastic or as sudden as in 1945, there have been dramatic changes. The Soviet Union has emerged as the coequal of the United States, which has a great deal to do with the resolution of the Cold War. More importantly, the gap between the superpowers and the rest of the world has narrowed considerably, mostly because of the nature of the new issues. China has risen as a power that seeks to compete, militarily if necessary, with the USSR on a potential critical issue. Western Europe ponders integrating its monetary systems to produce a currency that would rival, if not replace, the dollar in the international market. Various Third World regional powers have surfaced—Brazil, Mexico, Nigeria, Iran, India, Indonesia—and some have sought global power—the Arabs under the Saudis, and OPEC in a more general sense. Finally, the Third World, as a whole, makes up the bulk of the over one-hundred fifty state entities in the world, and through the UN controls one route to the global agenda.

The decline in the Cold War as an issue has given these new actors the opportunity to increase the salience of their concerns and has freed some of the older powers from the blinders of the superpower coalitions. A review of these concerns will give some idea of the various directions the future political order might take. As suggested by the model on actor coalescence, highly salient issues can bring actors together by suppressing differences on other questions. With the easing of Soviet-American tensions after the Cuban missile crisis, a relaxation which China militantly opposed, China challenged the USSR's ideological leadership of the communist world. The failure of Khrushchev to employ what China regarded as Soviet military parity with the West to support wars of liberation was seen as apostasy. To Mao and Zhou Enlai this was another example of putting CPSU interests before the interests of the world's exploited, reminiscent of Stalin's opposition to the 1949 revolution.

The raising of this highly salient issue, with its transcendent challenge, brought with it other stakes, including territorial disputes, which became symbolic of Soviet imperialism. The Chinese remember that Russia under the tsars seized what is today the Soviet Far Eastern Maritime Province (including Vladivostok) by "unequal treaties" with a weak China in 1858 and 1860, as part of the overall European imperial expansionism of the time and the incursions into China by the Europeans and Japan. Part of Sinkiang was seized in the 1860s, and additional areas were taken by force in the 1870s. Chinese weakness and exigencies of other critical issues, notably those of Chinese unification and civil war in the periods prior to and after World War II, World War II itself, and the Cold War, precluded any successful Chinese effort to rectify matters. Soviet economic influence in Sinkiang was continued until 1954 through the device of Soviet-dominated "joint stock companies," but even their abolition did not restore the entire area to China or bring agreement on other territorial differences. Anti-Soviet agitation in Sinkiang apparently began in 1958 during the Chinese "Great leap forward."[9] These tensions gained global publicity in March 1969 on the occasion of large-scale border fighting near Chenpao (Damansky) Island in the Ussuri River.

Soviet failure to march in step with China during the India border war, its failure to satisfy Chinese economic and nuclear aspirations, its later alliance with India, and competition with China in Vietnam, Africa, and other parts of the Third World began to fuse a number of stakes together on an actor dimension. This culminated in the Sino-American rapprochment, when the supposed cause of the initial ideological dispute (the United States) was sought as China's major (interim) ally, much like Stalin sought British and French support against Hitler.

By the time of the Chinese invasion of Vietnam in early 1979, with Russian military maneuvers near the Chinese borders and Deng Xiaoping's calls for an alliance with the United States against the USSR, it was clear that this issue is a highly salient and potentially critical issue on the global level. The latter is so because China seeks to compete with the Soviet Union for the friendship of the Third World and other communists, as well as for the aid of the West. Certainly, if the Soviet Union and China were the two most powerful actors in the world, there would be no doubt that this would become the new critical issue, because it has all the potential characteristics: it involves questions that are moral in character; it represents real differences in ways of governing; it is related to status competition; and it is relevant to many in the Third and Second Worlds because of its ideological content. But it will probably not become the critical issue for the entire system, because it is not salient to at least two major power groups—the United States and Western Europe. And unless it can be linked to one of the other potential critical issues, its crosscutting nature may prevent the Sino-Soviet cleavage from becoming the dominant critical issue in the near future.*

Just as Soviet hegemony became an issue with the decline of the Cold War, so has American hegemony, on a lesser scale in the West. De Gaulle first made this issue prominent by demanding gold for French-held dollars, trying to build Europe into a third force (without Britain), pulling out of NATO, and trying to deal directly with the Russians. The fracture reached a high point in 1974 with the Arab oil embargo, when the French government, even after de Gaulle, resisted American leadership and the attempt to build an anti-OPEC consumers' coalition, the International Energy Agency (IEA). Instead of joining IEA, the French government made its own arrangement with the Arabs and encouraged others, notably Japan and Italy, to do the same. France then tried to act as leader of a non-American West that was sympathetic to Arab concerns, but the effort failed. With that failure and American success with the IEA, the issue declined in salience and failed to link with the North-South cleavage to make it a United States–nonaligned cleavage. Nevertheless, economic competition for markets and goods, particularly in sensitive areas like weapons technology and nuclear energy, as well as political competition in former colonies, makes American hegemony an important second-order issue. A uniting of Western Europe, of course, would bring about a very drastic change in the status hierarchy, and only at that point would the possibility of this issue becoming a new critical issue become likely.

The issue that is most capable of becoming a new critical issue is the North–South dispute. The fundamental division represented by the North–South issue is between the wealthy and the poor of the world. This characterization, however, hardly does justice to a global cleavage which is becoming increasingly sharp. It suggests that the key stakes are concrete and reflect the single value of wealth. But this view fails to comprehend the manner in which a host of specific issues that were orginally based on concrete stakes—tariff concessions, foreign aid, terms of trade, loan policies, investment policies, technology transfers, and the like—have come to be fused with other specific issues like energy, multinational penetration, population control, and food distribution, and have come to be characterized by symbolic and even transcendent stakes as-

---

* This does not mean it will disappear from the agenda, but only that the other issues will affect it and hence the relationship between the USSR and China.

sociated with values like independence, equality, and esteem. The division itself is between a "small number of states, equaling some 20 percent of the world's population" which "controls 80 percent of the world's wealth" and the remaining four-fifths of the world's population.[10]

It is not merely that the poor are deprived in an absolute sense; revolutions in communication and travel have made the two sectors highly visible to each other, and the achievement of political independence by many of the poor with the decline of colonialism whetted appetites that cannot be sated. The sense of *relative* deprivation is, therefore, acute and is heightened by the fact that the gap continues to grow wider. "The affluent world," declares Barbara Ward, "adds each year to its existing wealth all and more of the entire income available to other continents" so that the poor "move at the speed of a bicycle" and the wealthy "at the speed of a moon rocket."[11]

If technological change has enhanced the capacity of the poor to communicate with one another, political independence, competitive wooing by the United States and Soviet Union during the Cold War, and the United Nations have provided leaders in the Third World with a sense of political efficacy. Their potential for identification and perceptions of similarity is high (though unrealized), because, in addition to their common deprivation, they are the heirs of colonial rule, geographically located in the Southern hemisphere, and nonwhite. This last point merits particular attention, because race is not only a potent trait around which the world's poor can identify, it is also becoming a transcendent stake in the North-South issue.[12] Perhaps even more than the numerous concrete stakes directly associated with wealth, race has served to link the domestic with the interstate arena in the North-South issue (just as communism did in the Cold War), so that nonwhites in wealthy societies (who are generally the most deprived in those societies) increasingly identify with the deprived elsewhere.*

While it is hard to measure precisely the degree to which the North-South issue, with its racial, social, political, and economic components, has come to embrace other issues, a rough idea can be had by illustrating

---

*See Harold R. Isaacs, "Color in World Affairs," *Foreign Affairs* (January 1969), 47(2):235–50. Tension between Jewish and Black groups in the United States over Middle Eastern and African questions illustrate the point.

its role in them and the consequent difficulty in encapsulating them for resolution. Questions like majority rule in Zimbabwe, independence for Namibia, and South Africa apartheid are commonly regarded as part of a piece, at least by many Africans and other citizens of the Third World. It is partly for this reason that Western proposals for resolving each of these issues separately have come to grief, regardless of their specific content. Indeed, the negative actor dimension that links these issues and stakes together is intensifying, so that proposals or statements made by an Andrew Young, or anyone else, are weighed in terms of whether they are pro-black and pro-poor, or pro-white and pro-status quo.

But it is not only stakes in southern Africa, or those involved in what is called the "New International Economic Order," that are embraced by the actor dimension of the North–South issue. The Palestine question, whatever the actual merits of the case, has also been drawn into the "critical" issue. Israel is regarded by Palestinians, Arabs, and many Third World leaders as a European interloper in the Middle East, the fruit of prior colonization. This impression is fostered by Israel's traditionally close ties with Western Europe and the United States, the European origin of many Israelis, the continuing friendly relations between Israel and South Africa, and the relative wealth and advanced technology of Israel in the midst of a sea of Arab poverty. The wedding of Palestine to the North–South issue was accelerated by the Arab oil embargo of 1973 and the growing importance of oil as a key stake in political questions of the Middle East and global economic matters. Thus, the Palestinian cause has been adopted by revolutionaries in a number of countries, including German, Japanese, and Irish terrorists. The growing cooperation among diverse terrorists and revolutionaries throughout the world is only understandable in terms of their generalized hostility toward the "forces of world imperialism" (Western governments). As in the case of Third World governments, each revolutionary group perceives the North–South issue in terms of a concrete stake that is highly salient to it, but which, in turn, is also symbolic of important other stakes.

It is likely that the North–South issue is not currently amenable to ritualization or dormancy, not to mention resolution. It is still in the midst of genesis; rules for interaction do not as yet exist, so that numerous ad hoc and formal rule-making games can be expected. The process that it follows will depend heavily on the ability and willingness of key actors to formulate acceptable rules. Since it is not likely that one or the other side can triumph easily, the outcome also depends upon whether, and when, key actors come to appreciate that mutual failure is probable. At that point, the choice will be one between encapsulating specific issues for settlement or engaging in a conflict spiral that might bring collective disaster. Imaginative leadership will then be called for. Timing is critical. If dramatic gestures, even concessions, are made too early, they may be taken as signs of weakness; yet the refusal to make such gestures under any conditions promises ritualization at best, and persistent crises at worst.

Whether the North–South conflict will become the next critical issue depends primarily on whether the Third World can remain unified as a group. This, in turn, depends on the ability to make the economic question transcendent rather than concrete, and the ability to link to this issue the Middle East and southern Africa issues. Making the economic question transcendent promotes solidarity and protects the cartel, the one weapon that has worked. If the North–South dispute is broken into concrete stakes, then it is more likely that divisions will occur between those who can be co-opted and those who cannot. To date, OPEC members have been generous in aid to selected "fellow" Third World actors, so that attempts to divide the Third World into fourth and even fifth worlds have not worked. The Middle East issue is important because it is this that keeps the Arabs, particularly the more conservative ones, in the coalition. Oil as a weapon, which has produced great shifts in wealth *and* status, was not used to bring about a new economic order but to save Egypt and Syria from defeat by Israel in 1973. The prospect of using oil to increase the status of certain Third World actors, and of employing resource cartels as a weapon against "imperialism," brought many non-Arab actors into active collaboration with the anti-Israeli forces. Finally, African actors were lured into the coalition by the tacit bargain of opposing Israel in return for Arab support against South Africa and Rhodesia.[13] Since both the Middle East and southern Africa issues are already actor-oriented and highly symbolic and transcendent, their linkage to demands for a new economic order has the effect of making the West a major enemy. Whether the Third World will move beyond an interdependence calculus to produce a real polarization in the world remains to be seen. From an American perspective, such a situation would be disadvantageous. However, such a development would benefit the USSR, because the *real* cleavage is West–South rather than North–South. If such an issue increased in salience, it might also swallow up the Sino-Soviet dispute, because both adversaries curry favor with the Third World.

The threat of a critical North–South issue emerging around the demand for a new economic order is grave, a fact reflected by the disruption of less salient issues in the UN. Thus, the West has raised a number of environmental questions which the Third World has literally refused to discuss, or has redefined in terms of the North–South dispute. Resolutions on the environment at the 1972 Stockholm conference included references to the just struggles of peoples against apartheid. At the 1974 population conference, Third World actors insisted that poverty, not population, was the problem. In the same year, at the World Food Conference, wasteful consumption in the West, particularly in the United States, was assailed. The need to write a new law of the sea was brought about partly because many Third World actors unilaterally claimed large areas of ocean space for themselves. The conference itself has bogged down over the question of whether the Third World will be able to mine deep-sea resources without having to share control and profits with Western corporations. Finally, condemnation of South Africa and Israel have become tests of allegiance and are almost ritualistic within the coalition.

Yet despite all of these efforts, the issues can be separated, and a shrewd American policy would seek to do precisely that. The Carter Administration has made several attempts along these lines. First, it has sought to defuse the Middle East question by encouraging an Israeli-Egyptian settlement, an attempt which has not fully worked but which has split the Arabs. Second, it has tried to resolve the southern Africa problem, particularly in Rhodesia-Zimbabwe, and in this instance, working with the British, it has enjoyed greater success. On each occasion, it has tried to keep the question of the new economic order separate. On that matter, it has reacted more sympathetically to Third World demands, adopting a more reformist approach than the previous Nixon-Ford Administration. In particular, American leaders have tried to co-opt the Saudis by giving them very high status roles, such as increased influence in the World Bank; the adoption of Arabic as an offical language of the United Nations; and the granting of military favors, including the sale of advanced weapons and the use of American forces, to support Saudi clients, such as the government of North Yemen. In addition, the United States has sought to generate support from non-Arab oil exporters like Nigeria and Indonesia, and to grant greater status to Mexico, Venezuela, and Ecuador. Actions of this sort may prevent the kind of hostile spiral that occurred between the United States and the USSR between 1945 and 1947. But again, domestic critics of Carter threaten to produce a new actor dimension. The narrow passage of the Panama Canal treaty shows that myopic jingoism is alive in the Senate, and further demands by a powerful actor to receive absolute deference from the Third World will go a long way to forging a unified Third World bloc, and making the North-South dispute a new critical issue.

It is particularly important to avoid this outcome, especially in light of the prospects of nuclear proliferation and resource scarcity. Little can be gained by strident American opposition to the Third World, and, although demands are sometimes extraordinary, final resolutions of particular issues need not be so. The reason for this concerns the nature of elites in the Third World. Few Third World leaders are authentic Marxists or revolutionaries. More often, they are members of a privileged elite, who are seeking a bigger slice of the pie, not only for their societies but for the interests they represent. Johan Galtung's idea of imperialism—where an elite in the Third World is in collusion with the West, the local multinational corporation, or CIA representative—may be accurate, but, even if it is, this does not make members of that elite servile clients or prevent them from demanding more. This is evident in Brazil and Chile, where the CIA was instrumental in eliminating elected leftists and in supporting rightists. American penetration of such countries will not end the demands.

Whether the issue will be resolved, and whether moderate elites can maintain power in the face of true revolutionaries, depend on whether economic reforms can meet the real demands of both elites and masses in the Third World. Herman Kahn and Robert Heilbroner represent two poles of opinion on this question. Kahn argues that within the next two hundred years most of the world will enjoy a standard of living comparable to that of the West today. Heilbroner believes that rapid population growth will deplete the world's resources and that the resulting period of scarcity will engender wars for the few resources that remain, bringing about the end of democratic governments in the West, owing to the need to suppress demand. Since neither author provides hard evidence for his forecasts, these works must be seen as primarily polemical in intent.*

Heilbroner's book is a tocsin, but its pessimistic tone lessens its value for policy making and renders it a potential danger lest it becomes a self-fulfilling prophecy. Kahn's book provides a program for action, but it is so optimistic that it may encourage complacency, and it greatly underestimates some of the political difficulties inherent in Third World development. Basically a polemic against imperialism and dependency theories, Kahn's book emphasizes a "trickle down" theory of development, with multinational corporations and Western investment serving as the catalysts. In his analysis, little mention is made of revolution or repression, although current efforts in the Third World to follow this path of development—e.g., Brazil—clearly suggest that coercion accompanies it. The question of fundamental social change within the Third World in order to end poverty, then, provides the explosive base of the North–South dispute, not only for the West and the East but for the current Third World elites in power as well. Revolution and/or repression have already played significant roles in this issue. How much of this will continue, and what form it will take, remain unanswered questions. Nevertheless, it is clear that the issue in some manner will dominate the global agenda. Its exact form will depend not only on perception, but on how well political decisions work to satisfy deprived values.

In this regard, the model of economic development that is adopted will have an important effect on political interactions. If the world market prohibits development that can alleviate poverty then the prospects for global and domestic stability are not good.[14] Yet even if the world market limits opportunity, the room for Third World actors to maneuver is probably greater than is usually believed to be the case.† It is for this reason that alternative modes of development that do not follow the advanced indus-

---

* In this regard, Heilbroner is somewhat more honest in that he acknowledges that he is not presenting any evidence, because, he says, no amount of evidence would convince the unconvinced and those who already share his position do not need evidence. Kahn's book is written in the same vein, but the author is prone to try to convince his readers with pseudo-scientific evidence or by substituting strong assertions for evidence. Cf. Herman Kahn, *The Next 200 Years* (New York: William Morrow, 1976), pp. 49, 54–57, 62, and Robert L. Heilbroner, *An Inquiry into the Human Prospect* (New York: Norton, 1974), pp. 23–27.

† This is a point made by a number of critics, and it is not entirely rejected by various dependency theorists themselves; see Tony Smith "The Underdevelopment of Development Literature: The Case of Dependency Theory," *World Politics* (January 1979), 31(2):257ff.

trial model, such as those promulgated by the Chinese or put forth by Ivan Illich, have attracted attention.* Clearly, the theory presented in this study is not able to predict which model of development will work, since it does not purport to explain economic behavior. However, it is clear from the model that frustration and failure lead to an escalation of hostility, which produces more disagreement, more negative actions, and more hostility. The longer any model of development fails to produce the prospect of alleviating economic dissatisfaction, the greater is the likelihood that the North–South issue will become a critical issue like the Cold War.

If development begins to succeed, however, that does not mean that conflict will disappear, only that this particular issue will not be the source of conflict. In the absence of a highly salient North–South dispute to keep the Third World unified, a number of regional struggles may increase in salience. The Arab–Israeli and Indian–Pakistani wars have already demonstrated the salience of such disputes, and have shown that they encourage the proliferation of nuclear weapons. Disputes and potential nuclear deterrence games between Brazil and Argentina, India and Pakistan, South Africa and the rest of Black Africa, and Iran and its neighbors, will not produce a peaceful world, but will prevent the North–South issue from becoming a critical issue. The prospect of a world composed of regional nuclear struggles poses a different and more long-term potential critical issue. The fact that the proliferation issue is already linked to energy, pollution, the North–South dispute, economic competition within the West (American hegemony over nuclear energy), and specific regional disputes is a portent of the future complexity of this issue.

The absence of a salient global critical issue may also have the effect of increasing domestic discord, particularly in an era when social change is promoted (but not caused) by a contagion effect. It is not surprising that a decline in the Cold War has coincided with an increase in the salience of a number of separatist and ethnic issues like Quebec separatism, Croation nationalism, Welsh and Scottish nationalism, Kurdish independence, Irish unification, cultural and linguistic autonomy in India,

*See Ivan Illich, *A History of Needs* (New York: Pantheon, 1978). For an excellent review of the issue positions on the New Economic Order, see Robert W. Cox, "Ideologies and the New International Economic Order," *International Organization* (Spring, 1979), 33(2):257–302.

Sri Lanka, and Belgium; tribal or religious rivalry in Burma, Chad, Nigeria, Uganda, Angola, and Zaïre; and racial conflict in Trinidad, the Sudan, and in Southeast Asia with the "overseas" Chinese. An examination of this last issue illustrates how such issues can become linked to larger global questions.

The issue of the "overseas" Chinese has its roots in the establishment of large Chinese communities in Southeast Asia during the late sixteenth and early seventeenth centuries, the final century of the Ming dynasty and a period of Chinese expansionism. In time, these communities became a source of nationalist sentiment and of opposition to the Manchu conquerors of China. The overseas communities grew and flourished during the era of European colonial dominance as a source of educated administrative and economic skills. In time, they came to dominate the urban and more modernized sectors of local economies, forming exclusive and advanced concentrations in predominantly agrarian and rural societies. Although communal conflicts exploded from time to time in Malaya, Burma, Indochina, Thailand, the Philippines, and Indonesia, the colonial presence in much of the area largely shielded the Chinese communities from the hatred and jealousy of ethnic majorities. With independence, this, of course, changed, and communal strife became endemic in these countries.

Local communal questions became deeply embedded in Cold War hostilities, particularly after the triumph of communism in China itself. Looked upon as local "fifth columnists" in Southeast Asia, the communities were utilized by the Maoist regime to acquire leverage in local politics. Declaring itself the protector of the overseas communities, the People's Republic provided aid in various forms to them and encouraged unrest during moments of deteriorating relations with local governments.* Ethnic Chinese were responsible for the Huk uprising in the Philippines, as well as the Malay Emergency, and constitute the bulk of the communist insurgents in Indonesia, Burma, and Thailand that continue to conduct operations against local regimes (which are dominated by non-Chinese ethnic groups). Local repression of the Chinese communities was largely undertaken in the name of anticommunism, the most

---

*Though the majority of overseas Chinese were ideologically anticommunist, they were proud of the growing status of the new regime and the cultural and political resurgence of China that it symbolized.

memorable of which was the wholesale slaughter of Chinese in Indonesia in 1965, after the overthrow of Sukarno, and the resulting seizure of Chinese property and businesses. In some respects, the issue of the overseas Chinese has become sharper with the decline of the Cold War, though it remains obscured by local fears of a united Vietnam and the growing shadow of Sino-Soviet competition. The fundamental ethnic hostility that underlies the issue is resurfacing (as Malaysian hostility to Chinese refugees from Vietnam reflects) without the "cover" formerly provided by the Cold War.

The appearance of all these issues, from racial conflicts to nuclear proliferation, is occurring in the absence of established rules to govern interaction, and as a consequence has stimulated numerous ad hoc rule-making games. The absence of rules accounts in part for the frequent recourse to force and the tendency of actors to behave unilaterally. This sense of disorganization has led all major actors, including Third World governments, to try to develop a new global order for making decisions. Consequently, a number of major planned rule-making games have been held to cope with the emergence of new problems. These include the convention on the Law of the Sea, the New International Economic Order talks, and the conferences on the environment, population, and food. This universalistic discussion marks a sharp break with previous rule-making games in history, which were confined to only the most powerful actors, and it remains to be seen whether less universalistic arrangements such as détente and OPEC-IEA will supplant these larger conferences.

The frequency of these conferences itself is further indication of the changing global order and the need to redefine the agenda. Whatever the eventual result of these formal and ad hoc rule-making games, the shape of the new political order will depend on three factors, or variable clusters—the nature of the issues under contention, the affect among the major contending actors, and the institutional setting in which decisions have to be made.

AN END AND A BEGINNING

Goethe once declared that "all theory . . . is gray, but the golden tree of actual life springs ever green." Yet, without theory, the tree of life remains a mystery, and with poor theory it is likely to wither. For the most part, the study of world politics remains without adequate theory at the present. For better or worse, the paradigm which held sway for centuries is irretrievably flawed. Less a guide to reality than a doctrine, its continued acceptance promises premature theoretical closure at best and misguided policy at worst. Global change is so swift, and the problems it brings in its train so complex and menacing, that incorrect theory is a luxury that is not easily afforded.

It is perhaps better to have no map of the world than to be guided by one that is badly flawed. The former condition at least encourages humility and caution. But the human mind will not permit itself to remain without models of the world for long, and humility, no matter how desirable, tends to disappear until or unless catastrophe strikes. Moreover, with or without models to understand them, the problems of global politics are real and will not be overcome by intellectual modesty or fatalism.

The work presented here has sought to produce the outlines of a new paradigm of global politics by identifying key stages and variables in the political process and the relationship among these. Turning from a definition of global politics as a struggle for power to a definition of it as the attempted authoritative allocation of values, the processes of actor and issue development, and the persistently tight relationship between these, are seen to be the components of a new paradigm and the elements of a new map to guide thinking about it. Whether the specific relationships identified or the hypotheses posited in the book are falsified or not, they do promise the bases of dynamic rather than static theory. Nor do we believe that everything we have asserted will be borne out by further research. If we did, we would be the victims of unconscionable hubris. What has been presented has profited from recent insights in a number of areas of political science and other disciplines, which have been wedded to one another. The result is something of a new map, the value of which remains to be determined.

REFERENCES

PREFACE

1. Kenneth N. Waltz, "Theory of International Relations," in Fred Greenstein and Nelson Polsby, eds., *Handbook of Political Science,* vol. 8, *International Politics* (Reading, Mass.: Addison-Wesley, 1975), p. 2. See also Waltz, *Theory of International Politics* (Reading, Mass.: Addison-Wesley, 1979), pp. 1–17.

2. Hubert M. Blalock, Jr., *Causal Inferences in Nonexperimental Research* (Chapel Hill: University of North Carolina Press, 1964), p. 6.

1. THE DECAY OF AN OLD PARADIGM

1. "Nature does not proceed by leaps," Linnaeus, *Philosophia Botanica,* sec. 77.

2. See Arnold Wolfers, *Discord and Collaboration* (Baltimore, Md.: Johns Hopkins University Press, 1962), p. 19; and Hans J. Morgenthau, *Politics Among Nations,* 5th ed., rev. (New York: Knopf, 1978), p. 4.

3. For a sample of this literature, see E. H. Carr, *The Twenty Years' Crisis, 1919–1939* (London: Macmillan, 1946); Thomas I. Cook and Malcolm Moos, *Power Through Purpose: The Realism of Idealism as a Basis for Foreign Policy* (Baltimore, Md.: Johns Hopkins University Press, 1954); John H. Herz, *Political Realism and Political Idealism* (Chicago: University of Chicago Press, 1951); Hans J. Morgenthau, *Politics Among Nations;* Morgenthau, *In Defense of the National Interest* (New York: Knopf, 1951); Morgenthau, *Scientific Man vs. Power Politics* (Chicago: University of Chicago Press, 1946); Kenneth W. Thompson, *Political Realism and the Crises of World Politics* (Princeton, N.J.: Princeton University Press, 1960); Robert E. Osgood, *Ideals and Self-Interest in*

America's Foreign Relations (Chicago: University of Chicago Press, 1953); Nicholas J. Spykman, *The Geography of the Peace* (New York: Harcourt, Brace, 1944); and George F. Kennan, *American Diplomacy, 1900–1950* (Chicago: University of Chicago Press, 1951).

4. Clive Parry, "The Function of Law in the International Community," in Max Sorensen, ed., *Manual of Public International Law* (New York: St. Martin's, 1968), p. 14. See also Leo Gross, "The Peace of Westphalia, 1648–1948," in Robert S. Wood, ed., *The Process of International Organization* (New York: Random House, 1971).

5. Morgenthau, *Politics Among Nations,* pp. 315, 316. See also Richard W. Mansbach, Yale H. Ferguson, and Donald E. Lampert, *The Web of World Politics* (Englewood Cliffs, N.J.: Prentice-Hall, 1976), pp. 7–19.

6. Thomas S. Kuhn, *The Structure of Scientific Revolutions,* 2d ed. (Chicago: University of Chicago Press, 1970), pp. 174–75. See also pp. 176–210 of the second edition, which clarify Kuhn's original statement.

7. Morgenthau, *Politics Among Nations,* p. 10.

8. Robert O. Keohane and Joseph S. Nye, Jr., eds. *Transnational Relations and World Politics* (Cambridge, Mass.: Harvard University Press, 1971).

9. J. P. Nettl, "The State as a Conceptual Variable," in Wolfram F. Hanreider, ed., *Comparative Foreign Policy: Theoretical Essays* (New York: McKay, 1971), p. 57.

10. Oran R. Young, "The Actors in World Politics," in James N. Rosenau, Vincent Davis, and Maurice A. East, eds., *The Analysis of International Politics* (New York: Free Press, 1972), p. 126. Emphasis in original.

11. Richard W. Mansbach, et al., *Web of World Politics,* p. ix.

12. Chadwick F. Alger, "The Impact of Cities on International Systems," *Ekistics* (November 1977), 44(264):246.

13. Karl Kaiser, "Transnational Politics: Toward A Theory of Multinational Politics," *International Organization* (Autumn 1971), 25(4):790–818.

14. Robert O. Keophane and Joseph Nye, Jr., *Power and Interdependence: World Politics in Transition* (Boston: Little, Brown, 1977), p. 5.

15. Graham T. Allison, *Essence of Decision* (Boston: Little, Brown, 1971); Morton H. Halperin, *Bureaucratic Politics and Foreign Policy* (Washington, D.C.: Brookings, 1974); and Graham T. Allison and Morton H. Halperin, "Bureaucratic Politics: A Paradigm and Some Policy Implications," in R. Tanter and R. H. Ullman, eds., *Theory and Policy in International Relations* (Princeton, N.J.: Princeton University Press, 1972), pp. 40–79.

16. Cf. Charles E. Lindblom, "The Science of 'Muddling Through,' " *Public Administration Review* (Spring 1959) 19:79–88; Sidney Verba, "Assumptions of Rationality and Non-Rationality in Models of the International System," in Klaus Knorr and Sidney Verba, eds., *The International System* (Princeton, N.J.: Princeton University Press, 1961), pp. 93–117; Allison, *Essence of Decision,;* Irving L. Janis, *Victims of Groupthink* (Boston: Houghton Mifflin, 1972); and John D.

Steinbruner, *The Cybernetic Theory of Decision* (Princeton, N.J.: Princeton University Press, 1974).

17. Cf. Charles F. Hermann, "Decision Structure and Process Influences on Foreign Policy" in Maurice A. East, Stephen A. Salmore, and Charles F. Hermann, eds., *Why Nations Act* (Beverly Hills, Calif.: Sage, 1978), p. 74.

18. James N. Rosenau, "Introduction: Political Science in a Shrinking World," in Rosenau, ed., *Linkage Politics,* (New York: Free Press, 1969), p. 2.

19. James N. Rosenau, "Pre-Theories and Theories of Foreign Policy," in R. Barry Farrell, ed., *Approaches to Comparative and International Politics* (Evanston, Ill.: Northwestern University Press, 1966), pp. 53–92.

20. John W. Burton, *World Society* (Cambridge: Cambridge University Press) 1972, p. 20.

21. *Ibid.,* p. 42.

22. See, for example, Fred W. Riggs, "International Relations as a Prismatic System," in Knorr and Verba, eds., *International System,* pp. 141–81.

23. James N. Rosenau, "Pre-Theories," and "Foreign Policy as an Issue Area," in James N. Rosenau, ed., *Domestic Sources of Foreign Policy* (New York: Free Press, 1967), pp. 11–51.

24. See Robert A. Dahl, *Who Governs?* (New Haven, Conn.: Yale University Press, 1961).

25. Theodore J. Lowi, "American Business, Public Policy, Case-Studies, and Political Theory," *World Politics* (July 1964), 16(4):677–715.

26. Robert O. Keohane and Joseph S. Nye, Jr., "Transnational Relations and World Politics," in *Transnational Relations and World Politics,* p. 734.

27. Michael K. O'Leary, "The Role of Issue," in James N. Rosenau, ed., *In Search of Global Patterns* (New York: Free Press, 1976), pp. 318–26.

28. Mansbach et al., *Web of World Politics,* pp. 285ff.

29. William D. Coplin, Stephen Mills, and Michael K. O'Leary, "The PRINCE Concepts and the Study of Foreign Policy," in Patrick J. McGowan, ed., *Sage International Yearbook of Foreign Policy Studies* (Beverly Hills, Calif.: Sage, 1974), 1:73–103. For a more general treatment, see William D. Coplin and Michael K. O'Leary, *Everyman's PRINCE* (North Scituate, Mass.: Duxbury Press, 1972).

30. John Handelman, John A. Vasquez, Michael K. O'Leary and William A. Coplin, "Color It Morgenthau: A Data-Based Assessment of Quantitative International Relations," (paper presented to the International Studies Association, New York City, 1973), and William D. Coplin, *Introduction to International Politics,* 2nd ed. (Chicago: Rand-McNally, 1974), ch. 13.

31. Kuhn, *Scientific Revolutions,* pp. 52–53.

32. Imre Lakatos, "Falsification and the Methodology of Scientific Research Programmes," in Imre Lakatos and Alan Musgrave, eds., *Criticism and the Growth of Knowledge* (Cambridge: Cambridge University Press, 1970), p. 116.

33. Kenneth N. Waltz, "Theory of International Relations" in Fred Green-

stein and Nelson Polsby, eds., *Handbook of Political Science;* vol. 8, *International Politics* (Reading, Mass.: Addison-Wesley, 1975), p. 73.

34. John A. Vasquez, "Colouring It Morgenthau: New Evidence for an Old Thesis," *British Journal of International Studies* (October 1979), vol. 5, table 10.

35. *Ibid.,* table 11.

36. Mansbach et al., *Web of World Politics,* pp. 214–17.

37. John A. Vasquez, "Statistical Findings in International Politics," *International Studies Quarterly* (June 1976), 20(2):196.

2. FROM THE ISSUE OF POWER TO THE POWER OF ISSUES

1. Robert O. Keohane and Joseph S. Nye, *Power and Interdependence: World Politics in Transition* (Boston: Little Brown, 1977), p. 25. Emphasis in original.

2. David Easton, *A Framework for Political Analysis* (Englewood Cliffs, N.J.: Prentice Hall, 1965), p. 50. See also Easton, *The Political System* (New York: Knopf, 1953), pp. 129–42.

3. David Easton, *A Systems Analysis of Political Life* (New York: Wiley, 1965), p. 48.

4. See Donald E. Lampert, Lawrence Falkowski and Richard W. Mansbach, "Is There an International System?" *International Studies Quarterly* (1978), 22(1):143–67, and P. Dale Dean, Jr., and John A. Vasquez, "From Power Politics to Issue Politics: Bipolarity and Multipolarity in Light of a New Paradigm," *Western Political Quarterly* (March 1976), 29(1):7–28.

5. James N. Rosenau, "Pre-Theories and Theories of Foreign Policy," in Rosenau, *The Scientific Study of Foreign Policy* (New York: Free Press, 1971), p. 99.

6. *Ibid.,* pp. 143, 145.

7. *Ibid.,* p. 145.

8. *Ibid.,* p. 145. Emphasis in original.

9. *Ibid.,* pp. 146–47.

10. Theodore J. Lowi, "American Business, Public Policy, Case Studies and Political Theory," *World Politics* (July 1964), 16(4):677–715.

11. Theodore J. Lowi, "Making Democracy Safe for the World: National Politics and Foreign Policy," in James N. Rosenau, ed., *Domestic Sources of Foreign Policy* (New York: Free Press, 1967), footnote 61, p. 325. Other efforts by Lowi to expand his original typology include "Decision Making vs. Policy-Making: Toward an Antidote for Technocracy," *Public Administration Review* (May/June 1970), 30:314–25; and "Four Systems of Policy, Politics, and Choice," *Public Administration Review* (July/August 1972) 32:298–310. For a review of efforts to elaborate the Lowi typology, see Lewis A. Froman, Jr., "The Categorization of Policy Contents," in Austin Ranney, ed., *Political Science and Public Policy* (Chicago: Markham, 1968), pp. 41–52.

12. Theodore J. Lowi, "American Business, Public Policy, Case Studies and Political Theory," pp. 689–90.

13. See Charles F. Hermann, "Some Issues in the Study of International Crisis," in Charles F. Hermann, ed., *International Crisis: Insights from Behavioral Research* (New York: Free Press, 1972), p. 13. For an alternative definition of crisis that de-emphasizes time constraints, see Glenn H. Snyder and Paul Diesing, *Conflict Among Nations: Bargaining, Decision Making, and System Structure in International Crises* (Princeton, N.J.: Princeton University Press, 1977), pp. 8–9.

14. Lowi, "American Business, Public Policy, Case Studies and Political Theory," pp. 690–91.

15. William Zimmerman, "Issue Area and Foreign-Policy Process: A Research Note in Search of a General Theory," *American Political Science Review* (December 1973), 67(2):1204–12.

16. Arnold Wolfers, "The Pole of Power and the Pole of Indifference," in Wolfers, *Discord and Collaboration: Essays on International Politics* (Baltimore, Md.: Johns Hopkins Press, 1962), pp. 81–02.

17. Arnold Wolfers, "The Actors in International Politics," in *ibid.*, p. 14.

18. *Ibid.*, p. 16.

19. *Ibid.*, p. 16.

20. See Graham T. Allison, *Essence of Decision: Explaining the Cuban Missile Crisis* (Boston: Little Brown, 1971), pp. 10–38.

21. William Zimmerman, "Issue Area," p. 1205.

22. James N. Rosenau, "Pre-Theories and Theories of Foreign Policy," p. 141.

23. See Robert A. Dahl, *Who Governs?* (New Haven, Conn.: Yale University Press, 1961).

24. M. Brecher, B. Steinberg, and J. Stein, "A Framework for Research on Foreign Policy Behavior," *Journal of Conflict Resolution* (March 1969), 13(1):75–101.

25. *Ibid.*, p. 88.

26. On this project, see James N. Rosenau, Philip M. Burgess, and Charles F. Hermann, "The Adaptation of Foreign Policy Research: A Case Study of an Anti-Case Study Project," *International Studies Quarterly* (March 1973), 17(1):119–44; and James N. Rosenau, ed., *Comparing Foreign Policies* (Beverly Hills, Calif.: Sage, 1974); and *In Search of Global Patterns* (New York: Free Press 1976) for examples of the research produced.

27. Charles F. Hermann, "Decision Structure and Process Influences on Foreign Policy," in Maurice East, Stephen Salmore, and Charles Hermann, eds., *Why Nations Act* (Beverly Hills, Calif.: Sage, 1978), p. 76.

28. Thomas L. Brewer, "Issue and Context Variation in Foreign Policy," *Journal of Conflict Resolution*, (March 1973), 17(1):89–115.

29. Charles F. Hermann, "International Crisis as a Situational Variable," in James N. Rosenau, ed., *International Politics and Foreign Policy*, rev. ed. (New York: Free Press, 1969), pp. 409–21.

30. Brewer, "Issue and Context Variation," table 6, p. 107.

31. *Ibid.*, p. 95.

32. *Ibid.*, pp. 103, 105–7.

33. R. J. Rummel, "U.S. Foreign Relations: Conflict, Cooperation, and Attribute Distances," in Bruce M. Russett, ed., *Peace, War, and Numbers* (Beverly Hills, Calif.: Sage, 1972), pp. 71–115.

34. Theodore J. Lowi, "American Business, Public Policy, Case Studies and Political Theory," p. 689.

35. Michael T. Hayes, "The Semi-Sovereign Pressure Groups: A Critique of Current Theory and an Alternative Typology," *Journal of Politics,* (February 1978), 40(1):138.

36. See Walter Lippmann, *The Public Philosophy* (Boston: Little Brown, 1955) and George F. Kennan, *American Diplomacy, 1900–1950* (Chicago: University of Chicago Press, 1951).

37. Mancur Olson, Jr., *The Logic of Collective Action* (Cambridge, Mass.: Harvard University Press, 1965), p. 14; and Norman Frolich, Joe A. Oppenheimer, and Oran R. Young, *Political Leadership and Collective Goods* (Princeton, N.J.: Princeton University Press, 1971), p. 3.

38. Robert Salisbury, "The Analysis of Public Policy: A Search for Theories and Roles," in Austin Ranney, ed., *Political Science and Public Policy* (Chicago: Markham, 1968), p. 157.

39. Theodore J. Lowi, "Making Democracy Safe for the World," pp. 325–26.

40. William D. Coplin, *Introduction to International Politics,* 2d edition (Chicago: Rand McNally, 1974), p. 86.

41. See *ibid.*, p. 88.

42. *Ibid.*, p. 89.

43. See Thomas Sloan, "Dynamics of Conflict Reduction in the Middle East: An Exploratory Study," (Department of Political Science, University of North Carolia, Chapel Hill, n.d.), pp. 13–14.

44. See Michael K. O'Leary, William D. Coplin, Donald J. McMaster and Esther L. Booth, "A Codebook and Brief Description of Issue-Coded WEIS Data (1966–1969)," (International Relations Program Reference Group Theory Working Paper #2, Syracuse University, 1975); and Michael K. O'Leary and Howard B. Shapiro, "Instructions for Coding Foreign Policy Acts," (PRINCE research Studies, Paper #8, International Relations Program, Syracuse University, 1972).

45. Richard W. Mansbach and John A. Vasquez, "Coding Issues in World Politics: A New Approach" (Rutgers University, 1977). Manuscript.

46. Keohane and Nye, *Power and Interdependence,* p. 65.

47. Bruce M. Russett, *International Regions and the International System: A Study in Political Ecology* (Chicago: Rand McNally, 1967), p. 63. See also Hayward R. Alker, Jr., and Bruce M. Russett, *World Politics in the General Assembly* (New Haven, Conn.: Yale University Press, 1965), chs. 3–6. Russett performed a similar analysis for the 1963 General Assembly Session. Russett, *International Regions and the International System,* pp. 63–65.

48. *Ibid.*, p. 63.

49. See Roger W. Cobb and Charles D. Elder, *Participation in American Politics: The Dynamics of Agenda-Building,* (Boston: Allyn and Bacon, 1972) p. 40, footnote 17. This is very similar to the list provided by Harold J. Lasswell and Abraham Kaplan, *Power and Society* (New Haven, Conn.: Yale University Press, 1950), pp. 55–56.

50. See Ted Robert Gurr, *Why Men Rebel* (Princeton, N.J.: Princeton University Press, 1970), p. 25; and Lowell Dittmer, "Political Culture and Political Symbolism: Toward a Theoretical Synthesis," *World Politics* (July 1977), 26(4):558.

51. Gurr, *Why Men Rebel,* p. 25.

52. See Murray Edelman, *The Symbolic Uses of Politics* (Urbana: University of Illinois Press, 1964), pp. 133–34.

53. Cited in Kenneth N. Waltz, *Man, the State, and War* (New York: Columbia University Press, 1959), p. 188.

54. Inis L. Claude, Jr., *Swords Into Plowshares,* 3d ed. (New York: Random House, 1964), p. 313.

55. See, for example, Bruce M. Russett, *What Price Vigilance? The Burdens of National Defense* (New Haven: Yale University Press, 1970), pp. 59–72.

3. THE ELEMENTS OF A NEW PARADIGM

1. Thomas S. Kuhn, *The Structure of Scientific Revolutions,* 2d ed. (Chicago: University of Chicago Press, 1970), p. 15.

2. Robert E. Osgood, *Ideals and Self-Interest in America's Foreign Relations* (Chicago: University of Chicago Press, 1953), p. 9. The author goes on to "reinterpret" major events in the history of American foreign relations in light of realist "insights."

4. AGENDA POLITICS

1. Roger W. Cobb, Jennie Keith-Ross and Marc Howard Ross, "Agenda Building as a Comparative Political Process," *American Political Science Review* (March 1976), 70(1):126.

2. Roger W. Cobb and Charles D. Elder, *Participation in American Politics: The Dynamics of Agenda Building* (Boston: Allyn & Bacon, 1972), p. 14.

3. See Anthony Downs, "Up and Down with Ecology—the 'Issue Attention Cycle'," *The Public Interest* (Summer 1972), 28:38–50.

4. See Hedley Bull, *The Anarchical Society* (New York: Columbia University Press, 1977) and his earlier article, "Society and Anarchy in International Relations," in Herbert Butterfield and Martin Wight, eds., *Diplomatic Investigations* (London: Allen and Unwin, 1966), pp. 40–48. See also Oran R. Young, "Anarchy and Social Choice: Reflections on the International Polity," *World Politics* (January 1978), 30(2):241–63.

5. Wolfgang Friedmann, *The Future of the Oceans* (New York: Braziller, 1971), p. 2.

6. J. L. Brierly, *The Law of Nations,* 5th ed. (New York: Oxford University Press, 1955), p. 176.

7. *Ibid.,* p. 185.

8. Theodore J. Lowi, "American Business, Public Policy, Case Studies and Political Theory," *World Politics* (July 1964), 16(4):713.

9. See, for example, Evan Luard, "Who Gets What on the Seabed?" *Foreign Policy* (Winter 1972–73), no. 9, pp. 132–47.

10. See Dennis L. Meadows et al., *The Limits to Growth* (New York: Universe Books, 1972).

11. Winston S. Churchill, *Their Finest Hour* (Boston: Houghton Mifflin, 1949), p. 133.

12. Cited *ibid.,* p. 129.

13. C. Fred Bergsten, "The Threat from the Third World," *Foreign Policy* (Summer 1973), no. 11, p. 108. For a dissenting view, see Stephen D. Krasner, "Oil Is the Exception," *Foreign Policy* (Spring 1974), no. 14, pp. 68–84. Bergsten reiterates his position in "The Threat Is Real," *Foreign Policy* (Spring 1974), no. 14, pp. 84–90.

14. Cobb and Elder, *Participation in American Politics,* pp. 103–9.

15. William A. Gamson, "Reputation and Resources in Community Politics," *American Journal of Sociology* (September 1966), 72:122. See also Peter Bachrach and Morton Baratz, *Power and Poverty* (New York: Oxford University Press, 1970), p. 58; and Thomas C. Schelling, *Arms and Influence* (New Haven, Conn.: Yale University Press, 1966), pp. 69–91.

16. Peter Bachrach and Morton Baratz, "Two Faces of Power," *American Political Science Review* (1962), 56:947–952; Bachrach and Baratz, "Decisions and Nondecisions: An Analytical Framework," *American Political Science Review* (1963), 57:632–42; and Bachrach and Elihu Bergman, *Power and Choice: The Formulation of American Population Policy* (Waltham, Mass.: Lexington Books, 1973).

17. Peter Bachrach and Morton Baratz, *Power and Poverty,* p. 44.

18. See Sidney Verba and Norman H. Nie, *Participation in America* (New York: Harper & Row, 1972), pp. 13–22, 263–64.

19. See Robert O. Keohane and Joseph S. Nye, Jr., *Power and Interdependence* (Boston: Little, Brown, 1977), p. 35.

20. See, for example, Joseph S. Nye, Jr., "UNCTAD: Poor Nations' Pressure Group," in Robert W. Cox and Harold K. Jacobson, *The Anatomy of Influence: Decision Making in International Organization* (New Haven, Conn.: Yale University Press, 1973), pp. 334–70.

21. See, for example, the role of nonstate actors in raising the pollution issue in John A. Vasquez, "Alternative Views of the U.N. Conference on the Human Environment," in John Handelman, Howard Shapiro, and John Vasquez, *Introductory Case Studies for International Relations* (Chicago: Rand McNally, 1974), ch. 4.

22. Roger Cobb, et al., "Agenda Building as a Comparative Political Process," pp. 131–32.

23. E. E. Schattschneider, *The Semi-Sovereign People* (New York: Holt, Rinehart & Winston, 1960), p. 1.

24. See Richard W. Mansbach et al., *The Web of World Politics: Nonstate Actors in the Global System* (Englewood Cliffs, N.J.: Prentice-Hall, 1976), pp. 104–35.

25. Robert A. Dahl, *Who Governs? Democracy and Power in an American City* (New Haven, Conn.: Yale University Press, 1961), p. 305.

26. Hans J. Morgenthau, "Another 'Great Debate': The National Interests of the United States," *American Political Science Review* (December 1952), 66(4):961–68.

27. Glenn H. Snyder and Paul Diesing, *Conflict Among Nations: Bargaining, Decision Making, and System Structure in International Crises* (Princeton, N.J.: Princeton University Press, 1977), p. 25.

28. Thucydides, *History of The Peloponnesian War,* trans. Rex Warner (Baltimore, Md.: Penguin, 1954), pp. 182–83.

29. James Sundquist, *Dynamics of the Party System* (Washington, D.C.: Brookings, 1973), pp. 28–36.

30. Anthony Downs, "Up and Down with Ecology—The 'Issue Attention Cycle'," 38–50.

31. Charles A. McClelland, "The Beginning, Duration, and Abatement of International Crises: Comparisons in Two Conflict Arenas," in Charles F. Hermann, ed., *International Crisis: Insights from Behavioral Research* (New York: Free Press, 1972), pp. 83–109.

32. Charles F. Hermann, "International Crisis as a Situational Variable," in James N. Rosenau, ed., *International Politics and Foreign Policy,* rev. ed. (New York: Free Press, 1969), pp. 409–22.

33. See Dean G. Pruitt, "Stability and Sudden Change in Interpersonal and International Affairs," in Rosenau, ed., *International Politics and Foreign Policy,* pp. 393–94; Oran Young, *The Politics of Force* (Princeton, N.J.: Princeton University Press, 1968), Ch. 4.

34. See Robert Dubin, "Industrial Conflict and Social Welfare," *Journal of Conflict Resolution* (June 1957), 1(2):187.

35. Richard N. Rosecrance, *Peace or War?* (New York: McGraw-Hill, 1973), p. 34.

36. Cited in Inis L. Claude, Jr., *Swords Into Plowshares,* 3d ed. (New York: Random House, 1964), p. 201.

37. "The wound unuttered lives deep within the breast," Vergil, *Aeneid,* iv, 67.

38. See Theodore Caplow, *Principles of Organization* (New York: Harcourt, Brace, 1964), pp. 326–65.

39. Frank H. Denton, "Some Regularities in International Conflict, 1820–1949," *Background* (February 1966), pp. 283–96; Richard N. Rosecrance, *Action and Reaction in World Politics* (Boston: Little, Brown, 1963).

Appendix

40. Jean Lacoutre, *Ho Chi Minh: A Political Biography* (New York: Vintage Books, 1968), p. 3.

41. Adam B. Ulam, *The Rivals* (New York: Viking, 1971), p. 12.

42. Clark M. Clifford, "A Viet Nam Reappraisal," *Foreign Affairs* (July 1969), 47(4):603.

43. Cited in *The Vietnam Hearings,* with an introduction by J. William Fulbright (New York: Vintage Books, 1966), p. 9.

44. Cited in U.S. Senate, Committee on Foreign Relations, *The United States and Vietnam: 1944–1947* (Washington, D.C.: Government Printing Office, 1972), p. 21.

45. See also the documents in *The Pentagon Papers* as published by the *New York Times* (New York: Bantam Books, 1971), pp. 27–38, esp. 37–38.

46. Wilfrid Knapp, *A History of War and Peace 1939–1965* (New York: Oxford University Press, 1967), p. 215.

47. *The Pentagon Papers,* p. 38.

48. For a general description of the events, see Chalmers M. Roberts, "The Day We Didn't Go to War," in Wesley R. Fishel, ed., *Vietnam: Anatomy of a Conflict* (Itasca, Ill.: Peacock, 1968), pp. 28–36.

49. Dwight D. Eisenhower, *Mandate for Change* (Garden City, N.Y.: Doubleday, 1963), p. 373–74.

50. *The Pentagon Papers,* p. 39.

51. *Ibid.,* pp. 10, 11.

52. *Ibid.,* p. 14.

53. Bernard B. Fall, *The Two Viet-Nams,* 2nd ed. (New York: Praeger, 1967), p. 233.

54. *The Pentagon Papers,* pp. 15ff.

55. Robert Scheer and Warren Hinckle, "The Viet-Nam Lobby," in Marcus G. Raskin and Bernard B. Fall, eds., *The Viet-Nam Reader* (New York: Vintage Books, 1965), p. 68.

56. *Ibid.,* p. 68.

57. For more on Lansdale's activities on Diem's behalf, see David Wise and Thomas B. Ross, *The Invisible Government* (New York: Bantam Books, 1964), pp. 167–69.

58. Cited in *The Pentagon Papers,* p. 23.

59. *Ibid.,* p. 164.

60. *Ibid.,* p. 67.

61. *Ibid.,* p. 432.

62. *Ibid.,* p. 128.

63. *Ibid.,* p. 459.

64. Townsend Hoopes, *The Limits of Intervention* (New York: McKay, 1969), p. 92.

65. Cited in *ibid.,* pp. 93–94.

66. Cited in William M. Safire, *Before the Fall: An Inside View of the Pre-Watergate White House* (Garden City: Doubleday, 1975), p. 452. For a fuller discussion, see Henry A. Kissinger, *White House Years* (Boston: Little, Brown, 1979), pp. 163–94, 684–783, and 1049–96.

67. Cited in Tad Szulc, "Behind the Vietnam Cease-Fire Agreement," *Foreign Policy* (Summer 1974), no. 15, p. 35.

68. Cited in Michael Roskin, "An American Metternich: Henry A. Kissinger and the Global Balance of Power," in Frank J. Merli and Theodore A. Wilson, eds., *Makers of American Diplomacy* (New York: Scribner, 1974), p. 698.

69. Frank Snepp, *Decent Interval* (New York: Random House, 1977), pp. 29, 51.

70. *Ibid.*, p. 28.

71. *Ibid.*, p. 579.

72. See Tai Sung An, "Turmoil in Indochina: The Vietnam-Cambodia Conflict," *Asian Affairs* (March/April 1978), 5(4):245–56.

5. THE BIRTH AND DEATH OF POLITICAL ACTORS

1. J. P. Nettl, "The State As a Conceptual Variable," *World Politics,* (July 1968), 20(4):560.

2. Polybius, "The Histories," in William Ebenstein, ed., *Great Political Thinkers,* 4th ed. (New York: Holt, Rinehart, & Winston, 1969), p. 116.

3. *The Politics of Aristotle,* translated by Ernest Barker (New York: Oxford University Press, 1969), p. 1.

4. See Lester W. Milbrath, *Political Participation* (Chicago: Rand McNally, 1965); Alex Inkeles, "Participant Citizenship in Six Developing Nations," *American Political Science Review* (December 1969), 63(4):1120–41; Norman H. Nie, G. Bingham Powell, Jr. and Kenneth Prewitt, "Social Structure and Political Participation: Development Relationships," *American Political Science Review* (June and September 1969), 63(1, 2): pp. 362–78, 808–32; Marvin Olsen, "Social and Political Participation," *American Sociological Review* (1970), 35:682–96; Sidney Verba and Norman H. Nie, *Participation in America* (New York: Harper & Row, 1972); Sidney Verba, Norman H. Nie, Jae-On Kim, *Participation and Political Equality* (New York: Cambridge University Press, 1978).

5. Nie, Powell, and Prewitt, "Social Structure and Political Participation."

6. For size, see Maurice A. East, "Size and Foreign Policy Behavior: A Test of Two Models," *World Politics* (July 1973), 25(4):556–76; Rudolph J. Rummel, "Some Empirical Findings on Nations and Their Behavior," *World Politics* (January 1969), 21(2):226–41. For development, see Stephen A. Salmore and Charles F. Hermann, "The Effects of Size, Development, and Accountability on Foreign Policy," *Peace Research Society Papers* (1969), 14:15–30.

7. Maurice A. East and Charles F. Hermann, "Do Nation-Types Account for Foreign Policy Behavior?" in Rosenau, ed., *Comparing Foreign Nations,* pp. 269–305.

8. *Ibid.,* p. 290, table 2.

9. These findings can be found respectively in East and Hermann, "Nation-Types," tables 6, 6, 8, 3, and 4.

10. James Kean and Patrick J. McGowan, "National Attributes and Foreign Policy Participation: A Path Analysis" in Patrick J. McGowan, ed., *Sage International Yearbook of Foreign Policy Studies,* vol. 1 (Beverly Hills, Calif.: Sage, 1973), p. 226.

11. See Johan Galtung, "A Structural Theory of Aggression," *Journal of Peace Research* (1964), 1(2):95–119; and R. J. Rummel, "A Status-Field Theory of International Relations," in R. J. Rummel, ed. *Field Theory Evolving* (Beverly Hills, Calif.: Sage, 1977), pp. 199–255.

12. See Daniel Lerner's description of traditional village life in Turkey in *The Passing of Traditional Society* (New York: Free Press, 1958), p. 24.

13. Milbrath, *Political Participation,* p. 113.

14. William D. Coplin and J. Martin Rochester, "The Permanent Court of International Justice, the International Court of Justice, the League of Nations and the United Nations, A Comparative Empirical Survey," *American Political Science Review* (June 1972), 66(2):529–51.

15. Verba and Nie, *Participation in America,* chap. 10.

16. See Robert C. Angell, "The Growth of Transnational Participation," *Journal of Social Issues,* (1967), 23(1):122–24.

17. See, for example, Alexander J. Groth, *Comparative Politics: A Distributive Approach* (New York: Macmillan, 1971), pp. 24–25.

18. Sheldon S. Wolin, *Politics and Vision* (Boston: Little, Brown, 1960), p. 275.

19. Karl W. Deutsch, et al., *Political Community and the North Atlantic Area* (Princeton, N.J.: Princeton University Press, 1957), p. 7.

20. See *ibid.*

21. See Edward T. Hall, *The Silent Language* (Garden City, N.Y.: Doubleday, 1973).

22. See Karl W. Deutsch, *Nationalism and Social Communication,* 2nd ed. (Cambridge, Mass.: MIT Press, 1966).

23. Richard W. Mansbach et al., *The Web of World Politics* (Englewood Cliffs, N.J.: Prentice-Hall, 1976), p. 5.

24. See, for example, Amitai Etzioni, *A Comparative Analysis of Complex Organizations* (New York: Free Press, 1961), pp. 17–18.

25. See, for example, William H. Riker, *Federalism: Origin, Operation, Maintenance* (Boston: Little, Brown, 1964); Thomas N. Frank, ed., *Why Federations Fail* (New York: New York University Press, 1968); and Carl J. Friedrich, *Trends of Federalism in Theory and Practice* (New York: Praeger, 1968).

26. James P. Sewell, *Functionalism and World Politics* (Princeton, N.J.: Princeton University Press, 1966), p. 3. See also David Mitrany, *A Working Peace System* (London: Royal Institute of International Affairs, 1943); Ernst B. Haas, *Beyond the Nation-State: Functionalism and International Organization*

(Stanford: Stanford University Press, 1964); and Ernst B. Haas, "The Study of Regional Integration: Reflections on the Joy and Anguish of Pretheorizing," *International Organization,* (Autumn 1970), 24(4):607–46.

27. See, for example, Lucian W. Pye, *Aspects of Political Development* (Boston: Little, Brown, 1966).

28. See Fred W. Riggs, "The Nation-State and Other Actors," in James N. Rosenau, ed., *International Politics and Foreign Policy,* rev. ed. (New York: Free Press, 1969), p. 91.

29. Oran R. Young, "The Actors in World Politics," in James N. Rosenau, Vincent Davis and Maurice A. East, eds., *The Analysis of International Politics,* (New York: Free Press, 1972), p. 136. For a discussion of the variety of actors in global politics, see Mansbach et al, *Web of World Politics.*

30. See Adam Przeworski and Henry Teune, *The Logic of Comparative Social Inquiry* (New York: Wiley, 1970), p. 30.

31. Roger Morris, *Uncertain Greatness: Henry Kissinger and American Foreign Policy* (New York: Harper & Row, 1977), pp. 123–130.

32. See, for example, Graham T. Allison and Morton H. Halperin, "Bureaucratic Politics: A Paradigm and Some Policy Implications," in Raymond Tanter and Richard H. Ullman, eds., *Theory and Policy in International Relations* (Princeton, N.J.: Princeton University Press, 1972), pp. 40–79.

33. James N. Rosenau, "Introduction: Political Science in a Shrinking World," in Rosenau, ed., *Linkage Politics* (New York: Free Press, 1969), p. 5.

34. John H. Herz, *International Politics in the Atomic Age* (New York: Columbia University Press, 1959), pp. 96–108 and *passim.*

35. James N. Rosenau, "Pre-Theories and Theories of Foreign Policy," in Rosenau, *The Scientific Study of Foreign Policy* (New York: Free Press, 1971), pp. 116–32.

36. For a theoretical elaboration of this process see Johan Galtung, "A Structural Theory of Imperialism," *Journal of Peace Research* (1971), 8(1):81–117.

37. See Alpheus Thomas Mason and William M. Beaney, *The Supreme Court in a Free Society* (New York: Norton, 1968), pp. 57–59.

38. See Sidney Verba et al., "Public Opinion and the War in Vietnam," *American Political Science Review* (June 1967), 62:2; and John E. Mueller, *War, Presidents and Public Opinion* (New York: John Wiley, 1973).

39. See "70,000 to 100,000 Young Men Could Face Prosecution," *New York Times,* December 28, 1971.

40. See Morton H. Halperin, Jerry J. Berman, Robert Borosage, and Christine M. Marwick, *The Lawless State: The Crimes of the U.S. Intelligence Agencies* (New York: Penguin, 1976).

41. James A. Nathan and James K. Oliver, *United States Foreign Policy and World Order* (Boston: Little, Brown, 1976), p. 572.

42. For analyses of subagencies of government as potential competitors, see Morton H. Halperin and Arnold Kanter, eds., *Readings in American Foreign Policy: A Bureaucratic Perspective* (Boston: Little, Brown, 1973), *passim.*

43. Martin Wight, "Why Is There No International Theory?" in Herbert Butterfield and Martin Wight, eds., *Diplomatic Investigations* (Cambridge, Mass.: Harvard University Press, 1968), p. 21.

44. Karl Kaiser, "Transnational Politics: Toward a Theory of Multinational Politics," *International Organization* (Autumn 1971), 25(4):792.

45. Charles F. Hermann, "International Crisis as a Situational Varible," in Rosenau, ed., *International Politics and Foreign Policy,* p. 146.

46. Irving L. Janis, *Victims of Groupthink: A Psychological Study of Foreign-Policy Decisions and Fiascoes* (Boston: Houghton Mifflin, 1972), p. 5.

47. Roger H. Hull, *The Irish Triangle: Conflict in Northern Ireland* (Princeton, N.J.: Princeton University Press, 1976), p. 19.

48. Henry A. Kissinger, *The Troubled Partnership* (Garden City, N.Y.: Anchor, 1966), p. 9. On a theoretical level there is some interesting empirical evidence for this proposition. See Ole Holsti, Terrence Hopmann, and John Sullivan, *Unity and Disintegration in International Alliances* (New York: John Wiley, 1973).

49. See, for example, K. J. Holsti and Thomas Allen Levy, "Bilateral Institutions and Transgovernmental Relations Between Canada and the United States," *International Organization* (Autumn 1974), 28(4):875–901.

50. See Mancur Olson, Jr., *The Logic of Collective Action* (Cambridge, Mass.: Harvard University Press, 1965).

51. Alan Bullock, *Hitler, a Study in Tyranny,* rev. ed., (New York: Harper & Row, 1964), p. 313.

52. Ted Robert Gurr, *Why Men Rebel* (Princeton, N.J.: Princeton University Press, 1970), p. 134.

53. *The Federalist,* No. 10 (New York: Modern Library, n.d.), p. 54.

54. Lewis Coser, *The Functions of Social Conflict* (New York: Free Press, 1956), p. 151.

55. Ted R. Gurr with Charles Ruttenberg, *Cross-National Studies of Civil Violence* (Washington, D.C.: Center for Research on Social Systems, American University, 1969).

56. See Terry L. Deibel, "A Guide to International Divorce," *Foreign Policy* (Spring 1978), no. 30: pp. 17–36.

57. See Allison and Halperin, "Bureaucratic Politics: A Paradigm and Some Policy Implications," for an overview.

58. Charles F. Hermann, "Decision Structure and Process Influences on Foreign Policy," in Maurice A. East, Stephen A. Salmore, and Charles F. Hermann, eds., *Why Nations Act* (Beverly Hills, Calif.: Sage, 1978), p. 74.

6. DETERMINING ISSUE POSITIONS

1. William D. Coplin, Stephen Mills, and Michael K. O'Leary, "The PRINCE Concepts and the Study of Foreign Policy," in Patrick J. McGowan, ed., *Sage*

International Yearbook of Foreign Policy Studies, vol. 1 (Beverly Hills, Calif.: Sage, 1973), p. 74.

2. Richard C. Snyder, H. W. Bruck and Burton Sapin, eds., *Foreign Policy Decision Making* (New York: Free Press, 1962).

3. Richard C. Snyder and Glenn D. Paige, "The U.S. Decision to Resist Aggression in Korea," *Administrative Science Quarterly* (1958), 3:341–78; Glenn D. Paige, *The Korean Decision* (New York: Free Press, 1968); Charles F. Hermann, "Threat, Time, and Surprise," in Hermann, ed., *International Crisis* (New York: Free Press, 1972), pp. 187–211; and Ole R. Holsti, Robert C. North, and Richard A. Brody, "Perception and Action in the 1914 Crisis," in J. David Singer, ed., *Quantitative International Politics* (New York: Free Press, 1968), pp. 85–123.

4. James N. Rosenau, "Comparative Foreign Policy: Fad, Fantasy, or Field?" and "Pre-Theories and Theories of Foreign Policy" in Rosenau, *The Scientific Study of Foreign Policy* (New York: Free Press, 1971), pp. 67–94 and 95–149 respectively.

5. See James N. Rosenau, ed., *Comparing Foreign Policies* (New York: Halsted, 1974), and Maurice A. East, Stephen Salmore and Charles F. Hermann, *Why Nations Act* (Beverly Hills, Calif.: Sage, 1978).

6. William D. Coplin and Michael K. O'Leary, "A Simulation Model for the Analysis and Explanation of International Interactions," (paper presented to the International Studies Association, San Juan, Puerto Rico, 1971). See also Coplin, Stephen Mills, and Michael K. O'Leary, "PRINCE Concepts," pp. 73–103.

7. David Vital, *The Inequality of States: A Study of the Small Power* (New York: Oxford University Press), 1967, p. 8.

8. See Bruce M. Russett, *International Regions and the International System: A Study in Political Ecology* (Chicago: Rand McNally, 1967), pp. 41–46.

9. See Graham T. Allison, *Essence of Decision* (Boston: Little, Brown, 1971).

10. See William A. Gamson, "A Theory of Coalition Formation," *American Sociological Review* (1961), 26(3):373–82; and Joseph H. de Rivera, *The Psychological Dimension of Foreign Policy* (Columbus, Ohio: Charles E. Merrill, 1968), pp. 107–12.

11. William H. Riker, *The Theory of Political Coalitions* (New Haven, Conn.: Yale University Press, 1962), pp. 32ff.

12. John Steinbruner, "Beyond Rational Deterrence: The Struggle for New Conceptions," *World Politics* (January 1976), 28(2):236.

13. Theodore H. von Laue, "Soviet Diplomacy: G. V. Chicherin, Peoples Commissar for Foreign Affairs, 1918–1930," in Gordon A. Craig and Felix Gilbert, eds., *The Diplomats 1919–1939,* vol. 1 (New York: Atheneum, 1965), pp. 243–44.

14. Cited in Elie Abel, *The Missile Crisis* (New York: Bantam, 1966), p. 95.

15. Cited in Holsti, North, and Brody, "Perception and Action," p. 137.

16. Coplin, Mills and O'Leary, "PRINCE Concepts," p. 77.

17. Oron J. Hale, *The Great Illusion, 1900–1914* (New York: Harper & Row, 1971), p. 255.

18. See for example, Glenn H. Snyder, " 'Prisoner's Dilemma' and 'Chicken' Models in International Politics," *International Studies Quarterly* (March 1971), 15(1):93ff.

19. See Lawrence Juda, *Ocean Space Rights: Developing US Policy* (New York: Praeger, 1975).

20. Richard N. Rosecrance, *International Relations: Peace or War?* (New York: McGraw-Hill, 1973), p. 221.

21. Richard N. Rosecrance, *Action and Reaction in World Politics* (Boston: Little, Brown, 1963), p. 156.

22. De Rivera, *Psychological Dimension,* p. 19.

23. Karl W. Deutsch, *The Nerves of Government* (New York: Free Press, 1963), pp. 258–60.

24. See Morton Deutsch, *The Resolution of Conflict* (New Haven, Conn.: Yale University Press, 1973); and Jeffrey Rubin and Bert Brown, *The Social Psychology of Bargaining and Negotiation* (New York: Academic Press, 1975).

25. Roger Cobb and Charles Elder, *International Community* (New York: Holt, Rinehart & Winston, 1970), pp. 93–115.

26. See, for example, Warren J. Phillips, "The Conflict Environment of Nations," in Jonathan Wilkenfeld, ed., *Conflict Behavior and Linkage Politics* (New York: McKay 1973), pp. 124–48; Warren Phillips and Robert Crain, "Dynamic Foreign Policy Interactions," in Pat McGowan ed., *Sage International Yearbook of Foreign Policy Studies,* vol. II (Beverly Hills, Calif.: Sage, 1974) pp. 227–269; Jeffrey Milstein, "American and Soviet Influence, Balance of Power and Arab-Israeli Violence," in Bruce M. Russett, ed., *Peace, War, and Numbers* (Beverly Hills, Calif.: Sage, 1972), pp. 139–67; and Dina A. Zinnes, "The Expression and Perception of Hostility in Prewar Crisis: 1914," in Singer, ed., *Quantitative International Politics,* pp. 85–123.

27. See Charles A. McClelland, "The Beginning, Duration, and Abatement of International Crises," in C. Hermann, ed. *International Crises,* pp. 83–105. See also Raymond Tanter, *Modeling and Managing International Conflicts: The Berlin Crisis* (Beverly Hills, Calif.: Sage, 1974).

28. Edward Azar, "Conflict Escalation and Conflict Reduction in an International Crisis: Suez, 1956," *Journal of Conflict Resolution* (June 1972), 16(2):183–201. See also James M. McCormick, "Evaluating Models of Crisis Behavior: Some Evidence from the Middle East," *International Studies Quarterly* (March 1975) 19(1):17–46.

29. O. Hobart Mowrer, *Learning Theory and Behavior* (New York: Wiley, 1960).

30. John Raser, "Learning and Affect in International Politics," *Journal of Peace Research* (1965), 2(3):220. Emphasis in original.

31. See Morton Deutsch, *Resolution of Conflict,* pp. 62–65.

32. Emory Bogardus, "Measuring Social Distances," *Journal of Applied Sociology* (March 1925), 9:299–308, and "A Social Distance Scale," *Sociology and Social Research* (January 1933), 17:265–271.

33. Albert F. Eldridge, *Images of Conflict* (New York: St. Martin's, 1979), pp. 35–37.

34. Lewis F. Richardson, *Statistics of Deadly Quarrels* (New York: Boxwood Press, 1960).

35. Cobb and Elder, *International Community*, pp. 39–44.

36. John A. Vasquez, "Statistical Findings in International Politics: A Data-Based Assessment," *International Studies Quarterly* (June 1976), 20(2):203–4.

37. Michael P. Sullivan, *International Relations: Theories and Evidence* (Englewood Cliffs, N.J.: Prentice-Hall, 1976), p. 141.

38. See R. J. Rummel, *The Dimensionality of Nations* (Beverly Hills, Calif.: Sage, 1972).

39. R. J. Rummel, "Dimensions of Conflict Behavior Within and Between Nations," *General Systems Yearbook* (1963), 8:1–50; and Raymond Tanter, "Dimensions of Conflict Behavior Within and Between Nations, 1958–1960," *Journal of Conflict Resolution* (March 1966), 10(1):41–64. However, somewhat different results were obtained by Jonathan Wilkenfeld, using Rummel's data, in associating regime type with conflict behavior. Wilkenfeld, "Domestic and Foreign Behavior of Nations," *Journal of Peace Research* (1968), 5(1):56–69.

40. R. J. Rummel, "The Relationship Between National Attributes and Foreign Conflict Behavior," in Singer, ed., *Quantitative International Politics*, pp. 187–215.

41. Vasquez, "Statistical Findings," pp. 200–2. The findings on demography-violence are from Robert C. North and Nazli Choucri, *Nations in Conflict* (San Francisco: Freeman, 1975); those on economic characteristics are from Hayward Alker, Jr., "Supranationalism in the United Nations," *Peace Research Society (International) Papers* (1964), 3:197–212; and those concerning integration may be found in several studies including Karl W. Deutsch, "Shifts in the Balance of Communication Flows," *Public Opinion Quarterly* (Spring 1957), 21(1):143–160; and Sullivan, *International Relations*, pp. 207–252.

42. See Kurt Lewin, *A Dynamic Theory of Personality* (New York: McGraw-Hill, 1935); Kurt Lewin, *Field Theory in Social Science* (New York: Harper Torchbooks, 1964); and Quincy Wright, *The Study of International Relations* (New York: Appleton-Century-Crofts, 1955), pp. 530–69. For interim assessments of the DON project, see Gordon Hilton, *A Review of the DON Project* (Beverly Hills, Calif.: Sage, 1973); and Francis W. Hoole and Dina A. Zinnes, eds., *Quantitative International Relations: An Appraisal* (New York: Praeger, 1976), pp. 149–243.

43. R. J. Rummel, "U.S. Foreign Relations: Conflict, Cooperation, and Attribute Distances," in Russett, ed., *Peace, War, and Numbers*, pp. 71–115. See also Sang-Woo Rhee, "China's Cooperation, Conflict and Interaction Behavior viewed from Rummel's Field Theory Perspective," in R. J. Rummel, ed., *Field Theory Evolving* (Beverly Hills, Calif.: Sage, 1977), pp. 371–403.

44. See Philip E. Jacob and Henry Teune, "The Integrative Process for Analysis of the Bases of Political Community," in Philip E. Jacob and James V.

Toscano, eds. *The Integration of Political Communities* (Philadelphia: Lippincott, 1964), pp. 8–23.

45. Coplin, Mills, and O'Leary, "PRINCE Concepts," p. 83.

46. For a review of the literature on power in these two fields, see Roderick Bell, David V. Edwards, and R. Harrison Wagner, eds. *Political Power: A Reader in Theory and Research* (New York: Free Press, 1969).

47. For an excellent review of the various meanings of power, see Dorwin Cartwright, ed., *Studies in Social Power* (Ann Arbor: Institute for Social Research, 1959), especially John R. P. French and Bertram Raven, "The Bases of Social Power," pp. 150–167. See also Robert A. Dahl, "The Concept of Power," *Behavioral Science* (July 1957), 2:201–15; and J. David Singer, "InterNation Influence: A Formal Model," *American Political Science Review,* (1963), 57(4):420–30.

48. Cited in Steven Rosen and Walter Jones, *The Logic of International Relations* (Cambridge, Mass.: Winthrop Publishers, 1974), p. 148. Generally, "wealth" and military victory are closely associated. See Steven Rosen, "War Power and the Willingness to Suffer," in Russett, ed., *Peace, War and Numbers,* p. 171.

49. See Wayne H. Ferris, *The Power Capabilities of Nation-States* (Lexington, Mass.: Lexington Books, 1973), pp. 115–166.

50. See William H. Riker, "Some Ambiguities in the Notion of Power," *American Political Science Review* (1964), 58:341–49.

51. See John W. Kingdon, *Congressmen's Voting Decisions* (New York: Harper & Row, 1973), for examples of this kind of "idiographic" use of influence.

52. John Spanier, *Games Nations Play* (New York: Praeger, 1972), p. 104.

53. R. J. Rummel, "A Status-Field Theory of International Relations," in Rummel, ed., *Field Theory Evolving,* p. 213.

54. *Ibid.,* p. 203.

55. *Ibid.,* p. 203.

56. For a review of this literature, see Norval D. Glenn, Jon P. Alston, and David Weiner, *Social Stratification: A Research Bibliography* (Berkeley, Calif.: Glendessary Press, 1970). Specific studies relevant to this model include Dorwin Cartwright and F. Harary, "Structural Balance: A Generalization of Heider's Theory," *Psychological Review* (September 1956), 63:277–93; Irving W. Goffman, "Status Inconsistency and Preference for Change in Power Distribution," *American Sociological Review* (June 1957), 22(3):275–81; Ralph V. Exline and Robert C. Ziller, "Status Congruency and Interpersonal Conflict in Decision-Making Groups," *Human Relations* (1959), 12(2):147–62; Gerhard Lenski, *Power and Privilege: A Theory of Social Stratification* (New York: McGraw-Hill, 1966); Morris Zelditch, Jr. and Bo Anderson, "On the Balance of a Set of Ranks," in Joseph Berger, Morris Zelditch, and Bo Anderson, eds., *Sociological Theories in Progress,* vol. 1 (Boston: Houghton Mifflin, 1966).

57. Johan Galtung, "A Structural Theory of Aggression," *Journal of Peace*

Research (1964), 1(2):95–119, and "A Structural Theory of Imperialism," *Journal of Peace Research* (1971), 8(1):81–117.

58. Galtung, "Summit Meetings and International Relations," *Journal of Peace Research* (1964), 1:36–54; "East-West Interaction Patterns," *Journal of Peace Research* (1966), 3(2):146–77; "Social Position, Party Identification and Foreign Policy Orientation: A Norwegian Case Study," in James N. Rosenau, ed., *Domestic Sources of Foreign Policy* (New York: Free Press, 1967), pp. 161–94.

59. Galtung, "East-West Interaction Patterns," p. 149.

60. Galtung, "A Structural Theory of Aggression."

61. See J. C. Davies, "Toward A Theory of Revolution," *American Sociological Review* (February 1962), 27(1):5–19.

62. Rummel, "A Status-Field Theory of International Relations," p. 213.

63. *Ibid.,* pp. 252–56.

64. Galtung, "East-West Interaction Patterns."

65. Rummel, "U.S. Foreign Relations."

66. Maurice A. East, "Rank-Dependent Interaction and Mobility: Two Aspects of Stratification," *Peace Research Society (International) Papers* (1970), 14:113–28.

67. Michael Wallace, "Status, Formal Organization, and Arms Levels as Factors Leading to the Onset of War, 1820–1964," in Russett, ed., *Peace, War, and Numbers,* pp. 49–71.

68. Manus Midlarsky, *On War* (New York: Free Press 1970), p. 131.

69. See Leonard Solomon, "The Influence of Some Types of Power Relationships and Game Strategies upon the Development of Interpersonal Trust," *Journal of Abnormal and Social Psychology* (1960), 61:223–30.

70. Morton Deutsch, *Resolution of Conflict,* p. 46.

71. Robert O. Keohane, "Lilliputians' Dilemmas: Small States in International Politics," *International Organization* (Spring 1969), 23(2):296.

72. Robert L. Rothstein, *Alliances and Small Powers* (New York: Columbia University Press, 1968), p. 29.

73. See Marshall R. Singer, *Weak States in a World of Powers: The Dynamics of International Relationships* (New York: Free Press, 1972), p. 367.

74. Lloyd H. Strickland, "Surveillance and Trust," *Journal of Personality* (1958), 26:200–15.

75. Roger Morris, *Uncertain Greatness: Henry Kissinger and American Foreign Policy* (New York: Harper and Row, 1977) discusses this for Biafra; and Anthony Lake, *The "Tar Baby" Option: American Policy Toward Southern Rhodesia* (New York: Columbia University Press, 1976), pp. 67–68, makes this point about Rhodesia.

76. Lake, *"Tar Baby" Option.* p. 63.

77. *Ibid.,* pp. 85–87.

7. THE LABYRINTH OF CONTENTION

1. J. David Singer, "The Global System and its Sub-Systems: A Developmental View," in James N. Rosenau, ed., *Linkage Politics* (New York: Free Press, 1969), p. 37. Emphasis in original.

2. See Charles A. McClelland and Gary D. Hoggard, "Conflict Patterns in the Interactions Among Nations," in James N. Rosenau, ed., *International Politics and Foreign Policy,* rev. ed. (New York: Free Press, 1969), p. 713.

3. Edward Azar, "The Analysis of International Events," *Peace Research Reviews,* (November 1970), 4(1):1–113.

4. R. J. Rummel, "U.S. Foreign Relations: Conflict: Cooperation, and Attribute Distances," in Bruce M. Russett, ed., *Peace, War, and Numbers* (Beverly Hills, Calif.: Sage, 1972), pp. 71–115.

5. John A. Vasquez, "Statistical Findings in International Politics: A Data-Based Assessment," *International Studies Quarterly* (June 1976), 20(2):171–218.

6. Richard W. Mansbach et al., *The Web of World Politics* (Englewood Cliffs, Prentice-Hall, 1976).

7. David Easton, *The Political System* (New York: Knopf, 1953), p. 53.

8. See Karl W. Deutsch and J. David Singer, "Multipolar Power Systems and International Stability," *World Politics* (April 1964) 16(3):390–406.

9. J. S. Coleman, *Community Conflict* (Glencoe, Ill. Free Press, 1957), p. 14.

10. See R. J. Rummel, "U.S. Foreign Relations," in Russett, ed., *Peace, War, and Numbers,* pp. 95–110.

11. See William D. Coplin and Michael K. O'Leary, "A Simulation Model for the Analysis and Explanation of International Interactions," (paper delivered to the International Studies Association, San Juan, Puerto Rico, 1971).

12. Morton Deutsch, *The Resolution of Conflict* (New Haven, Conn.: Yale University Press, 1973), p. 46.

13. Richard N. Rosecrance, *International Relations: Peace or War?* (New York: McGraw-Hill, 1973), pp. 93–94.

14. David J. Finlay, Ole R. Holsti and Richard R. Fagen, *Enemies in Politics* (Chicago: Rand McNally, 1967), p. 84.

15. President Eisenhower as cited in Bernard B. Fall, *The Two Viet-Nams: A Political and Military Analysis,* 2d rev. ed. (New York: Praeger, 1967), p. 321.

16. Dwight D. Eisenhower, *Mandate for Change: 1953–1956* (Garden City: Doubleday, 1963), pp. 348, 371.

17. D. Griesinger and D. Livingston, "Toward a Model of Interpersonal Motivation in Experimental Games," *Behavioral Sciences* (1973) 18:173–88; and C. G. McClintock, "Social Motivations in Settings of Outcome Interdependence," in Daniel Druckman, ed., *Negotiations: Social-Psychological Perspectives* (Beverly Hills, Calif.: Sage, 1977), pp. 55–59.

18. McClintock, *Social Motivations,* p. 59.

19. See, for example, Herman Kahn, "The Arms Race and Some of Its Hazards," in Donald G. Brennan, ed., *Arms Control, Disarmament and National Security* (New York: George Braziller, 1961), pp. 102–8, for a discussion of the "Doomsday Machine," the "Doomsday-in-a-Hurry Machine," and the "Homicide Pact Machine."

20. Leon Festinger, *A Theory of Cognitive Dissonance* (Stanford, Calif.: Stanford University Press, 1957), p. 10.

21. *Ibid.*, p. 12.

22. Leon Festinger, ed., *Conflict, Decision, and Dissonance* (Stanford, Calif.: Stanford University Press, 1964), pp. 155–56.

23. See, for example, Milton Rosenberg, "Some Limits of Dissonance: Toward a Differentiated View of Counterattitudinal Performance," in Shel A. Feldman, ed., *Cognitive Consistency* (New York: Academic Press, 1966).

24. See Ole R. Holsti, *Crisis, Escalation, War* (Montreal: McGill University Press, 1972), pp. 17–18.

25. Robert Jervis, *Perception and Misperception in International Politics* (Princeton, N.J.: Princeton University Press, 1976), p. 392.

26. A. J. P. Taylor, *A History of the First World War* (New York: Berkley Medallion Books, 1966), pp. 118–19.

27. *Ibid.*, pp. 122–23.

28. *Ibid.*, p. 125.

29. Morton Deutsch, "Vietnam and the Start of World War III: Some Psychological Parallels," presidential address before the New York State Psychological Association, May 6, 1966, cited in M. Deutsch, *The Resolution of Conflict*, pp. 356–57.

30. Roger Ashley Leonard, ed., *Clausewitz On War* (New York: Capricorn, 1968), pp. 61–62.

31. James N. Rosenau, "Foreign Policy As An Issue-Area"; and Theodore J. Lowi, "Making the World Safe for Democracy," in James N. Rosenau, ed., *Domestic Sources of Foreign Policy* (New York: Free Press, 1967), pp. 11–51, 295–333 respectively.

32. Lowi, "World Safe for Democracy," pp. 315–323.

33. John E. Mueller, "Trends in Popular Support for the Wars in Korea and Vietnam," *American Political Science Review* (June 1971), 65(2):366.

34. Festinger, *Theory of Cognitive Dissonance*, pp. 231–32.

35. Jervis, *Perception and Misperception in International Politics*, pp. 404–6, and M. Deutsch, *Resolution of Conflict*, pp. 357–58.

36. Milton Rokeach, *The Open and Closed Mind* (New York: Basic Books, 1960).

37. Festinger, *Theory of Cognitive Dissonance*, p. 13.

38. *Ibid.*, p. 264.

39. Karl W. Deutsch and Richard L. Merritt, "Effects of Events on National and International Images," in Herbert C. Kelman, ed., *International Behavior* (New York: Holt, Rinehart, and Winston, 1965), p. 183.

40. See Ole R. Holsti, "The Belief Systems and National Images: A Case Study," *Journal of Conflict Resolution* (September 1962), 6(3):247.

41. See Jack Brehm and Arthur Cohen, *Explorations in Cognitive Dissonance* (New York: Wiley, 1962), p. 308.

42. Festinger, *Theory of Cognitive Dissonance,* p. 17.

43. Charles Osgood, *An Alternative to War or Surrender* (Urbana: University of Illinois Press, 1962).

44. Townsend Hoopes, *The Limits of Intervention* (New York: McKay, 1969), pp. 139–40.

45. See Robert Axelrod, "The Analysis of Cognitive Maps," in Axelrod, ed., *Structure of Decision: The Cognitive Maps of Political Elites* (Princeton, N.J.: Princeton University Press, 1976), p. 72. Also, John A. Vasquez, "A Learning Theory of the American Anti-Vietnam War Movement," *Journal of Peace Research* (1976), 13(4):304–305.

46. See, for example, J. Merrill Carlsmith and Elliot Aronson, "Some Hedonic Consequences of the Confirmation and Disconfirmation of Expectancies," *Journal of Abnormal and Social Psychology* (1963), 66:151–56.

47. See, for example, Lewis F. Richardson, *Arms and Insecurity: A Mathematical Study of the Causes and Origins of War* and *Statistics of Deadly Quarrels* (Chicago: Quadrangle, 1960); Charles Osgood, *An Alternative to War or Surrender;* and Ole R. Holsti and Robert C. North, "The History of Human Conflict," in Elton B. McNeil, ed., *The Nature of Human Conflict* (Englewood Cliffs, N.J.: Prentice-Hall, 1965).

48. Jack Sawyer and Harold Guetzkow, "Bargaining and Negotiation in International Relations," in Kelman, ed., *International Behavior,* p. 485.

49. M. Deutsch, *The Resolution of Conflict,* p. 47.

50. See, for example, Thomas C. Schelling, *The Strategy of Conflict* (New York: Oxford University Press, 1963), pp. 21ff.

51. M. Deutsch, *The Resolution of Conflict,* pp. 158–59.

52. James N. Rosenau, *The Scientific Study of Foreign Policy* (New York: Free Press, 1971), p. 108.

53. *Ibid.,* p. 113.

54. See Charles F. Hermann, "Threat, Time and Surprise: A Simulation of International Crisis," in Hermann, ed., *International Crises: Insights from Behavioral Research* (New York: Free Press, 1972), pp. 187–215. Hermann's work, however, suggests that surprise may be a less relevant factor than the other two variables.

55. Ernest R. May, "The Nature of Foreign Policy: The Calculated versus the Axiomatic," *Daedalus* (Fall 1962), no. 4:662. See also May, *"Lessons" of the Past: The Use and Misuse of History in American Foreign Policy* (New York: Oxford, 1973), pp. 52–86.

56. See Joseph H. de Rivera, *The Psychological Dimension of Foreign Policy* (Columbus, Ohio: Merrill, 1968), p. 129ff.; Fred I. Greenstein, *Personality and Politics* (Chicago: Markham, 1969), pp. 46–56; William Wilcox, *Portrait of a*

General (New York: Knopf, 1964); and Daniel Levinson, "Role, Personality and Social Structure in Organizational Settings," *Journal of Abnormal and Social Psychology* (1959), 58:170–80.

57. Margaret G. Hermann, "When Leader Personality Will Affect Foreign Policy: Some Propositions," in James N. Rosenau, ed., *In Search of Global Patterns* (New York: Free Press, 1976), p. 328.

58. Edward Shils, "Authoritarianism: 'Right' and 'Left'," in Richard Christie and Marie Jahoda, eds., *Studies in the Scope and Method of "The Authoritarian Personality"* (New York: Free Press, 1954), pp. 44–45.

59. Ross Stagner, *Psychological Aspects of International Conflict* (Belmont, Calif.: Brooks/Cole, 1967), p. 3.

60. Margaret G. Hermann, "When Leader Personality Will Affect Foreign Policy," pp. 329–31.

61. Otomar J. Bartos, "How Predictable Are Negotiations," *Journal of Conflict Resolution* (December 1967), 11(4):495.

62. For an excellent summary of the work in this area, see Margaret G. Hermann and Nathan Kogan, "Effects of Negotiators' Personalities on Negotiating Behavior," in Daniel Druckman, ed., *Negotiations: Social-Psychological Perspectives* (Berverly Hills, Calif.: Sage, 1977), pp. 247–74.

63. G. W. Baxter, Jr., "Prejudiced Liberals? Race and Information Effects in a Two-Person Game," *Journal of Conflict Resolution* (March 1973), 17(1):131–61; and J. I. Tedeschi et al., "Social Desirability, Manifest Anxiety, and Social Power," *Journal of Social Psychology* (1969), 77:231–39.

64. Lloyd S. Etheredge, *A World of Men: The Private Sources of American Foreign Policy* (Boston, Mass.: M.I.T. Press, 1978), ch. 6; N. H. Berkowitz, "Alternative Measures of Authoritarianism, Response Sets, and Predictions in a Two-Person Game," *Journal of Social Psychology* (1968), 74:233–42; Morton Deutsch, "Trust, Trustworthiness, and the F-Scale," *Journal of Abnormal and Social Psychology* (1960), 61:138–40; and L. S. Wrightsman, "Personality and Attitudinal Correlates of Trusting and Trustworthy Behaviors in a Two-Person Game," *Journal of Personality and Social Psychology* (1966), 4:328–32.

65. A. H. Kelley and A. J. Stahelski, "Social Interaction Bases of Cooperators' and Competitors' Beliefs About Others," *Journal of Personality and Social Psychology* (1970), 16:88.

66. J. G. Phelan and E. Richardson, "Cognitive Complexity, Strategy of the Other Player, and Two-Person Game Behavior," *Journal of Psychology* (1969), 71:205–15.

67. M. J. Driver, "Individual Differences as Determinants of Aggression in the Inter-Nation Simulation," in Margaret G. Hermann, ed., *A Psychological Examination of Political Leaders* (New York: Free Press, 1976), pp. 337–53; O. J. Harvey et al., *Conceptual Systems and Personality Organizations* (New York: Wiley, 1961); Margaret G. Hermann, "Leader Personality and Foreign Policy Behavior," in James Rosenau, ed., *Comparing Foreign Policies* (New York: Halsted, 1974), pp. 222–25.

68. L. S. Wrightsman, "Personality and Attitudinal Correlates."

69. G. H. Shure and R. J. Meeker, *A Personality/Attitude Schedule for Use in Experimental Bargaining Studies* (Santa Monica, Calif.: Systems Development Corporation, Report TM-2543, 1965), p. 11.

70. Hermann and Kogan, "Effects of Negotiators' Personalities," pp. 254–55.

71. D. P. Crowne, "Family Orientation, Level of Aspiration, and Interpersonal Bargaining," *Journal of Personality and Social Psychology* (1966), 3:641–45.

72. Hermann and Kogan, "Effects of Negotiators' Personalities," p. 266. See also M. Hermann, "Leadership Personality and Foreign Policy Behavior," p. 223 for the likelihood of dogmatism to produce policy shifts.

73. C. Faucheux and S. Moscovici, "Self-esteem and Exploitative Behavior in a Game Against Chance and Nature," *Journal of Personality and Social Psychology* (1968), 8:83–88.

74. Osgood, *An Alternative to War or Surrender*.

75. W. Clay Hamner and Gary A. Yukl, "The Effectiveness of Different Offer Strategies in Bargaining," in Druckman, ed., *Negotiations,* pp. 140–41.

76. S. Siegel and L. F. Fouraker, *Bargaining and Group Decision Making* (New York: McGraw-Hill, 1960), p. 2.

77. Otomar J. Bartos, "Determinants and Consequences of Toughness," in P. Swingle, ed., *The Structure of Conflict* (New York: Academic Press, 1970), p. 14; and W. C. Hamner, "Effects of Bargaining Strategy and Pressure to Reach Agreement in a Stalemated Negotiation," *Journal of Personality and Social Psychology* (1974), 30:458–67.

78. M. Pilisuk and P. Skolnick, "Inducing Trust: A Test of the Osgood Proposal," *Journal of Personality and Social Psychology* (1968), 8:121–33. See also W. J. Crow, "A Study of Strategic Doctrines Using the Internation Simulation," *Journal of Conflict Resolution* (September 1963), 7(3):580–89.

79. Amitai Etzioni, "Disarmament and Arms Control Agencies," in P. F. Lazarsfeld, W. Sewell, and H. Wilensky, eds., *The Uses of Sociology* (New York: Basic Books, 1967), pp. 806–38; and Amitai Etzioni, "The Kennedy Experiment," *Western Political Quarterly* (June 1967), 20(2):361–80. See also L. Jensen, "Soviet-American Bargaining Behavior in the Post-War Disarmament Negotiations," *Journal of Conflict Resolution* (September 1963), 7(3):522–41.

80. Cf. Bartos, "Determinants and Consequences of Toughness."

81. Cf. O. J. Bartos, "Concession-making in Experimental Negotiations," in J. Berger et al., *Sociological Theories in Action* (Boston: Houghton Mifflin, 1966); and Bartos, "Determinants and Consequences of Toughness."

8. THE COHERENCE OF CONTENTION

1. I. William Zartman, *The 50% Solution* (Garden City, N.Y.: Doubleday Anchor, 1976), p. 484.

2. Thomas C. Schelling, *Arms and Influence* (New Haven, Conn.: Yale University Press, 1966), p. 1. Emphasis added.

3. Fred C. Iklé, *How Nations Negotiate* (New York: Praeger, 1967), p. 3. Emphasis omitted.

4. Dean G. Pruitt, "Methods for Resolving Differences of Interest: A Theoretical Analysis," *Journal of Social Issues* (1972), 28:144.

5. Edward Vose Gulick, *Europe's Classical Balance of Power* (New York: Norton, 1955), pp. 89, 90.

6. See Robert O. Keohane and Joseph S. Nye, Jr., *Power and Interdependence: World Politics in Transition* (Boston: Little, Brown, 1977), ch. 3.

7. Morton A. Kaplan, *System and Process in International Politics* (New York: Wiley, 1957), p. 17.

8. Richard N. Rosecrance, *Action and Reaction in World Politics* (Boston: Little, Brown, 1963), p. 97.

9. Iklé, *How Nations Negotiate,* p. 92. See also Oliver J. Lissitzyn, "International Law in a Divided World," *International Conciliation* (March 1963), no. 542.

10. H. G. Nicholas, *The United Nations as a Political Institution,* 5th ed. (New York: Oxford, 1975), p. 214.

11. John G. Stoessinger, *The United Nations and the Superpowers: China, Russia, and America,* 4th ed. (New York: Random House, 1977), p. 20.

12. For a fuller explanation of learning theory as applied here, see John A. Vasquez, "A Learning Theory of the American Anti-Vietnam War Movement, *Journal of Peace Research* (1976), 13(4):299–314.

13. John Raser, "Learning and Affect in International Politics," in James N. Rosenau, ed., *International Politics and Foreign Policy,* rev. ed. (New York: Free Press, 1969), p. 434.

14. O. Hobart Mowrer, *Learning Theory and Behavior* (New York: Wiley, 1960).

15. E. C. Tolman, *Purposive Behavior in Animals and Men* (New York: Appleton-Century-Crofts, 1932).

16. See Raymond F. Hopkins and Richard W. Mansbach, *Structure and Process in International Politics* (New York: Harper & Row, 1973), pp. 410–12.

17. James T. Tedeschi and Thomas V. Bonoma, "Measures of Last Resort: Coercion and Aggression in Bargaining," in Daniel Druckman, ed., *Negotiations: Social-Psychological Perspectives* (Beverly Hills, Calif.: Sage, 1977), p. 214.

18. Vasquez, "Learning Theory," pp. 304–5.

19. Robert Jervis, *Perception and Misperception in International Politics* (Princeton, N.J.: Princeton University Press, 1976), p. 233.

20. See David Braybrooke and Charles Lindblom, *A Strategy for Decision* (New York: Free Press, 1963), p. 69.

21. For an overview, see J. David Singer and Melvin Small, *The Wages of*

War, 1816–1965 (New York: Wiley, 1972); and J. David Singer, ed., *The Correlates of War*, vols. 1 and 2 (New York: Free Press, 1979, 1980). For an appraisal of this project, see Francis W. Hoole and Dina A. Zinnes, eds., *Quantitative International Politics: An Appraisal* (New York: Praeger, 1976), pp. 21–145.

22. Stuart Bremer, J. David Singer, and Urs Laterbacher, "The Population Density and War Proneness of European Nations, 1916–1965," *Comparative Political Studies* (October 1973), 6:329–48; Melvin Small and J. David Singer, "The War-Proneness of Democratic Regimes, 1816–1965," *Jerusalem Journal of International Relations* (Summer 1976), 1(4):50–68.

23. See J. David Singer and Melvin Small, "Alliance Aggregation and the Onset of War, 1815–1945," in Singer, ed., *Quantitative International Politics* (New York: Free Press, 1968), pp. 247–86; Michael Haas, "International Subsystems: Stability and Polarity," *American Political Science Review* (March 1970), 64(1):93–123; and P. Dale Dean, Jr. and John A. Vasquez, "From Power Politics to Issue Politics: Bipolarity and Multipolarity in Light of a New Paradigm," *Western Political Quarterly* (1976), 29(1):14–16.

24. Brian Healy and Arthur Stein, "The Balance of Power in International History: Theory and Reality," *Journal of Conflict Resolution* (March 1973), 17(1):33–63. See also Hsi-sheng Chi, "The Chinese Warlord System as an International System," and Winfried Franke, "The Italian City-State System as an International System," in Morton A. Kaplan, ed., *New Approaches to International Relations* (New York: St. Martin's Press, 1968), pp. 405–25 and 426–58.

25. J. David Singer, Stuart Bremer, and John Stuckey, "Capability Distribution, Uncertainty, and Major Power War, 1820–1965," in Bruce M. Russett, ed., *Peace, War, and Numbers* (Beverly Hills, Calif.: Sage, 1972), pp. 19–48.

26. Michael Wallace, "Status, Formal Organization, and Arms Levels as Factors Leading to the Onset of War, 1820–1964," in Russett, ed., *Peace, War, and Numbers*, p. 63.

27. Michael Wallace, "Arms Races and Escalation: Some New Evidence," *Journal of Conflict Resolution* (March 1979), 23(1):14–15.

28. Manus Midlarsky, *On War* (New York: Free Press, 1970), pp. 100, 129–44.

29. See James Lee Ray, *Status Inconsistency and War Involvement Among European States, 1816–1970* (Ann Arbor: University of Michigan, Ph.D. dissertation, 1974) and "Status Inconsistency and 'Aggressive' War Involvement in Europe, 1816–1970" (paper prepared for delivery to the Annual Convention of the International Studies Association, Washington, D.C., February 22–25, 1978); Charles S. Gochman, *Status, Conflict, and War: The Major Powers, 1820–1970* (Ann Arbor: University of Michigan, Ph.D. dissertation 1975) and "Status, Capabilities, and Major Power Conflict," in J. David Singer, ed., *The Correlates of War* (New York: Free Press, 1980), 2:83–124.

30. J. David Singer, ed., Introduction, *The Correlates of War*, 2:xxxiii–xxxv.

31. Ole R. Holsti, Richard A. Brody, and Robert C. North, "Measuring Affect and Action in International Reaction Models," *Journal of Peace Research*

(1964), 3(4):170–90. On the hostile spiral see Ole R. Holsti, Robert C. North, and Richard A. Brody, "Perception and Action in the 1914 Crisis," in Singer, ed., *Quantitative International Politics*, pp. 85–123; and Dina A. Zinnes, Joseph Zinnes, and Robert McClure, "Hostility in Diplomatic Communication," in Charles F. Hermann, ed., *International Crises: Insights from Behavioral Research* (New York: Free Press, 1972), pp. 139–65. For any appraisal of this project see Francis W. Hoole and Dina Zinnes, eds. *Quantitative International Politics*. pp. 349–463.

32. See Nazli Choucri and Robert C. North, *Nations in Conflict: National Growth and International Violence* (San Francisco: Freeman, 1974), pp. 25, 168–69, 244–54.

33. Rummel, "U.S. Foreign Relations: Conflict, Cooperation, and Attribute Distances," in Bruce M. Russett, ed., *Peace, War, and Numbers* (Beverly Hills, Calif.: Sage, 1972), p. 99.

34. Karl von Clausewitz, *On War,* trans. J. J. Graham (New York: Barnes and Noble, 1956), bk. II, ch. 3, p. 121.

35. *Ibid.*, bk. I, ch. 1, p. 2.

36. *Ibid.*, I p. 23.

37. See Peter R. Moody, Jr., "Clausewitz and the Fading Dialectic of War," *World Politics* (April 1979), 31(3):417.

38. Clausewitz, *On War,* book I, ch. 1, p. 4.

39. See, for example, Anthony Storr, *Human Aggression* (New York: Atheneum, 1968).

40. Bernard Berelson and Gary A. Steiner, *Human Behavior, An Inventory of Scientific Findings* (New York: Harcourt Brace Jovanovich, 1964), pp. 267–69. See the classic study by Carl I. Hoveland and Richard R. Sears of the relationship between the price of cotton and the number of lynchings in the American South: "Minor Studies of Aggression: VI. Correlation of lynching with economic indices," *Journal of Psychology* (1940), 9:307.

41. Clausewitz, *On War,* book I, ch. 1, p. 20.

42. Robert Butow, *Tojo and the Coming of the War* (Princeton, N.J.: Princeton University Press, 1961), p. 267.

43. Thucydides, *History of the Peloponnesian War,* Rex Warner, tr. (London: Chaucer Press, 1954), bk. v, ch. 7.

44. Max Jakobson, *The Diplomacy of the Winter War* (Cambridge, Mass. Harvard University Press, 1961), p. 28.

45. See, for example, K. J. Holsti, *International Politics: A Framework for Analysis,* 2d ed. (Englewood Cliffs, N.J.: Prentice-Hall, 1972), pp. 31–62.

46. See Raymond Aron, *Peace and War,* (New York: Praeger, 1968), pp. 484–87.

47. Jervis, *Perception and Misperception in International Politics,* pp. 62, 63.

48. John H. Herz, "Idealist Internationalism and the Security Dilemma," in Herz, *The Nation-State and the Crisis of World Politics* (New York: McKay, 1976), p. 73.

49. Thomas C. Schelling, *The Strategy of Conflict* (New York: Oxford, 1963), p. 207. See also pp. 208–29. Emphasis in original.

50. Cited in Alan Bullock *Hitler, A Study in Tyranny,* rev. ed. (New York: Harper & Row, 1964), p. 315.

9. REASSESSING THE PAST: GLOBAL HISTORY FROM A CHANGED PERSPECTIVE

1. David Hume, ''An Enquiry Concerning Human Understanding'' (1748) in Nicholas Capaldi, ed., *The Englightenment: The Proper Study of Mankind* (New York: Capricorn Books, 1968), p. 136.

2. Hans Reichenbach, *Experience and Prediction: An Analysis of the Foundations and the Structure of Knowledge* (Chicago: University of Chicago Press, 1938), p. 357.

3. See James A. Field, Jr., ''Transnationalism and the New Tribe,'' in Robert O. Keohane and Joseph S. Nye, Jr., eds., *Transnational Relations and World Politics* (Cambridge Mass.: Harvard University Press, 1971), pp. 3–22, for an examination of modern history in light of the insights of transnationalism.

4. R. R. Palmer, *A History of the Modern World,* 2d ed. revised with the collaboration of Joel Colton (New York: Knopf, 1956), p. 126.

5. Paul Seabury, ''The Status Quo and the Balance,'' in Seabury, ed., *Balance of Power* (San Francisco: Chandler, 1965), p. 202.

6. Edward Vose Gulick, *Europe's Classical Balance of Power.* (New York: Norton, 1967), pp. 52–91. See also Emmerich de Vattel, ''The Law of Nations or the Principles of Natural Law,'' in M. G. Forsyth, H. M. A. Keens-Soper, and P. Savigear, eds., *The Theory of International Relations* (New York: Atherton, 1970), pp. 103–25.

7. Gulick, *Balance of Power,* p. 35.

8. Sir Harold Nicolson, *Diplomacy,* 3d ed. (New York: Oxford University Press, 1963), p. 24.

9. W. H. Lewis, *The Splendid Century: Life in the France of Louis XIV* (Garden City, N.Y.: Doubleday, 1953), p. 36.

10. William Wordsworth, ''French Revolution As It Appeared to Enthusiasts at Its Commencement,'' in *The English Parnassus* (Oxford: Oxford University Press, 1961), p. 314.

11. Edmund Burke, *Reflections on the Revolution in France* (Garden City, N.Y.: Doubleday, 1961), pp. 50, 52.

12. Cited in Crane Brinton, Gordon A. Craig and Felix Gilbert, ''Jomini,'' in Edward Mead Earle, ed., *Makers of Modern Strategy* (New York: Atheneum, 1967), p. 77.

13. Cited in Palmer, *A History of the Modern World,* p. 407.

14. Cited in J. F. Bernard, *Talleyrand: A Biography* (New York: Capricorn, 1974), pp. 325–26.

15. René Albrecht-Carrié, *The Concert of Europe* (New York: Harper & Row, 1968), p. 4.

16. Cited in Hans J. Morgenthau, *Politics Among Nations,* 5th ed. rev. (New York: Knopf, 1978), p. 449.

17. *Ibid.,* p. 223.

18. Richard B. Elrod, "The Concert of Europe: A Fresh Look At An International System," *World Politics* (January 1976), 28(2):161.

19. Cited in Morgenthau, *Politics Among Nations,* p. 450.

20. W. A. Phillips, *The Confederation of Europe* (1914) as cited in Albrecht-Carrié, *The Concert of Europe,* p. 31.

21. Cited in Gulick, *Europe's Classical Balance of Power,* p. 32.

22. Richard N. Rosecrance, *Action and Reaction in World Politics* (Boston: Little Brown, 1963), pp. 79–148.

23. Albrecht-Carrié, *The Concert of Europe,* p. 32.

24. Elrod, "Concert of Europe," pp. 163–67.

25. See Morgenthau, *Politics Among Nations,* pp. 451–52.

26. Elrod, "Concert of Europe," p. 166.

27. Cited in Albrecht-Carrié, *The Concert of Europe,* p. 43.

28. Quoted by Phillips, *The Confederation of Europe,* as cited in Albrecht-Carrié, *Concert of Europe,* p. 48. See also pp. 49–57.

29. Gulick, *Europe's Classical Balance of Power* p. 295.

30. Cited in Palmer, *History of the Modern World* p. 453.

31. See Carl E. Schorske, *German Social Democracy 1905–1917* (New York: Wiley, 1965), pp. 263–64.

32. Cited in William L. Langer, ed., *An Encyclopedia of World History,* 5th ed. (Boston: Houghton Mifflin, 1972), p. 712.

33. Cited in R. W. Seton-Watson," A Trois in a World Governed by Five," in Theodore S. Hamerow, ed., *Otto von Bismarck* (Boston: Heath, 1962), p. 56.

34. A. N. Carr-Saunders, *World Population* (Oxford: Oxford University Press, 1936), p. 49.

35. Albrecht-Carrié, *The Concert of Europe,* p. 309. See also Rosecrance, *Action and Reaction in World Politics,* pp. 140–41.

36. Albrecht-Carrié, *The Concert of Europe,* pp. 310–11.

37. Oron J. Hale, *The Great Illusion 1900–1914* (New York: Harper & Row, 1971), p. 226.

38. F. S. Northedge and M. J. Grieve, *A Hundred Years of International Relations* (New York: Praeger, 1971), p. 28.

39. *Ibid.,* pp. 26–27.

40. Hale, *Great Illusion,* p. 268.

41. Northedge and Grieve, *Hundred Years* p. 30.

42. *Ibid.,* p. 31.

43. A. J. P. Taylor, *The Course of German History* (New York: Capricorn, 1962), p. 157.

44. Cited in Hale, *Great Illusion*, p. 270.

45. Cited in *ibid.*, p. 284.

46. G. P. Gooch, *History of Modern Europe* (New York: Henry Holt, 1922,), p. 559.

47. E. H. Carr, *The Twenty Years' Crisis 1919–1939* (New York: St. Martin's, 1962), p. 27.

48. Cited in Seabury, ed., *Balance of Power*, pp. 141, 142.

49. See Carr, *Twenty Years' Crisis*, p. 118.

50. Elmer Bendiner, *A Time for Angels: The Tragicomic History of the League of Nations* (New York: Knopf, 1975).

51. John Maynard Keynes, *The Economic Consequences of the Peace*, Harper Torchbook ed. (New York: Harper & Row, 1971), pp. 3–4.

52. Cited in Bendiner, *Time for Angels*, p. ix.

53. *Ibid.* p. 141.

54. Raymond J. Sontag, *A Broken World 1919–1939* (New York: Harper & Row, 1971), p. 19.

55. Winston S. Churchill, *The Gathering Storm* (Boston: Houghton Mifflin, 1948), p. 6.

56. Inis L. Claude, Jr., *Power and International Relations* (New York: Random House, 1962), p. 153.

57. Cited in Seabury, ed., *Balance of Power*, p. 147. Emphasis in original.

58. Cited in Theodore H. von Laue, "Soviet Diplomacy: G. V. Chicherin, People's Commissar for Foreign Affairs, 1918–1930," in Gordon A. Craig and Felix Gilbert, eds., *The Diplomats 1919–1939*, vol. 1 (New York: Atheneum, 1965), p. 235.

59. Cited in Churchill, *Gathering Storm*, p. 7.

60. A. J. P. Taylor, *The Origins of the Second World War* (Greenwich, Conn.: Fawcett, 1961), pp. 105–6.

61. John Toland, *The Rising Sun: The Decline and Fall of the Japanese Empire 1936–1945* (New York: Random House, 1970), p. 5.

62. See Christopher Thorne, *The Limits of Foreign Policy* (New York: Capricorn, 1973).

63. Benito Mussolini, "The Doctrine of Fascism," in William Ebenstein, ed., *Great Political Thinkers*, 4th ed. (New York: Holt, Rinehart & Winston, 1969), p. 629.

64. Churchill, *Gathering Storm*, p. 175.

65. Cited in Alan Bullock, *Hitler: A Study in Tyranny*, rev. ed. (New York: Harper & Row, 1964), p. 55.

66. *Ibid.*, p. 250.

67. Taylor, *The Origins of the Second World War*, p. 196.

68. Andrew M. Scott, *The Revolution in Statecraft: Informal Penetration* (New York: Random House, 1965), p. 10.

69. See George F. Kennan, *From Prague After Munich* (Princeton, N.J.: Princeton University Press, 1968).

70. John W. Wheeler-Bennett, *Munich: Prologue to Tragedy* (New York: Duell, Sloan & Pearce, 1948), p. 437. For a detailed analysis, see Roger Parkinson, *Peace For Our Time* (New York: McKay, 1971).

71. Sontag, *Broken World,* p. 284.

72. Churchill, *Gathering Storm* p. 128.

10. THE COLD WAR

1. Harry S. Truman, *Year of Decisions* (Garden City, N.Y.: Doubleday, 1955), p. 552.

2. See David V. Edwards, *Creating a New World Politics* (New York: McKay, 1973), pp. 11–27.

3. See Louis Fischer, *The Life of Lenin* (New York: Harper & Row, 1964), p. 109.

4. Cited in David Shub, *Lenin: A Biography* (Baltimore, Md.: Penguin, 1967), pp. 210–11.

5. Edmund Wilson, *To the Finland Station* (Garden City: N.Y.: Doubleday, 1940), p. 461.

6. Cited in Fischer, *Life of Lenin,* p. 131.

7. Cited in Peter G. Filene, ed., *American Views of Soviet Russia, 1917–1965* (Homewood, Ill.: Dorsey, 1968), p. 3.

8. Cited in *ibid,* p. 22.

9. Theodore von Laue, "Soviet Diplomacy: G. V. Chicherin, People's Commissar for Foreign Affairs, 1918–1930," in Gordon A. Craig and Felix Gilbert, eds., *The Diplomats 1919–1939,* vol. 2 (New York: Atheneum, 1965), p. 243.

10. Secretary of State to Italian Ambassador, August 10, 1920, *Papers Relating to the Foreign Relations of the United States, 1920,* vol. 3, cited in Filene, *American Views of Soviet Russia,* p. 45.

11. Philip S. Gillette, "Conditions of American-Soviet Commerce: The Beginning of Direct Cotton Trade, 1923–1924," *Soviet Union* (1974), 1(1): p. 76.

12. John W. Wheeler-Bennett, *Munich: Prologue to Tragedy* (New York: Duell, Sloan & Pearce, 1948), pp. 280–81.

13. Cited in Roger Parkinson, *Peace For Our Time* (New York: McKay, 1971), p. 123.

14. Cited in *ibid.,* p. 123.

15. *Ibid.*

16. George F. Kennan, *Russia and the West Under Lenin and Stalin* (Boston: Little Brown, 1960), pp. 310–11.

17. Elmer Bendiner, *A Time for Angels: The Tragicomic History of the League of Nations* (New York: Knopf, 1975), p. 395.

18. See John L. Gaddis, *The United States and the Origins of the Cold War 1941–1947* (New York: Columbia University Press, 1972), p. 9.

19. *Ibid.,* p. 65.

20. See Adam B. Ulam, *The Rivals* (New York: Viking, 1971), pp. 3–4.

21. *Ibid.*, pp. 13–14.

22. See Lynn Etheridge Davis, *The Cold War Begins: Soviet-American Conflict Over Eastern Europe* (Princeton, N.J.: Princeton University Press, 1974), pp. 78–79.

23. Ulam, *The Rivals*, p. 12.

24. Joseph P. Lash, *Roosevelt and Churchill 1939–1941: The Partnership That Saved The West* (New York: Norton, 1976), p. 237.

25. Gaddis, *Origins of the Cold War*, p. 205.

26. See Robert A. Divine, *Second Chance: The Triumph of Internationalism in America During World War II* (Baltimore, Md.: Penguin, 1970), pp. 57–58.

27. Stephen E. Pelz, *Race to Pearl Harbor* (Cambridge, Mass.: Harvard University Press, 1974), p. 223.

28. See B. H. Liddell-Hart, *History of the Second World War*, vol. 1 (New York: Capricorn Books, 1972), p. 312.

29. Cited in Anthony Sampson, *Macmillan: A Study in Ambiguity* (New York: Simon & Schuster, 1967), p. 61.

30. Joseph Frankel, *British Foreign Policy 1945–1973* (New York: Oxford University Press, 1975), p. 175.

31. Frankel, *British Foreign Policy*, p. 320.

32. See Cordell Hull, *The Memoirs of Cordell Hull* (New York: Macmillan, 1948), 2:1652ff.

33. See, for example, Davis, *The Cold War Begins*, pp. 144–52.

34. Cited in Gaddis, *Origins of the Cold War*, p. 154.

35. Cited in George F. Kennan, *Memoirs: 1925–1950* (Boston: Little, Brown, 1967), p. 222.

36. Ulam, *The Rivals*, pp. 18–19.

37. See John W. Spanier, *American Foreign Policy Since World War II*, 7th ed. (New York: Praeger, 1977); and Arthur M. Schlesinger Jr., "The Origins of the Cold War," *Foreign Affairs* (October 1967), 46(1):23–52.

38. Richard W. Mansbach, *The Soviet-Yugoslav Rapprochement of 1955–8; Its Ideological and Political Implications* (D. Phil. dissertation, Oxford University, 1967), p. 1.

39. Jan F. Triska and David D. Finley, *Soviet Foreign Policy* (New York: Macmillan, 1968), p. 346.

40. The best description of postwar developments in Eastern Europe remains Zbigniew K. Brzezinski, *The Soviet Bloc*, rev. ed. (New York: Praeger, 1967).

41. Frank P. Chamberlain, *This Age of Conflict*, 3d ed. (New York: Harcourt, Brace and World, 1963), p. 673.

42. Isaac Deutscher, "Stalin's Dilemma," in William Appleman Williams, ed., *The Shaping of American Diplomacy*, vol. 2:*1914–1968*, 2d ed. (Chicago: Rand McNally, 1970), pp. 320–21 (selected from *Russia: What Next?* [1953]).

43. Warren Eason, "Population Changes," cited in Ulam, *The Rivals*, p. 6.

44. Nigel Nicolson, ed., *Diaries and Letters of Harold Nicolson*. vol. 3: *The Later Years, 1945–1962* (New York: Atheneum, 1968), p. 116.

45. Deutscher, "Stalin's Dilemma," p. 322.

46. Winston S. Churchill, *Sinews of Peace: Post-War Speeches* (Boston: Houghton Mifflin, 1949), p. 94.

47. For a more complete description of Potsdam, see Herbert Feis, *Between War and Peace: The Potsdam Conference* (Princeton, N.J.: Princeton University Press, 1960).

48. H. Stuart Hughes, *Europe: A Contemporary History* (Englewood Cliffs, N.J.: Prentice-Hall, 1966), p. 388.

49. Herbert Feis, *From Trust to Terror: The Onset of the Cold War, 1945–1950* (New York: Norton, 1970), p. 37.

50. See James F. Byrnes, *Speaking Frankly* (New York: Harper, 1947), pp. 187–91.

51. Lucius Clay, *Decision in Germany* (New York: Doubleday, 1950), p. 354.

52. *Ibid.*, p. 360.

53. Arthur H. Vandenberg, Jr., ed., *The Private Papers of Senator Vandenberg* (Boston: Houghton Mifflin, 1952), p. 406.

54. See Peter Calvocoressi, *World Politics Since 1945*, 3d ed. (London: Longmans, 1977), p. 14.

55. Feis, *From Trust to Terror,* p. 4.

56. *Ibid.*

57. Gaddis, *Origins of the Cold War* p. 355.

58. David Horowitz, *The Free World Colossus,* rev. ed. (New York: Hill & Wang, 1971), p. 31.

59. Theodore J. Lowi, "Making Democracy Safe For The World," in James N. Rosenau, ed., *Domestic Sources of Foreign Policy* (New York: Free Press, 1967), pp. 320–23.

60. See Murray Levin, *Political Hysteria in America* (New York: Basic Books, 1971).

61. Dean Acheson, *Present at the Creation* (New York: Norton, 1969), p. 356–57.

62. *Ibid.*, p. 366.

63. Cited in Howard Zinn, *Vietnam, The Logic of Withdrawal* (Boston: Beacon Press, 1967), p. 156.

64. See Harry S. Truman, *Memoirs,* vol. 2: *Years of Trial and Hope* (New York: Doubleday, 1956), pp. 332–33; Glenn D. Paige, *The Korean Decision* (New York: Free Press, 1968), pp. 114–15; and Ernest R. May, *The "Lessons" of the Past* (New York: Oxford, 1973), pp. 52–86.

65. Spanier, *American Foreign Policy,* p. 70.

66. For the general's views, see Douglas MacArthur, *Reminiscences* (New York: McGraw-Hill, 1965), pp. 357–393.

67. See Alan Whiting, *China Crosses the Yalu: The Decision to Enter the Korean War* (New York: Macmillan, 1960).

68. Dwight D. Eisenhower, *The White House Years: Mandate for Change: 1953–1956* (Garden City, N.Y.: Doubleday, 1960), pp. 180–81.

69. Walter LaFeber, *America, Russia, and The Cold War, 1945–1971* (New

York: Wiley, 1972), p. 142. For a contrasting view, see Marshall Shulman, *Stalin's Foreign Policy Reappraised* (Cambridge, Mass.: Harvard University Press, 1963).

70. LaFeber, *America, Russia, and The Cold War*, pp. 143–44.

71. *Ibid.*, p. 144.

72. *Ibid.*, p. 149.

73. Urie Bronfenbrenner, "The Mirror Image in Soviet-American Relations: A Social Psychologist's Report," *Journal of Social Issues* (1961), 17(3):45–56. See also Ralph K. White, "Images in the Context of International Conflict," in Herbert C. Kelman, ed., *International Behavior* (New York: Holt, Rinehart & Winston, 1965), pp. 255–58.

74. See William A. Gamson and André Modigliani, *Untangling The Cold War* (Boston: Little Brown, 1971).

75. See James N. Rosenau, *The Scientific Study of Foreign Policy* (New York: Free Press, 1971), pp. 116–32, 197–237, and 275–303.

76. See Philip Agee, *Inside the Company: CIA Diary* (Baltimore, Md.: Penguin, 1975).

77. Cited in Leo Gruliow, ed., *Current Soviet Policies II: The Documentary Record of the 20th Communist Party Congress and Its Aftermath* (New York: Praeger, 1957), pp. 36, 37. See also Nikita S. Khrushchev, *For Victory in Peaceful Competition with Capitalism* (New York: Dutton, 1960).

78. R. J. Rummel, "U.S. Foreign Relations," in Bruce M. Russett, ed., *Peace, War, and Numbers* (Beverly Hills, Calif.: Sage, 1972), pp. 98–99.

79. Cited in LaFeber, *America, Russia, and The Cold War*, p. 173.

80. See, for example, David Wise and Thomas Ross, *The Invisible Government* (New York: Bantam, 1964); Victor Marchetti and John Marks, *The CIA and the Cult of Intelligence* (New York: Dell, 1974); Agee, *Inside The Company;* and Frank Snepp, *Decent Interval* (New York: Random House, 1977).

81. LaFeber, *America, Russia, and The Cold War*, pp. 152 and 204. The best summary of American use of deterrence is Alexander L. George and Richard Smoke, *Deterrence in American Foreign Policy: Theory and Practice* (New York: Columbia University Press, 1974).

82. See Glenn H. Snyder, " 'Prisoner's Dilemma' and 'Chicken' Models in International Politics," *International Studies Quarterly* (March 1971), 15(1):66–103. See also Glenn H. Snyder and Paul Diesing, *Conflict Among Nations: Bargaining, Decision Making and System Structure in International Crises* (Princeton, N.J.: Princeton University Press, 1977), pp. 79–129, for a sophisticated analysis of selected crises as game variants.

83. Cited in Elie Abel, *The Missile Crisis* (New York: Bantam Books, 1966), p. 134; and Roger Hilsman, *To Move A Nation* (Garden City, N.Y.: Doubleday, 1967), p. 215.

84. LaFeber, *America, Russia, and The Cold War*, p. 235.

85. See Hans J. Morgenthau, *Power Among Nations*, 5th ed. rev. (New York: Knopf, 1978), ch. 11.

86. See P. Dale Dean, Jr. and John A. Vasquez, "From Power Politics to Issue Politics," *Western Political Quarterly* (1976), 29(1):27–28, for a more detailed discussion of these agreements and their impact.

87. Henry A. Kissinger, "Détente with the Soviet Union: The Reality of Competition and the Imperative of Cooperation," in Robert J. Pranger, ed., *Détente and Defense: A Reader* (Washington, D.C.: American Enterprise Institute for Public Policy Research, 1976), p. 158.

88. Simon Serfaty, "Brzezinski: Play It Again, Zbig." *Foreign Policy,* (Fall 1978), no. 32, pp. 20–21.

89. Reproduced in Pranger, ed., *Détente and Defense,* pp. 114–16 and 145–47.

90. Cited *ibid.,* p. 181.

91. Cited *ibid.,* p. 161.

92. See, for example, William W. Whitson, "The Global Security Environment of 1977: Security Concepts for National Leadership," in Whitson, ed., *Foreign Policy and U.S. National Security* (New York: Praeger, 1976), pp. 12–13; and Seyom Brown, "A Cooling-Off Period For U.S.-Soviet Relations," *Foreign Policy* (Fall 1977), no. 28, pp. 4–5.

93. See Daniel Yergin, "Politics and Soviet-American Trade: The Three Questions," *Foreign Affairs* (April 1977), 55(3):531.

94. Gamson and Modigliani, *Untangling The Cold War, passim.*

95. *Ibid.,* p. 88.

96. Graham T. Allison and Morton H. Halperin, "Bureaucratic Politics: A Paradigm and Some Policy Implications," in Raymond Tanter and Richard H. Ullman, eds., *Theory and Practice in International Relations* (Princeton, N.J.: Princeton University Press, 1972), pp. 40–79.

11. THE FUTURE

1. Jimmy Carter, "Address to a Joint Session of Congress, SALT II Treaty," *New York Times,* June 19, 1979, p.A13:1.

2. See A. J. Ayer, *Language, Truth, and Logic,* rev. ed. (New York: Dover, 1948).

3. Charles Taylor, "Neutrality in Political Science," in P. Laslett and W. Runciman, eds., *Politics, Philosophy and Society,* third series (Oxford: Basil Blackwell, 1967). For a refutation of Taylor, see Fred Frohock, *Normative Political Inquiry* (Englewood Cliffs, N.J.: Prentice-Hall, 1974), pp. 35–43.

4. Kenneth L. Adelman, "Report from Angola," *Foreign Affairs* (April 1975), 53(3):560.

5. Paul H. Nitze, "Assuring Strategic Stability in an Era of Détente," *Foreign Affairs* (January 1976), 54(2):207, 227. See also Paul H. Nitze, "The Strategic Balance Between Hope and Skepticism," *Foreign Policy* (Winter 1974–75), no. 17, pp. 136–56; Paul H. Nitze, "Deterring Our Deterrent," *Foreign Policy* (Winter 1976–77), pp. 195–210; Albert Wohlstetter, "Is There A Strategic Arms

Race?'' *Foreign Policy* (Summer 1974), no. 15: pp. 3–20; Albert Wohlstetter, ''Rivals, But No 'Race','' *Foreign Policy* (Fall 1974), no. 16, 48–81; and R. J. Rummel, *Peace Endangered: The Reality of Détente* (Beverly Hills, Calif.: Sage, 1976).

6. Jan M. Lodal, ''SALT II and American Security,'' *Foreign Affairs* (Winter 1978–79), 57(2):255–56.

7. Aaron L. Friedberg, ''What SALT Can (And Cannot) Do,'' *Foreign Policy* (Winter 1978–79), no. 33, p. 93.

8. *Ibid.*, pp. 99–100.

9. William E. Griffith, *The Sino-Soviet Rift* (Cambridge, Mass.: MIT Press, 1964), p. 15.

10. Barbara Ward, *The Lopsided World* (New York: W. W. Norton, 1968), p. 11. See Charlotte Waterlow, *Superpowers and Victims: The Outlook for World Community* (Englewood Cliffs, N.J.: Prentice-Hall, 1974), pp. 1–2.

11. Ward, *Lopsided World,* p. 12.

12. See James N. Rosenau, *Race in International Politics: A Dialogue in Five Parts* (Denver: University of Denver, Monograph Series in World Affairs, vol. 7, no. 2, 1969–70).

13. Tom Farer, ''The United States and the Third World,'' *Foreign Affairs* (October 1975), 54(1):79–97.

14. For this view see André Gunder Frank, ''The Development of Underdevelopment,'' in James D. Cockcroft et al., *Dependence and Underdevelopment: Latin America's Political Economy* (New York: Anchor, 1972); and Immanuel Wallerstein, *The Modern World System* (New York: Academic Press, 1974).

AUTHOR INDEX

SUBJECT INDEX

tions, xxii, 72; model of, 78-79, 240-54; defined, 232, 234-35; feedback, 253-80
Interaction games, 80, 136, 281, 319, 332, 344, 400, 434; selection of, xxiii, 81-82, 293-98; shifts in, xxiii, 81, 298-301, 309-13, 316, 320; creation of, xxiii, 81, 301-4, 408, 422, 431, 442; defined, 287-93; and World War I, 369; in the Cold War, 388-89
Interdependence: actor, 60, 99, 109, 118, 128, 201, 216, 227, 271, 445; and actor emergence, xxi, 75, 144, 149-51, 154-55, 157; and coalescence/fragmentation, 162, 175; and Cold War, 388-89, 399, 401, 403, 407, 409-10
Interdependence calculus, xxii, 193, 212, 229, 270, 294-95, 334, 335, 348-49, 357, 362, 381, 383, 385, 411, 413, 480; determinants of, 77, 197, 199-200, 224, 250; defined, 192, 196-97, 221-28
Internal strife, 10, 21, 101-2, 177-79
International Court of Justice (ICJ), 153, 194
International Energy Agency (IEA), 181, 477, 486
International law, 3-4, 29, 88, 290-91, 300, 320, 333, 393
International Monetary Fund (IMF), 162, 169, 433; *see also* Monetary policy, international
International organization, 6, 114, 158, 161, 219, 227, 288, 301, 306-7, 403, 442; and the agenda process, 96, 99-100, 103; and participation, 148-49, 152n, 154
International regimes, 8, 13, 100, 119n, 122, 158, 161, 289, 300, 442
International relations enquiry, 158, 186-88, 431
International system, 6, 70, 96, 99, 219; structure of, 95, 97, 144n; the emerging, 474-86
Inter-University Comparative Foreign Policy project, 36
Investment policies, 477, 483
Iran, 201, 414, 430-31, 434, 457, 468, 475, 484; overthrow of the shah, 467
Ireland, 101, 173, 180, 337, 479, 484
Iron Curtain, 415, 432
Islam, 111, 487
Isolation, 318-19, 423-24
Israel, 440, 484; participation in UN, 54, 154; and U.S., 99, 222, 472, 479; and Lebanon, 107n, 118; and Egypt, 118, 193,

480, 481; as viewed by Third World, 479; and South Africa, 479; and Syria, 480; and the North-South dispute, 481; *see also* Middle East dispute
Issue, xiii, 95; defining issues in politics, xiii, 11, 51-52, 55, 72, 128, 142, 172, 179, 202-3, 234, 242, 262, 320, 400, 426; importance of in theory, xv, xix, xx, 10-12, 14-15, 23-27, 30, 87, 94-95; genesis of, xv, xx, xxi, xxiv, xxv, 73-74, 87-92, 115, 124, 232, 389-99, 442, 452; defined, xx, 54-55, 57-59; research on, 11, 23-27, 36-47, 55; measurement of, 14-15n, 54-55, 60; hierarchy of, 28-29; concurrent, 36, 76, 196, 203; characteristics, 38-49, 59, 69-72, 172, 176, 235, 312; conceptualization of, 47-67; and actor variation, 95, 143, 161-62, 442; change, 113-14, 161, 211; role of outside issues, 120; and coalescence/fragmentation, 170, 172, 175-76, 178; number of, 178, 236-37, 242-43, 442; and cooperation/conflict, 240-54; and interaction games, 298, 300, 311; *see also* Issue area; Single issue
Issue area, 10, 14, 67, 72, 162; research on, xix-xx, 7, 36-47, 211; typologies, xix, 23, 30, 298; Rosenau's 10, 30-31, 33-50, 56-57; Lowi's 31-42, 47-48, 50-53, 57; Zimmerman's, 32-35, 38-40, 42, 50-53, 57; substantive approaches, 35, 40, 53-57, 95; defined, 35, 56; Brecher et al., 35-36, 38-40, 53, 56; operationalization, 37, 38-39
Issue cycle, xxi, 73-74, 88, 113-24; *see also* Administration; Crisis; Decision making; Dormancy; Ritualization
Issue dimension, xx, 71, 211; effect on coalescence/fragmentation, xxi, 170-72, 175-78, 181-82; effect on issue position, xxii, 197-201, 294, 297, 310; determinants of, xxii, 199, 202-3, 207, 221, 253-80; defined, 60, 197-98; effect on cooperation/conflict, 60-61, 66, 78-79, 240-54; and friendship-hostility, 170-71, 240-54; and agreement-disagreement, 170-71, 229, 240-54; and positive-negative acts, 170-71, 240-54; and types of stakes, 240, 243-50; and nature of issue proposals, 240, 249
Issue linkage, 19, 60-61, 73, 78, 121, 172, 174, 207, 211, 220, 364; research on, 43-47; during the Cold War, 61, 391,